A HISTORY OF THE WORLD

A History of the World

HUGH THOMAS

HARPER & ROW, PUBLISHERS

NEW YORK

Cambridge
Hagerstown
Philadelphia
San Francisco

1817

London
Mexico City
São Paulo
Sydney

FIRST U.S. EDITION

ISBN: 0-06-014281-2

LIBRARY OF CONGRESS CATALOG CARD NUMBER: 79-1688

79   80   81   82   83   84   10   9   8   7   6   5   4   3   2   1

This book is dedicated to
Rómulo Betancourt

Contents

BOOK III
AN INTELLECTUAL TRANSFORMATION

BOOK IV

INDUSTRIAL TRIUMPHS

BOOK V
POLITICAL FAILURES

the past by excessive taxation — General conclusions on the modern state

Preface

The main purpose of this book is to provide a short history of the world arranged so far as possible on thematic, rather than chronological, lines. I wrote it because I had spent a great deal of time investigating specialised subjects and thought that I should like if possible to consider the background against which those occurrences had taken place. At the end of the book, I have allowed myself to be drawn into a discussion of the nature of the crisis which appears to affect the world in the last quarter of the twentieth century. My suggestion is that the best way of dealing with these difficulties is to place them against what appear to be their historical roots.

It will become evident that the 'world' mentioned in the title is not so large as some would expect. There is much more here about Tuscany than Tobago. Sir Henry Maine wrote, in his once famous book *Ancient Law*: 'It is difficult for a citizen of western Europe to bring thoroughly home to himself the truth that the civilisation which surrounds him is a rare exception in the history of the world. The tone of thought common among us all, our hopes, fears and speculations would be materially affected if we had vividly before us the relation of the progressive nations to the totality of human life.' I have tried to keep that caution in mind. Still, it is obvious that it is western Europe with North America which, since the fifteenth century at least, for good or evil, has provided the world's dynamism. Even the 'vulgar Marxism' which so fatally attracts so many students from poor parts of the world is a European product. I can still hear Professor Fernand Braudel explaining to some astonished students at the University of Reading his theory that the Mediterranean was a sea which 'psychologically' surrounded Brazil. North America is also, of course, a Europe-over-the-water. That this era of European dominance may one day come to seem a comparatively short one, lasting from about 1400 AD till 1945 (or perhaps 1973), is certainly possible. The modern statesmen, such as Charles de Gaulle or Jean Monnet, who, in contrasting ways, have sought to regenerate Europe since the Second World War, may come to resemble the later emperors of Rome whose titanic efforts to resist decay were doomed to failure. On the whole, I think that catastrophic interpretation of the future of Europe and its civilisation rather premature, not, it is true, because of our greater self-confidence but because, firstly, it is hard to see new ideas on the horizon which could effectively challenge ours in a free and open encounter; and, secondly, because the West still has leaders with a sense of the historic past. The world's demoralisation, wrote Ortega y Gasset at the end of the 1920s, derives from the demoralisation of Europe. Despite everything, and despite the further decline of Europe's political power, that still seems to be true.

This book is an unfinished history. I consider that I have cut out a few chunks of rock and given them certain shapes, and I present them to the reader as if to say 'this is how a history of the world should be shaped, in my opinion, if such a book could, in fact, be written'. The shapes are these. First, I have tried to bring together what seem to be the most interesting elements in the pre-history of the world and to notice how the age referred to by anthropologists as the age of hunters was, slowly, transformed into an era when agriculture began to affect some part at least of the cultivable regions of the world. To the layman, such divisions in time are more comprehensible than such concepts as the 'stone' age, the 'neolithic' age or the 'bronze' age. In Book II, I discuss the Age of Agriculture in the hope that a fresh look at the history of so long a time may be found by treating it as if it were a single epoch. I justify this by the suggestion that, to most people, those years were indeed really the age of grain, or the age of rice rather than the age of Egypt, Rome or Chivalry. Book III discusses the intellectual transformation which occurred in Europe between the Renaissance and the Enlightenment. The impression that I hope I will have left is that the forward movement which then characterised European life derived from a reinvigoration of ideas first formulated during antiquity but snuffed out after the conquest of the Mediterranean world by a Roman version of eastern despotism which itself derived from many diverse roots. In Book IV, I discuss the achievements of the industrial era and, in Book V, I notice how, and consider why, the innovations concerned have not as yet resulted in the creation of Utopia. The last chapters of Book V discuss some of the political problems of the present, and speculate how the liberal heritage of the West can best be preserved. The book attempts to take the story up till about 1973 or 1974, which was when I began seriously to write it: the subsequent tremors are not really considered.

A book of this sort is likely to be an educational adventure for its author. Having written several books about modern times, I felt a strong desire to consider our relation to antiquity; and, having spent a great deal of time in my other books discussing armies, anarchists and governments, I wished to consider, for a change, such often neglected topics as the history of brandy, of the thermometer and of the radish.

I need to make a number of acknowledgements: first, to the historians whose works I have pillaged in order to write this book. The names of most of those persons and of their books, along with general indications of sources, are given at the back of the book.

Secondly, I must thank Marjorie, Virginia and Lorenzo Scaretti for making available to me for so many summers at Il Trebbio an incomparable window from which to look at the world. So many great travellers passed through the valley beneath and so many exemplary men have lived at, or been to, Il Trebbio, that any person with a historic sense can be forgiven if, from time to time, they persuade themselves that, even though remote, they are living at the heart of civilisation. If some find it easy to imagine Lorenzo de' Medici walking under the pergola with Politian or Luigi Pulci, his country neighbour, others can as easily imagine Dante plotting in the neighbourhood with the Ubaldini, Giotto walking with his sheep, Becket, Montaigne or Boswell travelling past, Hannibal or Totila the Ostrogoth or General Mark Clark (with the 84th Indian division) preparing their armies. In this 'folding of the Apennine', as Matthew Arnold put it in a line of *Thyrsis*, it is certainly possible to approach that 'undisturbed, innocent, somnambulatory' reflection which, according to Goethe (who once spent a rather uncomfortable night in the valley, too), is essential for the production of anything worthwhile.

I am also grateful to Anne Somerset, who worked for me as a research assistant in the last stages of the book, who is responsible for the accuracy of many of the statements which I venture to make, and who typed, retyped and, on occasion, retyped again and again sections of the book; to my wife Vanessa, who also typed and retyped page upon page and made innumerable helpful suggestions as well as reading the proofs: to Cass Canfield Junior, of Harper and Row, always enthusiastic; to Christopher Sinclair Stevenson, of Hamish Hamilton; and to Lord Gladwyn, Daniel Johnson and Phyllis McDougall for their kindness in reading sections of the book in manuscript or in proof. Phyllis McDougall is also responsible, as with some of my earlier books, for the Index, which she has constructed very fast.

H.T.
April 1, 1979

BOOK I

The Foundations of History

'The investigation of a single detail already requires profound and very penetrating study . . . (But) historical research will not suffer from its connection with the universal. Without this link, research would become enfeebled, and, without exact research, the conception of the universal would degenerate into a fantasy'.

von Ranke

'The writing of history, as Goethe once noted, is one way of getting rid of the weight of the past . . . the writing of history liberates us from history'.

Croce

'The future of history and historians is to cleanse the story of mankind from . . . deceiving visions of a purposeful past'.

J. H. Plumb

'For it is history alone which, without involving us in actual danger, will mature our judgement and prepare us to take right views, whatever may be the crisis or the posture of affairs'.

Polybius

1

The Birth of the World

Genealogy has its satisfactions, but how disconcerting to those who worship ancestors to find that, in the direct male line, men derive from in ascending order, a monkey, a newt, a sea-lily and a bacterium. The legend that the Earl of Northumbria in Shakespeare's *Macbeth* was descended from a fairy bear seems, once the principles of evolution are accepted, only mildly misleading.

Life, however, is far from the first ingredient to take into account. The solar system of which the Earth is a part is now known to be a galaxy of 100 billion stars in an archipelago of galaxies perhaps comparable to ours, adrift in space. It is now thought that the universe was begun 15 to 20 billion years ago as a result of an explosion which propelled all the galaxies away from each other. The nearest galaxy to our own is held to be two million light years away. Our galaxy and the Earth apparently came into being almost simultaneously, following the contraction, by rotation, of clouds of dust, between 4 and 5 billion BC. The Sun was a concentrated core at the centre of this rotation. The planets formed around pieces of débris.

No one suspected until recently that the Earth and the Universe were anything like as old as this. In the seventeenth century, the Anglo-Irish theologian James Ussher, archbishop of Armagh, reflected a widely held attitude when he spoke of the world as having been created in 4004 BC. The French naturalist, Georges Buffon, thought that the world might be 'at least 70,000 years old'. In 1755, the philosopher Kant speculated that the figure might be 'a million, or even millions of, years old'. But the timetable now regarded as approximately correct was only discovered in 1935 by an inspired astronomer, Edwin Hubble, of Missouri. The considered study of the skies, however, began long ago in Babylon where much data were gathered together, and analysed, by means of relatively advanced mathematics (1).

The Earth's crust wrinkled for a long time, creating mountains and seas, the latter caused by the further condensation of vapours. The sea and the land were, it is now believed, once absolutely divided into entirely separate dimensions in a planet which thus had one ocean and

3

one continent, but the latter, known to geologists as Pangaea, split into something like the present continents about 2000 million BC. Much movement of land, however, continued afterwards. The creation of the Channel, which divides England from Europe, and the Bering Straits, which cut off Asia from America, were, for example, the product of later commotions. India was separated by sea from northern Asia for a time before 45 million BC, as was, till about 2 million BC, North from South America (2). Africa was once, it seems, as close to South America as was North America. The Mediterranean became a desert about 6 million BC and became a stretch of water again a million years later, while the Black Sea too was once the arm of a great ocean (3).

The early years of the Earth belong to chemists, not to historians. For a historian, it is enough to know that a metallic core, 3,750 miles wide, came into being within the Earth — mostly liquid iron and nickel, though solid in the centre. Between that core and the Earth's crust, a 'mantle' of iron and magnesium 1,875 miles deep took shape. The crust, which is of diverse composition, varies between twelve to thirty miles in depth on land, and only four miles under the sea.

Before the coming of anything recognisable by the name of 'life', many fundamental matters had already been decided: the Earth began to rotate clockwise, creating westerly winds; some latitudes were already cold, some hot; the tilt of the Earth's axis created seasons; mountain ranges already affected climate; and seasons had begun to be clearly differentiated (4).

Life, in the form of bacteria and micro-organisms, apparently began between 3.2 and 3.4 billion BC. The first plants, descendants of bacteria, grew in seas or on their edges. Their immediate descendants were worms (which came into being about 1000 million BC); shellfish; jawless fish; scorpions; and vertebrate fish, which were probably living by 450 million BC. The worms were the first living things which, unlike their predecessors, plants, had to seek food from outside themselves: plants can make for themselves the chemical elements which they need in order to survive. From the vertebrate fish, descended reptiles, large and small, which came into being about 350 million BC. Some of these were dinosaurs, pleiosaurs, or ichthyosaurs, the ancestors of turtles, lizards and snakes. Other extinct reptiles, known as therapsids, resembling the duck-billed platypus, could walk on two feet and had teeth. Whether they had fur, warm blood and laid eggs is obscure. From them, nevertheless, the mammals descended, at first being small and insect-eating, weighing less than 20 pounds, and seeming comparable to lemurs, bushbabies, shrews, or squirrels. For many millions of years, these ancestors of all the more successful animals of the world today lived side-by-side with the dinosaurs, who dominated the world for 150 million years.

The eclipse of the dinosaurs about 65 million BC was probably due to an unidentified climatic change which destroyed all large animals. Mammals perhaps survived since, apparently, they were then all under twenty pounds in weight. By that time, mammals had multiplied their species. Primates, the direct ancestors of men and monkeys, had appeared. So had insects and birds, while most flowering plants had assumed something like their present shape (5).

About 30 million BC, an animal was born which is believed to be a common ancestor of man and modern ape. These two species apparently diverged between then and about 5 million BC, though the date is a matter of dispute. Some anthropologists of distinction believe that men were already different from apes by 20 million BC. Others put the date nearer 4 million BC. At all events, between 10 and 5 million BC, the ancestors of men were still usually living in trees. They were still basically herbivorous and do not seem to have been carnivorous much before about 4 million BC. Then, or perhaps about 3 million BC, ancestors of men began to walk upright, as their usual mode of locomotion, and to carry things in their arms (6). By then, too, man was beginning to be regularly carnivorous – a differentiation from other primates perhaps caused by a shortage of nuts, berries and fruit. That, perhaps, was the main reason for the descent from the trees, though our closest relative among the other primates is also primarily a dweller on the ground (the African chimpanzee), and though the chimpanzee can use objects such as stones with great agility and effectiveness. There were shortly other differentiations from other primates; such as the more subtle possibilities of man's use of his hands; and his greater fertility. There are minor differences in sexual behaviour between humans and apes and, while chimpanzees and gorillas mate only during the female's ovulation, women, like female gibbons, can mate at any time. Gibbons, like most humans, live customarily in monogamous families, while male chimpanzees and gorillas seek to establish harems of females, which they try to dominate until overthrown by a younger rival. All the apes are close to men in blood, and an almost political sense of co-operation can be discerned in monkeys, though, unlike men and indeed birds, they do not as a rule co-operate with each other in the pursuit of food. Chimpanzees seem, though, to share food on the rare occasions when they eat meat. On the whole, however, apes eat vegetables or fruits, and do so on the spot. Some regard the change of habits of food-gathering from individual scavenging to co-operative search for game as the determining one in human evolution from apes (7).

The main distinctive characteristic of human beings, however, derives from the size of their brains. That may have followed man's change to an erect posture. The human brain needs a large skull and also a large cortex. Yet plainly it is not the size of man's brain alone which has been responsible for his place in the world; porpoises and whales have larger ones (8). Even so, the brains of men's ancestors doubled in size between about 3 million and 1,500,000 BC from 450 to 900 cubic centimetres. Meantime, these bipeds were making stone tools and hunting animals by 2,500,000 BC and, by 1,500,000 BC at least, the stone tools had begun to be flaked on both sides, perhaps to cut up elephants and mammoths, which could hardly have been eaten without some such implement. All these dates may be a little ungenerous, if that is the correct word. It may be, for instance, that upright walking evolved earlier than 3 or 4 million BC, and nearer 10 million.

Subsequently, that is after the beginning of both hunting and the making of stone tools, man's brain developed further to its present approximate size of 1400 cubic centimetres and the history of *homo sapiens* proper begins, or indeed of what anthropologists now call *homo sapiens sapiens*. The coming of this being seems only to have occurred about 40,000 BC. The main subdivisions, subspecies or races of men probably made crossings at different times of the 'threshold' from a more brutal to a more sapient state (9). Where the line was first crossed, and by whom, is unknown. Probably it happened in several continents at the same time. Perhaps the decisive change causing the brain to grow further was made possible because the early tools already in use enabled, as we would now put it, a better standard of living.

The differences between *homo sapiens* and *homo sapiens sapiens* were considerable: for example, the first, who was in the past often known as 'neanderthal man', from the fossilised remains found in the Neander valley in Germany in 1856, had a brain the same size as modern man, but slightly differently shaped. Most of the tools of *homo sapiens* which survive derive from flakes of flint. *Homo sapiens sapiens* had a less tough skull than his predecessor. His tools were slender and sometimes already shaped for ritual uses. Harpoons, needles, awls, complicated weapons and long voyages all followed fast, or at least fast in comparison with what had gone before. In comparison, *homo sapiens* pure and simple seemed closer to his predeccesor, to whom the name *homo erectus* is now given (10). That *homo erectus*, remains of which were found in Java in the 1890s and subsequently in Africa and China, had a thicker skull than *homo sapiens* had. His frontal lobes were not well developed, and his brain was small. His jaws and teeth were larger than modern man's. Even so, he used a stone axe. He even had fire, about 450,000 BC, in both Hungary and China. It was first used for keeping warm, giving light, and sharpening sticks at the ends to ward off enemies (the absence of early traces of fire in hot countries, such as Africa, suggests that the first use of it was the need for warmth.) *Homo erectus* used caves for shelter. Some of the late versions of this primate, such as those whose skulls have been found at Swanscombe in Kent, dating from 250,000 BC, have been thought of as 'virtually *homo sapiens*'.

It seems possible that the change occasioned by the coming ot *homo sapiens sapiens* about 40,000 BC may have been inspired by language. No doubt men were not silent before. Apes communicate with one another, but without language. Even simple tools must have needed speech for them to be made well. But the use of clear speech must have constituted a decisive change, making possible a whole range of activities previously unthought of. Among primates without language, there are no religions, no politics and no works of art. Speech is usually the main element of cohesion among human beings, even among the few primitive ones that have survived (11). But its origins are a mystery.

Thirty families of languages have been identified as existing in historic times. They embrace 2,500 main languages and dialects (12). But many languages avoid classification: when the Europeans discovered Australia, 500 tribes were found there, each with 500 to 600 members, and each one with their own language of several thousand words. Europe must once have been the same. In South Africa, the differences were even greater when the Europeans arrived: some tribes there spoke different languages among the men and women. Probably many people talked to each other effectively by whistling languages, such as the Silbo, which survives on the Canary island of Gomera, at Ans in the Pyrenees, and, in a slightly different manner, at Oaxaca in Mexico. Some think, with Carleton Coon, that the 'social requirements of a group of hunters made speech necessary' (13). Possibly the first languages were without parts of speech, with most phrases and thoughts expressed by a single word (14). Was speech perhaps a single invention, by a single tribe and did others imitate it imperfectly? (15) Over 20,000 years, two sister languages may be expected to deviate and to lose all semblance of relationship. But if all language derives from a single mother tongue, the original separation would have been many tens of thousands of years before 20,000 BC. Thus probably more than one breed of men discovered speech independently (16).

The questions posed by all these happenings go to the roots of the problems of human life and of history: what caused the deviation of man from animals? What was the cause of evolution within life? What caused life? What caused the occurrences which themselves caused the birth of the Earth and of the solar system? Was it really a 'spark from heaven', as Matthew Arnold put it (17), which caused the beginning of life? If the 'man monkey' became man because of a mutation in a single person, perhaps causing a change in the size of the brain, is there any reason to suppose that this mutation was caused by God, or a god, or some other extra-terrestrial 'creative agent,' in Lewis Mumford's phrase (18)? Was there some fortunate cross breeding? Did life originate at some time or has it, in some way, here or elsewhere, always existed as J.Z. Young posed the question (19)? Were there precedents for life on Earth or elsewhere? Was life on Earth brought by meteorite, or even by design, as some have argued, from another planet? Or from another solar system? Did God wind up the universe and then leave it to its own devices, as once argued by one Christian Bishop, Nicolas Oresme, at about the time that the clock was invented? (Oresme, who was bishop of Lisieux and tutor to King Charles VI of France, is also believed to have been the first European to use vulgar fractions and apparently came close to discovering Newton's concept of natural forces.)

These questions have not been solved satisfactorily by geologists or chemists any more than they have by theologians and philosophers. Since the questions are open, they give grounds for hope, or fear, of the existence of God or of the validity of religion but scarcely give any proof of the greater closeness to truth of one religion more than another. The sceptical may take comfort from the realisation that religion (which itself has, in a sense, 'evolved' from nature worship and polytheism to monotheism) began when the real early history of the Earth was unknown. But even the sceptical must accept that no other system anything like so intricate as that of life has occurred by mere chance. The achievement of Sir Isaac Newton was to prove that the force which causes a stone to fall is the same as that which keeps the planets in their path. But that does not divorce the universe from a spiritual order (20). Even the sceptical scientist Laplace, who told Napoleon that '*il n'avait pas besoin de cette hypothèse-là*' (that is, religion), agreed with Newton that the way that the planets revolved all in the same direction round the Sun was unlikely to be a matter of chance.

The relation of the earth with the Sun, and of man with animals, was widely known to the Greeks in classical times. Thus Aristarchus of Samos wrote, about 250 BC, that 'the Earth (and other planets) revolve round the Sun in the circumference of a circle, the Sun lying in the middle of the orbit'. He also calculated, fairly exactly, the relative distance from the Earth of both the moon and the Sun (because of these insights he, like Galileo later, was persecuted. Astronomy was thus started on the right path but little more was done for 1800 years, though Eratosthenes of Alexandria, who died in 194 BC, calculated the circumference of the Earth at 24,650 miles (it is 24,875) (21).

Similarly, man's relation to animals, and his evolution from them, was guessed by Anaximander of Miletus who, in the sixth century BC, saw that the structure of fish resembled humans', and argued both that men were descended from animals and that life began in the sea or in slime. The members of Pythagoras' colony at Croton had to forswear eating the flesh of animals since they too believed men to be related to animals. That idea was also held by many African tribes, who knew apes at first hand. But it was a point of view unacceptable to Christianity and other religions founded about the same time as the birth of Christ, and apes were rare in countries which adopted universal religions. Between Anaximander and Darwin, the only major scientific work achieved in biology was that undertaken in the eighteenth century by the Swedish master-classifier, Carl von Linné (Linnaeus) who divided two million or so different living things (800,000 plants; 800,000 insects; 400,000 animals) into species. Earlier, in the seventeenth century, the English chemist, Robert Boyle, 'the father of chemistry and the uncle of the Earl of Cork', recognised the true nature of the elements to constitute the simplest form of matter; then another Englishman, John Dalton, established that every element consists of its own variety of atom. (22).

Evolution, of course, seems to continue. The teeth and jaws of human beings become smaller as cooking rids them of some of the gastronomic troubles of early man. There were alterations in glands, brain and reproductive organs during the age of the hunters. The movement of the Earth's crust also continues: India is pushing against Asia, so is Italy against Northern Europe. These things cause tremors such as those which brought the great Chinese earthquakes in Tang Shan in 1976. The universe is also presumably continuing to expand.

Kant, who first argued that the Earth might be millions, rather than just thousands of years old, thought that the factor most distinguishing men from animals was an intuitive awareness of an inner moral law embodying Reason. Conduct, he believed, is to be judged in respect to whether it can be regarded as motivated by Reason. The test for an act should be, can the principle implied by it be applied universally? Unless it can, the act cannot be disinterested (23). Were such categorical imperatives always present? Did such concepts follow automatically from the increase in the size of man's brain? Did they have any effect before hunting, while man was still in the trees, and when the making of a stone axe was as remote from his capacity as is our capacity, in the twentieth century, to envisage, say, an infinite universe? How early did it, for instance, become evident that 'man rarely remains in his customary level in . . . critical circumstances: he rises above it or sinks below it' (as de Tocqueville said, comparing men to nations) (24)? When did man first appreciate the truths remarked on by one of the characters in Malraux's *Les Noyers d'Altenburg*? 'We know we have not chosen to be born, that we will not choose to die. That we have not chosen our parents. That we can do nothing against time.' (25). Were 'the timid . . . always cruel,' as Gibbon argues (26)? 'I have been specially disgusted with Rousseau since I went East,' said Napoleon, 'Savage man is a dog' (27). But did 'savage man' have any connection with an Egyptian of 1800 AD? Did those early men of about 2 million BC — 'protohuman hominids' as those who study them in the crevices of the Rift valley speak of them — forage and hunt as a troop of baboons do today (28)? Was there a division of labour even then between men and women? Doubtless the combined factors of females having repeated (and sought-after) pregnancies of nine months, and the habit of a carnivorous diet, began an allocation of tasks along lines which have dictated the behaviour of humans ever since.

Any comment on the early history of man, finally, ought to notice the critical invention, in the course of the twentieth century, of a technique for dating ancient remains based on measuring the content of carbon within the object concerned. This brilliant method was devised by Willard Libby, a chemist from Colorado, during the 1940s. It has had two limitations: first, that dating of objects older than 40,000 years is almost impossible since the carbon dies; second, that, the samples needed are relatively large. Doubtless new methods in future will remove these deficiencies (29). Various other methods of dating fossils and meteorites have also been devised which have enabled even the most remote dates mentioned in this chapter to be roughly confirmed.

This book is a study of history. There is one desirable corrective to any undue parochiality, however, about the development of our own species. There are now about two million species living on the Earth. But almost certainly, those two million species represent far less than one per cent of the species that have ever lived, the rest being now extinct (30). Then, though man is now more or less in control of the Earth, his era of dominance is measured still in terms of thousands of years in comparison with the millions of years during which the dinosaur held sway. Though this book lays a certain emphasis on the part played by men in history, the reader should beware of forgetting that one of the most beautiful of creatures, with an exquisitely made apparatus for feeding off human blood, is the most dangerous of all the 3,000 types of mosquito: the Aedes Aegypti.

2

Man as a Hunter

Most of man's time on Earth as a recognisable human being has been passed as a hunter. This hunting, which lasted until at least about 10,000 BC, is held to have been based on the stone hand axe which gave to the era its Greek name: 'palæolithic' or 'old stone' — a word invented, along with 'neolithic' or 'new', that is, polished stone, by Christian Thomsen, a Danish pioneer archaeologist, in 1836. Those who lived in the age of hunting would probably have been surprised to have been thought of as people of a 'stone age', for many of their weapons, as well as their houses, boats and bridges were made of wood, which, however, could not survive so easily as stone. The yew lances found at Clacton (England) or Lehringen (Saxony) perhaps suggest the nature of the age of hunters as much as do the stone axeheads in museums all over the world. 'Well may ours be called a wooden century,' wrote a pioneer of America in the nineteenth century AD, pointing to the wooden houses, bridges, fuel, pins (instead of nails) and latches which marked his days, thereby marking too a continuity rarely interrupted, before the twentieth century, among pioneering peoples (1). Still, the stone axe made possible the cutting and shaping of wood, and other stone implements enabled the scraping of skins for an early version of clothes and the cutting of meat for better food. As with most great innovations, no one can decide whether stone implements were invented in several places independently, or whether there was an original centre, from which the idea radiated. Common sense suggests a diversity of invention. Further, the surviving stone axes show not only a definite pattern of development and improvement, but also that, in some countries at least, early hunters went to great lengths to get good stone.

The stone from which the early hunters made their tools naturally varied from region to region: granite, basalt, quartz, obsidian and flint were all extensively used. Large numbers of these ancient tools have been found and many names have been given to them from 'hand axe' and 'chopper', to 'flaked axe', 'blade' and 'scraper'. Most of those names are inadequate. Microscopic traces of wear on the edges of flints

11

have recently been brilliantly analysed to show more accurately the real purposes of those ancient implements. 'Butchering', wood-working, working on hides, cutting material other than wood such as reeds or bracken have been activities carefully identified. The old 'hand axe' turns out to have been used as much for cutting meat as wood. 'Scrapers' were concerned with dressing hides (2). 'Blades' began the age of spears, arrows and harpoons, their handles being sometimes later decorated with beads, stone, bone, antler or ivory (obtained from mammoths, then widely dispersed in the northern hemisphere). There were also, by then (say 30,000 BC), special tools for special activities — for example, for engraving designs, and for working bones or antlers. The 'late stone age man' or the 'late hunter' was busy with perforation, with awls; rubbing or polishing; and the shaping of antlers. Needles of bone were already in use, as were spades of mammoth bone, spoons of mammoth ivory, and clubs of antler from reindeer.

Some hunting tribes survived a long time and some still do so, in rather artificial circumstances. The lands which they hunted were remote. Australian aborigines, San ('bushmen') in South Africa, Eskimoes, some hunters of Northern Siberia, and some tribes of southern Chile are characteristic representatives. Some South American Indians in tropical regions might just also still be called 'hunters'. The San people of South Africa live normally in packs of one large family strong but, sometimes, in gatherings, of up to a hundred. None of these peoples is now isolated and some live, on the one hand, nomadically, without much clothing but, on the other, use pottery as well as basketwork. The Kwakiutl Indians of British Columbia led, until the twentieth century, an elaborate but primitive cultural life, built around fishing. Their boats, of great cedar trunks, survive. Most of the North American Indians, now settled or extinct, lived, in the fifteenth century AD, much as they did in 10,000 BC. The 50,000 or so Eskimoes now living reached their zone from Alaska or Greenland between about 100 BC and 1200 AD. Their tents of caribou or sealskin; their permanent winter villages and temporary snow summer houses; their boats and kayaks and dog-drawn sledges of wood; their methods of hunting seals, caribou, foxes, ptarmigan, with weapons and hooks (of stone, antler, driftwood and latterly iron); their movements during the seasons; their clothes of caribou hides and fur, and their knives of antler or whalebone; are indications not only of adaptation to circumstances but of a society older than most others, even if the primitiveness is now mitigated by some modern implements.

Another picture of life in a human pack can be guessed at from what the Europeans saw when they began to colonise Australasia. In Tasmania, for example, about 1770 AD, between 2000 and 4,000 people ranged over 25,000 square miles in bands of fifty, sheltered from the weather by windbreaks, using chipped stones as tools, and wooden clubs and spears (the tips hardened by fire) as weapons. Tasmanian hunters rarely stayed in one place, though they lived mostly on the coast, avoiding the rain forest of the interior. Good hunting needs space: to be sure of food, hunters in Tasmania had to live at a density of no more than ten people to the square mile.

The species of animals killed by early hunters were numerous, ranging from elephant and rhinoceros to horse and deer, depending on the part of the world. Bone harpoons made fishing as rewarding as killing animals. Fishing was also often done by building dams in rivers. Hunters knew the usefulness of cords and threads (for fastening, binding and even sewing, using needles of horn or bone) and they also made baskets.

Hunters evidently often killed each other, both thoughtlessly and by design, within and outside the tribe. Many were cannibals or, at least, ate the brains and marrow of the bones, if not the flesh, of their enemies. About 15,000 BC, the bow and arrow were apparently invented, in central Asia — an improvement on both the axe and the stick, in the hands of a skilful archer. Hunting man sometimes had some sort of boat from which to fish. He may not have had the sail, but he probably had the oar by about 20,000 BC. Hunters had a more varied diet, probably, than most non-humans now surviving and perhaps even than some modern peoples too.

Modern man certainly descended from early hunters at different times, in different places. False starts probably occurred. The wonder is as much that there are not more sub-species of man, white, black, mongoloid, as that there are more than one.

The colour of skin and climate are clearly connected. Black skins keep the body cooler and protect the skin from sunlight better than white ones. But there is little differentiation of colour among American Indians or Chinese or Mongoloid peoples generally. Black was, for a time, believed to be the original colour of man, with other colours arising through mutation. Now some argue that the original colour was yellow. Such ideas do not seem to be very firmly based. Some such changes may have been caused by variations in climate. Thus the Earth is now known to have been warmer at the time of the eclipse of the dinosaurs, in 50 million BC, than it is today, and more of it was covered by forest than is the case now. By 25 million BC the climate was cooler. Much of the Earth was covered by grass: a condition which favoured the evolution of the horse, among other animals.

The different races of men probably arose as a result of gradual genetic diversification following widespread colonisations of new territories during the 'final glacial circle' — that is, the last ice age — between 60,000 and 10,000 BC, when a great deal of now inhabited land was permanently under ice. Climate determined (though presumably did not alone inspire) ethnic characteristics: blond, fair-skinned people survived in cool conditions; dark skins did well in hot, non-forested regions; yellow skins prospered in tropical rain forests, and Eskimoes probably gained their flat noses through the need to mitigate the temperature of the air before drawing it into their lungs (3).

At all events, as everyone now knows, pink, sallow and pale-skinned people gathered eventually in the northern hemisphere. Black and dark brown people lived in the tropics (in Africa and South East Asia but not, to begin with, in tropical America.) Yellow, brown or mongoloid people were to be found in Central Asia and Malaysia, Japan (after 7500 BC), Australasia (after 14,000 BC), parts of Polynesia and the Americas, both North and South, (inhabited as far south as southern Chile by 15,000 BC). The Earth had thus already been colonised, almost completely, by roaming tribes, save for some islands which could only be reached later by skilful seamanship (New Zealand, and some Caribbean islands, Hawaii, and even some Mediterranean islands).

During this long era, while man was establishing his primacy over other animals, most of the characteristic human habits and qualities must have come into being, including the beginnings of family life; humour, art and love; and attitudes to disease and to education. Hunting people must have known best which wood was the toughest, and which the most supple, much better than most twentieth century people. They naturally knew animals well, and their seasons for breeding. They knew plants, and their uses as poisons as well as foods and drugs. Tribes sometimes depended on single herds of animals and pursued them from cool to warm places, according to season, almost as shepherds later led sheep in that fashion. Though hunting man did not read or write, practise agriculture or manufacture anything for profit, most of the human virtues and vices, as they are normally reckoned to be, must already have existed by 20,000 BC.

Most tribes of early man were probably no more nomadic than the Indians of North America, the Scythians, or the Huns of central Asia, before they attacked westwards. That is, they had regular hunting grounds, from which they were only displaced by stronger tribes who attacked them. Within those hunting grounds, there were regular stopping places, in caves or artificial dwellings scooped out of soil, huts of poles and skins held together by mammoth bones and, later, by mud walls (4). In size, such tribes varied. Perhaps there were some tribes larger than those 500 to 600 strong met by Europeans when they got to Australia. Perhaps the average was twenty to forty: 'Fifty would be the limit,' wrote Carleton Coon (5). These groups would consist essentially of groups of a few families in which the adult men, perhaps five or six in a group of fifty people, would hunt and the rest would depend on them. While the males hunted, the females would perhaps be gathering plants, cooking (by roasting in pits) or looking after children — though boys perhaps went hunting from the age of ten as assistants to their fathers. The long childhood of humans confirmed the desirability of a permanent union between man and woman greater than among other animals.

Many remains of primitive man suggest that the person concerned met a violent death. A low density of population perhaps kept down epidemics; but there was clearly high infant mortality. Expectation of life was well under thirty years, and few would attain the age of fifty.

On death, hunters were, towards the beginning of historic times, usually buried, sometimes in a cave, with sometimes the limbs being flexed to save space (and so economise the effort of digging graves) or perhaps to ensure against the dead man's return as a ghost. The beginning of regular burials suggests respect for, and anxiety in respect of, the transitoriness of life. Thus, even before the age of agriculture, man evidently believed in some deities, subscribed to some magic, perhaps even had hope of life after death: what else, otherwise, is to be made of the burial place found in Uzbekistan, where a dead child of the era of hunting was surrounded by a ring of goat horns, pushed downwards into the earth floor? The first record of man being anxious to conserve the memory of the dead dates from at least 70,000 BC. Neanderthal man buried his dead regularly and, from 15,000 BC, men began the habit of leaving prized objects in graves. Sometimes, the dead might already be buried in the fur of the skins which they had worn in life, perhaps sprinkled with red ochre to preserve them; and, the nearer to historic times the burial, the more likely that the bodies would be accompanied by ornamental objects, such as shells, or jewellery, made perhaps of ivory, horn, snails' shells or the vertebrae of fish (6). Objects found in those ancient graves give ample support to the remark of Bernard Berenson that, 'in the fear of death all the arts have their roots' (7). The first aesthetic act of all, however, was perhaps the making of stone axes with an elaboration beyond functional needs: patterns of geometric shape, for example, or herringbone patterns, criss-crosses, and chevrons. Figurines of mammoths, of other animals, and of women began soon to be modelled from clay – particularly of women – for use in graves. Those 'Venus figurines', which robustly emphasise breasts, thighs, buttocks and pregnancy, if rarely heads, legs or arms, are the earliest real artistic creations which have yet been found. They have been discovered in the western Pyrenees and south west France, on the Italian Riviera, in Bohemia and the Ukraine, made from clay by hand, of course, but nevertheless fired in heat to ensure a finish. Artists in caves also used the unevennesses in rocks, marks of drips and stalagmites, as elements in elaborate, perhaps magical paintings. Those artists used fingers, but also probably branches, and brushes of fur or feather. Unusual powers of observation were needed for such works of art: qualities which must have made for better hunting and perhaps helped ultimately to lead to agriculture in those very areas which were then favourable to grazing animals (8).

Most primitive communities which survived into historic times had a marked if incomplete idea of equality and freedom within the group concerned, combined with exclusiveness, suspicion and prejudice towards the outside. Thus, though no one in such tribes usually married a sister or a brother, or a father or mother, they usually married distant cousins. Prohibitions on exogamy gave these people their coherence. There was sometimes no chief in such tribes and sometimes even no explicit authority. The most experienced might guide the community, but they often did not have the power to rule it. Common ancestors would be likely to be worshipped. Kinship, genealogy and myth were usually matters of concern. All older people might be regarded as parents: all children, a communal responsibility. Some German tribes in being in Tacitus's day certainly lived in a rough state of democracy. Primitive tribes described by Herodotus did the same. There are signs that, in the early days of Babylon, some of the villages had their affairs ordered by councils of elders, rather than by despots.

Beyond these things frequently common to 'primitive' peoples, there was, and is, a wealth of diversity. Among some tribes, it is permissible to marry aunts, while some can marry only aunts on the mother's side. Some communities recognise matrilinear descent, in order to maintain purity of blood. Inheritance through the sister's son, as practised by the Ashanti monarchs of West Africa, was a well-known custom in many ancient communities. Patrilinear and matrilinear communities appeared early on, each with distinct characteristics.

Was this, we wonder, the golden age described by the most influential of modern philosophers, Rousseau: 'While the Earth was left to its natural fertility and its immense forests whose trees were never mutilated with the axe, it could afford, on every side, both sustenance and shelter for every species' (9).

Or was Rousseau's less famous contemporary, Vico, more accurate when (as recalled by Isaiah Berlin) he saw these early men as 'like the Cyclops Polyphemus, in the Odyssey, fathers of primitive families, despotic, savage, violent, ferocious, able to survive only by means of the most terrifying discipline, by enforcing absolute obedience' (10)?

There is nothing of which to be sure. Such evidence as there is can certainly be arranged to persuade oneself that most hunters lived in a near-anarchist paradise. Jean Jaurès described the 'open field in mediaeval agriculture as constituting primitive communism' (11). This early communal living in tribes, in competition with each other, might also be made to seem like the conditions of a small capitalist enterprise. Naturally, there is no certainty that there was religion: yet it is easy to imagine hunting men enjoying a primitive worship of sun and moon, and a general flight of the whole tribe into the bushes at a clap of thunder. What does seem obvious is that there must have been some political co-operation. Careful planning must have been necessary to secure the right food at the right time. Among hunting people who survived into historic times in America, each species of game was believed to be ruled by a spiritual leader — some great white beaver, for example, who ruled over all beavers. Similarly, hunters themselves had to regulate their killing to prevent over-hunting (12). Thus political life has an ancestry older than agriculture and perhaps should be granted to have had some kind of existence from the earliest days of hunting.

3

The Coming of Agriculture

The decisive changes during the age of the hunter were probably
decided by alterations of climate. Those were, of course, caused by the
same inexplicable drives as caused life itself. Long 'ice ages' succeeded
false dawns of warmth. The last ice age lasted most of the early part of
the last hundred thousand years. During that time, the sea was
probably about 600 feet lower, as a rule, than it is now. Arabia, the Gobi
Desert, North Africa and the Sahara were much less dry. Both England
and Japan were still territorially linked to the continents near to them.
Asia and America were joined over the Bering Straits — a fact which
enabled the Americas to be populated — as were Asia Minor and the
Balkans, over the Bosphorus. The Adriatic was dry. But, halfway up
England, the Arctic began. That embraced northern Germany, northern
Russia and nearly all Canada.

The 'retreat' of the last 'ice age' occurred because of the shrinking of
the polar ice cap, between about 12,000 BC and 6000 BC. It caused some
geographical changes which now seem of very great importance, as well
as some climatic changes which led, in turn, to all sorts of opportunities,
including agriculture and, in the end, as a result, to settled political
systems. It also cut off, through the narrow strait of deep water between
Java and Bali, the Australasian fauna and flora from the Oriental. So the
Australian aborigines were isolated and had no more contact with the
rest of the world until the Chinese investigated their coastline in the
fifteenth century and the Dutch a little later (1). The sea also rose to cut
off Britain from Europe, Scandinavia from Germany, Russia from
Alaska (2). But many places in the north of the Earth were at that time
opened up for settlement. Forests of oak, elm and alder in central
Europe took the place of the open grazing lands formerly occupied by
reindeer. The people of central Europe turned from hunting reindeer to
fishing, as well as to more varied forms of hunting, while the peoples of
the Near East probably racked their brains in order to find a way of
surviving in their established habitats. Many doubtless died, others
perhaps emigrated. Perhaps we can see, in Herodotus's story of a
people whom he knew as the Psylli, a distant memory of that lost time:

'The Psylli, a people of North Africa, had all their water ponds dried by the South West wind. They declared war on the wind, went out to the desert to meet it where it came from, and were buried in it by heaps of sand' (3). That time saw the origin of the myths of the golden age and of the Garden of Eden: a time in the past when food was abundant, and no effort was needed to live. Afterwards, 'man could only eat by the sweat of his brow' (4). The change of climate as well as over-hunting led to the extinction of large game, such as mammoth, and that in turn caused, probably, a drop in population. Some tribes died out, defeated by the need to find new game day after day. Others returned to the berries and fruits of the days before hunting, or intensified the search for fish or molluscs. Perhaps the reindeer, which gave horn and bone as well as meat, and moved, then as now, in herds hundreds of thousands strong (where several herds join up, the numbers have been known to be a million), was already half-domesticated. That probably gave men ideas as to what might be done with other animals if they could be captured (5). (Reindeer had been drawn to man as much as man to them, because of their taste for the salt that they found in human urine (6).)

Agriculture began with the domestication of the dog about 15,000 BC, an event characterised by the formation of regular packs for hunting in which man and dog collaborated (7). Dogs, descended from wolves or dingos, were taken by the first invaders of America with them, apparently not as completely domesticated animals (the earliest domesticated dog in the Americas seems to come from Idaho, about 9000 BC). Early dogs were mostly sheepdogs, the many varieties of modern dog being bred more recently. Perhaps some kind of stock keeping had preceded this, for that could be done by nomads (8). This began the long era of collaboration between men and animals on terms laid down by the former.

Robust historians in the past felt confident enough to speak in terms of an 'agricultural revolution' occurring between about 12,000 BC and 7000 BC but it is eccentric to speak thus of a series of changes which extended over several thousand years. The invention of agriculture is thus a historical phenomenon like the Renaissance: its beginning is not where it seemed to be fifty years ago. Furthermore, every year, a new discovery gives evidence of an earlier agriculture than was once considered likely. The presence of large peas, beans, cucumbers and water chestnuts has, for example, been held to prove that cultivation of those vegetables began in Thailand and Burma about 9750 BC (9). South East Asia, China, India, and Africa are less well studied in these matters than is the Near East, where agriculture has been customarily regarded as having been conceived. China, in particular, although plainly populated by very early man, has few traces of human life, except in Manchuria, between the earliest times and about 2500 BC, where what had previously seemed an empty land began to support a comparatively large and busy population. Still, by about 13,000 BC, wild wheat fields, themselves brought about by warm winds previously unknown, were apparently beginning to be harvested regularly by men from permanent settlements of farmers in what is now southern Turkey, east Syria and northern Iraq. The wheat concerned was emmer wheat, an ancestor of modern wheat, which, along with rye (originally a weed of the early wheat fields), barley, oats, millet and perhaps spelt, grew wild in the eastern Mediterranean. There, too, it was domesticated. That meant encouraging the cross-breeding of the tougher tamed plants whose grains have to be regularly sown, since, unlike wild ones, they do not disperse automatically (10). Like many modern plants (and other things), domesticated wheat would die out soon enough if not tended by man, for domestication means not simply a 'taming', but a genetic change in order to make the plants concerned better suited for man. (Wild animals, of course, can be tended, but that is not the same as domestication.)

Other agricultural innovations included weeding; digging soil with a hooked branch or an antler; the use of fire to complete the clearing of a tract of land and to fertilise it — the idea being presumably gained by seeing the effect of accidental fires; and the use of a flint-bladed sickle, perhaps with a bone handle, with which to cut the harvest though, in the earliest days, the harvest was accomplished by pulling out stalks by hand. Still, flint blades, adapted from ancient weapons, were being used, apparently near the Nile, for reaping by 12,000 BC.

From pictures of a later time, it is possible to guess roughly what an early harvest was like. The reapers formed a line, cutting the corn, and laying the cut sheaves on the left. Their neighbours did the same, but left the sheaves to the right. Others bound the sheaves, which would then be spread on the threshing floor, the tips toward the centre. The grain would be trodden out, to begin with by men, a few thousand years later by animals. The corn would then be ground by pestles (11). In this style, the Near East, particularly Egypt, began her long history as a granary to the Mediterranean. The grain would be boiled in a pit, subsequently beaten into a paste, and mixed with water to make the first flatbreads, perhaps baked with a crust. Iraqi civilisation had a barley flatbread made from paste, spread out and cooled on a hot surface — and it is still eaten there. These heavy early breads might be helped down with sesame oil, fish or sauces of various kinds. The grinding naturally played a large part in these undertakings, since, while corn can be kept for a long time, flour cannot be. Therefore, grinding is necessary almost all the time.

Did agriculture begin in one or two places, result in the establishment of villages, and then become diffused over the whole earth, early seized upon by weary hunters who had been seeing their game die and were anyway only too glad to find a way of not going on their travels again?

Or did it occur at the same time in many places? In the valleys of the Tigris and Euphrates, the Nile, the Indus and the Yellow River, perhaps the Mekong, perhaps in central America? Caution suggests a diverse origin, even though it is indeed 'hard to accept,' as Christopher Wrigley puts it, 'that men should have lived for tens of thousands of years during which the idea of putting seeds or tubers back into the ground should have occurred to no one, and that it should then have occurred to several people independently' (12). Yet it is equally hard to escape the realisation that many things were learned independently in America and in the old world, at a time when there was no contact between the two. The dog was domesticated in both the Near East and in the Americas at much the same time in the two places and, equally, maize was planted in both places, again without agricultural pioneers from one world playing a part in the achievement of the other. By all accounts, the radish was separately domesticated in many places. Then the whole process of agricultural innovation was stretched over thousands of years. If agriculture radiated as an 'idea', perhaps even in a world without means of communication it would have developed faster than it did in practice.

Five rivers (the Nile, the Euphrates, the Tigris, the Indus, and the Yellow River) were clearly foci of early agriculture. Cattle may have crowded towards these rivers because of climatic changes. The muddy deltas were good places to discover that nutritious plants could be deliberately sown. Possibly, planting began in places where game or wild fruit were short. The Euphrates and Tigris, admittedly, lacked an alluvial plain. The agriculture which grew up between those rivers was dependent on the timing of the thaw in the Armenian mountains and the spring rainfall. Hence, perhaps, the intricacy of the politics there. All the same, ancient Iraq had a high productivity: 200 grains grown to one sown. In Egypt and in China, the deposit of mud left by the rivers could be cultivated again and again without treatment.

The main Egyptian crop continued to be wheat, the early Chinese crop was millet (rice did not appear till many generations later, being a native of south China or Indo-China and is anyway grown best in the Yangtze Valley) while, in Iraq, barley was more common. Though some semi-horticultural agriculture was practised in the Americas by 6000 BC (beans, squashes, chili peppers, gourds), the earliest maize was probably cultivated in Mexico between 6000 and 5000 BC.

The tools of this early agriculture need a little investigation. Thus the foot-plough of the Scottish Highlands was no more than a stick put into the ground and pulled towards the cultivator. It has been in use in the twentieth century AD, but would have seemed already quite primitive in the twentieth century BC in Egypt. A Peruvian plough, the same instrument of the Andes, made of very hard wood, and sharpened by fire, is said to be still in use. At all events, the early ploughs were little more than hoes, but soon harrows and rakes, in much the same form as modern ones, were introduced. The foot-plough became, about 7000 BC, a two-man plough, in Egypt, with one man pulling on a rope, in front, and a second man pressing the plough's point into the ground. A cross-beam gave this plough more sophistication. But eventually the use of animal power transformed matters.

Reindeer may have been ridden occasionally, or milked, as they still are in Lapland. The much maligned wolf taught man many things in the way of rounding up cattle. Perhaps wild goats also hovered near the new agricultural settlements in the hope of finding grain till they invited capture. The 'omnivorous goat' must have been used to clear scrub soon after the extension of agriculture away from the natural gardens of the river valleys. Goats also provided milk, hair and a waterproof skin for use in human clothing, whether or no those benefits were realised before the conscious control of breeding started to ensure more productive strains. The use of milk by human beings also probably began with the goat, in the Near East, about 8000 BC. Then, even before agriculture, nomads had herded sheep for meat, for milk and for skins: since, even before the invention of spinning and weaving, sheep were recognised as being able to provide a good natural felt. Pigs were probably domesticated in several places, at much the same time. It is possible that they, like goats, took some initiatives in securing their own domestication. Once villages began to be formed, the shining virtues of the domestic pig must have become quickly apparent, for it can give abundant supplies of meat and fat (and bristles as well as skin) and can be kept in very restricted places. Pigs are as good as goats at destroying undergrowth. They soon became the staple domestic animal of China, as they have remained in all uncultivated territories for many generations. Hog breeding furnished the main food of uncleared parts of America even in the nineteenth century (13). All these animals were taken in a domesticated form throughout the old world, including Africa. In the Americas, the still entirely nomadic tribes continued an unrelenting war against wild animals, much as Europe and Asia had done before 10,000 BC: mammoth and giant sloth were still being hunted in 6000 BC but probably the destruction of all large types (except reindeer) was complete by 5000 BC and the cultivation of crops was, perhaps in consequence, beginning.

Probably all these early domesticated animals were used for a time as beasts of burden. Even sheep were made to tread in the seed sown by shepherds in Egypt. But these animals only made a minor impact on how the harvest was gathered, in comparison with cattle, whose domestication was the most important step taken by human beings in their exploitation of the animal world. This seems to have occurred in Turkey, Macedonia and Greece about 6000 BC. The innovation seems to have taken a long time to be carried elsewhere. Egypt and Iraq did not have cattle as beasts of burden before 4000 BC; central Africa not before 3000 BC, north west Europe not before 2500 BC and China only by 2000 BC. (From the beginning, China used cattle mostly for traction, hardly at all for milk; in Africa, cows were mostly used for meat.) At least by 2500 BC, and probably before domestication, there were different breeds: humped cattle in India and Iraq, piebald in Egypt and among the lake dwellings of Switzerland and Denmark. Many theories, some beguiling, explain differences between the fighting bulls of Spain, the hornless Angus, and the white cattle of Italy. In that first society of which there is a detailed memory, namely Egypt, there were certainly two types of cattle: lean cattle, with powerful horns, living on grass, used for the plough, with bulls being used for heavy loads: and the other, *Bos africanus* (14), for meat.

Agriculture began on light soil where the early scratch plough had worked well. The first cattle-powered version of this used in Egypt (as in the Yellow River delta in China) was pulled by two cows, though the plough itself was little more than a stick. In Sumer, a heavier stick was dragged diagonally across the earth, throwing up loose earth at the sides and, there, a stone-edged plough was first used with a yoke binding the animals firmly to the shaft. But even that more powerful method of cultivation was inadequate for the heavier soils of northern Europe. Agriculture indeed came there late, and hesitantly. The castration of the bull, and his conversion into the ox, which has played such a part in agriculture, followed in the Near East about 4000 BC, probably in one of the cities of northern Iraq, symbolising the successful harnessing of the power of animals for man's needs very obviously. That too seems to have followed only very slowly in northern countries (15).

Several more animals began to be used in agriculture during the thousand years between 2000 BC and 1000 BC. First of all, the ass (of African origin) began to be in regular use in caravans for trade between Iraq and Egypt. The north African dromedary was also beginning to be used for the same purpose by 1600 BC in Palestine. The process was assisted by the invention of wheels, in use in Iraq as early as 4000 BC (16), and employed for ox carts only a few hundred years later, both there and in Egypt. Wheels were being used in China by 2000 BC.

Finally, there came the domestication of the horse, though that word seems inappropriate for the early use made of that animal in the great plains of the Russian steppe, where hunting tribes were long celebrated as bold and skilful riders. Their constant practice 'had seated them so firmly on horseback that,' wrote Gibbon of their descendants, 'they were supposed to perform the ordinary duties of civil life there . . . even to sleep without dismounting' (17). But though clearly in the steppe men learnt how to ride horses, all the earliest pictures of domesticated horses show them drawing light carts or chariots, rather than being ridden. By 2500 BC, for example, carts were in use in Turkestan, and in

Macedonia and Troy by 1800 BC. By 1700 BC, chariot-borne nomads or hunters able to make use of this superior equine technology were sweeping regularly towards the settled communities. The spoke (four were normal to begin with, six later) seems to have been invented at the same time. By 1500 BC the horse chariot had become recognised as a decisive weapon of war, just as, 3000 years later, horses alone were decisively used against the Aztecs and Incas.

Horses reached north west Europe slowly, perhaps not before 1000 BC, presumably as an already domesticated animal. Was the horse taken to Greece about 2000 BC and to India about 1500 BC by the first Aryan invaders, in the shape of a pony (18)? In China, the ox-cart was at any rate known by 2000 BC, and the horse and cart, or chariot, not much later, though the 'horses' were small Mongolian ponies with heavy heads, or even 'half asses' comparable, no doubt, to the true wild horse which existed till recently in Mongolia (19). Not till much later did the Chinese use the larger, more graceful, smaller-headed horses, the expedition to obtain which from central Asia is commemorated in the legend of the heavenly horses of Ferghana: an emperor needed horses to carry him to Heaven (20).

These early horses were ridden and driven without saddles, stirrups, or horseshoes and, though they had, from early on, primarily a military use, and a use for transporting the great, they were eaten too. Mares' milk and blood were drunk extensively in central Asia – indeed, in some circumstances are drunk there to this day. On the other hand, the use of horses for traction was rare, for the heavy harness used on oxen throttled horses. No one had the ingenuity to think of a different method until someone did so in China in the third century AD.

These cattle, carts, asses and horses continued to revolve round a wheat civilisation in Egypt; a barley one in Babylon; a millet one in China; and a mixed cereal one in India. In the Americas, maize would subsequently establish itself almost as decisively, in the small areas where there were settled communities, but there were no comparable beasts of burden there.

The merit of those staples was that, unlike fruit, meat, berries and all other food known till then, the grain so obtained could be stored for a long time without deterioration. The effect of this on the stabilisation of societies can thus easily be imagined.

Beyond the borders of the settled agricultural regions, however, nomads continued their old existence, constantly attracted by the prosperity of the settled regions which they sometimes laid waste and sometimes sought to capture. At that time — between 10,000 BC and 2000 BC — the majority of the 5 to 10 million people in the world were, indeed, surely nomads. They included even in 2000 BC the ancestors of the Greeks, Romans and Indians, the so-called 'Aryans' who lived near the Caspian Sea, surviving chiefly by rearing cattle, and talking some version of ancient Sanskrit which was the ancestor of Hindustani as well as of Greek (21). For a long time too, even 'settled' agricultural kingdoms had very uncertain borders; as suggested by the Indian horse-sacrifice where a horse was permitted to wander at will, the king claiming all the land over which it wandered (22).

For thousands of generations, real settled life and agriculture were only established in a few limited regions. Thus in central Asia, among the forests of what is now Russia, the agricultural technique which lasted into the sixteenth century AD and till the twentieth in the north, was half-nomadic in type: having made a clearing in the woods, the peasants set the undergrowth and stumps on fire. Ashes left after the fire were rich in potash and lime. The soil so treated yielded some good harvests. After it ceased to do so, the peasants would move on to another part of the forest and there put into effect this 'slash-burn' method anew (23). Much of the world at least lived thus almost until the industrial revolution, and thus many nomads approached the age of industry without the recollection of a long, settled agriculture. The abundance of wild life was certainly still a determining factor in the food supply of most of the world in 1750, certainly so in 1500. Nor should one forget 'the many primitive peoples who,' as Karl Wittfogel put it, 'endured lean years and even long periods of famine, without making the crucial changeover to agriculture, and who thus demonstrate the immense attractions of non-material values when increased material security can be attained only at the price of political, economic and cultural submission' (24). The gypsy and the bandit, that is, have a place in history. Nomads constantly battered at the doors of settled communities, often forcing an entrance, capturing the states concerned, as the Mongols captured China in the early thirteenth century AD, but, as a rule, were absorbed by the vanquished. Indeed, in many remote places, such as the Tibetan plateau, shepherds still move their herds of yaks from one area of sparse grass to another (25), even if they have ceased to menace China. The Scythian, Pecheneg or Hungarian nomads who drank mares' milk or blood, and threatened western Europe in the ninth century, and the Mongols who for so long menaced both China from the west and Russia from the east, have as much claim to represent continuity in history as the owners of a Tuscan villa. In mediaeval France, Marc Bloch tells us, semi-nomadic men of the forests prowled round the edges of the *grandes domaines*: huntsmen, charcoal burners, gatherers of wax and wild honey, dealers in woodash or simply woodmen — men who were from the beginning more traders than agriculturalists (26). The white pioneers in the American Mid-West depended in the 1830s for their subsistence on 'the natural growth of vegetation and the proceeds of hunting' (27). So, too, did their Indian opponents. In Western Spain, in the early twentieth century, the typical peasant was still the *yuntero*, a landless man with a team of mules which he would graze on common land. Even in France, in the nineteenth century, a few regions belonged to hunters (28). Those who lived from the forest were always opposed to an extension of the land under the plough and, even in Europe and other major agricultural regions, there were only modest additions to the acreage under cultivation between pre-history and the Middle Ages (c.1050–1300 AD), and then afterwards only sporadically and in special areas (England during the early enclosures, Tuscany in the fifteenth century). Most agricultural revolutions after 1300 till the twentieth century were concerned with a better way of using existing soil, not with cutting down more of the greenwood.

4

Early Social Bonds

The settled societies of the early agricultural age were, as it were, held together by several further innovations: pottery, for example, which had been anticipated by wooden vessels which had the same original aim of carrying water, and by the clay ornaments of the late hunting era. Pottery was first made in Iraq, where clay vitrifies easily and forms a hard product difficult to break even with a hammer * (1). Monochrome pottery was being made by 7000 BC, painted by 6500 BC and, within a few hundred years, all the ancient cities of Iraq boasted decorated bowls, drinking flasks, and cylinder seals carrying diverse patterns, fired in well-built kilns, whose temperatures already reached 800° centigrade (2). (Clay beads, bricks made from clay, and clay for mortar as well as clay figurines anticipated the use of clay for pottery.) By 4000 BC, the Egyptian potters knew that a glaze could be put on pottery by treating it with sand, potash, and soda, and that they could make the colour blue by adding salts of copper (3). About 3000 BC, at Uruk (Erech in the Bible), the potter's wheel was devised, making it possible to do in two minutes work that had previously taken several hours — perhaps being invented at the same time as the brick mould. By 2000 BC, the wheel had been so improved that it could be turned by the foot or a stick. Henceforth, a professional potter (first known 2000 years earlier) was normal, being closely connected in Iraq with early metallurgists (4). This wheel was taken through Europe, Africa and the East but it made fairly slow progress: it did not reach southern Britain till about the time of the birth of Christ (5). In China, it may not have arrived till about 1600 BC (6), but probably that is too late an estimate.

By a coincidental development to which, perhaps, inadequate attention has been paid, pottery was also invented in the Americas. The American peoples did not achieve the potter's wheel, it is true, before Columbus and the Spaniards took it there in the fifteenth century AD 3200 BC. The work there was more laborious than in the near East, since Ecuador, and beautiful painted pottery was being made by the Mayas by 3200 BC. The work there was more laborious than in the Near East, since pots had to be built up from coils of wet clay as they still are

* Claims have recently been made, however, for an African origin.

27

sometimes even in the old world (7).

All early pottery was developed alongside brickmaking. Bricks were shaped in moulds and dried in the sun, afterwards in kilns. In consequence, early houses seemed little more than large pots — as Sir James Jeans put it (8). Before the wheel, after all, potters made both houses and pots with their hands.

An activity which complemented pottery was spinning. That began with the use of vegetables such as reed, palm fibre and esparto grass. The making of baskets, ropes and matting has had a continuous history since about 6000 BC in Egypt. Hemp was also used in China before records began (say, 4000 BC). By 3000 BC flax was established in Egypt as the main material for clothing. The fibres of that carefully cultivated crop were soaked, then spun, a stick being used, first simply to avoid entanglement, and subsequently as a spindle, with a whorl or weight on top. Less important was the distaff, for holding the fibres ready to spin. The loom was apparently invented by about 5000 BC, providing a frame on which threads were stretched parallel to form the warp, to be crossed at right angles by the continuous woof (9). As with pottery, the new world independently, though later, worked out the act of spinning and weaving, making use both of its own cotton and the wool of alpaca and llama. Though fleeces continued to be worn without spinning — Herodotus spoke of 'Fair Libya abounding in fleeces' (10) — wool was regularly used as well in the Eastern Mediterranean by 3000 BC.

Sheep (and wool) were probably taken from the Near East to India, thence further east. Cotton, on the other hand, was probably carried from India to Egypt, though some suppose that the crop itself came from Africa. It seems not to have been known in China till 700 AD. But two out of the four types of cotton usually cultivated were native to the new world. Elaborate and finely woven cloths were made in Mexico and Peru long before the coming of Columbus. The colour of the weaves of Nazca, in Peru, for example, were striking in comparison with all products of the old world. At the same time, China developed the use of silk from the silk worms feeding from white mulberry trees long before the Shang dynasty. Did this 'sericulture' begin in the time of the legendary Emperor Fu-shi, about 3000 BC? That is now thought unlikely. Another mythical Emperor, Huang Ti, was supposed to have encouraged the silk worm about 2630 BC, since he believed silk clothes would enable him to escape from frost. By 1000 BC, anyway, China had already vast regions carefully drained for the mulberry plantations.

The significance of these developments was, of course, that, thenceforth, the use of clothing was no longer confined to those who could scrape skins effectively. It is hard to think of a more important change. Its effect upon population must have been decisive even if, in hot countries, the earliest clothing was merely a 'lower garment' and a cloak (11).

The birth of agriculture, paradoxically, by modern considerations, saw the birth of the city. It was to serve agriculture, too, that mining began.

What were they like, those early 'cities', primarily of farmers, set up around the early fields of wheat or millet in 8000 BC? Probably simply overgrown villages, a collection of mudhuts, 'baked mud and baked reeds, comparable to a beaver's nest', says Lewis Mumford (12). Such no doubt was Jarmo in Northern Iraq, which, in 7000 BC had a population of only 150; such also perhaps were Catal Hüyük, in Turkey, and Jericho which, about 1800 BC had populations of 2000, living in houses which had walls of baked mud and reeds, floors of beaten mud, and roofs of carefully plastered branches (13). By then, other villages in the Near East had rectangular houses with several rooms, stone foundations, clay ovens with chimneys, and clay basins in the floor. A thousand years later, unbaked brick had become the characteristic building material in Iraq, being used to make a typical oriental house, its rooms grouped round a courtyard. By 4000 BC, such places had cobbled streets, and circular temples: the architects had mastered the principle of the vault. Those architects only used stone, which was rare in Iraq, for doors, fireplaces, and drains. Some temples were painted, while the ziggurat had been invented at Uruk (14). By 3000 BC, some cities boasted about 50,000 people or even, as in the case of Ur, perhaps twice that (in 2200 BC).

Sumer, the most famous of the early cities of Iraq, was a town of thick, walled, windowless, mud huts. Rooms were fitted together to suit the site, rarely with a masterplan but with low doors and common walls. Many cities of ancient Iraq had some town planning for military purposes on a gridiron pattern (15). One can compare those villages with a more primitive city, Catal Hüyük, which had no streets, only a series of rectangular houses contiguously interspersed by courtyards. The walls in Catal Hüyük were of the same dried clay as they later were in Sumer, but the houses were bungalows with flat roofs and no doors. Entry was through holes in the roof made by stepped timbers. The rough lamps used by hunting man, an open stone container for animal fat, including a wick of twisted dried grass or moss, had given way to lamps of metal or pottery. The oil used was probably the same olive oil or sesame oil as was used for cooking in Egypt and Iraq respectively.

In Egypt, houses were more often built with wood than they were in Iraq. The public buildings were using stone by 2500 BC. The capital of Egypt was by then surrounded by a stone wall while the royal palaces had columns and colonnades. By then, already, the essential characteristics of city life had taken form: walls, streets, blocks of houses, workshops, an organised market, the temple and its precinct, the administrative area. To construct these things out of unbaked clay, or mud, or wood, or stone, copper tools of an elaboration not surpassed until the Renaissance were devised. There were also pull-saws and bow-drills, as well as glue (made by boiling down bones, skins and hooves), useful not only for shaping buildings but also for making boxes, chair frames and tables (16). Some ancient cities, such as the first version of Troy (c. 2300 BC), had walls of sun-dried bricks 12 feet thick. Stone in Egypt was cut from cliffs in great courses by masons using wedges, being taken away by a huge force of labour. All blocks could be dressed and squared by hand, and huge buildings could be built: the exceptional Great Hall of Karnak at Thebes, for example, measured 329 feet by 170.

Both agriculture and cities, formerly villages, came into being in regions which were, through much of the year, uncomfortably hot in the day and uncomfortably cold at night. It was very early realised, however, that thick walls could, and can, act as both insulators against, and reservoirs of, heat. Curved roofs had similar effects, as did a limitation of the number of windows, the growing of plants in courtyards and the existence of narrow streets.

The early houses of temperate zones, such as Europe, differed in that there was not only less need for heavy walls in houses but also less of a demand for city walls since, among other things, the system of irrigation did not have to be so meticulously defended. Houses seemed to be individual units, often round (for example, Sesklo). There were also lake dwellers who lived on platforms of timber in the middle of lakes. Crete, meantime, had two-storey houses from 1700 BC — a typical house there being supported by stone piers, with frames of timber, facing inwards on to courtyards approached by cloisters. The Cretans had staircases, probably before anyone else did. Mycenae, more exposed to attacks from pirates, was surrounded by limestone fortress walls, the light coming through high windows. The Mycenaeans, like the Egyptians (but unlike the Babylonians) did not have an arch. But the 'Treasury of Atreus' had one, all the same, with a span of 40 feet (17).

All these urban achievements were far from the felt tents, wool pile rugs and waggons of the Scythian nomads and others who constituted the most serious threat to all these societies (18). But they were close enough to the cities built, from adobe bricks, by the Nazca and Moche people of ancient Peru. (Though the arch did not reach America before Columbus, the Mayas did have a form of vaulting to support their roofs. Two legs of the vault were drawn close together until the space could be bridged by capstones (19).

By 3000 BC, most settled communities were establishing semi-religious authoritarian monarchies, whose rulers already customarily succeeded their fathers, and whose purpose, even if half forgotten, was to ensure that ploughing was regularly done and to make military arrangements to prevent the nomadic hunters from seizing the harvest when it was in. Irrigation was usually a main function of these king-doms. For most of them depended not on rainfall (it was believed in antiquity to have rained only once in Egypt, on the day, Herodotus tells us, that the country was invaded by Cambyses, King of Persia) but on water from rivers or wells, which had either to be allowed to flood the fields, as in Egypt, or to be artificially, intelligently and, above all, regularly diverted. The preparation and then the maintenance of these hydraulic systems needed the labour of hundreds of disciplined, hard-working, and co-operative men. Small-scale irrigation can be managed by independent peasants but, if large rivers have to be dammed and floods taken advantage of, a large administration is essential. Hence one reason perhaps for the early Chinese despotism, whose first ruler, the founder of the legendary Hsia dynasty, is supposed to have risen to his kingly rank from the position of supreme hydraulic functionary (20). The kingdom of lower Egypt — though not Egypt of the Delta — was also apparently made into a single unit because a change of climate forced the until then separate and still partially nomadic tribes about 5000 BC to move close to the Nile and depend absolutely on it for water (21). In historic times, the construction of reservoirs, tanks, canals and wells was looked upon as one of the most important of the functions of government in India, with careful distribution and measuring of water (22). Irrigation is still, and has perhaps always been, the most time-consuming single item in the farmer's calendar in both China and India (23). Probably the same was true in the past of Iraq, the lake area of Mexico, Mayah Yucatan, and of all countries dependent on rivers whose overflow, properly handled, brings fertility and life and whose unchecked waters leave death and devastation in their wake. 'The dikes,' Karl Wittfogel points out, 'have to be repaired in the proper season so that they will hold in times of inundation; and the canals have to be properly cleared so that the moisture will be satisfactorily distribu-ted' (24). Doubtless the entire history of oriental despotism cannot be attributed entirely to the needs of irrigation. But plainly irrigation necessitated, and made for, a source of central authority in a way which agricultures dependent on rainfall do not.

To carry out these arrangements, as well as to invent (as they did) the windlass, pulley, crank and lock with a key, all complicated beyond the dreams of hunting man, the pioneer agricultural kingdoms also needed adequate methods of calculating, accounting, reckoning, recording and, finally, writing. As Gordon Childe put it, 'When a society has possess-ions in greater numbers than it can use immediately, it needs numerals' (25).

Like many other of these achievements, the citizens of the towns of what is now Iraq were responsible for the fundamental innovations. There, the first calendar and the first, hieroglyphic, script were devised. There too were worked out the first system of numbers and the first system of weights and measures. In the schools of ancient Iraq, multiplication, division, square and cube roots, algebra and geometry were all taught. Those schools knew of the theorem, now called after Pythagoras, in 1700 BC and were close to quadratic equations — reaching, indeed, a mathematical level of achievement not touched elsewhere until the Renaissance (26). This ancient Iraqi mathematics used both a decimal and a sexagesimal system. So far as the first system was concerned (invented, perhaps, because we have ten fingers), they employed the so-called 'place-value' system, which modern Europeans also use — by courtesy of the Hindus and Arabs, it is true — whereby the symbol depends on its position relative to other symbols. Thus '5' equalled (and equals) '5' when thus written and '50' when placed in front of a '0'. But some of the cities of Iraq used the sexagesimal system. It is for that reason that, in mathematics and chronology, the circle is divided into 360 degrees, the hour into 60 minutes, the minute into 60 seconds, while the day has 24 hours. The ancient Iraqis also knew that the value of π was 3 1/8, whereas the inhabitants of Israel about 1000 BC believed it to be exactly 3 (27). In these matters, the Egyptians learned from their neighbours and altered their systems for their own benefit. They used the decimal system but only that. Units were indicated by strokes and 10s, 100s and 1000s by signs. They multiplied and divided by 2, occasionally by 3, but used hardly any higher table. They used fractions in a primitive way. Their system of so-called 'unit fractions' was also adopted by the Greeks and Romans, and greatly delayed progress in mathematics. On the other hand, the Chinese had a good understanding of fractions, which they were using effectively at the time when their history begins to be separable from folklore (28). The Hindus, who were in touch with China from a very early time, had a more elaborate version and it was from them that Europe, ultimately through Islam, gained the use of the modern fraction, as of other mathematical innovations.

Still, much could be done with Egyptian mathematics. The Great Pyramid of Gizeh, built about 2900 BC, shows the dimensions of the Egyptian mathematical achievement. Its base is a perfect square, the sides run exactly north to south and east to west. All the surfaces have the same slope of 50°, being built of stones so well fitted that it is impossible to insert a blade between them (29).

The Iraqis in 4000 BC, meantime, had made the day when the moon was full, as well as the day of the new moon, a day for religious ritual: thus there were 'moondays' on the 1st or 28th (or 29th) of every month. Later, half 'moondays' also became feast days. But this lunar month does not, unfortunately, coincide with the solar one (the latter is 29½ days). Sumer therefore replaced the lunar calendar with a solar one. That remained inaccurate. For a time, a year of twelve months each of thirty days was used, but every six years there was a thirteenth month, occasionally a fourteenth one. This irregularity was adequate for Iraq, but the Egyptians, desiring greater accuracy, in order to know when the flood of the Nile was going to reach them, had twelve months of thirty days each, plus five extra days. In the end, the Egyptians worked out their calendar by reference not to the rising of the Nile, which was occasionally unreliable, but to Sirius, the Dog Star, which rose once every year at dawn at the same moment. The discrepancy with the true year, as it is recognised now, was slight.

Perhaps the Egyptians' mistakes were due to their belief that the Earth was flat and the sky a table held up by four pillars, while the stars were supposed to revolve round a celestial pole. Also, they worshipped, rather than studied, heavenly movements, while their geometry was based on surfaces and volumes, not on lines (30).

More accurate than either of these two peoples were the Mayas, who, a little later, employed a fulltime priesthood to collect astronomical facts and predict the future by mathematics based on the use of the *Quipu*, an arrangement of knotted strings which enabled them to calculate. The settled Indian societies of old central America all had calendars, but the Mayas had the best one, since they knew that the year was a little more than 365 days. Indeed, the later Mayan calculation of a year of 365.2420 days was closer to the modern evaluation of 365.2422 days than the Gregorian one — which was 365.2425 (31).

Mayan priests owed their influence to their control of the calendar and to their ability to predict everything, from full moons to eclipses. Their temples were established with astronomical considerations in mind: the shrine of Uaxactún, for example, was so laid out that anyone standing on the steps of the largest pyramid could, at the Equinox, see the sun rise in the dead centre of the main temple.

The ancient Iraqi civilisation also devised the first hieroglyphic script, about 3500 BC. This apparently occurred at the city of Uruk and was soon copied elsewhere. Numerals, pictographs and ideographs were inscribed by a sharp reed pen on specially prepared clay tablets. No transaction was regarded as having validity unless it was recorded on tablets. About 1,500 separate signs were used, mostly abstract and mostly still undeciphered. The tablets which can be read record business transactions by the temples and sales of land. One should, however, no doubt beware of thinking that the invention of writing seemed at the time as sensational an event as it may now appear: the illiterate brain is, after all, capable of great feats of memory, of calculation and of wise judgment (32). Also, it may be that some system of accounting, at least, if not a form of writing, antedated the inscriptions at Uruk by several hundred years. It is even possible that writing was actually a development of reckoning (33). By about 3000 BC, at all events, the end of the reed used to inscribe the tablets had begun to be shaped like a wedge, a *cuneus* in Latin — hence the word 'cuneiform'.

The language in which this innovation was first embodied was Sumerian, a difficult tongue, without much relation to others then known. Later, Akaddian became the *lingua franca* of ancient Iraq, despite its 600 written signs, being succeeded later still by Aramaic, the spoken language of a greater number of cities than Akaddian. Aramaic later began to use an alphabet, of twenty-two letters, an idea which apparently was devised by some Semitic people – were they the Jews? – about 2000 BC. A linear form was in use in Crete, and Mycenae, by about 1400 BC in order to express Greek (34).

The Egyptians had by then their own hieroglyphs. Each hieroglyph was with them a separate ideogram and, in the hands of their best scribes, almost a different painting. That continued to be the handwriting of priests for many generations. Soon, a simpler 'hieratic' Egyptian came to be used in secular documents. The Egyptians made no steps, however, towards an alphabet (though pen, ink and papyrus were being used on the Nile from 3000 BC), perhaps since, in the beginning, they only needed (or their priests only wished them) to record the yearly height of the Nile's flooding, the genealogy of Memphis's priests, and the names of kings (35). Papyrus, a reed which grew in the Nile, was, nevertheless, soon in demand throughout the Eastern Mediterranean, because, when the pith of the reed was cut into strips laid across one another, dried and stuck together, a roll of something close to writing paper could be formed. Ink from lamp black was first used upon it (36).

Later on, the Egyptians realised the inconvenience of having a gap between priestly and written language. A 'demotic' tongue was devised (in the fifth century BC). That simply added another layer of language, for both the two previous tongues survived. A subsequent form, Coptic, which is demotic Egyptian with a Greek alphabet, also later had a brief heyday.

Indian writing, during the civilisation of the Indus and much later in the Aryan era, plainly had connections with that of Iraq, and it would be reasonable to assume that it reached India as a result of commerce. But the idea of ideograms came to the Chinese, apparently independently, and apparently first too in the form of signs engraved on scapular bones of sheep, or shells of turtles, as a means of asking questions of heaven. Probably by 1500 BC, the Shang dynasty had a written script of some 5,000 ideograms, though only 1,500 of them are now readable (37). With modifications, this script became a basis of modern Chinese, which has always remained faithful to ideographic, as opposed to alphabetic, script. The Chinese also had figures probably by 1200 BC. Japan, on the other hand, only began to write and read a script which was modelled on an offshoot of Chinese, though based on a separate language, about 400–500 AD.

In the Americas, writing came later still. Indeed, there was no real writing before 1492, though the Mayas had a few numbers and hieroglyphs which seem only to indicate dates. As yet, the few surviving Maya inscriptions have been incompletely translated (38). The Aztecs had only a few curious and also still unread hieroglyphs.

An alphabet, once acquired, did not necessarily survive conquest: when Homer spoke of a letter being entrusted to a traveller, writing was a dim memory in Greece. The idea, known in Mycenae, had died out. Thus, Dr John Chadwick points out, Homer described it as something 'almost magical' (39). Like the Phoenicians (who carried the alphabet of twenty-two letters back to them), the Greeks of the classical age began by writing from right to left but, when they developed the simpler Ionic script, they were already writing from left to right (40). From Greece, the alphabet was taken to the Etruscans in Italy and thence passed to the Latins. By then writing was being used to tell stories as well as merely to render accounts of what was owing. In 2100 BC, the poem of Gilgamesh, King of Uruk, was written down. A novel is believed to have been written by Simibet, in Egypt, not much later. Mythological poems of ancient Phoenicia date perhaps from 1400 BC, while the song of Deborah apparently dates from about 1150 BC. The biographies of David and Saul, included in the later biblical Book of Samuel, are held to be of much the same date. A thousand years before Christ, therefore, the long history of written literature, and even the history of history itself, had begun.

5

Early Dealings Between Peoples

These early settled agricultural city monarchies were, from a very early stage indeed, in touch with each other through commerce, and through war.

Stone was perhaps traded in some countries before anything else. Thus many axes have come to light at sites far away from where the stone of which they were made derives (1). On the other hand, the tribes needing, for example, Cornish or Cumbrian stone perhaps merely went to seize it. Was salt the 'primordial narcotic' and sought by agricultural man from the very beginning? Perhaps, since the Chinese began taking brine from deep wells in Szechwan from the earliest days of settled life (2). The most important metal traded in ancient Iraq in the beginning was obsidian, a dark, volcanic, rock-like bottle glass carried from the mountains of Asia Minor by river. It was used (as by the Mayas in Yucatan) for knives or spearheads, before copper was mined for the same purpose. The traders might best be described as pedlars. Malachite and turquoise were desired for decoration. Baskets, carpets, and other textiles were sold before 3000 BC along the Euphrates and by then, commerce had begun between Iraq and Egypt. Sargon of Agade in Iraq spoke of ships full of goods being moored outside his capital, in 2370 BC (3). A caravan route employing 200 donkeys, travelling twelve to fifteen hours a day, was soon in existence between Armenia and all the cities of Iraq.

This commerce, and comparable trade with Africa, to begin with, was financed by Iraqi temples, but private capitalists, seeking a profit, were also involved from the very earliest times, establishing a system of exchange which has never really ended. Since the State or the priesthood controlled much of the commerce – for example, the iron exported by the Hittites was a royal monopoly – these commercial enterprises can hardly be said to have constituted a free economy (4). But only rarely has the State been completely inactive in commercial enterprise and, if some peoples, such as the Hittites (and the Mycenean Greeks), left their trade to be organised by officials, many Iraqi merchants were really entrepreneurs buying private estates with their profits, and even lending money – for a type of currency, in the form of silver bars or rings, was already in being, in the Near East, as it was in the form of cowrie shells, in China (5).

Sales of slaves, food, wine, wool, metals and bricks occurred in Iraq, probably on the quayside (since so much of the trade was river-borne). As the generations passed, political control in Iraq passed from Ur to Sumer, from Sumer to Assur, from Assur to Nineveh, from Nineveh to Babylon, but trade continued regardless, the ships being improved, the donkey caravans becoming slowly better organised. Sometimes trade caused wars, it is true, but though the Bible recalls the military achievements of Tiglath Pileser and Shalmaneser, it somewhat neglects the trade which brought them cotton from India, silver from Cilicia, and which may have caused the wars (6). Assyrian merchants had, for example, established their own quarters in numerous cities of Turkey by 1950 BC, regulating the traffic of copper, ensuring the regular departure of the caravans, making their Akkadian tongue a *lingua franca* throughout the Middle East, and using Akkadian cuneiform to record transactions (7).

Egypt was more favoured agriculturally than were the cities of Iraq, and limestone was available from the mountains nearby for its lavish building schemes (including the Pyramids). But some imports were sought, all the same; particularly timber. Egypt went to Byblos in Syria for trees, to Lebanon for cedar, later to Crete for olive oil, and, in exchange, sold salted fish, flax and papyrus, ox hide and rope, alabaster and lentils — and above all gold, a state monopoly (8).

For by this time mines, smelted and hammered metals, had already begun to affect commerce, agriculture and war.

Metallurgy began to play a part in commerce and war at an extremely early date. Gold, for example, was probably being worked in Egypt before 4000 BC (9) as was copper probably as early as 6000 BC in much the same place or region, and at much the same time, as pottery was initiated.

Metal has usually to be separated from those other elements with which it is organically combined. That was usually done, to begin with, by burning charcoal at a high temperature in a furnace in which the right circumstances were achieved for, first, reducing the metals to their elementary state and, second, achieving a chemical reaction in order to secure the separation of all extraneous matter and metals not required. Metal came soon to be worked into objects, either by shaping it with the anvil, perhaps heating it if it was needed to be soft; or melting it, so that it could be poured molten into a mould, and thus given a rough shape to be finished again with a hammer. These processes were first learned in Asia Minor between 6000 and 4000 BC, before writing, that is, and long before the domestication of the horse.

As suggested above, the first metal to be mined, smelted and then traded was copper. By 4000 BC, smelting was being carried on in the

Balkans and, by 2500 BC, in Spain and the Aegean (10). These early coppersmiths used stone tools, pursuing a vein of ore horizontally into the
rock for many yards. Copper much improved the quality of all tools
both for mining itself and for agriculture. In the great days of Babylon,
about 2000 BC, copper was being carried there from Africa and parts of
Asia in great quantities (11). By 1500 BC, the coppersmiths, perhaps by
accident, had discovered that if, while copper is being melted, molten
tin, or lead, or antimony is poured in, the ensuing mixture, bronze, will
be harder than, and, above all, remain sharp longer than, stone (12).

Bronze greatly improved both tools of agriculture and weapons in
war, and the minute supplies of tin possessed by Asia Minor were, in
consequence, for many years regarded as fifty times more desirable
than silver. The prayer of the wife of the first great Bolivian tin miner,
Patino, 'Lord, may it be tin not silver' when a seam was discovered in
the nineteenth century AD, was perhaps foreshadowed in 1500 BC (13).
Tin was soon also discovered in northern Europe and exported to
Babylon from there. (Flints from Britain also had a considerable market,
dug up from thirty-foot mines between 3000 and 2000 BC.) Iron was
being forged by 2500 BC, also in Asia Minor (14). That final elimination
of all waste which enables iron to become steel, with its sharper edge
and greater durability, was embarked upon there too about 1400 BC
(15).

Among the founders of metallurgy, the Egyptians should not be forgotten. They had no iron, no copper and no tin but they did have gold
and, from the earliest days of the united kingdom, the goldsmiths of
Memphis (a famous clan of dwarfs), the scribes who weighed their products, the bellowsmen who heated the open fires through pottery
pipes, the men who poured the liquid gold into moulds or hammered it
on the anvil — were the exporters-in-chief of ancient Egypt even if they
were not essential in the economy (16). The Egyptian state was strong
and settled, commerce was an affair of state and, therefore, both less
effective and more cautious than the trade of Babylon. It was perhaps
that which, in the end, made it easy for Greek merchants, following in
the steps of the Phoenicians, and living like the Phoenicians in ghettoes
outside the ports, to capture the trade of Egypt, as they later captured
that of much of the Eastern Mediterranean by the time of Herodotus.

These metallurgical developments reached India and China, through
traders, within a few hundred years of their achievement in the Near
East. There was much bronze in China by 1800 BC, for example, but
used only, it seems, for war and ritual, not agriculture. Iron-working
has also been, for a long time, associated with the disintegration of the
early Chou dynasty about 500 BC (17).

Among the earliest of commodities exchanged for profit there were
also slaves. It may very well be that slavery, like politics, anticipated
agriculture. But the very earliest societies seem, in fact, not to have

relied greatly on slave labour. More important in such societies was the forced labour demanded of the people themselves. Thus neither the economy of the earliest days of Iraq nor that of China employed slaves on a large scale. But, though slaves were always fairly rare in China, that ceased to be so in the Near East by about 2000 BC at latest. By then, Egypt, for example, was importing huge numbers from 'Nubia' in the south and even re-exporting them to Iraq. Thenceforth, most references in antiquity to agriculture or large-scale building in antiquity must imply the employment of slaves. The King's Chamber in the Great Pyramid of Gizeh (2900 BC) was roofed by 56 slabs of stone, each weighing 54 tons. Slaves in thousands were responsible for moving them, as they were for many of the other great works of ancient Egypt which survive to puzzle, as well as to impress, the visitor with their monumental grandeur. Equally, long before that, slaves had begun to be imported to Iraqi cities as regular objects of commerce, and so a process began which, in one form or another, has continued ever since. Female slaves in particular were sought for work in Iraqi temple-spinning workshops. Soon, slaves who had, for a time, all been the property of the State, could be bought by private persons. Eventually, many households in Iraq had three slaves each (18). That pattern was copied elsewhere.

Most of such slaves began as prisoners of war, or were slave girls procured by raids into the hills from among nomads, but were subsequently quite often bred in captivity. People also became slaves because of debt or hunger, or were sold as children by poor parents. Sometimes too, people might be seized by creditors to become slaves. Even on occasion, they might sell themselves. Crimes were sometimes punished by enslavement.

These early slaves were rarely members of an unbreakable caste, for they could often work their way to freedom. A free woman might marry a slave; and slaves could acquire property. Slavery did much to mingle the races, as has happened throughout history.

Contact between all these ancient peoples also came from war, as well as from commerce, and war, from the beginning, played a decisive part in establishing them. The village states of Iraq came into being when several tribes wished jointly to guarantee their defence as well as their production of food. Doubtless that was so in Egypt too. The unification of both (never properly assured in Iraq) was secured by force and, in Egypt, the fighting (about 3000 BC) is thought to have lasted for many generations.

Antler and stone axes had assisted hunting tribes against each other, as well as against animals and trees. Bows and arrows, like slings and lances, preceded the sowing of the first wheat seed by the first farmer. Afterwards, copper axes were used for war at least as soon as they were used against scrub oak and wild acacia. By 3000 BC, war had, indeed, assumed an almost familiar shape. Iraqi kings organised their men in the form of a phalanx, while the Egyptians preferred the horde, relying on pastoral tribes near them to do most of the serious fighting on their behalf. In Egyptian practice, a day would be fixed for the battle rather as if it were a lawsuit, the fighting would be postponed if the enemy were not ready, and it was formally accepted that the gods would give victory to the better army. Such forms were sometimes followed in ancient China and in the European Middle Ages. But how to apportion the claims of a good army, or a good weapon, was as hard then as at any later time. Thus the long bow and arrow, introduced from central Asia, is held to have given the Semites of Akkad their victory about 2500 BC over the lance-carrying soldiers of Sumer, while the triangular bow, helmet and coat of mail are regarded as having helped them to defeat Egypt about 1200 (19). The horse and two-wheeled chariot allegedly developed by the Milani, a tribe of Asia Minor, were used to decisive effect by the Hittites and Kassites, who conquered Iraq about 1500 BC. Subsequently, the Assyrian empire at its grandest depended on the battering ram and the siege engines, later perfected by Rome, as well as on a method of organisation whereby every able-bodied man knew that he was liable to be called up to serve, and whereby engineers, officers and shock troops each knew their allotted tasks as if they constituted regular professions. Later, Babylonian kings had huge standing armies which fought continuously for years. Organisation, technology, courage and good leadership, as much as good luck, contributed to victories then as now. The Hittites, for example, won victories for many years largely because of their possession of iron weapons, the secret of which the royal smiths kept to themselves for as long as they could. In the end, they collapsed, but apparently not at the hands of people with a superior technology. Bronze weapons' superiority over those of copper and stone was great, perhaps comparable to the advantage given by gunpowder. Iron and steel followed. But even now none will say that the victories of the numerous sea-raiders which caused such upheavals in the Mediterranean about 1200 BC were due primarily to the use of special weapons.

The importance of war in early history is shown by the fact that the epics of almost every country deal with a conflict of one sort or another. The longest poem in the world, for example, the Hindu *Mahabharata* 'revolves round the famous struggle at Murukshetra between the Kauravas and the Pandavas over land rights and is set in the fertile and strategic region north of Delhi'. In this and every other epic, the story told is essentially how the foundations of the kingdom concerned were established by war and heroism by legendary warriors. The end is usually happy: 'the Pandavas ruled long and peacefully. They finally renounced the kingdom . . . and went to the city of the Gods in the Himalayas,' (20).

6

The History of the Innovators

Of the early major innovating societies, a stable despotism was first established in China. Though not always able to resist conquest, China was as a rule able to absorb conquerors. Under the Han dynasty, after 202 BC, Chinese landowners consolidated their claims on the peasants, as the State did upon the landowners who were really bureaucrats, but Confucianism* restrained them from the systematic misuse of power. Hence a political structure which enabled the monarchy in China to expand throughout the valley of the Yellow River, and then south to the Yangtze. Neither landlord nor tax official under the Han dynasty demanded so much from the peasant that he could not survive. The essence of the Chinese method of agriculture was a dependence on the methodical cultivation of a single crop, rice; a fixed system of water supply; and strong defences, such as the Great Wall of the third century BC, behind which a network of roads and canals could be constructed to ensure good rice crops and the swift carriage of imperial orders. Egypt survived as an independent state till its conquest by Persia in 525 BC but, after some vicissitudes, continued recognisable as the old Egypt till it fell to Rome in 30 BC. Thereafter, Egypt was merely the richest part of the Roman Empire, but its method of despotism contributed a great deal of the style to the Empire which was established by Augustus on the ruins of the old city republic. It also marked the history of Africa indelibly: the Sudanese principality of Kush, for example, with its capital at Meroe, copied Egypt's political system. Egypt continued to act as an example to all black monarchies in Africa and, till the first century AD, carried on a vigorous trade with the Mediterranean world. Other African monarchies copied it in turn and others them, the torch of the Pharaohs thus being passed on continuously: even perhaps by the same families, since it has been suggested that the royal family of Kush, themselves descendants of Egyptian rulers, established a new government, after the fall of their original fief, in the region between Lake Chad and the Nile.

The cities of Iraq, meanwhile, became the basis for the Assyrian and

* See below, page 137.

41

Babylonian Empires before being conquered by Persia in 539 BC. That region remained far the richest part of the Persian Empire, which itself survived till conquered by Alexander in 333 BC at the battle of Gaugamela. That battle handed over most of the Near East to European rulers till the coming of the Arabs in the seventh century AD, for whom the region survived also as a granary and, indeed, as a centre of government for many generations, until the depleted irrigation works were allowed to fall in at the time of the Mongol invasions in the thirteenth century. The civilisation of the Indus valley, meantime, spreading a thousand miles along the river and several hundred on either side, particularly along the coast, became the focus for a congeries of Indian monarchies established in imitation of it, along other rivers. From the start, in what Mortimer Wheeler called its 'exacting and minatory environment', it traded, thereby acting as an essential geographical link with the West and China (1). True, the 'Aryan' invaders who descended upon India about 1500 BC, as they did upon Greece and Asia Minor, emerging from pasture lands near the Caspian Sea which they had exhausted, were ethnically different from those of the ancient dwellers in the Indus civilisation. But though the manner of their victory led to the unusual system of segregation known as 'castes', the survival of several gods and goddesses from the Indus valley suggests that the Aryans were probably half absorbed by those whom they conquered. This in turn led to the establishment of tribal monarchies, which were gradually institutionalised to form the basis of ancient Indian political society, whose unique feature, however, remained the castes which, in the words of a modern Indian historian, Romila Thapar, 'localised many of the functions which would normally be associated with a truly oriental despotism' (2). The subsequent political history of India is partly the history of dynastic power; partly that of village councils and guilds; and partly that of castes and how they interacted. But, at all events, by the fourth or third century BC these different political manifestations had been overtaken by the establishment of imperial authorities which, under the Mauryas or the Moguls, lasted in one way or another, feebly or forcibly, until the Europeans came.

As for the Mayas in Yucatan, their ancient civilisation based on the calendar and the irrigation ditch continued in, latterly, a degraded form until the fifteenth century. They did not, however, quickly evolve a unified empire and remained an agglomeration of city states comparable to those of the early days of Iraq.

Outside these founding civilisations, as it were, many peoples sought successfully to emulate the forerunners. Most of them also strove to achieve predictability of crops by insisting on despotic monarchies whose ambitions were to plan the economy with great care. But in the wet northern regions of both Europe and Asia, as in the wet southern ones of Africa and South America, where limited agriculture could be organised without elaborate hydraulic arrangements, many of the customary freedoms and much of the mobility within hunting tribes survived — and even survived a settled agriculture.

However agriculture was organised, no serious change in the way of living of these peoples and their neighbours who imitated them occurred till after 1700 AD. Until then, a majority in every settled community were concerned with tillage. The opportunities for barter and exchange were exceptional. They arose primarily in connection with the exploitation of natural products of woodlands and wastes. In that respect, 'the needs of most people were indeed equal', as the Orwins* put it (3). The kings, noblemen, courtiers, priests of this religion or that, knights, artists and craftsmen, were a small minority, all supported by workers on the land (4). The men who made history were, Gibbon says, enabled to survive by eating the produce which was 'the result of the patient toil of the husbandmen' (5). The fields, which produced these fruits so successfully over so many generations, were literally the work of men's hands. Even the fields of Europe represent the subjugation of Nature by men after a long struggle 'often with inadequate weapons, and at a cost impossible to measure', again in the words of the Orwins (6). The pioneering process of clearing the land by girdling, cutting and burning trees, the planting of corn amid the stumps of dead trees, was still a major endeavour in the nineteenth century AD (7). So was the business of turning treeless prairie into wheat fields (8). The history especially of Rome was an elaboration on the theme of how the minority who lived in towns fed themselves by the labour of the great majority who did not.

Change was modest. The Egyptian priests of the sun might not have found themselves immediately at home at the court of the Sun King, Louis XIV, nor among the Inca worshippers of the sun conquered by Pizarro, but they would nevertheless have recognised, in those comparatively modern countries, the absolute dominance of religion, as well as the unquestioned territorial and agricultural basis of the absolute hereditary monarchy. True, such priests would have been baffled by the change towards mystical, as well as intellectually inquisitive, religion which occurred about 500 BC (leading to Zoroastrianism, Buddhism, Confucianism, the Eleusinian mysteries, and Christianity) and perhaps would have been astonished at the ease with which Jehovah, the god of the Jews, had inspired an international religion (though not one recognised by Jews) long after Moses had led his band of followers out of Egypt. But they would have been at home with the plough, the sickle, and the ox, as well as the wheat, barley and fruit whose cultivation occupied the majority of men in 1800 AD as in 1800 BC; as with the vast peas-

---

* C. S. and C.S. Orwin, authors of *The Open Fields*, a great work of historical investigation into agricultural economics.

antry, which still in 1800 AD constituted between 80% and 95% of the population even of Europe (9). They would have recognised the roles of the great estate and the small farmer, the tenant and the landless labourer; the vineyards and the wine; and, though the plough would have differed a little from the one with which they were familiar, they would perhaps have understood more than we would today a society in which 'agriculture, in the great majority of the provinces . . . may be considered a huge factory for the manufacture of corn' in the words of the commissaries of the provincial assembly of Orléanais in 1789. They would, too, have recognised a world in which little happened: 'from the beginning of the sixteenth century, agricultural life in the province of Córdoba was a slow, sulky life, without accidents, without emotions, a life without history,' as Díaz del Moral, a historian of Spanish anarchism, put it.

Furthermore, it seems evident that many of those changes that there were in these agricultural societies continued to be caused, like the opportunity for the beginning of agriculture itself, primarily by natural phenomena or by climate. The wet warm climate of the Ganges always had a pervasive effect on Indian history (10), enabling the establishment, on the large plain, of strong, unitary kingdoms (11). In Spain, only 40% of the soil is cultivable: the rest mountainous or barren. So the 'cruel winters and the burning summers,' wrote Claudio Sánchez Albornoz, '. . . uneven and uncertain rains, limited fertility of the majority of the soil . . . have hardened the . . . peasantry forced to suffer the inclemency . . . during millennia' (12). The lack of a frontier has been the deciding feature of Russian history: indeed, 'Russia *is* the frontier', wrote Tibor Szamuely (13). Russian farmers must confine livestock indoors two months longer than European farmers; and the network of navigable waterways, poor soil in the north, vagaries of rainfall (heaviest where it does least good), as well as the belt of fertile black earth (250 million acres), deriving from humus (vegetable mould) have been the main motors of Russian history: the black earth area has always produced 70% of Russian wheat, though, over the course of its recorded history, Russia has averaged one bad harvest out of every three (14). The 'barbarian' invasions of the Roman Empire in the third and fourth centuries AD derived, Joseph Needham speculated, from the 'progressive or cyclical dessication' of the Gobi and steppe regions (15).

Some too have alleged that declining rainfall about 250 BC was the explanation for the end of the rural simplicity (and discipline!) which characterised the life of early Rome. Since there was not enough rain to maintain an adequate flow of water in the rivers, pools and marshes were formed which became breeding grounds for mosquitoes. They in turn brought malaria. When the rain came again, in the late second century, the character of the countryside had already been changed, and the vine and olive had been introduced into the best fields of Italy, thereby causing Rome to depend on imports of corn for her bread — hence the grain imported, the trade from Egypt, with its despotic tradition, the free loaves, the crises of the last hundred years of the Republic, and the establishment of the Principate. The clarity of Greek light obviously influenced Greek art, and explains the clarity of Greek philosophy in ways which historians who primarily interest themselves in the 'economic and social forces which underlie the history of peoples' (16) may overlook. The fourteenth century AD in Europe saw the beginning of a cold wet period, caused by a small advance of the glaciers. Heavy rain ruined innumerable harvests and wrecked the English vineyards of the early Middle Ages (17), and fishing replaced agriculture as the chief economic activity of northern countries such as Scandinavia and Iceland (18). Some have called the centuries after the fourteenth the 'little ice age'. The first English economic historian, Thorold Rogers, 'never noticed, in any earlier century, such a continuity of dearth as from 1630 to 1637, from 1646 to 1651, from 1658 to 1661, and from 1693 to 1699, in each case inclusive' (19). The winters of 1709 and 1740 were arctic in intensity in Europe, and were followed by very cold springs and summers: Saint Simon paints a chill picture of Louis XIV's courtiers pressing their noses to the windows of the Château at Versailles, shivering, waiting for the news, which they rightly suspected of being bad, from the battle of Malplaquet (20). In 1316, 1675, and 1816, Le Roy Ladurie wrote, 'all Europe spent the summer round the fire' (21). Doubtless there were compensations. Long cold winters encouraged more people than just the men of Iceland to stay at home and read, or than just the Scots to listen to family prayers: 'Snow and cold weather can . . . help to explain the high degree of literacy in Alpine populations', says Professor Cipolla (22). The hailstorm of July 13, 1788, devastated the harvest of that year in France, helping to cause the famous shortages of 1789 (23); and the earthquake of 1756 in Lisbon caused men to question the idea of progress. 1816 was perhaps the worst summer ever recorded in northern Europe: there was frost in July. There was scarcely a harvest at all. The consequence was famine, the last major such event in the northern hemisphere until the government-inspired famine of Russia in the 1930s (24).

About some natural occurrences or climatic changes there will always be speculation. Were the lake villages of central Europe of 500 BC built because of the rise of the lakes themselves, and was that rise itself the result of the well known cold spell of that era? And was the decline of the Maya civilisation explicable by changes in the weather (25)? Did the earthquake on Thera about 1500 BC really smash the entire Minoan fleet and thus also the 'first empire which built its fortune on the waves'; or was it perhaps some other natural disaster? Did the first civilisation of the Indus valley collapse because of an excessive flood from the great river, a failure in hydraulic arrangement which China, Egypt, Babylon and the Mayas managed to prevent?

These speculations border on tautology. Civilisation began in river valleys. Both Egypt and Babylon depended on seasonal floods to bring back fresh soil, to irrigate and to fertilise the land. Rivers were everywhere, till the age of railways, the motors of both commerce and (through the waterwheel) industry. The modern industrial age even began with the creation of false rivers: canals. Nor is a geographical explanation of history, such as was favoured by Montesquieu (and more recently, indirectly by Fernand Braudel) (26) particularly new: in the fifth century BC one Greek follower of Hippocrates attributed the alleged mildness of Asiatics to the tamer conditions in which they lived, and the capacities for endurance and high spirits of Europeans to their hard struggle for existence (27). Madame Curie, on return from a visit to Spain, said that, if she had been born in Andalusia, she would never have invented radium (28), a judgement which overlooked the frequently unpromising atmosphere for medical research in Madame Curie's own birthplace, Warsaw. Two points can perhaps be made: first, naturally, weather has had a greater effect in countries which have, on the whole, depended on rainfall and less on those which have had to establish hydraulic administrations; second, as many have been stimulated to great achievement by the idiosyncrasies or harshnesses of geography as have been bowed down by them. The Attic Greeks are a good example of this. Who, too, would have thought it likely that so many achievements of civilisation were begun in a desert between two rivers, with a hot climate, where there was no building stone, no minerals, and no timber (save palm trees)? Yet Sumer and Babylon triumphed over these deficiencies because the soil was fertile, because there was water for irrigation if only that could be organised, and because the rivers gave access to valuable stone and metals in remote highlands. Israel, Rome, Venice and the Netherlands as well as Athens and Sumer, responded to natural deficiencies with resource. A master-key to the understanding of history is not so easily, nor so early, available.

BOOK II

The Age of Agriculture

'The doctrine that our remote ancestors had simple law dies hard. Too often, we suppose that, could we get back to the beginning, we should find that all was intelligible, and we should then be able to watch the process whereby simple ideas were smothered by technicalities. But it is not so. Simplicity is the outcome of technical subtlety — it is the goal, not the starting point. As we go backwards, the familiar outlines become blurred: the ideas become fluid and, instead of the simple, we find the indefinite.'

(F. W. Maitland, *Domesday Book and Beyond*).

'We always get back to the same questions: who was talking about gear wheels in −1st century Bactria? Did the Roman-Syrian merchant Chin Lun who visited China in +226 happen to take an interest in cartography . . . ?'

Joseph Needham, *Science & Civilisation in China*

During the ten thousand years between the birth of agriculture and the industrial revolution, the three most important changes were first, an increase in the population of the world; second, an increase in the acreage of land placed under the plough; and third, the growth of a number of communities in which it was accepted that the individual had rights as well as duties.

The first two of these changes form the frame for a consideration of the developments in the history of agriculture. One should never, however, overestimate the amount of land cultivated.* Even in 1870, only a quarter of the acreage of so advanced a country as the German Empire was under the plough (1). Similarly, the mind's eye, when looking at the past, should not imagine a countryside of cultivated prairies. Rather should it imagine a field cut out on high scrubland or perhaps from out of a forest, or indeed a group of small fields,

---

* *A population of 730 million (such as the world had in 1750) would perhaps need about 1,200 billion acres to support it. (This does not take into account the 'rice' population (2).)*

possibly protected by some kind of defensive structure, against bandits or marauders, as was the case in Africa until recently.

The third change occurred primarily among certain European peoples which depended on rainfall to water their crops, in cities, and among people influenced by Greek thought and by Christianity.

7

Population and its Increase

The best estimate of the numbers of the 'very rare food-gathering biped' that man seemed to be in about 2 million BC (1) is the brave one of 100,000 (2). At the birth of settled agriculture, about 10000 BC or 8000 BC, there were perhaps already 5 or 10 million people in the world (3). The figure might have been 100 million at the time of the first dynasty in Egypt (4), in 3000 BC, and it then perhaps rose to 250 million by the time of the birth of Christ (5) and to 500 million about 1500 AD (6). In 1750, when the age of industry began, the population of the world was probably a little under 750 million (7).

None of these figures can be expected to be at all accurate. But the population of the world was certainly higher in the eighteenth century than it had ever been before, and the most recent increase had been the fastest. In 2 million BC, the world's population was something like the size of a single English parliamentary constituency; that at the time of the birth of agriculture, something like that of London about 1980 AD; and, in the time of Christ, something comparable to the present population of Russia. In 1750 AD, the world's population was still less than the number of people who now live in the single state of China.

The population of the world has not grown to these levels by a steady process. There have been setbacks. The best known of these is what happened in the New World after the arrival of the Spaniards in 1492. Mexico had before then a population of about 25 million. That population fell to 6 million by 1548 and, by the end of the century, was only 1,350,000, of whom 100,000 were Spaniards (8). Mexico's population only recovered to its levels of 1492 in the mid-twentieth century (9). Probably the population of Peru began to fall before the Spaniards conquered it, since smallpox preceded Pizarro there (10). On a longer time-scale, the history of Egypt is a better example of irregularity: the population at the time of the Middle Kingdom (1991−1570 BC) was 7 to 8 million, much the same as it was in 150 AD (11). It fell to 3 million by 550 AD (12) and was less than 2½ million between 1600 and 1800 (13). It had probably got back to 7 million by the time of the British occupation in 1882 and is perhaps now 40 million (14). China experienced a similar decline and recovery, on a larger scale, between the first century and the sixteenth century AD.

Most of the great countries of the past about which conventional history is constructed had what would now seem small populations, at the time of their greatness, comparable to that of Scotland in 1980. Iraq perhaps had 4 to 5 million in 2000 BC, Egypt (as noticed above) 7 to 8 million at that time. Greece in the fifth century BC had perhaps 2 million, and Rome, in Caesar's day, a maximum of a million (15). Germany had 4 million at the time of Otto the Great, France 5 million under Charlemagne (16). Italy had anything between 5 and 10 million during the lifetime of Leonardo (17); Spain, 7 million under Ferdinand and Isabella (18); and England had 3 million under Elizabeth I (19) and nearly 8 million at what seems to have been its zenith, in the eighteenth century (20).

The populations of the East, though small by modern standards, were always larger: India perhaps had a population of 100 to 140 million in 300 BC, China nearly 60 million in the first century AD (21). The comparative size of those populations, and the relative inability of the people concerned to create anything in the way of free institutions, shows the folly of supposing that large numbers are a benefit in themselves.

Often too, peoples which have been invaded have attributed their ill luck to the supposed influx of a vast number of enemies. In that way did the Mediterranean peoples explain their defeat at the hands of the Celts and Germans. The romanised Germans of Charlemagne's time said the same of the Vikings. Their grandchildren spoke thus of the Hungarians. In most cases, such expeditions were, however, not caused by 'pressure of population'. They were mounted by 'small numbers of warriors seeking booty', as Marc Bloch put it (22).

The question which needs to be answered is: why did not the population of the world increase faster? At, for instance, the rate that it is increasing in the twentieth century? After all, the world's population may have been 250 million in 1 AD. If so, it took 1500 years to double. But it rose from 500 to 1000 million between 1500 and about 1825. It doubled again between 1825 and 1925; and yet again, between 1925 and 1976, from 2000 million to 4000 million.

The first thing to be said is that the expectation of life did not rise greatly between the era of Neanderthal man and the eighteenth century AD. It was probably 29 years in the stone age (23), and perhaps did well to average between 25 to 30 between 1700 and 1750 (24).* England

---

*The expectation of life for anyone who had already reached 30 years in the seventeenth and eighteenth centuries seems to have been about 22 to 26 years, in England, which meant a man's death coincided, as Lawrence Stone pointed out, with the marriage of his eldest son (perhaps making an inverse causal relation between the adult mortality and the age of marriage).

between, say, 1300 and 1750 was apparently exceptional in having an average often rising to 35 years (25). In comparison, in the late 1970s, the expectation of life was believed to be 71 in Europe, 62 in Latin America, 56 in Asia and 48 in Africa (26). Asia, Africa and Latin America thus have a life expectation a third higher than that of Europe in the eighteenth century. Sweden is today apparently the nation with the highest expectancy of life (75 years): Guinea the lowest (27 years) — that is, below that of Neanderthal man (27).

A rise in the birth rate, not a fall in the death rate, however, seems to have been the immediate cause of the rise of the population during the eighteenth century at least, and perhaps that was usually the case before.* In the sixteenth and seventeenth centuries, a birth rate of 35 per 1000 was normal in Europe (28). In the eighteenth century, that rose almost everywhere. By 1800, most European countries had a birth rate of 40 per 1000 (France was 33 in 1802, Russia over 50 in the 1860s). The highest figures for birth rates in recorded series for European countries all occur at different times: Austria being 43 per 1000 in 1820, Germany averaging 40 between 1872—79, Britain reaching 36 in 1878 and Italy reaching 39 in 1836 (29). Now these figures are often exceeded in the 'Third World' today. Few African countries have a birth rate under 40 per 1000. The average Latin American birth rate is 38 to 40 per 1000, while India, Indonesia and China average respectively 43, 48 and 33 (30).

We need to speculate on why these high figures for birth rates began to be achieved in the eighteenth century. Was it the coming of better medicine, or some other changes in the character of disease? A better climate and hence, for that reason, better food? An end of civil wars and other improved arrangements for public order? Or other factors, contributing to a revival of optimism? In the nineteenth century (figures for earlier times are not reliable), the highest rates of birth coincide with times of high self-confidence in the country concerned: France had its highest birth rate in the year of the Peace of Amiens, in 1802; Germany, in the year immediately after the formation of the Empire, in 1871; Russia, in the year of the emancipation of the serfs; Italy, at the time of reunification; and so on. The same was true of other countries in the twentieth century (31).

From these modern instances, it is necessary to go back further and ask again, what, in the remote past prevented the birth rate from being higher? First of all, there were numerous attempts in the past to limit births by one form or other of contraception. For example, there were clear contraceptive benefits in the requirements of Lamaist Buddhism that every family should contribute a son to one of the great monasteries. Tibet also practised for many hundreds of years a system of polyandry which also restricted births (32). The Chinese employed

*See below, page 230.

abortion and infanticide before Christ, and evidently sought, if they did not achieve, a contraceptive pill in the seventh century AD. Ancient Egypt, concerned to maintain the family, also wished to keep the population stable. Paste made from crocodile dung used as a pessary, honey and natron (a carbonate of soda) placed in the vagina, medicated tampons of lint dressed with tips of acacia were all used in the seventeenth or sixteenth centuries BC. Soranus of Ephesus, in the second century BC, discussed different methods of contraception, including recommendation of 'abstention from coitus at times which we have indicated' (33). It should thus be evident that it is foolish to suppose that the idea of contraception as such is a modern one.

It seems obvious, also, that many families throughout the world, despite the Church, the King, the hope of having young people to look after the old, and the need of hands in the harvest, limited their families by, for example, *coitus interruptus*, postponement of marriage, abstinence, abortion and infanticide (34). Henri II's law shows that abortion must have been sufficiently practised for it to be legislated against (35).* There were doubtless also many who would have liked to have said to their sons-in-law what Madame de Sévigné, in the seventeenth century, said to hers: 'Listen to me, son-in-law, if, after this boy's birth, you do not give my daughter a rest, I shall assume you do not love her [and] . . . take her away from you. Do you think that I gave her to you to be killed?' When the son-in-law obeyed, she wondered: 'Do I owe this to his temperance or to his real affection?' (36). Careful investigation of families in the days of the Renaissance has shown that fewer families had a large number of children than is often believed. After all, the age of agriculture was an age of peasants who, at a certain stage, have a greater inducement to limit children, in order to avoid the division of properties than to produce them to work the land (37). In France, by the eighteenth century, children were also already competitors with other luxuries which were then available. Perhaps women's desire to keep their figures, in an aesthetically aware society, played its part. Perhaps that had been the case in Egypt, Greece and Rome before. The use of wet nurses in the first place shows that maternity was not chic.

No doubt *coitus interruptus* was the most common method of contraception used, since no foreign body put into the uterus could then have been hygienic — even though hygiene was not recognised. Since this practice is held to require self-control, the early decline in the rate of French growth of population has been attributed to greater self-control

*Henri II of France insisted on *'déclarations de grossesse '* (that being tantamount to saying that the government wished the child to be born), and the parishes in England were ordered to collect vital statistics by Thomas Cromwell in 1538, in order to establish information about descent needed to maintain rights of inheritance firmly (38). But that system was not thoroughly maintained and it was not until the nineteenth century that it could be said to be so: a good example of the length of time that it often takes human societies to implement ideas even when they know them to be good ones.

among the French (39). French historians, however, doubt that: *'L'unique problème est celui du "pourquoi" et non celui du "comment",'* wrote Pierre Chaunu*, *'parce que le "comment" les singes anthropomorphiques le connaissent . . . et les sociétés primitives sont celles qu'ont été les plus efficaces . . . les recherches sous ma direction en Normandie montrent que la diffusion d'un certain malthusianisme latent dans les campagnes Normands se situe . . . dès 1730—40 . . . il s'agit d'un problème de motivation, et non pas de téchnique'* (40). Such devices as there were seem indeed to have been more used against disease than against conception.

But probably the most obvious way in which population was limited in the past is illustrated by the history of infant mortality. Statistics will, doubtless, never be found which explain this accurately for the remoter past. The main points to notice, however, are firstly, that, before the eighteenth century, there was never any alternative to breast feeding and, second, that there was no knowledge of the desirability of hygiene. Mothers and nurses, therefore, effectively poisoned children in thousands. Some knowledge of what happened can be gleaned from the experience of the eighteenth century itself.

Where possible, the rich then were in the habit, in Western Europe as elsewhere, of turning over their babies to wet nurses. That admittedly necessitated, in the families of the upper class, much care in the choice of a wet nurse, since it was thought that a child's character would thereby be influenced (41). Nevertheless, many wet nurses were inadequate. Babies were passed from one to another, and then, in the end, were often distressed to return to the real mother: 'who has not seen these banished children?' asked Cobbett, 'when brought and put into the arms of their mother, screaming to get from them and stretching out their little hands to get back to the arms of their nurse?' (42). As for the poor, whenever they could, they turned over their unwanted children, legitimate or illegitimate, to foundling hospitals, to which, even in 1750 — perhaps particularly in 1750 — thousands of children were sent. On the eve of the French Revolution, 40% of births in France were believed to be *enfants trouvés*. A majority of such children died. An American historian, William Langer, commenting on these events of only 150 years ago, wrote: 'In the light of available data, one is almost forced to admit that the proposal seriously advanced at the time that unwanted babies should be painlessly asphyxiated in small gas chambers† was definitely humanitarian' (43). 'The survival of the wet-nurse in France, into the eighteenth century, ensured a high rate of infant mortality,' wrote Lawrence Stone, another historian of the modern family (44). In precolumbian America, the lack of milk from animals meant that mothers had to nurse their children till three or four years old. That must have

---

*Pierre Chaunu has recently used his great prestige as a demographic historian to appeal for more births in the advanced world, particularly in France.
† Gas was invented about 1800. See below, page 303.

decreased feminine fertility even if it may have helped the children.

The slow growth, and occasional decline, of population in the age of agriculture worried most societies. Homosexuality was widely rendered illegal essentially for that reason, as in Babylon (45). Europe and the Mediterranean were primarily influenced in respect of population by Christianity and Judaism and by God's reported adjuration to Adam and Eve 'to be fruitful and multiply' (46). Indeed, most societies had policies towards population one way or the other. (It is left to the modern democratic state, otherwise so much of a busybody, to have no policy on the subject, except those it adopts on behalf of Asia or Africa.)

The golden age of Greece had unambiguous, but different, attitudes. The discrepancy between Genesis's 'Be fruitful and multiply' and the Greek anxiety about over-population could not have been wider. The Greeks had too many people for their supply of food from 700 BC onwards. Hence, their colonisation of the Mediterranean, their reliance on imported wheat from the Black Sea, and the proposals of Plato for an ideal city of 5040 people. Aristotle also wanted to keep population stable. He thought that over-population would increase the poorer classes, not the intelligent ones, and, therefore, lead the city to anarchy and, afterwards, to despotism. Plato considered population on eugenic grounds: 'nuptial inspectors' would ensure that the best wedded the most beautiful (47). These views (which had no successor till the twentieth century AD) were held against a background in which, in all Greek states, abortion or abandonment of children was permitted. The only difference among them was that, in Sparta (where, uniquely in history, it was provided that no member of the élite should be able to identify his children or parents), it was the state which would decide whether a child would be permitted to survive, while, in Athens, that duty was the responsibility of the father.

These to us stony-hearted policies, along with a public cult of homosexuality, were successful. By the second century BC, Greece was short of men. Polybius complained that people were preoccupied by money and food and wished neither to marry nor to have children. The kings of Macedon passed a law trying to persuade their subjects to breed. Sparta changed its laws to give a bias against bachelors. It even encouraged the wives of old men to have children by others. In vain; the decline of population and the decline of Greece continued apace.

The Romans carried out censuses from about the sixth century BC and, for the next five centuries, their population rose, encouraged by a flow of slaves captured in wars and by the frequency of marriage by girls from the age of twelve onwards. But, by the time of Augustus, fashionable families practised a cult of childlessness. The first Emperors had few or no children: after all, as Gibbon recalled, of the first fifteen Emperors, Claudius was the only one whose taste was 'entirely correct' in sexual matters (48). Old Roman law had given unlimited power to the *paterfamilias*, even to the extent of permitting him to expose new born children on rubbish dumps if they were not desired — earlier, even to slay or to sell a child (49). From the first century AD, however, the State began to try to encourage the population to grow. Laws were passed which almost obliged the young to marry. The continuous flow of slaves and other non-Roman immigrants seemed to make no difference: the population declined. Celibates suffered loss of inheritance: again, to no avail. Gibbon wrote, 'Pious maids who consecrated their virginity to Christ were restrained from taking the veil till their fortieth year. Widows under that age were compelled to form a second alliance within five years by [the threat of] the forfeiture of half of their wealth' (50). To kill a child was proclaimed to be the same crime as parricide. Probably, Septimus Severus' law of 212 AD proclaiming all citizens of the Roman Empire to be free and equal within it was decreed with one eye on the size of the population. But, as previously in Greece, these laws were to no avail. All who write of the decline of Rome notice the shortage of men for armies, and the deserted farmlands (51).

The coming of Christianity seems, despite its message that marriage was, as with the Jews, intended for the procreation of children, to have exacerbated Rome's problems in this regard. For the Church also exalted virginity, condemned adultery, insisted on the maintenance of marriages (however badly they were working and however unequal the partners were in age) and, of course, in the end extolled monasticism. Some fathers of the Church (Tertullian, Origen) even condemned marriage as impure. Meantime, the burden of taxation meant that 'the horrid practice of exposing or murdering the new born infants' became ever more frequent (52). The increased importance of the eunuch was symbolic. Soon afterwards, the Western Empire fell.

The subject of population, like most things of the mind, was not raised in a new form till a thousand years later, although St Thomas Aquinas had made clear that, in his view, 'any carnal act which could not result in generation is unnatural' (53). The humanist, Leone Battista Alberti, in his *Treatise on the Family*, written in Florence in 1432, agreed, and suggested that the state should honour those with large families (54). Luther, Muhammed and Machiavelli said the same. Bodin in Paris in the sixteenth century argued that '*il n'est ni force ni richesse que d'hommes*'. Juan de Mariana, Vauban and Frederick the Great thought the same. True, foundling hospitals had been established in many mediaeval towns for unwanted children to be handed in at a revolving window, sometimes identified, sometimes not. But that was the town, not the country. On the whole, and despite the contradictory evidence cited above, the intellectual climate during most of the age of agriculture was one where most religions encouraged large families. The Greek experience was exceptional in this matter, as in others. Most people were encouraged to marry and people were more afraid of the population dying out than growing too fast. In the eighteenth century even, just when the world's population was beginning to leap forward at an unprecedented pace, even the cleverest men believed that the world was less populated than it once had been. Montesquieu wrote, in his *L'Esprit des Lois*, 'il y a peine sur la terre la dixième partie des hommes qui y étaient dans les anciens temps. Ce qui'il y a d'étonnant, c'est qu'elle se dépeuple tous les jours. Si cela continue, la terre ne sera plus dans deux siècles qu'un désert' (55). The Abbé Raynal, another intelligent man, thought in 1781 that it would be odd if the USA could support a million people (56). David Hume thought much the same.

A typical family in the world of agriculture is no doubt impossible to define. Was such a thing to be found in India, at almost any time between the Aryan and the European conquest? There, the family was often a large one, generally extending over several generations with sons and their families living in the patriarchal centre. Early marriage was unusual, most people had some choice in their mate, but a wife had to practise first a symbolic self-immolation at the death of her husband, and among the upper classes of central and east India later a real sacrifice (*Suttee*) — the first instance of which is believed to be in 510 AD. The Indians banned any incestuous relationship very strongly. Polygamy and polyandry were known but monogamy was more usual. The position of women was always subordinate, even if, as very often in old societies, idealised in literature. The only women who had any real freedom in India in its golden age were those who became Buddhist nuns, prostitutes, or actresses (57). Yet to know what really happened in this model family, in truth, it would be necessary to ask an endless number of questions comparable to those posed by Burckhardt in his chapter on morality in *The Civilisation of the Renaissance in Italy*: 'Was the marriage tie really more sacred in France during the fifteenth century than in Italy? What eye can pierce the depths in which the character and fate of nations are formed? in which even those intellectual capacities which, at first sight, we would take to be primary are, in fact, evolved late and slowly?' (58). Literature tells something of the realities of the past, but poetry and novels even of the same period sometimes give different pictures. Still, some truths emerge: 'Among the Massagetae, wives were held in common,' said Herodotus, 'but the Egyptians, like the Greeks, had only one wife' (59). In mediaeval Europe girls were often really nuns in their own house. Despite immense varieties of ways of living, some facts seem to stand out:

First, the world was managed, and most families, by people who would now be regarded as young men.

Second, the more primitive the society, the larger the group: Marc Bloch tells us that 'vast kindreds' or 'patriarchal families' characterised Europe till the sixth century AD at least, and only slowly did the idea of such clans begin to count less and individuals or small 'nuclear' families count more (60), though few of those professionally concerned in demographic history would agree as to when that began to be so.

Third, what Gibbon calls the 'iniquity of primogeniture' was a comparatively late development, even among monarchs and noblemen (61).

Fourth, a great many families, certainly much more than today, found themselves, because of early deaths, without either their fathers or mothers fairly early on in their childhoods (62).

Fifth, probably about half the population at any one time were under age. That is approximately the percentage of a country such as Venezuela today. But then there was only rarely a school. Dr Laslett adjures us, therefore, to 'imagine our ancestors in the perpetual presence of their young offspring' (63), some of whom were, of course, working, even if that merely meant hovering around the loom.

It is very tempting indeed to regard population and its growth as a key to human history. After all, the numbers concerned in the age of agriculture were very much smaller than they are today. Time and again, 'population pressure', a useful if somewhat vague and Germanised expression, has been given as the explanation for this or that occurrence. The inflation of the European sixteenth century was caused by the import of gold and silver from South America, it was once, it seemed, proved by Earl Hamilton. But that argument forgot the growth of European population. Have not those who attributed the Russian Revolution to the First World War forgotten the great increase of population in Russia since 1861? On the other hand, much of history was a time of very slow growth of population indeed. There were also very serious setbacks due to disease, war and famine as the next few chapters will try to show.

8

Population: Disease and Medicine

When David committed what to Jehovah seemed the disgraceful crime of making a census, he was offered a choice of three punishments: war, famine, and disease (1). He chose disease.

The part of disease in keeping down the growth of population in the age of agriculture was considerable and obvious. What the great killing microbes actually were is more difficult to decide: could the disease which devasted Athens in the fifth century really have been measles — a measles in its prime, a newly brought infection arriving amid a population lacking immunity or powers of resistance, as suggested by W H McNeill? (2). What were the plagues which carried away thousands in Rome during the second and third centuries AD? At that time, after all, smallpox and measles were recognised as being separate things, and the name of leprosy was given in the past to many skin infections. The word 'plague', too, was attached to almost anything, from influenza to dysentery.

In the absence of exact knowledge of the various epidemics, the precise effect of disease on history can scarcely be studied. But some general comments seem worth making. First, many maladies which had been mastered by those who lived with them for generations gained new leases of life when travel made possible their rebirth in new continents. Hunting man met fewer diseases than modern man. Though peripatetic, he came into touch with fewer centres of bacteria. He adjusted himself to local illnesses which he and his ancestors had long known. A good example of that process was the way in which the natives of the Caribbean and northern South America were immune to the only serious disease of that continent, syphilis. The legends of old Cuba before Columbus, for example, were full of tales of heroic canoers finding the cure for that disease in remote jungles (3). Travel and commerce, however, since 1492 in particular, have spread nearly all diseases world-wide. Man has been a much more effective carrier of some diseases than rats: irrigation, for example, which, from the early days of Sumer, was the hallmark of civilised agriculture in the West, encouraged the mosquito and the many diseases that it carries. Similarly, when the Spaniards first sailed down the Amazon, they met no fever of any sort: within a hundred years such a journey would have been most risky, for yellow fever prospered in the New World as well as did malaria. It was only taken there in 1648 from West Africa, no doubt in a slave ship. It ruled the countries of the Caribbean as firmly as did any viceroy. Hookworm also came from fertilised fields. Larger, and more, cities meant more rats: and more rats meant more plague bacilli in the fleas on the rats' backs. Indeed, diseases, such as measles, mumps, smallpox, and influenza, depended on the large populations of settled agricultural man. They derived, it seems, from modified versions of diseases which affected animals and are mostly probably about 6000 to 8000 years old.

Secondly, some diseases have been actually created by man. For example, gas gangrene, the worst complication to affect a patient suffering from a gunshot wound (4), naturally had no history before the general dissemination of firearms in the sixteenth century.

A third point is that it seems reasonably certain that the lives of great diseases are controlled by elements not as yet fully known but perhaps comparable to those of civilisations. This seems certainly the case in respect of plague, the epidemic which probably caused more distress than anything else in history and which, because of its unmistakable symptoms, even in literature, can be more easily chronicled than any other. It is an exemplary tale, and worth a certain diversion.

There are two plagues: bubonic, caused by bites of fleas, and resulting in large tumours, or buboes, in the groin, or the armpit, and pulmonary plague, transmitted by spit or breath. Most plagues in history were bubonic plagues.

With this illness, the flea feeds on the blood of an infected rat and takes into itself a quantity of plague bacilli. These lodge in the forestomach of the flea which becomes blackened by a solid mass of bacilli. Thereafter, whenever a flea feeds, the blood does not pass to the stomach but goes into the hole made by the flea's bite. The bacilli flood the hole with regurgitated blood, whether it be that of a man or another rat (5).

The rats concerned are black ones which originally came from India. The disease itself may have been endemic there for thousands of years. It was, apparently, unknown in Europe before about 300 BC. Perhaps it was brought to the Mediterranean by Alexander's army. The opening of a regular land route to the East (ensured by Alexander) anyway made possible the transmission of a disease whose incidence in the West was, partly at least, a consequence of Mediterranean man's desire for silk and spice. Even so, the 'plagues' of Rome may not have been such. The first unquestioned incidence of plague in the West was the epidemic which affected Constantinople in Justinian's day: 10,000 were said to be dying from bubonic plague there in 542. The sporadic return of this disease was probably a cause of the subsequent weakness of the Eastern Empire (as perhaps of the Persian one too), so helping the easy victories of the Arabs in the seventh century (6). About that time, the plague was first seen, apparently, in China. It returned there again and again. Half the population of Shantung seem to have died from it in the 760s (7).

The plague then became quiescent for reasons as obscure as those which caused its subsequent revival. Did it revive as a result of the slave trade from the Black Sea to Italy? Was it transmitted by the Tartars, who, in 1346, were besieging the Genoese at their factory at Kaffa in the Crimea, and who threw their infected corpses over the walls into the town? At all events, the plague quickly swept into Europe: 'It began,' wrote Boccaccio, 'both in men and women with certain swellings in the groin, or under the armpit. They grew to the size of a small apple or egg . . . These spread all over the body. Soon after . . . black or purple spots appeared on the thighs or any other part of the body . . . most people died within 3 days . . . most of them without fever. Some thought that moderate living would preserve them. They formed small communities living entirely separate from everybody else. They shut themselves up in houses where there were no sick, eating the finest food . . . [while] others thought the sure cure was to drink and be merry' (8). Whatever evasive action was pursued, a third of Europe's population died, two-fifths by 1400. Poland largely escaped, but no other country in Europe did. The Near East lost huge numbers too. The loss of population was not made up for a century or more. Economies declined. Farms were abandoned. Labour was short. Prices rose. Many were ruined. At the first suspicion of a recrudescence of plague, the rich fled to their country houses. Magistrates and prelates abandoned their duties. It sometimes seemed, therefore, that the poor suffered worse. The psychological reaction was curious: flagellants beat each other furiously to propitiate God's supposed wrath, some accused Jews of spreading the disease. The optimistic and humane Christianity of the thirteenth century gave way to mysticism. Painters depicted the dance of death, instead of the serene pastures loved by Giotto. The failure of Church and Bible to have anything effective to say encouraged lay scepticism. Perhaps the death of the clerics may have encouraged the use of the vernacular in literature. The cult of St Sebastian grew, for the world saw itself as being dealt terrible blows by unseen arrows. The plague in England even led to the first attempt at a statutory incomes' policy — the 'Statute of Labourers'. It sought to fix wages at or near the rates prevailing in 1346. In the event, the shortage of labour almost everywhere made wage-labour more attractive and, in the west of Europe, most escaped from feudal restrictions in consequence.

The plague returned often to Europe between then and 1750. The 'Great Plague' is remembered in England in 1666, but that was only one of several visits, and not the worst. Spain suffered a terrible visitation of plague between 1647 and 1654, probably the most severe catastrophe in her modern history, almost half the population of Seville died, giving Cádiz the chance to restore her ancient position as the greatest trading city of the South (9). Italy suffered equally in the seventeenth century, and again in 1743. Russia suffered terribly in 1709 and 1720, while 90,000 died in 1720 in Marseilles and nearby (including all the policemen, most public servants, and thirty two out of thirty five surgeons). Then, though there continued to be epidemics in Egypt, and though a million died of the plague in India in 1895, the bacillus withdrew, as it were, from Europe and has not been seen since. Why? Did the black rat find the new stone houses of absolutist Europe less friendly than the old wooden ones of feudalism? Was that black rat overthrown in a secret civil war of the animal world by the brown or grey rat? Did people wash more? Were the quarantine arrangements begun in Venice and which ensured the insulation of Marseilles in 1720 actually effective? None of these explanations is quite satisfactory: Italians had stone houses in the fourteenth century, and plague can be passed on by squirrels. Whatever the reason, despite occasional panics (the steamship was believed likely to bring back plague to Europe from China in the 1870s), the life of the plague, in Europe at least, simply came to an end. No change in technology and no great sudden turn in the 'class struggle' was the explanation.

It was not till long after the plague ceased to be a menace that its cause came to be known. A connection with rats was suspected, it is true, but the role of the flea was not realised. Only in 1898 did Paul Louis Simond suggest that the flea might be the transmitter. Only in 1914 was that hypothesis proved.

When plague disappeared, other diseases took its place. A roll of succession comparable to a list of monarchs could be devised showing that bubonic plague was followed in the eighteenth century as the reigning malady by smallpox (though that had been known, in a minor way, since the days of Justinian), in the nineteenth by tuberculosis — briefly challenged by cholera — and in the twentieth by heart diseases, cancer and, as a cause of death, accidents in cars. Similarly, leprosy, the malady *par excellence* of the early Middle Ages, was never able to re-establish itself in Europe after the Black Death.

These diseases did not, however, have such devastating effects, both in terms of numbers killed and of psychological disturbance caused, as did plague.

The eclipse of plague was not secured by doctors, nor by an international medical plan. It died. Its death coincided with a general improvement in climate, which itself did much perhaps to revive a spirit of optimism in European affairs. Perhaps the increase in the world's population in the eighteenth century is directly related to both the climate and the optimism, as much as to the better health.

The history of malaria, another historic disease, is a further exemplary tale, with a less happy outcome. It is still in 1980 probably the world's worst disease. Between a million and two million die of it every year (out of total deaths per year of about 50 million) and perhaps 250 million are continuously affected by it (10). There are several strains, of which the one known in Europe is mild in comparison with that which has caused havoc in Africa. In Africa, malaria is probably as prevalent in the twentieth century as it ever was, while recent irrigation (like early hydraulic agriculture) helped the mosquitoes, which need stagnant water in which to breed. Known once as 'ague', and deriving its modern name in English from the false assumption that it derived from the bad air, *mal aire*, of Italian swamps, this disease was known in antiquity and was accurately described by the great Greek physician, Hippocrates. Many African tribes believed that the disease was carried by mosquitoes. But that view was not recognised as true by Europeans till the nineteenth century. (A Tuscan proverb argued that 'the best remedy against malaria is a well filled stewpot' (11).)

Though Hippocrates knew of malaria, it is not evident that it was a serious disease before the late Roman Empire (12). In the last years of that extraordinary enterprise, the shortage of manpower and the prevalence of invasions led to the neglect of the drainage in the city and of the once highly developed irrigation in the nearby farmland of the Campagna. The stagnant water afforded an opportunity to the mosquitoes which remained there for 1500 years, making malaria the characteristic disease of the region, and being the main cause of the decline and depopulation of Rome for so long. The draining of the marshes was, however, begun by Pope Pius VII in the eighteenth century and completed by Mussolini in the 1930s. The population of Rome had grown from about 130,000 in 508 BC (13) to 750,000 in 70 BC (14), and reached over a million during the third century (15). It fell back to 700,000 in the days of Constantine the Great (16), and numbered apparently a mere 35,000 in 1050 (17), before rising to 100,000 by 1600 (18), 160,000 by 1800, 300,000 by 1880 and only reaching a million again in the time of Mussolini (1930) (19): the life of the city was probably determined more by malaria than by any other factor.

Meantime malaria, taken to the Americas by the Spaniards, completed the destruction of the indigenous population in the tropical low lands already begun by smallpox. Malaria dominated the tropical parts of South America till the twentieth century, causing an inertia which perhaps explains the ease with which the Spanish Empire maintained itself. Many victims felt that, when they had 'water in the blood', as one of them in Venezuela put it, they might as well give up all attempts at resistance to the problems of maintaining life (20). Nor was malaria only tropical in its incidence. The Fens and Romney Marsh were formidable breeding grounds in England. Cromwell, Alexander Borgia and Dante all died of malaria.

In the seventeenth century, it became known that malaria could be suppressed, if not cured, by applying to the patient the bark of the chinchona tree, a South American plant first used by the intelligent Condesa de Chinchón, wife of the Governor of Peru in 1638. Hence the name of that delightful town of Castile passed to the healing tree. The bark had been used by Indians before but, since it was disseminated in Europe by the Society of Jesus, it was known for a time (and characteristically suspected by Protestants) as 'Jesuits' bark'. Since the forests where the chinchona flourished were in the hands of His Catholic Majesty, Protestants had to wait many years before they could assure themselves of a regular supply of this precious wood: a serious drawback to the Reformation. The Dutch, in the end, established plantations of chinchona in Java in 1854, however, and, after that, Protestant Europeans were able to insulate themselves against malaria. That enabled them to penetrate Africa for the first time (21).

Every time that malaria is mentioned, Africa comes back to the discussion. That continent has been so influenced by the effects of the disease that it might well have been called after it. The curious frontiers of existing countries there derive ultimately from the desire of both Arab and European conquerors to base their colonies on the coast (22). Malaria also ensured that, while Africa could be circumnavigated by a European, in 1487, it was not till 1853–6 that it could be crossed by one: Livingstone.

The history of both plague and malaria recalls one fundamental point in history; which is that, before the nineteenth century, no serious contribution was made to the relief of the disease either by medicine or doctors. Certainly population did not increase because of what was done in that respect before the nineteenth century.

Of course, doctors and surgeons have existed for many generations. Some may even claim that those generations of experience were essential to the recent medical achievements of the industrial age. It seems dubious. The benefits of surgery were equally modest till the nineteenth century.

The earliest known medical or surgical activity was the trepanning of skulls. It often occurred between 7000 BC and 5000 BC. To relieve pressure on the brain, or to let out devils? Perhaps both. At all events, in ancient Iraq, the piece of bone cut out was often prized and hung round the neck as an amulet. Bones of even remoter times have often shown signs of disease though not of surgery (23). The Chinese, perhaps as a result of information passed from the West, used trepanning to cure blindness caused by benign tumours (24).

Ancient Babylon and Egypt both had doctors and doctor-gods, and Ningizzida, son of the god Ninazu, was the first, it seems, to have been identified by a rod of entwined serpents. In Egypt, doctors were often priests. Epidemics had goddesses. Many diseases were held to be the work of demons. All doctors were specialists: there were no general practitioners. Both Babylon's and Egypt's doctors had innumerable instruments and prescriptions, most with magical or semi-religious qualities. The laws of Hammurabi in Babylon, of about 1800 BC, named punishments for doctors who failed to cure diseases. In its heyday, Babylon cultivated 250 medical plants, used 150 mineral substances, and bred animals for medical purposes. Emetics were used to sicken demons. Tablets which survive preserve many diagnoses: 'If a man's body is yellow, if his eyes and his face are yellow, and if his skin is flabby — it's jaundice' (25). Egypt had a good reputation throughout the ancient world for doctors, and great families of surgeons were established — nearly all professions became hereditary — who, among other things, opened abscesses and stopped bleeding by cauterisation, using a kind of adhesive plaster on wounds. Though they possessed many recognisable implements, including an early form of scalpel, they did not amputate.

In Greece, medicine showed, to begin with, little advance on Egyptian and Babylonian practice, even though the art of bandaging was early well developed there. An important change came with the great Hippocrates of Cos, who, in the fifth century BC, devised his famous method of taking and keeping notes on patients. He also started the clinical lecture and the bedside instruction. He insisted that doctors had to behave honourably: an idea embodied in the Hippocratic oath which binds doctors to work for the patient's benefit, not to give deadly drugs, not to misuse their position (for example, to seduce female patients), and to keep silent about what they may learn in the course of their treatment.

These rules were challenged by Hippocrates's contemporary, Plato, who thought that doctors should not only concern themselves with the prolongation of life but should consider the interests of the State. On the whole, despite many generations of incompetent doctors, the Hippocratic idea was not seriously challenged by educated physicians until the twentieth century when, in both Communist Russia and Nazi Germany, Plato's ideas were partially put into effect.* Even in democracies, doctors have individually been known to break the oath of secrecy about what they have learned from patients. Doubtless, there have been many instances of physicians refusing to treat patients (or insisting on so doing) before the twentieth century. It is hard to think of previous occasions when such malpractice became a governmental policy. But then medicine has never been so much discussed as it is to-day.

Many books were attributed to Hippocrates, but only his aphorisms remain: for example, 'Life is short, art is long, opportunity fleeting, experience fallacious, judgement difficult', or; 'Those naturally very fat

* See below, page 398.

are more liable to sudden death than those that are thin'. Hippocrates's studies of actual cases were without parallel, like many Greek innovations, till the seventeenth century AD. Other Greeks also did great things in medicine. Herophilus, in the third century BC, for example, dissected a human body in public, and recognised the brain to be the centre of the nervous system. Erasistratus of Chios, grandson of Aristotle, about the same time, thought that disease was caused by excess of blood, a truly disastrous error. (He was said to have discovered, by the motion of his pulse, the love which the Emperor Antiochus had conceived for his mother-in-law, and was rewarded with a large sum (26).)

Rome, on the other hand, was as uninventive in medical matters as indeed it was in most affairs of a reflective kind. But the Empire did develop an effective system of medical organisation, based principally on greater attention to sanitation. Imperial Rome had numerous public lavatories, drainage was good, and the first public hospitals were created, beginning as private nursing homes in doctors' houses. The Emperor Vespasian, for example, in the first century AD, gave doctors a salary at the public's expense for the first time. The Army also took care to secure an adequate supply of doctors (27). Otherwise, Rome's contribution to medicine merits the neglect that its method of imperial succession also deserves, were it not for the extraordinary figure of Galen, who died in 200 AD, and who was probably the most influential doctor of all time.

Galen is a good example of a strong character all of whose most important ideas were wrong. His energy, learning and friendship with the humane Emperor Marcus Aurelius, gave him a great reputation in his lifetime and control over the imagination of medical Europe for a thousand years. As a student of anatomy, Galen knew where the bones are in the human frame, though he knew animals better than men. There was little he did not know about muscles, so he may genuinely be looked upon as the founder of experimental physiology. But he was ignorant of the brain and of the vascular system. He thought that blood was made in the liver. He believed that suppuration was an indispensable part of healing, and in the 'miraculous' powers of certain substances. He and his followers endeavoured to heal wounds by numerous methods of constant interference, such as changing bandages, an error that was not finally dismissed until the twentieth century. Galen lived at a time of decreasing rationalism and an increasing desire to believe, whatever the absurdity of the belief. He and his school brooked no criticism, and, unfortunately, conquered the medical schools of the Roman world. (Ptolemy, who re-established the Earth at the centre of the Universe, did much the same for astronomy as Galen did for medicine.*)

* This is perhaps unfair to Ptolemy who did list 1,022 stars and made serious contributions

The era known in the West as the Dark Ages was specially sombre in respect of the study of medicine. Byzantium kept what books it could. Few read them. The Nestorians, chased as heretics from the Eastern Empire, put many Greek medical books into Syriac and subsequently they were translated into Arabic. But in the West of Europe, monks relieved patients as best they could, innocent of theoretical knowledge, and worshipped St Cosmas and St Damian, patrons of 'medicine' allegedly murdered under Diocletian. Some trepanning was done with a thong-drill and a few dim recollections of the advances made during the pre-Christian era survived in remote, if pagan, valleys. Princes and priests meantime faced leprosy, with brutality.

That disease had previously been confined to the East. It apparently reached France and Britain in the sixth century (though some still claim that it was brought to Europe by the Crusaders). Lepers were isolated, declared legally dead, and often excluded from the Church — an impious act of cruelty for which the Bible gave no justification. 20,000 leprosaria were founded outside mediaeval towns in Europe, in which the shattered, white-faced patients, many of them only suffering (at least at the beginning) from chicken-pox, were forced to wait for a lingering death. These arrangements were the only medical innovation of the Middle Ages. They had, in the end, some good effects: the arrangements for quarantine used with success for plague derived from the special landing station where Venetian lepers were forced to wait for first a *trentaine*, then a *quarantaine* (forty days) in the open air.

One improvement in health does, however, date from the Middle Ages: spectacles, without which intellectual life in the twentieth century would be hard to imagine, were in use in a primitive form from the fourteenth century onwards (perhaps devised by Roger Bacon in England), making a substantial if often an unacknowledged, contribution to the revival of learning.

While Europe slept, and America lived a dream of innocence free almost both of disease and of physicians, Islam was at work. Arabic Spain, for example, knew all the old Greek books on medicine and made use of them. A school of medicine was established at Salerno, then a strong principality, near Naples, deriving its vigour from constant military contact with the Arabs. A few old Greek books were translated into Latin. Salerno also taught the desirability of a balanced diet (30) and revived memories of Hippocrates. Public dissection began again. A few adventurous spirits went to Spain to bring back the secrets of Graeco-Arab medicine to northern Europe. Though sometimes branded wizards, they persisted. Thus a Renaissance in medicine began in the end. But still the actual impact of medical science on life and death remained slight. It is hard to believe that population was much

to astronomical movements and to optics (28). His *Almagest* also seemed to be a breath of fresh air when translated into Latin from Greek about 1160 (29).

affected one way or the other by those ancient scalpels.

The medicine of China during classical and mediaeval days seems to have been at every point more successful than that of the West. That was partly because of the use of acupuncture, which, from a very early time, enabled the Chinese surgeons to be more ambitious in cautery. I-Ching thus wrote: 'In China, there are more than 400 different kinds of herbs, minerals, stalks and roots, most of which are excellent and rare in colour and taste . . . thereby, we can control any disease and control the temperament'. In treatment, we hear, 'I-Ching relied largely on abstention from food' (31). It is astonishing that Europe, which learned so much from the East during the Middle Ages, never seems to have considered the use of acupuncture as a means of securing the patient's insensitivity to pain. Chinese medicine, on the other hand, remained almost as unchanging in its character as in its methods of irrigation, being based on a series of special principles formally laid down, including a very elaborate way of listening to the pulse and the early use of mineral drugs.

The Indians included medicine from an early time in their curricula of education. It was however, entirely practical. It suffered no special setbacks in the Middle Ages but remained, on the other hand, as static as the system of castes, except for the beginning of work in veterinary science (32).

These considerations deal with the regular practice of medicine. In much of the world, however, including Europe, the age of agriculture was a time when disease was looked upon as an evil presence which could be exorcised or conjured out — by witch doctors, charmers, wizards, witches, or even kings. English wizards, for instance, in the sixteenth century, told their clients to dig holes in churchyards, boil eggs in urine, and tie staves, salt and herbs in cows' tails (33). Money retrieved from the offertory of a church was held to have magical power. Magic in the age of agriculture had many other uses: for example, detection of thieves, love philtres, to give foreknowledge of rebellions, pursuit of treasure. In the rational days of the nineteenth century, these ideas were dismissed as dangerous fancies. But today, the role of suggestion, faith in therapy, the power of ritual as well as the concept of psychosomatic disease have been reconsidered. In the late seventeenth century a French doctor had a patient who was convinced that he was possessed of the devil. The doctor called in a priest and a surgeon, while equipping himself with a bag containing a bat. The patient was told that a small operation was needed, the priest offered a prayer and the surgeon made a modest cut in the man's side. As the cut was made, the doctor allowed the bat to fly up and cried, 'Behold, the Devil is gone'. The man was cured (34). Possibly more people throughout the world were then effectively cured in this manner than was the case as a result of the weak working of a weak science.

9

Population: War and Battle

The second of the evils supposed in the Bible to have been linked to the expansion of population and a limitation on its rise was war.

Now, in the age of agriculture, people died because of war less in battle than as a result of marauding armies. In a contest as long-lasting as the Hundred Years' War, the devastation of crops was more destructive than the killing of men. Men also died from disease contracted in war, usually the consequence of crowding tired, ill-fed men into a small space, thus creating a fertile ground for microbes. How appropriate that Clausewitz, the greatest writer on war, should have died from cholera, in 1831, when stationed on the German-Russian frontier! Cholera also carried away, in the same epidemic, not only Clausewitz's chief, the great field-marshal Gneisenau, but the commander of the Russian army across the river and Hegel too. (That first great European outbreak of cholera seems to have been brought back from Bengal, where it had been for long endemic and destroyed, in its slow way, 18% of the population of Cairo, and thousands of Muslims on the way to Mecca. At that time, nobody knew that cholera was caused by a bacillus which can live a long time in water independently.) At the same time, the creation of large armies has often preserved peace, even if it has done so at a price. The history of war is, therefore, not entirely the history of killing by violence; and the Great Condé perhaps was statistically right to suppose that 'one night in Paris' would 'make up for the losses at the battlefield of Rocroy' (1).

The violence of savage peoples was, and is, expressed in head-hunting, assassination, man hunts and predatory expeditions, caused by fear, religion, hunger and cruelty. Can such killings be dignified by the name of warfare? Probably not: the idea of 'warfare' only applies when a 'special condition of hostility solemnly proclaimed is recognised, as distinct from individual quarrels and family feuds' (2). This definition has, however, not always been carried out by modern peoples who believe themselves civilised. Still, in African communities a fight over the succession to the chieftainship is a permanent feature of life (3). To men of the Stone Age, war was not the business of a few select

68

people. It was the occupation of every adult male, whose aim was to kill all enemy males and abduct the women and children. In some respects, people of the twentieth century have returned to a condition where discrimination between victims is impossible: slaughter is now on total lines (4). That sort of war must have been one reason for the failure of population to rise as fast as it might between at least the birth of agriculture and that of Christ. The Bible, the Homeric poems, Herodotus, and almost every work giving useful historical evidence, are all full of terrible wars to the death, heroes being almost always successful warriors, successful nations being almost always those successful in battle. Death in action was considered the noblest way to die throughout most of history.

What have been the causes of war? Over-population was often considered the likely reason in the remote past. But overpopulated China remained many years at peace, and the American Indians, who occupied little territory per head of population, were usually at war. The barbarian conquests in late Roman days were carried out by small but fierce tribes from places where the density of population was low. In 1939, Germany had less pressure of population than Poland. Italy had a lower birth rate than Ethiopia did when the former attacked the latter in 1935. The German desire for *lebensraum* was, one suspects, more an excuse for, than a cause of, the Second World War (5). In general, wars have seemed, like crime, more often than not to have been caused by the desire of the audacious to seize the goods of the comfortable.

Very often, the audacious have had such confidence in their weapons that they have believed victory to be theirs for the asking. Thus, the weapons in the Mycenæan age were, like those of the European 'Hallstatt culture', made of bronze: swords, just invented, double axes, spears, and javelins. Armour was sometimes made of bronze too, but also of leather, heavy linen (surprisingly good against swords) and shields of ox-hide, with metal bosses. Chariots were more often used for taking warriors to battle than actually in the fight (unlike the use to which the Hittites put their equipment). Cavalry was not used, since the horses of that time were small, unshod animals, which had no proper harness and whose few riders had no stirrups. These Mycenæan forces seem usually to have been prepared for use against seaborne raiders (6). The battering rams and siege engines devised by the Assyrians, afterwards perfected by the Romans, were decisive in sieges. The Hittites retained their knowledge of the secrets of how to make iron till their empire fell apart, but thereafter that precious information soon spread — to farming also. (Plough-shares and sickles, as well as sword and dagger blades, were soon being made all over the Near East (7).) Innovations in technology naturally were almost always decisive in their early stages. For example, the Persian conquests (of Assyria, Babylon, Media and Lydia) were achieved by mounted bowmen and camels from Bactria.

The 'long lances' of Scythia were thereby shown to be ineffective. Later, Arab camels were used — though, for many years, not as beasts of burden. The decisive battle between the Persians and the Lydians was won by the former since, according to tradition, the latter's horses did not like the smell of the Persian camels (8). Cyaxares, King of the Medes, was the first man, according to Herodotus, to give any real organisation to an army, dividing the troops into companies and forming distinct bodies of spearmen, archers, and cavalry who, before that time, 'had been mingled' (9). This innovation also probably preserved more life than it destroyed.

The numbers involved in the armies of the eastern empires were large in proportion to the populations, even if the figures for Xerxes' force given by Herodotus resemble the grand exaggerations of Spanish chroniclers in the sixteenth century in the New World. Sparta, the great military power of Greece, after the eclipse of the cavalry of Thessaly in the sixth century (and a state in arms rather than a strong country with a good army), had 5,000 warriors of the officer class, 5,000 shepherds, and 35,000 'helots' (10). Meantime, both Greece and Persia were, in the end, reduced by Alexander's 35,000 men, a force adequate to conquer half the world. It is said that the Roman army at Cannae was 50,000–80,000 strong. The Roman army at its zenith in, say, the second century AD, included thirty legions each of about 12,500 — or about 375,000 to 400,000 men in all with which to preserve the peace in the age of the Antonines. But the monarchies of the Middle Ages in Europe never approached such figures: the King of France commanded the largest army in feudal Europe at Crécy: 12,000 men (11). That number of Berbers was enough to conquer Spain for Islam in 711. The first crusade gathered only 25,000–30,000. The German Emperor's all-out offensive against the Turks in 1467 numbered a mere 18,500.

In comparison, oriental armies seem almost modern: Haroun al Rashid once conducted a summer campaign with 135,000 regular soldiers while, under the Sung dynasty, it is said, China had trained several million men (12).

How did all these armies really fight? Sometimes the parties (as in mediaeval China and ancient Egypt) might put their disputes to a representative test: Chalcis and Eretria fought by terms of a contract in which rules were laid down beforehand in the temple of Artemis. Time and place for the battle were specified, so were the weapons. A code of honour had grown up too. Even the King of Persia, Xerxes, according to Herodotus, refused to act 'like the Lacedaemonians who, by killing the heralds, had broken the laws which all men hold in common ' (13). All the evidence indeed is that, from a very early stage, regularly instituted states endeavoured to keep to certain rules in the actual battle. They as a rule treated captives, if not as specifically laid down in the Hague Conventions of 1899 and 1907, infinitely better than captives were treated on the Eastern front in 1941—45. Only after battles did violence as a rule become likely to be uncontrolled. The existence of certain rules to which all states within a certain civilisation adhered made of course the attacks from outsiders, 'barbarian hordes', all the more feared.

Sieges were devastating to civilians: in the Peloponnesian war, Sparta built two walls round Plataea, one against the besieged, one against any relief force, the two lines being sixteen feet apart (14). Such devices were intended to 'reduce' the populations concerned and often they did so, causing innumerable civilian deaths. When sieges ended in the besiegers' victory, the besieged were often 'put to the sword'. Such actions, even when carried out by peoples, such as the Greeks, who were more thoughtful than most, resulted in innumerable killings. Thucydides ascribed the breakdown of order and of democracy to the demoralising effect of war: 'Greek states lived on so bare a subsistence rate,' Maurice Bowra wrote, 'that a long war had a devastating effect . . . machinery for enforcing law was undermined by the absence of men on foreign service . . . and more violent politicians came to the fore' (15).

From the fourth century BC onwards, for about eight hundred years, large, organised armies were the decisive influences in the history of the Mediterranean world. First, there were the phalanxes of Macedon, the secret of whose success was that cavalry, for which northern Greece had been long renowned, was, for the first time, linked with infantry rather than scattered about. The infantry shed its heavy armour for greater mobility and greater ease in using the long lance in battle. Once Greece had been reduced by Philip, the Macedonian armies in Asia were also sustained by an irresistible Greek fleet. Alexander, it is said, was the first to use the torsion catapult to despatch arrows and stones, at the siege of Tyre in 323 BC. That was a great innovation, marking the beginning of an era in which such spring catapults would give attack an advantage over defence till the coming of stone castles in the Middle Ages.

The history of the Roman army, however, is the history of an armed institution which undoubtedly preserved life more than it destroyed it. It is so important in the history of war that consideration of it deserves a diversion. For the Roman army was, to begin with, really the State, inseparable from it and with no other institution comparable to it, with each class within the State obliged to play a military part, even more than was the case in Sparta. Thus, before entering the *cursus honorum*, the career for the leaders of Roman political life in the Republic, at twenty-eight years of age, a man had to have served ten campaigns. All magistrates and politicians were thus ex-soldiers. On the other hand, the rank and file of the Roman army were amateurs, farmers, who returned home at the end of the season's campaigning. That military basis for many years gave Roman life its coherence, and the recollection of that arrangement cast a shadow over the careers at least of the

European nobility till only recently. War followed war throughout the third and much of the second, century BC (16). Rome succeeded in dominating the Italian peninsula with its army, but thereafter large-scale foreign operations and Mediterranean-wide diplomacy seriously strained the old constitution, with its principle of annual office and colleges of electors.* War, for example, forced a change in the old law which prevented a man being a consul more than once in ten years. The establishment of the proconsulship, which led to the achievement of such power by Caesar and Pompey (and hence to the Empire), also began with the need, or the desire, for a commandership-in-chief, a post first filled by Scipio Africanus, for ten years (17). A century later, Marius, in the war against Jugurtha, found that, out of the old classes in the census, there were no citizens willing to fight. But there were innumerable extra *'classi'*: the proletariat of the city, ex-slaves, ex-captives, men perhaps Celtic in origin, and men never normally conscripted. Marius made of them a volunteer but professional army. Henceforward, soldiers ceased to expect to go home to their farms. A whole breed of men existed who knew only the Legion and its eagle.

The new legionaries extended the Empire. But there was not enough money with which to pay them. Hence their loyalty turned increasingly towards individual generals, who promised them rewards provided they won (18). Hence, the Roman civil wars, which destroyed the old constitution and doubtless killed many thousands of potential fathers of families. Peace was only achieved when Augustus decided to give smallholdings in Italy to thousands of his, and his uncle's, soldiers, at the cost, in many cases, of long-established smallholders. Augustus also paid his men a cash bounty equivalent to thirteen years' wages, a sum raised by sales and inheritance taxes.

The imperial task of the Roman army was to preserve, with these professional cadres, peace in the huge territories which the Republic had won. The main strength (sixteen legions†) lay on the Rhine and Danube, the next most important army was that constituted by the legions on the Euphrates. While Egypt, Africa and Spain had usually one legion each, Britain had three. Italy, at that time, was held by 20,000 men. This standing army was composed of volunteers at eighteen who served for twenty-five years. After that, they would get a grant of land or a gratuity, but land, far the best asset in the age of agriculture, was almost always preferred. Recruitment became local. Soldiers were theoretically not allowed to marry, but usually did so, so much so that, in the end, it seemed as if soldiering was on its way to becoming an hereditary calling. Equally characteristic of Rome during this long, defensive era were the famous fortified cities, whose ruins are so often visible, established in the form of a square or quadrangle, big enough to

* See below, page 158.
† Each of about 12,500 men.

hold 20,000 men, the praetorium or general's quarters rising high in the centre above the straight streets constructed on a gridiron pattern, a symbol both of Roman power in the provinces and of military power in ensuring Rome's authority. Over these years, the real authority in the Roman empire moved, indeed, to those defensive barracks: the old capital became increasingly a shell, the true capital was wherever the belligerent emperor kept his headquarters (19).

The wars against Picts, Germans and Parthians were the only inter-ruptions in the triumphant administrative achievements of the early Empire. But, at the end of the second century, at about the date which Gibbon chose as the starting point of his book, the main question in Rome became one of how to control the controllers of the peace. This is an occurrence which has affected many armies, particularly effective ones. Usually such events have led to destructive civil wars of an ex-tremely violent nature, affecting both population and national confi-dence. In Rome, the difficulties arose directly from the growth of the imperial guard (the nine praetorian cohorts stationed at Rome and in certain Italian towns, which had begun under Augustus and were later increased to ten). After the death of Caligula in 41 AD, the praetorians swiftly frustrated a patriotic move on the part of the enfeebled Senate to revive the Republic. In 69 AD, the guard gave the Empire to Otho who, however, lost it in four months. A hundred and twenty years later, after the relative serenity of the age of Vespasian and of the Antonines, the guard dominated the Empire for ninety years, from 193 to 280, killing Pertinax, auctioning the Empire to Severus Julianus and murdering two imperial candidates from the Senate in 238. Meantime, other armies had their imperial candidates and pretensions; for, from 68 AD, as Tacitus put it, it was known 'that elsewhere than at Rome an emperor might be created' (20). In the second century, the Empire was disturbed by a continuous civil war between the army of the East and that of the Danube, the Senate in Rome continually bowing to the wishes of which-ever proved stronger (21).

These disputes were the first occasion in history when military force unrelated to properly constituted power became the determining factor in a political system. After the fall of the Roman Empire, this military intervention in politics became again of minor importance to religious or royal considerations until the fall of the European empires in the nine-teenth and twentieth centuries, when military politics much like that of the praetorian era were revived:'the caprice of armies long habituated to frequent and violent revolutions might even raise to the throne the most obscure of their fellow soldiers' (22). Gibbon's contemptuous words characterise the history of Africa, Latin America and Asia after the European empires had withdrawn: old customary loyalties bound men no longer, but neither did imperial ones.

As the political power of the Roman armies increased, their military capacity declined. That also has been a mark of modern political life: the more political the army, the less professional and the less effective they have been militarily, since, as Gibbon put the matter in respect of the late Roman Empire, 'the relaxation of discipline, and the disuse of exercise, rendered the soldiers less able and less willing, to support the fatigues of the service; they complained of the weight of the armour which they seldom wore; and they successively obtained the permission of laying aside both their cuirasses and their helmets' (23). The consequence was the introduction of barbarians into the Roman armies: 'every day more universal, more necessary and more fatal' and the 'most daring of the Scythians . . . found it more profitable to defend, than to ravage, the Roman provinces' (24). The consequences included the general breakdown of order, the sense of pessimism and decay which characterised the second half of the Roman Empire, the continuous civil wars and the marked and steady decline in the birth rate.

The end of antiquity will always be, and indeed has been for two or three centuries, a fit subject for meditation by reflective historians. The role of war in causing it cannot be forgotten: indeed, the final collapse in the Eastern Mediterranean, and the end of Mediterranean commerce as it had been known for generations, was occasioned by the great Arab victories. But among the causes of the failure of population to grow faster, the place of war probably figures less greatly, at least directly, than may seem to have been the case at first sight. Great armies have been as often as not the instruments to preserve civilisations.

10

Population: Famine and Food

The threat posed by famine in the age of agriculture probably justified, in most minds, the disciplined despotisms of China, or Egypt, or the pre-Columbian New World. There, indeed, famine was largely avoided because of that discipline. In the Western world, however, failure of harvests was only an occasional threat but, when it occurred, there was usually no defence against it.

The first crop of the world in terms of importance has been, for several centuries, rice. Rice still provides the main diet for six out of ten people in the world today. Its likely original home was South East Asia but it is not clear who domesticated it first. Perhaps the Chinese were responsible, between 2000 and 1500 BC though rice is known to have been grown, wild, in all probability, in Siam about 3500 BC (1). To begin with, its cultivation was limited to one harvest a year instead of the two or three which have made the modern rice field almost a factory. But even one harvest of rice needs to be grown in muddy water which is constantly in movement. Clear water would attract mosquitoes, and stagnant water does not give enough oxygen.

Rice, since time immemorial, has actually been grown in nurseries, to begin with. The small plants reared there are transferred later to grow in soil which, when well-manured, gives a higher yield than wheat fields. Rice is both land-intensive and labour-intensive: fallow is never needed. Hence, there has never been a rotation of crops. Rice has never had its centre in the oldest focus of Chinese agriculture, the muddy estuary of the Yellow River valley, for there grain, millet, and wheat have been the characteristic crops. Rice had, and has, its centre in the plain of the River Yangtze. It is there that the greater number of China's canals were dug.

The Chinese developed their classic pattern of agriculture between 1500 BC, by which time rice was domesticated, and 500 BC, when their system of canals for irrigation was firmly established. Millet, wheat, buckwheat, sorghum and barley continued to be grown, but the Chinese did not leaven bread (partly because they did not have the

vine) and unleavened flatbread is highly unsatisfactory if eaten continuously. There was never much beef in China and so, while some
Emperors 'ate only game', pigs continued to be the main livestock. The
scarcity of both cattle (except for the invaluable water buffalo) and
horses meant that, in China, human excreta played as big a part as
animal manure in fertilising fields, as indeed it still does.

After its success in China, in the Yangtze valley in particular, rice was
cultivated everywhere in the Far East, in the Philippines, Indonesia,
Malaya and Japan (though not till 100 BC), displacing millet and
usually helping the establishment of sober, disciplined societies,
ruled by authoritarian monarchs. India also began to grow rice,
which, with some wheat and other grain as well, became the staple
crop there also. All these agricultures depended primarily on irrigation
rather than rainfall. All observed that rice harvests fail less often than
harvests of wheat, providing that the water supplies are properly
managed.

The first Chinese Empire was established around the need to ensure
these supplies of food: the actual manifestation being the city of Hsiao-
T'un (Anyang) a city carefully laid out in zones, the quarter of the palace
and that of the artisans being easily distinguished in their present state,
with rectangular houses of wood on terraces of beaten earth, pitched or
gabled roofs supported by stone, and even sometimes with bronze
bases. From this city, the Shang dynasty about 1200 BC ruled a stable
state, dominating a series of village communities. How that anyway
half-mythical dynasty gained power is a mystery, though presumably it
was by force – or by the manipulation of real, or imagined, fears of war.
Its more historical successors, the two Chou dynasties and afterwards
the Ch'in, established their great rice-driven state with meticulous
attention to maintaining regular supplies over generations. The security
which this ensured must have been the main explanation for the rise in
the population of China so relatively steadily in comparison with the
dramatic declines and uneasy recoveries in such peoples as Egypt or
Iraq. Other Eastern states copied China.

In comparison, the history of societies dependent on grain was far
more complicated. Consider some examples from the history of the
Mediterranean in classical days. In the days of the Mycenæan kingdoms, Greece had a good supply of wheat and barley, presumably
because its population was so small (2). In the fifth century BC,
however, the cultivable acres of Greece were given over to vineyards
and olive farms whose produce was exchanged with the 'barbarians',
above all those who lived in the Ukraine, for grain of numerous types.
Athens's empire was created out of the need to guarantee her supply of
grain by her navy. The silver from the mines of the Laurium financed
the navy which ensured the grain. The ensuing economic problems
resulted in the quarrels within Greece and the instability of the political

system there. Why did Athens fall? asked Maurice Bowra and answered, because she was too poor, the alliance which she directed was too diverse, her gods were overthrown by more profound cults, and her science turned sterile. 'Athens fell because she depended on corn from the Black Sea,' Bowra went on, 'and, when cut off, she had no choice but surrender' (3).

Even more restless was the history of grain in Rome. Italy about 500 BC was a land of small farms, though the cultivated area might not have been much greater than the 'built-up area' today. As noticed before, the landscape was without the olive, the vine or the cypress, as well as the tower and the bell, those characteristic sights of historic Italy, all of which were subsequently imported. A few rich proprietors might have had as many as 200 acres of fields, but even seventy acres was unusual, and probably over half the farms of the tribes of Italy were of five acres or less (4). This majority of the farmers grew wheat or barley, reared goats and pigs, perhaps a flock of sheep and, if rich, owned a pair of oxen or mules. Slaves would have been fewer than free labourers. Most Romans until 300 BC were farmers, working from their houses in the city or living in small, semi-fortified villages in the neighbourhood. The city of Rome was, of course, supplied by its own farmers. The disciplined way of life of early Rome was underpinned by a simple and efficient agricultural self-sufficiency.

The conquests by the Romans in central Italy, however, led to the formation of a state domain, *ager publicus*. Out of this conquered territory, large estates began to be formed. Legally all those estates were supposed to be less than 500 *iugera* (333 acres) but that rule was often broken.

In 232 BC, the then consul Caius Flaminius tried to carry out a programme encouraging prosperity by establishing allotments for poor farmers on conquered land, including land already farmed by rich landlords. The Senate was hostile, believing in the sanctity of private property, above all in their own by now large estates, and vetoed the plan. Flaminius ignored them and took the matter to the Assembly of the Roman people where his father, a senator, in the name of paternal authority, dragged him from the platform. But the law was eventually passed. Instead of prosperity, however, the era of demagoguery began (5). The government, to keep down the price of bread, encouraged the import of grain, and began to demand that commodity from all conquered enemies. This they distributed free or at a subsidised price, beginning a characteristic Roman food policy — probably learned from the East, for Egypt had a custom of giving away free boiled meat to the poor in a field outside cities known as 'the Table of the Sun' while, in 1064 BC, the Emperor of China had set up a store of grain to be sold cheaply if the harvest were bad (6). Thereafter, more and more Roman farms abandoned corn for vines, olives, horticulture and pasturage.

These changes were perhaps encouraged by a temporary change to a less rainy climate (7). (The olive, a native of the East Mediterranean, had been known in Greece for a long time, but seems not to have been seen in Italy before 400 or 300 BC.) All these new crops were best grown on large estates, often on a mixed farm. Small farmers frequently gave up the struggle (and went into towns) or were forced into the hands of usurers. The owners of large estates also preferred to employ slaves rather than free men, despite the difficulties which slaves always caused. The influx of destitute farmers to the city of Rome in turn increased that city's already grave problem of food (8). These events led to the main political crisis of Rome in the first century BC.

In the early part of that century, the price of grain in Rome rose: pirates on the sea were interrupting supplies between Africa and Italy. The Senate approved provisions of free grain but the Roman economy could not afford to issue them indefinitely. The tribune Gabinius proposed that a great command should be conferred on Pompey in order to put down the pirates. The Senate opposed the idea for fear of what Pompey would do with that command afterwards. The 'mob' thereupon stormed the Senate, and the 'people' confirmed Pompey's appointment. That in itself lowered the price of grain. It fell further when Pompey beat the pirates off the sea in three weeks. Ten years afterwards, however, prices of grain were again rising. Cato, who was by then consul, distributed subsidised, but not free, grain, as did his enemy Clodius, the unscrupulous tribune who was the Roman agent of Pompey and Caesar during the years of their proconsulships and alliance. In a few years, a further crisis over grain brought Pompey to supreme power. But his reluctance to force recalcitrant suppliers to give up the grain that they were hoarding (some of them were his own old soldiers settled on new land) turned the populace against him. The scarcity continued (9) and led to the overthrow of the Republic.

After the consequent civil wars, Augustus introduced a regular distribution of grain to 300,000 citizens. This *annona*, the characteristic item of social security aid to 'lazy plebeians' (10), was eventually changed by Alexander Severus to the provision of loaves. Thereafter, all free men were eligible for tickets for loaves and the distribution continued, despite the failure of the imperial government to prevent both the sale, and the inheritance, of tickets for the *annona*. Other free issues from time to time at Rome included oil and pork. Wine was also sometimes sold at subsidised prices (11). 274 public bakeries produced both free bread and the loaves which were put on sale. About 350 AD, there were 120,000 daily recipients of six half-pound loaves in Rome, 80,000 in Constantinople where Roman practice was copied (12). Most of the grain used in these free issues, as well as the rest of Rome's needs, came from far away.

If Varrus's famous legions had beaten the Germans in 9 AD, no doubt the history of Roman grain would have been different. For there, as Tacitus put it, 'corn was the only produce required from the earth'. But the corn of Germany stayed beyond Rome's reach. Sicily and Egypt, and other parts of North Africa, remained the granaries of Rome, later supplemented by Britain and Roumania.

The collapse of Roman authority brought the civic munificence of the Empire to an end even though Pope Gregory the Great later revived the *annona*. In the meantime, a population used to free distribution had no more idea how to look after itself than a domesticated wheat could survive without cultivation. The reduction in the size of the Roman population to under 100,000 in 800 AD from a million in 400 AD must have been principally caused by famine, itself a consequence of the end of the free supplies of bread. Even the potter's wheel fell into disuse in Western Europe, pots being again made by hand.

From the early Middle Ages onwards, in Europe, civic authorities intervened in matters affecting the supply not only of grain, but of all food, which vaguely recalled the rules of Rome and might suggest to the unwary that something like a modern State then existed. In France, for example, special inspectors searched pigs' tongues for ulcers supposed to cause leprosy. In mediaeval Venice, fish was taken to a single place to be valued and examined. Several Italian cities employed inspectors who checked against the sale of underweight loaves of bread. There was indeed scarcely a town of importance which did not have what Venice described as its grain office, which controlled not only grain and flour, but also sales in the city. Thus in Venice, flour could only be sold in two places: near St Mark's, and on the Rialto. The Doge was always informed of the level of stocks and, if he discovered that the city had reserves sufficient only for a year or for eight months, he would investigate. In England, the Assize of Bread of 1266 stipulated weights, consistencies, prices and colours of bread which, to some extent, have remained in being ever since, while, in 1390, the authorities of London were doing what the Emperor of China had started to do in 1000 BC: buying quantities of grain to relieve the poor during the dearth, keeping large reserves (13). Similarly, Philip II of Spain was kept 'minutely informed of the variations in the weather from seed time onwards'. It was not just an economic matter, 'for' Braudel reminds us 'famine, real famine, when people died in the streets, was still a reality' (14).

In the sixteenth century, the small size of the area devoted to the production of grain meant that the Mediterranean world, despite its brilliance, was always near to famine. That dictated politics and war. As late as 1660, London, the richest city in Europe, was still so short of food that 50 out of 250 people buried in a prosperous parish had died of starvation (15). The last great European famine was that in Andalusia in 1882. The Balearic islands could scarcely support their cities at all till the eighteenth century (16). There were numerous crises of subsistence in

France in the seventeenth century (17), resulting in local famines which, on occasion, trebled the normal death roll. In short, famine was characteristic of history even in purportedly rich places till the age of modern agriculture – or rather, modern transport, which enabled food to be carried from place to place quickly: 'And great was the famine in the land,' runs a chronicle of 1192 in Castile or, 'and people were dying of hunger . . . and the famine in the kingdom was severe until the summer . . . and they were eating the animals and the dogs and the cats and even the boys that they could steal', runs another chronicle, from Andalusia of 1213 (18). Very often in history, deaths were attributed to 'plague' when undernourishment or starvation would have been a more exact name. In the eighteenth century in northern Spain, an average meal was still held to be 'a little bit of black bread accompanied either by some kind of milk or some vile vegetable but, all in all, in such small quantity that there are those who get up from the table satisfied once in life' (19).

Famine apart, winter diets in wheat-powered continents in the age of agriculture were usually bad. It was that, rather than the cold, that made winter a difficult time. Salt bacon, dried fish, bread and dried peas gave no protection against scurvy. Many people must have been in a condition about to contract scurvy by March. Manors and monasteries had herb gardens, orchards and vineyards and some villagers had plots on which they could grow a few vegetables. But vegetables were usually neglected, partly out of a traditional belief that meat gave strength and passion – an illusion from nomadic life. The Tartars, for example, with their diet of raw horse flesh, scoffed at bread eaters – 'those who eat the tips of weeds'. Mediaeval Europe was anyway more carnivorous than it had ever been before, since the countryside remained open with huge pastures (20). Rich Englishmen may have eaten two or three pounds of meat a day, often raw.

Fish played a part, but mostly in ports. Drying, salting, smoking, as well as accidental preservation by frost, however, made preserved fish a major item of commerce. Salmon weirs and millponds were also maintained to enable Christians to fast in style on Wednesdays, Fridays, and in Lent. The German merchants of the Hanse in the Middle Ages made fortunes from salted herring — which lasted a year, provided the gutting had been done well. Subsequently, in the fifteenth century, the Dutch introduced fifty fathom nets for fishing at night, particularly off the English coast — one cause of the Anglo-Dutch wars of the seventeenth century. Cabot's discovery of a large supply of cod off Newfoundland gave New England its first major export, and supplied the British navy with salted fish for two hundred years (21).

The precise character of food in the age of agriculture is difficult to guess. Certainly, diets can be estimated for, for example, Venetian sailors of about 1320 calories *per diem* (2 pounds of bread, an ounce of cheese, three pounds of salted pork, washed down with a quarter litre of wine); or a sixteenth century 'man of property' in England (an ounce of cheese, 1½ pounds of meat, a pound of bread, 6 ounces of herring, a quart of ale) – again a day; or for a Polish peasant at the same time, also a day (four ounces of cheese, nearly two pounds of bread, four ounces of herring, three litres of beer, two ounces of butter, three ounces of 'husks', and an ounce each of peas and eggs) (22). But the trouble with these estimates is that it is impossible to know how typical they were, or how far the official diets were ever fulfilled: a similar official one for the British soldier in the First World War was rarely put into practice (23). How many people lived only on hard boiled eggs as did the Florentine painter, Piero di Cosimo (24)? According to Vasari, he cooked fifty at a time and ate them one by one when he was hungry. Don Quixote's habitual diet was 'a stew of hash more beef than mutton most nights, boiled bones on Saturdays, lentils on Fridays, a young pigeon as a Sunday treat'; on that, he spent 3/4 of his income (25). Was that characteristic? And how often would he have had that 'portion of badly soaked and worse cooked salt cod with some bread as black and grinning as his armour' (26)? A few impressionistic recollections from literature give as likely a picture of what food in the age of agriculture was like as statistics do: thus Montaigne said that, at the Crown Inn at Lindau, he enjoyed a 'double headed' cabbage, of which they made soups all the winter, broths without bread and rice* eaten from a big pot: 'There was great abundance of good fish which they serve up with the meat course: they disdain trout and eat only the roe . . . plenty of woodcocks and leverets . . . stewed plums, pear and apple tarts . . . sometimes, they serve up the roast first and the soup at the end, sometimes the other. The only dessert they have is pears, apples, which are very good, walnuts and cheese' (27).

One distinguishing mark between European and other diets – here Ancient Egypt, like other Middle Eastern civilisations, should be classed with the East – was the number of prohibitions in all civilisations other than the European, sometimes associated with early attempts at hygiene. For example, Egyptian priests were not permitted to eat fish, and not supposed even to look at beans. During the New Kingdom, pork was also forbidden to priests: a legacy it is said, from the Hyksos kings, who were believed to be of Semitic stock. Both Jews and Arabs, from the earliest days, were forbidden to eat pork – a characteristically nomadic view, it has been suggested by some, since the pig is so essentially an animal of a static culture. India gave the best example later of such bans. There, the priests listed a series of impure items by 500 AD: any meat cut with a sword; all carnivores; locusts, camels, and sour rice; any dish which had been sniffed; when food had been eaten from an earthenware dish, it was to be broken, not used again. By 200 AD each

* The arrival in Europe of rice is mentioned on page 233.

Indian meal was also supposed to consist of thirty-two mouthfuls. By then, too, the inelegant custom had arisen there whereby the wife waited on, and did not share the food of, the husband.

Perhaps, however, as so often, such regulations give an indication as to what was not done, rather than what was. A characteristic meal in India between 500 AD and 1750 AD for a labourer might have been no more than milk and *ghi* (purified butter), some half-cooked vegetable to give it flavour, barley porridge, mixed with a mustard stalk; and perhaps some fruit — all washed down with half-fermented water, in which the barley had been boiled. On the other hand, the rich ate as well in India as Trimalchio, the great gastronome, in Rome: and on all ceremonial occasions, even for poor people, elaborate meals were sought, including oxen, goat, and sheep, and every sort of spice and herb (which had the great merit that, when dried, they could be kept indefinitely), and washed down by intoxicating wines made from honey (28).

Obviously, it would be unwise to seek too sharp distinctions between the two main types of society, that based on grain and that based on rice, which grew up during the age of agriculture: and even more unwise to trace absolutely the difference in their politics from the nature of the crops grown. There were always, no doubt, individualistic Japanese, and disciplined Europeans. Yet it has now become known that many personal characteristics derive ultimately from diet and, in seeking the origins of historical differences, the character of staple crops is a good beginning.

During the age of agriculture, not only did peoples become accustomed to crops which were indigenous to other parts of the world — even the Chinese depended on rice, which certainly did not originate on the Yellow River — but to crops which were grown a long way from where they were eaten.

A good example of this is to be seen in respect of the production of wine. The wild vine flourished in the Caucasus. It was there, probably, that it was first brought into domestication. Disseminated perhaps by birds, it may have been widely distributed very early on: Noah, a 'husbandman', had not only a vineyard, but made himself drunk (29). Vines were grown in Egypt by 4000 BC in the Delta of the Nile, and wine was used as part of the rituals for Osiris. Subsequently, vineyards became common, the grapes were pressed by dancing, and the wine made in a way that did not change much until the twentieth century (30). Doubtless to begin with a drink for the rich — the Egyptian poor drank beer* — wine later became popular, perhaps under the influence of Greece or of Crete. In both countries, the vine was extensively cultivated, the wine

* The ordinary Egyptians used the foam of beer, it seems, rather than yeast to leaven their bread by fermentation, but unleavened flatbreads survived a long time in the ancient Middle East, not only for use in the Jewish Passover.

being well differentiated by place and year almost in the modern French style (31). It began to be exported. The Greeks kept wine in large pots smeared previously with resin and, when exported, placed it in goat or pig skins, or large clay amphorae.

These exported Greek wines were prevented from going bad by treatment with resin. Some wines for sale abroad were kept fresh by the addition of vine ash and other spices. Thus most of the wine exported by the Greeks was fortified, of 'a sherry type'. About 100 AD, the wooden barrel, with metal hoops, was introduced by the 'barbarian' Celts, to whom the Greeks had always exported a great deal of wine. Barrelled wine kept better than it did in amphorae (32). The barrel was thus an important Northern contribution to the life of the South, and one not usually acknowledged by the latter. Most early wine drinkers, incidentally, made their wine strong, and diluted it to drink. Only Scythians, it was said, drank it pure.

At the time of Christ, Italy was reckoned to be the best producer of wine. France was then held to be too cold a place for grapes to ripen properly there. But vines only need an annual average temperature of 22 degrees centigrade. So the French vineyards were founded, in the days of the Antonines. Wine was then widely drunk throughout the Roman Empire, though the monks of the Benedictine order received a modest half pint a day. The conquest by the Arabs of the Eastern Mediterranean ruined the estates where the vine had begun its history — it was forbidden to Muslims traditionally on the ground that some of Mahomet's generals had been found drunk on the battlefield (33) — but only one caliph of Muslim Spain ordered the destruction of the vineyards; and he was overthrown. (Wine was sold freely in Spain under Islam, lending support to the theories of those who argue that Muslim Spain was at heart Catholic and Latin (34)). Mediaeval Europe, meantime, regarded the heavy drinking of wine as a most knightly action:

'And drinks of wine a gallon at two gulps:
Pity the men on whom he wages war' (35).

Vines were widely planted in France in the Middle Ages, particularly when the new granaries of Germany were opened up by the expansions eastwards in the twelfth century. Frenchmen turned many wheat fields over to vines, and exchanged wine for cheap German grain. On the other hand, wine was as important in Christianity as it had been in the Egyptian ritual: without wine, there could be no mass nor, until the chalice was reserved to the priest alone in the thirteenth century, no communion for the faithful. Christianity considered wine to be essential for its mysteries and took it wherever it went, even to countries, such as England, where it had never been before (36). The South of Europe, however, continued to produce most of the wine and the North bought it. So a substantial trade followed, most of it carried in barrels. The bottles and corks now so associated with the wine trade were not used before the seventeenth century, and were not common till the eighteenth. It was also only then that special vintages began, the expensive vintages often owing their fame more to the routes which they took than to the quality of the wine concerned. The preservation of wine for long periods was, however, impossible before the exploitation of the great cork forests of Spain.*

An average consumption of wine in the late agricultural age might be 100 litres per year per person, as was characteristic of Valladolid in the sixteenth century. A similar figure has been quoted for Paris on the eve of the Revolution. Before the age of purification of water, it must be remembered, the drinking of alcohol was actually the best way to swallow liquid without risking being poisoned. Tea, chocolate and coffee were not known, save, to some extent, in the regions where the plants concerned were themselves indigenous: tea in China, and also in the Andes; coffee in Abyssinia; and chocolate in Mexico. The Indians had, it is true, various soft drinks — the juice of mangoes and limes, sugar cane and rose-hip juice — but fruit juices in Europe were very rare and, in northern Europe, where the orange and lemon were unknown, never experienced. Milk could be found, but the scraggy cows of the age of agriculture were needed for ploughing, not milking, and the thin milk available was often foul, though watery whey was drunk fairly widely. Milk in towns was always as unhygienic as water was, probably being responsible for scrofula. Cattle in many towns were diseased and usually kept in very bad conditions. Other societies arranged alternatives. The Mongol armies drank the blood of their horses: half a pint every tenth day could be taken from each animal through a vein — and every horseman had eighteen mounts. Blood, it was said, had the merit of not needing to be cooled nor did it involve transport costs. Other primitive herdsmen also drank blood: the Arabs drank camels' blood before the coming of Islam, the Irish, it is said, drank cows' blood mixed with milk, in the seventeenth century. The Masai do the same in the twentieth (36). Many nomads also made a kind of wine (kumiss) out of fermented mares' milk, and similar alcoholic juices were concocted out of the milk of camel, tiger, deer, dog, yak and sheep.

Various forms of beer were also drunk from the earliest time. Technically, it was usually ale, in the sense that it was beer without preservative herbs such as hops, which were not introduced till the late Middle Ages, at least in Europe. In ancient Babylon, 40% of the grain in some cities went on the manufacture of beer. A workman at Sumer might

---

* A line of Horace's makes clear that the properties of cork were known in antiquity, but it does not seem as if it was much used until the seventeenth century.

receive about 2.2 pints a day, and senior officials might get five times as much. Indeed, beer was sometimes used in Sumer in lieu of wages and probably evolved from bread-making there. (It was discovered early that bread made from sprouted grain which had been dried, and then pounded, kept better than bread made from ordinary flour.) Both ancient Iraq and Egypt had numerous types of beer, some very strong. In the end, Babylonians found that they did not have enough barley to feed their population with beer as well as bread and so, Dr Tannahill tells us, took to wine as Egypt had done before (37). Tacitus found the Germans also drinking a very strong beer (which some have mistakenly supposed to be an early gin) (38), and the Chinese had as many beers as they had crops. Peasants in Russia were brewing *kvass*, beer usually made from rye, from the Middle Ages onwards. Most beer was brewed domestically: something which could be done by any peasant family, though beer was sold in mediaeval Europe and was an early target for government regulation. Then, there was cider, which began to be made in the Basque country, it is said, for there the cider apple is apparently indigenous.

Agriculture in the Americas, meantime, continued to be based on maize and, to a lesser extent, on potatoes until the coming of Columbus. Maize is a crop as bounteous in its returns as rice and gives less trouble. Its grain is edible even before it is ripe. One grain of maize sown can produce almost a hundred grains in the following harvest, even in dry soil and more in well-watered land. Not much weeding is necessary. Harvesting is easy. Two harvests are possible with irrigation. Grown on the edges of lakes or on the terraces of the Peruvian Andes, maize therefore became, over many centuries, the staple food of the Americas, often eaten with tomatoes, or peppers, or fish. Maize also enabled production, particularly in the Andes, of the delicious *chicha* or maize beer and, latterly, of 'Bourbon' whisky.* Maize was well established by 1000 BC, but that does not quite stifle the speculation that it came late to the New World from the East with the mysterious white god Quetzalcoatl, as some Mexicans supposed (39).

Potatoes, indigenous to the Andes, were grown on high land everywhere between Chile and Columbia before 1492. They never competed with maize, however, and were regarded usually as a substitute for it in land above 11,000 feet, where maize cannot grow.

Bread was also made, in that remote America before Columbus, from the tapioca plant, manioc or yucca, the roots of which were grated, squeezed free of juice, and boiled. The pulp was then sieved into cakes and cooked, on a griddle, to become 'cassava bread'.† Indigenous to Brazil, tapioca was also cultivated in North America and the Caribbean

---

* Usually made from a mixture of rye and maize.
† Cassava is an old Caribbean Indian (Taino) word and bread from it for a very long time formed the main diet of poor people of all races living round the Caribbean.

before the Spaniards arrived. Another bread was made in the Americas from the palm-like zamia, by grating the stems of that plant, shaping the pulp into a ball and leaving it in the sun, till it began to ferment. It was then flattened and baked. Meantime, early Californians were gorging themselves on obscure molluscs, groundnuts, avocadoes, chili peppers and some game, such as guinea pig or duck (40). The guinea pig later on was to be seen running in and out of houses in Peru in the days of the Incas, combining edibility with fearlessness (41).

The Aztec peasant's food was porridge from maize as a beginning to the day, perhaps sweetened with honey and red peppers. More important as a staple was an omelette, made of dough from a dried crushed kernel of maize, boiled with water, charcoal and lime, with other skins added, and probably often eaten with tomatoes and chili peppers. The Aztecs used no cooking oil from seeds. Their main meat was game (though they sometimes ate dog), and they continued to eat insects and other forms of life long ago dismissed from the tables of the old world: tadpoles, larvae, winged ants, white worms, newts and iguana. Turkey and avocado also played a part in their diet (42), both being indigenous to the Americas.

Now, societies based on maize needed effective control of water as much as those based on rice. Hence once again in America, irrigation canals were constructed to divert water which, as in China, derived from sources other than rainfall. Hence too, the foundation of 'hydraulic monarchies' necessitating disciplined work by large labour forces.

Many people look at old maps, glance at old figures for populations, and exclaim, how wonderful to have lived in such an empty world! Such nostalgia is misplaced. The world before the railway in the nineteenth century could not, as has been seen, carry food very quickly from place to place. Even if it could be carried, most foods — meat, vegetables, fruit — went bad soon unless salted or dried. Grain could be carried far and stored — hence, indeed, its importance — but, even so, grain fleets might fail and so famine was constantly feared, even in civilised countries such as Italy, even during the Renaissance: particularly, perhaps, in civilised countries, for cities and civilisation have grown up together. The provisioning of a great city was, in the past, always a great feat.

The question of why population did not grow faster between 8000 BC and 1750 AD is not one which will ever be satisfactorily resolved. Nor is the question of exactly how much land was under the plough or at any rate farmed at any special time. But agriculture must always have cut a modest figure on any realistic map of the world before 1750 AD. The character of this agriculture in the broadest terms — technology, landowning, types of labour and produce apart from food — is the subject of the next few chapters. It occupied most people most of the time and is, therefore, the central theme of this part of this book.

11

Agriculture: Techniques

The history of the age of agriculture may perhaps seem to some partly an elaboration on the history of the plough. The first 'scratch' plough, as has been seen earlier, was an enlarged digging stick or downward pointing spike, drawn by men, to begin with, and then by two oxen which were attached to it by a pole. The triangular 'share' of this plough did not, as a rule, turn over the soil, and left a wedge of earth undisturbed between the furrows. Cross-ploughing — sometimes more than once — was, therefore, necessary. The consequence was usually a fairly square field. Cross-ploughing also breaks up soil well, and brings more stones to the surface.

It was soon realised that the wooden, often oaken, blade of the share worked better if protected by a hard edge: so the Egyptians began to use a flint edge. The idea came into general use and later bronze and iron shares were generally used. The Romans had many iron ploughshares. Others used pebbles skilfully pushed into holes in the wood. A bough of a tree with an iron tip was used in Britain before Caesar landed. That was also used by the ancient Germans (1). This primitive plough in almost its old form was still to be seen in France in 1913, in Russia till 1930 and in other places in the Mediterranean and the East till even later, particularly in places where it is dry (2).

The Chinese, meantime, had, about 1000 BC, developed a curved 'mouldboard' to overturn the sliced sod. Used continuously for the cultivation of rice thenceforward, it was not, however, appreciated in Europe for another 1400 years (3).

Actually, the scratch plough (as has been seen) was not very effective in northern Europe, with its heavy soils and fairly wet summers. So agriculture, when it was taken north was, till about 500 AD, largely confined to drained hillsides or plateaus, with light soil. The teams of two oxen or mules used for ploughing in classical times were also too weak for heavier work (4).

The corn of Greece and Rome was grown on soil which grew increasingly worse, being scorched by drought in summer, and drenched by a rain in winter which washed away the natural nutrients. Conditions were worsened by the denuding of hillsides by woodcutting. The soil was held together neither by dead leaves nor by dry roots. Hence the poverty of Greece, which, about 650 BC, led very quickly to debt once coinage had been introduced and subsequently to colonisation. Cattle were scarce; so, therefore, was manure. The yield of Roman corn was poor, 4 grains to 1 sown compared with 200 to 1 in Babylon (5).

During the first century AD, a bigger plough began to be used in Italy (perhaps being invented in France) for heavier soil. It was usually wheeled and pulled by eight oxen. This had several advantages. It was naturally more easily moved from field to field. Ploughmen could regulate more easily the depth of the furrow. But it needed peace, stability, and predictability. So it did not come into general use, even in the northern European parts of the Roman Empire, until re-introduced, modified, by the Slavs about 600 AD. This heavy plough, the Slavs' only contribution to human improvement until the Russian novel of the nineteenth century, had three new elements: first, a knife-like iron blade in front of the plough, the so-called coulter, which slashed vertically into the ground; a ploughshare in the form of a blade which cut horizontally through the ground at grass roots; and a mouldboard, like that devised in China, which turned over the soil or turf on to one side. This plough was sometimes set on wheels and drawn by a team of oxen, sometimes four, sometimes eight in number. It coped well with heavy soil, and permitted the clearance of forests much more easily than the simpler, old ploughs. Soil was thrown up with such force that crossploughing was not necessary, with a consequent saving of labour. Since these fields were usually ploughed clockwise, with the sod turned over inwards to the right, they often came to look like a long low ridge, assuring a crop on the crest even in wet years, and one in the trough or furrow in the driest (6). The old squarish fields gave way generally to long ones.

The disadvantage of this heavy plough was that it needed a team of oxen to pull it and, while it did well on large estates, it was much too unwieldy as well as too expensive for small holdings. Poor farmers, therefore, had to work in co-operation. Sometimes, this had the effect of assisting indirectly the creation of large estates, sometimes leading to something close to co-operatives. The heavy plough also encouraged the process by which manors created from virgin land in northern Europe were divided into common fields, themselves divided into strips, usually about 220 feet by 20 feet, and usually divided one from another in a disorganised manner* (7).

In many parts of the world this plough was never used. African agriculture, for example, remained based upon the scratch plough till the twentieth century, as did that of Asia and America, until after 1492.

---

* See page 107, below.

In Africa's case, the unavailability of a good animal for traction was the main reason: oxen did not live long in the tropics.

The use of the heavy plough of northern Europe accounted for the increase of food and, therefore, probably of population in Europe during Carolingian times and also, therefore, at one remove, provided the incentive for Viking expeditions. It also led to the great extension of arable land throughout Europe between the eleventh and the four-teenth centuries, the transformation of the Po valley from marshes and forests into the great flat prosperous plain which it now is, with its drainage regulated (as a result of the initiative of the Benedictine and later Cistercian monks). Perhaps too the Crusades and the expansion of religious orders in Europe may indirectly be explained by this growth of population and hence by the new plough.

Within a few hundred years too, the greater efficacy of this plough had been enhanced by changes in the energy driving it: the horse became a competitor of the ox. Here again, northern Europe differentia-ted itself from the rest of the world.

The horse, in a previous chapter, was shown as drawing chariots effectively for war, being ridden for hunting, but apart from bits and bridles (known before 1000 BC in Europe, as in the Mediterranean world) the only aid to horsemanship was the spur. Light horseshoes only became common in the Mediterranean about 100 BC, when the Gauls and then the Romans adopted iron shoes. Though the Greeks had a saddle cloth of sorts, the earliest regular saddle in the West seems not to have been seen earlier than the first century AD and perhaps later, though 'barbarians' in central Asia may have used saddles long before that (8).

The discovery of the stirrup in the West transformed the history of the horse and of war. Spears needed no longer to be thrown, but could be held as lances and rammed home. Horsemen became the directors of the battlefield. Hence the equestrian knight, symbol of chivalry. In 732, Charles Martel held the Arabs at the battle of Tours, his cavalry equipped with stirrups (9). A century later, Charles the Bald, summon-ing his tenants-in-chief to the feudal host, ordered that they should attend mounted (10). Horses were bred to be as big as possible. By 900, nomadic tribes and settled monarchies alike used stirrups, though not always iron ones: the Sassanids who crossed the Oxus about then with 10,000 horses were 'so poor that their stirrups were made of wood' (11). (Horses too were never cheap: in the time of the Cid in Spain, about 1000 AD, a horse cost the equivalent of fifty oxen (12)). The conse-quence was the organisation, over the next generation, in much of Europe of what is now called 'feudalism'.* Under this system, nobles held land from kings in return for military service and sub-tenants held

* The word was invented in France about 1720.

land from nobles on the same understanding. Anyone who could not, or would not, fulfil his new military obligations forfeited his grant of land (13). So the households of lords became schools in which boys were trained in chivalry, the creation of a 'self-conscious cosmopolitan military caste aware of its solidarity and soon aware of its traditions', as Marc Bloch describes it, kept in good morale by *chansons de geste*, and trained by tournaments to keep fit. These knights wore heavy armour which became heavier, as time went by: hence, pennons, shields, hereditary arms to enable recognition. Entry into knighthood (as in crafts or priesthoods) became a rite, often enacted in church, perhaps after a long vigil of prayer, with swords blessed, the Church accepting knightly oaths. Horses were carefully trained and they, as Persian horses had been, were protected by mail. Each knight was the captain of a small team of squires, grooms and servants, together with several horses, as a bullfighter is the 'sword' of his *cuadrilla* (14).

The idea extended at first no further than the Carolingian empire. The Anglo-Saxons knew the stirrup. But they did not recognise its military uses. Harold and his men rode horses with stirrups but dismounted to fight, while William's charged. After his victory, William established a horse-powered autocracy based on knights' service (15). Byzantium, Islam and other societies copied Europe, as did the Germans eventually (though the ceremonies of initiation for knights derive from ancient German practice) (16). The wars of the Reconquista in Spain were also fought, on both sides, mostly by cavalry with stirrups: for example, the Almoravides in 1094 were said to have had 150,000 horse, only 3000 foot.

Last among Europeans to become aware of the need for a professional class of cavalry were the Italians: in mediaeval Florence, armies all still consisted of footsoldiers, and (as in modern Europe) all able-bodied citizens could be called upon to be soldiers at a moment's notice. No horses decided a battle in Italy before the battle of Montaperti (1260) (where Manfred and the Siennese Ghibellines inflicted a great defeat on the Florentine Guelfs because of the former's judicious use of a few German cavalrymen) (17).

This apotheosis of the horse had important agricultural consequences. Sometime in the late ninth century, heavy horseshoes of iron, like the light Roman ones but much stronger, followed the stirrup into Europe from the East. They reached Byzantium by 900, by 950 they were habitual in the West for long journeys, and by 1000 they were already cheap enough to be afforded by peasants (18).

The heavy horseshoes meant that hooves could stand up to previously difficult wet soil. The size of the horses bred for war (the *destriers*) made them competitive with oxen in agriculture, if only a new sort of harness could be found which, unlike the old yoke, did not press against the horse's windpipe and jugular vein. Another weakness of the yoke, was that the drawing came at the withers: too high for a maximum effect. So, even with new shoes, horses could not really be used for ploughing, nor harrowing, nor even heavy hauling.

At some time, in the early Middle Ages, also from the Eastern source whence all the great equestrian innovations have come, far on the windy plains of the central Asian steppe, and accompanied, it would seem, by the cross bow and the wheelbarrow, the modern horse-collar arrived. If its coming was unrecorded, its effect was great. It allowed the horse to pull as hard as the ox. But the horse can move faster, and is actually stronger, than the ox. So it can both cover twice the ground the ox can, and can work two or three hours more a day. The question of speed was probably decisive in making farmers turn to horses in northern Europe, for the weather is temperamental, and the success of the crop depends on taking advantage of a good opportunity. This change, together with the use of shafts attached to the breast band, and traces to link teams of animals, enabled a series of major agricultural changes in northern Europe. In the twelfth century, ploughing from Kiev to Normandy was usually done with horses, while, in the Mediterranean, oxen continued, with lighter ploughs. At the same time, the wagoner and the carter carrying goods by horse assisted the revival of the mediaeval European economy.

These changes were less marked elsewhere. China devised the horse collar, but did not use horses to agricultural advantage since water buffaloes, then as now, seemed more appropriate for rice farming than horses. In the Americas, there was no plough before 1492 AD, indeed no metal tools at all, save for a few bronze instruments among the Incas. In Africa, horses were always expensive since, like oxen, they did not like tropical circumstances: in the sixteenth century, horses were costing three times as much as slaves in central Africa: the decisive reason for Africa's continuing slow development.

The horse helped the beginning of a real rotation of crops in Europe. It had been long known that crops would exhaust the soil if the same crop were grown on it year after year. Only Egypt, with its fertile loess, had been able to avoid some kind of rotation. Civilised countries of antiquity, such as the Roman empire, had used a rotation of two years: one year grain, one year fallow. Occasionally, the field not in use for wheat might be used for pasture. Though both Greeks and Romans observed that peas and beans restored exhausted soil, they did not make a habit of alternating them with other crops. Partly, that was because some believed that beans contained the souls of the departed. The main agricultural improvement of mediaeval Europe, so far as crops were concerned, was the substitution in many places of a rotation of three crops for two. That coincided with, indeed was probably inspired by, the increase in size of fields and estates, as more and more forests in Europe fell before the axe (19). As with irrigation, the great abbeys were among the first to adopt the change. Thus, very often, in mediaeval northern Europe, good land was divided into that which grew spring corn, winter corn such as oats (for horses) and fallow; while, in the south, corn and fallow continued to take turn and turn about. In northern Europe, peas and beans began to be grown regularly alongside the oats, imparting certain desirable acids to the soil (20). Later on, in Flanders, cereals and fodder alternated, while Dutch fields began to have five years of crops, then five years of pasturage (21).

These changes in methods of cultivation were not complemented by changes in methods of harvesting. Corn was, almost from its first appearance, cut by a sickle, one of the oldest and most continuously used tools of all. When collected up, it was threshed by a wooden flail or trodden out on an earthen threshing floor by oxen or horses. After threshing, the grain was separated from chaff by being tossed in the air, the wind carrying the chaff away. All these usages, which began in the Near East, in its golden age, continued almost unchanged everywhere till the nineteenth century AD and, in many places, even in Europe, till the twentieth.

The grinding of grain also early developed the principles which characterised it till the nineteenth century, between a fixed and a rotating stone (22), though refinements were added (grooves, for example, incised in both stones, by the miller, or by the itinerant crafts-man; while the texture of the stones themselves was often considered very important, being frequently brought from remote places). At first, Egypt and Babylon used a small bun-shaped stone for use on large, saucer-shaped stones, for their grinding. This was soon replaced in Egypt by the 'saddle quern', the best maker of flour for thousands of years: a miller sat at one end of a rectangular, slanted stone and pushed his rubbing stone backwards and forwards. This was in use among the Celts in Britain between 550 and 300 BC. Later, the rubbing stone was made more square, to allow the grain to trickle through a slit to the grinding surface, so saving the trouble of lifting up the stone whenever another handful of grain was needed.

Though, in ancient Egypt, there were a few professional bakers in towns, most people made their own bread until the Roman Empire. The full rotary motion made possible by driving donkeys or mules around a mill gave the professional baker in a city such as Rome an advantage over the housewife, thus enabling large-scale and semi-mechanical grinding. By 100 BC, in Rome, bakers were becoming millers, the millers mass producers. These rotary querns were widespread in Europe by about 200 BC, to judge from remains from Celtic Britain (23).

The millers were pioneers in other ways. They were, for example, the first to make use of the water mill, apparently developed in Pontus, in the first century BC at much the same time that it was devised in China — a simultaneity that suggests a greater connection between the two regions than is usually realised. The earliest type of mill used an axle which was horizontal, in China, and vertical, in the West. The lower end of the vertical axle had a wheel immersed in a stream. The upper end passed through the lower millstone and was fixed directly to the upper stone, which it turned. This mill, mostly used for the grinding of corn, could only work well with really fast-flowing water. In the first century BC, the great Roman architect Vitruvius designed a vertical 'undershot' waterwheel which connected the wheels' horizontal axle with the vertical axle of the stones, so permitting faster rotation. The idea was probably influenced by the Persian *noria* or *saquiya* by which pots were arranged round the circumference of a wheel, turned by a man or an animal, and dipped into water. Within a hundred years, a mill of this sort surely would have been in wide use in Rome, had it not been for the availability of slaves. By the end of the Roman Empire, in the fourth or fifth centuries, the more powerful 'overshot' wheel also existed, both in Rome and in China, but neither civilisation showed much imagination, to begin with, in applying it to an industrial process. These wheels were kept for grinding corn, and that they did well. For example, a wheel at Arles in late Roman days had sixteen overshot wheels, which ground three tons of corn an hour. Chinese water wheels, on the horizontal principle, perhaps an extension of the rotary quern, were very often constructed and, in India, water wheels for irrigation were 'a familiar part of the rural landscape' by about 650 AD (24).

There were some further Western innovations in the Byzantine era. Some experiments were made with tide mills. Still, only in the tenth century AD was there any serious use of watermills for activities other than the grinding of corn (probably on the Serchio near Lucca) (25). But from then on, there certainly was such use, specially encouraged by the Cistercian monks, so that soon and until the nineteenth century there was scarcely a village between Moscow and the Atlantic which did not have its wheel, used for an increasing diversity of actions. The grinding of grain was a priority but the wheel could also lift and tilt hammers used in forging, pump bellows for ovens, launder, saw, crush olives, full cloth, reduce paper to pulp, pigments to paint and malt to beer. Domesday Book records already nearly 6000 mills in England at the time of the Norman Conquest. There were said to be 60,000 watermills in France in the sixteenth century — and perhaps 500,000 in Europe on the eve of the industrial revolution (26). In 1534, a mill was set up in Paris for polishing precious stones, but its owners found it taken over by the King for use as a royal mint, to produce 'milled' coins (27). Probably the biggest wheel of all was established in France at Marly, to feed the fountains of Versailles, generating at best seventy-five horse-power (28). But by then the age of agriculture was already in its dying days.

Just as commerce began in earnest when obsidian was carried down a river (the Euphrates) to Jarmo in Iraq about 5000 BC, the waterwheels of mediaeval European towns made the rivers into real engines of prosperity for a whole era. A Benedictine monk recalled that 'the river enters the abbey as much as the well, acting as a check, allows. It gushes first into the corn mill, where it is very actively employed in grinding the grain under the weight of the wheel, and in shaking the fine sieve which separates flour from bran. Thence, it fills the boiler to prepare beer for the monks' drinking . . . it is then drawn into the fulling machines, where its duty is to make the cloth for the monks' clothing [by] raising and alternately lowering the heavy hammer and mallet* . . . next, the river enters the tannery, where it devotes much care and labour to the materials for the monks' shoes; then it divides . . . and passes through the various departments of cooking, crushing, watering, or grinding . . . At last, it carries away the refuse' (29). Every river, indeed, in the age of agriculture was a river of life. Thus, the ancient Egyptians depended so much on the Nile that it was worshipped in innumerable guises, above all as Hâpi, depicted as a well-nourished man, with huge breasts hanging over his chest, and a vast belly bulging over his belt. Hâpi was permitted to seem to be dead much of the year, when nature in Egypt was exhausted, the trees being grey with dirt, and only a few vegetable plots being kept alive with the greatest difficulty. Then, in June, the great river would rise again, driving forward mud and debris which first coloured the water green. The rising of the water could be seen at Aswan about June 7th, it was at Cairo about the 17th, and in the Delta two days later. The green Nile had by then turned red, as the river spread over the banks to cover the countryside and, in late September, the whole valley would seem a shallow lagoon between deserts, the towns becoming little Venices, joined by causeways. Sebeh, the crocodile god, was detected by the pious. The protection of causeways and walls became the main work, though pilgrimages would be undertaken to holy places. The cultivable area was divided into rectangles varying between 1000 and 40,000 acres and they were fed with water, by sluices, so as to be flooded to a depth of three to six feet. The water was then drained off back to the Nile by a system of canals, when, in October, the Nile began to shrink and return to its 'normal' bed (30).

These two periods, *perit*, when the river was going out into the fields, and *shemu*, when it was withdrawing, were, actually, the first well-identified seasons, the river being thus the father of the calendar, as well as of most undertakings, both industrial and agricultural in the age of agriculture. Aside from any industrial use, water, of course, plays a decisive part in agriculture everywhere. For example, it is now estimated that 1500 tons of water are needed to grow a ton of wheat, 4000 tons

---

* 'Fulling' is to beat or tread cloth in order to cleanse or to thicken it.

of water to grow a ton of rice, 10,000 tons of water to grow a ton of cotton fibre (31). The availability of water seemed, a generation ago, to be indeed the decisive element in all agrarian productivity and land reform. A traveller looked at, for example, west Valencia in Spain to see weed-choked crops on rocky hillsides, badly pruned mulberries, olives caught by frost, and mean, terraced wheat. Only a few miles away, there was the richly irrigated coastal plain which has given five crops every two years for hundreds of years because, it seemed, it had a good system of irrigation. Vines, carobs, rice, fruit, all flourished — in the thirteenth century, as they do today (32). The worship, almost, of water has thus good credentials. An automatic device to raise water, the *shaduf*, enabled vines, date palms, flowers and vegetables of Egypt to be watered since 2000 BC. A continuous chain of buckets was apparently in use in the Hanging Gardens of Babylon to water the flowers there. Wells lined by rough stone and with a rope pulley existed in Egypt by 1500 BC, while water was being conserved by damming as early as 1300 BC on the Orontes in Syria.

Only the wind is really comparable to water. Yet the windmill has a far less interesting history than the waterwheel. Originating in Persia or Afghanistan, perhaps derived from the revolving bookcases of China or the wind-driven prayer wheels of central Asia, windmills, by the tenth century, were being used in Persia for irrigation and, later, for grinding corn. There was a Western copy of this by 1180, in England. It was once held that these windmills were brought back by the Crusaders, but there were apparently no windmills at that time in the Holy Land. The earliest mills turned horizontally and they continue thus in China, but a vertical wheel was being used in Europe in the thirteenth and fourteenth centuries and afterwards.

For a time, windmills actually seemed to have an advantage over waterwheels, for they could not be stopped by freezing and could be built almost wherever needed. But Mediterranean people found waterwheels more reliable. Windmills thus took a long time to reach, for example, central Castile, where they were still a novelty in the days of Cervantes. Hence Don Quixote's surprise at seeing them looking so white against the parched earth, much as they look today. By the fourteenth century, tower windmills had been devised, bodies built of stone or brick, and sails adjusted to the tops of the buildings. Many of these were used for pumping water as well as for grinding corn. Holland, whose flat land was specially good for this type of energy, at one time had 8000 windmills. The average strength of a windmill was much the same as that of a watermill — five to ten horsepower (33).

The plough, the ox, the horse, the waterwheel and the windmill, the water buffalo and the irrigation ditch: these were the motors of the age of agriculture. Yet we now know very well that a lack of technology, pure and simple, is not the only reason for unproductive agriculture. Gunnar Myrdal, in his famous study of the causes of poverty in the twentieth century, Asian Drama, *singled out innumerable other explanations for change and undevelopment, health and ill-health, in economics. The character of ownership, the type of lease, the political system, seemed to him at least as important as the availability of a tractor or the existence of a farm-to-market road. Doubtless if that analysis is true of the present century in Asia, it must have been true of most of the world in the past. The next chapters, therefore, discuss the way that land was held in an age when most of the populated world was managed by landowners.*

12

Agriculture: Landlords and Labourers

The small portion of the world already being farmed in the days of classical antiquity was being looked after by, in a rough ascending order of status: slaves, who could be sold at will by a master, though their rights, like their duties, differed from era to era, and from place to place: serfs, or labourers who, though more free than slaves, had their freedom of movement constrained by law or custom; labourers, paid in kind or cash for a set piece of work, or a set number of hours; modest farmers, owning their own land, perhaps able to employ one to two labourers, but whose livelihood depended on their own work and that of their family; farmers, some rich, some poor, who rented land, sometimes for money, sometimes by some form of sharecropping; small properties; and great estates, some in private hands, and some, in the East in particular, maintained more or less as state farms on which special groups of serving men, slaves or forced labour were, from the earliest days, employed (though most of the land even in those despotisms was probably farmed by smallholders (1)). Still, the characteristic economic and social holding of the age of agriculture was the large estate: not because of the charms of country life in agreeable circumstances, so well and so delightfully chronicled from the time of Horace onwards; but because of its political significance. All forms of landholding were, for several hundred generations, political forms, but none more so than the great estate.

In Egypt, in the Middle East generally in antiquity, in China and India, in Rome and feudal Europe, the large estate was what it had been in mediaeval France and would be in nineteenth-century South America: 'a unit both territorial and social' (2), in France, according to Marc Bloch, or a 'social and political organisation, a means of control, the basis of the ruling oligarchy' (3), in South America, according to John Lynch. The great estates of Andalusia which, for so long, provided Castilian noble families with their revenues, continued much the same under Romans, Goths, Arabs and Christians — huge latifundia growing wheat, olives or barley, or breeding bulls, and usually run by a bailiff. Of innumerable tyrants, kings, princes of the Church, and nobles, between 2000 BC and 1800 AD, it might have been said, as it was of General Rosas in Argentina, in the nineteenth century, 'Who was Rosas? An owner of land. What did he accumulate? Land. What did he give to his supporters? Land. What did he take from his enemies? Land' (4). Along the Ganges, everyone noticed, the large landowners were, from the time of the Aryan conquest, the potential traders as well as rulers, since they had both leisure and capital (5).

Where if anywhere can the great estate be most 'typically' found? Surely during the Roman Empire when the great estate, the *fundus*, an enterprise usually called after some long dead owner (for example, 'Fundus Claudius'), would be divided into tenancies and a home farm, ancestor of the feudal demesne farm which, in many places, survived till the present — in, for example, the 'administration cane' land of the Latin American sugar estate of the twentieth century. Large estates, such as that of Pliny the Younger at Tifernum in Tuscany, with its 3000 acres, would employ a big slave population and also much casual labour (6). In France, and perhaps in other outlying parts of the Roman Empire, the estates of the early centuries were a continuation of an even earlier system, going back to the days of domination by the Celts, for 'all points to the conclusion that the Gallo-Roman aristocracy was a caste of village chieftains, drawing part of their incomes from dues owed by their peasant subjects', the regime itself having its origin in an ancient tribal system, and the change from clan leadership to seigneurial authority being, for Marc Bloch again, 'relatively simple', comparable to what happened later in mediaeval Wales (7). In slightly similar circumstances, mediaeval Germany was a country which seemed not unlike Africa in the nineteenth century, 'where the Chief was only just becoming Lord' (8). Similarly, though the life of an estate might be interrupted (and land not cultivated) during a time of civil war, or invasion by nomads in the fifth and sixth centuries, or as a result of the marauding Vikings and Magyars in the ninth and tenth centuries, or the Hundred Years' War of the fifteenth, there was always continuity. The majority of great estates of Rome passed, without change in type of farming, though with change of ownership, from the Empire to the Middle Ages. Some of them were made over as gifts to the Church — perhaps many, for the Church did not as a rule accept waste lands. Some dominant mediaeval families may have had a connection with leading Roman subjects of early Frankish kings, but, if so, the direct line of descent was, in every case, broken: no blood connection seems to exist between mediaeval landowners and the holders of land under Rome (9).

When the Germans occupied the Roman Empire, they seized, or were given, substantial sections of the land (about two thirds of the acreage in France, half of the forest), so that a new race of German (that is, Frankish) landowners mostly ran old Roman estates. But the estates themselves probably did not change much in shape, nor, Henri Pirenne argues, was the area of cultivated land increased (10). Such estates retained their old characteristics: demesnes, or home farms; tenant farmers owing services and dues; the territorial intermixture of demesne land with those of tenants. But 'the constant unrest, the habitual resort to force, the insecurity which impelled everyone to seek a protector . . . the abuse of power fostered by the absence of government . . . all combined to draw an ever-increasing number of peasants into the hands of seigneurial subjection' (11). The anarchy of the end of the Carolingian state, for example (and the confusion of the time of the Vikings), gave many vassals the chance to seize outright lands which they had received as temporary grants (12), particularly those 'counts', originally perhaps 250 to 350, who had been organised as a bureaucracy, to begin with, but who, from the saddle of the new big horses of mediaeval Europe, made themselves the captains of feudalism. Afterwards, the enfeebled monarchs could only confirm the titles or indeed continue the process — arms, titles, exemption from taxes granted in return for knight service. In the fiefs so created, the lord was king. Feudalism imposed, however, obligations on all: the Earl of Stafford could not refuse his duties to the King; was he, in an absolute sense, therefore, no freer than the serf? All had some freedoms in the age of agriculture, some more than others. Most people had fewer than their ancestors had in the age of hunters.

Everywhere feudalism had different forms, with different effects. In England, it was installed by the deliberate plan of William the Conqueror; and assisted the growth of the monarchy. In Germany, feudalism, on the contrary, prevented the survival of a central monarchy. Spain's feudalism proper was confined to Catalonia, which Charlemagne reconquered from Islam: elsewhere, the powerful military orders, the availability of Muslim slaves, the royal grants of latifundia, made landholding in Spain more oriental in character than northern European. In France, the system lasted a long time, preserving its inconveniences and privileges, more than the benefits, due to royal interventions. The National Assembly after 1789 'totally abolished' the feudal regime; among the duties of those who hold the Légion d'Honneur is the task of combatting 'any enterprise tending to re-establish the feudal regime' (13). But, in many places, the end of feudalism meant the end of obligations by landlords (to the King, as to the serf), without freeing the labourers. Thus, after the wars of independence in South America, the latifundium* was a refuge against chaos, much as the early mediaeval fief was (14). Yet the great private estate of the nineteenth century rarely imposed irksome duties on landlords. Similarly, the Thirty Years' War enabled Junkers in Prussia to establish local despotisms over peasants,

---

* Never precisely a feudal enterprise.

who were often Slav in ancestry (15). The government of England in the eighteenth century, seemed, perhaps was, a committee of landlords. Landowners were the richest class in England till at least the 1870s (16) and financed much of politics as if it were one more private interest, only a little more important than their stud-book. In the nineteenth century, indeed, the large estate was probably at its most powerful — (as, indeed, was the hereditary monarchy): a tamed labour force was available to work at low wages for a lord who had no feudal limitations on his ownership and often still had real privileges.

The word 'feudalism' is not one which can be exactly used anywhere else save in western Europe. True, in India, in the early Middle Ages, a system existed in which the monarch granted the income from certain lands to certain tenants, whose responsibility was to provide levies (17). Equally, the Chinese system of land-holding was, for several hundreds of years at the very beginning of their history, apparently, based on the work of peasants who, in return for protection, did work on their lord's estate. Tribute was passed 'from rank to rank', ultimately reaching the imperial court where noblemen were expected to serve certain sojourns Later, both Indian and Chinese ranks acquired a hierarchical flavour, not unlike Western ranks of nobility, and later – though still not much before the fall of Rome in the West – the whole system gave way to one in which government officials rather than noblemen ran new territories and old ones as well (18).

This, of course, is an oversimplification of the diversity of the 'Great Estates': how can one begin to compare, it will be asked, the estancias of South America, founded by the Spaniards, with their hundreds of head of cattle (original grantees were entitled to seventy-four cattle, or 666 sheep, on an estate of a league* square), even with the farms in the same places based on the manpower needed before the Spaniards introduced their cattle-powered agriculture (19)? The tangle of rents, mortgages, tenancies and entails cannot, it will be said, be so simply dismissed. And what, anyway, is a 'large' estate? 130 or 250 acres, after all, would have been considered a large enterprise even for a monastery in mediaeval France (20), and so would five acres in the rich Valencian huerta (21). The biggest estate in fourth century Attica, apart from an exceptional case, was sixty or so acres (22). The huge farms of the early Roman empire — Pliny's 3000 acres have been mentioned — seem on a different scale. In Domesday England, a large manor, such as that at Staines in Middlesex, with its six watermills, fish weir, meadow for twenty-four teams of oxen, wood for thirty pigs, was 2280 acres, while the manor of Leominster (Hereford), held by Harold's Queen Edith, and her family, accounted for nearly 10,000 acres (23). Yet the fact is that the management of a great estate the world over has many similarities

---

* Two and three-fifths miles.

with others like it. Absentee and resident landlords, even bailiffs and *fattori*, even *mezzaiouli** and sharecroppers, the differences are of emphasis, not of fundamental purpose. Whether the estate was a part of the one fifth or so of France owned by the Church in 1789, or whether it was run by the Templars, estates owned clerically were much the same, too, in character.

For much of the age of agriculture, meantime, monarchs lived in their kingdoms as great landowners did on their estates, conforming to the customs of the property accepted by their ancestors, relying on their stewards, sons or chaplains for advice, seeking to enlarge their estates by marriage or, occasionally, conquest, fighting their cousins if they had unfairly taken their inheritance, sometimes lapsing into senility or vice and, therefore, temporarily leaving the running of affairs to brothers or scheming uncles. A king's court was a lord's household somewhat enlarged. In both, all dined together, privacy was non-existent, rooms such as libraries were few (only in the seventeenth century did the idea of the great hall begin to vanish in England, and lord and lady begin to dine apart). The King's property in England in 1100 resembled that of a lord of the manor in an open field, a huge enterprise dotted about the shires, some in bad soil, some in good, disorganised and not centralised, but often giving a substantial revenue; and, in Eastern despotisms, as in Western monarchies, the ruler was usually the largest landowner (24). The King of Prussia, for example, owned nearly a third of his kingdom as late as 1750 (25). Yet there were differences, not always evident to the observer nor even to the man who worked there, but profound, as will be seen.

The question of inheritance, of estates as of kingdoms, for example, varied. Consider again mediaeval Europe. Sometimes the lord of an estate would decide which of his sons, or, occasionally, daughters or other relations, would succeed him (26). Sometimes, the sons themselves would decide which of them was the best (27). Primogeniture only slowly became the rule in most European countries after the Carolingians, though there was no trace of it in ancient Roman practice and though Germans were slow to adopt what they called 'this alien trick' (28). For many generations, some petty lords continued to practise common inheritance and common cultivation. Sometimes, if a lord were defeated whilst fighting to extend his lands, he might be succeeded by an enemy; or the King, or other superior political authority (or a bishop), might grant the lands concerned to a new tenant, in return for certain obligations. In England, under the Anglo-Saxons, land was still being given to office holders, the title to which soon became hereditary (29). But the main difference in the West and the East was that, once possessed of an estate, an English lord became a person of local signifi-

* The operators of sharecropping leases in Italy.

cance, unlike his Oriental contemporary, who remained usually at bottom no better than a civil servant, and able to be dismissed at a moment's notice.

Here then there begin to appear in the era of early feudalism in Europe certain fundamental differences between customs prevailing in the feudal West and those in the East. Feudal Europe was poorer than Islam or India or China. Its monarchies had smaller armies. It was less quick to make use of innovations. But yet it had ceased to be nomadic. It was a congeries of settled communities within which noblemen, bishops and, to some extent already, merchants (as will be seen later) existed in their own right. Indeed, they had, or had obtained, rights. In their own localities, they were the masters. No matter that this derived from the almost universal, irremediable, recognised and regretted weakness of the central authority. It led to fundamental differences in the end. Properties in feudal Europe were admittedly still granted, and granted by kings not against an obligation to pay something (that was a secondary matter) but to do something. Such obligations, in much of mediaeval Europe, were sealed by a physical act of homage, hands submitted together, to the master: he who proffered hands made a declaration as a man. The chief would then kiss his subordinate, and on the mouth. This act had happened among the Germans before the fall of the Roman Empire but, during the Carolingian era, as indeed in India under the Gupta dynasty, an oath might be made, on the Gospel or on relics (30). Later still, the obligations were extended, in, for example, Normandy and England, to cover an obligation to hold, at the disposal of the superior, a prescribed number of knights and men. The vassal himself would, as a rule, decide how this service was to be fulfilled. He could, for instance, as some princes of the Church preferred, keep his vassals on the demesne and so, though having to provide for their board and lodging, at least maintain the estate intact (31); or, more usually, he could let out estates to them. But, in feudal society in its purest form, such as the kingdom of Jerusalem, tenure was dependent. Everyone who held land held it of someone else (32), though, on very few occasions, were there more than a few men between king and peasant, in the hierarchy of holdings: 'Four townsmen hold of Hugh de Lacy, who holds of S. de Furneaux, who holds of the Count of Brittany, who holds of the King' (33). These obligations would ultimately be commuted into rents (34).

Over-simplicity usually begets deception. Yet, even in the age of agriculture, there were never more than two types of monarch: first, despots, symbolised by the personality of Frederick II, Emperor and King of Sicily, foolishly over-praised in many works of nostalgic history, a man who sought in Burckhardt's phrase, to transform 'the people into a multitude destitute of will and of means of resistance'; who 'centralised . . . the whole judicial and political administration';

who collected taxes 'by those cruel and vexatious methods without which . . . it is impossible to obtain money from Orientals'; who crowned his 'system of government by a religious inquisition' (35); and who regarded everything within the state as his own property — just as Wang Mang, the Hsin emperor of China in the first century AD declared the entire land of the country to be the property of the State (36).

Second, there were rulers who regarded themselves, as they had to, as the trustees of a series of laws and customs by which they themselves were bound, even if gradually. Sovereignty over vassals and fiefs became the means whereby the Kings of England, France, Portugal and Spain gradually succeeded in establishing sovereignty over territory. In the differences, however, between the two sorts of rule lay the foundations of the different types of modern state. The combination of fief with vassalage, or feudalism, is unique to western Europe. The feudal lords of Europe were able to establish a degree of independence of, and separation from, the monarchy because the monarchy lacked the means, on the whole, to prevent them. The efforts of Frederick II were unsuccessful. Thus there emerged out of feudal Europe what Karl Wittfogel rightly speaks of as 'one of the strongest forms of private property known to mankind' (37). The great estate in the European West came to be, unlike such enterprises elsewhere, grand outposts of resistance to central power. In the East, and that unfortunately included Russia, the central power looked on the great estate as, as it were, one of its own dependent branches.

13

Agriculture: Co-operation

A system of tenancy popular with landlords for six hundred years in Europe, and still found in most parts of the world is share-cropping, or *métayage* (*mezzadria*). By that, the tenant, in return for a free house and plot, and perhaps implements, surrenders a half, a quarter, or another fraction of the crop. Established in Roman times, it was common in mediaeval French vineyards and also in central Italy, whose astute financial leaders realised that there could be no better hedge against inflation. There were Italian states where all those who leased land were obliged absolutely to employ that type of lease. Subsequently, it also became widespread in Europe and, for several generations, seemed the ideal manner of running an estate, after direct cultivation. But there were usually some difficulties. It was not clear how permanent the leases so obtained were, and the system did not absorb technological change very easily. Still, in many parts of Italy, a system which had its roots in Rome, and was first apparently practised formally in the seventh century by the Benedictine abbey of St Fiona, on Monte Amiata, lasted till the 1960s, when a combination of new and expensive machinery and the demand for labour in the cities destroyed it (1).

In France, *métayage* perhaps accounted for half the territory in 1789, above all in the centre and south (2). Stripped of feudal adjuncts, the system survived since, even in contemporary circumstances, the lord or proprietor could not gain his share of the produce without contributing his share of the working capital. But by the end of the nineteenth century, *métayage* in France had become simply the curiosity of certain provinces, and the same was the case in Germany, where it had once been common, especially in wine-growing districts (3).

The system has been used outside Europe too. Thus, in the US South, after the collapse of the great slave-powered cotton plantations at the end of the civil war in 1865, share-cropping was considered the best way of ensuring the labour to produce cotton: though the bargain was a harsher one than normal in Europe for, in order to receive half the crop, the cultivator, usually a freed slave, had to share the cost of all fertilisers, the baling and the ginning* (4). The region where this system of cultivation has worked best in modern times seems to have been in the Basque provinces. There, very often, the owner has lived in the nearby town, the rainfall is regular, relations between tenant and owner are good, and contracts are often oral. Hence the Basque country, till the twentieth century, was the 'satisfied area' of Spain, almost the only place, according to Gerald Brenan, where there was no social problem (5). Probably that was why one of the twentieth century's most encouraging features, the co-operatives, based on Mondragón, have begun so successfully there (6).

It is difficult to avoid a word or two about a different sort of co-operative, or, rather what seems to be on the surface a co-operative, namely the system known as the common (or open) field which, for nearly a thousand years, dominated northern Europe and still exists in a few isolated pockets. That system implied farming in common with three main elements: first, an arable area, growing corn, divided into three large fields, upon one of which, at any one time, winter grain might be growing; spring corn and some vegetables might be on another field; while the third would be fallow. Each of these large fields, however, would be divided into strips representing about a day's labour with the heavy plough, or 22 yards by 220 yards, that is, an acre in size, and the different plots would remain as if permanent freeholds, regardless of the crop. Treeless, hedgeless, cut up by balks and mere-stones into furlongs, gores and headlands, these open common fields were 'very ugly things' to look at (7), in William Cobbett's recollection, but they have become, nevertheless, the focus of deep nostalgia.

Secondly, there would be an area of meadowland, allocated among the community concerned exactly as the ploughland had been, each family having a strip on which to grow an annual crop of hay. Finally, there would be waste land (a common much like the open field during the fallow time), used for permanent grazing or for the possible expansion of the area under arable farming if the population should chance to grow. On this waste land, there might also be an area of wood, useful for firewood, acorns, and beechmast for pigs and so on. Very likely there would also be, in the nearby village, a mill, a pond, or a bog, where some would have rights of cutting peat. On the common, custom often enabled weavers to spread their cloth, and even squatters to establish huts.

It was the first of those three tracts which was of the most importance, since it had other uses than simply the production of grain. At any time other than when there were crops growing on it, for example, livestock could graze there, leaving behind invaluable manure for the future (8).

Now this system lasted in much of France, England, Germany and to some extent Spain, for 500 years or more, in one form or another. It had

*Ginning means the removal of seeds of cotton by a gin (engine).

many interesting consequences. First, for the system to work at all, the fairly disciplined adherence to it of every member of the community was necessary. Secondly, the right of common grazing on the stubble after the harvest made it impossible for any individualist to try to grow a crop which would be unharvested when neighbours had grown their corn. The farmer was thus so closely dependent on his neighbour that he could do little without his help or assent. His lands were also so mingled with those of others that the traditional 'peasant's memory' was needed to recognise what belonged to whom. No fences could be set up, save where a strip abutted on to the common way, since that would have interfered with grazing. The parcelling-out meant that cultivation had to be in common, even if the crop always went to an individual owner. Within what might have seemed on the surface an almost collectivist employment and control of land, however, individual rights were very strictly maintained (9). Finally, villages in the economy of the common field were compact, with few isolated homesteads. The system outlived the conversion of the villages into towns: the peasantry of Wiesbaden brought ploughs and dung carts to and fro across the town daily as late as 1845 (10). Even Berlin had its three fields in 1819 (11).

Land in Russia, until the Revolution of 1917, was also mostly held communally though not in fields comparable to those of West Europe. Scattered villages characterised it, not great estates, and the villages were often divided by waste. Each village, as a rule, divided its land into sections according to the quality of the soil and its geographical ease of access. Every household claimed, in every section, small strips of land corresponding to the needs of its adult members (the strips were usually nine to twelve feet broad, several hundred yards long, the shape and size being comparable to the strips in the West) and one man probably had some thirty to fifty such strips. From time to time, perhaps every ten years, the village would re-divide the strips according to new needs, an action often unpopular and, therefore, often usually having to be underwritten by the local authorities. These villages were run by a council of heads of family, and collaboration was the rule. Meantime, within every family, work was also traditionally done in common, since the father was usually assisted till his death by sons and grandchildren. This 'joint family' was often unpopular, particularly in modern times (probably due to over-population) and, in the generation between the emancipation of the serfs in 1861 and the revolution in 1917, many peasants broke away from their families, though as a rule remaining within their village (12).

Common fields of one sort or another, indeed existed almost every-where, in both the old world and the new, primarily since peasants without animals can be easily co-ordinated into something close to teams, even when they work irrigated fields with a digging stick, and even when they are working with ploughing teams on separate fields

(13). The exception seems to have been India. There, after the successful Aryan conquest about 1500 BC, land began by being owned in common by the village, and farmed in common, therefore, too. But with the decline of tribal units, land was divided between families and thus outright private property came into being at a very early date (14). Because of a multitude of hindrances in the development of a free market, poverty, and handkerchief-sized plots, that system survived many generations though to-day much of India is owned by large scale farmer-capitalists.

How these intricate systems of common farming began has been an interesting subject for argument. In Russia, the origins of the system have been endlessly debated for a hundred years (15). In Europe, the system is now generally held to have derived from the type of cultivation usually carried on by the Germans before they invaded the Roman Empire. Each year, the leading men of a tribe would meet and decide (as was later done at a court leet in England) which part of the land recently cleared should be ploughed, and planted with what. By the time of Tacitus (100 AD), the land was already being divided up between individuals, and the frequency of that division had declined (16). But when new lands were conquered, or new waste cleared, the process would begin again. The size of the strip would be decided by the action of the plough. Naturally, the land for cultivation would be that adjacent to the settlement concerned and, upon that, the men of the community would go to work, setting out a day's ploughing for each team working side by side. By the end of the working day, each would have ploughed one or more strips, according to the nature of the soil. Next day, the labourers would move on, to set out and plough the section beyond the first day's work. In the end, all would have land ready for sowing in strips, equally dispersed, so that, in theory, all would have the same opportunities, the same share of the different sorts of soil, and much the same hopes of avoiding the impact of national disaster.

In a typical village of old Europe, a farmer's year, as described by the Orwins, might be: about October 15, the winter sowing of wheat would be finished, and the livestock grazing on the wheat stubble in the second open field of the three would be driven off. There would then be twelve days of ploughing. This land would lie untouched and exposed throughout the winter. The farmer would then be concerned primarily with his cattle, which would be quartered near, or inside, his house. Ditches or fences would be mended, corn threshed. In March, there would be spring sowing. The stocks of winter food for the livestock (as for humans) would be finished, the cattle would be tethered on the commons or waste in April immediately there was any sign of young grass. That month and the next, the farmer would be occupied with sheep and lambs, cows and calves, and be beginning to plough the fallow ready for the autumn wheat's sowing. At the end of June, the grass in the common meadows would be ready for the hay harvest in which, after the swathes had been cut with scythes, women and children would share. That work would be finished by August 1, when the 'aftermath' on the by then harvested meadow would be open for common grazing (and manuring) till October. Then the corn harvest would follow. Young and old would repair to the cornfields, the men cutting the corn with sickles, the women and children binding the staves and building them into stooks. Finally, the corn would be stacked in barns and threshed there during the winter, the grain obtained being ground in a watermill or a windmill (17).

Even when there were no open fields, something similar occurred, with appropriate religious and other festive rites differing from country to country. Of course, there were innumerable local deviations (the harvest in northern France being in July, in England in September and, in the South, earlier). The French system of uniting all the stock into a common herd for grazing on stubble, regularly, was, for example, not usual in England (18). The division of land into small farms, themselves split into parcels, was nowhere more elaborate than in Spain where, by the end of the age of agriculture, a farm in, say, Guadalajara probably averaged twelve to forty acres, split into fourteen to twenty parcels (19). With all such harvests, there might be a combination of the efforts of many different sorts of landowners, some being rich, some not. For example, at Laxton, a village in Lincolnshire, the lord in the thirteenth century derived his living partly from his demesne farm of 250 acres, partly from his strips scattered among those of the tenants, and partly from services on three 600-acre open fields. Four hundred years later, in the same village, the lord's strip was larger but there were no services (or rents) due to him any more. The open fields were a little smaller too than they had been in 1232. On them, there were still innumerable strips, in every conceivable shape, two of the freeholders having land of over 600 acres, most having much smaller enterprises under forty acres in all (and divided up). The farms concerned, even the smallest, were busy with a mixture of arable and animal husbandry. Animals were needed for a great variety of purposes, but to feed them was a major undertaking. The scarcity of manure was a reason for what would now seem the low yield, and lords sometimes asked for pots of human excrement as part of their dues (20). Meantime, what seemed then, and have sometimes seemed since, in the minds of some historians, major revolutions often did not affect landowners much: for example, except in Ireland, the British civil war of the seventeenth century did not produce a major transfer of landed property from one group to another. Three quarters even of the properties sold under the Commonwealth probably returned to their original owners after the Restoration (21).

14

Agriculture: Slaves and Serfs

Every major project of agriculture in the Near East and Mediterranean in antiquity depended upon slaves. So did both those industrial under takings which depended on agricultural products, and those mines whose products were then concerned to improve agriculture as well as to furnish weapons for war. On the other hand, slaves were not so much employed in those projects in agriculture which depended on irrigation. There, as has been suggested before, the population would be more likely to be subject to various forms of forced labour. In the Mediterranean world, the Mycenæan kingdoms were perhaps a touch-stone of the general character of slave labour in the region about 1400 BC. There were many slaves there, especially female ones, some working in the textile industry or for bronzesmiths, and many in private households. Some were captured in war, most were bought (suggesting already that the traffic in slaves was probably the largest single commer-cial item at that time). Families and children of slaves were permitted to keep together (1). Much later, the slave population of Athens was perhaps decisive in enabling it to continue as a city of commerce (in slaves as in other items) (2). Chios, the first Greek democracy, was also the first Greek city to import large consignments of slaves from the 'Barbarian East' (3). Previously the slaves had come from the Scythian or Slavic north. By then, slaves were cheap: they cost no more to buy than a year's expenditure on their upkeep (4). It thus seems fairly clear that all the economic problems of a slave trade had been successfully res-olved: Greece needed slave labour, Asia (or the northern coast of the Black Sea) could provide the slaves.

The people who, in the end, established their rule over the ancient world, the Romans, had, to begin with, no large slave estates. Was that, perhaps, as some have suggested, the reason for Rome's success over Carthage, by then a bloated state, with her plantations filled with dis-gruntled slaves from all over the Mediterranean? If so, Rome fell into Carthage's mistake (5). The campaigns of conquest from the third century BC onwards brought territory but, even more, brought waves of slaves who went to work on new plantations in Italy: 25,000 slaves were gained from the capture of Agrigentum, 60,000 from Marius' victory in Germany, 150,000 from the capture of Epirus and, it was said, 2 million, no less, from Pompey's victories in Asia. By then Delos, the island which had been the centre of the Athenian Empire, had become the great slave emporium of the civilised world. 10,000 slaves a day were sold there, according to the geographer, Strabo (6). A special dock was built for the purpose. Even numerically, these undertakings rivalled the market in slaves in the West Indies in the eighteenth century.

This slave population transformed Roman society. Slaves, to begin with, made millionaires out of the great commanders. Caesar was poor when he went to Gaul but he returned rich, because of the booty of slaves which he had acquired. After his victory at Alesia in 52 BC, he even gave one slave each to his legionaries. As occurred in Russia in the Middle Ages, or in Africa in the eighteenth century, the profits available from slaves sometimes led to war to replenish slave markets. Captured slaves also sometimes weighed down armies (7). Furthermore, the availability of this type of labour force made possible, more than anything else, the creation of plantations (particularly in Sicily and South Italy) which were worked by gangs of slaves just as much as were the similar estates of colonial America. Then, the racial mixture of Rome was transformed. Anyone who was not a Roman citizen could be enslaved and, though certain races were favoured on the assumption that they provided the best workers, there were no specific slave races to the Roman mind. But innumerable slaves were freed for good service. Masters in Rome constantly spurred on their slaves to work hard by offers of bonuses with which they could buy their freedom (8). Sick slaves abandoned by their masters were also often freed, while the slaves of the Emperor became men of immense, if perilous, eminence. Hence a considerable social mobility in Rome. After the third generation, after all, any freed slave could regard himself as a full citizen. The eunuchs who managed the Empire in the East were often slaves. Their power derived from their control of imperial audiences and, with weak rulers, of which there was no lack, they thereby could direct the Empire (9). All imperial slaves had opportunities to better themselves. After centuries of manumission, 80% of Roman families, according to the French historian, Jérôme Carcopino, had, in the second century AD, once been emancipated from slavery (10), even if no one of importance seems to have reached the conclusion which modern man persuades himself would have come automatically to him, in the circumstances: that the institution of slavery ought to be abolished (11).

Roman slaves were often able to secure that they were well treated. Many of those in Rome itself had some hours of recreation during the afternoon, and so might have found the week of forty hours in the twentieth century irksome (12). It was accepted, from the days of the early Republic, that slaves had souls and hence, were allowed to worship the souls of their own predecessors. Magistrates were legally bound to consider complaints laid by slaves against the injustice of masters. The killing of slaves was considered to be murder (13).

The character of Roman slavery, as of Rome, was changed by the end of the wars of expansion. Roman slaveowners 'were reduced,' Gibbon wrote, 'to the milder, but more tedious, method of propagation' (14). Many landlords converted their estates to leasehold or paid their labourers to labour, when the slave prices rose. By the late Empire, in consequence, slaves were mostly in domestic service, rather than on estates (15). Some masters of estates in the late Empire comforted themselves (as did the owners of West Indian sugar plantations, later) that slaves worked badly in comparison with free men. After all, the death of a slave meant the loss of capital. That reassuring reflection did not prevent the decline of the Roman economy.

Nor did slaves vanish with the Roman Empire, nor with the coming of Christianity, despite the Roman Church's theoretical attitude that all members of the human species were potential members of *societas Christiana*. Throughout the Dark Ages, slave families continued as such in Europe. Slaves continued to be brought from the Levant or Slavic Europe until the seventh century. But the collapse of commerce after the Arabs captured the seas prevented a flourishing trade. There were many diversities of treatment among those who were actually slaves in the Dark Ages in Europe. Some *servi* were looked upon as human cattle in their master's house. Some were, in effect, 'tenant slaves', living like free tenants, though unable to participate in judicial assemblies, nor be summoned to the army (16). We hear of a king of Sussex giving land and '250 slaves' to a supporter (17). But slaves in early mediaeval Europe often had a cottage and yard of their own, even if the duties demanded of them were constant. Vikings looked on slaves as the richest plunder to be gained from their expeditions and, with those whom they caught, they quickly began to convert their own scarcely cultivated plots into slave plantations — as if the slaves were highly trained agronomists. The Viking realm in Russia, the monarchy of Rurik, was, also, built up on the sale of slaves to Islam through the Khanates of Kiev: a factor in Russian history not to be forgotten. That very active mediaeval sale of slaves (in Russia, in Sicily, perhaps above all in Islamic Spain) indeed resulted in the accidental use of the word *esclave* or 'slav' becoming a vernacular synonym for the Latin *servus*.*

---

* Slav derives from *slovo*, a word to signify (in Slav) people who can speak as opposed to *nemsty*, dumb people — a word also used for 'German'. The Slavs, a nomadic people of cattle grazers, lived in the third century AD between the Vistula and the Oder, with no political organisation, and first began to migrate in the sixth century eastwards towards Russia, southwards to the Balkans, being pressed by the Avars whom they later absorbed (18).

By the late Middle Ages, probably because of the increase in Europe's population, this European slave trade had, however, almost died out. But a few domestic slaves remained. The Black Death revived a demand for them when labour was hard to come by. In the late fourteenth century, Florence authorised the import of slaves, provided that they were infidels. By the end of the century in that city, Iris Origo wrote, 'hardly a well-to-do household was without at least one slave. Brides brought them as part of their dowry; doctors accepted them in lieu of fees' (19). The persons concerned were often girls (Circassians, Tartars, Greeks or Russians) bought in Ibiza or Majorca. So much for purity of blood in Tuscany! But they were slaves hired to wash dishes or to carry wood to the oven, not to work on farms. Their economic contribution was thus modest, though, in the Balearic islands, their agricultural work continued. Northern Europe had by then virtually forgotten slavery, though it was nowhere explicitly condemned. In Byzantium, on the other hand, the shrinking Empire, until its fall, had slaves much as Tuscany did while, every year from the Middle Ages till 1700, the Crimean cavalry would sweep into Russia, in pursuit of young Slavs, for the slave marts of Asia.

Asiatic slavery in the Middle Ages was comparable in its place in society to what it had been in Rome. A limited number of slaves were everywhere employed as manual labour in large-scale enterprises, in mines, draining marshes, on fleets. In Islam, Bernard Lewis explains, the growth, under the Abbasid caliphate, of many rich capitalists with 'considerable liquid capital at their disposal led to the purchase of slaves in large numbers in agriculture'. Most of these were negro, mostly from East Africa. They were treated very harshly indeed, and that led to numerous revolts, including a famous quasi-religious slave revolt in the ninth century which began among the slaves working on the salt flats east of Basra. For a time, the rebels controlled a great deal of southern Iraq and south west Persia. But the main basis of production in Islam was by free, or semi-free, peasants. Most Muslim slaves were used as domestic servants or in the army. The latter, the Mamluks, many of Slav or Christian origin, in the end formed a powerful military caste, almost dominating the state, as the old Roman Emperor's house slaves had sometimes dominated Rome (20).

It might even be represented that the overthrow of the Caliphate, weakened by excessive taxation and over-spending in Baghdad, was due to a rebellion of Turkish slaves. From the ninth century onwards, anyway, the caliphs used Turkish military slaves extensively, since their bowmanship and horsemanship were both unrivalled in Asia, and since, once converted into a kind of palace guard, the Turks were specially loyal to the persons of the caliphs. Ultimately, one Turkish tribe, the Seljuks, entered the Caliphate as conquerors, accepted Islam (the orthodox version) and came to dominate the Empire, of course making use of the Mamluk slaves who were already there (21). They did not abolish the Caliphate, however. Having become Muslims, the Seljuks allowed it to survive, rather as the Goths permitted the Western Empire to flicker on till 476 AD, leaving it finally to be destroyed only by the Mongols in 1258.

There were few slaves in the Chinese empires. Instead, all, at all times, owed labour to the emperor or lord. The canals which irrigated the country, and which allowed for the communication between provinces which, in turn, enabled the unification of the country, were mostly built by forced labour. To widen the canal between the Yangtze and the Huang Ho valley, about 5,500,000 workers, including in some places all commoners between fifteen and fifty, are said to have been concentrated under the control of 50,000 police in the seventh century AD. They were workers in a classic system of *corvée*, not slaves. Slaves were not numerous in ancient India, either, but they existed, both in mines and in domestic service, and also in service of the guilds. In the *Arthashastra*, a treatise on government of about 300 BC, it is said that a man may be either a slave by birth — that is, of low caste status; or by selling himself; or by being captured in war; or as a result of a judicial punishment (22).

The history of slavery has been written often but usually, understandably, in a mood of anger that such a thing could have occurred in the past for so long. Some of the best historians of it in the West Indies, for instance, have been its most polemical critics. What seem to be needed are two further considerations: first, a more considered study of the economic significance of the traffic in slaves in Mediterranean antiquity when it was evidently the most important item of commerce for so long; and second, the role of domestic slavery as a means of providing a career open to talented people, which contrasted with the immobility of an oriental system in which the whole population was subject to the demands of *corvée*. Perhaps it was this role of slavery as an institution which, like the Catholic Church, provided to the clever the chance to rise, that explains the otherwise rather mysterious 'universal acceptance of the principle of slavery' by that Catholic Church itself (23).

An intermediate position between slave and hired labourer was in the past filled by an individual known as the serf. This person had equivalents in many societies. Typical was the serf of the late Roman Empire, who was apparently chained by law to his holding, as was his son after him. Otherwise, he was free to do as he wished. Subsequently, however, in the Middle Ages in Europe, the position was altered. A serf, though he inherited the Latin name *servus*, a slave, was free save that he could not change his lord. He was attached to a man, not to a holding. True, some masters, like the abbot of Vézelay, thought that his serf was 'mine, from the soles of his feet to the crown of his head' while, in mediaeval England, a man was permitted to kill his serf with impunity ('if a man slay his serf, his is the sin, and his is the loss') (24). Equally, serfs were as a rule discouraged, in mediaeval Europe, to marry out of the circle of those serfs dependent on the lord in question: that ensured that the lord kept control of the children. Marriage outside the circle necessitated permission, and payment. Serfs had to make annual payments intended to formalise the fact of serfdom. Serfs could sometimes buy their freedom, while the sale of serfs was a means of obtaining money: after the battle of Poitiers in 1356, some French knights sold freedom to their serfs in order to raise their own ransoms (25).

This mediaeval European category of serf had an equivalent in Mexico immediately after the Spanish conquest, in the person of the *encomendado:* a worker allocated to a grantee of a great estate in return for teaching him the Catholic faith. The latter obligation could, however, seem a very modest return for years of unpaid service under the authority of a brutal overseer, one of the consequences of which was often the swift death from one of the innumerable diseases which the Spaniards brought to the New World. At the end of the Middle Ages, repeated enfranchisements, the growth of an economy based increasingly on wages, and a series of unprecedented difficulties (such as the Black Death) giving rise to shortage of labour, caused the decline of Western European serfdom, though it survived in remote parts until the nineteenth century. In Eastern Europe, however, where the land was cleared more slowly, where the economies were less dynamic anyway, where even the three-field system had scarcely begun before the fifteenth century (with lower yields from the crops), and where new land was still being aggressively sought, the bonds of serfdom were being increased. In 1417, towns in Prussia agreed to hand runaway serfs back to their masters, and Prussian landowners were given the right to have fugitives handed back to them in 1494. The bulk of Russia's population, too, were turned into serfs instead of tenants between 1550 and 1650. The monarchy in Moscow was then emerging as the undisputed master of that country, and the conquests of land previously in the hands of Tartars were opening up immeasurable opportunities for those peasants who could escape from Muscovy (26). Until then, peasants could move where they liked, providing that they were not in debt. In the end, the Tsar, concerned primarily about receiving what he considered his proper share of taxes, introduced a statute of serfdom which bound serfs absolutely to masters (that was in 1649) and slaves and serfs were then merged under the name of the latter (27). That system lasted till 1861. Elsewhere in eastern Europe, serfdom lasted nearly as long. The average village was still 'servile' in 1750 in East Germany. Serfs still owed their masters heavy services and payments in kind (28) and, in most German states in 1788, peasants were not allowed to leave their lord's estate (29). Even the Duke of Savoy, the King of Denmark and the princes of West Germany did not formally abolish serfdom before 1770 and the King of Prussia only even embarked on abolition in 1807.

Not everything generally supposed about the evil condition of serfs in East Europe is true. Thus even a Russian serf lived in his own house, not in a barracks, and the produce of his labour was his own. Serfs could not, it is true, leave their village without permission. Otherwise, they probably had better standards of living than Scottish or Irish peasants of that day, and they were certainly more free than slaves in the West Indies or in the US at the same time.

The small farmer, the private peasant, the family with three acres and a cow, has a mythical position in the history of agriculture. The sterling virtues of independence allegedly characteristic of such people, their self-reliance and austerity are held to have given some of the greatest states their most valiant men. Some regret the conversion of Rome from a land of small farmers to one of great estates (or the end of the free peasants in Russia in the sixteenth century), others point approvingly to the small size of the farms of Attica, or recall the 'bold peasantry' of England. Ernest Renan thought that the 'shrewd' peasants of Normandy incarnated all human virtues. Whether he would also have thought that the peasants of the valley of the Ganges were such admirable freeholders, though they had been so for many generations, seems improbable, for all his knowledge of the Orient. The truth is that smallholders have often been the most narrow-minded of those who have made any contribution to agriculture. With enterprises less than, say, forty acres in size, and often tending to fragment further because of the birth of too many sons, constantly on the verge of being degraded into dependent tenancies, indebted to larger landlords, such smallholders have been usually too poor to be able to introduce technological improvements: the essential distinction in the European Middle Ages was that between those who could afford a plough team and those who could not. Sometimes, smallholders without a plough might (as in northern Spain) create real co-operative ventures for themselves; or they might commend themselves to lords, seeking protection without conceding deference. On the whole, the small peasant occupies a more important place in what people have thought about agriculture than is evident in what happened. The 'yeoman' is more a figure in literary, than in economic, history and his virtues are more sung in poetry than in practice. He is probably also less frequent than literature would suggest. Thus in Spain in 1797, only 22% of all those involved in farming owned their own land (30). This compares with approximately one third of the Spanish labour force who, at the same time, were day labourers — men who, under most versions of feudalism, secured some extra benefits but did not do so under the system which replaced it.

Of course, there are exceptions to this rule, as there are to all rules. For example, the distribution of the lands of Visigothic noblemen in Spain by the Arab conquerors to the soldiers of the army of the faithful created a new class of smallholders who, according to Bernard Lewis, 'were largely responsible for the agricultural prosperity of Muslim Spain' (31). Similar claims have been made for the smallholders of the Ganges, the tobacco farmers of Cuba, and so on. In most instances, these prosperous smallholders were, however, men who devoted themselves to intensive labour on a single crop in exceptional circumstances. Many, such as the Arab smallholder of Almeria, were primarily concerned with producing a crop, such as silk, for manufacture.

Throughout history paid labourers have played a part in work on large estates. But, except in special circumstances, such as England in the eighteenth century, most labourers had *some* land. They worked for wages because their land, or their fathers' land, was too small to keep a family (32). That land might be tiny, but it was there. The landless labourer of Andalusia and Estremadura makes an important contribution to the history of rural protest in Spain but, as an individual in agricultural history, he was rare.

It will be asked, but what of the history of rural unemployment? In mainly agricultural countries today, the numbers of unemployed are usually not registered and many who are dependent on a wage from agriculture are often underemployed. Agriculture, by the very nature of its activity, has created seasonal unemployment during most of its history. Many families have lived all winter from what they have managed to secure during the harvest. Hence, therefore, there were always, through the ages, peasants' revolts: crushed, rarely publicised, usually not even recorded, there were always challenges to authority, however constituted. In Fuenteovejuna, in 1476, the land had been given by King Enrique IV of Castile to the knightly order of Calatrava. Their local administrator or comendador was Fernan Gómez de Guzmán who entered the city as into a conquered town. In 1476, the entire people, led, in this instance, by their mayor and aldermen, assaulted the palace of the comendador, whom they threw out of the window and killed. A few weeks later, a judge came. He asked: 'who killed the comendador?' 'Fuenteovejuna' came the answer (33), and one which inspired a legend, as well as a play by Lope de Vega.

In the last generation, the history of peasants' revolts has for the first time begun to receive attention. The research and findings of scholars such as Rodney Hilton have been illuminating, new and salutary. It is desirable to be reminded that the old world of agriculture seethed, under a surface of rhythmic serenity. Fugitive serfs, robbers and fugitive slaves have a place in history. In all probability, the best of us have several of them among our ancestors. The tiny armies of mediaeval Europe have doubtless attracted too much attention in the past. The longbowmen and their successors, the crossbowmen, were not machines. Yet the essential fact of history before the Renaissance in Europe, and before the twentieth century elsewhere, is that, except against nomads, the old regimes maintained themselves, and the poor remained patient; the poorer they were, the more resigned. Why that was so was a question which puzzled David Hume, who must rank as one of the cleverest Europeans, so it is no confession of weakness to say that it is not easy to answer. An attempt will be made later. What those regimes were has already been touched upon. They will be discussed again. In the meantime, a few words are needed to remind the reader that agriculture is not only concerned with the production of food. In the past, as today, many of its crops are concerned, for example, with producing raw materials for industry and providing means whereby populations clothe themselves.

15

Agriculture: Cloths and Clothes

Clothes in the age of agriculture began by depending on the furs and animal skins of the age of hunters. But dressed skins (leather) and then sheep's wool played an increasing part, followed by linen and silk and, to a lesser extent, cotton. Even in hot and prosperous countries, the use of hides and fur, however, never died out after the coming of textiles: the Japanese had a jimboar, or leather over-garment painted on the back, for wearing outside, at the time of the Renaissance (1). Fur was less expensive than cloth was in mediaeval Florence (2).

Textiles, including the vegetable fibres, linen and cotton, have, like some other commodities, been turned into fabric by four processes, all of them known from as early as 4000 BC: the cleaning and straightening of the fibres to make a roll of parallel strings; spinning, to create thread; weaving, to make the fabric; and finishing — bleaching, dyeing, fulling and pressing. All those processes were done by hand until the eighteenth century, though mechanisation had affected the process of finishing before that. Of these commodities, wool is the most important and most interesting to consider in detail.

Wool has been a commodity of value since at least the days of Crete, when the 100,000 sheep of Knossos were one of the sources of the wealth of that island (3). Then, as under Rome, spinning was carried out at home on a spindle stick. On the other hand, weavers were professional people from the earliest days, and even the poorest bought clothes ready made. The weavers bought yarn from private spinners and sold cloth either direct to clients or to merchants. There were a few weaving factories. The importance of sheep and their wool in antiquity is suggested by the investigation of a sheep's liver being, in both Babylon and among the Etruscans, a means of finding the will of God (4). Under Rome, too, certain wools already had special clients. Thus, the peculiar fineness of the fleece of sheep raised on the soft meadows of the Channel coast had been noticed, and Tournai had, by 400 AD, a factory for making the imperial army's cloaks. Afterwards, Friesian cloaks made Flanders famous: Charlemagne gave Haroun al Raschid a *pallia fresonica*. By the thirteenth century, Flemish workshops, directed

119

by 'capitalist entrepreneurs', as Pirenne put it (5), had come to be considered without rivals for the fineness of their weaves and the beauty of their colours. In that basic element of early mediaeval commerce in Europe, the wool trade, Flanders played the main part.

From the thirteenth century in Europe, the disentangling (carding) of the wool was done by a pair of wire-toothed brushes, the wool being worked from one hand to another, that task having been previously entrusted to a simple thistle (*cardus*). Combing, as an alternative to 'carding', by metal teeth mounted on horn with a wooden handle, allowed the comb to slip more easily through the wool. Then the spinning wheel came. Like most major mediaeval innovations, the spinning wheel was invented in China, being tried out in Germany in 1280 (at Speyer) for the first time in Europe. It doubled productivity, though spinning continued to be done largely at home, often merely occupying days when there was no work on the land for wives and daughters. Afterwards, a horizontal frame loom was devised, a great help to weavers. Finally, the fulling mill was devised, with power-driven mallets for the human foot, driven by water wheels (6). These new things seem first to have been tried in Italy, as was, in 1480, a means of permitting both spinning and winding thread to be done at the same time on a bobbin. By 1524, a crank, treadle and connecting rod for this purpose had been added (7).

Four European countries depended for their wealth in the late agricultural age on wool: in addition to Flanders, there were also England, Tuscany and Castile.

To begin with, English shepherds merely supplied the Flemish weavers. Then, after the Norman Conquest, Flemish artisans crossed the Channel and taught the English how to use wool. Eventually wool became 'the sacred staple and foundation of our wealth', in Andrew Young's words, though long after it had ceased to be so.

This industry became increasingly well-known in mediaeval Europe. Most of the work was done in scattered villages, in small cottages, a loom being placed in the main room of the house, the spinners being helped by hand cards for carding, by distaff and spindle. Often, this peasant wool worker would have clipped the wool from his own sheep. There might be water to remove the grease from the cloth, while a tub or two of dye and water would be placed at the door. Fulling and teasing might be done for a fixed payment at one or other of the many publicly maintained watermills. The father might sit at the shuttle, his wife and daughters at the spinning wheel, and his son be doing the carding. Such a house might have also an acre or two of land, on which there would be a cow for milk, some chickens, and a horse to fetch the wool from the shepherd. The horse would take the carded wool to the fulling mill, where, after a careful official inspection, it would be sold to a merchant whom the peasant might have known before and who might on occasion go direct to the peasant to place orders.

This long self-sufficient world eventually came to an end in Europe because of specialisation. There were some houses where only spinning was done, and some with several looms. Some weavers allowed themselves to get into debt, and merchants would lend them money on the security of their looms. Sometimes, those merchants would end up owning everything which the weaver possessed. The process known as 'putting out' meant that the weaver became more a workman, less a part-farmer. In some cottages, the 'sweating of labour' would, at the end of the age of agriculture, be worse than in a factory. Sometimes, perhaps often, specialisation was insisted upon by those peasants who preferred spinning to digging and, like those who produced wooden tools, such as scythes, had always hoped to concentrate upon it. Often, too, the weavers had enough work in their wool business to keep them from agriculture except during harvest (8).

Being one of the oldest industries, wool was everywhere more regulated than any other. Innumerable English Acts of Parliament, for example, laid down rules about length, breadth, weight of pieces and so on. Most of these rules were made to ensure quality. Most countries in Europe had a large number of wool inspectors to this end. These rules were, by the eighteenth century, an obstacle to all improvement in conditions of work. Colonies dependent on England, for example, were not allowed to produce wool. Ireland was prevented from developing a wool trade of her own. Only finished cloth was allowed to be exported (to prevent people copying) and in almost every country live sheep were banned from being exported (9).

The history of wool in Italy differed substantially from that in England. There the water from the streams and rivers running into the Arno, between Florence and the sea, gave such places as Prato and Lucca the chance to act as purveyors of cloth to Venetian merchants. In Prato, well-built canals provided water for fulling and dyeing. Tuscan wool workers all maintained their own speciality: weavers, carders, spinners, dyers, wool-sellers, wool merchants and yarn dealers were all separate careers. By the thirteenth century, all were embraced in guilds led by the merchants. The poorest group were the washers and carders (*i ciompi*, from the clogs that they customarily wore). Above them, were the other grades, mostly women who, though employed by merchants, were mainly working in their own homes, as in England. By that time, the best merchant sold Tuscan wool only to the poor, since it was rough. The best cloth, on which Tuscany became rich and so financed the Renaissance, was bought raw from Spain, Minorca, Africa or England, particularly from the Cotswolds. Thus the shepherds of Burford and Northleach made their contribution to the revival of commerce, and the great barns of the Cotswolds helped to create the fortunes of the Bardi, the Medici and the Frescobaldi (10).

The wealth of Florence was thus based on the import of raw, and the manufacture of finished, wool. This achievement of an economy entirely based on commerce had no parallel in the ancient world nor, it seems, in the East. The experience gained in this commerce led to the establishment of the great Florentine banking families and, indeed, to the whole paraphernalia of modern commerce, with its double book-keeping ('the Italian method'), and trading associations which led to modern companies, shares, representatives abroad, sleeping partnerships and credit systems.

Finally, among the wool trades of the Middle Ages, that of Spain deserves notice, since it derived from the exploitation of a single, especially desirable breed of animal, the *merino* sheep, an animal with white curly wool, probably introduced into Spain from Africa by the Muslims (its late discovery may have been due to its poor capacity for providing mutton) (11), though the semi-annual sheep migrations along fixed routes which characterised the history of Spanish wool were known under the Goths, probably even under the Iberians. Indeed, the keeping of sheep in the Mediterranean had for hundreds of years a similar pattern of life, often causing difficulties with farmers *en route*, an echo of ancient quarrels between herdsmen and husbandmen (12). Rome had had a special praetor to look after the routes. Those practices were not interrupted by the fall of Rome. Mediaeval monarchs in both Italy and Spain merely sought to codify old rules (13). Spain in the Middle Ages had, however, a more pastoral economy than any other country in Europe. On its broad grasslands, large herds not only of sheep but of pigs and half wild cattle grazed. This geography fitted better than did arable farming with a political background of a 'perpetual crusade', as Macaulay spoke of the Spanish Middle Ages (14), and shifting frontiers. The migratory cycle of sheep in Estremadura and South Castile during the winter, in the northern mountains during the summer, coincided with the alternation of winter peace and summer fighting. Shepherds made their way from Christendom into the land of the Muslims even in the earliest days (15). By about 1400, Spain was exporting raw wool all over Europe, especially to Tuscany, while English exports had dropped there. For Spain, wool had become the 'indispensable source of royal revenue'. The State sought, in the words of the historian of the Spanish wooltrade, Julius Klein, a 'carefully planned policy aimed persistently at one definite purpose, the export of those raw materials for which the greatest quantities of gold and foreign commodites could be secured in return' (16).

The Spanish wool trade was thus an export business, but there was no native cloth industry. King Ferdinand I tried to found one by introducing detailed regulations for guilds, even prescribing a form of 'putting out system', *à l'anglaise*, establishing standard grades and weights of wool and so on, but all to no avail. Foreign merchants even took over the selling of the wool with royal permission and, in the middle of the so-called 'golden century' of Spain, the Genoese had a monopoly of the export trade of wool from Spain (as of the sale of slaves to the Spanish Empire). Vast quantities were sold too to the Spanish Empire, and the woollen blanket, or *serape*, replaced the old *manta* of cotton or vegetable fibre of pre-Columbian America.

The Spanish failure to exploit a great natural resource must be attributed to one of the major Spanish institutions which, like many such, was a mixed blessing, despite its fame in history: the Mesta. Its history not only reveals a great deal about the economic failure of the Spanish people but also explains a little why the Latin American peoples have not benefited more from the advantages of being a part of the European community of commercial nations (17).

The Mesta (the word derives either from *mezclado* or 'mixed' — mixed that is, with strange flocks; or from '*mecht*'; meaning winter encampments in north Africa) was a guild of sheepowners which arranged the movements of sheep from summer to winter quarters, from north to south, along numerous well defined sheepwalks. The Mesta protected the sheep from landowners who might have enclosed rights of way. It ensured the marking of the sheep. It organised herding. It arranged the policing, and fixed the rests, for 2·6 million sheep in 1479, 3 million in 1519 and, in 1526, 3·4 million, who moved about 200 or 300 miles up and down Spain. The Mesta had its first letter of privilege in 1273, and it survived, latterly shrunken, till 1839. The daily march was sometimes fifteen miles, the average was five miles and usually travel took a month. The southbound journey was made to coincide with the fiestas of the towns concerned, and with harvest time (18).

Now, anyone who paid sheep tolls could join the Mesta, and such a person would not have to possess any specific number of animals. Far the largest number of sheep in the Mesta indeed, belonged to small farmers who themselves led perhaps a few hundred sheep down the route, though there were also grandees who employed a bailiff to lead their 30,000 sheep for them. Meetings of the Mesta were regularly held, in a democratic manner, with several hundred people being present (only a tenth of those allowed to attend), though, in the end, the richer landowners took over the organisation. Women sheep owners, interestingly enough, had all the rights of men.

The difficulty posed by the Mesta was that it was a protected organisation and was given every subsidy and political advantage that it required by the Crown, which in turn did all that it could to encourage the sale of wool abroad. This centralisation of management hampered most severely the birth in Spain of anything like free enterprise. Spain indeed, by insisting on governmental control of marketing, was behaving more like the Islamic despotisms that the Christians had conquered than a modern European society, such as Tuscany, to whom she was selling the wool. Every effort was also made, by the Crown, to extend pasturage at the expense of husbandry, and that too could not have been beneficial in the long run. Attempts by landowners to improve agriculture, even in the *vegas* of Granada and Murcia, were either forbidden or choked by taxes. 'Seldom, if ever, had the whole agrarian life of a nation been held in so firm a grip, or been made to follow so strictly the single-minded purpose of a determined administration,' Julius Klein concluded, adding that it 'was not unlikely that the Mesta pressed the Kings to expel both the Moors and the Jews' (19), people who, by then anyway, were more concerned with crops than with livestock. The history of the Mesta is, therefore, one of how a governmental organisation dominated the main raw material of Spanish clothing in the later stages of the age of agriculture. Its static organisation helps to explain why wool was not the material which would in the end determine the manufacturing age in its earliest stages — neither in Spain, nor elsewhere in Europe. That role was played by cotton. The impact of the experience of the Mesta was also decisive in the way that the Spaniards managed their trade with the New World after 1492, as will subsequently be seen.*

Almost as important as wool in commerce, and much more so in luxury commerce, was silk, mostly produced on mulberry trees by silk-worms,† the great discovery of the Chinese in the earliest times. The Chinese retained their monopoly of the manufacture of silk, by reeling, till about 300 AD, when the Japanese apparently discovered, or stole, the secret of the process. They were followed by the Indians. Long before that, however, caravans had begun to go regularly west from China to Syria in 243 days to carry their stuffs along the famous 'silk road', a path which, very roughly, lay along the south side of the Tien Shan mountains as far as Kashgar, and then crossed into Persia by Kashgar, Ferghana and Samarkand. Ten or twelve ships also went east from Suez every year. In China and, later, Japan, officials wore silk in public as a matter of course. In the Western mind, China was so associated with silk that the Greek and Roman names for China, Seres, indicated the cultivation of silk.

In the Mediterranean world, silk clothes were confined, to begin with, to women. From the time of the reprobate Emperor Heliogabalus onwards, about 237 AD, men came to like them too. The Emperor Aurelian complained that a pound of silk was sold in Rome in his day for twelve ounces of gold (20). The drain of gold in Rome in the later

---

*See below page 439.

†Some wild silk has been produced for very many generations in China, and also in Assyria, Syria and the Aegean, by worms feeding on the oak. The product was not precisely a silk since it was not made by reeling (the cocoons were collected after the moths had emerged) but by combing and spinning.

Empire was caused by what appears to have become an almost insatiable appetite for silk.

In the days of Justinian, in the sixth century, the Chinese secret reached the West. Some silkworms' eggs were apparently smuggled to Byzantium (21). From then on, Chinese silk lost its unique position. There were enough people in the West who could acquire knowledge of the technology of silk-growing to ensure that Mediterranean merchants could thereafter produce a silk equal to that of China in quality. The Byzantine state, however, maintained a monopoly of silk worms on the mulberry trees for about 500 years. Only when merchants from Genoa and Venice took over, as it were, the finances of Constantinople, after 1204, was Italy able to become a manufacturer. Lucca became the first Italian capital of sericulture, but other cities soon rivalled it. Muslim Spain, meantime, also made silk, particularly in Almería, then a great industrial city, which at one time boasted 5000 looms. The mountains behind, the magical Alpujarras, were covered with mulberry trees, and many Berbers were attracted to settle there. (Silk-worms like a light airy climate, but dislike noise, and bad smells: the smell of fried fish apparently makes them die.)

The two main vegetable fibres of the age of agriculture were linen and, though less importantly, cotton. Linen from flax was extensively cultivated in Egypt. Herodotus believed that all Egyptian clothing was linen, whether it was the long upper robe and short kilt of the men or the long robe of the women, and that priests wore a leopard skin over their linen dress. (Some priests, however, apparently wore cotton.) Used for linseed oil, sails and cordage, as well as for clothing, linen was grown all over Europe in the Middle Ages. It was much the most important vegetable fibre in the West till the eighteenth century, and was almost the only western crop to find a market in Peking. No great technical development affected its processing between the days of ancient Egypt and the Renaissance, save for a machine which broke up the tissues (22). Linen was particularly popular for underclothes for hundreds of years, from the time of the richer Greeks (23) to that of the merchants of mediaeval Tuscany (24). When Dr Johnson wrote that 'Kit Smart had no love of clean linen', he was referring to underclothes (25). Still, a sense of proportion is necessary: for the majority of the world, in Europe as in China, underclothes were almost unknown till the thirteenth century and, to a great extent till the nineteenth. Only manufacturing industry could produce such clothes in large enough quantities to make any impact, for the majority of the population, on the scabies, tinea and other skin diseases which derive from lack of cleanliness.

Cotton was indigenous in Burma and Sind: in Egypt (as tree cotton); and in the West Indies (in its 'sea island' form) (26). Egyptian cotton was apparently used for the dress of some higher Egyptian priests but, in its original form, Egyptian cotton was a poor product and no match for

Burmese cotton, which was widely worn in India in the fourth century BC (27). Alexander's armies carried that latter plant to Greece where it began slowly to be cultivated. Under Rome, it was cultivated more extensively, particularly in Malta. The Muslims took it to Spain and, mixing it with a coarse linen warp from Egypt, it became well known, in mediaeval Europe, as 'fustian' (from the Cairo suburb of Fostat) (28). This, together with cotton grown in the Mediterranean, was used in mediaeval Europe as alternatives to wool, but only when wool was in short supply (29). Sea island cotton was cultivated in the Americas long before Columbus arrived there: and cotton cloth (and some other cloths made from vegetable fibre) was much used, in very fine weaves, in many places before 1492, and indeed constituted a major item in assessments of tribute at the time of the Spanish conquest (30). In China, mandarins wore silk in public but cotton in private, while ordinary Chinese people, for thousands of years, simply wore at work a long white cotton shirt gathered at the waist (31).

From very early on, people wished to have their clothes coloured if they could. Hence the importance of dyeing, one of the most complicated of the early chemical processes, since the days of ancient Egypt. It was also known very early that cloth would take colours more deeply and permanently if it was first treated with the salts known as alum (32). In classical days, this was gained from numerous volcanic regions of the Near East, and by the thirteenth century from Yemen but, after the fall of Constantinople, in 1453, the West was cut off from those ancient stores. Then large deposits were discovered at Tolfa in the Papal States, the exploitation of which was entrusted by the Pope to the Medici family. Another large deposit was discovered near Volterra, a find which led to Lorenzo de Medici's brutal attack on that then independent Etruscan city (33). As to the dyes themselves, all, of course, came from an animal or vegetable origin — yellow from saffron, weld or fustic, while green and black both came from mixtures (34), particularly making use of indigo or of woad, grown throughout Europe. Purple came, for a time, from Tyrian purple, a brilliant dye derived from a crustacean indigenous to the coast of Syria (35). The secret of making it was lost after 1453. Red was derived from the madder plant, cultivated near both Rome and Avignon, the two papal cities of Europe, until the discovery of cochineal, a product of the Americas made from the dried bodies of dead insects on Mexican cactuses (36).

These processes are a good reminder that practical associations of techniques may often be used for thousands of years before the scientific principles behind them are recognised. The vast amount of trading of these cloths over thousands of miles in often difficult conditions is a reminder too that the desire for comfortable and attractive clothes, the subservience to fashion and elaborate treatments of raw materials are among the most deep-rooted of human activities and attitudes, influencing profoundly agriculture, commerce, war, technology and methods of government — particularly in Europe.

The third major change, it was earlier suggested, during the age of agriculture was the foundation of certain societies where individuals could be said to have rights. Here, we are on very treacherous ground. Words change their meanings over centuries. Rights as understood in the European Middle Ages are not the same things as are understood by that word in the twentieth century. Sometimes, even the mere definition of such a concept as 'individualism' seems too complicated an enterprise. Still, by the fifteenth century in Europe, these things had assumed certain similarities to — certain family connections with, shall we say — what we now understand by them. In discussing land holding, distinctions have already been drawn between societies which recognised private possession outright and those which, though rich and prosperous, did not. The word 'capitalist' has been mentioned in relation to Flemish wool merchants. In the next few chapters, the discussion of these and related ideas will investigate the religious background to all such abstract discussions, the legal and governmental foreground, and finally will turn towards some social and economic considerations.

16

Part 1

An Early History of the Soul

The coming of a society which respected the independence of the individual conscience can be traced to developments in certain parts of the Mediterranean and western European society during the age of agriculture. It is something still confined to a few parts of the world, and despised in others. The reasons for this transformation during the agricultural age can, firstly, be attributed to the evolution of certain types of landholding; secondly, to the memory of Athens; thirdly, to Christianity and the emphasis laid in Judaism upon law; and fourthly, to the growth of societies of merchants who, though oligarchic, managed to gain a short-lived independence of agricultural monarchies. Gradually, as a result, the belief grew that people's representatives had a right to choose their governments.

The role of religion in the transformation is the most important of the elements concerned. Religion has admittedly often been, and is still often, an impediment, rather than an encouragement to, independent enquiry. Enlightened scepticism is the impulse towards the study of truth. Yet the background to reason is a recognition of the uniqueness of the individual soul. The emphasis by the Greeks on this aspect of the world of the spirit was a real fore-runner to Christianity. But their agnosticism prevented such speculation becoming an accepted attitude of mind in a large society. Large societies have always demanded, and will probably always demand, complete explanation of past, present and future such as is contributed by religion. It was the achievement of Christianity to make possible an intellectual culture which not only gave to its followers the security of such a general interpretation of human life but ultimately, through the idea of personal salvation, gave an encouragement to a sense of individual responsibility. Self reliance as well as self denial, Lord Acton pointed out, are 'written as legibly in the New Testament as in the *Wealth of Nations*' (1), and the concept of modern political representation was more clearly worked out in mediaeval ecclesiastical law than in civil society.

Religion in the age of agriculture had four main characteristics. First, a

128

widespread worship of the sun as the chief among influences for fertility — apparently as important as rain. Second, a concern with death. Third, a gradual evolution from polytheism to monotheism. Fourth, the evolution in Christianity in particular, but also within Judaism, among monotheistic religions, of a concept of the world of the spirit as something distinct from, and critical of, the political and temporal world.

The sun was naturally more important to farmers than to hunters. To it, sacrifices were made all over the world, from the horses offered by the Parsees to the cattle offered, after testing to see if they were clean, by the Egyptians. The temple of the sun at On (Heliopolis in Greek) had a priestly class well established before the unification of the Egyptian kingdoms. But there also survived there, from earlier days, animal gods, such as the beasts of Anatolia. Quite possibly, hunters usually worshipped animals or rivers and those were ousted by the sun when the latter became needed to ripen crops.

The connection between death and religion now seems quite normal, though perhaps in times of secular funerals and neglect of ceremonial (as recently practised in the Anglo Saxon world) it may soon cease to be so. Still, when the expectation of life was so much shorter — perhaps thirty years as a maximum in both agricultural and nomadic societies, in 5000 BC — it was natural to be concerned by mortality. The worship of dead ancestors was probably as universal as the worship of the sun.

In Jericho, in what seem the earliest days of its history, about 7000 BC, the dead were buried under the floor, while skulls had their features restored by plaster and were buried separately from the bodies (2). Later, in the great days of Ur (about 2700 BC to 2500 BC), the tombs of the great, above all of kings, were vast rooms. Such monarchs' deaths would often be followed by suicide, on the tombs themselves, of their courtiers: perhaps ten or twenty of them would drink a cup of poison and die forthwith, to be covered by the king's horses and then by earth (3). Others in ancient Iraq preserved their dead in honey (4). In Egypt, even before the unification of the kingdom (about 4000 BC), bodies were buried in the sand of the desert, in which rainless land they would be preserved for thousands of years. From about 3500 BC onwards, royal and rich families among the Egyptians embalmed their dead. The numerous mummies now in museums commemorate a respect for death and the past combined. At the same time, everyone from kings to paupers took enormous trouble with their tombs: the former built their pyramids long before they were old men and, as dynasty succeeded dynasty, pyramids became grander, brick giving way to stone. Even as early as the IIIrd dynasty, the gods of the dead claimed 'the greater part of Egypt's resources' (5), according to Pierre Montet, the pyramids being lined by tiles, filled with pictures, alabaster, gold, resin and silver.

These entombments were religious acts of the first importance. The pyramid was not really a tomb. It was believed to be the king himself who, if generouslyprovided for, would not only be immortal but would ensure that all who had worked for him would also live forever. Life after death would be a 'perpetual domain', another, even more immobile Egypt, from which hail, locusts, epidemics, invasions, robberies and famine would have been removed. The individual would live there with his ever youthful wife, his ever gambolling children, and his staff of scribes, stewards and craftsmen, each man retaining the rank that he had gained in life. Thus the Egyptians who, apparently for the first time, devised the intoxicating idea of immortality, organised their entire brilliant society around the hope of it: an aim which could scarcely have been made more realisable by the humidity of the tombs, which ruined silver and bronze, and which caused much of the elaborate leather and linen used to rot (6). Still, if it were accepted that the soul were immortal, the society which accepted it, however hierarchical, naturally had to look on individuals in a new light. If the soul were so assured, to have to worship the king was a small price to pay. Souls of the wicked in Egypt were supposed to pass into animals and only return to human life, for another chance, after they had traversed through every species, a journey which was believed to last a mere 3000 years. The Egyptians also believed in some oracles, such as that of the goddess Latona, but that form of worship did not interest many people before the classical age of Greece.

For a long time, Egypt was alone in maintaining this original interpretation of life and death. Collective burials, perhaps associated with commerce or mining, continued throughout the Mediterranean, in caves or in orifices specially cut in rocks, between 4000 and 1500 BC (7). The rulers of Mycænae were placed in circular vaults (8). The kings of ancient Ethiopia were embalmed, painted to resemble the living, and placed in a crystal pillar, specially hollowed out (9), while burial mounds were built in 5000 BC in eastern Canada (10). Scythians, by 1000 BC, were being buried in chambers roofed by timber, themselves deep inside huge grass-covered barrows, their rulers being as usual embalmed and accompanied to the grave by wife, chief servants, horses, clothing and family possessions. Ordinary people, says Herodotus, were allowed to avoid causing a massacre of those dimensions by merely giving the corpse a banquet (11). The tombs of early rulers of Japan were, it seems, buildings up to eighty acres in size (12).

While most bodies, therefore, were buried, there were some variations: the Massagetae, for example, a people of Scythia who had wives in common, were killed when they grew old and the bodies were boiled and eaten. Only if people had died of disease were they buried, an eventuality which caused distress and much wailing (13). Among the Indians, the flesh of the dead among some tribes was removed but the bodies were buried (14). Romans were also cremated, to begin with: a practice which their Sabine neighbours abhorred.The Romans' predecessors as masters of central Italy, the Etruscans, were buried in tombs so elaborate as to persuade some scholars, perhaps falsely, that they were more obsessed than others by death or by life after death (15). Later, Romans in the Republic were buried, but Augustus changed the system back to cremation, for he feared the effects on health of the by his time overcrowded common burial pits (16). The concept of an immortal soul, meantime, stole, like a ghost in its own right, through Mediterranean religions. The desire of innumerable early religions for such a concept is summed up in a quotation in Greek on a flat gold leaf found near Catanzaro in southern Italy:

In Hades, thou wilt find on thy left a spring and, near the spring, a white cypress. Go not near. Thou wilt find another spring, an icy spring, that hath its source in the lake of Mnemosyne and, before it, thou wilt see guards. Then shalt thou say to those guards: 'I am a son of earth and the starry sky, but I come of a race of gods, as ye know: my lips are parched, I am dying of thirst: oh hasten, give me to drink of the icy water of the lake of Memory.' And they will allow thee to drink from the sacred source and, when thou hast drained each drop, thou wilt reign with the other heroes (17).

In the early days of the age of agriculture, all naturally accepted the religion, and the view of the purpose of life, of the people of whom they were a part. Not only priests but kings, civil servants, craftsmen, looked on the existence of the gods and goddesses adopted by their peoples at some remote time in the past as the explanation of life. Religion and race went together. A member of the Massagetae did not contemplate becoming a worshipper of Jehovah. He automatically believed in that people's gods just as he accepted the rule of its monarch. Each tribe and, often, each family, had their own gods and their own religion. Many walls of Çatal Hüyük, for example (8000 BC), were so richly decorated as to suggest that they were shrines. Their number, and their small size, suggest also that they were domestic in character: shrines built for the intimate worship of gods conceived of as ancestors, or ancestors as gods, long before the age of full-time priests in public temples (18). Only the establishment of cities and of organised communities limited the number of gods, or at least demoted many belonging to individuals. By 3000 BC, the ordinary people of Sumer, as of many other agricultural communities, believed that they depended upon deities who were the owners of the soil. To secure the favour of the deities, they paid tribute to the priests. The revenues so gained were used to provide the gods (doubtless the priests) with gigantic feasts, an ample supply of beer and specialist craftsmen (19). The earliest temple yet unearthed, at Eridu , not far from Sumer, (of about 3500 BC), a direct ancestor of the church and mosque, with a long central hall and an altar, had large flanking chambers for grain, while the earliest writing, at Uruk, dealt with the grain accounts of the temple there.

As the generations passed, these religions became associated with epics, prayers, myths, incantations, hymns, songs, dances and rites, as well as a panoply of gods arranged in uncertain, sometimes changing, hierarchical order. Most early settled societies had fertility cults of one sort or another, the increase of production being a matter of preoccupation, and probably antedating any consideration of what happens after death. Ladies of Heaven, gods of vegetation, fish gods, moon gods, water gods, gods of wisdom, love and war, all made their appearances in Iraq, anticipating comparable myths in other countries: thus in Sumer, about 3500 BC, Iranna, goddess of love and of war, set off to conquer the nether regions. While she was away, 'the bull sprang not upon the cow, the man impregnated not the maiden': an obvious prefiguration of the exploits of Persephone and of Baal (who descended into the underworld for seven years).

The Mayas, like the men of Stonehenge, were specially concerned to propitiate the gods at the right moment. Hence their meticulous concern with punctuality, their good calendars and their huge temples (20). The Incas in Peru ruled over a state which recognised the Sapa Inca as a descendant of the sun and thus as divine. The combination of religious and temporal power in the person of a divine emperor also characterised Rome after Augustus, while the emperor of China, 'the son of Heaven', played the critical part in all the great religious ceremonies (21).

Despite the great innovation implicit in Egyptian religion, what struck contemporaries in classical times about the gods of Egypt was their riches and their number. The god Amon at Thebes owned a tenth of Egypt, for example, including 433 gardens, 46 workshops, 83 ships, 65 little towns and 400,000 beasts. On Amon's estates, nearly 90,000 men worked. If other gods were less well off, the diversity of gods was astounding. The forty-two provinces of Egypt each had a separate deity. So did the smallest city. Most gods had innumerable cults. The forms in which the Egyptian gods were worshipped shocked Romans: 'What monsters are revered by demented Egypt?' asked the poet Juvenal, 'One part worships the crocodile. Another goes in awe of the ibis, which feeds on serpents. Elsewhere, there shines the golden effigy of the long-tailed monkey' (22). Still, the size of the religious buildings of Egypt impressed the Romans. They were surprised by the great temples (usually a rectangular walled enclosure of unbaked brick, sometimes 300 yards by 1500), the vast sacred gardens and orchards, the enormous parasitical staffs of the temple headed by shaved, circumcised and bemasked priests, men without any particular moral code save to respect the tradition into which they had been born. The great pyramids were each made of over two million blocks of stone averaging 2½ metric tons in weight, and had employed 4000 masons for twenty years continuously as well as perhaps 100,000 men for three months' work a year for the same period (23). The Egyptians' sense of immortality thus seemed often modified by strongly temporal considerations.

China was something of an exception to all these developments. Though the settled communities on the Yellow River and beyond were brought together under the Shang dynasty (after about 1500 BC) or perhaps under their mythical predecessors, the Hsia, neither the early agricultural societies, nor the monarchies which succeeded them, established a very elaborate religion. Sacrifices might be made to the king's ancestors, or to the gods of the soil. Questions might be asked of gods as to, for example, where a traveller should stay on a journey or whether the harvest would be good or bad but the replies to such questions were usually only 'yes', or 'no' or 'lucky' or 'unlucky'. Thus, the place of gods in society was less than it was in the West, and, in China, the gods were not served by a priestly bureaucracy. Why did China have no dominant religion? Perhaps because kings, priests and ordinary people knew that benefits derived from hard physical effort to maintain the irrigation canals, rather than waiting (or praying) for rain. So the beautiful painted pottery and silk of the earliest days in China were not always created in honour of a special deity. Nor, at the earliest stage of their religious history, can anything particularly interesting be said about the ancient Indians, preoccupied as the cities of Iraq were by a mother Goddess and by sacred trees. In America, the Mayas, concerned with a nether world which seemed 'a blood curdling vision of smoke and fright' seemed equally superstitious. Even the Etruscans, otherwise so intelligent, still sought, in the fifth century BC, the interpretation of the will of the gods in claps of thunder, lightning, bird flight, and livers of sheep.

By that time, however, such ancient forebodings, and indeed such a diversity of gods, had ceased to have a determining hold over the imaginations of a few richer peoples. For, in several such societies, the notion of a single god had been conceived, about 1500 BC. Most early agricultural societies usually had, besides the great miscellany of minor deities, one who was allowed precedence: for example, Enlil, the deity of Nippur, as of the atmosphere and of the earth, was early accepted as the dominant god of Iraq, identified in Babylon as Marduk, and as Bel (Baal) or Lord in neighbouring Iraqi cities. About 1400 BC, the Pharaoh Amenophis IV tried to abolish the minor gods of Egypt and confirm the sun in a unique position. Animal representations of deities were banned, and revenues of all gods were directed into a single royal treasury. These moves failed because of the attitude of the well-entrenched priests, the earliest known clash between Church and State and won by the former, whose financial interests were probably threatened by the king's decrees. But among a then nomadic tribe, the Jews, which had fled from Iraq precisely because its leaders had rejected the gods there, and then emigrated to Egypt, the cult of a single god, Jehovah, began to flourish, not long afterwards. The Jewish religion was the first to recognise an invisible and omnipotent deity with no wizards. That deity was not, like the later Greek gods, a superlative individual but was, rather, the father, creator, ruler of the universe, and the unique source both of all goodness and vengeance.

This early Judaism received about 1200 BC a formal theology from Moses, who had led the Jews out of Egypt, first to Mount Sinai and thence to Canaan, a beautiful territory about halfway between Iraq and Egypt, whose inhabitants had previously worshipped numerous local gods at open-air shrines. The priestly hereditary class of Judaism, traditionally descended from Moses' brother Aaron, could inspire political and religious deference among the 'Children of Israel' since (as in early Iraq in many cities) for a long time there was no monarch, only a succession of 'judges', but the revelation of the idea of the total transcendence of God was not confined to a few holy men but made manifest to the entire people. Religion, law and politics held the people together (largely by oral teaching, for it was a long time before Moses' law was written down). At Mount Sinai, the different groups were bound into a legal community by a 'covenant' with the God Jehovah, who was assumed to be the Jews' supreme commander in war, as well as the world's creator and judge. The exceptional legal position of Jehovah also distinguished the Jews from their neighbours, even if the laws proclaimed on Jehovah's behalf by Moses and his successors derived in part from Hammurabi and other legislators of old Iraq. Among many substantial conceptions attributable to the Jews, and subsequently passed on to Christianity, was the sense that Law was a concept which, originally given by God, bound rulers as well as ruled. Another was the dangerous, if inspiring, one that the Jews were a specially chosen community.

The Greeks of classical times had many deities, whose characteristic was that, like the deities of Iraq whom the Jews had rejected, they fought and quarrelled but did not die. There was a master god, Zeus, apparently brought by the Aryan ancestors of the Greeks from the Caspian Sea whence they originally came, while the other gods were indigenous (24). In Greek religion, there was no orthodoxy, there were no sacred books, no order of authority, nor even a link between the rumbustious gods of Zeus' court, with their magnificent good looks which never faded, and the Delphic, Dionysian, Eleusinian, Orphic and other mysteries. The Greeks in the classical age lived in a religious maelstrom. Many attributed all passion, rain, witty thoughts or qualms of conscience to the gods. All saw the gods as self-sufficient and, above all, successful, beings, the memory of whose extraordinary achievements glittered across the Mediterranean like swords in sunlight. With these gods men might be friendly, but they must never insult them: when Actaeon saw Diana naked, he was torn to pieces by his own hounds.

The Greeks shared with the Jews (unknowingly) the sense of 'destiny, vague, but sure', even if that destiny was not revealed, at least not in Homer (25). They believed in some ultimate order of 'necessity' or of 'fate' to which even gods (as well as great men) had to conform (26). They also thought that poetry, the first art of literature, but, with the Greeks, indissolubly linked with music, was the 'voice of a man who had a god to prompt him' (27). The Greeks were anxious to establish where man fitted in to the nature of the universe: they sought a harmony which was defined as 'keeping to one's place'. Finally, the Greeks allowed themselves to speculate about the chances of religion having a rational basis. That was a great step forward in freeing the intellect from superstition: 'when it comes to the gods, I am unable to discover whether they exist or not', wrote Plato 'or even what they are like in form. For there are many things which stand in the way of this knowledge — the obscurity of the problem and the brevity of man's life' (28). When it came to the point, too, the religious authority to which the Greeks paid, in the great days, most attention, was the Pythia, the priestess of Apollo at Delphi, who considered that most troubles could be settled by common sense.

The Greek philosophical imagination anticipated every problem of religion, (though not every experience) and drew some of its inspired thoughts from Egypt (though nothing directly from the Jews). Thus the Greek community at Croton thought that the body was merely a temporary prison of the soul, while Pythagoras, the inspiration of that colony, believed not only in immortality, but in the transmigration of souls, an idea which he had learned from Pherecydes of Scyros (who died in 515 BC). Further, 'like the Italian painters of the Renaissance who painted again and again the familiar stories of the Bible, Greek tragedians told again and again familiar myths,' using religion as a lens through which to glimpse all the problems of the world (29), fostering thereby, as Maurice Bowra put it, 'a new spirit of enquiry into the visible world . . . a desire to understand things exactly' (30).

At much the same time, equally thoughtful visions began to be glimpsed in other parts of the world, drawing men away from animal gods, or weather gods, towards a few more mystical and profound beliefs, perhaps remotely connected with Egyptian ideas. Thus the Indians of the Indus valley had originally worshipped gods of fertility. The Aryans who went to India — and perhaps that connected them with their Greek distant cousins — sensed forces around them which they could not control, and which they invested with divinity. These forces, they believed, could only be propitiated by sacrifice. Such views were commemorated in the Rigveda, a long collection of sacrificial hymns (*Veda*), dedicated to the gods of the Aryans, written down by priests, about 1000 BC. Later, a sect of poets, in the *Upanishads*, a mystical version of the *Vedas* (about 600 BC) taught that the soul could escape from the suffering inherent in earthly life by the realisation of its identity through an impersonal, if cosmic, soul. The doctrine of rebirth to a higher level, ensured by former acts (Karma), was also conceived. These ideas were welcomed by traditionalists on the grounds that they gave a sacred sanction to the system of castes already well-established in India.* The era between then and the fourth century BC was subsequently as reflective as, if perhaps less stimulating than, the same epoch was in Greece. Parsya, for example, argued that life could be organised best by the acceptance of four vows: to injure nobody; not to steal; to be truthful; and to possess no property. Another prophet, Mahavira, who was almost an atheist, added non-violence, chastity and rigid asceticism to those, and so founded Jainism, while the serene Siddhartha, the Buddha, an historic personage who lived about 500 BC, taught that meditation, morality, altruism and personal religious experience could lead to Nirvana, or a peaceful release from the continuous cycle of birth and rebirth (31). He also had an early version of the idea of the social contract for the origin of the state.

These views did not, however, overturn the by then well-established system of castes nor the old religions of India. The castes divided society completely and, though Buddhism and Jainism supported the lower castes, the priests, the Brahmins, continued skilfully to use the new ideas to underwrite the old castes. This combination evolved into what is now known as Hinduism by the third century BC, the original framework being modified to allow the birth of a new generation of gods: Siva, the god of destruction, change and rebirth; Vishnu, a god of sacrifice, the preserver, recognised as being embodied on earth by the hero Krishna; Rama, the spirit of conjugal devotion; and Brahma, the creator, the Indian equivalent of Zeus or Jehovah, though less important, save for Brahma's role in founding the castes. These revisions leading to modern Hinduism were embodied in the *Bhagavad-Gita*, a book written about the first century AD, which prescribed that every man should act according to the Law, regardless of the consequences.

Numerous other sects, some extraordinary, survived and prospered, sometimes splitting or coalescing, though occasionally, as exemplified by the case of Asoka in the third century BC, a great King might arise who was affected by one of India's beliefs (in his case, Buddhism) and let that belief dominate the peninsula for a time. The Jains, for example, believed in the transmigration of souls: if one lived well one would be

---

* See below page 517.

reincarnated in a higher state; if badly, lower; even insects may have been, and may again become, humans. That meant that it was desirable to avoid eating anything, in a fruit or vegetable, which might be alive. Hence the Jains' vegetarianism, and the evolution of a concept, shared by Buddhists, that cows (always prized by Aryans) were sacred. All these relatively new religions co-existed, however, with India's more ancient beliefs. Of the new sects, Buddhism and Jainism remained for good. Buddhism, indeed, became the dominant religion of Asia, establishing outside India a large system of monasteries and convents, which became the direct stimulus for hundreds of years of sculpture, poetry, architecture, education and sceptical reflection.

A similar intellectual vitality characterised China about the same time, that is, from 500 BC onwards. Many philosophers were able to obtain a hearing and to record their views. They were consulted by kings and noblemen. The mythical Lao-Tzu preached that man was part of a harmonious universe governed by law and that he could find his best ethical guide within himself. Mo Ti argued that self-discipline, clear thinking and, above all, the accurate use of words was the only guide to correct action. He suggested, however, that a benevolent paternalism was the only hope for effective government. Confucius (born about 550 BC) also taught the virtues of clear thinking, which, with self discipline, he believed could lead the superior man to correct action in all his relationships: above all, since that was an agricultural age, a good landlord would treat his peasants well. As a man of royal descent, Confucius gave a rather enthusiastic support to the Chou emperor as representative of the only unifying factor which he could see in his society. His hero, however, was Yu, the legendary founder of the equally legendary Hsia kings, who ate simple food and dressed poorly, but built irrigation canals to the public benefit. Mencius, who lived about 320 BC, more specifically urged monarchs to pursue the public welfare. When the Ch'in dynasty established itself in China in the third century BC, a 'golden age of Chinese philosophy' was inaugurated. All the thinkers associated with it lived in a society rendered stable by the iron rules needed for the production of rice, but whose people had only a feeble attachment to its old gods – perhaps because of the obvious fact that much of Chinese prosperity was due to human endeavour in husbanding water rather than, as occurred in the rainy West, to the emptying of the heavens. The Chinese Empire was, for many centuries, managed by Confucian scholars with a remarkable degree of tolerance of Buddhists, Taoists* and others, including, later, Muslims and Christians. (32)

The general movement towards intellectual religion was also experienced very strongly indeed in Persia, where Zoroaster, who lived about 660 BC, refined the religion previously prevailing in Persia out of

* Taoists were followers of Lao-Tzu with some elements of Buddhism added.

all recognition. The world, he believed, was a great battleground between good and evil. Good men were those who obeyed the good god Ormazd, lord of wisdom. If they did so, they would, after death, cross the bridge of the Requiter to paradise. The evil people, on the other hand, would fall off the bridge and be interned in the 'House of the Lie'.

These powerful and simple interpretations captured first Bactria, then Media (Zoroaster, whose name meant 'rich in camels', was a Mede) and, in the end, Persia. The great Achaemenid kings of Persia were Zoroastrians. The 'barbarians' of Greek history were thus led by men whose religion was as close to Christianity as was their own religion and, through the heresy of Manichaeism, affected Christianity directly. Indeed, a kind of 'vulgar' Zoroastrianism has almost had the longest life of all religious ideas (33).

The religion practised officially by the people who came to dominate the most civilised part of the Western world, Rome, was, however, less reflective. There, from the earliest days until the fourth century AD, priests, augurs, keepers of the Sybilline books and vestal virgins, maintained watch over the flight of birds and the sacred fire, predicting the future and imposing on the past a patina of gravity, not always justified by the events so embalmed.

'The deities of a thousand groves and of a thousand streams', representatives of 'every virtue and every vice, exercised a pantheistic authority' over nature while 'the various modes of worship . . . were all considered by the people as equally true, by the philosophers as equally false; by the magistrates as equally useful' (34). Thus Gibbon summed up Roman religion. No doubt there was a time when Mars, the god of war, and then Jupiter, the father of the gods, exercised a real authority over Romans but, by the time when they began to write of them, their hold was as modest as that of the river gods over China and they were used principally to inaugurate magistrates. The diversity of deities increased when Rome managed to conquer so much of the then settled agricultural world in the west. The conquerors brought law but, unlike the European conquerors of the world in the sixteenth century, they had no universal religion to propagate. Indeed, the religion of Rome could be, and was, easily assimilated to the Greek, of which it was, originally, an offshoot. Rome also accepted, without difficulty, the sacred springs and trees of Britain and Gaul, the heavenly goddess of Carthage, Baal in Syria and, in Egypt, the vast paraphernalia of temples, animal gods and professional priests. Mithraism, the worship of Isis, Stoicism, Judaism and Platonism all flourished, after their fashion. Their idiosyncracies were protected by law. Thus a Jew could not be sued on the Sabbath and was not pressed to serve in the army, since he could not there obey the law of Moses. This tolerance had been practised by the Achaemenid emperors of Persia and indeed, was the mark of all political units known as 'empires' in the ancient world. A cult of the Emperor himself began, it is true, in the time of Augustus, but, for many generations, its chief function was to provide an excuse for athletic festivals. Those were held throughout the Empire, with a devotion to ancient custom but with less religious feeling than in courtly ceremonies of conventional piety. Waves of mysticism, however, occasionally swept the Roman Empire: Domitian established a short-lived cult of Isis, while Hadrian's friend Antinous set up a cult of Diana. Diocletian, who restored the Empire, believed in Mithras. Hence his persecution of Christianity when he heard that Christians in the army were insulting the old gods.

After centuries of toleration, cynicism, agnosticism, mild polytheism, pessimism and a cult of the Emperor which fell far short of that constructed for the Pharaoh, the Roman Empire in the third century AD constituted an easy prey for Christianity. The ground for the acceptance of that faith had been prepared, regardless of the question of the divinity of Christ, by the blending of oriental mysticism with Roman wisdom and with a long term optimism embodied in the idea of the immortality of the soul.

16

Part 2

Universal Religions

Christianity had a radical and new conception of human destiny. With Pythagoras and the citizens of Croton, Christians believed, from the beginning, that the body was a prison. Life on Earth was a preparation for Heaven. Christians also accepted the Egyptian concept of immortality and considered both the end of the world and the Kingdom of Heaven to be imminent. Where Christianity differed, to begin with, from other religions was in the place that it gave to the individuality of the human being who, even if his spirit were the only thing that counted, had full responsibility to achieve his own fate, regardless of the demands of temporal power. A second element was the attention which it paid to the care for the poor, humble and sick. In place of numerous deities too, there was, at least to begin with, only one, paternal, God. Christians were ordered to follow a special rule of life, consisting of the eating of a common frugal meal, baptism by water and acceptance of the idea that answers were provided to all questions in a series of sacred books. But above all, the humane but austere character of the Redeemer, Jesus, son of God, born in Nazareth in what now seems to have been 6 BC, was a contrast with that presented by saviours in previous religions.

In the first and second centuries AD, Christians were more unpopular in the Roman Empire than were the Jews. They were believed to practise ritual infanticide. They appeared to enjoy the act of insulting old gods. Still, the tolerance of Rome prevailed for many generations. Two Jewish teachers, a tentmaker and a fisherman, St Paul and St Peter, seemed an improbable threat to the established gods, even if they had been executed by Nero. The Christian religion was also, to begin with, largely confined to Greeks and to urban merchants. The landowners and the peasants remained pagan. Innumerable other mystery religions competed for the minds of Romans: Mithraism, and Manichaeism, Egyptian and Syrian cults, many old, some new. Greek was the language of the Church of Christ till the fourth century, though Christians went East as well as West — even to India, where the apostle Thomas is supposed to have founded the Syrian Church in Malabar before being killed in 68 AD.

Persecutions under Rome were sporadic. They were due to working-class agitation against Greeks as much as anything else. About 250 AD they became more frequent, perhaps because of the need to find scapegoats for so many disasters. The Emperor Decius ordered everyone to worship the old gods. Perhaps that was one of the things that inspired St Antony, an Egyptian peasant, who died in 305 AD, to organise a group of Christians into collective worship, so beginning the monastic movement, carried further, perhaps on Indian inspiration deriving from Buddhism, by St Martin of Tours. Meantime, the organisation of the Church by bishops controlling dioceses, choosing priests and deacons, excommunicating and baptising, had begun. At that time, in a recollection of the democratic process which had characterised early Rome, as indeed many early societies, the bishops were elected by the clergy, and by the general body of Christians in the diocese.

Only a small percentage of the Empire could have been Christian before 300. If there were a twentieth, it would be surprising. What distinguished them from the followers of other religions was their self-confidence, self-sacrifice, hard work, austerity, determination and also selfless care for the sick at a time of increased numbers of plagues. They acquired particular following in the countryside, unlike the other mystery religions of the time (35). They also showed a unique willingness to challenge the temporal order in the name of a higher authority which was not even specifically political.

The triumph of the Christians was preceded by their violent persecution by Diocletian, who declared Mithras to be the protector of the Empire in 307 AD, and expelled the Christians first from the army (in which the cult of Mithras was strong) and then from the civil service. Next, on the prompting of the pagan Galerius, he closed the churches, confiscated books of scripture, and banned religious meetings. This reign of intolerance was less severe than those actions might suggest. There were few martyrs, and most of them became saints: for example, only eighty-three people were martyred in Palestine between 303 and 313 (36), according to the count of Professor A. H. M. Jones.

Constantine became a Christian because he saw, on one of his marches, with his own eyes, 'the luminous trophy of the cross placed above the meridian sun' and inscribed: 'By this, conquer' (37). He did conquer, but some would say that his Christianity derived more from calculation or from 'superstitious liking for a symbol which had brought him luck than out of moral conviction'. Still, once he had committed himself, he did not retreat. Constantine favoured Christians in the army and bureaucracy, endowed the Church with vast estates, buildings, and allowances of corn, and legalised bequests to the Church. He empowered bishops to make slaves of Roman citizens and permitted any party to a civil suit to transfer his plea to a bishop's court. These actions transformed the history of Christianity.

The income of the Church had originally depended on the faithful's first fruits of their harvest or freewill offerings. (Tithes were not demanded till the time of Merovingian Gaul.) Now the situation was changed, though there were sometimes difficulties in resolving the dividing line between a bishop's personal and ecclesiastical income. Monasteries came to be endowed, sometimes heavily. For the time being, the pagans suffered inconveniences only (confiscations of lands and of treasures from temples), though they were forced to ban sacrifices. But, once Christianity had become official, it spread fast. After many centuries in which the world had seemed free from magic, miracles began again. Chapels began to be built over the tombs of dead holy men. Their anniversaries were celebrated, and they themselves were worshipped as if they were minor gods. Their relics (if they could be found or invented plausibly) were venerated. Saints were held to protect especial cities as old gods had done. Pictures began to be painted depicting the Saints, at the right hand of God. Further privileges for Christianity were meantime introduced by Constantine's son, Constantius II. The Church was rendered immune from poll tax. Even grave-diggers were excused taxes on traders. It was accepted that clergy could only be tried by bishops. The Emperor Julian, Constantius's cousin, sought to restore a mild paganism but, though he nearly revived the Empire, he died too soon to be able to do much for the crumbling pantheon of the old gods. About thirty years later, Theodosius, the last great Emperor, put the question to the then much decayed Senate whether the worship of Jupiter or of Christ should be the religion of Rome. The Senate was full of aristocrats who doubtless preferred Jupiter. They were cowed by Theodosius's known preferences (invigorated by St Ambrose, Archbishop of Milan, then already almost as important a city as Rome). The Senate voted Jupiter out and voted Christ in: a rare example of religious change occurring after pacific debate. Thereafter, with a few exceptions, such as the Pantheon in Rome and the temple of Venus in Carthage, the Church of Christ took over the old buildings of the old religion. The temples were destroyed and their stones used for churches (38). In Egypt, Archbishop Theophilus not only destroyed the idols and the temples, but ruined the priests. He burned much of the great library of Alexandria, the greatest collection of books in antiquity. All these developments put the Jews into a most peculiar position: they were at once indispensable to, but at the same time a burden to, the triumphant belief. From the consequent ambiguities, Judaism has never escaped (39).

Unfortunately, the Church's triumph did not lead to harmony. Even Constantine had found, at the very first congress of the Church, that his new religion was rent by innumerable controversies. The followers of Bishop Arius, for example, argued that, God being indivisible, the Son must be a being later in creation than the Father ('There was a time, when He was not'). Bishops of Rome soon claimed primacy over other bishops. Even within Rome, within thirty years of Constantine's death, fighting and bloodshed broke out between the followers of two rival candidates to the Papacy (40). In the East, fanaticism burned in a hundred minor controversies. All the time, though, the Church increased in size, numbers, riches, and influence. Innumerable monasteries and churches dotted the Mediterranean world. Doorkeepers, singers, funeral attendants, grave-diggers, and male nurses, often counted as clerics. All had incomes and privileges. Pagans were excluded from posts in the government and in the law. Compared with these changes the eclipse of the Empire in the West seemed almost a minor occurrence.

Unfortunately too, though a spirit of humanity was always latent within the Church, Gibbon was speaking little less than the truth when he said that 'a boundless intolerance of all divergences of opinion was united with an equally boundless toleration of all falsehood and deliberate fraud that could favour conventional opinions. Credulity being taught as a virtue and all conclusions being dictated by authority, a deadly torpor sank upon the human mind which, for many centuries, almost suspended its action' (41). Even the design of churches of the early Middle Ages needed no invention, being based on pagan temples or Greek basilicae. Some would even say that the expensive edifice that the Church had become was a critical reason for the collapse of the Empire itself. Gibbon sourly commented that even the 'vices of the clergy' were then 'far less dangerous than their virtues' (42).

The most interesting characteristic of those days was the spread of monasticism, including the extraordinary phenomenon of the anchorite or hermit. Some holy men deliberately reduced themselves to the level of animals. St Simeon Stylites considered that he could serve God best by sitting for thirty years on the top of a pillar sixty feet high. Monasticism, nevertheless, when coherently articulated under the inspiration of St Benedict of Nursia (who founded Monte Cassino in 529 AD), led to the revival of the Church. For the monks of the early Middle Ages in Benedictine monasteries resembled colonists, isolated in a largely hostile world, thrown on their own resources, village states of literacy in a rural countryside. Christianity had been well established in the Roman country before Constantine. It became increasingly a rural religion as town life, independently, became less secure.

A few individual Christians stand out against a confused backcloth of divided loyalties, uncertain power, and authority depending upon nostalgia: for example, the first 'four fathers' of the Latin Church. The first of these was St Jerome, the great translator of the Bible from Greek into Latin — 'the Vulgate'. A hater of cities (and thereby typical of the character of Christianity at that time), and a persistent advocate of monasticism, Jerome had a decisive importance because of his austere but magnificent literary style which, as Walter Ullman says, dominated the writings on government as upon Christianity for many centuries, holding together Christian kingdoms as nothing else. Second was St Ambrose, the aristocratic Archbishop of Milan, who influenced the Emperor Theodosius, and who wrote *Duties of the Clergy* which, if based on Cicero's *De Officiis*, was, for centuries, the only generally available work on ethics. Then St Augustine, Bishop of Hippo, wrote *City of God* to argue, correctly, that the decline of the Roman Empire was not the fault of Christianity. In so writing, he also introduced a breath of Greek philosophy and even of Manichaeism into Christianity. He was on entirely good historical grounds to point out, at least by implication, that the decay of classical science had begun long before Constantine made the Empire Christian. The ideas of original sin, salvation through grace and a predestined universe either derived, in their mediaeval form, from him or were embellished by him.

A fourth early father, Gregory (who died in 604), was the first Pope to be an administrator. He began a Christian revival based on austere practice (celibacy, fair elections, and effective law), honest accounting, and rational administration in the city of Rome — the best since the Antonines. Gregory was able to establish for the first time that the Bishop of Rome was head anyway of the Western Church. With financial help from Byzantium, he seemed almost to have the powers of a new Emperor in the West. Many of Gregory's innovations affect the Catholic Church in the twentieth century: for example, the organisation of parishes, the distribution of festivals, the order of processions and the changes in sacerdotal clothes. His innovations in administration were to make possible the later mediaeval claims by his successors that the Pope of Rome was superior to the Emperor.

The low intellectual level and the slavish respect for custom of the Church at that time were, in the first place, due to the ambiguity of the relations between Church and State at a moment of weak temporal authority. It was also something that the powers of politics and of religion could be separated. To render to God what was God's and to Caesar what was Caesar's was not fully acceptable even under Rome: Caesar was expected to come first. Gregory the Great, however, represented what Hobbes described the papacy to be: 'the ghost of old Rome sitting crowned upon the grave thereof' (43). For many generations afterwards the Catholic church assumed explicitly or implicitly that it really was the Empire.

Into a demoralised and divided Christian world, the Arab invasions thrust like an arrow. Some attribute the collapse of both the Byzantine and the Persian armies before the Arabs to the prevalence of heresies which had destroyed the self-confidence of the two powers from within (44). The Arab tribes, many of them living as collective entities, led by a Sheikh without much authority, had, before Muhammad, the same simple worship of the sun, moon and stars, attended by rich priests, as had other peoples at a primitive stage. Though the new religion grew up from the rivalries of Mecca and Medina, two prosperous market towns run by oligarchies, where some Christian Greeks and Jews lived and traded spices. From those foreigners, perhaps, Muhammad derived some of his ideas.

Muhammad preached a religion which, in theory, at least, seemed quite close to Christianity, emphasising a single god, the last judgement and the efficacy of prayer. Regarding himself as the last of the prophets as well as the secretary of Allah, Muhammad himself played the part of a new Christ. He was a personage of decisive political importance in his own lifetime, however, and one, as Gibbon put it, 'distinguished by the beauty of his person, an outward gift which is seldom despised except by those to whom it has been refused' (45). There was much more belief in fatalism among his followers than in any Christian writing, however, even than in the works of St Augustine and of Calvin, while the duties of Muslims were both more precise and more numerous than those of Christians (reciting the profession of faith; attesting the mission of Muhammad; saying five daily prayers; fasting in Ramadan; going on pilgrimage to Mecca; and taking part in war when it was proclaimed to be holy). Muslims had also to turn five times a day in the direction of Mecca, their hands had to be clean, they had to go to the mosque on Friday, they were not supposed to drink wine and they had to give a tenth of their income to charity. Muhammad himself, though, of course, a historical personage, not a mythical one, is a rather mysterious being. Was he illiterate, as Muslim tradition suggests? Did he pass his early life in commerce? Did he have eleven wives, ten of them widows? Such matters are obscure. All that can be said with certainty is that he was half a warrior and half a prophet who, when his ideas were rejected in his native city of Mecca, organised the people of Medina, and some poor Meccan *émigrés*, under his own leadership, to become the core of an army of conquest. He went to Medina on that city's invitation to resolve their internal squabbles. He left it as its ruler. With him, there was no dilemma between religious and temporal power, nor, indeed, between civilian and military power. Church, State and Army were one. Evidently Bernard Lewis is correct to point out that he revived and redirected currents that already existed among the Arabs of his time, and that 'his career was the answer to a great political, social and moral need' for 'a higher form of religion' than that which the Arabs had had before then (46). But he himself only conquered a small territory in Arabia. His successor led the excited faithful into Iraq. In ten years of unrivalled conquests, Omar, the first caliph (the word meant 'the deputy to the prophet'), conquered Egypt and Syria (Jerusalem fell in 636) from the Byzantines, and Persia from the Sassanids. The Byzantine armies were overstretched, badly led and wracked by disease. They had been fighting the Persians for three centuries. Both sides in that ancient conflict were an easy prey to the Arab horsemen.

A century after Muhammad's death, the Muslims had pressed back the Eastern empire into Asia Minor, dominated all the fertile territory which lay between Morocco and the Indus, occupied Bokhara and Samarkand, conquered nearly all Spain, and penetrated France. A Muslim fleet, built in the late 640s after a brief Byzantine re-occupation of Alexandria had shown the caliph the importance of sea power, controlled the Mediterranean after 655. Well did the great Belgian historian Henri Pirenne argue that these events more than the German invasions marked the real end of the Graeco-Roman civilisation. It was not that the Arabs imposed their culture on those they vanquished. For it was only after Islam received a heady mixture of Persian thought that it was a culture at all. The various Christian sects in the Middle East survived almost intact under Arab rule. Islam was essentially a military empire to begin with.

What caused this expansion? Over-population? Religious self-confidence? Desire for glory? Doubtless a mixture of all three. The conquerors, though, were not holy men but generals, whose religious interest, on the whole, was modest. Glory was probably as important a motive as any. After all, the conquerors took over only state lands and lands of the enemies of the regime in countries which they conquered. They did not interfere in previous religions provided their leaders paid tribute. The old subjects of the Byzantine empire apparently found the charge light to bear. Bernard Lewis claims that the Christian populations of Syria and Egypt preferred the rule of Islam to that of orthodox Byzantium (47). Probably the Jews thought the same. Much to the surprise of the Arabs, many of these Levantines became Muslims. Indeed, they soon began to contribute to what Islam became.

Christian churches remained open in Al-Andalus, the Muslim kingdom in southern Spain (48). Nor did Islam stifle scientific enquiry. Hence the preservation of chemistry, hence the early universities, hence the extension of the craftsmanship of antiquity, hence the skill with which the caliphs made use of men of many nations and faiths. Hence indeed the intellectual and commercial superiority of the Arab world in the ninth and tenth centuries which were the golden age of Islam, particularly in Spain. There the spirit of Muslim toleration was seen at its best. There music (elsewhere condemned) was prized. There, there were numerous marriages, at every level, the royal one included, between Christian and Muslim: would any Christian king of 880, other than a Spanish one, have sent his son (as Alfonso III sent the future Ordoño II) to be educated at the Muslim court of Zaragoza (49)? This tolerance even survived a disdain on the part of Spanish Muslims for the 'polytheists' of the North, even survived the semi-sacred character of the Caliph of Córdoba. Under the cloak of Islam, too, the multitude of ancient Near Eastern peoples began to speak Arabic and, in the end, particularly after the Turkish conquests gave both Arabs and Levantines a new common master, to think of themselves as Arab.

Even so, neither the tolerance towards different creeds expressed by Islam, nor its role in preserving the memory of classical knowledge, should cause us to forget its autocratic nature, and its denial of the right of individuals to seek their own destiny. The fatalism which predestination always inculcates stifled the Arabs' capacity for individual initiative. The concept of a holy war such as that waged even by Muhammad is the reverse of humanitarian. Muslim punishments were, indeed are, harsh. Redemption by good works scarcely existed in the Muslim mind, which was also encouraged to concentrate on a sybaritic picture of what Heaven might be for those who believed and were just: 'For them are prepared gardens . . . they will be covered with gold bracelets, and shall be clothed in green silk and brocades . . . Youths who will continue in their bloom forever shall go round to attend them with goblets and beakers and a cup of flowing wine. . . . They shall not hear therein any vain discourse or any charge of sin but only the salutation "Peace! Peace!"' (50). But in the Bible and the Christian Sacred books, the precise nature of Heaven is largely left to the decision of God the lawgiver, and neither the diet nor the quality of the staff are so lovingly described.

Furthermore, Islam remained a state religion: the caliph was the head of the cult. None of the sects, neither Sunnis nor Shi'ites, nor their derivatives into which Islam soon became divided, engaged in anything like a serious struggle to limit the power of the Muslim state (51). Indeed, the idea would have been incomprehensible. Nor were there many political innovations in the way that the caliphs exercised power. They ultimately, under the Abbasids, moved their capital to what had previously been the Persian village of Baghdad, and they drew inspiration from the old Persian customs of relying on governors to manage revenue. They used innumerable Persian Muslims as civil servants, and were anxious, like the Sultans in Delhi, to display, deliberately exaggeratedly, the difference between ruler and ruled (52). The Abbasid caliphs, indeed, seemed as much the descendants of the Sassanid, Parthian or Achaemenid great Kings of Persia as of the prophet. Disputes multiplied within Islam from then on, but it is difficult to see many points of abstract principle at stake. Religion was persistently invoked but probably in order to fill the gap left by the lack of radical Arab thought. Later, the divisions which destroyed the unity of Islam certainly had some religious, and strongly felt religious, implications: Zoroastrianism, for example, lingered on in Persia and, perhaps, at one remove, was probably the background to the heresies leading to the establishment of autonomous principalities in the east of the Islamic empire. But peasants' hostility to taxes, ancient noblemen's reluctance to become peasants, slave resentments, and ambitions of governors who knew that they were indispensable as collectors of taxes all played a part. Further, the definition of Islam as articulating a total identification of Church and State meant that all these things were naturally posed differently than they were in other, less all-embracing, creeds.

The Christian Church did challenge temporal claims. In the early Middle Ages, the Church was a legal class, protected by its own law and courts, but not primarily a social class. It drew members from all sections. There were divisions within it: monks; priests, who were permitted to marry until the eleventh century, with dynasties of priests being as common as they had been in Egypt; prelates, equal in authority and riches to great lords, and some of them as adept in war as in peace.* All these persons' relations with civil authority were ambiguous. Some would doubtless have liked to have dispensed with civil power altogether. After all, as Walter Ullmann put it, 'for the greater part of the Middle Ages, government and its underlying principles were controlled first and foremost as integral parts of applied Christian doctrines' (53). But churches needed armed, if usually barefoot, soldiers to protect them. Others, from the grandest to the poorest, were appointees of the barons, who also sometimes constituted themselves abbots. Even when they did not do so, there was an open sale of offices. Kings meantime claimed to be descended sometimes from pagan gods, but they desired ritualistic coronation, and soon were found claiming miraculous powers. They were often advised by clerics: between the eighth and thirteenth centuries, all the chancellors of France were clergymen (54). The ideology of this mediaeval Church was rather amateurish, somewhat illiterate, Manichaean, with many nature rites, and much magic. Many still believed that the end of the world was close: 'the fear of Hell was one of the great social forces of the age' (55), Marc Bloch remarked. At the same time, the Papacy in Rome reached the nadir of its history with the reign of the family Crescenti, who exercised a rule known to historians as the 'pornocracy'.

Revival began when a pious duke of Aquitaine founded the monastery of Cluny in Burgundy. The aim was a reforming organisation within the Church under the Papacy, though (because of the Crescenti), 910 was an inauspicious moment for such an event. Cluny and its daughter houses stood for the celibacy of the clergy, for an end of lay influence over clerical appointments, particularly bishops, and an end too of the sale of ecclesiastical offices, for an abandonment of work in the fields, and, as a substitute, prolonged services. These ideas dominated not only the organisation of Cluny's own network of monasteries

* Class is a matter discussed on page 517. But some influential modern thinkers have written misleadingly about the clergy as a 'class' in the Middle Ages, e.g. Gramsci: 'the category of ecclesiastics can be considered the category of intellectuals *organically* bound to the landed aristocracy'. But the main problem of the Middle Ages was specifically the disharmony between clergy and laity.

which regarded Cluny's abbot as their leader, but many other Benedictine houses. Their ideas assisted the Church's integrity but, even so, the inclination of the Abbots of Cluny was to restrict the little classical learning that remained: Abbot Odo saw Virgil, the most famous classical writer during the Middle Ages, as 'a beautiful vase full of vermin' (56). 'My grammar = Christ,' said Peter Damian, who introduced flagellation into the hermitage of Fonte Avellana, about 1043. He believed that a monk's role was to mourn, not to study.

Among the monasteries affected (in architecture and behaviour) by the Cluniac reformation most important perhaps were those along the route to the shrine of St James at Compostela where St James's cult had become, in Américo Castro's words, 'a positive creed' in Spain against Islam, after the legendary appearance of the brother of Christ, on a white horse, at the battle of Clavijo in 822. The pilgrimage of so many to Santiago made León and Castile turn their eyes to France. French knights animated the Reconquista. Indeed, the main line of the Spanish kings in the late Middle Ages derived from the Capetians through that Count of Burgundy who 'liberated' Portugal and founded a kingdom there; and the first bishop in reconquered Toledo (1085) was French (57).

Cluny was a remarkable achievement. It offered an 'exalted daily round', the companionship of noble buildings and distinguished men, the daily recital of the Bible in regular sequence followed by elaborate rituals: what Sir Richard Southern described as 'a majestic life, perhaps superior to any form of Christian life, before or since', while the lovely hills along the valley of the Grosne in Burgundy lay behind. The abbots themselves also moved on a grand scale, respected among kings, dukes, popes, even emperors (58).

Somewhat earlier, meantime, the divisions between Western and earlier Christianity which had dogged the Church since the collapse of the Western Empire, broke into the open. 338 Eastern bishops said in 754 that all visible symbols of Christ were blasphemous. The worship of images would lead to paganism. The controversy inspired the severance between the Greek Orthodox and the Roman churches. Long expected, the only curiosity was the ground of the dispute, since the slant-eyed beauties who passed for the Virgin Mary on ikons continued to play a greater part in the imagery of the East than in any other branch of the Christian family. Behind the dispute, too, lay a difference in the attitude to temporal power: the Byzantine emperors had a truly oriental view of the Church as a branch of the national bureaucracy; the Western Church, long independent of imperial control, regarded itself as superior to all temporal power, just as, as they put it, in a dangerous metaphor, the head is to the body.

Eventually, in the persons of Popes Leo IX and Gregory VII, and after the breach with Constantinople, the ideas of Cluny reached Rome, causing the bitter, if intellectual, controversy over episcopal investiture. Though forced to concede defeat in some arguments with the Emperor, the Popes were effective in renewing the Church. The Popes' victory was marked by the Crusades, called for in 1095 by Urban II (previously Abbot of Cluny), and by the movement to build the 'Gothic' cathedrals begun after the monastery of St Denis in 1137 (Cluny had been started in Romanesque style). These great churches both calmed and inspired the spirit, though (in keeping with Cluny's tradition) they gave grounds for dreams, not speculation. In Gothic churches, music sounded well but words rang out no more than they do in opera. Mediaeval Christians were thus offered an aesthetic, but not an intellectual, experience. The Gothic movement was slow to mature: the pointed arch did not generally appear till the thirteenth century, enabling cross-vaulting, and leading to great new heights to the naves and choirs. The mason, entering his golden age, was thus caused to do much work in the limestone or sandstone quarries.* In the meantime, there was a ban on the sale of offices. Laymen, kings and squires were excluded from the choosing of churchmen, while bishops were, in theory, selected by a college of canons. Clerical marriage was also banned, for the first time formally, though higher clergy had usually restricted themselves from such a union.

The papal administration which grew out of this reformation was a competent one and influenced modern government in a variety of important ways. An expert staff ensured fast correspondence. Papal legates maintained obedience, and contact. Popes held regular courts of justice (60). In cathedrals, canons established a common life comparable to that in monasteries and, particularly in England, many cathedrals were turned outright into the churches of Benedictine monasteries. From the twelfth century, cathedrals were also asked to provide masters to teach poor scholars and clerks and, as an unsuitable accompaniment to this educational reformation, a new catalogue of miraculous stories spread across Europe — particularly those about the Virgin Mary who, until then, had played a minor part in such tales. The Crusades, embarked on in a mood of religious frenzy but carried out for commercial benefit, also brought back many new objects of veneration: the Crown of Thorns, the Holy Blood, a part of the True Cross, and the skull of John the Baptist. Military orders too were founded, inter-

---

* As a rule, the mason was the director of a mediaeval building, being concerned with every important structural problem, from the counter-poise of buttresses to the design of the tracery. 'Minor' matters, such as carpentry, slating, glazing and plumbing were all incidental. Masons also filled the countryside with stone castles instead of wooden ones. Countess Albereda of Bayeux was so pleased with the mason who built her castle that she had him executed to prevent him building another (59). The person of the 'architect' remained anonymous as a rule till the Renaissance. Even then, it is not clear who designed most of the châteaux of the Loire, or Fontainebleau, though the detailed, 10,500 word specification for the latter survives.

national like the Templars and the Hospitallers, or local, like the Teutonic Knights or the Order of Calatrava, fusing the ascetic life with the life of combat and powerful enough to dominate kingdoms. Alfonso I of Aragon even named the Hospitallers and the Templars heirs to his kingdom. Never had the Church militant seemed more determined: 'God has fixed a day for you to be at Edessa:* there the sinners will be saved who hit hard and who serve him in his need.' It was as if, as one song of the crusades put it, God had organised a tournament between Heaven and Hell (61). Another revival of the time of the crusades was the statue: sculpture had vanished in Europe after 500 AD, but the Europeans who reached Palestine and the Near East in the train of the crusaders could see the statues of the past for themselves. Before 1100, life-size saints reappeared in the recesses of great churches (62). If the crusades in the east Mediterranean were in the end fruitless, they were much more successful in eastern Europe or southern Spain. Abbeys followed the sword.

The recovery of the Church was continued by the foundation in the eleventh century of the Cistercian order which, to begin with, in the days of its English founder, Stephen Harding, aimed at a return to the simple life, as prescribed by the then half-forgotten St Benedict. Also founded, in 1098, like Cluny in 'watery Burgundy' at Cîteaux, amid vines and sheep, the white-habited 'Cistercians' grew fast so that, as a result of the determination of St Bernard of Clairvaux, there were 500 houses by 1200. The return to the manual labour which Cluny had scorned enabled the Cistercians to make a greater mark in cattle-, horse- and sheep-breeding than they did in theology. The export of English wool by the Cistercians was a determining element in the English economy. Lay brothers were recruited to do the heavier work in the fields, while the abbots remained in loose touch with Cîteaux, whose lord was the spiritual commander of an enterprise which was, to the colonisation particularly of East Europe, what the East India Company would be to India.

The Franciscans and Dominicans, grey and black friars, followed, in 1209 and 1225 respectively. They spread at a rate comparable to the orders based on Cluny and Cîteaux. These friars had, as their chief purpose, the preservation of the mediaeval city for the Church and the defeat of the numerous heresies which seemed so attractive to many in the prosperous thirteenth century. St Francis and his followers preached the beauties of humility, and devotion, in simple, large churches to big audiences who sang cheerful hymns written in the vernacular. The followers of these orders were to possess nothing and to beg when they could not work. They were priests of the age of troubadours, wooing my Lady Poverty with good humour. The Fran-

* The principality of the Norman crusader, Bohemond, which was captured by the Turks in 1144.

ciscans used oratory, for the first time, as a means of making propaganda for the Church, an approach made possible by the revival of cities where large audiences could be found. The Dominicans were also devoted to charity in towns, but, above all, to preaching (they were commended originally by the Pope as 'Friars Preacher'). Their founder's passionate hostility to the heresies of the Albigensians, and his success in destroying them, secured for them the control of the newly founded Inquisition (1233), an institution intended to ensure intellectual conformity throughout Christendom. The Dominicans, thereafter, had a great influence on the subsequent history of education. Large churches, such as Santa Maria Novella, Santa Croce and even the Duomo (built by the guild of wool merchants) in Florence, made a marked contrast with the great high Gothic cathedrals contemporaneously spreading over northern Europe. In Dominican churches, as in Roman law-courts, the words of the orator were meant to be heard. Both these orders might under other circumstances have become heresies. Instead, they became the most reliable first line of defence of a Church determined to maintain unity even if it had to persecute (63).

Mediaeval Europe was a religious society: even movements of dissent, like that of the well-organised Albigensians, with its Manichaean or Persian ancestry, never questioned the essential truth of the Christian revelation. Wicked princes were explained away as bearing the mark of the Antichrist, whose dreadful empire would precede the coming of the Kingdom of God (64). Frederick II, Stupor Mundi, it is true is said to have suggested that Christ, Moses and Muhammad were imposters: he was almost alone to do so in the thousand years between 400 and 1400 (65).* He also raised the question of whether he was, legally or technically speaking, the owner of the possessions of his subjects; to receive the answer 'no' (66). It was that legacy of independence which Christianity contributed to the 'liberal heritage' of the West. It was perhaps characteristic that it was left to the prince who doubted the validity of Christianity to seek intellectual justification for tyranny. Yet the various questions raised by the movements of dissent — doubts about transubstantiation or whether it was permissible to study pagan works — led the way to a revival of scepticism which, in the end, would destroy the unity of Christianity and indeed of every other universal religion.

The desire to keep scepticism at bay was the chief motive for the Church's support for Universities. Those schools began as groups gathered round the person of some prominent teacher — Ivrenius, a teacher of Roman law, the inspiration in the twelfth century of the first university, Bologna, or Vacarius, who taught the same subject a little later, to inspire Oxford. When these institutions began, they were as peripatetic as were the Dominicans. But they soon became fixed in one

* Though Moses was portrayed as a sorcerer in some mystery plays (67).

place and have been a permanent part of the intellectual world ever since (68). At much the same time, the Friars ceased to be respected for their poverty and became popular, because of their wealth, and Saint Francis's austere ideas were even condemned as heretical in 1322. By 1500, the Friars were large and prosperous landowners and the Church itself seemed corrupt, luxurious, murderous, even, according to Burckhardt, 'satanic', and practically secular (69).

Further, if the basic tenets of religion were rarely contested anywhere, the Europeans, at least, had an equal reliance upon the idea of a fixed universe in which the four elements — earth, air, fire and water — were maintained in ceaseless permutation by the distant but predictable movements of the universe. That, at least, went for the majority of educated people. The uneducated majority had a variety of magicians and fairies in whom to place their trust at least from time to time. The prophets in the minds of many people in mediaeval England, for example, were not confined to those mentioned in the Old Testament. They included Merlin, whose prophecies were reissued in manuscript in the fifteenth century to justify the claims of one participant or another in the Wars of the Roses. People also believed in the Devil. The early Hebrews attributed evil to the existence of rival deities. But the triumph of Monotheism made it necessary to explain why there should be evil in the world if God were both omnipotent and good. So the notion of Satan was a necessary complement to that of God. 'Possession' by the Devil survived as a fairly common complaint.*

Equally, one belief which survived the days when organised religion dominated society was that in spirits and ghosts, superstition and magic, demons and chiromancy, sorcery and alchemy. Towards the end of the end of the age of agriculture, at all events during the days of the Renaissance, theism, or deism, platonic mysticism and even a kind of revived paganism all revolved in the minds of the seekers after truth. Some branches of Christianity and other religions collaborated, in practice, with these beliefs. Thus the mediaeval Church used the lives of saints in one form or another to find a method to prophesy the future and control it. Over 500 miracles were, for example, associated with St Thomas à Becket at Canterbury, while local saints, prayer, and sacraments were invoked in ways that often suggested magic more than faith (70).

One other concept which made its appearance during the age of agriculture, in several continents, in one form or another, was Honour. Europeans like to suppose that this idea was a combination of Christianity and Feudalism but, though it played an essential part in chivalry, its roots may be sought in Persia or in ancient Greece as much as in the works of the early fathers.† By the fifteenth century, it plainly meant as

* The purely medical significance of this side of religion is discussed on page 67.
† Herodotus wrote that, in his time, the Arabs were known to 'keep pledges more than any other people' (73).

much to many people as religion did. Guicciardini, the historian of Italy, wrote: 'He who esteems honour highly succeeds in all that he undertakes, since he fears neither trouble, danger nor expense' (71). The early history of this concept would repay attention, since Jacob Burckhardt, the nineteenth century historian of the Renaissance, was probably right when he suggested that, in his day, 'the decisive rule of conduct' for cultivated Europeans was 'a sense of honour' – that 'enigmatic mixture of conscience and egotism which often survives in modern man after he has lost, whether by his own fault or not, faith, love and hope' (72).

In Islam, as in the West, a universal empire survived in name long after its regions were in effect separate kingdoms more than principalities. As in Christianity, a single language kept together and largely diverted the ethnically divided peoples who subscribed to the creed. Pilgrims went to Rome (or Jerusalem) or to Mecca because of the collapse of the political unity which had once made those holy places the hearts of great communities embracing continents. Islam's legacy, however, to the age of technical and intellectual revival which began in Europe in the late Middle Ages and ultimately affected the globe was a different one from Christianity's in three clear ways: first, Islam was in very many respects more tolerant because a good Muslim knew that people who supported other religions, even ones comparable to Islam, were likely to burn in hell whatever happened; second, it was more fatalistic; third, the theology, wrote Bernard Lewis, was 'determinant, and authoritarian, demanding the unquestioning acceptance of the Divine Law'. A book, Bernard Lewis continued, in Islam was 'often presented not as an individual and personal creation of the author but as a link in the chain of transmission'. Hence, when the era of expansion came to an end, it was easy for Islam to go to sleep, as it were, and remain in an intellectual torpor which was to last till the nineteenth or twentieth century when it and other ancient faiths met the modernising challenges of the West (74).

In 1500 AD, a few river gods and magical memories survived in remote if sacred groves. But international religions had imposed themselves on a large proportion of the world's richer, and more thoughtful, peoples. These religions had all of them local characteristics and local manifestations. But they had ceased to be associated primarily with single peoples or even, in the case of both Buddhism and Christianity, single cultures; and, as will now be seen, the laws and governments beneath these systems greatly differed. Even so, the main preoccupation of all but a few eccentrics continued for many years yet to be religious: 'Heaven made the sovereign for the sake of the people', wrote Hsun Tzu, a philosopher of the third century BC in China, but he did not question heaven's existence.

17

Law, Government and Liberty

Government arose for three reasons: to assist the community concerned to provide defences against enemies; to preserve the religion of that community; and to provide law. The third of these actions became more important still, at least while the communities were at peace, and it is that aspect of the political life of peoples which will be discussed in this chapter.

The earliest codes of law which have survived seem more like the rules of a game than anything which we now speak of as law: but law is itself an attempt to give to life the rhythm, the certainty, and the predictability of a game: and games are not superficial things* (1). When a king died in Persia, before the Achaemenid line, there was, according to tradition, five days' anarchy to show people the advantage of having kings and laws (2). That principle did not mean that kings were supposed to be subject to laws. But it was already appreciated by priests, noblemen, 'elders', merchants and even rulers that the knowledge of law could not be confined to the king and to his agents and so kept secret. Codes of law, from an early time, were, therefore, made known by being carved in stone in a public place. In this respect, kings in Greece and those in Iraq behaved similarly.

In the ancient Mediterranean, these codes of law were intended to clarify old customs, themselves conceived as unalterably decided. Of course, such codes could not be promulgated before the coming of writing and perhaps the evolution of writing was closely connected with the beginning of the codification of law. At all events, in ancient Iraq, collections of laws were common by 2000 BC. Perhaps every city had one. In Ur, for example, in 2100 BC, the code makes it plainer than any surviving pot or pyramid that the human beings of that time were fully recognisable to modern man: 'If a man has broken another man's bones, he shall pay one mina of silver', the code specified and went on, 'if a man has hired an ox and damaged its eye', he would have to pay

---

* The seriousness of games is discussed on page 605.

half its price. Other laws made provision for inheritance, prevention of cruelty to children, illegitimate children, and property. Judges were professional, and court procedure was carefully worked out, as were rules for the treatment of witnesses, testimony on oath, rules for a clash of evidence (including trial by water; though, somewhat more logically than in Europe, the guilty person sank, the innocent floated) (3).

The precious intellectual achievement of a rule of law had not yet been achieved. The laws of Hammurabi of about 1750 BC, however, show that it was realised that if, for example, the requital for a murder were left to the family of the murdered person, a long vendetta might follow. To replace that by a system in which the state was the impartial arbitrator was an achievement as great as the invention of pottery. The people of ancient Iraq also probably knew that 'when justice is both certain and mild, it is more efficacious' (4), in de Tocqueville's words. Another sign of their individuality, perhaps, is the fact that, as soon as law began to be written down, personal names began to be noticed. Perhaps, indeed, the name, in the form which we know it, as well as writing, is a consequence of law (Herodotus knew of only one African tribe, the backward Atarantes of Morocco, who used no names at all) (5).

In contrast with Iraq, the ancient Egyptians had no code of laws, and no professional lawyers. They did have contracts, wills, decrees, judges, reports of proceedings, and punishments. The Indians — in the Indus valley or in the early days of Aryan dominance — were also slow to develop legal institutions very early. The kings, chief priests, and certain elders of the community concerned acted as judges in accordance with custom. By classical Indian times, say about 500 AD, the guilds of artisans and local assemblies had also gathered to themselves judicial powers. Chinese statesmen too were always averse to any kind of codification of law, even their philosophers believing that each case should be judged on its merits and that the abstract should be avoided. In the eighth century AD, there was, nevertheless, some codification of Chinese criminal law on a modest scale. But civil law remained little used, on the grounds, argues Joseph Needham, that 'a genius for compromise had long been characteristic of private and commercial life' in China.

Where the attitude of the Greeks to law is considered, we are immediately conscious of a fundamental divide between them and others. It was not simply that in Greece, particularly in Athens, people felt increasingly free, and intellectually imaginative enough, to speculate on any subject. After all, speculation might lead anyone anywhere. The decisive matter is that the Greeks realised that men had risen from brutish levels. They attributed that, not to any abstract idea of progress, evolution or any other vague force, but to the power of law. Secondly, they made elaborate comparisons with the law as practised by themselves and by barbarians, whose laws they regarded as being based on the whim of an irresponsible, and often arbitrary, barbarian ruler. Their laws, they thought, protected their lives and property and enabled them to plan their lives as they wished. The Greeks were wrong, no doubt, to dismiss the laws of Babylon as worthless (much less the law of Moses of which they do not seem to have heard), even to set them on a par with the unwritten customs of, say, the Scythians, but they were right to argue that (as with China and ancient Mayan society too, had they known it) in both instances, 'the ruler's will had the force of law' (as the Roman legist Ulpian would later formulate it). The Greeks fully appreciated the paradox that they obeyed laws 'in order to be free', as Cicero (and later, in slightly different terms, Goethe) put it. The explanation of this change was, of course, political. The kings in Athens and in other Greek communities had given way to oligarchies largely commercial in outlook. So the states concerned required a concept of law other than that which was simply the command of the lawgiver.

Greek law, though reflecting the will of the gods, gave much attention to the question of how people should behave in relation to one another. Justice, on the other hand, was conceived of as indicating, in Maurice Bowra's words, 'a natural tendency to obey the rules of a civilised society and also as giving every man his due' (6). The word was indeed considered one of the four cardinal virtues (along with courage, wisdom and temperance). The Athenians, according to Thucydides, respected laws 'whether they are actually on the statute book or belong to that code which, although it is unwritten, cannot be broken without acknowledged disgrace' (7). In Athens, too, knowledge of the law was part of the business of being a citizen since, in any litigation, each man had to plead his own case. Though litigation was rife in the fifth century BC, advocacy was not practised professionally. That meant that there were great advantages if, through education, a man could acquire a detailed knowledge of the law (8). It was, after all, a considerable achievement to be able to plead effectively, as was the need, before a jury of about 500 persons (9).

In modern life, many languages (including the English) leave an ambiguity between laws which describe regularities of nature and laws which are prohibitions or commandments. These two kinds of laws in the twentieth century have hardly more in common than the name (10). But in all ancient societies, including the Greek, that was not the case, and the ambiguity, as we may see it, explains what such societies thought laws should be.

The consequence of these attitudes in Athens was the achievement of a democracy which, whatever its shortcomings, was direct, not representative. This was possible primarily because the population was small. All power was vested in the open-air meetings of all male citizens held on the Pnyx. Probably 45,000 were entitled to attend. One sixth of the total population, that is, perhaps 4000 to 5000 people, customarily went to the meetings (11). A council of 500 was selected by lot to judge what needed to be judged, while the assembly elected ten generals to defend the State. There was no permanent officialdom (12). Power was 'judicial and administrative'. But the administrative was a tiny part of the business transacted on the Pnyx. Nor was legislation needed. The laws had been dictated by Solon long before. Those who claim to be influenced by Athens should not forget these facts. The 'legislature' was more like a jury than a parliament.

In the Italian peninsula, a system prevailed which, to begin with, had certain similarities with the Greek one. The Etruscan kings were thus elected for life by a consultative assembly, and the election was confirmed by a council of elders, an anticipation of the Senate of Rome. In Rome, as in Athens, there was, to begin with, a democracy, not so direct as the Athenian one, not so 'representative' as those which modern large states have achieved. The propertyless poor were less powerful than their numbers would have ensured in a full democracy but nevertheless had a vote on critical decisions as a 'century' in the so-called *comitia centuriata* (13). In addition, the power of the executive, in the hands of consuls, was limited to one year. A 'dictator' could be named, but only in an emergency, and only for six months. Weighted voting gave patricians advantages over plebeians, but the plebeians could sometimes impose changes such as, for example, the provision in 265 BC that no one should be elected to the same magistracy twice (a law subsequently altered). The Roman democracy had many other qualifications (14) but the essence of it was that it was complex. It was the gradual simplification, decay and ruin of ancient complexities that led Caesar to the Principate, an eventuality ensured by the use of violence in the so-called *comitia tributa*, the public 'committee of clans', and by the exploitation by Augustus of the fear of renewed anarchy in Rome (15).

Against this background, Roman law began in much the same way as did Greek or ancient Iraqi law, but the subsequent development was quite different. Inscribed, according to tradition, by the decemvirs on the famous twelve 'tables' with the usual intention of making clear what the rules of the society were, the law was continuously and regularly modified, from the earliest days until the time of Justinian. Even so, however, law in Rome was a slave to its code. It had nothing to do with morality. That gave it its force. The most just complaint could not, and never did, move the judges, unless specially permitted by the praetor, whose task was to introduce some consideration of equity. Motives could not as a rule be discussed in Roman courts. As early as the time of Caesar, there were complaints about the law's pedantry. Further, while, in the beginning, Roman trials had been held, as in Greece, in front of large gatherings, a multitude of laymen proved incapable of dealing with complicated cases when law itself had become so refined. Thus a special profession of 'jurisconsults' grew up. Latin literature is full of impressions of how they worked: 'the clients from the country flocking to the great man's antechamber in the early morning and the students standing around with their notebooks to record his replies,' as Sir Henry Maine described it (16). Roman magistrates fortunately remained amateurs. They were assisted by assessors who were professional.

Some historians of Rome give the impression, it is true, of an Empire increasingly riddled with restrictions. Laws were often ignored, and bribes given in order to ensure that they should be (17). Rome seemed more litigious than law-abiding: already, in the first century AD, the Emperor Vespasian was wondering how the system could cope with the flood of suits, criminal and civil, which occupied the time of the hot and crowded courts (18). Legal practice too, left much to be desired: criminal justice, for example, was inefficient and brutal. The injured party, not the State, was supposed to bring the guilty to the dock. On the other hand, it is evident that, in their speculation as to whether or no there was a law of nature, Roman lawyers devised the then original and now fundamental concept of the equality of citizens before the law, and Marcel Reinhard is right to argue that the Romans were administrators before they were conquerors, jurists more than administrators (19).

The law of Rome had actually become obscure by 500 AD. It could only be established from a vast array of sources: from the works of classical writers on law, imperial decrees, decrees of prefects, or edicts contained in many thousands of volumes 'which,' says Gibbon, 'no fortune could purchase and no capacity could digest' (20). By the later Empire, too, the municipal courts had mostly faded away, and the court of first instance was the provincial governor's. Later, minor cases were dealt with by a specially appointed *defensor civitatis*, while Constantine took the bold step of empowering bishops to decide civil cases at the behest of both parties. The bishops gave a quick, cheap and consequently popular service. Around these courts grew a whole tradition of scholarship and practice which, particularly after the eclipse of the Empire, profoundly marked the political as well as the legal evolution of Europe (21).

Essentially, the Roman law that we know is Justinian's. In his day, an effort was made to make the law consistent. But it was unsuccessful. 'Instead of a statue cast in a simple mould, by the hand of an artist,' wrote Gibbon, again, 'the works of Justinian represent a tessellated pavement of antique and costly, but too often of inconsistent, fragments' (22). Perhaps the chief element which survived the subsequent untutored age was what Gibbon refers to as the 'exclusive, absolute and perpetual domination of the father over his children', and, indeed, over his wife (23). But behind that and innumerable other concepts, was the idea that the law derived from certain clear, well-defined principles and not directly from custom: the essential contribution of Roman law to the modern world.

Under the Empire, however, Rome was transformed politically from a democratic republic to something close to an eastern despotism, echoing Alexander's and the Pharaohs' systems. The victory over Egypt completed a process which had originated with Scipio Africanus's conquest of Carthage. But Egypt could claim to have influenced Rome. In Egypt, the Roman emperor was an absolute monarch. He was served there by a prefect himself served by the large staff of the Pharaohs. Between the first and the fourth centuries, Rome took upon itself many Egyptian characteristics, political and administrative. From Egypt, came the theocracy of Caligula, the idea of a large bureaucracy, the idea of separating civilian and military power; from Egypt too came both the grain to feed Rome and the largest quantity of taxes — for it was the richest province. The bureaucracy established itself because the senatorial class ceased to serve the Empire as competent administrators. The Emperor Gallienus sought to extend the Egyptian model of rule to the whole of the Roman empire. The Illyrian Emperor Aurelian wore a diadem and golden costume, with precious stones, copied from the Persians (24). The emperor in the late Empire was personally absolute, making all appointments down to those of provincial governors (25), and dominating the law. Once the Emperor could at least be challenged. When the villainous Emperor Commodus sentenced Appianus, an Egyptian priest of Alexandria, to death for rebellion, the latter protested. The following exchange then took place:

Commodus: 'Do you realise whom you are addressing?'
Appianus: 'Yes, a tyrant.'
Commodus: 'Not so, you are speaking to the Emperor.'
Appianus: 'Certainly not. Your father, the divine Marcus Aurelius, had every right to call himself Emperor because he cultivated wisdom, despised money and loved what was good. But you have no such right since you are the antithesis of your father. You love tyranny, vice and brutality.' (26)

Such an exchange could not have occurred after about 250 AD and certainly not after 300. The forum for such a thing did not exist.

Under the Empire there were always, however, distinctions in the income of the state which never occurred in such simple despotisms as those of the Tartars. Thus, this income was divided into *res privata* (crown lands gained by confiscation, or old royal lands, such as parts of Cappadocia, and much scattered property in towns and agricultural land which was let and which paid for the general purposes of the state); *res summa* (customs duties on frontiers, taxes, fines); and special levies for wars or emergency (27). Till 212 AD, emperors were gods only to provincials, not to Romans. After the Empire became Christian under Constantine, the Church also limited imperial authority. The Senate, though impotent, was always influential. Emperors who defied it seldom died in their beds, A. H. M. Jones pointed out (28). The secretariat of Roman emperors was also small and, for a long time, despite Egypt's influence, personal. The office of imperial correspondence *(ab epistolis)*, the office of petitions *(a libellis)*, the enquiry office *(a cognitionibus)*, and the chamberlain running the household *(a cubicule)* each contained fewer than ten people, headed by a man of distinction (Suetonius, for example, was head of *ab epistolis* and Ulpian of *a libellis* under Septimus Severus). Magistrates, such as prefects of the city (in control of the urban cohorts or police and the corn supply, water, etc), and the governors of provinces only slowly established secretariats of any size. From the time of Constantine, civil servants increased in numbers and pretentiousness. They began to wear uniforms and to hold ranks in fictional regiments. Many were corrupt, pedantic and rapacious. They also became hereditary — a rule which, in the end, applied to workers in royal mints, weaving and dyeing factories, gold mines, and to town councillors. Yet, even in the fifth century, the numbers of bureaucrats or men working for the Emperor were infinitesimal in comparison with the present day, never exceeding 40,000 in both parts of the Empire* (29), and private property was guaranteed.

The Roman system of law and politics thus evolved from what was, in the early days of the Republic, a direct democracy, with a bias towards aristocracy, to what became in the end a despotism, with some major qualifications uniting the power of the Emperor and preserving the person of the individual. The Emperor, even at the disgraceful end of the Empire, was expected to keep his own laws.

This was not the case in the ancient East nor, indeed, in pre-Columbian America. The Inca Empire had, for example, many advantages in respect of governmental organisation. Great post roads carried the Inca's orders everywhere, while conquered people were organised in tribes, under a *cacique*, whose task was solely to labour for the Inca state (30). But there was no private property and no freedom under any law. The Persian empire of the Achaemenid dynasty was also a bureaucratic state, in which provincial governors and satraps were not aristocrats, but high officials. The Persian bureaucratic tradition was indeed one of the most continuous of Middle Eastern institutions, affording, after 650 AD as before, invaluable service to the Caliphate as to the Sassanids (31). Naturally, Persians interpreted Islamic law according to their own judgment. Equally, the unified Chinese empire, established by the Ch'in dynasty after 220 BC, and essentially preserved ever since, was a bureaucratic form of government. Holders of estates which might

---

* Apart of course from the army of, say, 375,000.

have deserved the name of 'feudal' beforehand all vanished. The nobility had to live in the capital, and the country was divided into 36 (later 41) prefectures. Everything was standardised, merchants discriminated against, roads and walls meticulously built for defence and for supervision.

Similar developments, though on a far more modest scale, can be glimpsed in Africa. There were in that continent, during the age of agriculture, a large number of monarchies based upon tribes but looking back, institutionally, at a remote remove, as suggested before, to the Egyptian monarchy. These states were, as a rule, run by a king who, says J. D. Fage, 'led a life sedulously secluded from the common people: he gave audience from behind a curtain; not even the most intimate of his courtiers might see him eat and drink'. Such monarchies, numbering anything from a few thousand to over a million in population, were almost always based on the hereditary position of the King and the bureaucrats around him were also nobles, a bureaucracy without paper, reading, and writing, but one in which power was exercised by officials who held office by the king's pleasure, could be dismissed at will and who, as a rule, managed such external trade as there was as a royal monopoly (32).

The development in India, from very complex institutions based on custom to a simpler system based on personal power, is observable and even comparable, superficially, to the evolution of political power in Rome. Among the Aryan invaders, the original chiefs seem to have been elected as leaders in battle. Those chiefs eventually assumed privileges associated with kingship. Their power, to begin with, was often restrained by tribal assemblies, such as a council of elders and a general assembly of the tribe. Some tribes were directly managed by these assemblies, just as Athens was by the meetings on the Pnyx. Gradually, partly as a result of alliances between priests and rulers, partly as a result of the growth of administrative systems, kings became hereditary, the assemblies' powers diminished and, finally, monarchs became regarded, or caused themselves to be regarded, as divine (33). Some semi-democratic republics, however, did survive a long time, especially in hilly regions, in the foothills of the Himalayas or in the Punjab. Meetings of heads of families discussed policies and elected leaders (34). One day, perhaps, some of these institutions will seem almost as worthy of as careful a study as those of Greece. They were, however, always coincident with monarchies in which the usual simple rules of absolute government survived and which, in the end, prevailed everywhere, resulting in something like an imperial system by about 250 BC, under the dynasty of the Mauryas. Those monarchs set up a monarchy, a regime whose chief interest is that it created a system of secret police agents within the nation whose mission was to gain information. This system declined for the reason that many great polities do in the end – excessive taxation – but left behind in India a desire and a memory of empire which it never quite lost. Nor was the memory of general assemblies of the populace quite lost either. Thus, within the empire of the Pallavas about 800 AD, assemblies of villages, of guilds and of professional groups were all held annually and representative committees of those assemblies – a very modern touch – met more often. In that regime, indeed, it was possible to detect again the glimmerings of what promised to be a democratic life sometimes under the supervision of an official, but sometimes not (35).

The courts, armies and such other political apparatus of many of these ancient states were already financed largely by taxation. This included poll taxes on citizens, often payable in kind, and often collected by headmen in villages, who were, in countless countries, the most important political and judicial local personages, but also by other tax farmers. It included customs, such as the 20% demanded on all goods which crossed frontiers in the Roman Empire; and inheritance taxes, such as the 5% in the Roman Empire paid on wills worth more than 100,000 sesterces, other than by direct heirs. There were also indirect taxes, such as the excise of 1% demanded in all Roman markets. Income derived also of course, from loot in war, as well as from profits from national enterprises, such as mines. Nearly all these taxes and ways of raising money survive. But most taxes were on spending. Income tax as such was apparently not conceived of till the fourteenth century in Italy, but, from Babylon to China, from India to Aztec America, all despots sought their percentage of every crop, which, of course, is much the same thing. That indeed was the distinctive tax of the age of agriculture as income tax is of our industrial age. In India, in the earliest days, the king alone could sanction clearance of waste and took a percentage, usually a sixth, of the crop, as a tax. The Muslim and Ottoman Empires also acquired the bad habits of simple confiscation of goods under the guise of poll taxes and also of using provincial governors as tax farmers, who often became the independent rulers of their provinces, rendering a purely formal homage to the caliph, whose function was increasingly reduced to giving formal and often retrospective approval to things done in their name (36).

Almost everywhere people who had no money had to serve certain days of labour, as was the case in Egypt during the Middle Kingdom, and the more efficient despotisms had recourse to censuses to ensure that that service was performed, from the earliest days of agriculture. Such censuses might be accompanied, as in Rome under Diocletian, by what seems to us to be the modern device of a careful estimate, by the appropriate authority, of how much money would be needed in the coming year, how many horses and uniforms, say, or how many recruits needed for the army.

Could it really be that, as is very clearly implied in the work of the best of modern historians of Rome, that overtaxation of the Roman Empire was the chief reason for its collapse? That beguiling theory leaves out consideration of the fact that many other large, overtaxed despotisms, such as the Chinese Empire, lasted a very long time despite their fiscal systems. The French doctor Bernier, who lived in both the Ottoman Empire and the Mogul Empire in the seventeenth century, noticed that there was 'little encouragement to engage in commercial pursuits', since tax-hungry despots had the 'power and inclination to deprive any man of the fruits of his industry'. So anyone who managed to acquire wealth sought to conceal it for fear of confiscation on arbitrary grounds (37). But, Bernard Lewis explains, 'one of the primary causes of economic decline' in the caliphate 'was undoubtedly the extravagance and lack of organisation at the centre' (38).

To turn from those powerful despotic monarchies to a consideration of nomads or feudal Europe, or any other society where the paraphernalia of government was modest, is like turning from the present system of the State to that of ancient Greece. Yet, even in feudal Europe, men were not living in prefiscal innocence. Pepin, Charlemagne's father, for example, confirmed the application of the Mosaic principle that lords and estates should pay a tenth part of their harvest to the Church — a principle which often meant that the lords, who controlled the local churches, took the 'tithe'. One principle of the Gregorian reform in the eleventh century was the provision that tithes should definitely go to the Church — though that usually meant the monasteries and chapters of cathedrals, not the village priests. Hence the accumulation of sacks of grains in tithe barns up and down Europe (39). Kings also collected a poll tax, the *geld*, to pay for their preservation from the Vikings, and the Normans in England maintained it, even though they were really the Viking danger institutionalised. Domesday Book was considered to be a 'geld book', by the great historian Maitland (40) and it clearly had many fiscal uses even if modern mediaevalists would frown on so simple a judgement as that (41). Yet it is the modest incidence of taxation which strikes the student of mediaeval Europe as being so remarkable — tiny in comparison with the Caliphate or the Byzantine Empire as well as with Rome or the modern state. The only way that the Carolingians, for example, could raise money effectively was through profits on their own lands, from tributes from conquered peoples, from booty, and from a few tolls on the roads from the insignificant commerce (42). Only in the late thirteenth century were even the most powerful kings of the Middle Ages, those of France, able to institute a regular tax, the *taille*, for which the authority of their people was not needed and which was used to finance the expensive army.

The general rule seems to have been, in the age of agriculture, that the settled communities evolved from diversity to simplicity, often from some degree of government by consultation towards government by decree. Kings remained supreme magistrates, as well as commanders-in-chief and high priests but increasingly, particularly in rich and stable societies, that is, particularly in what would have seemed in modern language to have been the 'advanced countries', they interpreted the law in their own interest. Yet, beyond the settled communities, among nomads or, even, more primitive agrarian monarchies, such as 'the ancient Germans' (while they were still 'ancient'), more free practices survived. Lord Acton, in a fanciful passage in his essay on Liberty, recalled that Tacitus pointed to the Germans of the first century AD 'with a vague and bitter feeling that to the institutions of these barbarians the future of the world belonged'. Their kings, when they had kings, did not always overrule their councils. They were sometimes still elected. They were sometimes deposed. They were also sometimes bound by oath to act in obedience to the general wish. As among the early Babylonians — and the later Vikings — they enjoyed real authority only in war (43). Modern historians agree that, among the matters resolved by the Magna Carta by the king of England was that 'authority should be subject to law which the community itself defined' (44). The idea of liberty thus shone brighter in England by 1215 than it did in more sophisticated places.

The history of the world is not, actually, the story of liberty; otherwise, it would be shorter. But it is plain that, in the era when agriculture was the main preoccupation of most people, that concept, however fumblingly, was often raised. Peoples believed themselves to be free when, in their collective organisation, they were free from foreign rule. Individuals believed themselves to be so when they had obtained recognition of laws which restricted governments as well as themselves. Of course, liberty implied order, just as rights are worthless without obligations. During the last few hundred years of the age of agriculture, certain communities in Europe began to obtain new formalisation, through parliaments, of ancient liberties and limitations of power which had been roughly conceived in tribal days. Such customs may have been in origin German. A great deal of the philosophy which was used to describe them was Greek. The idea of representation was contributed by mediaeval ecclesiastical law. The circumstances in which these ideas were worked out, principally over the matter of the power of parliaments to accept or deny the government's power of taxation — were Western European. It was, in the end, Britain and Holland, and afterwards their neighbours, which were able to take best advantage of a whole range of new opportunities which came to be available to them between the fifteenth and eighteenth centuries as a result of the phenomena which we have become accustomed to think of as the Renaissance, the Scientific Revolution and the Enlightenment — concepts which endure, and with a worldwide significance, despite some well-intentioned complaints about their parochiality.

BOOK III

An Intellectual Transformation c.1450 – c.1750

But see! Each muse in Leo's golden days,
Starts from her trance, and trims her wither'd bays,
Rome's ancient Genius, o'er its ruins spread,
Shakes off the dust, and rears his rev'rend head.

Alexander Pope, Essay on Criticism

And new Philosophy calls all in doubt,
The Element of fire is quite put out;
The Sun is lost, and th'earth, and no man's wit
Can well direct him, where to look for it.

John Donne

The fourteenth century peasants had been at once more oppressed and better cared for. The great seigneurs may have sometimes treated them harshly, but they never abandoned them to their own devices.

Alexis De Tocqueville, French Revolution

Cosimo de' Medici to Santi Bentivoglio who had lived as a wool merchant in Florence, though the heir to the Bentivoglios of Bologna:
   'Weigh well, young man, this matter which you must consider: wherein resideth, to the philosophic mind, the greater advantage: the delights of a private citizen's estate, or the pleasures which the government of a city can afford?' Santi hesitated, and, on the advice of Nero Capponi, chose Bologna.

Stendhal, Journey to Italy

   'Most of us, when we visit Rome, go up on the morning after our arrival to the heights of the Janiculum . . . . there it all lies beneath us, the heart of Europe and the living chronicle of man's long march to civilisation. . .

Trevelyan, Garibaldi and the Defence of the Roman Republic:

'It is well to observe the force and virtue and consequences of discoveries. These are to be seen nowhere more conspicuously than in those three which were unknown to the ancients . . . . namely, printing, gunpowder and the magnet. For these three have changed the whole face and state of things . . . . the first in literature, the second in warfare, the third in navigation'.

Francis Bacon, Book I, aphorism 129, *Novum Organum,*
[All three derived from China]

The word 'Renaissance' was apparently invented by the great French nationalist historian, Jules Michelet, in 1840. The expression 'Middle Ages' was invented by the German, Christoph Keller, in the seventeenth century. These labels seemed helpful once. They do not seem valueless now, they have not been rejected, yet each generation of cultural historians throws the origins of the Renaissance back earlier and earlier while economic historians often date the end of the Middle Ages in the seventeenth century. In this Book, those ideas, innovations and discoveries are discussed which, in the last few centuries of an age when most men and women lived on the land, led to the achievement of an 'industrial age, in the eighteenth century – a phrase which really means an age of machinery and mass production.

18

The Renaissance in Europe

The word Renaissance implies the recovery of the achievements of Rome and Greece and, in the process, some fundamental changes in the society which subsequently developed in consequence of the quickening of the human spirit that followed. No sign of such reinvigoration of old achievements occurred in China under the Ming dynasty. China, in the fifteenth century, though rent by civil war, had earlier seemed far more innovative a society than Europe. Certain factors, speculated upon by Joseph Needham in many learned volumes, made Chinese society more favourable to the application of science in early times than European mediaeval society. The same factors inhibited China from inspiring a development of modern science in Asia comparable to that inspired by Italy in modern Europe, even though Corsalis, writing to Lorenzino de' Medici in 1515, recognised the Chinese were *'di nostra qualità'* (1). First in the development of many artefacts from gunpowder to paper, from the magnetic compass to cast iron, Chinese endeavour continued to be thwarted by the survival of despotism. No independent cities established themselves even in the chaos following the eclipse of the Mongol Empire — and the Mongol conquest in 1279 was destructive — just as the Turkish conquest was in India. The only well-established traders in China were the Muslim and, therefore, alien communities of North China and Yunnan. The Chinese naval expeditions of the early fifteenth centuries to the Persian Gulf and the embassies sent abroad to the Near East at that time, were never pursued and, indeed, were less concerned with the spirit of enquiry than with a desire to defend the despotism; were perhaps undertaken simply out of uneasiness lest a deposed nephew, known to be in the South Seas, reappear from thence to claim a disputed throne.

The Renaissance in Italy took men infinitely further into the realm of ideas than the Romans (whom the men of the *quattrocento* in Italy sought to emulate) had dared, or sought, to venture. The recovery of antiquity took a form, indeed, which Rome herself would have despised. Romans were great lawgivers, engineers, administrators, soldiers and mechanics, but they did not excel in the realm of abstract thought. Theirs was

169

the world of affairs. That applied, also to those whom Romans prized in the Greek world. Aristotle, for example, was good at biology, but bad at anything which needed experiment: observation was his speciality (2).

What was it, China aside, that caused these changes to occur primarily in *'ce petit cap du continent Asiatique'* which Paul Valéry liked to call Europe (3)? Marc Bloch, the greatest French historian, believed that the comparative immunity of Western Europe from invasion (since the Vikings and Hungarians) played a great part. He recalled the Russians and Chinese, overwhelmed by the Mongols; the Indo-Chinese, crushed by Khmers; East Europe, never free of the Turks and 'steppe people' (4). But what of the Japanese? The Aztecs? Surely insulation could not be the only explanation for the European Renaissance. Otherwise, the Tasmanians might have invented the wheel. Nor was Europe wholly isolated.

The European Renaissance was, of course, far from being a matter of a number of artists such as Brunelleschi or Michelozzo going down in the *quattrocento* from Tuscany to Rome in order to copy ruins. That comment in no way reflects on the quality of classical copies, such as Brunelleschi's Santa Maria degli Angeli in Florence, and Michelozzo's chapel in the church of Santissima Annunziata, nor on the seriousness with which artists of the Renaissance took their work. But the recovery of urban life, the revival of scepticism, the retrieval of the histories of Livy, and the rediscovery of art, had all begun in the eleventh or the twelfth centuries, had caused a widespread commercial reinvigoration of Europe in the thirteenth and had only been interrupted in the fourteenth century by disease and its consequences.

The element of recovery in this Enlightenment was, of course, important. This did not take the shape only, or even primarily, of a renaissance in art. For example, it is now generally agreed that the seventeenth-century French mathematician Pierre de Fermat was the founder of the theory of numbers, the branch of mathematics that deals with the properties of numbers. Fermat was originally inspired by Diophantus of Alexandria, whose *Arithmetica*, written in the days of the Antonines, was rediscovered in the sixteenth century. Fermat's experience was typical of all leaders of thought during the Renaissance. His own work depended on a classical model, though he excelled his mentor in breadth of understanding (5). Orators, preachers, and professors studied Cicero, Quintilian and the imperial panegyrists and no accomplishment was 'more highly esteemed than the power of improvisation in Latin' (6). Students of herbs in the sixteenth century studied Dioscorides' *Materia Medica*. Perhaps most important of all in the Renaissance in Europe, there was a rediscovery of technology long forgotten or abused. Thus mediaeval man had tended to look down on mines and mining — almost as if it was a kind of rape of the soil. The pick was held to remove the irreplaceable soil from God's earth. But in *De re metallica*, in the sixteenth century, Georgius Agricola called the miners' profession 'higher than that of merchants' (7). Admittedly, in technology, the process of recovery had begun long before the days of what has come to be called the Renaissance. For example, the potter's wheel had been lost in Europe after the fall of Rome. It was revived in the ninth century. Thereafter, pottery (which had never declined in China) gradually recovered its ancient quality. True porcelain had begun to be made in China at Wen-chou in Chekiang about 400 AD when it was found, probably by accident, that a crystalline white mineral, feldspar, could be incorporated in the body of the pottery, to create a glaze, so enabling 'stoneware'. By 900, this art had been perfected in China and the famous jade green ware of the T'ang dynasty began to be exported (8). Stoneware also began to be made in the Rhineland after 900, and a salt glaze was begun in the fifteenth century.

Another critical change was that people knew where they were more accurately in the Renaissance. That was not only because of the discovery of America nor of spectacles (in the thirteenth century), nor because of the invention of the telescope about 1600 (probably in Middleburg in the Netherlands* (9)), but also because of the coming of the clock to Europe in the fourteenth century. Earlier, there had been a great vagueness about time, which even affected dates: when precisely *was* the year 1000? How old was the king? As for the hours of the day, waterclocks were rare and froze in winter in the north of Europe (10), though elaborate, even striking, waterclocks had been known in the Near East for a long time – the great Mosque of Damascus had one by at least 1186, and Procopius of Gaza saw one there about 500 AD (11). Sundials were unsatisfactory because they depended on fine weather. Hour glasses were not much used, since after a time, the sand enlarged the opening through which it flowed. But after the invention of the counterpoise clock in Germany, no European city felt proud of itself unless it had an elaborate public clock, with angels, planets, and prophets, as Lynn White tells us, 'marching and countermarching', often attached to churches, sometimes to town halls (12). Among the first clocks were those of Strasbourg (c.1354), Wells (c. 1375–80), Salisbury (c. 1386), and Rouen (1390). These clocks usually had only an hour hand. A minute hand followed, about 1400, and a second hand, about 1550, though even the minute hand took a long time to come into general use: the clocks depicted in Brueghel's paintings of about 1550 have only one hand. The pendulum was devised by Galileo in 1581 (on seeing a lamp in Pisa) but it only began to be used in 1641. It was not till 1670 that Christiaan Huygens invented the grandfather clock. Portable clocks were invented in the fifteenth century. Huygens also devised the balance spring about 1675. Jewel bearings began to be used about 1700

* Galileo exploited this brilliant idea, and made a modest telescope to observe the sky in 1608, but there seems little doubt that the inventors were Dutchmen.

and small watches came into general production about 1750. As important in telling people where they really stood was the adoption of the Gregorian calendar, which was much more accurate than the old Julian one.

Renaissance man is also reasonably recognisable in innumerable small ways to his modern descendants. The autobiography of Benvenuto Cellini, for example, is plainly the work of a modern man, respecting himself more than God, Pope or Duke, and out for himself. Even the exaggerations — his personal killing of the Constable de Bourbon, his escape from the Castello San Angelo — are similar to amiable boastings of men of the modern age. The great Burckhardt believed that the Florentines of the fifteenth century were 'the pattern and the earliest expression of modern Europeans generally'. A few jokes of the early Middle Ages amuse us, it is true, but they are certainly few. Chaucer has some good moments, but from the days of the Renaissance, humour becomes much more recognisable. Wit, as long dormant in literature as style, reappeared as a weapon even in theological disputes. In Boccaccio, Madonna Oretta was bored by someone telling her a long story and going back to the beginning: 'Sir,' she remarks, 'your horse trots too roughly. I beg you to allow me to go on foot' (13). The long discussion of types of humour at the court of Urbino as reported by Castiglione would not seem out of place in the twentieth century: 'On three counts I have to go to Bologna,' said Giacomo Sadoleto, a learned jurist. 'The three counts are, Count Ludovico de San Bonifacio, Count Ernesto Rangole and the Count of Pepoli,' interposed Professor Filippo Beroaldo. 'Think how generous he is,' said Niccolo Leonice, of an aquaintance, 'for he gives away not only his own things but those of others' (14). Thus the jesters, fools, *buffone*, parodists, and satirists of antiquity were revived as much as the dome of the Pantheon.

The individuality of the Renaissance is also expressed in the resumption of the use of a surname as well as a personal name – a habit which had existed in Rome but been forgotten by commoners. (In Herodotus's day, the custom had already existed of taking the father's name to distinguish a man from others with the same Christian name: and even then some people took a matronymic.) In the twelfth century in France, it was already common to add a nickname, or perhaps a second Christian name, to the original single name. By the thirteenth century, the second name, whatever its form, began to become hereditary in grand families. But the process was slow: in Burgundy, for example, people took their mothers' names; new branches of a good family might take a brand new name. Servants and slaves sometimes took the names of their masters. Only modern Europe would begin to insist that all had surnames as well as Christian names (15), and the world here followed Europe slavishly.

Alongside these events, it may seem perverse to single out so modest an invention as Catherine de' Medici's of the side saddle. Yet that device, inspired by the most powerful woman in Europe between 1559 and 1580, symbolises more than anything another change lying ahead of humanity at the end of the era of Enlightenment: the beginning of the freedom of women from their old subservient role. Italian families of the Renaissance among the upper classes insisted that daughters and sons should alike receive education. The sixteenth century saw the beginning of the modern recognition of women's individuality as expressed in the lives of Isabella of Castile, Vittoria Colonna, Caterina Sforza, Isabella Gonzaga, Elizabeth of England, and even poor Mary of Scotland. They are commemorated in the characters of the noble women who dominate so many of Shakespeare's incomparable plays.

19

The World Re-opened

The most astonishing change brought about in the days of the Renaissance was the opening of the whole world to European shipping. This was an innovation beside which the Reformation, for example, seems at first sight a minor matter local to Christianity in Europe until we remember how few of the world's population took advantage of the new journeying or could do so.

This innovation in travel can be dated as beginning when the Portuguese, under King Diniz the Worker, about the year 1300 started, with Venetian and Genoese guidance, to finance long sea journeys. The best known of those descendants, the mysterious stay-at-home, Henry the Navigator, sent out many expeditions after 1418 to discover the African coast, perhaps with the intention of propagating religion, perhaps to find a route by sea to Ethiopia as well as to Guinea, though his motives are hard to be certain of. At the end of the fifteenth century, Columbus was beginning to set off for America and, within twenty years, the Europeans were to be found everywhere. The technological bases for these journeys were: the stern-post rudder, the astrolabe, the magnetic compass, new sails, and ships with three masts.

Mediaeval ships in Europe, like those of antiquity, mostly hugged the coasts. Only exceptionally were they out of sight of the land. Merchant ships of that era, Braudel tells us, were more like travelling bazaars than the great destination-conscious vessels of the nineteenth century. They stopped almost daily to buy and to sell, daily renewing their supplies, and dropping into small ports a day's voyage apart (1). Usually powered by oars, they might put up a square sail with which they could make headway given a fair wind. No such ship could do anything against an adverse wind, though the square sail gave stability on large ships (2). Even the most powerful ships of the ancient world had a sailing season limited to the months between April and November. Few boats could expect to survive the effects of the wind in the winter on the sea. No ships of the ancient world, even those which, regularly at the summer solstice, set off from Myos-Hormos, the port of Egypt on the Red Sea, to sail to Malabar (in forty days), were larger than about 330 tons, the average being between sixty and 130 tons, a fifteen-ton ship being quite frequent, while Pliny wrote that, in his day, a large Indian ship was fifteen tons only (3).

The rise of Islam transformed communications in both Africa and Asia. The Arabs had conquered Persia by 652 AD and their first embassy to China was in 651. In 758, Arab pirates looted Canton. Later in the eighth century, they reached Malaya. About that time the great Muslim general, al Hajjáj al Thadafí, even contemplated the conquest of China (4). Within the next few centuries much of north Africa became part of the Islamic world, to begin with as part of the Caliphate under governors, who subsequently made themselves independent. Some of them, particularly in northern Africa, were able to reconstruct something of the agricultural and economic life which they had inherited from Rome. The ships which made these journeys and, therefore, made possible such a successful economic revival were powered by a triangular sail which, despite its name of 'latin' (lateen) effectively challenged the old square sail since with it a vessel could beat into an adverse wind.

Northern Europe, however, had some mediaeval innovations too. Indeed, in the end, their ships proved the best vessels when put to the test for they had to face a sea more turbulent than the Mediterranean. The Viking ship, a 'deckless masterpiece of joinery' as Marc Bloch put it, had a keel, a steering oar with a tiller, a square sail and thirty, or sometimes even sixty, oars a side. In the twelfth century, the Scandinavians also developed the cog: a clinker-built* ship with a square sail, and probably a development of the 'round ship' of North Sea trade. The Vikings, like the Arabs, began as pirates and ended as merchants. For the Norsemen were not destructive barbarians, as they used once to be depicted. They wished to seize the wealth of the warm and prosperous South, not to destroy it. Their most remarkable accomplishment was the establishment of their commercial sites for the better carrying on of the slave trade in the Varangian state in Russia. Gradually, along all the rivers of Europe up which the Vikings sailed, in those incomparable vessels, made by a race of great craftsmen (5), commerce was reinvigorated. Cloaks from Flanders began again to be exchanged for wine at fairs at Lille or Ypres, or in the other, increasingly prosperous, cities of the Low Countries. The Venetians, meantime, increased their contacts, which had never been wholly dropped, with Byzantium. Genoa copied them. Venetian ships began to challenge the Islamic command of the Mediterranean from the early eleventh century by making use of the Arabs' own methods of seamanship.

Before the end of the thirteenth century, the Genoese organised regular sailings between Italian ports and the North Sea. They did that

---

* External planks overlapping downwards and fastened with copper nails.

largely by making use of the stern post rudder, by which a helmsman could manage the rudder at the rear of the boat rather than the middle. This idea apparently had been devised in China before 1100 (6). The Arabs then introduced to the western Mediterranean both the astrolabe* (originally Persian), and the magnetic compass (originally also Chinese), whose needle was allowed to float on a straw, but, by the late thirteenth century, was already mounted on a pivot. The first sea chart dates from that time too (7). During the course of the next few generations, Mediterranean merchants began to use vessels with three masts, with a square sail on their main mast but triangular ones on the other two. Then, in the fifteenth century, western European and northern ships began also to use this type of vessel. This enabled them to begin to face the Atlantic with much greater confidence, since they could meet an adverse wind but, at the same time, expect a measure of stability from their square sail.

Almost as important was the sea quadrant (invented about 1456) by which the sailor measured the elevation of the pole star by a plumb line passing over an engraved scale. That transformed nocturnal sailing. The combination of these changes enabled sea captains to envisage, for the first time, long journeys across the sea without sight of land.

The country which first made use of these innovations in seamanship and boatbuilding was, as earlier indicated, Portugal. Portugal, a thin slip of a country founded by commoners during the Second Crusade, managed to escape the stagnation and civil war which characterised much of Western Europe in the fifteenth century. Indeed, the mercantile forces were powerful enough to dominate the monarchy (8). Portugal's great achievement was the carrack, the characteristic modern sailing ship of the age of discoveries. In addition to the stern-post rudder, this remarkable new vessel had its tiller in the hull. The forecastle had high bows. With these ships, the Portuguese discovered a far larger world than anyone in Europe previously thought even existed. They brought Africa, America and Asia within reach of European commerce, conquest and colonisation. Already, in 1418 the Portuguese had reached Madeira. In 1427, Diego de Sevilla found the Azores. (The Canary Isles had been assigned by the Pope to Spain in 1344.) After great struggles, the Portuguese rounded the difficult West African Cape Bojador, with its high winds, in 1434. Then, in 1444, Nuño Tristram reached the Senegal river. In 1445, Dimis Dias rounded Cape Verde. In 1469, King Alfonso leased the Guinea trade to a private entrepreneur, Fernão Gomes, with the stipulation that he carry forward the exploration a hundred leagues a year. He did so: Guinea, and the Gold Coast were reached in 1470. The Portuguese established their fort at El Mina in

---

* An instrument which enabled a ship's position to be determined from calculating the height of the sun.

1482. In 1484, Diego Cão reached the Congo River, and, in 1487, Bartolemeu Dias rounded the Cape of Good Hope. Ten years later, Vasco da Gama left, with four ships, to chart the route to India round southern Africa.

European ships reached America long before that. Portuguese and perhaps English fishermen looking for cod had reached the Great Banks at least by 1480. Even earlier, the Vikings had settled parts of Greenland, and one of them, Leif Ericson, was driven on to the coast of Newfoundland, where he settled about 1000 AD. Thorfinn Karlsefric and three ships also spent three winters in the Americas between 1003 and 1006. Where exactly were their shadow 'Hellulands' and 'Marklands'? Labrador and Cape Cod? At all events, Norsemen were known in the Americas, if only in Labrador, between then and about 1350. After the Latin translation of Ptolemy's *Geography* in 1410, the idea of the sphericity of the earth, which had never been quite forgotten, also spread rapidly in European scientific circles. Columbus heard of the idea as a young man.

Christopher Columbus was the son of weavers from Genoa. He began to make journeys by sea about 1472. He went to England, Portugal and Madeira, and perhaps to Guinea. His enthusiasm commended him to Queen Isabella of Spain, whom he met, through her confessor, at La Rábida near Palos (Huelva), in south-west Andalusia. He gained financial support both from the Crown and from private merchants in Cataluña and Valencia. He set off to find a westward route to India. The expedition was largely composed of people from Palos and the neighbourhood. He went with three caravels, 280, 140 and 100 tons respectively. This journey opened up a new world to Europe as well as the old one to America. It also gave to shipping the invaluable idea of the hammock, one of the most useful Caribbean inventions.

Columbus's four journeys (1492, 1493, 1498 and 1502) led to the European colonisation of the Americas. Other Italians followed Columbus, in the service of kings of other nations. John Cabot, another Genoese, thus reached Newfoundland and Brazil in 1498 (in the service of England) while Amerigo Vespucci, a Florentine and an agent of the Medicis living in Seville, discovered the Amazon. He got as far down the coast of South America as the Cape de São Roque, with Alonso de Ojeda (in the service of Spain). In 1500, Pedro Cabral, a Portuguese sailing to India from Lisbon, was diverted and landed in Brazil. In 1501–2, Vespucci sailed along the Brazilian coast at least as far as the Rio Grande. His Christian name was soon given to the continent. In 1513, Balboa crossed the isthmus of Panama to discover the Pacific. In 1519–22, an expedition led on behalf of Spain by, first, a Portuguese, Fernão de Magalhaes (Magellan) and then a Basque, Juan Sebastián del Cano, circumnavigated the globe, going westwards. Meanwhile, Cabral had sailed via South Africa from Brazil to India. Francisco de

Almeida established Portuguese forts on the Indian coast. At the battle of Diu in 1509, one of the world's decisive engagements if ever there were one, he destroyed the Muslim galleys by the skilful use of light sailing ships manned with guns. Against them, the old galleys of the East, like those of Venetians and Turks, were no match. That began the era of European domination for the next four centuries – or rather of western European domination. The mounting of cannon on the upper as well as the main deck by the French in 1506 was the fundamental innovation which really destroyed the old art of war at sea which had been largely based on ramming and boarding. After 1550, the Europeans also produced effective mobile artillery for use on the land which they had conquered. Meantime, in 1513, a native of Lisbon, Jorge Alvarez, put in to Canton and, in 1542, Antonio de Mota, another Portuguese, reached Japan.

These journeys, and the conquests which followed, altered the history of the world. Francisco Grande in 1585 even offered Philip II the conquest of China with 5000 men (9). He was dissuaded, but Europeans now controlled the Eastern trade. Until then, the Mamluk beys, who governed Egypt, had kept prices of pepper and other Eastern spices high by insisting that the annual consignment be small. After 1509, a Portuguese thalassocracy blocked the Egyptian trade, which had mostly gone through Venice, and opened their own more effective commerce.

The decisive element in these journeys was that they led to settlement as well as conquest and trade. In spirit, they had something in common with the Crusades. The crusaders, like the conquistadors, were preoccupied by God as well as mammon. But the journeys of the Renaissance led in the new world to the establishment of a permanent conquest of an under-populated new world into which the vitality and enterprise of old Europe was poured for four centuries (10).

From the sixteenth century, there were always regular sailings between the old and new worlds. From the beginning, ships sailed from Spain in convoys, so as to combine defence and navigation. From 1543, ships were forbidden to leave Spain for the Indies with less than ten vessels in the fleet. The fleet outwards left every May, the crews would bid farewell to Europe at Tenerife, with its towering cone. Then, for forty days, they would see nothing of land till they crossed the Windward Islands, close to the wild, rocky island of Dominica. Thereafter, there would be Santo Domingo, Vera Cruz and Nombre de Díos, sometimes Havana. The fleets would usually sail from Seville (though, from 1492 till 1500, also from little ports of the Río Tinto, Palos and Moguer). That established an effective monopoly of control. (The Río Tinto ports were silted up by 1500. Málaga and Cartagena were concerned with the Italian trade. Ships from Corunna and Bilbao had to go a long way south to Portugal to pick up favourable winds.) Only Cadiz could really have been a rival to Seville, but Cadiz was more exposed, both to pirates or enemies and to winds. So Seville both imported and re-exported, though it was a far from ideal spot. Few great ships could be launched there. The services of maintenance for big ships were poor. The harbour was small. Ships above a certain draught could not cross the bar at Sanlúcar fully loaded. Thus wine destined for the Americas was put on board at Cadiz. Passengers often embarked at Sanlúcar. Yet Seville was the centre of the bureaucracy, and remained the seat of the school of navigation founded by Vespucci.

In the Americas, Vera Cruz and Nombre de Díos came to life only when the fleet sailed in. The captains-general came down from the hills to take over the towns. When the fleet left, those cities returned to being shanty towns sunk in malarial torpor, housing a few officials only. The fleet would stand well to the north, out of the winds, before the Atlantic crossing began. The captains would seek a westerly wind near Bermuda and then run down to the Azores (11). After 1562, the fleets would always meet at Havana and there pick up a naval escort to help them cross the Atlantic free from pirates.

Not least among the consequences of the voyages of the sixteenth century was the beginning of accurate geography. The people of the Mediterranean in the Middle Ages knew little more about the world than Herodotus, who had not realised that there was a sea border to the north of Europe (12). A Catalan atlas of 1375 had given to India its proper shape, and some Egyptian and Greek maps were locally accurate. But no one — least of all their own inhabitants — knew the extent even of the three then familiar continents — Europa (named after the daughter of King Agenor seduced by Jupiter); Asia (called after Prometheus' mother, it seems); and Africa, a word used by Romans to designate Tunisia, probably deriving from a lost tribe, the Aourigha, of Berber origin, driven by the Carthaginians into the desert, which ended in what was believed in Europe to be nothingness. After the sixteenth century, cartography improved enormously. The great Mercator, whose real name was Gerhard Kremer, a Flemish mathematician employed by the Emperor Charles V in his military campaigns, made the first modern map projections. His maps were indeed the first to be known as an atlas, a word taken from one of the Titans whom Greek legends made another son of Asia. It is thus appropriate that the greatest of Renaissance Popes, Pius II (Aeneas Sylvius), should have been a keen geographer as, indeed, was Petrarch, the first true reviver of learning in mediaeval Europe, in the judgment of John Addington Symonds (13). It is equally appropriate that the works of the historian of antiquity who was the most conscious of geographical matters, namely Herodotus, should also have been revived at the time of the Renaissance. Herodotus was not perhaps a direct inspiration. But, as Arnaldo Momigliano suggests, the new historians did as Herodotus had done: they travelled, 'questioned local people, and went back from the present to the past, by collecting oral traditions' (14). The first Latin translation of Herodotus was done about 1452 and the translator was none other than Lorenzo Valla, the librarian of the Vatican who proved that the idea of a gift of temporal power by Constantine the Great to the Papacy was a fraud.

20

The Revival of Commerce

The innovations of the Renaissance, in the meantime, might have been ineffective, comparable to the innovations of the Hellenistic age, if European commerce had not been able to market the goods which industrial invention and improvements in communication had made possible. For, Paul Mantoux wrote, the progress of commerce and industry had become so interwoven that 'it is difficult to discover on which side a new development started, progress in industry seeming impossible unless preceded by progress in commerce' (1). Holland, in the seventeenth century, became the leading commercial country in the world. But it traded few Dutch goods. Everything was carried everywhere by the Dutch, regardless of make. England also afterwards became a great commercial country long before she was an industrial one (2). The gradual transformation of the old hierarchical society into one where men could begin to shape their own life, with the chance of choosing between different forms of profession and consumption, was, therefore, closely associated with the growth of commerce, the increase in the use of money, and an elaboration of the ways that both commerce and money were manipulated.

Money had, of course, existed in one form or another for many generations and in almost every type of society. Almost everything under the sun has been for a time used as money — beans of the cacao tree in ancient America, seashells off the Canary coast, cowries in both China and on the Gulf of Guinea, cows in India, beer in Sumer, salt in Senegal, on the Niger and in Abyssinia, copper bracelets, horses, chickens, cylinders cut from coral (in Etruria), dried fish (Iceland), furs (Russia), tobacco, grain, sugar and cocoa. In Canada, playing cards would be used for money in the eighteenth century, nails were still being used in Scotland in 1775 (3), while Japan used rice in the seventeeth century. But the money mostly respected through history has been coinage of gold, silver and copper — and latterly, though not till well into the age of industry, nickel, other base metals and paper (paper was used as money in China from the ninth to the fourteenth century, and was then abandoned, since it brought inflation) (4).

181

The concept of metal as a means of exchange is thus ancient. It was apparently developed in both the Far and the Near East independently. Silver was used in ancient Iraq as a standard of value, without any silver changing hands. The price of an object about 2000 BC in Babylon might be stated in silver but be paid for in cloths, or bronze objects or beer (5). The first regular silver coins appear to have been struck by the Hittites about 1500 BC. They were well supplied with silver, which was also used as a medium of exchange by those Assyrian merchants who, for a long time, dominated commerce (6). Coins were later used by the Lydians, another people of Asia Minor, whose kings stamped a lion's head as a badge on ingots of electrum with a standard weight. From Lydia, the idea of stamped coins passed to Greece, many of whose towns, soon after 700 BC, were minting silver, particularly at Aegina, where silver pieces were given heads of turtles, each with a given weight (7). It also seems possible that coins, in the sense of round pieces of metal, officially stamped as a token, for a value, may have been used by the Chinese as early as this (8).

Long before this, both gold and silver had begun to be admired, worked and prized for aesthetic reasons. As many as a hundred gold mines were established in Egypt. The discovery that gold can be plated thin to cover stone or wood was made by the Egyptians before the establishment of the Egyptian state. Most of the gold of Egypt passed through the hands of Pharaohs at least for a time, and much of it was immobilised in tombs, though robbers from the earliest times sought to break them open. Babylon also acquired, even if it did not produce, a great deal of gold, while Crete was the home of men of legendary skill with that metal. There was, however, a legend that even Minos came from Egypt. Gold was certainly carried to the East Mediterranean from Spain, the Danube, perhaps ancient Rhodesia, and even Ireland, long before 1000 BC. A gold goblet was said to hang from a chain on Hercules's bow (9). To the Greeks, the beauty of gold, with its brightness and permanence, was indissolubly linked with the gods, whose palaces, thrones, chariots, lyres, arrows and armour were all said to be made of it. The fact that gold is as malleable as lead and can be beaten when it is cold added to its appeal. The gods of Greece themselves were always said to be 'golden' because of the divine light shining from them, and the legendary time when men were closest to gods was known to the Greeks as the golden age (10).

The Greeks, however, chose silver as their currency for they had plenty of it in the silver mines of Laurion and never had enough gold even though King Croesus of Lydia sent 7,500 pounds of it to Delphi (one reason for the prestige of that sanctuary in a gold-less land). Currency there created inflation immediately. Instead of borrowing grain, peasants started to borrow money in order to buy it at high prices. To repay the loan, the peasant either had to raise the cash or to hold on till the market revived. Either way, he was in a weak position. The Athenians, meantime, realised the importance of having a gold reserve to back their silver currency. Thus Pheidias made the chryselephantine statue of Athena so that 2,000 pounds of gold could be taken off it in an emergency (11). Alexander's conquest of Persia caused gold to be more plentiful in Greece. Not only did he conquer Persia but he also captured remote, rich sources of gold in the far east of Persia which even the Achaemenids had not touched. The subsequent Hellenic age was therefore characterised by an unprecedented quantity of gold objects for personal use – hammered, cast, engraved, embossed, or applied with paste on to glass (12). Even so, most commercial transactions continued to be by barter.

Rome began its rise to prosperity almost without gold, on the fringe of the Greek silver world. That changed when she conquered the Etruscans. The Etruscans had brought their gold techniques from Lydia to Etruria. Their goldsmiths had in particular developed filigree. Other Roman conquests in the south of Italy and afterwards in the Val d'Aosta caused Roman reserves to stand at 4,000 Roman pounds in 218 BC. That hoard quadrupled by the end of the third Punic War. But the reserves remained reserves: for many generations, the Romans, like the Greeks, kept their currency silver (in the silver *denarius*). There was, under the Republic, little gold in private hands. The use of silver as the day-to-day currency also meant that the Romans had as much need for silver as for gold when they sought their war indemnities.

Yet Rome had a gold coinage before the end of the Republic (the *aureus*). In the early Empire, there was not only a lavish display of personal gold, but vast expense of gold on luxuries from India, as the number of Roman gold coins found in India proves. Spain was then the main source of this gold. The Roman coinage was of a high quality to begin with but, by the third century AD, became debased. Silver ceased to be used at all. The Empire then tried out a coinage of bronze and copper. By that time, all the precious metals of the Empire had been converted into plate or jewellery. Inflation and monetary instability ensued, and those familiar things characterised the crisis in the Empire of the third century AD, almost as much as did civil war. That era was perhaps the only time before the sixteenth century when the use of money was so widespread as to make the shortage of it a serious inconvenience or even a misery for more than a minority of people. Otherwise, the vast majority lived on their own produce, served their masters according to their status, and rarely saw a coin from one year's end to another.

The later Roman Empire was given financial stability, in the end, by Constantine, who obtained gold by robbing the pagan temples in the name of his conversion to Christianity. Constantine issued a gold *solidus*, seventy-two of which were held to equal a pound of gold. This 'solid' object (also known in Constantinople as the 'Byzant') remained unchanged in weight and purity well into the Middle Ages. Constantine's silver *milliarensis*, of which 24 were supposed to equal one *solidus*, was less successful, and was later abandoned. Afterwards, the collapse of the administration in the West left the mines for these precious minerals without skilled labour, guards, transport or a central market. Mine shafts were abandoned to floods, and looting was rife. Even so, the Visigoths, Burgundians, Merovingians, and Anglo-Saxons all operated mints, producing gold coins which, like their political pretensions, feebly, slavishly and badly echoed old Roman practice. Thus the Merovingians had a *sou*, instead of a *solidus*, and a *denier*, for a *denarius* (13). New gold could not be obtained, but there was enough in circulation to permit a gold coinage theoretically to limp on.

Paradoxically, the economic revival of c.700 AD in Western Europe led almost to the disappearance of the gold currency. Gold was scarce in the Carolingian Empire because of a revival of Byzantium backed by a large, pure gold currency. The currency of Charlemagne was, theoretically: £1 or *libra* (*lira*), a pound's worth of gold. That was equivalent to 20 *soldi* (sols), or shillings, of silver. Each *soldus* was worth 12 copper *denarii*, pence, or deniers. In practice, gold was not current, and a silver penny, or denier, was the only real coin. Charlemagne tried to ensure that his coins should only be coined in the royal mints. Then Louis the Pious allowed certain churches to coin money (14). In England, the King was not so ambitious: 'No one is to coin money except in a port,' decreed Athelstan, but that word then included many inland towns (15). Minting continued anarchic and English *denarii* had many different alloys and weights (16). That comment could be made about a great many primitive countries whose coinage seems at first sight to be sound.

The Caliphate, on the other hand, had always had both gold and silver coins, the gold being brought from as far away as the Niger and Senegal. Timbuktu became in the early Middle Ages 'a city of gold' linked by camel to the Mediterranean, to which spices, gold, slaves and ivory were carried in bulk. El Andalus, or Moorish Spain (independent from the Caliphate in the mid eighth century) also had an elaborate money economy, with silver-plated *dishemes* minted early, and gold *dinars* minted in the eighth century (17). Those currencies were the heart of an economy which was as far superior in the volume of its trade to western Europe as was its ostentation and culture, though, by the late Middle Ages, the repeated ravages of Turks and Mongols, as well as the caliph's own extravagances, had caused the collapse of that system and the virtual return in the Near East to subsistence agriculture, and to barter. But, by then, large numbers of Arabs (or perhaps they were really Persians) had settled in Chinese and other Eastern ports, and their descendants were playing a part in the Chinese imperial administration. Chinese merchants visited Baghdad. From the East, Islam had imported silk, paper, porcelain and a little steel, not to speak of such useful things as 'Arabic' numerals, from India (18). The commerce and finance of the time of the Abbasid caliphs developed banking, a system of cheques and letters of credit, and loans (including loans made to governments) on a scale which seems not to have been equalled under Rome and which probably directly led to Italian emulation: after all, most of the bankers themselves were Jews or Christians because of the Muslim ban on usury. Arab conquests in Sicily, as well as the prosperity of Egypt under the Fatimid caliphs, made Italy very close again to the East Mediterranean.

The system of numbering which the Abbasid empire took from India quickly passed into general use in the Muslim world and moved to Europe apparently through Spain. Adelard of Bath, the great translator, first used arabic numbers, with the invaluable use of the zero, in his translation of Al Khwarizmi's *Algebra* in the early twelfth century, and Leonardo of Pisa, in his *Liber Abaci*, in 1202 asserted that the 'Arabic' system was better than the Roman one (19). But it took some time before that method passed into general European use.

The European gold currencies revived, as did commerce and banking generally, after the Crusades. The Italian cities who financed the latter soon had enough gold to produce the florin — in Florence — in 1252, the *janarius* in Genoa the same year, and other coins in Venice and elsewhere. Even England eventually, in 1330, had a florin. Probably, mediaeval currency was made from Arab gold melted down, though by then there was some new gold mining in Europe, especially in Hungary. The Serbian monarchy of Stephen Dushan also mined silver successfully, enabling that state to be quite strong for a few generations. The Bohemian silver mines were opened in the fourteenth century.

By that time, however, several major alterations had occurred in the way that Europeans, especially Italians, managed their commercial transactions. Everything seems to point to the Crusades as having been the 'motor' of the changes. Thus the Crusades undoubtedly offered, as has been suggested earlier, great opportunities to merchants, principally Italian merchants, if they could only work in proper collaboration. Hence, the single merchant or pedlar acting alone was less characteristic of the Mediterranean later Middle Ages than an association of merchants (20). Such merchants of the twelfth century were usually men who could write, could use a system of credit, and operate internationally. Perhaps a majority of early merchants were children of non-free parents. Their meeting places were fairs: that of St Denis (actually known from 629); the six fairs of Champagne; Foggia (which sold the pastoral products of southern Italy); and Danzig (a great fair from the mid-tenth century, where grain was exchanged for saffron from Armenia, cattle from Moldavia, cloth from England); and, in England, there were important fairs at Stourbridge, Winchester, Beverley, Greenwich and Boston. Though other associations of merchants were founded (for example, that of the merchants of the Hanse who linked England and the Low Countries with the Baltic and Scandinavia), the trade of the Middle Ages was dominated by Italians. Merchants were soon found directing most of the Italian cities which had managed to escape, during the wars of the Guelfs and Ghibellines, from direct control by either the Pope or the German emperor. Those cities may have thought that they were operating 'in the name of God and profit', in the closing words of letter-writers from Prato of the fourteenth century (21), but the latter motive seems often to have been strongest. Those merchants devised the beneficial customs of underwriting and insuring bills of lading, and providing separate letters of advice. In the footsteps of the Italians came the Jews (whose exclusion from Spain in 1492 amounted to the expulsion of the business community of the country) and the Armenians (whose dispersion for commercial reasons in the sixteenth century perhaps lost them forever the chance of achieving an Armenian national state) (22). But the concept of the company, the share, the capital market and the stock market, began in Italy in the thirteenth or fourteenth century. Indeed, the 'company' – the word in most European languages perhaps derives from an association of those with whom a man breaks bread (*conpagne*, signifying 'with bread') – probably owes its origin, in the form that it is now known, to innovations specifically undertaken at the time of the Crusades in Italy. Men had, of course, often sought profit before. Indeed, they had always done so. But it seems doubtful whether they associated it in any form remotely comparable to the modern company before the age of the Crusades, or elsewhere than in the Mediterranean.

The second important development was the birth of banking. This cannot in itself be attributed to the Crusades. For, after all, the Crusades themselves were financed by banks. But it does seem fairly obvious that the renewed contact with the Eastern Mediterranean brought modest Italian financiers into contact with those Christian or Jewish money-merchants who handled the financial arrangements within the by then disintegrating Muslim world. At all events, there were, in the thirteenth century, in Italy, three classes of traders in money: first, petty money-lenders; second, money changers who dealt in the exchange of currency, precious stones, and bullion; and, third, bankers who were also merchants (23). Among these last, the Amalfians, Venetians and Pisans were the oldest established and the Florentines the newest and later the most energetic. Buying wool, and making and selling woollen goods, these Italians began to operate on so large and so international a scale that they soon became moneylenders to kings; and not only to kings. With Peter's Pence and other ecclesiastical taxes pouring into Rome in the late Middle Ages, the question of who held the papal account was a matter of great importance: for example, the Pazzi family's conspiracy in Florence in the fifteenth century, would not, probably, have got under way if that family had not already secured the transfer to themselves of the papal account from the Medici (24). By the mid-fifteenth century, at all events, Cosimo de' Medici was sitting in his office in the Via Larga in Florence at the headquarters of an international bank with branches in Rome, Milan, Geneva, Bruges, Ancona, Pisa, London and Avignon, trading in almost every known luxury and necessity, on the general principle, says John Hale, of 'spreading risks through diversity' (25).

A third development, whose connection with the Crusades is a good deal less obvious, was the beginning of a tendency throughout feudal Europe, particularly in England, for all lords to turn their feudal dues into rents and to realise their incomes in cash. Merchants in new towns encouraged this, and labourers in times of labour shortage such as occurred in the fourteenth century encouraged it too.

It is easy to compare the lively financial system reviving the West with the failure of the Chinese, otherwise so inventive, to develop an adequate banking system. The individual merchants in China under the T'ang dynasty were the only source of credit. All emperors and bureau-crats were frightened of the idea that capitalists might accumulate huge fortunes. On the other hand, emperors in China did not mind bureau-crats accumulating riches, however they did so (26). Paper money was introduced into China about 910 AD; but the efforts of an inspired reformer, Wang An Shih, a minister of finance under the T'ang dynasty (he died in 1086), to introduce taxation in money, rather than in grain, failed (27). In that failure, itself a reflection of innumerable signs of stagnation within old China, is to be seen one important reason for the failure of China to profit from her undoubted technological superiority over the West. It is something which, if very remotely, recalls the relation of a technologically imaginative Europe and a commercially more ingenious USA in the twentieth century. In ancient India and China, usury and the lending of money, the exchange of goods for cash and manufacture, had all occurred in a way to rival in sophistication anything which happened in Europe till the thirteenth or fourteenth century. But in any nation which was rich, that state was always strong, strong enough at any event to control prices to limit profits by mer-chants even if they were reasonably independent men, or even, as occurred in the Mauryan empire about the third century BC, to fix the percentage of profit (28). Now for the first time, in Italy, an undoubtedly rich region, states were controlled by merchants, and not *vice versa*.

When the Spaniards reached Mexico, they found there a class of small-scale but apparently private professional merchants (29). In India, by that time, independent merchants also existed, after a fashion. But, like the merchants used by the Tsar in Russia, their status was always inferior. They were really more the ruler's commercial agents than they were capitalists. Perhaps for this reason, the astute Spanish jurist Vitoria would have preferred an empire based more on commerce than conquest since he thought that commerce as effective as conquest in spreading the Gospel (30).

The discovery of America — appropriately by a Genoese, for Genoa was the leading financial centre of the world in the sixteenth century — gave Europe access to vast new sources of gold and silver. The Aztec goldsmiths had been expert in casting gold. They used silver with it to produce a polychrome effect 'more magnificent than exquisite', as the historian of gold, C.H.V. Sutherland, put it. Old Mexico had innumerable gems. Little survives, for most went into the Spanish melting pot. Atahualpa's offer to fill a room with gold to secure his ransom from Pizarro was fulfilled with plates of gold. The gold was then boiled down. In all, 750,000 pounds of gold were sent from Spanish America to Spain between 1492 and 1600 (31), of which at least 10% became royal property. This gold was so great in quantity as to offer many opportunities, above all to the Spanish economy, but also to the rest of Europe. It also provided many disturbances. The price level in Spain rose in the sixteenth century 400%, partly as a result of the import of precious metals, though partly also because of an increase in population and because of lavish spending on war by the government. The significance of the import of precious metals was probably at least as great in that it enabled all European countries of any importance to have a gold currency, which factor in turn allowed, in the prevailing circumstances of reliance on gold, a vast expansion of the credit available to both states and private people (32). Indeed, the significance of the Spanish inflation of the sixteenth century, so meticulously chronicled by Earl Hamilton, is that it was the first currency crisis in a Europe becoming used to transactions in cash, and on a scale larger than the great inflation of the late third century (33). (The attribution of the rise in prices in the sixteenth century entirely to the import of gold and silver now seems extravagant to most careful students of that era, since the large scale exploitation of the silver mines of Potosí did not begin till after the beginning of the inflation.)

The gold of America offered great opportunities to the brilliant Renaissance goldsmiths, of whom Cellini was supreme. But it also caused kings to default on debts. The long-term effect of the coming of American gold was to inspire a major, beneficial and, in the short term, decisive, shift in the character of commerce towards private merchants. Hence the foundation of the first great banks: the Bank of Palermo (1551), the Banco della Piazza di Rialto (1587), the Banco di S. Ambrogio (Milan, 1593), the Monte de Pietà (Naples), Santo Spirito (Rome) and, in the seventeenth century, the Exchange Bank of Amsterdam (founded 1609), and the Bank of England (1694) (34).

The supply of gold from the Americas also made possible a vast expansion of trade with the East which had considerably died down since the fall of Rome. The golden *cruzado* of Portugal revived contact with the East as effectively as if it were a real renaissance of the *aureus* of old Rome.

The mining of these ores declined in the depressed seventeenth century. But the second silver age in the eighteenth gave to Spain apparently inexhaustible supplies of silver, from Mexico. How natural that the Spaniards should look on the New World as enacting the miraculous adventures described in old books of chivalry and that the names of the two extremities of the Spanish dominions should be taken from those books: 'Patagonia', in *Primaleón*; California, in *Sergas de Esplandián* (35). Brazil meantime made a major contribution to the economy of Portugal. Her golden baroque city of Ouro Preto seemed later the most prosperous in the world. But northern Europe had been productive too. Silver was found in Bohemia at Joachimsthal, in the valley of the river Thaler, in such profusion that the word 'thaler' was given to a new Bohemian coin: hence, at one remove, the better-known word 'dollar', a contribution to the world's vocabulary for which Bohemia has not always been adequately credited.* Meantime, Genoese, Flemings, Germans and Portuguese (Jews) had so established themselves as to dominate Spanish commerce by the late sixteenth century. Companies of Flemings could even be formed to defend Cadiz against Drake in 1590. The Dutch trade in Cadiz transformed Amsterdam as Europe's major money market. A stream of French artisans into Spain became so great as to cause popular outbreaks against them.

Banking developed late in England. Private persons for a long time were happy to entrust their money to merchants, merchants to goldsmiths of Lombard Street. The notes issued by these men began in the mid-seventeenth century to take the place of cash in some transactions. The first Bank of England was simply a group of people who had agreed to lend £1,200,999 to William III at 8%. In return, they received the title of corporation and the right of receiving deposits, discounting commercial bills or doing, that is, what the Exchange Bank of Amsterdam or the Bank of St George at Genoa had already been doing for some time (36). This bank not only issued the first bank notes in England but, more important (paper money played little part in the ordinary life of most people till well into the nineteenth century), guaranteed the price of gold at £4 4s 11½d per ounce, at which price it was fixed till 1914. Although that was only made possible by the increase of production of gold during the next two centuries (about seven times more gold was produced in the eighteenth and nineteenth centuries than was produced in the sixteenth and seventeenth) it meant that, for the first time, gold was established as the key commodity in international trade.

* The Spanish *dólar* was the best known silver coin in the newly independent colonies in the 1780s and hence was adopted as the currency of the US.

Thereafter, too, for 200 years, every reputable bank issuing a bank note had enough gold or silver in its vaults to make it fully convertible on demand: the root of an unparalleled public confidence. That had not been the case before.

Three other aspects of the revival and reinvigoration of European commerce in the course of the Renaissance need to be noticed. First, the new states of Italy, or rather Venice, embarked upon the modern science of statistics. Feudal states knew only the catalogues of rights and possessions and tended to look on production of goods as fixed. But Venetians began to reckon men from the early sixteenth century in souls, not hearths, and the speech of the dying Doge Mocenigo in 1423 gave something like a statistical account of the resources of Venice (37), almost in the style of a modern annual of statistics. Florence was soon even more sophisticated.

Secondly, the same Italian states began to develop a rational admini-stration of taxation which made mediaeval Europe seem amateur (38) though, as a result, by the end of the sixteenth century, familiar com-plaints were heard: 'all states of Europe groaned under taxes in the late sixteenth century,' Braudel tells us, and, in Florence, considered 'a model of administration', the burden of taxes was so great that, in 1582, it led to an exodus of population (39).

Thirdly, the combination of better communications, new forms of trading, banking and an increase in goods made possible the creation of a wholly new method of financing trade and investment. This was the market in prices, stocks, shares and commodities which has been so misunderstood, often wilfully misunderstood, in the twentieth century. Was it the invention of Jewish refugees from Spain, Huguenots, or sober Dutch burghers? Whoever is to be credited with this remarkable work of Renaissance art, it was created in the Netherlands in the early sixteenth century on the basis of what Dutch merchants had learned in Italy, particularly in Venice and Florence.

By the mid-sixteenth century, speculation on 'grain futures' was current in Amsterdam. In the early seventeenth century, herrings, spices, and whale oil were also objects of speculative trading (40). Purely financial speculation in shares of companies began in Amster-dam about then too – the one financial innovation of the Dutch, for everything else they did was an improvement on Italian practice. The idea took on 'like a rocket' (in the words of Violet Barbour) in London, though only in the 1690s. Brokers, whose whole life was spent dealing in shares, began business. It was already observed in the early seven-teenth century that, 'without possessing shares, or even a desire to acquire any, one can carry on a big business in them . . . the seller so to speak, sells nothing but wind, and the buyer receives only wind' (41). This began a new custom of managing commerce which played a decisive part in financing the Industrial Revolution. It only began to falter to any marked extent when governments took to intervening regularly in markets, during the First World War and after the collapse of the Russian market in 1917. In the meantime, public and private loans, and foreign investments, came to be more and more important in economic life. The financial network founded by the Dutch was far from a narrowly national one. Even in the Dutch revolutionary war, merchants of Amsterdam traded with Spain, as they did with Britain in the Anglo-Dutch wars. The famine which struck France in 1709, after the terrible harvest, was relieved by Dutch grain carriers, even though Holland was at war with France. Dutch merchants always agreed to finance enemy powers (42).

In the twentieth century, tourists, in search of art, travel in numbers superior to the population of all Europe in the fifteenth century to see the 'great cities of civilisation', Venice, Florence and Amsterdam. How few of them realise that they are visiting the places where the modern system of finance was born or that the works of art before which they stand delighted were themselves made possible by a financial revival as remarkable as anything recovered during the Renaissance!

21

Slow Journeys by Land

One means of communication which was in no serious way improved during the Renaissance was travel by land. Indeed, there was no serious revival of Roman achievements till the nineteenth century.

The reason for this is that the real changes of the Renaissance were carried out by men of cities, private merchants who, however rich, were not the masters of great labour forces, and by small rather than large states — Florence, Venice, Portugal, the Netherlands, England, not, as such, France, the German Empire, Russia or the Ottoman Sultanate. The great roads of antiquity had been the achievement of great despotisms and, as a result, had really been built to enable the ruler's messengers to travel fast, rather than to assist private merchants to seek profits. Thus, the freedom-loving Greeks had bad roads. Their streets were unpaved and undrained, even if they did prepare a wheel rut to help carts and chariots, particularly on the way in and out of mines and quarries. Their charioteers were prized, the Cyreneans in particular being noted for their skill at chariot driving (1), but chariots were for sport or a useful assistance in war rather than a help to trade. In Egypt, Herodotus considered the great road which carried the stones of the pyramids to be scarcely inferior to the pyramids themselves. But that road was a road for slaves, not for free men. Long before the era of Herodotus, the Near Eastern roads of tyranny had been brought to their best by the Assyrians, whose provincial governors remained in day-to-day touch with their lords through professional messengers. These travelled along post roads by horse or mule, exchanging steeds at specific places — thus originating a system of imperial control which lasted till the nineteenth century AD (2). They were in particular used and extended by the Persians, whose empire was consolidated by good roads (3). These constituted the glory of the Middle Eastern public service until the Arab conquest in the sixth century AD (4). Thereafter, the increasing use of horses and camels rather than wagons, and the subsequent collapse of the Caliphate, caused them to fall into disuse. Meantime, a few bridges were also built in the ancient Near East. Most of those were decorative, however (the 36-foot wide bridge at the palace of Minos, for example, or the bridges of Nebuchadnezzar at Babylon, resting on a hundred brick piers), or were used for aqueducts. Fords usually served the purposes of modern bridges. Xerxes carried his army across the Hellespont by joining about 700 ships, anchoring them and tying them to land. Planks were then laid across, then brushwood and then earth (5).

For a few hundred years, it is true, the trade routes to India by land were probably as good as those achieved by sea. They ran through Afghanistan either via Kabul or Kandahar, Persepolis or Susa. Within India, elaborate roads had also been built by that time and Afghanistan linked India as well as the Hellenic world with Kashgar and China along what became known as the 'old silk route'. Along these roads, soldiers and missionaries travelled as well as merchants and the sea route to China from Egypt probably carried more goods, as a rule; but that undoubtedly was one good example of an ancient mercantile land path.

Such a judgment could not have been passed on the famous system of Roman roads. The concept of good roads reached Rome through the Etruscans. Perhaps they brought the idea from Lydia. Such Roman improvements as there were were based on hard work more than original thought. The ground was dug up and set with stones. The middle part of the road was raised to allow drainage, and topped with gravel. Bridges were built with stone for the first time (for example, the fine bridge still in use at Rimini). Main roads were caused to run straight from city to city, with little account taken of hills or obstacles. There were major and minor post stations every ten or twelve miles along the main roads. Each station kept horses, vets, ostlers, surgeons, cartwrights, carriages and wagons. The upkeep was maintained by provincial taxes. The horses (whose average life was four years) were provided by a regular levy. Each station was managed by a retired official from the imperial service. Inspectors paid regular visits. Expensive though the system was, particularly in the outer provinces, it enabled travellers on horseback to go easily 100 miles a day (6). There was also a wagon post, which provided ox wagons with two pairs for heavy goods. In the outer Empire, pack donkeys and camels were also maintained. There were in all 54,000 miles of Roman roads, a network of communications which maintained the Empire, enabling the legionaries to march their 10,000 paces a day or their 9½ miles or sometimes more (7). Still, on these roads, civil servants had priority and the bulk of internal Roman trade went by the sea or rivers. It was always far cheaper to ship wheat from Syria to Andalusia than to carry it from south to north Spain overland (8). Inland, the life of the Roman Empire consisted of the provisioning of little oases, 'drops of water on a drying surface' (9), as Peter Brown put it.

The eclipse of the Roman civil service meant the eclipse of the roads and posts. Armies of barbarians travelling in vast caravanserais could force services from captured towns on old post routes. No one else could. Those who travelled to Rome in the early Middle Ages on pilgrimage, for example, would stop at monasteries, or perhaps large, half empty, castles, taking with them bedding and cooking things. Inns were as risky as that where Theseus was nearly murdered by Procrustes. But the old road network of the Assyrians and Persians continued to be kept up in the Near East, though the Arabs travelled by horse or in caravans of camels, 'ships of the desert' as they became called, and so did not need the roads: the role of the camel had earlier also been destructive to the old Roman civilisation of northern Africa. Introduced into the region by Septimus Severus about 200 AD, that animal was, thereafter, mastered by nomads of the desert, who used it to raid the old pleasant cities and gardens of the Mahgreb and then return into the pathless desert (10): a means of communication which favoured banditry rather than administration or commerce.

In the Middle Ages, both the Caliph and the Emperor of China had roads which made the poor horse-tracks of Europe seem very inferior. In the ninth century, the Caliphate boasted 900 relay stations, and the postmaster-general was often, appropriately, the head of the intelligence service (11). The Chinese system of roads (as of canals) naturally also survived. Marco Polo described the Emperor's secretariat receiving despatches from places ten days' journey off in one day and one night (12). In the nineteenth century, the postal service of China would have 2,000 express stations, 30,526 horses, and nearly 50,000 foot messengers, with about 70,000 service personnel (13). Probably that reflects the state of affairs earlier too. But these elaborate services were used not as a means of communication, but as one of control by the government.

Some quickening of transport on land in Europe admittedly came with the horseshoe and the carthorse, in the eleventh or twelfth centuries.* Peasants could then think of selling their surplus, if they had one, at a fair or market. Previously such a thing in old Europe was as unthinkable as in those many countries of Africa or South America in the twentieth century where there are no roads from farm to market, where motor traffic is impossible, and animals of traction inadequate or unavailable. Some other technical improvements of wagons, such as the pivoted front wheel (and perhaps the brake), derived from the early Middle Ages. Most Roman vehicles, except postchaises and ceremonial chariots, had been two-wheeled. But, by the twelfth century, a four-wheeled *caretta*, capable of carrying heavy loads, very slowly, was in being (14). By that time, 'international' travel by road had recovered. Priests or monks went from northern Europe to Rome, took back with them the idea of Romanesque architecture, and often indeed took back craftsmen too from Italy. By the fourteenth century, Chaucer could

---

* See above page 91.

write that, every April, people longed to 'go on pilgrimage' – adventures which would not have been safe very much more than a hundred years before.

Reliance on the horse meant that seasonal interruptions of many communications were henceforth often due less to bad weather than to difficulties of obtaining forage: Carolingian *missi* never began their tours of inspection till the grass had grown (15), cavalry armies waited till the hay was cut. Such journeys 'internationalised' several peoples. Hungary, for example, lay on a land route to Jerusalem which the *destrier* and horseshoe had made a possible alternative to the pirate-infested seas (though Richard Coeur de Lion found it had its risks too). Frederick Barbarossa was received in Hungary by a king, Bela III, not unlike himself in habits. Bela's queen was Margaret, a sister of the King of France, and widow to the heir apparent of England. A Frenchman in the eleventh century wrote the first history of Hungary (16). Meanwhile, the builders of Gothic cathedrals also threw many bridges across the rivers of Europe (17). Not far away in Asia, the Mongol Empire, which, from 1279 till 1350, embraced all China and most of Russia (except for Novgorod) and even stretched to Budapest, was kept together by horsemen capable of riding at the Roman pace of a hundred miles a day for days on end (18), thus maintaining the tradition of good communications and despotism till the dawn of our own times.

In the European Renaissance further changes making for good communication inland are hard to discern. The wheel, it is true, had been improved by making it concave. Coaches in towns appeared in the late fifteenth century.* Neither invention made any contribution to long-distance transport till roads were improved to bear that delicate innovation. Roads in the sixteenth century in Europe consisted mostly of tracks a yard wide, satisfactory enough for horsemen, alongside which flocks and walkers had sometimes beaten out footpaths (19).

The only real innovation of the Renaissance in respect of transport was, however, seen in the Americas. One of the many groups of llama tenders who lived in the highlands of the Andes, the Incas, had, in the fifteenth century, established a monarchical system, and constructed a network of fine roads for couriers, made partly of stone, partly raised on causeways if they crossed marshes or rainy regions, partly simply of earth but always well marked (20). Rivers were crossed by monkey bridges of cables of plaited agave fibre, or floating bridges, or pontoons of reeds. Up and down the Andes, too, went caravans of llamas, bred as beasts of burden even though they could only carry a hundredweight, and could only travel fifteen miles a day (21). These were the only

* The coach was an Hungarian invention, the word deriving from Kocs, a town between Raab and Buda. The key to this innovation was a body suspended on straps, with a bogie. The front axle was attached to the chassis by a pivot, a device revived for war in the fifteenth century.

important domestic animals of the Americas before 1492 (22), and they were quite inadequate. Though their wool was too coarse to be spun, it could be used for fibres (23).

Spaniards on horses conquered America, mules sustained the conquest. The introduction of the latter provided, within only a few years of the Spanish conquest, essential links between Vera Cruz and Mexico, Lima and Cuzco, Pánama and Nombre de Díos. Without these animals, the gold and silver of the new continent would never have reached the Caribbean, much less Spain. The owners of the convoys later financed the production of cotton and coffee, being pioneers of early South American capitalism (24). In the eighteenth century, Braudel estimated, South America was a continent powered by two million mules, though, in the Argentinian pampas, as in North America, ox carts were used, and, in the mines of Brazil, slaves carried the gold.

In Europe, the French began the revival of communication by land. Grants for new roads and state coaches were agreed by Louis XIV in 1664. A series of *'pavés du roi'* began to underpin the communications within what was already the most centralised state of Europe. In the mid-eighteenth century, an *École des Ponts et Chaussées* was set up. The engineer Trésaguet was, in the 1760s, beginning his famous system of roads of three layers: foundations, contours hammered in, small hard stones on top.

Equally famous was the French government's lack of compunction in seizing all the private land which it needed for roads and tearing down all the houses which stood in its way. The French Department of Highways was already fascinated by the straight line, carefully avoiding the use of existing roads if they showed the slightest deviation from this ideal rectitude (25). By 1789, France had achieved a good system of stone roads radiating from Paris. The idea was copied in Spain, and inspired the use of long-distance coaches in both countries. Even so, all goods in the eighteenth century were still sent by sea for preference. These French roads were also inspiring Catherine the Great and Joseph II in Russia and Austria. Britain then had what seemed on the map a very elaborate system of communications, with an endless series of well-established roads. But most such roads were really impassable. The only good ones were those which still had some Roman stones left. The parishes were responsible. They were incompetent. Carts sometimes took five hours to travel ten miles, or were held up for a day or more by floods. In the seventeenth century, the different regions of England were thus utterly cut off one from the other. A great North Road, with a turnpike, was begun in 1663, but the tolls were unpopular. The rebellion of Bonnie Prince Charlie, in 1745, proved the need for better roads for strategic purposes: the bad going had made the concentration of the royal army difficult and a network of turnpike roads on the

French pattern was then financed, also on the French pattern. Those roads were still far behind French ones, which were anyway being further improved, as the Revolution drew nearer, by the great eighteenth century bridge-builder Perronet. The last of his works was begun in 1787 and ended in 1793. The earliest users were the mob assembling for the execution of King Louis XVI: some of the stone used was taken from the Bastille, the symbolic fortress of the old regime of the agricultural age.

Along these roads a post service was also revived. For much of the Middle Ages, the only regular post in Europe had been that between Venice and Constantinople. The last attempts at a royal post vanished after the end of the Carolingians. Merchants and others who wished to communicate over long distances financed their own messengers. Servants before the nineteenth century spent much of their time carrying letters. In the seventeenth century, the German family of Thurn und Taxis employed 20,000 people to provide a post service which was reliable though not quick (a letter took nine days to get from Frankfurt to Berlin). From intercepted readings of those letters the Emperor, like later tyrants (particularly those eavesdropping by telephone), gained his impression of what was happening in his realm (26). He did not expect thereby to stimulate commerce.

Nor did armies travel any faster after the Renaissance than they had done before. Napoleon's army moved no faster than Caesar's, as the poet Valéry was later fond of pointing out. Few armies covered more than thirty miles in twenty-four hours in the sixteenth century. But 120 miles a day were then covered on the sea in good weather. The truth is that, until the invention of the internal combustion engine in the 1880s, the road played a minor part, in the exchange of both ideas and commerce.

22

A Revolution: Printing

Communications are not simply a matter of journeying. The pen since the fourteenth century has often been mightier than the horse and the sail. That was due to printing. If any innovation deserves the over-used word 'revolutionary', printing is it.

Until the fifteenth century AD, the best way to communicate with many people was either by oratory or drama: at all events, the spoken word. Some tried to improve on this. Atticus, Cicero's friend, tried to found a business by getting slaves to make copies of books. In Rome, authors, though, hoped at best for a public reading in a private house. Augustus and Claudius encouraged that. Hadrian built a special 'Athenaeum' for it (1). The Romans made several contributions to the art of printing, for they cut patterns out of wooden blocks and stamped them in plaster. They were prevented, probably, from going any further in respect of printing for the communication of ideas, not only through lack of technological invention, but through the absence of a cheap material on which to print. The Egyptians had used papyrus, but that was in short supply. The ancient Babylonians had had pressed seals but no papyrus. The Greeks based their life on oral communications. There is little evidence of private reading then being a regular practice.

The Romans substituted parchment (untanned leather) for papyrus, the invention of 'parchment' originating in the state of Pergamum, which had devised it when Ptolemy Epiphanes banned the export of papyrus, in order to try to check the growth of a library which could be a rival to that at Alexandria. The Church first adapted parchment, then lawyers. Before that, the custom had begun of folding up a large rectangular sheet to form pages and then binding them together as a 'volume'. The early Christians apparently invented the idea of the modern book. But since 200 quarto pages of parchment would require the skins of twelve sheep, the material on which writing was done was then sometimes more valuable than what was written on it.

The Chinese had had paper since 105 AD.* They made it from

* The name of the inspired inventor of paper should not be idly forgotten by Westerners who use it all the time. It was Tshai Lun, who died in 114 AD.

decayed vegetable matter, and, like silk, kept the method of making it for a long time a secret. In the ninth century, an Arab expedition took some Chinese papermakers prisoner at Samarkand. The secret of paper then passed to the West. Arab paper manuscripts survive from the ninth century. By 1150 AD, there was a paper industry in Moorish Spain, probably in Morocco and Sicily. Thence, the idea was taken northwards, though the Arabs used rags instead of vegetables. Játiva, some miles south of Valencia on the borders of Al-Andalus, had a paper mill using cloth, wood and straw by 1150. It was first turned by hand, then by wind and water. By 1200, there was another such mill in France, and in Italy one at Fabriano in Tuscany by 1300. A watermill was employed to tear rags to shreds.

Meantime, the Chinese had also devised a method of printing. That was probably a result of the Buddhist expansion about 500 to 700 AD. The Buddhists had always felt the necessity for the endless repetition of famous names. Textbooks by the thousand were also needed for the public examinations. At all events, the first block printing known is that of a Buddhist charm of about 770 AD (2). That type of printing did very well. Several hundred years later, under the Sung dynasty, and perhaps as a result of a demand for scholarly works by provincial civil servants starved of literature in their remote posts, the Chinese devised printing with moveable type in something like the modern manner about 1040, and the idea spread in the East. But since the languages of the East were ideographic, the type could only be made for words not letters. Still, a currency in paper was devised (as earlier noticed), making use of printing, and Marco Polo observed, in the thirteenth century, the Chinese block printing of playing cards. These were soon copied in the West, while punches were also devised for marking metal by goldsmiths and silversmiths. By 1410, Jan van Eyck was using oil paints which adhere to metal and enabled engravings (3). By then, the woodcut had already been devised in China, in 1406 or before.

Printing proper came when a moveable type was devised which could be used repeatedly, combined at will, removed easily, and produce uniformity of lettering. Types had to be available in large numbers even for a single sheet. They were needed by the thousand for a whole book. To obtain them, casting in replicas was devised. A single letter engraved in relief and sunk into a slab of brass would provide the intaglio, or matrix (female die), of that letter in reverse. From that, any number of replicas could be cast by pouring molten lead on them (4). Was it Johann Gutenberg, the goldsmith of Mainz, who first did this? Or Johann Fust, his partner? Or Schoffer, a Dutch inventor of Haarlem? Or Procope Waldfogel, of Prague? At all events, by 1448, a large printing office had been established by Gutenberg and Fust at Mainz, with type made from an alloy of lead, tin and antimony. They settled down to produce the Vulgate Bible in St Jerome's translation. The first scientific work, Pliny's

Natural History, was published in Venice in 1469. The proof reader made much the same marks as he does today, against thick black Gothic letter type: 'roman' type was not introduced till 1500. The ink used at the beginning was also much the same as now: an oil-bound liquid made by grinding linseed oil with lampblack, or powdered charcoal. (Probably the linseed oil derived from its use as a varnish by Flemish painters). The composing was completed by locking up the lines and the spaces, inking them and then pressing them on paper.

By 1500, 40,000 editions of books were in being, and 20 million books. Printing presses had been set up throughout Europe, the first books being printed in Venice (as indicated earlier) in 1469, in Florence, Naples and Paris in 1471, Cracow in 1474, and in Spain in 1475. Few changes had such dramatic consequences. Pope Sixtus IV founded the Vatican Library to house the new flow of books and others followed suit. By 1500, it was hard to remember the days when Federigo da Montefeltro kept thirty or forty *scrittori* always employed and Cosimo il Vecchio in Florence had hired forty-five men to copy, in the beautiful light Italian hand of the day, 200 books for the library at the Badia of Fiesole — or that the great book-collector, Poggio, passed thirty-two days copying the works of Quintilian, which he had found in the Benedictine abbey of St Gall (5). It was no longer only the rich who could aspire to possess books. Even the first news-sheets were published before 1500 (for example, the Nuremberg Chronicle). Such broadsheets were often seen during the next century. The printing press soon crossed the Atlantic. Small presses were established in Mexico in 1534 and in Lima in 1584 (6). During the sixteenth century, 200 million books were printed and, in the seventeenth, publishers were printing between 500 and 2000 copies of a book (7). For a few bestsellers such as the tales of chivalry which so went to the head of the Spanish nobility, as to that of Don Quixote, they printed as many as 4000. By the end of the seventeenth century, printed news-sheets had become, as Keith Thomas says, 'an indispensable feature of London life' (8), and the same was soon true of the Netherlands and Germany.

There were thereafter very few technical innovations for several hundred years, though the letters in a press could wear out. The early press remained mostly unchanged till the eighteenth century. The first etching dates from 1500: Dürer's (and Rembrandt's) steel point engravings by drypoint represented only a small advance. The illustrated book, with its woodcuts and elaborate drawings, came to be seen in all courtly houses. The standard of printing probably decayed in the seventeenth century, but the rate of output increased and, in the eighteenth, the consumption of paper tells its own story. In England, for example, paper charged with duty totalled 2.5 million tons in 1713 and 12.4 million in 1800 (9). By that time, there were numerous semi-newspapers: in 1760, even forty provincial journals in England (10).

Many journals of one sort or another were being printed in Italy. Within a few years of the beginning of the Industrial Revolution proper, Tom Paine's *Rights of Man* sold in tens of thousands and Byron's *Corsair* could be sold in an edition of 10,000 on publication. It could soon be fairly said in Europe that, in Lewis Mumford's words, 'the swish and crack of paper is the underlying sound of the metropolis' (11). Ideas could immediately be communicated to large numbers of people, provided they could read, and the availability of books was the greatest stimulus to people to teach themselves to read. The majority of the population could eventually be shown the existence of general as well as particular issues.

One further consequence of the printing press was a government's grant of an exclusive privilege of making new inventions called the patent, first introduced into Venice in 1474, among glassmakers. It spread thence to Florence and was first used in England in 1542. Another was the vast number of 'romances of chivalry' which stimulated the imagination of the Spanish conquistadors and, indeed, of the whole Spanish upper and middle class (12). But by far the biggest consequence of printing was the collapse of the unity of Western Christianity known as the Reformation.

Christianity had already split, into an Eastern and Western branch, by the eighth century. Within the Western branch, there had been numerous minor heresies, which were partly social protests, which in the end were quelled (the Albigensians, Lollards, and Hussites). Now, with printing, the increasing availability of the Bible, the wide circulation of religious polemics, and the awakening of the differences between the Church's practice and its intellectual foundations, transformed Western Christianity. The editions of the Church fathers and the Greek text of the New Testament translated by Erasmus of Rotterdam made evident in 1516 the shortcomings of basic ecclesiastical writings. Erasmus's *Praise of Folly*, published in 1509, satirised all institutions, especially the Church. The basic Lutheran doctrine of justification by faith alone was an essential corollary of the diffusion of printing. Had it not been for printing, the Church of Rome would probably have been able to crush the Reformation as it had crushed the Albigensians: the Elector of Saxony was able to protect his protégé Luther as the Count of Toulouse was not able to defend the heretics of the twelfth century, since the printer's block, if not the pen, was shown to be mightier than the sword. Luther's translation of the Bible, completed in 1534, also did for German what St Jerome's had done for silver age Latin. It may seem superficial to attribute the series of intellectual disruptions known as the Reformation to technological causes. Yet the outpouring of religious tracts which characterise the sixteenth and seventeenth centuries in Europe cannot be imagined without the presses which, readily, long before newspapers became general, printed everything which came to them, and the history of religious persecution in the seventeenth century is above all the history of the suppression of printed tracts. The Counter-Reformation was also assisted, at least, by the presses: the first book printed in the Americas was the *Doctrina Breve* for the use of priests. The men of imagination who carried out the conversion of the Indies, the most remarkable achievement of the modern Church, could not have performed their task without the accompaniment of thousands of copies of that work, as of the Bible. But the most successful institution of the Counter-Reformation was doubtless the Society of Jesus and its most extraordinary achievement was certainly the Jesuit colony on the upper Parana. Cloistered jungle missions were founded there in the early seventeenth century. It was a society kept together by reading and writing, in which *The Spiritual Exercises* of St Ignatius played the decisive part. It was *The Spiritual Exercises* too which gave Matteo Ricci, the great missionary to China, 'one of the most remarkable and brilliant men in history', as Joseph Needham refers to him, his successes at the Chinese court in the latter days of the Ming dynasty (13).

The most curious aspect of the Reformation was that it occurred when, thanks to the rediscovery of antiquity and the reinvigoration which that gave to painting, the Church of Rome was served by the most gifted artists who have ever lived. Painting, however, was a product of illiteracy. The Church could thereby impose dogmas, relate legends and stimulate devotion, without submitting anything to critical enquiry. Printing posed something of a challenge, therefore, to the 'propaganda by sight' upon which preachers had relied for so long (14). It also raised a fundamental question about the need for an institutionalised Church: if all who could read could understand the Bible what need was there of a middleman, so to speak, between God and man, in the form of a priest? Yet, while painters turned away from the grotesque improvisations of the Middle Ages, they secularised their subjects more than their patrons seem to have realised. They transformed every scene into a pageant. Saints became humble scholars. St Ursula looked as if she were a village girl, the Virgin Mary, an ordinary mother, while the spectators of the Crucifixion looked often as if they were uninterested.

The Reformation gave a religious justification to the local disputes between the Holy Roman Emperor and the German princes. It divided the emerging nations of Europe into two at a time when some of those nations had both established order at home and were interested in long-distance trade. It caused the decline, into innumerable parts, of half the European population, so that each Protestant could be said to be able to found his own Church while, in the beginning, it also divided the positive German Reformation from the corrupt Italian hierarchy. It also in the end inspired the Counter-Reformation, which caused a rebuilding of learning in the Catholic Church as imposing as that in the

Protestant. Thinking independently about the headship of the Church led to thinking independently about the nature of politics, science, art, and learning. The country which Francesco Caraccioli (not Voltaire, as is often supposed) believed to have a hundred religions and only one sauce — namely, England — was naturally in the forefront of all forms of intellectual adventure during the seventeenth century. The Reformation also increased the gulf between those who believed that one should find one's own way to God by intellectual endeavour and those who, on the contrary, thought that all such effort was pointless or even heretical, since, in the words of Muhammad (and some Andalusians), 'it is written' ('*estaba de Díos*'). It also began the slow dissolution of social bonds which, after the collapse of others such as loyalty to neighbourhood and family, in the twentieth century would cause a major social crisis. Some indication of the shape of the future was given when Protestant churches abandoned the confessional, since the personal confession and interrogation of every layman had been, to quote Keith Thomas again, a most 'compulsive system of social discipline' (15). Even the Church of Rome introduced a private confessional box after the Counter-Reformation whereas, before, all confessions were public ones.

We should beware, however, of supposing that Protestantism represented scepticism, while Rome and the Counter-Reformation spelled prejudice. For example, Nicolaus Koppernigk (Copernicus), a Catholic Pole working at the episcopal palace at Helisberg, agreed with the long-dead Aristarchus of Samos that the Sun, 'as if sitting on a royal throne, governs the family of stars which move around it'. The Pope (to whom Copernicus dedicated his book) was not at first critical. But Luther and Melanchthon were hostile. Copernicus's disciple, Giordano Bruno, believed the universe to be infinite and so 'nobody can be said to be in the centre of it'. He was burned for his attitude towards transubstantiation and for attacking the Pope, rather more than for his astronomical attitudes. Servetus, who anticipated Harvey's theory of the circulation of the blood, was burned at the instigation of the Protestant Calvin.

Another consequence of printing perhaps was the beginning in the sixteenth century of a widespread concern for self-education which has since never ceased. Before printing, few people were in a position to teach themselves anything. Subsequently, it has been usually accepted that, in the words of Dr Johnson, 'you can never be wise unless you love reading' (16). Printing stimulated nationalism as well as religious scepticism: the first patriotic utterances of German literature belong to the humanists of the time of Maximilian I (17). Few such opportunities were open without books and printing. Nor were they open at all in China where, despite the serenity of the life, the character of the script still prevented the exploitation of the invention of moveable type, already achieved in the eleventh century. But in Europe, all politicians, artists, leaders of opinion, even soldiers, now read voraciously. Libraries came into being in every 'gentleman's residence', and one of the great forms of art, the novel, was soon born.

23

City Life

The Renaissance revived the idea of living in cities. Partly this was a consequence of the revival of Greek learning and writings. The Greeks, after all, had seen the city state as the natural unit for society. They believed that such states did not exist in their time (between 900 and 400 BC) among other peoples, and considered that fact just one more sign of their Persian opponents' barbarism. The city state seemed, however, to the Greeks a natural development of family and of village. Even Plato and Aristotle, so far-sighted in so many things, saw the city state as the desirable, even the logical, end of all political development. Neither foresaw the multinational empires of the future, though Aristotle was the tutor of Alexander. A sense of self-sufficiency was the main characteristic of Greek cities. But there was naivety in that view: Athens herself expanded and, had she not been thwarted, her empire might have grown as did that of Rome, a city state originally populated by urban farmers which established Mediterranean unity. Nor did the Greeks seem to know that, in ancient Iraq, the most remarkable achievements had occurred when that society was concentrated in cities as independent as, and for longer than, those of classical Greece. The Greek cities were, however, of special interest to the Italians during the Renaissance for the obvious reason that contemporary Italy seemed in so many ways a reincarnation of the old Greek world. Originally, the Greeks had been a single tribe, nomadic and hunting, a branch of the Aryan, or Indo-European, family, no doubt, but with a long separate identity, as their language suggests. Under tribal leadership, they fell on Greece from the north (much as the 'barbarians' did on the Mediterranean world at the close of antiquity) and divided to form cities, each under monarchies, though most of those, like the line of King Cecrops, in Athens, died out. Athens always retained its hinterland, Attica, as its source of wine, meat, and other crops but, as earlier noticed, depended on grain from the Ukraine for which the Athenians paid with silver from the Laurion mines and with other objects which they had themselves imported from elsewhere, such as Egypt.

This was a general political condition so similar to the state of affairs

205

in Italy in the fifteenth century that the parallels were very obvious indeed. The Italian cities, like Greek cities, were, in every sense of the word, close to the country. Their inhabitants still usually had nearby estates or, if poor, gardens of vegetables, and their streets were full of sheep, straw and hay, cattle and pigs. Around the cities of the Renaissance, throughout Europe, a great number of festivals, mystery plays, processions, pantomimes, illuminations, carnivals, balls, boat races and games came to occur regularly and ritualistically, symbols of continuity with rural life, interplay between religion and paganism, art and religion, beside which our modern pageants and festivals are pale, if formal, shadows, without ritual significance (1). This was a reminder of the fact that the birth of agriculture really coincided with, and was made possible by, the village and the city perhaps at the same time, built for defence as well as for occasional commercial exchange. In this respect, James Mellaert, discoverer of Çatal Hüyük, warns us to avoid thinking that cities developed out of villages: 'the reverse seems far more logical'. Early agriculture was built round the fortified group of homesteads and had nothing to do with the isolated farmhouse which constitutes the idea of 'the country' to many minds in the twentieth century.

The Roman Empire, in the mind of the Renaissance, represented an urban achievement above all. The Empire seemed to have been a mosaic of cities which governed their surrounding hinterlands. All Roman citizens belonged to a city, even if they lived somewhere else. Some Roman imperial cities were commercial (for example, Carthage, known after its eclipse as a centre of cheap woollen goods), or semi-colonial (such as Trier and Arles). All had the same administrative structure, the same magistrates, prefects, curators of aqueducts and of drains, managers (*comes*) of ports — the same methods of taxation, amphitheatres, baths, public services. But, by the fourth century in the West, many citizens withdrew, if they could, into the country to take up agriculture. Many once well-established cities began to lack the public services to which they had been used. In Rome, the 'urban cohorts' which had constituted a police force disintegrated, leaving the prefect with a few night watchmen and clerks to assist him to maintain order and law. In the east of the Mediterranean where the land had remained more fairly distributed, and where urban life was more deeply rooted, many cities were still fairly prosperous in the sixth century. They then looked, of course, to Constantinople as the imperial city. It was, however, badly built, out of old ransacked buildings, and with a bad water supply, even if well situated strategically (2).

The idea of the city greatly suffered during the Dark Ages. Even the Christian Church derived its strength from the countryside. Nevertheless, that Church had based its diocesan boundaries on those of Roman cities. That held together the ancient municipal tradition. Bishops' power increased as States' power decreased. Some cities survived with many habits and traditions barely interrupted in the Byzantine Empire, even when conquered by the Arabs. Perhaps Italy never wholly lost the idea of what urban life could aspire to. Elsewhere in Europe, towns consisted of little more than groups of clergy attached to the cathedral, or monks of the urban monasteries, together with a few students at the ecclesiastical schools and some artisans needed for the cathedrals' upkeep. There might be weekly markets and an annual fair. At the city's gate, a toll might be levied, a mint might operate within the walls, and there would be huge granaries. Bishops had *de facto* temporal, as well as spiritual, power, judicial as well as police activities. It was they who kept up the walls against both Vikings and Saracen pirates, or against other bandits. Kings and noblemen seemed, against this setting, purely rural beings, usually inhabiting remote castles.

The way that cities declined and managed to revive in Europe is exemplified by the history of Florence. Florence, founded as a Roman camp about 50 AD, was laid out in a square (not now distinguishable) and surrounded by a wall (still visible) like other Italian cities. Florence recovered from long decline, as a result of the Crusades, in the shadow of Venice. It was a good stopping place on the Arno at the cross roads on the way from Rome to Bologna and from Pisa and Genoa, and near the foot of several passes across the Apennines. Municipal life began following the death in 1115, without heirs, of Matilda, Grand Duchess of Tuscany, leaving Florence, like other cities, able to pursue its independence between Pope and Emperor. For a time, a general assembly of citizens was the source of political power. That came to mean an upper stratum of 150 merchants. If noblemen with large estates nearby (such as the Ubaldini in the Mugello) or others of Lombard stock had joined forces, they could have prevented the emergence of an oligarchic but independent Florence. But they did not. Had Florence, like Pisa and Lucca, been in a plain, or like Siena and Arezzo, on a height, the feudal nobility might have settled inside the walls. But they preferred to remain outside, on fortified mountains nearby. Thus the distinctive character of Florence: its lack of old nobility, its *grandi* being merchants. Long civil wars followed during the twelfth and thirteenth centuries, the Pope, the French and the Emperor by proxy taking part, despite the cultural revival associated with Giotto (born 1266) or Dante (born 1265). The heroes of the latter were anyway imperial nobles such as the Cardinal Ottoviano degli Ubaldini who confessed, 'I lost whatever soul I had in the Ghibelline cause' (3). Florence experimented with annually elected consuls and then had a system of eight priors who ruled for two months, living, while they did so, all together in the Signoria. The subsequent papal victory in the south of Italy did not alter these new Florentine liberties. They in turn were accompanied by the great commercial boom based on manufactured, coarse woollen cloth or later wool itself imported from the north and locally refined.

Meantime, political control, as in some other free Italian cities, was accumulated by the craft guilds (in Florence's case the seven major guilds and fourteen minor ones). A form of organic oligarchy thereafter lasted till about 1530, though the Medici family established a real domination (though not a formal one) before that, and though there were some difficulties with mercenary commanders-in-chief (*condottieri*). The rebellion of the lowest paid wool workers (the *ciompi*) in 1378 promised to create a genuine democracy, but this political system was one of rule by merchants through guilds – nothing like a syndicalist state managed by workers. Indeed, from 1378 onwards, single men without official position (Maso degli Albizzi, Gino Capponi, Niccolò da Uzzano and then Cosimo de'Medici) dominated the town and the enlarged province of which it was the centre. The Florentine constitution continued to be based on the essential principle of distrust to prevent power being concentrated in too few men for too long. But, in the end, the Medici gained political power, in order to protect their bank (4). By then, families such as the Medici constituted, in effect if not in name, a new aristocracy: 'a gentleman can be made with two yards of cloth,' Cosimo de'Medici remarked presciently (5).

The struggles between rich and poor in Florence, were, in many ways, a rehearsal for the 'class struggles' of the nineteenth century more than a repetition of those of Rome, or of other places during the Renaissance. In Florence, towards the end of the fourteenth century, according to Werner Sombart, 'We meet the perfect bourgeois for the first time' (6). The frequent depiction of cities in the art of the Renaissance in Florence, however, is a reminder that many saw the city which they were constructing as the summit of *virtù*, very much as the Greeks had done, and the supreme political achievement (7). People began to think again about how to organise the ideal society – and that seemed more like an Italian city state than anything else achieved before (8). The idea has never ceased to exert a certain charm.

The house of a merchant in Tuscany about 1400 might have consisted of twelve to fourteen rooms if he were a successful man (only the Medici and Strozzi had more). Its roof would be tiled and the windows would have small, heavy, wooden shutters. It might have glass which, though no longer rare, was a luxury (in 1332, a Franciscan included glass in his list of luxuries which had drawn God's wrath on the city) (9). By the sixteenth century, glass had become cheap and easily available in Italy (it had been used for decorative solid objects from at least 2500 BC). There might be a loggia built on the side of the house for entertaining, with a vaulted ceiling. Perhaps there might also be a fireplace, a modern luxury devised in France, usually made of stone, and set against the wall with a chimney. (In England, a fireplace in the wall was still a luxury in the days of Shakespeare.) These fireplaces, if they were there, would probably be the main decorative element in the room, being much prized and, since few even in the Renaissance recalled Roman systems of heating, the only refuge in a cold house (in Europe until the twentieth century, it was often desirable to wear furs, if you had them, inside the house during winter). A Florentine merchant might also have warming pans, as well as *scaldini*, little jars containing charcoal which one might hold when cold, on the knee or in the hand. For light, there would be horn lanterns, wax torches on long poles, tallow candles, and brass oil lamps — identical to those of Rome – in which olive oil burned. The walls of such a house might often be hung with French serge or linen, perhaps a carpet. Carpetings for floors were rare, though not unknown (in the thirteenth century, the carpets used by a Toledan bishop travelling to London were a curiosity (10)). The bed would be the most important piece of furniture, often curtained and canopied, with a mattress perhaps covered with striped French cloth. Pillows, sheets and blankets were already in general use (11). Most rooms would have large chests as their only furniture, being used for baggage as well as furniture, in which clothes, linen, jewels, furs would lie (the cupboard was a later device) and a truckle bed for servants to sleep on. By then, in rich families, dining rooms were beginning to be separate from kitchens, as they had started to be in monasteries because of the scale of the preparations (12), while the use of the common table for all the household was dying. Servants, after the Renaissance, would everywhere have their meals separately below stairs (13)

Even rich men's dining rooms would be barely furnished in Florence at the turn of the fourteenth and fifteenth centuries. They usually contained a dining table perhaps five yards long, with still only one glass as a rule from which all would drink (as with a loving cup) and then pass on. There were no forks save for serving and only a few spoons. Most people still brought and used their own knives. Benches would be far more common than chairs, which were regarded as rare, honorific items till at least the sixteenth century (14). Kitchens would have a wooden sink, a safe for dry meat, cauldrons, and many pots and pans still familiar in the twentieth century (15).

The coming of the chair as a piece of furniture for every day indeed marks the Renaissance as much as anything else. The turner and the joiner who made this furniture with wheel-lathes, pole-lathes, mechanical saws, worked usually in oak till the sixteenth century when all sorts of other woods, from walnut to beech, elm to pine, began to be used. Joiners were not really independent of carpenters till the high Renaissance. The Renaissance also revived the plane, known to Rome, but forgotten for centuries. With these tools, benches gave way to stools, stools to chairs, in Italy first, but then afterwards everywhere in Europe. For the joinery of the Italians soon spread to northern Europe. France was a centre of fine work by the sixteenth century and was preparing, even then, to surpass Italy. By the seventeenth and eighteenth centuries, chairs were as important in the lives of any who could afford them as they are today, large fortunes being made by those who marketed or designed them.

Furniture and panelling were only two of the household uses of wood. No means of heating existed apart from firewood. All carpenters' tools derived from wood, as did spinning wheels, wine presses, ploughs and navies. (Was Europe's power perhaps attributable to her great forests? Braudel once asked, was Islam's eclipse due to her lack of them?) The vast demands for wood in late mediaeval Europe are hard to picture. Most of the supply was floated down the rivers. Every fleet needed a great forest to build it, so all mercantile nations needed access to the Baltic and the tall pine trees grown there for their masts. The huge quantity of wood meant a continuous danger of fire, in mediaeval and Renaissance towns. As early as 1276, Lübeck issued an ordinance enforcing fireproof ceilings, London in 1189 gave privileges to those who built roofs of tile and in 1212 ordered thatched roofs to be whitewashed to resist the fire better (16). Even so, fires happened often, and they spread easily once they had begun. Most ceilings of rooms were only the floors of the rooms above, straw was used on floors in winter (and flowers in summer) and burned merrily. In such cities, the domestic life of responsible families began, however, to flourish.

These cities of the Renaissance had all begun to have paving again. In this, they copied the cities of Moorish Spain, for Córdoba, the capital of Al-Andalus, with its half million inhabitants (and 300 mosques, 80,000 shops and workshops) had paving from the ninth century (17). Paris laid down slabs of stone to guard against the dust in 1185, Florence in 1240 and London in 1280.

As early as the thirteenth century in Europe the land around prosperous towns, particularly in Italy, was beginning again to be built upon, as it had been in the days of Rome. The slopes of the hills round Florence filled with villas, and the Venetians began to design their beautiful, if melancholy, houses on the Brenta. Such houses took advantage of the better water and air in a well chosen spot in the country, and often (as with the Medici houses at Castello or Careggi) served as a place to escape the plague. The construction of such houses indicated too a degree of confidence that their owners would not be disturbed by bandits or barbarian noblemen from the hills; the Medici villa at Cafaggiolo, for example, was the first example of a house where the castellation was entirely decorative. These innocent beginnings would lead in the end to suburbia, the commuter, and their attendant *grandeurs et misères*, but in the Renaissance that was still far away.

The Italian and German cities of the Renaissance were, in many ways, impractical and backward-looking. Alberti's treatise on city planning in the fifteenth century in Florence, for example, took no account at all of cannon (18). Fortifications played little part in his consideration. But gunpowder would sound the death knell of free cities as it did of chivalry. A typical Russian city of the seventeenth century was neither a priestly nor a commercial place but, according to Richard Pipes, a 'military and administrative outpost, run by the state, where a few governmental buildings were set amid a rambling agglomeration of low wooden houses, churches and bazaars set in vegetable patches with wide but unpaved streets and unregulated river banks' (19). Such would characterise only too many cities of the future. Moscow in 1701 had 16,000 households of which no less than 7,500 were lived in by officials of the state, and 1,500 by clergy (20).

Nor was the scale of Renaissance cities such as for them to need to anticipate the difficulties of modern megalopolises. Naples, with 300,000 people, was the largest Christian city in 1600, exceeding by far London's approximately 200,000, not to speak of Paris and Moscow (which both had perhaps 150,000). No other European city was of this size except Constantinople, still a huge distended urban monster with over 700,000 people, and none remotely approached either the size of Rome at its height, with about a million, or even some of the Chinese cities: Yangchow, capital of South China in Marco Polo's day, had about a million to a million and a half inhabitants in 1280 (21) – a strange spectacle for a native of Venice which, in the thirteenth century, probably had only 80,000 people, for all its prosperity.

Nor did any European city of the Renaissance, for all the attention paid to antiquity, approach the arrangements for drainage and water supply which had been worked out by the ancient Iraqis and Romans. Ancient Babylon, for example, showed a knowledge of the elementary principles of drainage and there were both sewers and cess-pools; and even main drains leading to the river. In Assyria, palaces had lavatories and bathrooms as modern as some still found in much of Europe, and superior to those which exist in the twentieth century in half the world (22). Water might be procured by wells or by means of aqueducts. Sennacherib brought water to Nineveh along a 300-yard aqueduct and a six-mile canal to water his orchards and parks. Calah had wells 90 feet deep, one of which could still yield 5,000 gallons a day in 1952 (23). Similar admirable conditions existed in Mycenae: water reached flushing lavatories and bathrooms, through terracotta pipes, and vanished through sloping gutters (24). Later, the Greeks used aqueducts often and devised the principle of the siphon to carry water in pipes over heights. Their contemporaries, the Etruscans, paid a greater attention to drainage than any other early people: thus the *cloaca maxima*, built in the sixth century BC, was on a scale so large that it seems almost as if they had some inkling that that group of villages which was the core of Rome would become the capital of a million people (25). Though most Romans collected their excreta in jars or pots which they carried downstairs to empty into a vat at the foot of the stairs to be emptied by manure merchants, or to be taken to a cess-pool, and though urine was often simply poured out of top windows (26), Rome was more hygienic than many cities even of today because of the number of her pipes for drainage, themselves due to the availability of cheap lead (27).

As hydraulic engineers, the Romans were certainly supreme in the ancient world. Rome was supplied by twelve aqueducts carrying water along largely underground courses. These fed the 1,352 fountains — of the fourth century AD — from which most people drew their water, the large number of public baths (1,000 in Pliny's day, including eleven giant ones (28)) in which the Romans spent the better part of their leisure, not only bathing but indulging in sports, cultivating physical fitness and beauty (most large baths had hot and cold air rooms, swimming baths, tubs and, from the Empire onwards, mixed bathing) (29). Other Roman cities had less elaborate aqueducts and some (at Segovia, or Pont du Gard) survive. The Romans were also adept tunnellers: the tunnel which took water to Rome from Lake Fucino, in the Apennines, stretched three and a half miles: the longest in the world till the great railway tunnels of the 1870s (30). For Romans living in the old capital, the fall of the Empire dated from the moment when the public slaves no longer maintained such things and when the fountains ran dry.

The world took many generations to recover Rome's standards of water supply. That was one reason for the small size of Western cities. Another was the perpetual difficulty of provisioning cities larger than a few tens of thousands. William Dunbar, in a famous poem, spoke of London as 'the flower of cities all'. But where could a nation with more than one London get its meat, its game, and its grain, in a community still largely pastoral? Constantinople in Dunbar's day ate 300 to 500 tons of grain a day, thereby necessitating the constant use of the Ottoman fleet and the command of the Black Sea, for access to the Ukraine.

Several developments did, however, occur in European cities as a prelude to industrialisation: carriages effectively arrived in Europe as a means of urban transport; and it was realised that a column of men can only be led in martial order through a straight, flat street. Several cities were thus refurbished along Vitruvian lines. The great Palladio wrote: 'The ways will be more convenient if they are made everywhere equal; that is, there will be no place within them where armies may not easily march' (31). That accurate, if subservient, comment from Europe's greatest architect meant that there would be no more street battles in higgledy-piggledy towns between townsmen and apprentices. Along the wide boulevards, or avenues, of the new Rome, inspired ultimately by the first-century architect Vitruvius but reconstructed by Bramante, according to Sixtus IV's master plan, in the seventeenth century, or the new Paris begun by Henri IV, or even the new London (fortunately prevented by civil war from being fully palladianised by Inigo Jones), the glittering uniforms of the new absolutist states of post Renaissance Europe could swagger, inspiring respect and fear. Was it instinct or design that caused public opinion in London to refuse Wren's grand plan for the rebuilding of London after the great fire, which had devastated 436 acres of London and had given England's greatest architect such a unique opportunity? Would liberty have survived if he had had his way and he had made London one of the world's most beautiful cities? Perhaps, since a pattern had already been set whereby in England even great noblemen regarded their town house as a *pied à terre* (perhaps in a square as favoured by Jones) and their country houses as their real home. In France, on the other hand, noblemen, in their detached Parisian hôtels, looked on the country as a place of disgrace. In that attitude, they were slavishly copied by the rest of continental Europe.

Most European towns were beginning to cease to have just one or two functions (commerce, defence or government). They were becoming again, as they had been in antiquity, centres of living for tens of thousands, including many who, like the Neapolitan *lazzaroni*, the most famous beggars in Europe, were there simply to pick a living where they could. There had clearly been little point in being a thief or a beggar in the country, for the people there were too poor. But in Naples, or in Amsterdam (a physical proof that the growth of a post-mediaeval city need not raise intolerable problems of design) or London and Paris, there were enormous opportunities for the crooked and the shiftless. The age when the city became a lure for everyone ambitious, rich and poor, honest and dishonest, had begun – or begun again.

Then, during these last generations before industrialisation, the urban house of the West, if not the city, attained something like the character it retained till the transformations wrought by air-conditioning and central-heating in the twentieth century. Rooms were differentiated. The pantry began to differ from the kitchen, the dining room from the drawing room (a room for conversation, meeting, reception, 'withdrawing'). Doors, previously narrow, opening inwards and letting one person through at a time, became double – presumably a sign of self-confidence. Even impoverished Germany had glass in windows in the sixteenth century. A curved chimney shaft was found to prevent smoke more effectively than a straight one and the better draught gave more heat. That was helped too by the large cast-iron stoves, often manufactured in England, often decorated elaborately as in Germany or bare in France, but used in most places from Russia to the Atlantic. In these rooms, or at least among the richer ones, mahogany panelling began to be introduced from the West Indies and South America, a fine wood so hard that it could only be worked by steel tools of the best quality. It was that which led to the finest achievements of the rococo age, with cabinet-making (itself a new profession) in the hands of Boulle, Chippendale, Sheraton and Hepplewhite – though South America's contribution in providing the wood for this finery is often forgotten. A major change in European building materials also occurred. The sandstone and limestone quarries of France were opened to enable stone houses to be built like the Roman houses, for endurance, in place of wood. In England, brick took over from wood. Other European nations copied one or the other. This process, complete by the end of the seventeenth century, helped to cause another great change in the character of northern European peoples, marking them out even more from dwellers in the wood and bamboo houses of China and the East in general (good against earthquakes). The felt tent of the nomad seemed further away than ever.

Urban achievement at its height seemed to be expressed, to many travellers in the eighteenth century, in the home of mahogany, the Spanish imperial cities of the New World. Officials, planters and priests lived in cities, themselves planned on classical principles, with fine municipal buildings and splendid palaces. Already, in the late sixteenth century, Mexico City astonished visiting Englishmen. It was much larger than Madrid or Seville or indeed any Spanish town and it was unfortified because of being far inland. Enemies could only come from the sea (32). Other Spanish American cities were similarly undefended, unless they were on the sea, as were Havana or Cartagena. In some ways, those bureaucratically run imperial cities seemed more 'modern' than those of Spain itself. Seventeen cities, and a third of the villages of Spain, were still under seigneurial jurisdiction and control about 1800 (33), while Spanish American ones ran themselves with oligarchic merchants as municipal councillors.

Urban life in the eighteenth century can be seen, from one point of view, at its height. A decline in crime made going out safer. A network of systems of communications provided by good messengers ensured swift delivery of everything from state papers to love letters. The cities were small enough for people to be able to walk out from them into the country. Their small size enabled the give-and-take of casual conversation between acquaintances who met by chance. Hence Dr Johnson's famous comments on the charms of London. On the other hand, the life of the city as a work of art, as a self-conscious achievement complete in itself, was in decline. In the seventeenth century, cities such as Genoa still had vast financial empires (Genoa had become the centre for the redistribution of Spanish silver as well as of silk and spices from the East) and Venice remained rich. By the eighteenth century, neither was so. Some cities survived as states (including, indeed, Genoa and Venice till 1798) but the 'nation states', Britain, France and Prussia in the eighteenth century, were by then determining events. Even Florence had abandoned itself to becoming a satrapy of the Habsburgs. By Louis XIV's time, the torch even of fashion had passed from Italy to France. Boulle's methods of glueing brass or shell to other materials to make furniture had no equal in Italy. Britain began to make as fine glass as Venice ever had (even if she was thwarted by taxation by weight). German cities, particularly, suffered badly in the eighteenth century. Many were independent still. But they were not well placed to take part in world trade, and the Treaty of Westphalia gave foreigners control of many German rivers. The Thirty Years' War had physically ruined many old cities. England dominated Germany's woollen industry and supplied Germany with manufactured goods through merchant adventurers. Even the trading organisation known as the Hanse was dissolved in 1669. All the northern German cities, save Hamburg, lost importance. Hamburg was, for a time it is true, an exception to the general decay in Germany. Its trade increased after the fall of Antwerp, to the Spaniards. It became, as Antwerp had been, a centre of refuge for exiles of all sorts. Hamburg had the first coffee house, and the first masonic lodge in Germany. A Dutch bank was effectively founded there in 1619. Yet, in the fifteenth century, it had seemed as if German painting, German scientific invention, and German trade might steadily have grown in importance. By the eighteenth century, that was plainly not to be for another hundred years and it then unfortunately came more under the inspiration of the country-minded Junkers, than of city fathers.

Those who live in cities have usually enjoyed higher incomes, better access to schools, doctors, and professions linked to literacy. Magistrates have been fairer. Cities have been as a rule also more impersonal than villages. In the country, the tyranny of local opinion and lack of tolerance towards any deviation is normal. In the city 'no man there marketh another's doings', as a traveller said of Venice in the sixteenth century (34). Eccentricity and individualism were thus easier there.

Still, as in respect of the discussion of land-holding, over-simplicity or the pursuit of a general rule begets deception. In Italy, in the Middle Ages, for example, there were many towns run by despots who sought to organise the entire population, as if it were their private servants. In comparison with these towns, feudal domains, like those of Charles the Rash of Burgundy, seemed almost dominions of consent (35).

The link between urban growth and freedom of conscience was often tenuous. But agricultural communities were always governed by landowners. Urban ones needed a different organisation. In the East, the large cities of India and China were used as administrative capitals by omnigerent rulers. In the West, more particularly in Europe, the cities grew into the market-places for ideas as well as for commodities.

24

Gunpowder Wars

The sixteenth century was the century of Leonardo and Erasmus but it was also the first century of the effective use of gunpowder. The origins of this commodity, like that of other characteristic things of the Renaissance, are to be found in the Middle Ages and not, primarily, in Europe.

In the late seventh century AD, Callinicus of Heliopolis (Syria) devised a fireball, made of naphtha or liquid bitumen which, when mingled with sulphur and pitch, and hurled at the Arab armies besieging Constantinople in 716–718 AD, helped the Greeks to victory. This 'Greek fire' was an ancestor of gunpowder. Its success resulted in experiments with other combustible powders and liquids. The older Greek 'artillery', based on twisting of hair by torsion, and used by the Romans, was inadequate for northern Europe, for it worked only in dry summer campaigns; otherwise the fibre lost its elasticity. Once commerce revived, many clever ideas came to Europe from the East. The first of these was the *huo p'ao* known in Europe as the *trebuchet*, and used in China by the eleventh century AD. This tilting engine for throwing missiles by the use of weights began to be used in Europe by the early twelfth century (1). By that time, a hand gun for throwing Greek fire was being used in Byzantium. It also seems that, from the ninth century, the Chinese were using saltpetre, sulphur and crushed charcoal, thrown by catapults to cause an explosion, in order to frighten demons. A tube to throw spears, not just fire, was in use in China in 1232 (at the siege of Loyang). In 1252, something close to a rocket was being used in Cologne. Saltpetre, known as 'Chinese snow', was in use for war in Egypt by then.

The critical invention in these matters was the combination of the right mixture of ingredients to make true gunpowder, with the realisation that, if it were made to explode in a tube, a ball of stone or iron might be ejaculated. Greek fire had resulted in the elaboration of copper tubes strong enough to contain the explosion. Metallic guns were being used in both India and China by about 1275, spreading thereafter to the rest of the East. Perhaps the Philippines saw gun-fire before France did.

Gunpowder was in use in Flanders by 1314, at Metz by 1324, and in a

216

bronze gun near Florence by 1326. King Muhammad IV of Granada apparently attacked Alicante with artillery, in 1331. Cannon balls took longer to be invented but iron shot was being made at Lucca by 1341. England had two calibres of gun firing lead shot by 1346, and cannon balls were being made at Toulouse by 1347. Petrarch speaks of gunpowder as being common about 1355. Cannon were in use in China by 1356, and played a decisive part in the wars of the rebellious Ming against the Mongol emperors between that date and 1382 (2), although it seems not to have been used in India till taken there by the Portuguese, in the sixteenth century (3). In 1389, cannon were first used in a decisive battle, at Kossovo, causing Serbia to become a vassal state of Turkey.

These early cannon were inefficient. Even at Kossovo, they were extremely unwieldy and difficult to manage. The guns were huge, wrought-iron or bronze monsters, either welded into crude tubes and strengthened by iron hoops or, if bronze, cast direct by craftsmen who knew the art from making bells. The shot was small. The gunpowder was loosely mixed, and that retarded the explosion. These guns were installed in ships early on — a consequence of navies' mobility; in 1377, the first naval battle with artillery occurred, off La Rochelle: a Spanish naval victory over England, in which twelve Castilian galleys destroyed thirty-six English ones (4). Even so, the Venetians had bowmen as their main naval armament till 1450. Actually, till about 1450, when mobile artillery was devised, drawn by oxen in Italy, or mounted on gun-carriages drawn by horses in France, the new developments had little effect. Swords, charges and archery were still deciding wars till the mid-fifteenth century, and castles remained almost invulnerable. Then, gun-founders altered their techniques. They ceased their concentration on increasing the size of guns, which were useful only in sieges, and moveable only with great difficulty. (The crowning achievement of that era had been the great brass cannon made for Sultan Muhammad II by the Hungarian gunmaker, Orban, to throw huge, stone, thousand-pound balls into Constantinople. It needed 60 to 140 oxen to pull it, 100 men to manipulate it, and two hours to load it. It cracked and never worked properly (5). Even so, other such guns helped the Turks batter down the walls of Christian cities which had resisted them for hundreds of years and the French versions enabled Charles VII of France to drive out the English monarchs at long last at the end of the Hundred Years' War.*

Still, the real impact of gunpowder was not appreciated till King Charles VIII of France's famous 'first modern army' invaded Italy in 1494. It included batteries of light, mobile, bronze, field artillery, firing iron cannon balls, rather than stone ones. They destroyed every castle they could aim at. The battles of Ravenna (in 1512) and Marignano (in

* Hand-guns as well as cannon were used by the French in the 1450s.

1515) were won by superior artillery. These opened a new age in warfare. Heavy siege artillery with gunpowder (firing 900 paces and clearly distinguished from field artillery) meant that cities could no longer rest peacefully behind their stone walls, secure in the knowledge of their invulnerability before horsemen. Nor could independent-minded barons. Field artillery was decisive at Belgrade in 1521, at Mohacs in 1526 and in Ivan the Terrible's conquest of Kazan and Astrakhan from Islam during the 1550s. The first two of those victories gave the Turks much Christian artillery, to their great advantage later. Thereafter, the European states depended absolutely for survival on foundries such as Spain's ones at Málaga (established in 1499), and Medina del Campo (established in 1405), or those at Innsbruck, Venice, and the Tower of London. These state workyards, in which individual craftsmen collaborated, were helped by the growth of central European mining and metallurgy which, in the end, gave Germany an advantage over Renaissance Italy. The casting of iron for the first time effectively in West Germany in the fourteenth century transformed European iron technology and further assisted the methods of warfare which were to dispense with castles, chivalry and the Renaissance in Italy as well, inaugurating the modern state, with its clearly defined frontiers, internal order, and strong institutions (6).

These developments are likely to be deplored by those who, like anarchists, see in the modern state little but evil. But still the new state of the sixteenth century, modest in its pretensions compared with its descendant of the twentieth, had beneficial effects. It removed, in the end, men from fear of barons and marauding armies and most probably helped the growth of population almost as much as the eclipse of the plague. It is hard to feel nostalgic, for example, about the internecine wars of the Italians during the generations before mobile artillery: immortalised though the fights between the Oddi and Baglioni of Perugia may be in the paintings of the young Raphael (who observed the combats as a pupil with Perugino), the terror, bloodshed, treachery and murder involved made even conquest by a foreign power seem a blessed release (7). The same might have been said of France, at the time of the Hundred Years' War, a time of continual struggle in which, while the losses in battle were slight, armies, public and private, mercenary and monarchical, lived for years on or off the local inhabitants, committing innumerable thefts and acts of indiscipline, and creating a culture of war from which the country took generations to recover.

Naturally, war has never really ceased being influenced by innovations in technology. The bow-and-arrow, the discovery of copper and of iron, the manufacture of bronze, the invention of the sail have all been already noticed. All successful peoples have appropriated the good ideas of others. Thus Rome made excellent use of the large Celtic forts which they adapted so successfully to create their own castles. They copied the catapult and the hand-cross-bow from Carthage — and it was their loss that they did not also copy the Parthians' wooden towers which were moved forward on wheels till the soldiers within them, who were provided with every species of missile, could engage, almost on the level, any troops who defended the ramparts of a castle (8). They were, on the other hand, influenced in their wall-building in Britain and elsewhere by the Chinese who sought in 300 BC, through their famous wall, to insulate themselves from invaders in that way. Then, as has been amply shown, the stirrup, devised in central Asia some time in the sixth century, made it possible for the first time for horsemen to ride fast and to meet a shock with the possibility of survival. The stirrup was known in France by about 730 and was presumably the reason for the 'sudden and urgent demand for cavalry' — big horses — which led to Charles Martel's confiscation of ecclesiastical lands and their redistribution to noblemen on the condition that they should despatch mounted and trained knights to the royal armies, recalling the horsemen of Persia who had for so long withstood Rome (9). The old Frankish battleaxes and javelins, both infantry weapons, disappeared, while the lance, with its heavy stock and spurs beneath the blade (to prevent too deep penetration and so cause difficulty in withdrawing the weapon), became usual in Frankish armies. Hence Charles Martel's victory at Tours over the Arabs. The cross-bow also reached Byzantium from central Asia about 600 AD. The long-bow, whose value was first shown in the wars between the English and the Welsh (in Wales, traditional cavalry had been shown to be useless, but archers could bring down enemies with long shots), followed about 1200. Longbowmen, though their reach was less far than crossbowmen, could fire five to six arrows to the crossbowman's one and could still pierce chain mail (10) — a factor which led the defeated French chivalry to take up plate armour.

True, the Arab conquests, one of the real turning points of history (11), were due less to technological innovation than to what Marc Bloch, speaking of the Vikings, described as a 'social' superiority (12). Their victories were due to a skilled use of cavalry (though initially still without the stirrup), in combination with archers; they had no infantry. But the Ch'in emperors established the unity of China chiefly because of the cast-iron swords which they alone possessed. (Cast iron had been developed in China soon after the idea of forging, though the invention did not reach the West till 1500 AD.) Equally, the axe and the pike created the invaluable Swiss mercenaries of the fifteenth century.

Even so, there can be little doubt that the use of cannon and shot fired by gunpowder was the most striking adaptation of any invention by societies which did not themselves have the original idea. War, the preservation of governments, riots and crimes have all been transformed by gunpowder. The French knight in armour, the Ritter of the Middle Ages in Germany, the increasing use of rules of war, the distinctions carefully made between *guerre couverte* (private war) and *guerre publique* (public war between states) not to speak of *guerre mortelle* (when the populations in vanquished territories could be 'put to the sword'), all vanished for good or evil – though perhaps the French knights' great days had been in decline since their decimation by longbowmen at the battle of Crécy in 1346. Also in decline henceforth were the professional mercenaries, Swiss or German, who had often in mediaeval Italian wars come to look on war as a tactical exercise in which the aim was to capture an enemy's army, not to defeat him by expensive battles: *Condottieri* were even sometimes suspected of settling beforehand what was to happen; even of arranging beforehand to draw the game (13). Such sportsmanship now vanished, though, as will be seen, the benefits cannot be dismissed altogether and though mercenary captains lasted until well into the seventeenth century – the greatest of them all, the Czech nobleman, Wallenstein, being murdered on the brink, it would seem, of establishing a great kingdom. The most successful army of the fifteenth and sixteenth century, however, was a national one, nationally led and financed, that of Spain: an army of infantry not cavalrymen, with noblemen sometimes in the ranks and carrying hand guns. They dominated Europe from the defeat of François I in 1525 till their own eclipse at Rocroy in 1646.

In the sixteenth century cannon were still individuals, and often had names. They usually were made differently one from another. Their expectancy of life was short. Bells were often melted down to make them. The best guns were usually German or Venetian, and German ones were exported in large numbers, particularly to Portugal and to Spain (whose rulers thereby spent much of the gold of the Americas). Many gunners aboard Portuguese and Spanish ships were Germans or Flemings. Though Spain founded arsenals of her own, she often depended on the enemy's manufacture. England, too, though making iron guns in the Ashdown Forest, also bought many from abroad, particularly from the Flemings (14). Later, the English cast-iron guns, because of the phosphorus in the soil of Sussex, turned out to be more robust than those cast on the continent. They did not blow up so often at the wrong moment. They remained heavier than bronze guns, but they did not heat so much, and were three or four times less expensive. English guns thus became items for export, particularly to the Dutch, in their wars against Spain.

Meanwhile, for the first time since the era of the Vikings, a Scandinavian country began to count in the 'world's game', as Pope Julius II put it. This was Sweden, which, with her charcoal forests and ample copper, tin and iron, began also to make guns. At first they were wrought-iron guns, then bronze, then cast-iron, in the English style. In the seventeenth century, Swedish cannon were sold all over Europe, numbers enough to 'equip a small fleet' often being exported in a single year. In contrast, the French arms industry, despite the efforts of Colbert, was sluggish, and the armies of Louis XIV bought abroad.

By now, artillery was not the only use for gunpowder. There was also the hand gun. This recalled the blow pipes used for Greek fire but it played a small part till the sixteenth century. The first hand gun was a weapon fired with a slow match applied to a touch hole in the barrel, in order to light the fire-priming powder on the firing pan. A match lock followed, with an arm, which, when the trigger was pulled, brought the match down on to the priming. That was a faster method, but the match had to be kept alight. That was difficult to assure in the middle of a battle. Some of these weapons nevertheless were effective: Talbot, Earl of Shrewsbury, was actually killed with a hand gun in the last battle of the Hundred Years' War, in 1452 (15). Rifled hand guns, as devised in Leipzig in 1498, were common in central Europe during the sixteenth century.* Then, about 1525, the Italians devised a pistol with a wheel lock, which was favoured for a long time for use mounted. A key was used to wind a spring, whose release turned a rough wheel against pyrites. The sparks so caused touched the priming. But the winding meant that the weapon could not be fired quickly twice. So its use was confined to cavalrymen. They would fire and then charge, sword in hand. Other hand guns were soon made: for example, the arquebus (from the German *Hakenbuhse*, or hookgun, from the hooked shape of the butt); and the musket. The first may have been in use in the late fifteenth century. At all events, Spanish arquebusiers were in action at Pavia in 1525, so originating the modern infantry force. Filippo Strozzi of Milan enabled that weapon to be effective from five hundred paces. Muskets (from the Italian *moschetto*, a sparrow hawk) were heavier and more powerful than the arquebus (they were effective from 600 paces), firing, to begin with, from a rest stuck into the ground, and using a matchlock.

The rifle, meantime, had probably been devised about 1475, though it was scarcely used for military purposes till the Thirty Years' War. Until then, rifles had mainly been for rich sportsmen who could afford to pay for accuracy when shooting at birds — a new sport — and did not mind the slow business of filling up the barrel by a ram-rod — activities far too time-wasting in war. But, about 1630, something like a modern rifle was made possible when a flintlock rifle was devised in France. A flint was pulled back and, when the trigger was released, it was driven by a strong spring against a rough metal plate over a firing pan, into which

* A 'rifled' gun is one with spiral grooves in its barrel.

sparks flew. That system was quickly adapted to the musket and, when made lighter, it could be used simply from the shoulder, without a stand.

The rifle of those days could only expect to be accurate for one hundred yards. It was not, therefore, yet a battle-winning weapon. Even so, it was introduced into the French army by Louis XIV. It was copied by both the English and the new German army of the Great Elector of Prussia, who also invented paper cartridges about 1670. The bayonet, a sword blade devised at Bayonne, and fixed on to a musket for use in infantry charges, completed the characteristic equipment of European soldiery of the eighteenth century, though a steel-headed pike on a shaft of wood remained the main weapon of foot soldiers till 1700.

These new weapons were all used previously outside Europe and by non-Europeans. Jewish gunsmiths helped the Muslim armies of Suleiman the Magnificent to develop field artillery. Field guns and siege guns were used in India by 1500. Chinese artillery was as good as European in the sixteenth century. But they did not make bronze guns as satisfactorily as was done in the West, and their cast iron was by 1600 less well made than the British or Swedish type.

The explanation of this failure by the Chinese to exploit their great advantages has been touched on before. It will remain one of the great problems of history and no explanation is entirely satisfactory. The careful system of supplies, training, and tactics, in, for example, China during the Tang dynasty (618–907 AD) would have made their forces superior to those of any Western army of that time. But, in the seventeenth century, by a bizarre irony, the Portuguese tried to prevent the knowledge of modern foundries passing to the East, as the Chinese had tried so often to do with their own best inventions. Eventually the secret was communicated to China, apparently by the Jesuits, who are understood to have offered to pass on what they knew in return for the right to set up missions. Even so, the Chinese continued to make only small iron guns, able to attack castles yet inadequate against the big walls of new fortified cities. Perhaps the Chinese government feared internal bandits as much as foreign invasion. There was, of course, also no internal arms' trade in China – unlike, say, Italy, where Francesco Datini, 'the merchant of Prato', in Iris Origo's book of that name, was busy as an arms' dealer in the early fifteenth century (10). In England, the ironsmiths who wished to sell guns abroad won their arguments successfully against an initially sceptical Crown. They had no equivalent in China, where the all-powerful rulers controlled every craftsman in their country's arsenal. The low social status of the craftsman was yet one more reason for the failure of China to take advantage of her early advanced technology.

Admittedly, Chinese junks were able to compete against Western sailing ships for mercantile activities, though they never made effective men-of-war. The Korean navy in the sixteenth century put long-range artillery on their ships, an idea which was taken over by the Japanese. But that era of Japanese expansion was short and ended in the 1630s, when Shogun Tokugawa Iemitsu, who desired to avoid all foreign influences, both banned his countrymen from sailing anywhere, and prohibited the manufacture of ocean-going ships. That decree, short-sighted or sagacious as it may alternately seem, delayed Japanese inter-national action for 250 years. Though the Chinese governments were more open, Chinese society was equally resistant to change. Chinese gunpowder remained curiously second-rate in the late sixteenth century. Their firearms were bad, while their old bamboo pikes, shar-pened by fire or with iron tips, like their scimitars of iron or tin cui-rasses, were no match for those of the West. Even Western manufacture overseas could not compete with European products (17).

In the late sixteenth century, some 70% of Spanish state revenue was spent on weapons, and two-thirds of the revenue of other European countries probably also went thus (18). Yet, by both the standards of antiquity and of the modern era, numbers concerned in battles were still small: at Lepanto, 208 Christian galleys faced 230 Turkish ones (19). The total English fleet at the Armada in 1588 numbered 2000 ships. Fairfax had only 26,000 men at Marston Moor: but that was, as Dr Laslett says, 'one of the largest crowds assembled before Napoleonic times in England' (20). The Spaniards at Rocroy also numbered 26,000 (21). That did not mean that wars were modest affairs. The Thirty Years' War cost Mecklenburg 80% of its population and other parts of Germany not much less. The murders, the loss of harvests, the thefts, the epidemics, the 'sackings' of towns reproduced for Germany, on a worse scale, the troubles experienced during the Hundred Years' War in France (22). In Bohemia, only 6000 villages out of 35,000 were considered habitable after the Thirty Years' War, and the population there is said to have fallen from 2 million to 700,000 at that time (23).

A great effort, meantime, was made in the sixteenth century to revive the fortress against the new threat of artillery. Cities in zones of war went to enormous trouble to create new systems of defence, such as Perugia's projecting towers 'spread out like a man's hand' – thereby, it was hoped, putting the heart of the city beyond the reach of enemy guns. These elaborate fortifications, the *traces italiennes*, as they were known, designed by engineers, mathematicians and artists (Michel-angelo helped to plan Florence's fortifications in 1527) took over from simple walls of masonry, placing a great burden of expense on the local municipality, and everywhere rendering more difficult the survival of small states and cities which did not have powerful friends. Because of them the siege and not the pitched battle became the characteristic form of European land warfare for nearly a hundred years.

The elaborate grandeur of these fortresses began to be rendered ineffective after the development of the telescope in 1590, which vastly improved the accuracy of artillery. The concurrent increased mobility of supplies, on slowly improving canals and roads and better organised commissariats, gave an impetus to the mobile army such as had not been seen since the early Middle Ages. In reply, military engineers discovered that earth was a better fortification against cannon than brick. Outworks suddenly counted far more than traditional ramparts.

The civil wars of the late sixteenth and seventeenth centuries, (the French and English Civil Wars, the Fronde, the Thirty Years' War, the Eighty Years' War between Spain and the Netherlands), saw in many countries the establishment anew of standing armies. It is true that England, then the most vigorous country and the one most commercially successful, ultimately avoided such a development. But most other strong countries usually set up such armies, and thereby simplified the art of government. Military barracks had the same place in baroque Europe as monasteries had in mediaeval Europe. *Champs de Mars*, arsenals, and large squares designed for review became the characteristic of the new fixed capitals, while turning, drilling, parading, blaring of the bugle and beating the tattoo, were, as Lewis Mumford suggests, the new ceremonial in an age when the Church had lost its greatest appeal (24). The big guns of the new artillery meant that force was concentrated in fewer hands. The artillery-powered empires needed, in return, heavy and regular taxation. Perhaps that was less destructive than chaos (25). Jacob Burckhardt, indeed, regarded the introduction of firearms as doing 'its part in making war a democratic pursuit' because, henceforth, the skills of humbly-born technicians, such as engineers, were as important as that of noblemen (26).

In old books of history, the role of war was often exaggerated, and even those who wrote of war often neglected the ordinance and the sources of energy needed. But war determined the frontiers of states, and decisively affected the character of governments which, in the age of enlightenment as in that of agriculture, remained primarily (perhaps indeed, in the seventeenth century, increasingly) organisations for managing armies, though not necessarily for the waging of war. It also benefitted the revival of capitalism (27). Firms such as De Geer and Trip of Amsterdam established themselves as munitions' merchants of the Thirty Years' War, supplying not only Sweden and the States General in Holland but also sometimes their own Spanish opponents. In the English Civil War, the same firm supplied both the King and the Covenanters, and later supplied the Tsar of Russia (28). Critics of military investments by governments sometimes forget that the era before standing armies was one of private armies, often creating a most savage series of conditions even in years of formal peace. Standing armies, coming in from the seventeenth century onwards, helped to humanise war, since they were disciplined, and accepted rules. They emphasised a distinction between civilian and military targets. Everywhere where big guns were established, the effect was originally to concentrate force in fewer hands and, despite the bloodshed when one cannon-owning state quarrelled with another one, more responsible ones. In the eighteenth century, 'gunpowder empires' undoubtedly led to a superior level of peace, by assisting the growth of the idea that 'all damage done to the enemy unnecessarily . . . is a licentiousness condemned by the law of nature' (29). Thus though war was certainly ceasing to be chivalrous, it could not be said to have returned immediately to barbarism.

Appendix to Chapter 24

POPULATIONS OF CITIES IN 1800

Canton 1,236,000
London 1,117,000
Constantinople between 300,000–1,000,000
Madras c.800,000
Calcutta 700,000 (1814)
Paris 547,000
Nanking 500,000 (approx estimate, 1843)
Ningpo 500,000 (approx estimate, 1843)
Soochow 500,000 (approx estimate, 1843)
Naples 427,000
Shanghai 270,000 (approx estimate, 1843)
Moscow 250,000
Vienna 247,000
St Petersburg 220,000
Amsterdam 201,000
Cairo 200,000 (approx)
Hyderabad c. 200,000
Peking 200,000 (approx)
Lisbon 180,000
Berlin 175,000
Dublin 165,000
Rome 163,000

Madrid 160,000
Bombay 150,000
Delhi 150,000
Palermo 139,000
Mexico c. 137,000
Milan 135,000
Venice 134,000
Hamburg 130,000
Rio de Janeiro 125,000
Marseilles 111,000
Lyons 110,000
Cadiz 100,000
Copenhagen 100,000
Valencia 100,000
Warsaw 100,000
Florence 78,093
Lima 64,000 (1812)
Havana 51,037
Philadelphia 42,444
New York 33,121
Boston 18,028
Alexandra estimated at a few thousands

25

People, Medicine and Food of the Renaissance

Another consequence of the 'revolution' in communications brought by printing was the beginning of modern medicine. For, in the sixteenth century, the world was enabled by the wide circulation of medical tracts to shake off at last the effects of over a thousand years of the influence of Galen. As a result, Paracelsus, a Swiss of wide culture, to whom humanity is indebted for the word 'alcohol', sensibly wrote, 'It is nature's balsam, not the surgeon's interference, that heals wounds.' Girolamo Fracastoro worked out in Verona a rational theory of infection, which he rightly regarded as being caused by the passage of minute bodies to the affected person. (Fracastoro also wrote a poem, '*Syphilis sive morbus gallicus*', a fantasy about the shepherd Syphilis, who insulted Apollo, and, therefore, received a vile disease. Hence the name of the venereal disease then beginning, as a result of the discovery of America, to make its mark on Europe)*. At the same time, Miguel Serveto (Servetus), a brilliant Navarrese (born in Tudela), discovered that blood was pumped to the lungs by the arteries. He was, however, as has been earlier indicated, burned alive in Geneva, after being tried for religious eccentricities which he had expressed in some private letters addressed to Calvin. Vesalius of Brussels, professor at Padua, then revived the study of anatomy and had an immediate effect on surgery. Above all, he influenced military surgery, that being the sphere where most good surgeons then gained their experience – so much so indeed that all surgery seemed, for a long time, to be military; otherwise, a few barbers pretended to 'chirurgeonly' expertise. That became even more the case after the French wars in Italy confirmed the importance of gunpowder – an innovation with effects at first so alarming that it was even supposed that wounds caused by it might be poisoned. Ambroise Paré, a French military surgeon, who served King

* Syphilis seems not to have been known in Europe before Columbus brought back some Indians from Cuba on his first voyage, in 1492. Taken to Naples, it caused devastation in Charles VIII's army there the following year (1).

François I, was the first to appreciate the importance of an understanding of anatomy for effective surgery. He also realised that wounds healed better if they were not cauterised with burning oil, or otherwise treated with fire, as had happened ever since the remotest days (Aeschylus refers to it in his *Agamemnon* in 450 BC), and saw that dead tissue in the wound was itself a danger. Paré's realisation of such simple, but previously unrecognised, truths, as well as his unerring skill in finding exactly where a bullet lay in the body, made him a genuine pioneer. His contemporary, Alfonso Ferri, proved that all foreign bodies in a wound had to be removed for an effective cure to be possible. Painters of the Renaissance, meantime, concerned themselves with the anatomy as much as the doctors did. Leonardo, for example, realised that Galen was wrong about the interconnection of heart and lungs (2).

The medical advances of the sixteenth century were largely the work of the Southern Europeans. But Italian intellectual life declined after the Spanish conquests. Spanish life also itself became stagnant — even if Don Quixote was wise enough to realise that 'a tooth is more important than a diamond'. The innovators of the next generations were mainly Protestants, from England and Holland. Thus Zacharias Jansen, a spectacle-maker, of Middleburg in Holland, discovered the microscope and William Harvey, an ex-student at Padua, built on Serveto's groundwork to show that the arteries pump the blood away from the heart, while the veins carry it back again. Thus the movement of blood was shown to be continuous and in the same direction. It was an Englishman too, Thomas Sydenham, a Dorsetshire physician, a protégé of Cromwell's, who wrote that 'disease . . . however prejudicial soever it may be to the body is no more than a vigorous effort of Nature to destroy the mortific matter and thus recover the patient' (3).

During the following century, a Dutch Protestant scientist, Leeuwenhoek, using a magnifying glass, picked out bacteria, and showed that muscles are made up of fibres of their own. His German colleague, Kepler, explained that short- and long-sightedness derive from the crystalline lens of the eye bringing rays of light to a focus which is not in the retina (4). Robert Hooke found the cells, Jan Swammerdam found the red corpuscle. Boerhaave founded a great medical school at Leyden. The reign of the surgeon who was more barber than scientist came to an end. Since then, surgeons have had to have proven training for their work. Next, John Hunter, a British army surgeon, described the nature of shock and of inflammation. Pierre Fauchard wrote the first serious book on the care of teeth. Other Frenchmen gained great if often undeserved reputations for their operations to extract stones in the bladder, a characteristic complaint of the seventeenth century, mostly caused by a bad diet. Still, effective surgery was confined to that, along with trepanning, amputation, incision of abscesses, and cataracts. Operations for these were performed better in the eighteenth century than ever before.

But they had little effect on the death rate.

The same was true of all medicine. Even in Florence, the great city of the Renaissance, the ignorance was still such that, in the eighteenth century, the population believed that the two last representatives of the house of Medici, Grand Duke Gian Gastone and his sister, the Electress Anna Maria Luisa, were carried off in a 'hurricane of wind': 'The Devil came for them in a *temporale*,' wrote the English consul ironically. Casanova thought that, in his day, more people perished 'at the hands of doctors than are purged by them' (5). Cellini's doctor, Maestro Francesco, two centuries before, seeing his patient improve, without much effort by him, said wisely, 'O powers of nature! She knows her own needs; the doctors know nothing' (6). Maestro Francesco was unusual only in his recognition of his ignorance. In the eighteenth century, a few drugs were used but probably fewer and less effectively than in old Babylon or Egypt. Nothing was known for use against typhus or puerperal fever. Charms were still widely believed in, even in Europe. King Charles II purported to cure thousands by the ancient technique of touching in the 1660's (7). The bleeding and purges proffered by many doctors were worse than useless for most patients (8). True, there was a marked increase in the number of hospitals in the eighteenth century. England, for example, had only five in 1700, of which two were in London, and, in 1800, there were fifty. But those frightful institutions were, to begin with, worse than useless. No one, for example, knew at that time the importance of isolation or of hygiene. As late as 1854, cholera patients were admitted to a general ward in London. Any patient admitted to hospital then ran a severe risk of contracting a mortal infection (9). Death risks in the early lying-in hospitals were usually greater than at home. The beginning of the use of forceps, in the eighteenth century, and other artificial means for assisting the delivery of babies, also had a bad effect for the same reason, that nobody realised the desirability of cleanliness.

The fall in the death rate which did occur in the eighteenth century was probably due less to medicine than to 'improvements in the environment' (10) as some modern scholars put it, and to better food. Obviously, the questions of death rates and birth rates are interrelated, for any increase in the birth rate is rendered ineffective by very high mortality among infants. As a rule, a decline in the birth rate follows, in most societies, a decline of the death rate, by several generations. During the generations when the rates differ, the population goes up. The least prolific of couples can easily double their number in twenty years. If that were to happen always, high increases in population would occur everywhere. But that expansion in the remote past met resistance from the environment: wild species usually multiply up to a point where mortality and fertility are equal. That balance was achieved in human history too. It was disturbed in the eighteenth century, apparently by, as is now generally accepted by demographic historians, an increase in the birth rate.

Why should that have occurred? It cannot have been the consequence of an increased demand for labour. On the contrary, the rise led to rural poverty in England and occurred everywhere in Europe and elsewhere too, so far as can be seen. In England, the population's increase expanded the labour available at a rate faster than agriculture could absorb it and produced the large number of landless, often unemployable, labourers observable in all sorts of villages, both enclosed and open (11). Actually, industrialisation in the eighteenth century probably saved Europe from the effects of over-population, as emigration to the Americas would do in the nineteenth.

The rise in population in the eighteenth century was, in fact, comparable to that of the thirteenth, of which it was, to a great extent, a continuation, after a long interruption. It was assisted (as seen earlier) by a decline in great epidemics, such as plague, and by the optimism which the disappearance of plague itself betokened. It may have been affected by the improvement in diet following the discovery of America, and must have been assisted by the improvements in European agriculture, though it is as well to notice that the increase in population was as great, indeed even greater, in the eighteenth century, in Russia, where the improvements in both diet and agriculture were scarcely noticeable. Perhaps the creation of strong states and an end of private wars were as important as anything. (Yet the strongest state in the eighteenth century was France, which grew in population less than any other country.) Asia, and particularly China, was also better administered in the eighteenth century than before. The population of the Americas was being increased by interior immigration and continual movement, though not yet keeping up with the ravages of plague. At that time, only in Japan were there any official restrictions on birth, such as encouragements to celibacy, late marriage and even abortion. But, in the East in general, newborn children were often abandoned, and some African tribes and Pacific islands still practised infanticide.

The country which increased its population least in the eighteenth century, so far as we know, was France; that which grew most as a result of natural increase, rather than immigration, was Russia. Did France's population fail to grow in order that holdings might not be subdivided? Did Russia's grow because of the realisation that there was land available in the east and south, newly conquered? Neither country anyway made substantial contributions to the coming of industrialisation, though France did more than Russia. If, though, the population of France had multiplied at the same rate as did that of the French settlers in Canada, it would be to-day far greater than the population of the whole earth (12).

Europe was, of course, by the eighteenth century, the focus of the world's vital forces. Its population was, however, still modest in comparison with modern times. France and the Empire each then had about 20 million people, Italy 15 million, Russia 14 million and Britain and Spain had about 7 million each. The biggest states in Germany, Prussia and Bavaria, numbered only 2 million and 1½ million respectively. As for cities, by 1750 London and Paris each numbered about 600,000 to 700,000. Lyons was the only other French city over 100,000 (it was about 110,000). No other English city was larger than 100,000. Glasgow and Liverpool would number 80,000 each in 1801. Naples was then the only Italian city over 150,000, and Rome was a little less than that, Venice had dropped to 140,000, Milan 100,000, Florence and Genoa and Turin almost 70,000 each. Only three central European cities had populations over 100,000 − Vienna (225,000), Hamburg (150,000) and Berlin (140,000). In comparison, both China's and India's populations were probably over 100 million each, and a total population of 450 million already for Asia might be a correct estimate (13).

Africa's population in 1750 is hard to guess. 100 million? It could not have been much more. The Americas were the emptiest of the big continents, in 1750 perhaps numbering 2 million in the North, 15 million in the South. Half the population of the North were white, but only a fifth were so in the South. The rest were Indian, Negro, or mixed, in one way or another. Australia's population was still negligible.

There are, however, some special points to be made about population in the eighteenth century, particularly in respect of marriage where Europe (and the US), as in so many other things, begin to be differentiated from the rest of the world. First of all, in most of the world and probably as in mediaeval Europe, too, people married young, and the vast majority married. Very few people remained single: perhaps 2% or 3% at most. But in western Europe about 1500 or 1600, and certainly by 1750, people married late, and the number of bachelors and spinsters in their late forties approached 16% or 17% (14). This pattern was reversed somewhat, for the first time, after 1945,* so that Dr Laslett can tell us provocatively that 'despite Romeo and Juliet, all records declare that in Elizabethan England, marriage was rare at fourteen and not as common in the late 'teens as it is now' (15).

The first question which occurs to someone who is not a student of demography is, how was it possible in primitive societies and indeed apparently in nearly every society except Western Europe between 1500 and 1945 to arrange that nearly every woman married? That seems specially difficult to imagine since most people lived in small communities of a few hundred and the number of possible partners, small at the beginning, was reduced by conventions and castes. Was the profes-

---

* Perhaps because of the fall in the age of sexual maturity of women during the last few generations which has been widely noticed, never explained.

sional marriage broker responsible? Or polygamy? Or the fact that, in primitive societies, remarriage was, and is universal – as indeed it was in mediaeval Europe, despite the Church's disapproval (16)? This question is not easy to answer unless it is appreciated that one of the main preoccupations of primitive society was to arrange marriages, while a great deal of attention was paid to marriage rituals which played, and play, a critical part in the entertainment of the population, partly because bridesmaids and pages, in whatever form they took, appeared as the potential bridal pairs of the future. A marriage feast was an occasion to show off the potentialities of other daughters, as well as to celebrate the wedding.

The second question is, why did the change away from marriage occur in western Europe? Now to this, Professor Hajnal of Oslo has an answer. He attributes it to a change in landholding. The collapse of feudalism created small holdings with single heirs who often naturally waited for their fathers to die and leave them the farm. Large estates and large households, such as still existed in eastern Europe, could absorb the youngest married couple much more easily (17). This may be part of the explanation. But there is another one: and that is the cult of romantic love which was the most striking change in the western world since the Renaissance.

Dr Johnson dismissed love as an artificial emotion invented by novelists and adopted, by both men and women, as a cover for sexual desire (18). The cult was certainly invented in Europe by the Provençal troubadours (perhaps deriving from the Arabs), stimulated by chivalry and began to be diffused (despite Dante's passionate views on the matter*), it would seem, to a wide audience, only after the invention of the printing press. It was an idea further embellished, as Johnson implied, by writers, in the seventeenth and eighteenth centuries, and made into a mass cult by popular novelists, mass circulation magazines, and films in the twentieth century. Certainly, the concept of romantic love made old-fashioned ideas of arranged marriage more and more unacceptable and that interpretation began earlier than is generally supposed: Benvenuto Cellini's father, for example, married for love in the late fifteenth century (19). At all earlier times, and in most primitive societies subsequently, marriages have been arranged or even settled by lot, as was the case with the Moravians in the US, in the eighteenth century, against whom Benjamin Franklin complained. (Franklin said, 'If the matches are not made by the mutual choice of the parties, some of them may chance to be very unhappy.' 'And so they may,' answered his interlocutor, 'if you let the parties choose for themselves.' 'Which indeed, I could not deny' (20).) Laurence Stone points out that, before the Renaissance, marriage was not an intimate association, based upon choice, but a

* I refer to the history of Paolo and Francesca.

means of tying together two families (21). He also argues that this concept of a marriage, as an alliance between two families, was itself a development of the later Middle Ages since, earlier, marriage seemed a very informal affair in Europe with much casual polygamy and even polyandry, many bastards and relatively easy divorce (at least till the Hildebrandine reforms).*

Now Professor Hajnal suggests that we should see, in these European 'marriage patterns' of the Renaissance and afterwards, the real reason for the growth of modern capitalism. For, he says, these habits gave many people, even most people, a period during which savings would be easier since they had no responsibility for children. Those who did not save demanded goods other than what might be needed for immediate survival. From the Renaissance onwards, the whole culture of Europe, particularly northern and Protestant Europe, stimulated the growth of an attitude of mind in which people were persuaded not to marry until they were able to support a family. No doubt Professor Hajnal is correct to mention this as one cause, as important as Protestantism or coal, of the birth of the new capitalist spirit. But we must beware of finding a new idea attractive because of itself, particularly in this complicated arena; Confucius also believed marriage should be delayed till thirty for men, and twenty for women (23); Aristotle thought men should marry at thirty-nine (24).

Furthermore, a state of affairs comparable to that which prevailed in the Renaissance probably for the first time prevailed in Rome too. In the time of Hadrian, Professor Carcopino assures us, a father did not dream of forcing his daughter to marry against her will (25). In Rome between about 100 BC and 100 AD, the concept of romantic love certainly had, as it were, an early demonstration, as the poems of Catullus suggest. Love poems were similarly written in ancient Egypt (26).

The most likely single explanation for the swift increase in the world's population in the eighteenth century was the improvement of food almost everywhere. That was partly a result of better and more enlightened agriculture, as will be discussed later.† However, a more striking agricultural change than anything in the sixteenth century was the transformation caused by the export of certain plants to America and the import of some American crops to the old world, Europe, Asia and Africa included. Like most events of the Renaissance, this history has its origins in the Middle Ages.

Rice, for example, had been carried to Europe by the Arabs from China. In the early Middle Ages, it was being sold at the fairs of Champagne. Though grown in several Mediterranean countries and, there-

---

* For example, the daughters of the Cid were divorced, the daughter of the first count of Castile was married three times etc, (22).
† Considered in detail below, see page 353.

fore, well established in Italy by the time of the Renaissance, it was regarded as a supplement to corn in an emergency, never tempting those (the rich) who decided the fashions and owned the land. Rice was thus grown in Mediterranean countries only sporadically. But the Spaniards' discoveries and conquests in America had a greater effect. They brought to Europe maize, tomatoes, potatoes,* turkeys, jerusalem artichokes and chocolate.† The discoveries in America also led to the cultivation there, on a large scale, of sugar and coffee, which are plants indigenous to the South Seas and Ethiopia respectively. The more regular journeys eastwards stimulated a trade in tea from China and later stimulated the cultivation of tea elsewhere in the East. Both were encouraged by imports of sugar from the West Indies.

Nor was the benefit Europe's alone. Indeed, if such new foods in Europe are considered against those made available to Africa and America as a result of the discoveries, the greater gain might seem to accrue to the latter. American crops such as papaya, sweet potatoes, pineapples, and potatoes, not to speak of maize, manioc (cassava) and groundnuts, were taken to Africa, while wheat, chickpeas, sugar cane, beans, bananas, rice, citrus fruits, yams, coffee, breadfruit, and coconuts, as well as sheep, horses and cattle, went to the Americas and, ultimately, to Australasia. These changes were probably the most important ones ever in the history of agriculture and, therefore, in that of food. The staple crops of the Guinea and Congo forests are today maize and manioc, for instance.‡ The changes were, ironically, the result of journeys serviced by sailors who themselves lived on dried cod, jerked (*charqui*) beef, salt pork, dried peas and ships' biscuits often alive with weevils. Much of the food of those who themselves inspired the world's greatest dietary revolution was probably damp, too. Wood absorbs much water when it floats. Thus it was hard to keep anything dry in old ships. Ships' biscuits, dried to hardness so that they were impossible to break by hand, were edible for fifty years if mixed with water, but fresh water was rarely in lavish supply. Then, it was realised by physicians in 1600 that citrus fruits were effective against scurvy. But it was not till the late eighteenth century that anyone took any action. Ships, thereafter, issued a daily ration of lemon juice after the fifth or sixth week out.

The immediate effect of this revolution in European agriculture and diet should not be exaggerated. Bread, cheese, meat and beer continued to be the regular foods of the poor in eighteenth century England. Gruel

---

* See below page 377.
† Chocolate was introduced to Europeans as a drink. Though slabs of chocolate were known in Spain c.1520, it took the mass manufacturers of the nineteenth century to make solid chocolate popular and cheap.
‡ The banana and both the Asian Yam and the Coco Yam were South Eastern Asian plants which probably reached Africa about 100 AD.

or soup, bread, cider and bad wine, fish and meat, dominated French food till the Revolution. Only in the late eighteenth century did sugar and potatoes begin to have a serious effect in a few countries. Tomatoes, though domesticated in Mexico before 1492, and taken to Europe before 1550, were unpopular for several centuries, for they were looked on as potentially poisonous because of their connection with the nightshade family (27). But the effect on the Americas of the Spanish import of horses and cattle was immediate. The horse even changed the North American Indian from being a farmer to becoming a nomad once again. Of course, there were many other extraordinary consequences: once the Europeans began offering European goods, for example, in exchange for furs, the Indians began to hunt wild animals with unrestrained energy and so destroyed the old equilibrium which they had attained in the past. The beaver in particular was almost killed off.

The Reformation and Renaissance in northern Europe also had some interesting effects on habits of drinking. Thus the use of hops began in Holland for brewing as a development of its other market gardening activities. It was said that: 'Hops, Reformation, bays and beer, Came into England all in one year' (28).

This enabled beer to be kept much longer and, after initial suspicion, it began to be popular in northern Europe from the Renaissance onwards (the ale of the past could not be kept more than a few days unless it was brewed strong) (29). From that time, a great variety of beers became available, from 'stout' to 'small beer' – a table drink for children (an allowance at Christ's Hospital school in London in the seventeenth century allocated each boy about 2½ gallons a week (30)). Though home-brewing somewhat declined, a very great deal of it apparently continued.

Britain was the first country to decide that the sale of alcohol was a different matter from the sale of other foods and drinks, and acts regulating the sale of beer characterise the English statute books, from the fifteenth century onwards. (Edward VI also devised a law whereby drink could only be sold at licensed places (31)). Towards the end of the age of agriculture in the 1720s, Benjamin Franklin recalled a typical occurrence in London: 'We had an alehouse boy who attended always in the house to supply the workmen. My companion in the press drank every day a pint before breakfast, a pint at breakfast . . . a pint between breakfast and dinner; a pint at dinner; a pint in the afternoon, about 6, and another when he had done his work'. He did this because he thought it made him strong. Franklin said that it couldn't be so, but he was unpersuadable 'and spent four to five shillings out of his wages every Saturday night' (32). By that time, however, beer, even in England, was being challenged by a new form of alcoholic drink: spirits.

Spirits were not known to the Romans. Their origin is obscure. Alchemists perhaps knew of the principle of distillation in the first century

AD. But the best claim to have invented them is that of Arnau de Vilanova, a Catalan physician who distilled alcoholic spirits from wine in the late eleventh century, in order to treat wounds. He also discovered that, if mixed with aromatic plants, the spirit would become palatable (33). The Chinese, on the other hand, are also believed to have invented a still even earlier.* At all events, stills in Europe are not known to have existed before the early Middle Ages. Arnau de Vilanova gave his drink when made from grape juice or wine the name of *aqua vitae* since, he said, it 'preserved youth, revived the heart, cured colic, dropsy and paralysis, calmed toothache and gave protection against plague' (34). (The Germans called this 'brande win' – burnt wine –, hence brandy in English.) The appeal of these 'spirits' was, however, slow to spread. A few monastery gardens began to experiment with mixing exotic herbs with spirits, and began the long tradition of monastic liqueurs. Spirits were given a stimulus of a sort by the Black Death. Physicians prescribed brandy for psychological as well as therapeutic reasons (35). But by the end of the fourteenth century, little was being drunk for pleasure. It was left for the countries of the reformed Christian Church to bring in the diversity of alcoholic spirits which have altered the drinking habits of the modern world so strikingly.

The inspirers of this innovation were the Dutch. It was they who, in their commercial activities, helped to make available a new range of spirits: not only those distilled from wine, such as cognac, armagnac, marc, but also calvados, from apple juice or cider, kirsch from cherries, gin from juniper berries (*ginevra*), vodka from grain (the Russians learned little from Europe in the sixteenth century, but they did learn the art of distilling), *aguardiente*, from the juice of sugar cane, and, finally, whisky, an Irish and Scottish spirit, distilled from malted barley or rye for the first time apparently in the sixteenth century. Everywhere in that century, it is evident, drunkenness increased, encouraged by the Dutch. Several old drinks such as mead (previously drunk a good deal in both England and Russia) disappeared after distilling became a well-known process (37).

Thus, in the last part of the age of agriculture, a new world opened to lovers of alcohol. Peasants such as those in Russia could 'pass', says Richard Pipes, 'quickly from abstinence to stupor' (38). In the Americas, brandy, rum and *aguardiente*, as well as a brandy (*mezcal*), made from the Mexicans' own drink of *pulque* (the juice from the heart of the maguey cactus) rivalled smallpox as Europe's 'poisoned gifts' to the New World (39). European stills were probably carried to China at the same time (40). Rum, another, lighter, product of sugar cane through

---

* Though beware of too early an accreditation: thus Joseph Needham writes, 'Dependence on the translation of a deservedly eminent sinologist could lead to an entirely unjustified belief in the knowledge and the use of distillation in the 1st century' (36).

molasses, was also developed in the seventeenth century. It became the standby of the British Navy.*

Everywhere the Dutch Empire extended, the desire for spirit went too. The Dutch wars of the seventeenth century might have been won by the English but, English drinkers were soon conquered by the Dutch taste for gin.

The seventeenth century also saw the emergence of such refinements as champagne, port and other lightly-spiced wines, the second being preservable almost indefinitely, like spirits. Thus the drinker in the eighteenth century had a wider range of choice than at any previous time. Furthermore, the age of the discriminating drinker was now beginning. Corks were used to stop bottles and enable even unspiced wine to be kept for years. Bottles were laid on their side in racks. The cylindrical bottle of the present-day size came into being during the eighteenth century. Special vintages began to be sought. But eighteenth century London was also recklessly bibulous. Spirits could be sold everywhere without licence and little tax. It was said that, about 1750, every fourth house in St Giles's Circus sold gin (41). Special 'straw houses' existed where anyone could get drunk for a few pence and where the landlord gave straw to those unable to walk home. Beer drinking suffered a severe drop. Nor was it only England that sold vast quantities of spirits: there was so much cheap brandy in Catalonia that, for a time, the world price was set by the market at the little town of Reus (42). Brandy was, with cotton, really the basis of a Catalan Renaissance. Rum too had an empire of its own, based on Jamaica. Vast quantities were available to all the navies and armies which haunted the Caribbean. Benjamin Franklin recalls that, in his expeditionary force to Canada in 1757, it was agreed that the chaplain, a Presbyterian, should give out the rum ration – a gill of rum a day – after morning prayers: 'Never were prayers more generally and more punctually attended' (43).

Drunkenness greatly increased in the generations following. Most observers thought that it increased in particular in Paris and Madrid, in whose popular taverns much could be drunk without paying the urban tax levied on wine. Later, the wine trade became the subject of politically inspired tariffs: for example, the Navigation Acts in England in the seventeenth century excluded much brought from France or Germany in Dutch ships, while Lord Methuen's Act of 1702 in England imposed a tariff on French wines, to inaugurate the era of 'port' (44). The drinking went on apace.

Why did not the Spaniards take the vine to the Americas, except, very

---

* Rum was given out neat in the British Navy till 1740. Then Admiral Vernon issued rations of rum and water which, since he wore a cloak of 'grogram' cloth in bad weather, was known as 'grog'. In the Napoleonic wars, lemon was added and, later, lime: hence, limey.

late, to Chile and California? Whatever the reason, Spanish America preferred to import its wine, like most other things, including flour and olive oil; and native America continued to subsist on maize, manioc and pulque. The colonists presumably preferred the importing of wine to its propagation, while the shippers wanted the colonists' custom.

Europe and the Mediterranean became, in the last stages of the age of agriculture, a civilisation based almost as much on wine as on wheat. Like grain, wine could be, and, in many instances, had to be, traded. Christianity, with its emphasis on the sacramental part played by wine, emphasised its necessity. From the days of ancient Egypt, wine also played a steady role in European commerce. In other civilisations, men have been content to drink what has been locally available. No great trade has ever been necessary in pulque or rice wine — nor in the fermented water which served as an alcohol in many parts of India.

The days of the Renaissance began, however, another 'revolution' in food apart from the growth of spirits, vegetables and the potato. That was the beginning of a change in the physical way that people ate their food. That had definite consequences on health.

Most people in the age of agriculture in Europe carried a knife for general purposes. Forks, on the other hand, had been used for hundreds of years only in kitchens, with two prongs, like garden forks. In Byzantium, it is true, small, two-pronged forks were employed at dinners from the tenth century. But they were not known even in rich houses in Italy till the sixteenth century, then being taken to France, it is said, by Catherine de' Medici on the occasion of her marriage, in 1533. They did not become popular, since they were expensive, difficult to make, and rare. Until the eighteenth century, most people in Europe went on eating with their fingers and a knife. Then mass-produced forks became possible, like knives, and indeed spoons, though those had always been common for serving soup. Men such as Matthew Boulton, whose other contributions to the Industrial Revolution in combination with Watt were so signal*, made their original fortune, it seems, in the manufacture of these small objects which are now taken for granted but which played so little part before 1750. Nor, before the eighteenth century, did many people have their own plates or drinking cups. People usually ate in pairs, one cover being enough to serve two. Poor diners in mediaeval Europe often had, instead of a plate, a thick slice of stale, unleavened bread, the 'trencher' of England's stout 'trenchermen'. It absorbed juice and might afterwards be eaten, or sometimes thrown away. By the eighteenth century, a wooden plate with a circular depression in the middle became common enough, and, by the early nineteenth, mass-produced 'china' followed: a vast benefit.

China, in this as in most things, had been early innovative and then

*See below page 251.

conservative. Chop-sticks were used there by at least 400 BC, and they thence spread to Japan. Nothing much changed afterwards. In the Americas, people had nothing more than a knife. In Africa the majority did not have even that, before 1750. India had knives but escaped the chop-stick, despite her use of rice.

The consequences for the growth of population of some of these developments must seem tenuous. New foods, new spirits, knives and forks, like the cult of love, may all be interpreted in different ways. One major occurrence of the sixteenth century, though, needs to be noticed because of the shadow that it caused to fall across the future history of Africa and America for the next few centuries and is continuously being reinterpreted.

Better roads undoubtedly enabled large numbers of French workers to go to Spain in the sixteenth century and from then onwards, of course, the Americas were a challenge and a magnet for the enterprising and ambitious left out of the banquet of life in Europe. The most extraordinary movement of labour, however, was that which took about nine million Africans to the Americas in what is known as the slave trade (45).

Slavery had almost ceased in Europe by the fifteenth century, but it had done so nowhere else, neither in the Eastern Mediterranean nor in North Africa. The idea was revived in Europe, primarily for domestic use, by the Portuguese when they began their travels around the west coast of Africa in the 1440s. Between then and the end of the fifteenth century, they established a flourishing trade. Sales to Spain began too. When the Spaniards founded plantations on which to grow sugar in the Canary Islands, they employed black slaves there. Though some slaves may have been kidnapped, most were sold by African chiefs, the slaves themselves being, as in antiquity, debtors, or prisoners captured in war, or criminals. The European interest vastly stimulated trade in slaves from Guinea, a territory which was previously a place mostly of subsistent farming and no large undertakings: but a trans-Saharan slave trade to the Red Sea from West Africa had been in existence since the tenth century for the benefit of Arabs (46).

Naturally, in the circumstances, Columbus, who had anyway interests in the Canaries, took slaves with him to the Americas and, by the end of the sixteenth century, the traffic in slaves to the Spanish colonies was already a profitable enterprise. Perhaps 275,000 slaves had gone by then to the Americas. The slaves worked in all sorts of undertakings, but especially in the mills founded for the grinding and manufacture of sugar from cane, which also was an import into the Americas from the old world. This industrial use of slaves reinvigorated an institution which, for some time, had been built around domestic employment. Slave traffic, in vile conditions, became more and more important, particularly when the French, British and above all Dutch colonists established themselves in the West Indies, alongside the Spaniards and Portuguese. According to an inspired historical statistician, Philip Curtin, probably about 340,000 slaves were carried to the Americas in the seventeenth century, perhaps 6 million in the eighteenth and perhaps 2 million in the nineteenth (47). The production of sugar remained the biggest slave enterprise. The gold mines of Brazil, the coffee fields of Sainte Domingue, the tobacco plantations of Virginia, and later those of cotton in the same place, also depended on this labour force, carried at great expense but even greater potential profit, from west or south-west Africa, where the trade had become much the most important commercial activity in the world by the eighteenth century. Probably the colonists of what became the US played a modest part in these imports: 400,000 slaves in all were probably imported there, for the large US black population of the present derives mostly from natural increase (48).

This revival of slavery by Europeans in the Americas was unexpected. By the fifteenth century, only the Spaniards and Portuguese among Europeans had anything like a slave code still in existence. Some have suggested that slaves received better treatment in Spanish colonies in America than in the Protestant North (49). That case is hard to sustain: Spanish slave laws, like other laws of that nature, and like so much other Spanish legislation, were indications of what might be hoped for, not what was actually done. Still, the small size of Spanish operations till the nineteenth century probably made conditions for slaves better in their colonies for many generations than they were in the huge plantations of the British and French West Indies. Spanish slaves, like Roman ones, could also buy their freedom. Domestic slaves throughout the Americas were in a privileged position and often gained their freedom in the end.

Sugar was mostly grown by slave labour till the nineteenth century and, for well over a hundred years at the most critical era of the world's commercial history, sugar was the most important item of commerce. To an old world previously used to the sparing use of sucrose provided by honey, West Indian sugar transformed diets. The merchants responsible for both sugar and slaves often accumulated fortunes – in Bristol, Liverpool, Nantes, Cadiz, Lisbon – and undoubtedly that helped to finance some part of the great capital enterprises of the Industrial Revolution (50), though detailed analysis would probably show that the greatest fortunes of the eighteenth century were made by men who equipped armies, not slave plantations (51).

Revolts of slaves in the West Indies often occurred. The small size of the islands, accompanied by the unmistakeable colour of the slaves, prevented any being of consequence until the late eighteenth century. The revolt in Sainte Domingue was successful. It ruined the French colony there. Out of the richest colony in the world, the rebels created the poorest republic (52). The result was to put the slave owners of the rest of the Americas on their watch. Revolts of slaves in North America were fewer. The consequence was ultimately to make the issue of the extension of slavery one of the main causes of the worst war the Americas have yet experienced; though the origins of the American civil war were at the time not so clear as they subsequently have seemed.*

The effects of the slave trade on Africa need to be measured too. During the early years, the African monarchs profited from the trade and the weapons, cloth, metal and spirits which they obtained in exchange had the effect of increasing the wealth of the peoples concerned. Harsh and insensitive comment though it may seem, the loss of population — which might have been about 40,000 persons a year at most — was economically acceptable (53). The loss, if loss it was in an economic sense, was more than compensated for by the wealth that accrued to the Gulf of Guinea as a result of trade with Europe. Angola and East Africa did suffer as a result of their losses of population, since they were less populous. But Guinea suffered political consequences. Large kingdoms came to be established just inland from the coast — such as Ashanti and Dahomey — in the creation of which firearms played a critical part but which were as much the creations of the slave trade as were Jamaica or Barbados (52). Arab slave traders, meantime, continued to ply their commerce generations after the British abandoned it; indeed, there seems every reason to believe that the trade flourishes still.

The Atlantic slave trade symbolises to many people the evils which they believe that the European expansion after the fifteenth century caused the world. Europe is held by some to have sacked the world in search of gold and forced remote continents into a humiliating dependency. Now, it is understandable that, in the late twentieth century, peoples which were, for many generations, subservient to western Europe should seek the reasons for that state of affairs, particularly if their new independence has brought many unresolved difficulties. It is also comprehensible that some good hearted North Americans and Europeans should look back in anger and astonishment at the ruthlessness with which their ancestors conducted their business. Yet these points of view seek to give a modern moral dimension to events in the past which are not really susceptible of such satisfying pigeon-holing. The course of action undertaken by the Europeans in the sixteenth and seventeenth centuries was comparable to that of all self-confident peoples in the past, and doubtless of the future. It is no use expecting a handful of squabbling European peoples to behave better than any

* The growth of the US slave population as a result of the cotton industry is discussed on page 290. The US also, in the course of the early nineteenth century, absorbed large territories such as those embraced by the 'Louisiana purchase' and the 'Missouri territory' which were already full of slaves.

other group has ever behaved in history. Nor can the benefits of European expansion be so easily brushed aside. The slave trade was recognised at the time by the Anglo-Saxons at least to constitute a moral retrogression. Otherwise, European intervention in continents far from home certainly transformed the politics of those regions, but it sometimes foiled the attempts of one aggressive local people to impose a tyranny over others which might have exceeded in brutality and destructiveness anything which even the Spaniards, 'the last of the warrior nomads', as Michael Howard speaks of the conquistadors, brought with them (54). If the Spaniards had not conquered the Caribbean, in the fifteenth century, the cannibalistic Caribs might easily have done so. That Europe was a disturbing force in the world between, say, 1450 and 1914 is obvious. But they brought with them ideas as well as naval guns and merchants. The Europeans did not always act in the tropics as if they were the fit representatives of the ideas of Christianity and the Rule of Law. But at least they brought those ideas within the reach almost of the entire population of the globe.

BOOK IV

Our Times I — Industrial Triumphs

.... From all these valuable presents which she had received from the gods, the woman was called Pandora, which intimates that she had received *every* necessary gift. . . . . Jupiter after this gave her a beautiful box which she was ordered to present to the man who married her. . . . Epimetheus opened the box . . . . there issued from it a multitude of evils and distempers which dispersed themselves all over the world and which, from that fatal moment, have never ceased to afflict the human race. Hope was the only one who remained at the bottom of the box. . . .

Lemprière's *Classical Dictionary*.

Few persons in the old world ever found themselves in groups larger than family groups and there were few families of more than a dozen members (including the extended family of uncles etc.). There was no object in England larger than St Paul's or London Bridge.

Peter Laslett, *The World we have lost*.

When Morland was appointed Minister of the Interior, a certain courtier who chanced to witness his arrival at Versailles exclaimed aghast:
'Merciful Heaven! Do you see? No buckles on his shoes.'
'Ah', returned General Dumouriez, 'Then all is lost.'

Stendhal, *Rome, Naples, Florence*

The French historian Rulhière, now forgotten, said, on being elected to the Academy in 1787, that 1749 was the year when the love of belles lettres was exchanged for philosophy, when the desire to please was replaced by the desire to instruct.

As recalled by Michael Levey, in *Rococo to Revolution*.

Talking of London, he observed, 'Sir, if you wish to have a just notion of the magnitude of this city, you must not be satisfied with seeing its great streets and squares, but must survey the innumerable little lanes and courts. It is not in the showy evolutions of buildings, but in the multiplicity of human habitations which are crowded together, that the wonderful immensity of London consists.'

Boswell, *Life of Johnson*, Vol. II

Since 1750, the world has been transformed by machines. Agriculture has benefited as much as manufacture. It requires an effort of imagination to realise that, in the lifetimes of the grandfathers of our grandfathers, the overwhelming majority of the world's population lived in the country and that was so in the lifetimes of even the grandfathers of most people now living*. In the course of these two hundred years, new empires and new creeds have risen and fallen fast. Final solutions have everywhere turned out to be provisional. Words have taken on new meanings and then lost them, and the complexity of problems has given support to absurd simplifications.

Beware of supposing that progress has been continuous or that all agree that it has occurred: 'Compared to most twentieth century societies,' wrote Richard Pipes, 'the Russian countryside of the imperial age was an oasis of quiet' (1). A constant theme of events since 1750 has also been the apparent incapacity of people of different origin to live side by side: compare the tolerance of twelfth century Spain where Christians, Jews and Muslims lived in comprehension as neighbours in a way to make it, not the seventeenth or eighteenth centuries, deserving of the name the 'Age of Tolerance'.

The age of industry coincided with Romanticism: Goethe's romantic writings and Byron's life coincided with the start of the factory system, and the beginnings of 'mass culture' were not far behind. Yet, alongside the industrial achievement, the anonymous work of thousands of engineers and millions of labourers, we have known a cult of the individual, and of the individual achievement. Biography as a work of art has in modern industrial society overtaken fiction in popularity. Respect for the individual conscience as directed by God without the need for an intermediary in the form of a church was an element in Puritanism which survived in modern Europe, via Holland and England (2). The great inventions of the eighteenth and nineteenth centuries were private masterpieces in many instances: but there were many ambiguities. Was individualism even in the nineteenth century too stern and lonely a creed? Is it so now? Matthew Arnold believed that it had been so in the days of ancient Greece. The hellenic conception of human nature (spontaneity of conscience), he argued, in Culture and Anarchy, was unsound at that moment of man's development; it was premature; 'the indispensable basis of conduct and self control, the platform upon which alone the perfection aimed at by Greece can come to bloom was not to be achieved by our race so easily; centuries of probation and discipline were needed' (3). Have we reached again a time when individualism is bound to falter? That is a pessimistic conclusion: Keynes posed the problem thus: 'I think that capitalism wisely managed can probably be made more efficient for attaining economic ends than any alternative system yet in sight, but that in itself is in many ways extremely objectionable. Our problem is to work out a social organisation which shall be as efficient as possible without offending our notions of a satisfactory way of life' (4). Capitalism, since Keynes, has developed vigorously but it is still often its own worst enemy, it lacks morale and it still seems to be

* My grandfathers were born in 1850 and 1857 respectively.

outmanoeuvred in debate – which, in an age more conscious than ever of presentation, affects its morale. Keynes's problem has not yet been resolved.

Most of the labour of the industrial countries remained, for many years after the coming of industrialisation, outside the factories. More people, it is true, worked in trade, manufacturing and handicrafts in England than in agriculture in 1811 but that did not become true of Germany till about 1895, of the US about the same time and of France and other European nations, till after 1945. By that time, every year an increasing proportion of the labour force in rich countries was already working in service undertakings of one sort or another. The factory was the symbol of the new era. It never employed morc than a modest proportion of those who lived through it.

26

The Age of Machines

The essential characteristic of our times (that is, the years since 1750) is the manufacture of goods for sale outside the neighbourhood concerned, in a factory, and by a machine. This development began in England in the eighteenth century. It was the equivalent of those agricultural innovations in the Near East of about 8000 BC. The critical innovation in the early history of agriculture was the realisation that crops could be made to grow again and again. The decisive innovation in the eighteenth century was a combination of four things: first, the mechanisation of the textile industry, causing a change in the clothing habits of the world, subsequently spreading to most other industries; second, a series of organisational innovations, in particular the factory system; third, a series of inventions in power; and fourth, a series of new commercial opportunities, relating both to the purchase of raw materials and to sales.

The technical changes in the textile industry were associated with cotton, rather than wool. Before the eighteenth century, cotton had nowhere been an important textile. For a variety of reasons, it now so became.

The substitution of machinery for individual manufacture was the fundamental change. Everything else which seems to characterise the industrial age had existed in the agricultural past: capitalism and long-distance commerce; the widespread use of money; the concentration of large numbers in a single place;* but the use of machinery meant mass production.

Mass production, in its turn, meant a new method of organisation of labour: the factory, the initiator of all modern things. It implied innovations in the use of energy, with steam taking the place of animal, wind or water power; and it resulted in innovations in transport, though, to begin with, those were confined to the construction of artificial rivers (canals) and the improvement of roads.

The least confusing way of explaining the phenomenon of industrial-

* See below, page 250.

isation is probably to indicate exactly what occurred in respect of the English cotton industry.

In the seventeenth century, the British and the Dutch East India Companies began to import cotton (both calicoes and muslins) from India on a scale sufficient to worry wool merchants (some Indian manufactured cotton cloth had been imported into Europe since time immemorial, and there had been a few feeble attempts to copy it). In the early sixteenth century, the Venetians were selling raw cotton to Antwerp, and, from there, Dutch cotton manufactures went to England. Still in 1700, nearly all the cotton goods sold in Europe came from India or elsewhere in the East: Manchester produced a poor imitation (1). When, in 1721, Indian cotton goods were banned, on the insistence of the wool merchants, an opportunity opened up in England, particularly when Liverpool, a developing port, growing rich on the slave trade, began to import raw cotton from the West Indies and Brazil.

The spinning of cotton needs a damp but stable climate. Lancashire could offer that. Manchester began first to produce fustian (a mixture of linen and cotton), and imitation Indian patterns using engraved plates. This cotton industry began as a subsidiary of agriculture comparable to that of wool. Then the fustian masters began to buy the raw cotton in bulk (the linen being in thread) and to 'put it out'. As a rule, these merchants were self-made men, with a weak system of guilds. The industry which they formed was more free of taboos than was the wool one. It was, therefore, able to take advantage of a number of changes in technology offered by several inspired, though in the main personally unfortunate, inventors.

Doubtless it would not have seemed likely to the men and women of the eighteenth century in Europe, with their high, powdered head-dressings and wigs, their hooped skirts, knee breeches and silk stockings, their coat tails and their négligés, that the sphere of life which would lead to the transformation of society would turn out to be a revolution in the manufacture of clothes; but so it was. Textiles were the chief manufactures already, in all rich countries, and the machines which now began to make them would lead to a transformation of the whole of industry.

For centuries, water-driven or horse-drawn fulling stocks had thudded down on to wet cloth of all sorts, beating and thickening it (2). The 'finishing' stages of the preparation of the cloth had thus been 'mechanised' for a long time. But now the more complicated earlier stages were mechanised too.

Until the 1730s, weaving had usually been done by throwing the shuttle through the alternate threads of the cotton. The weaver did that with one of his hands, and caught the shuttle with the other hand. In weaving broad pieces of cloth, two men were needed. They threw the shuttle back and forth to each other. The cross stitch (the 'weft', as opposed to the 'warp') was closed up after each throw of the shuttle by a layer of wood extending across the piece of cloth being woven. In the early 1730s, John Kay, the son of a wool merchant from Bury in Lancashire, added to this layer a grooved guiding board in which the shuttle could be thrown fast from side to side by a mechanical shuttle driver. This 'flying shuttle' needed only one hand, the other being available for closing up the weft. The output of a single weaver was thereby doubled and the quality was also improved. This enlightened device was rejected by the wool merchants. Kay himself was intimidated by mobs who broke up his house and all within it, and he apparently died in poverty in France. But his weaving machine began to be used about 1760 by cotton manufacturers (3).

Meantime, spinning machines began also to be made. The first of these was patented in 1738 by John Wyatt and Lewis Paul, and built in London by Edward Cave, a printer from Rugby, using the power of the Turnmill Brook which flowed into the River Fleet. This machine seems not really to have been used. The 'Spinning Jenny'* as devised by James Hargreaves and patented in 1770, was the first mechanical spinner. This was a rectangular frame on four legs. At each end, there was a row of vertical spindles. Between them, the previously 'carded' cotton would be passed backwards and forwards. The thread could be drawn and twisted at the same time. A single workman could thus spin several threads. His productive power was multiplied by eight. The jenny was immediately denounced by those who believed that such machines would damage employment. But, since the jenny needed no motor power, it seemed, to begin with, to be likely to revive, rather than bring an end to, cottage industry. Hargreaves, the inventor, was a carpenter and hand-loom worker at Standhill, near Blackburn in Lancashire. As with Kay, the inventor's house was sacked. The first jenny was burned and Hargreaves fled to Nottingham (4).

The decisive innovator, however, in the cotton industry was Richard Arkwright, an organiser, rather than an original inventor. First, he devised a machine very like Wyatt's and Paul's. Then he put several of them in a single workshop at Nottingham. He went next to Cromford near Derby. There he used water power to work the machines in another factory. This 'water frame' produced stronger thread than the most skilled spinner could do. He could thus make pure cotton goods more easily, instead of the fustian mixture of his predecessors — the earliest spinning machines produced a cotton thread which broke unless mixed with linen. Arkwright was later shown to be a pirate. 'His' spinning machine had apparently been first devised by Thomas Highs, a mad inventor with no business capacity. But Arkwright only lost his patent. He still had his factories. He continued to build these in

---

* The reason for the name is not known.

numerous places, sometimes in collaboration with others (for example, Strutt of Belper, or Peel of Bury) or a group of shareholders. He was also quick to use the steam engine after Watt's invention of it (5).

Arkwright's achievement was the factory, a social device which has dominated history ever since, making possible the mass production of innumerable goods, not just cottons. For the complicated, delicate, expensive, largely wooden, hand-made, and high-powered machinery which now made the best, and most sought after, cloths could not be managed in cottages. So factories were soon built to employ first tens, then hundreds, of people, as often as not in hamlets or on hills outside old towns, leading to the establishment of new communities without previous history, which gradually themselves turned into towns. There was, for a long time, an immense variety of systems: a fustian master might gather numerous hand-machines in his workshop; sometimes the plant and the raw material might be owned by different people, sometimes small spinning mills might receive cotton raw and send it back as yarn. Factories for a time competed with cottagers. Meantime, the import of printed cottons remained forbidden, hence giving protection (even if muslin, yarn, and undyed material continued to be brought in), while a bounty was given to all calicoes or muslins *exported* from England.

The concentration of labour in one place in a factory had, of course, occurred before in numerous nations: even in England, in the sixteenth century, Jack of Newbury employed 260 men, 100 women, 150 boys and girls together with fullers and dyers in Berkshire. In the early eighteenth century, something very like the factory system was also nearly invented by pioneers of the English silk industry. About 1715, the son of a Norwich weaver, Sir Thomas Lombe, sent his brother John to learn how to throw silk at Livorno in Tuscany and, on his return, the two brothers set up silk-throwing machines on the Italian pattern on an island in the River Derwent, or rather in a huge factory, 500 feet long, five to six storeys high, with nearly 500 windows — a building resembling a huge barracks. The machines were worked by a water wheel from the Derwent. Their task was to give the threads a twist by a rapid rotary movement. The 300 workers had to reknot the threads. Later, there were even larger silk factories in England. But the industry never did well, for the raw material was too expensive, particularly after the King of Sardinia forbade the export of silk because of the competition of the then thriving Spanish, French and Italian silk industries.*(6)

Then, at the same time, concentration on factory lines was normal among slaves in the sugar plantations of the West Indies: indeed, the

* The best silk in Europe was then grown at Valencia, the Spanish government encouraging domestic producers by banning the import of raw silk and the whole business being organised on a 'putting out' basis. There were 5,000 looms in Valencia in 1787. Meantime, the Spanish colony of the Philippines had been built around a Spanish settlement at

word 'factory' had, previous to the late eighteenth century, been used principally in English for an establishment for traders abroad such as traded slaves in West Africa. In the English dominions in 1750, slave-powered plantations were the largest single units. Very often, governments had also, as in Rome, established large arsenals, to make arms and armour, linen mills, woollen mills, dye-works, and even silk factories (8). Perhaps, indeed, Rome was on the brink of achieving a modern factory system, like so much else, before its disintegration in the fourth century. Then, in seventeenth century France, Colbert established several state factories. Some of those were run directly by the state. Others were undertaken by private people with state subsidies. Under Louis XIV, these foretastes of twentieth century practice produced two-thirds of the cloth of France (9). They were copied in Spain. At Guadalajara, a state wool factory was set up: and there was also one for tapestries at Madrid (10). The difference between all those factories and those founded by Arkwright was that the former lived by protection, subsidy, and bureaucratic direction. The same was the case with the textile plants set up in Italy in the eighteenth century. In all those places, at those times, the genuine merchant, who did not have a subsidy, operated by 'putting out' the material, which in turn was worked for a wage by an artisan (11).

The characteristic institution of society during the age of industry has certainly been the factory, just as the large estate and the hunting tribe were the characteristic forms in earlier ages. The factory's main features are: all the processes of manufacture are concentrated in a single plant. The larger the factory, the more economic the enterprise, and the larger the machine. The machines are specialised, and driven by non-human power. The workers are directed, and their work supervised by skilled management, for stipulated wages and fixed hours (not piece work), and the production is for the general market.

The size of the early factories doubtless seemed at the time the largest single innovation in comparison with past practice. Thus Matthew Boulton (whom Boswell named an 'Iron Captain in the middle of his troops') in the 1770s employed about 700 to 800 workers in his factory at Soho for the manufacture of everything metallic from steam engines to nails and screws. Josiah Wedgwood had several hundreds, making 'china', at his splendid works, 'Etruria', near Hanley in Staffordshire. This compared with, say, 500 employed on the largest sugar plantation in the West Indies, about 1770 (in the French colony of Sainte Domingue). But there was no immediate rapid growth in the size of

---

Manila, which exchanged American silver for Chinese silk. The long and dangerous ten-week journey from Acapulco to Manila led to a great profit, and, at one time, even exceeded the Atlantic trade in its quantity. Much silk flooded into Peru and Mexico and some went from Acapulco to Spain (7).

factories. In the 1830s, English flax mills still employed an average of only nine persons per plant; silk mills, twenty-five; wool factories, forty-five; and even cotton mills, only 175. The average coal mine in Britain then employed about fifty people above and below ground. The exceptions to this still modest scale of operation in the nineteenth century were iron works, of which the biggest, Richard Crawshay's iron works at Cyfarthfa, outside Merthyr, employed 2000 during the Napoleonic wars. Shipbuilders also employed many people. The average shipbuilding yard occupied 570 men, far more than any other enterprise, and the largest competitor in size was the iron manufacturer (who averaged 219) (12). But, of 8,500 factories using steam or other types of new power, in London, in 1898, the average number of workers was still only 41. The average size even of US factories was only 41·8 in 1929. In Germany, proportions were even smaller – 12 per manufacturing business in 1910 (13) while, in 1848, most French workers worked in firms of only five people.

The earliest factories have become known as 'dark satanic mills' because of William Blake's eloquent hostility to them. Unpleasant though some certainly were, beneficial changes were introduced into factories regularly and steadily almost from the beginning. First, great improvements in conditions of work were achieved in all industrial countries, as a result of the activities partly of philanthropists, partly of governments and, much later, of trades unions. Lighting, ventilation, schemes for the absorption of shocks, improved places for eating or resting, medical advice and increased safety, had been started by a few high-minded employers and their example was insisted upon by inspectors. The substitution of electricity for steam in so many undertakings later also caused beneficial changes. Many laws protected employees against the use of processes likely to be a danger to health. Reading aloud and, latterly, music (and in some countries, patriotic exhortations) varied the monotony.* But the enforcement of such rules was imperfect. Work in factories became less interesting. In the 1870s, typical factories in 'modern' countries began to be equipped with overhead conveyor belts. They had some precedents earlier in the century but it was not till after the American civil war that the meat-packing houses of Chicago showed the way (14). The mass assembly plant designed for the Chicago mail order plant of Sears Roebuck, in the 1880s, was another step towards complete mechanisation. This process was then brought to a logical conclusion in 1910 by Henry Ford (who carefully studied Sears Roebuck's innovation), when he set up a plant at Highland Park, near Detroit, for the manufacture of the Model T car, the first motor car financially within the reach of ordinary workers.†

* After the 1920s, the radio.
† See below page 321.

Finally, there came in the 1920s, the fully automatic assembly line, whereby the worker, no longer condemned to repeat his movements endlessly, merely supervised an intricate process which functioned, and had to function, like a watch, accurate to the split second (15). Meantime, managers (in particular, in the automobile industry) have gone to great trouble to make conditions in their plants more agreeable, and recently, at least in the industrial West, and probably elsewhere, the more modern the plant, the more money the worker within it receives, and the better general conditions there are.

A second development in the history of the factory has been the increasing scale and scope of the company which operates it. This has had three dimensions: economics of scale; stability made possible thereby in prices; and a means of standardising different items. The corporate form of organisation with limited liability seemed to point the same moral. Industrial enterprises operating over a wide market — and, since 1945, over several nations — began to spread. This process was started on a major scale by J.D. Rockefeller's Standard Oil Company (1879), which included several competitors which afterwards ran plants in harmony. Legislation also began to benefit large firms in most industrial states. There soon came not only 'horizontal' but 'vertical' combinations, which drew successive stages of industry into a single organisation. The US Steel Corporation, for example, brought under one management sources of ore, mines, furnaces and ships for the carriage of ore.

The personal consequences of these changes were summed up in 1863 by a man working in Chubb's factory in London for locks: 'I was a master locksmith for twenty-two years . . . . but we all work in large shops now'. Men who had been master craftsmen in innumerable minor trades became, as a result of factories, mere overseers in large establishments. Factories also, in the end, took away the rural base from the worker, who was cut off, therefore, from an auxiliary source of food and the sense of independence which comes from even the smallest holding (16).

Specialisation, with its benefits and miseries, is, however, not a wholly new problem: Xenophon, for example, in the fourth century BC wrote: 'In small towns, the same man makes couches, doors, ploughs, tables, and often he even builds houses. . . . In large cities, one man makes shoes for men, another for women, there are even places where one man earns a living by just mending shoes, another by cutting them out' (17).

Many of these inventions were obstructed at the beginning by riots and protests over possible unemployment. The uproar caused by the work of Kay and Hargreaves has been noted. There are many other instances, and earlier ones. Thus the practice of knitting, for example, had been known among the Arabs for hundreds of years and was widely undertaken as a domestic art in Europe during the Middle Ages, as it is now. In 1589, William Lee, curate of Calverton, Nottingham-shire, invented a machine for knitting socks and stockings.* He was discouraged from pursuing that by the Crown (on that matter, at least, Elizabeth I and James I saw eye to eye), and poor Lee (like Kay later) had to take refuge in Paris (where he died of grief) for fear of armed rioters outside his house. Similarly, a ribbon loom, devised in Danzig in the sixteenth century, reached London by 1616. But its use was also delayed by rioters. The stocking frame was, nevertheless, beginning to displace knitting by hand by the late seventeenth century. Knitting was already an 'industry', the frame being as a rule 'rented' by the worker who used it at home, the 'rent' being deducted from his wages. But the clash between innovators and suspicious labour continued. The determi-nation and willpower of men like Arkwright was essential to force through the changes in the cotton industry which were needed if people were really going to be clothed cheaply and well. Even so, about 1812, Yorkshire was said to have been reduced to an 'insurrectional state' by rioters 'the chief of whom, be he whomsoever he may, is styled General Ludd' (18). About 12,000 troops were posted in the 'disturbed counties'. Doubtless, if the governments of the early industrial age had wished, or been forced, to please the workers, the factory movement and the indu-strial revolution would have been brought to an end. No doubt even an enlightened despot would have agreed with Diocletian: when an engineer offered to design a machine to raise the columns of a temple, the Emperor refused, saying, 'Let me rather feed the common folk' (19). That reply perhaps explains more than anything else why the Roman Empire failed to industrialise. The Emperor could not conceive that the population might be better fed than through back-breaking work. Equally, even Montesquieu, one of the cleverest men in the eighteenth century went so far as to criticise the water-mills for 'depriving labou-rers of their work'. When Jacquard invented a power loom in France in 1803, Napoleon sent for him from Paris. He was in doubt as to whether he was going to be rewarded, or arrested (20). Adam Smith, however, argued that mechanisation spelled no danger and that those displaced would find other jobs (21). That has proved to be true. By and large, and making every allowance for a great deal of short-term and local unhap-piness, as well as the fact that the history of unemployment is ill-chronicled, the active or employed population of rich countries, such as those in Europe, though not always fully employed, is far larger than it was in the days of those who rioted in Robert Peel's cotton printing factory in the 1770s.

In the age of agriculture, most people worked as hard as they could,

---

* It is said that he devised the frame because a girl to whom he was paying court devoted more attention to her knitting than to him.

from dawn to dusk, and from childhood to old age. That is doubtless the same with most agricultural enterprises of the twentieth century. Whether a peasant, or rural wage earner of 1914, or even 1975, did less work than those who worked on the land before 1750 it is difficult to

EMPLOYED POPULATION OF EUROPE IN '000s
(1970 FRONTIERS) (2)

	1770	1970s
France	13,000	20,400 (1968)
West Germany	8,700	28,400 (1971)
Britain	5,500	25,800 (1975)
Italy	8,700	18,750 (1971)

say. Mechanisation has lightened work in agriculture,* but many agricultural workers now work alone. So the work may be even heavier and more boring than it used once to be. A day's management of a combine harvester can scarcely be lighter work than a day's harvesting was on the same estate in 1750.

Still, in 1750, there were few prescribed hours of work anywhere in the world, in any profession. In cottage industries, many women and children in summer worked a twelve-hour day. In winter, they may have worked eight. Many children began to work at the age of five. In Venice, true, a ban on child labour in dangerous trades was introduced in the Middle Ages, and, in England, a statute of 1563 provided that all craftsmen and labourers should, if hired by the day, between March and September, be at work by 5 a.m. and go on till 8 p.m. save for half an hour's 'dinner', sleep of one hour, and drinking of half an hour. This twelve-and-a-half hour day was to be five days a week (23). Such statutes were, however, introduced as much to exhort the workers to work as to prevent their exploitation. The difference between work and play was not recognised. Kings and slaves, like priests and farmers, were, on the other hand, most of the time on duty. Thus, when the era of the factory began, no one thought that anyone's hours should be altered: whether the factories increased any hours or lowered the age when children began to work, is doubtful, as Sir John Clapham tells us (24).† To request my people may be at work as soon as it is light, work till it is dark, and be diligent while they are at it can hardly be necessary,' reflected George Washington, in, of course, a rural setting, adding 'the presumption is that every labourer does as much in 24 hours as his health . . . will allow' (25).

---

* Mechanisation of agriculture is discussed in Chapter 34 below.
† John Locke, writing in 1697, said that children of the poor should work for some part of the day when they got to the age of three (26).

This applied at first to the innumerable men, women and children who went willingly into factories — willingly since, otherwise, they might have starved, as they had done in the remote past. The new large industries of the late eighteenth century were a godsend to overseers of parishes who increasingly had had their work cut out to find work for destitute children by the rise in population.* In innumerable cotton factories, boys were taken in return for their keep, though, after 1784, magistrates, as a rule, forbade parishes to place children in factories where there was work at night, and some philanthropic manufacturers, such as David Dale, built good housing for their workers (there was the famous model village of New Lanark, of which Robert Owen became manager in 1797). Even so, the industrial revolution was, to begin with, partly powered by people who, in the conditions of the seventeenth century, would simply not have grown to maturity. The work of women and children in the early industrial revolution was, meantime, adequate for the tasks concerned, since spinning is easily learned and no strength is needed. Indeed, children were prized because their touch was thought delicate (27).

The invention of gas by William Murdock, Matthew Boulton's foreman at Soho, at the end of the eighteenth century, altered the complexion of things. It meant that the factories could be lit at night. Workers could be made to work long hours even in winter. The consequence of lighting, however, was immediately to bring legal limitations of hours and conditions of work. As a result of the activity of certain Mancunian philanthropists, in 1802, Sir Robert Peel, a rich cotton-mill-owner of Bury and associate of Arkwright's who was also a member of Parliament,† introduced a Bill which insisted on new standards for at least those children in factories for which the state had accepted responsibility. Working hours for children under fourteen years were generally not to exceed twelve. Sexes were to be separated. One free suit was to be provided yearly by the state in maintained factories. Every such factory was to be whitewashed twice a year. There were only to be two children to a bed. Education, the learning of the three Rs, and religious education once a week, was made obligatory. This law established also the principle of the inspection of factories.

On the whole, since Britain (unlike her neighbours) lived under a state of law‡ those modest rules slowly began to be carried out (28). Further modifications.followed. Thus an Act of 1819 banned children under nine from working at a cotton mill. In 1849, in a typical factory in Britain or America, work averaged twelve hours fifteen minutes a day for six days a week — that is, a working week of 73½ hours (29). The following year, a new Factory Act in Britain limited the working week to

*That critical matter has been discussed on page 399.
† Father of the Prime Minister.
‡ See below page 434.

60 hours for women. From then on, a half holiday on Saturday was normal (though Lloyds would remain open on Saturday afternoons till 1854). In the meantime, a campaign for a ten-hour day began in the US. A limit to those hours for workers in all state establishments had already been imposed by President van Buren in 1840 (30). A ten-hour day was also considered a maximum for all women by a law of 1869, and for everyone under the age of eighteen (31). In the 1860s, most workers in the US were, however, still working about 63 hours a week, or slightly over ten hours for six days a week. That figure had fallen to nine by 1915. In the USA, probably about 18% of all children in the country were still employed between 1890 and 1910 (32) – unlike even Russia, where the employment of children under twelve had been banned from factories in 1882 (33). French and German workers in factories were still then working ten hours a day as a rule (34). In Russia, a legal maximum working day of 11½ hours for all, regardless of age or sex, was introduced in 1897. Ten hours for nightwork was also the Russian limit (35). In England, the working week had been cut to 56½ hours for textile workers in 1874 and, in 1900, the country as a whole probably averaged a little over 54 hours. But shops in England were then open seventy-four or even eighty hours a week – a great source of drudgery for children (as, of course, was both domestic service and the use of errand boys). By 1914, children under fourteen in most industrial countries had usually been withdrawn from the factory in order to go to school, though children over twelve were still found 'half time' in English factories till 1914, that is, thirty-three hours a week: the rest of the time, they went to school.

After the First World War, the economies of the industrialised countries moved steadily towards the idea of a day of eight hours or a week of forty hours (achieved in the US by 1938, with half days on Saturdays) and also towards a world in which children under fourteen or even seventeen were never employed. Agricultural workers began to demand such conditions also. The only people who stood out were the admittedly still resilient self-employed, along with scholars, soldiers, doctors and politicians – though such a comment ignores the vast numbers who, in all industrial countries, now work many hours for payments in cash after their official hours in order to avoid income tax, a new menace which only began to affect average people after 1945. Whether those secret hours of 'moonlighting' point the way to a new pattern of employment seems uncertain. It is possible. But, at all events, less work is plainly done in the twentieth century in rich countries than ever before. Both entertainment and education have, therefore, given rise to large industries of their own. In the nineteenth century, most people worked at least 3,500 hours a year (the German figure for 1877 was 3,300) (36). In the 1970s, most people in the industrialised countries have an official working year of about 1,800 hours. The majority of people in the US or West Europe thus probably do less work now (again officially) in their seventy odd years of life than their ancestors did in their forty or fifty years. In a single week nowadays, the average worker has nearly twice as many hours of 'leisure' (seventy-two hours) than officially he has of work (forty hours) not to speak of fifty-six hours' sleep.

Most advanced countries would probably profit by having longer official working hours. The proof of this lies in what happened in France between 1936 and 1939. In 1936, a forty-hour week was introduced. Industrial output fell, unemployment and inflation increased, and purchasing power was cut. In 1938, the hours of the working week were increased by the abandonment of regulations curtailing them. The number of unemployed dropped. Production rose 15%, exports 17% and the increase in prices slowed down. The lesson implicit, wrote the French sociologist Alfred Sauvy, should be taught to students of political economy as the battles of Austerlitz and Tannenberg are taught at military academies (37). It never has been.

The preceding chapter may read as if it is being suggested that the 'dark satanic mills' of the industrial age were oases of 'sweetness and light'. That is not its point. But it is suggested that the really evil conditions castigated by, for example, Mrs Gaskell, in her novels or Dickens in his, affected only a minority of the employed population and that it is wrong to found any general theory of human behaviour on the basis of evidence collected in Manchester in the 1840s. Furthermore, in deploring the conditions in which cotton-workers lived, we should not forget the cloth which they produced and which served to keep millions of people clean and warm; in regretting that children were employed by even the greatest potters, we should not forget the pots.

27

Steam and Coal

The machine age has largely depended on an intensified use of irreplaceable energy (coal, lignite, gas, oil) instead of (as until then) inexhaustible replaceable sources (wind, water, wood, or animal or man power).

Industrialisation began, however, with old sources of energy. The first factories of England, for example, including Arkwright's first cotton mills at Cromford, Wedgwood's factory for pottery at Etruria, on the Grand Union canal, Lombe's silk factory on the Derwent, all used water-power and water-wheels. Indeed, as late as 1848, France still had 22,500 water-mills in use (17,300 for corn) against only 5,200 steam engines (1). The first US factories were powered by water (2). Seventeenth century Holland, by far the most industrialised region on earth, was run by wind. In addition, a vast increase in the numbers of horses and oxen (Europe had 14 million horses and 24 million oxen about 1789) had also recently increased Europe's animal energy resources (3).

Still, the use of steam very soon gave the factory system a new dimension.

Anaxagoras (a mentor of Socrates and Pericles), who died in 428 BC, had shown that water can only enter a vessel when the air goes out of it (4). Hero's *Pneumatica* showed that the expansive force of steam was perfectly known in the first century BC. But nothing was done to make use of it for 2,000 years. Did the brilliant Gerbert (later Pope Sylvester II) build a steam organ in 1000 AD, as suggested by William of Malmesbury? Probably not. Still, some steam-powered sprayers existed in the thirteenth century. Leonardo sketched steam-powered bellows and cannon. In his day, some experiments were also carried out to try and turn a spit by steam (5).

The power of atmospheric pressure was nevertheless only fully realised during the seventeenth century, when Denys Papin, in Holland, was able to write, about 1690: 'Since it is a property of water that a small quantity of it turned into vapour by air has an elastic force like that of air . . . I concluded that machines could be constructed wherein water, by the help of no very intense heat, and at little cost, could produce that perfect vacuum' (6). Not long after, Captain Thomas

Savery of Devonshire, an army officer, devised a pump powered by atmospheric pressure to get rid of water which had flooded copper mines (7). A blacksmith of Dartmouth, Thomas Newcomen had the same idea, for a more developed 'atmospheric machine' first used in 1712 at a colliery at Dudley Castle. It lifted 10 gallons of water 153 feet in a minute. It was much sought after, and two such machines were built per year for two-thirds of a century, many being exported to Europe and the colonies. One Newcomen machine worked continuously from 1750 to 1900 at Bristol.

The efficiency of these and other comparable mechanisms was limited by the impossibility then of boring accurate cylinders, such as were needed for good pumps. Thus the growth of precision proved to be as great a development as any other of the late eighteenth century.

James Watt, the son of the borough treasurer of the modest Glaswegian suburb of Greenock, was the father of the most famous device of the early industrial revolution, the steam engine proper. He first learned French, German and Italian, in order to be aware of all the contemporary developments in his subject of study. Watt considered that the reason for the weaknesses of the Newcomen engine was that the cylinder cooled between each stroke. About 1765, he suggested two critical improvements; the chamber in which the steam was condensed should become a separate vessel different from the cylinder; and the steam should act on a piston, not simply by atmospheric pressure. This last idea came to him suddenly, as if by intuition, on Glasgow Green, during a Sunday walk; since steam was 'an elastic body, it would rush into a vacuum and, if a communication was made between the cylinder and the exhausted vessel, it would rush into it and might there be condensed, without cooling the cylinder'. (8).

During the next few years, Watt was busy completing a machine embodying this idea. His difficulties were both technological and financial: first, he had to bore an accurate cylinder to avoid any escape at all between its wall and the piston. Only millwrights were skilled engineers at that time. Watt consulted the then prince of these, John Wilkinson, whose new boring mill (designed for cannon) could serve his purpose. Watt's financial problems were first helped by John Roebuck, who wanted pumps for his coal mines. Roebuck thus set up the first steam engine at Kinneil House, Edinburgh. Unfortunately, Roebuck went bankrupt. Matthew Boulton, the pioneer of accurate workmanship, of Soho, Birmingham, was willing to take Roebuck's place. Boulton, who already employed 600 workmen, was renowned as a manufacturer of buttons, knives, watch chains and shoe buckles.

By 1775, Wilkinson had ordered one of Watt's machines to blow his furnaces. In 1777, Périer Frères ordered one for the water supply in Paris. In the 1780s, Watt's machines had begun to be commercially profitable. All the ironmasters began to use them. Brewers followed, and then manufacturers of china. A steam engine was used experimentally in Cuba for sugar manufacture in 1797 (9). The steam-powered Albion flour mills in London became a great sight from 1785 and, the same year, a steam-powered cotton spinning mill was set up at Papplewick. The future German statesman Stein went from Prussia to England in 1787 to take back a steam engine, and Catalonia had one by 1790 (10).

Boulton and Watt built 496 machines in all, of which 164 supplemented the work of Newcomen engines as pumps in coal mines, 24 were used as blast furnaces, and 308 were directly used as machines. Steam was by then on its way to freeing industry from the shackles of geography. Unlike water power, it did not depend specifically on valleys (11).

The Napoleonic wars for a time interrupted commerce. In 1815, even in England, the steam engine was confined to the wool and cotton industries and a few blast furnaces. But, afterwards, trade revived. Watt's patent had run out in 1800 and the technical difficulties of making accurate and, therefore, safe machines were beginning to be overcome. Watt had thought that a further refinement, the high pressure steam engine, would prove too dangerous. But that was nevertheless patented in 1802, simultaneously by Richard Trevithick in Coalbrookdale (Shropshire) and Oliver Evans, in Delaware in the US. This engine, with a cast-iron boiler 1½ inches thick, developed steam pressure of 145 pounds per square inch (ten times the pressure of the atmosphere). It allowed Trevithick in 1804 to build the first steam locomotive. Oliver Evans drove an amphibious steam boat in 1804. Regular trips were possible by steam along inland waterways in the US, from 1807 onwards (12). A German steam engine was also made in Berlin, in 1812 (13).

After Waterloo, steam began to conquer all forms of machinery. The first packet boat (from Dover to Calais) ran regularly from 1821; the railway engine after 1829; the ocean-going steamboat after 1850 (the delay there was caused by inadequate knowledge of how to carry sufficient coal); and there was also soon the steam reaper.* *The Times* in London was printed by steam from 1814. Cuba had 55 steam engines by 1860, making it the largest exporter of sugar and the richest colony the world had ever seen (14), though it was still attached then to a rather poor metropolis.

There were no real further major innovations in the world of steam till the turbine (a kind of steam windmill) was created to drive a dynamo at a speed which the by then old steam engine could not attain. Charles Parsons, one of the few great engineers to be the son of a nobleman, took out a patent for that in 1884. The same year, the turbo-generator came into being. It became soon established as the main motor for the

*See below, page 360.

then growing electrical industry, and then after 1894 for large ships. By 1910, both British passenger liners and the large ships of the navy were using these elaborations (15).

An important contribution to industrialisation, meantime, was made by the then old profession, already noticed in passing. This was the work of clock-makers and scientific instrument makers. They used accurate screw-cutters, dividing machines and lathes (much improved in the early eighteenth century). Such machinery was, of course, made by hand until the nineteenth century, as were the essential parts of steam engines. In 1759, John Harrison made a watch-sized timepiece which determined longitude to an accuracy of half a degree. That enormously stimulated the craft of watch-making in England. The fifty cylinders made in 1776 by John Wilkinson at his works in Denbigh for Matthew Boulton, to use in his steam engines, did 'not err the thickness of an old shilling' in any part (16). That accuracy was an absolutely essential contribution to the success of steam engines and subsequent machines.

These changes took a little time to have a general effect. In 1824, an English parliamentary committee of enquiry on the subject of monopoly asked: 'A great many manufacturers make their own machinery?' 'They do,' was the reply from a Lancashire manufacturer (17). Most machinery was then still wooden, fitted perhaps with a few metal tips like the iron parts of a plough. The Spinning Jenny and Flying Shuttle were originally made by craftsmen living at home. But soon machines began to be regularly made by manufacturers and put up for sale. Once precision was achieved, individual parts could be made separately. By 1856, Sir Joseph Whitworth had, in his workshop at Manchester, machines capable of measuring one millionth part of an inch, enabling the standardisation of screw threads. Soon, above all in the US, fully interchangeable parts of machines were produced: an improvement originally associated with spare parts for muskets. Few developments were so important.

One benefit was the effect on coinage. That was the idea of James Watt's backer, Matthew Boulton, to defeat forgers. Boulton built a coining press powered by steam in which the coins, held in place by steel clamps, were stamped automatically, with an accuracy never previously achieved. Each press could stamp 50 to 100 coins a minute. This was a great success, and Boulton received orders from all over the world, including revolutionary France, Russia and finally, in 1797, from his own government (18).

This achievement emphasised the boon of accurate instruments and precise machinery.

Although cotton was the raw material *par excellence* of the early days of industrialisation, the history of pottery has its lessons also. Again, English history is generally indicative.

In the mid seventeenth century, the main workshops of England were producing coarse stoneware, earthenware cups and plates, and pots of various sorts. The largest of these workshops employed six men — one man to shape the pots, another to make handles, while the others did decoration, glazing and firing. A few, saltglaze, workshops were begun near Burslem in Staffordshire in the late seventeenth century by the Elers brothers, potters of German origin, but English pottery was still inferior to that of the continent (19).

About the turn of the seventeenth and eighteenth centuries, an unprecedented quantity of Chinese ceramics began to be brought back — blue and white porcelain, transparent enamels — to be admired in every fashionable city of Europe. A chemist to Augustus the Strong, king of Saxony, Johann Friedrich Böttger,* copied the process success-fully at Meissen, and a French state factory at Sèvres in 1768 began to use the Chinese method too. Copies began also in England, in the Staffordshire potteries, where John Astbury's† translucent stoneware began to make the fortune of that region by bringing the chance of obtaining 'china' to a mass market. By 1750, double firing began to produce the characteristic earthenware of Staffordshire. Then, in 1759, Josiah Wedgwood, a connection of Astbury's, founded his business at Burslem and, ten years later, he established his factory, 'Etruria', not far away, as has been seen, bringing the clay from Cornwall and elsewhere, by means of the great Trunk Canal which he helped to finance. He was inspired by the recent discoveries at Pompeii and elsewhere in Italy. Steam engines soon began to be used for mixing clay and grinding flint. Josiah Spode began in 1797 to add bone ash in his factory at Stoke-on-Trent. These huge factories, and others soon founded like them on the continent and in the US, fast transformed above all the eating habits of the world, since china and pottery are much easier to clean than wood and pewter.

The result was that, by 1850, the latter had vanished in all but the most impoverished homes. Cheap china, usually earthenware, had taken their place, an immense sanitary achievement which benefited millions even though the master potters are to be condemned for employing child labour, as they undoubtedly did for many years later than other enterprises (20). The final shaping of pots meantime contin-ued to be done by hand till the 1840s, while steam was not applied to the potters' wheel before the 1870s (21).

The steam engine could perhaps have been introduced with fuel

* He believed that he could turn base metals into gold and was accordingly kept a prisoner.
† He gained the secrets of the Elers brothers' factory by pretending to be an idiot.

other than coal. But coal was the main source of power everywhere during the first half of the industrial revolution and, indeed, is still a major contributor to power in most nations. Production of coal in the 1970s is over 2,000 million tons a year, and contributes perhaps a third of the world's production of energy.

Actually, coal had been used for heating houses in China on a modest scale for 3,000 years, and in blast furnaces too. In the Middle Ages in Europe, coal was found in limekilns, was used to heat houses sometimes, and was also to be seen in some iron works, though never on a scale to rival charcoal. Liège had started to use coal mines in the fifteenth century, for its already well-known metallurgical works. Coal was also exported, down the Meuse. Similarly in the sixteenth century, Newcastle began to use the coal mines of Durham in order to fire its salt industry (made from sea water), afterwards for other local industries, and, finally, in bakers' ovens. Then, carried by sea to London, coal was used in houses when the shortage of wood began to be acute in the days of Elizabeth I. By 1660, Britain was producing half a million tons of coal a year, probably five times the produce of the rest of the world (22). The river Tyne was always full of colliers ready to leave for London, where windows of glass were being built in new houses to keep in the heat of the new coal-burning fireplaces. Mortar from coal-burned limestone helped to keep together the houses themselves, which were increasingly built of brick and stone. Meantime, boring rods had been devised to ascertain the whereabouts of seams of coal.

The coal of that time was not much used generally for manufacture, though a little smelting of lead, tin and copper was done. Coal was held to impair the quality of iron when employed for smelting, and was believed to have a bad effect on malt when employed to dry it in breweries.

In Derbyshire, the brewers started to char their coal in order to make coke and then to use coke to dry their malt. This experiment worked. Abraham Darby, son of a farmer near Dudley, a town in Worcestershire long known for its seams of coal, was serving an apprenticeship to a malt mill manufacturer. In 1709, he began to use coke in a blast furnace at Coalbrookdale, on the Severn in Shropshire. His son, of the same name, studied how to make cast iron acceptable to forges. He found that there was little phosphorus in the ore of coal. The coke which he subsequently made began to be used continuously for the smelting of iron, a turning point in the history of that and all metals. From then on, coal was recognised as a raw material whose abundance in Britain enabled her to benefit from a long lead in other inventions.

Canals enabled this raw material to be carried to inland cities. Had it not been for them, the shortage of fuel other than coal would have prevented the growth of industry. In England, there had until recently been no interest in those artificial rivers, unlike the state of affairs in

France, where the Languedoc canal, linking the Atlantic with the Mediterranean, was constructed between 1666 and 1681.

Both seas and rivers had, from an early time, been supplemented by canals, which criss-crossed ancient Egypt, Iraq and the Yangtze valley as if they were cobwebs. Of those canals, the best known were the Pharoah Necos' attempt to link the Red Sea with the Nile, upon which project 120,000 Egyptians are said to have died between 609 and 623 BC, and Sennacherib's stone canal, which brought water to Nineveh from fifty miles away with a fall of 1 in 80. Wide valleys were crossed by aqueducts. Roman aqueducts were famous. But they were used only for the supply of water to their great cities, not for the shipment of goods. The idea of a canal between the Saône and the Meuse, or the Rhine and the Danube occurred to Charlemagne ('their execution,' wrote Gibbon 'would have vivified the Empire, and more cost and labour were often wasted in the structure of a cathedral'), but nothing was done. Carolingian France was less far sighted than T'ang China. In the Middle Ages, northern Italy was, however, converted into a criss-cross of irrigation canals, which compensated Milan for being surrounded by land. They could ship all manner of goods to the Po and to Ferrara (23). But Britain had had neither money nor inclination for such plans before the eighteenth century. Contemporaneously with the first English concern with these matters, Charles III of Spain was trying to introduce canals to make up for the bad roads and unnavigable rivers which held up Spanish commerce. Hence his plan for a canal from Tudela in Aragon to the Mediterranean, or from Segovia in Castile to the Biscay coast at Santander. The first of these got under way in the 1780s (24). But lack of private capital, political disturbances and courtly negligence prevented any further action there.

In England, in the early eighteenth century, both the Lancashire river Douglas and the Sankey river in the same county were deepened, in order to carry coal to the sea more easily. An inspired engineer, James Brindley, suggested to Francis, Duke of Bridgewater (perhaps on the example of the Languedoc Canal) that, instead of carrying coal the seven miles to Manchester from his colliery at Worsley, at nine shillings a ton, a canal might be created. That was done. The water was kept at one level by aqueducts (one over a river, the Irwell) and tunnels, and the coal was carried by barges. The result was that the price of coal fell by half. The Duke and Brindley went on to finance and build a canal from Manchester to Liverpool and then one from the Trent to the Mersey. The latter linked the North Sea to the Irish Sea. Brindley next sketched out a whole network for an English canal system. Though that was not carried out in full, England was transformed by the growth of canals. Between 1760 and 1800, a new cheap and easy system of transport was established which enabled the natural resources of all parts of the country to be concentrated. 4250 miles of inland waterways were built. The work was all done either by private persons or joint stock companies. The Government limited itself to enquiries and granting permissions.

The creation of canals meant that all the new sources of coal could be exploited: in Lancashire, South Wales, Staffordshire, Yorkshire and Scotland. Coal output increased from 6 million tons in 1770 in England to 66 million in 1856 (and ultimately to a maximum of 287 million in 1913) (25).

The increase in production of coal was made possible in the first place by cheap labour (partly the consequence of an increase in population but including many Irish immigrants), and because of the availability of steam engines to pump deep mines free of water. Subsequently, steam engines were also used to hoist both coal and miners. Still, in the early nineteenth century, women were still being used to carry coal up (as much as a hundred feet) on ladders while their husbands were cutting at the mine's face. Conditions in Scotland were specially bad. Workers in coal mines and in salt pits were still legally serfs, bound to the mines for life. They could be sold with them, and even wore the visible sign of slavery in the shape of a collar (26).

In the early days, new seams of coal were opened up by fairly haphazard blasting, by use of black powder. The miner worked with handpick and crowbar and simply put his coal on to a sledge to be pulled by women, children or ponies. Thomas Wilson of Tyneside introduced iron rails in the 1780s to alleviate the work of the haulier. Indeed, rails had been used above ground for many years. But even so, every large mine had innumerable miles of paths, at increasingly great depths, down to 1,000 feet by 1825, 2,000 in the 1830s. These depths were achieved as a result of the efforts of a series of outstanding engineers, who devised winding machines to raise the coal on hemp cord, and then wire rope (an innovation first used in Germany in 1834). But these early mines were ill-lit by dangerous lanterns, which often caused disasters. In 1816, however, the lamp invented by Sir Humphry Davy enabled a naked flame to be kept alight safely under ground, even in damp and gassy mines. A safety shaft was also usually introduced by the middle of the nineteenth century. But the evils of coal dust and the diseases which it causes were not appreciated for many years while safety precautions were often ignored, at least until after terrible disasters had given gruesome warnings. It seems strange that water wheels and windlasses were not employed more often: pumps for drainage were used in Bohemia in the sixteenth century (27).

By 1880, most coal was being raised from the pits by machine, not by women, but the actual hewing remained a handicraft similar to that of cane cutting. Coal-cutting machines took a long time to be introduced. No effective conveyor to take the coal from the face to the surface was introduced before 1912. Till then, miners had to spend a great deal of time at work filling tubs.

By then, the coal miners were among the most formidable of labour forces, proud of a long tradition of exhausting and dangerous work, conscious of their importance in the economy, united in their organisation, and numerous: in 1911, there were 1.2 million miners in Britain, in comparison with 20,000 in 1829 (28), more than in any other single trade except the workers in agriculture and metallurgical trades. Kaiser Wilhem II in Germany conceded the importance of the coal industry by siding with the miners against the coal owners in a great strike in 1889, to Bismarck's disgust (29).

In 1789, Belgium already had mines 600 feet deep at Mons. Belgium's membership of the French Empire under Napoleon gave her coal the run of the French market. In 1830, Belgium had about 300 collieries, each employing 100 men (30). France, however, was not so competitive in respect of coal. Her coal was hard to work, the seams were thin, the prices high, and the coal itself inferior to that of England. Though French coal production increased, it only attained 41 million tons by 1913, and a maximum of 60 million tons in 1958 (31). France imported during the twentieth century twice as much as she raised (32). France's relative industrial backwardness in the nineteenth century cannot be entirely explained by her shortage of coal, but it was certainly a disadvantage to her at that stage of the age of manufacturing.

Equally, the fairly early success of Germany can partly be explained by her possession of vast stores of coal, partly in the Ruhr and Roer (at the eastern end of the Belgian fields), and also in Silesia, the broad finger of territory won for Prussia by Frederick the Great — and later lost, to Poland, by Hitler. The impact of railways gave particular importance to German coal. Having never made much use of coal before the age of industry, and being comparatively uninterested in canals, German production of coal was only at the French level in the 1830s (about 3 million tons). But, after the coming of railways, production moved ahead fast. (She was only just behind Britain in 1913 and she overtook Britain in 1921). During the Nazi era, Germany was regularly producing much more than Britain (380 million tons in 1938 to Britain's 230 million), a superiority she maintained after 1945, even during the high days of the era of oil. Indeed, in the 1970s, East Germany alone was producing far more than Britain. US production of bituminous coal first exceeded that of Britain in 1902, was almost twice British production in 1913 (478 million tons) and never fell below that since (33).

The importance of coal in the first stages of industrial development can equally well be seen from the history of the coal-less countries. Their mechanisation was delayed. They had to import coal at great expense, just as the highly mechanised countries have to import oil in the late twentieth century. The need to import coal also limited the internal and external politics of the countries concerned. In 1920, the

Italian communists believed that they could carry through the same type of revolution which Lenin had managed in Russia in 1917. 'Do you take into account that Italy has neither wheat nor coal?' Lenin asked. Lenin advised against revolution (34). Italy under Fascism, up to the 1930s, still imported nearly 60% of her coal from Britain. In 1936, as a result of sanctions under the League of Nations, the proportion of coal imported from Britain fell to 1% of Italy's needs. Thereafter, though Russia sold her a certain amount, the bulk of Italian imports came from Germany: 'As soon as the Italians adapted their factories to . . . German coal,' wrote Denis Mack Smith, 'they found that the change was, for technological reasons, as well as political, almost irreversible' (35). In 1913, coal was the third most important British export (£54 million, against £55 million iron and steel manufactures, and £127 million cotton goods) and the *entente cordiale* between Britain and France was based as much on the coal trade between the two countries as on joint fears of Germany.

Long before the days for which these statistics have been given, coal had surrendered to oil as the main impulse behind continuing mechanisation. A symbolic alteration was the action of Winston Churchill as First Lord of the Admiralty in changing the fuel of the world's largest navy from coal to oil in 1911 (36). Even so, the part played by coal continued to have much significance in all industrial countries. Even in the 1970s, the use of coal in electricity power stations gave coal miners enough power to shake governments.

The world was nevertheless by the 1970s using more coal in one year than had been generated in a hundred years through carbonisation; so that some were saying, as early as 1940, that the 'use of fossil fuel' could only be 'an episode' (37). But those hundreds of years of carbonisation were a very long time ago indeed and the 'episode' of coal seems like continuing a long time, for large reserves still exist, while the future of oil seems far more unpredictable. A recent study of world coal production suggested that the US might, by the year 2000, have to be mining three times more coal than it is in the late 1970s; that while the world's annual coal production was 3,400 million tons, reserves were no less than 11,500 billion tons though only 740 billion are held to be recoverable. But even that is five or six times the current estimates of proved reserves of oil (38). The 'energy crisis' is thus really a relatively short-term and manageable crisis in the sense that the word is usually employed. Of course, the massive increase of the burning of coal would pollute the atmosphere. The recovery of coal from beds under the North Sea would be difficult. The demand for coal will naturally outrun the production of many nations, resulting in the necessity for an elaborate commerce. Coalfields will continue to be ugly and dangerous places in which to work. The despoliation of large tracts of beautiful or agricultural land is disagreeable. Nevertheless, these things can all be overcome.

One paradox, however, is that the economically recoverable resources of coal are mostly in those countries which are already rich or becoming so: the US, China, Russia and Western Europe. All the same, coal is a fuel certain to remain abundant at reasonably low cost until well into the twenty-first century and new methods of recovering it – machines at the coal face – will surely remove its ugly legend.

27

Part 2

The New Iron Age

If steam and coal were the characteristic sources of energy of the industrial age in its first stages the raw material concerned was, primarily, iron.

Though the nineteenth century was an age which used iron more than ever before, iron had been used continuously from its discovery in Asia Minor before 2500 BC until 1750 AD, when its history was transformed in an important variety of ways.

Iron is a harder metal to work than is copper: a pure iron melts at 1,535° centigrade, while copper does so at 1,083° centigrade. Thus, until the development of the blast furnace (in China before Christ, but in the West not until the fourteenth century AD) (39), molten iron could not be produced for casting. Iron could, admittedly, be made red-hot by a great fire. The heat could be increased by bellows or by natural draughts. But then repeated hammerings were needed to create wrought iron from the crude iron. The consequent product could be neither sharp, nor pure. Hence, to begin with, iron was used primarily for ornaments, and only later for swords, axes, helmets and daggers. Those warlike refinements were made easier by hinged tongs which assisted the smith's work. They were probably developed at the same time as the hand tools which have remained the same in shape ever since: such as small saws, files, and anvils (for making nails) (40).

Tubal-cain, who figures early in *Genesis*, was said to be an instructor of 'artificers' of brass and iron (41). Despite that, for a long time, iron working was a secret of the Hittites. Their empire was indeed partly based on their possession of iron weapons (42). Other contemporaneous civilisations, such as that of Mycænae, knew of iron, but it was rare, and was mentioned by Homer still only as an ornament. Both the Mycæneans and the Trojans lacked the technical skill to exploit it (43).

The Hittite empire collapsed in 1200 BC. The ironsmiths were scattered. Iron began to be mined and worked in many parts of the Mediterranean. 'Heaven sent' iron from meteorites, in particular, was used for tools in the ancient Mediterranean, just as was iron from one which fell in Greenland in the nineteenth century. Though Asia Minor remained the main source of the metal in the old world (44), iron from the Eastern Alps was being worked by German and Celtic tribes very early on. The Assyrian empire was based on iron weapons, in particular the iron-capped battering ram. The Etruscans were equally preoccupied by iron, having discovered large deposits at Piombino-Populonia (a mountain range full of useful metals such as lead, copper and tin). Their smelting was done in furnaces of clay or stone, stoked with wood. They exchanged iron products in Greece and elsewhere in Italy for gold (45).

Iron also began to be used in Africa by the Carthaginians about 800 BC, and from thence, or from Egypt, the art of making it was slowly taken south into Africa proper. Iron was thus being smelted probably in the Nok kingdom in Nigeria by 300 BC, in the Congo perhaps earlier, in Kenya by 100 AD and in Rhodesia by 300 AD. Iron was of special use in those countries for clearing the ground for Africa's early agriculture. The gardens first created there for yams and bananas were made possible by iron tools (46). Much later, central Africa enjoyed a 'great burst of iron engineering' after 500 AD, leading to the organisation of kingdoms whose chief weapons were iron spears (47). The iron age in the Congo may even have preceded agriculture (48).

Iron smelting, meantime, began in India certainly not later than 516 BC when Darius the Persian made North India his twentieth satrapy. Some believe that iron reached there as early as 800 BC. Then, in the Mediterranean, iron weapons and armour equipped the armies of both Greeks and Romans. Roman agriculture had, of course, iron parts for ploughs, spades, sickles, axes, hatchets, chisels, mallets, hammers and lathes (49). Vast numbers of these iron implements were passed down from the Roman to the mediaeval world (50), and were still in use at the time of the Renaissance.

All this time, China was casting iron freely, though she did not develop forging before the third century AD. Why should she have? Cast iron is more useful than wrought iron (51). The reason for the Chinese success in casting iron so early was, probably, that they could heat their blast furnaces at a higher temperature than anyone did in the West till the fourteenth century AD. That in turn was probably because the ores of China had a high phosphorus content. Chinese blast furnaces were heated by bellows, with pistons which were themselves worked by paddle wheels (52). The West still could not melt iron fully, though certain Catalan furnaces managed in Roman days to produce malleable iron by using two pairs of bellows to maintain a constant blast (53).

The decline of Rome and of the Roman civilisation was marked as much as anything else by the decline of metallurgy. The recovery of the art of smelting in Carolingian Europe coincided with the opening of many new mines along the Rhine and Meuse in the Ardennes; and also in England. The mediaeval peasantry in Europe used an amount of iron 'inconceivable in any earlier age', according to Lynn White (54) for the tools which were made by blacksmiths, the indispensable supports of mediaeval agriculture. In particular, there was the heavy axe for felling trees which accounted as much as anything else for the great extension of arable land in the tenth century (55). The symbolic figure of the early Middle Ages was the knight in iron armour, equipped with iron weapons and supported on his horse by iron stirrups. His efficiency was secured by a great number of little ovens for iron dotted around Europe (for there was iron in innumerable European hillsides), to which the broken-up iron would be taken to be smelted, and afterwards removed to forges, there to be beaten on the anvil (56).

Blast furnaces, in which iron could be rendered properly liquid, were first set up in Europe in Germany during the fourteenth century. A direct connection with China is hard to find. Doubtless it will be. At all events, and almost certainly a result of war, the blast furnaces transformed Europe's technology.

In the course of the Renaissance, the frequency of war increased the demand for, and the price of, iron. The demand for new agricultural tools, cooking pots, forks, knives, fire-backs, fire-irons (for the new chimneys), and anchors for ships (a demand specialised in by the Basque country) was all considerable. At the same time, charcoal was short, thus causing a further geographical shift of iron industries. Though cast iron, from England and Styria,* from huge blast furnaces, dominated the market for weapons, wrought iron continued for a long time to be more popular because of the impurities which the large furnaces left behind (57). Slowly, however, blast furnaces spread, to Sweden, as to Spain. The iron works established during the seventeenth century in Santander and Vizcaya (in the Basque country) were, to the great Catalan historian Vicens Vives, 'one of the few encouragements of that moribund century' (58). In the eighteenth century, 'almost every village in the Basque country seemed to have a forge,' reported Richard Herr (59). The same was true of Santander. The smelting was still by charcoal. That exhausted the forests. But then these were small ovens in a mediaeval style, not blast furnaces. Despite the increase in demand for iron, production in Europe was probably no more than 150,000 tons a year in 1600 (60), a figure exceeded by England alone about 1800 (61). Yet Don Quixote thought that, in the seventeenth century, he lived in an iron age already (62). Even in 1800, the world's production of iron was a mere 2 million tons (63), a figure produced in 1972 by Algeria alone, which was responsible then for less than 0.5% of the world's ore (64).

Sixteenth century England was running out of wood for fires. So, as has been seen earlier, coal began to be used instead.† But ordinary

* Lower Austria.   † See above p. 264.

English coal was unsuitable for smelting iron, since it had a bad chemical effect on the ore. About 1700, England was still importing iron and, though plainly a rising power, was still far less important as a producer of that mineral than Sweden, Germany, or even Russia. English iron works were small, scattered and specialist, chiefly employing shoe bucklers, sword cutlers, and nail makers. Abraham Darby* transformed this state of affairs. He had noticed that Dutch smelters used sulphur. He experimented in Coalbrookdale, his Shropshire valley which was full of iron. By making the right mixture of sulphur with coal, he invented coke. Using carefully selected ores, he cast, in his blast furnaces, an iron far more liquid than any previously achieved outside China. With those, he made cast-iron pots. His son, Abraham Darby II, improved on his father's process, and was making iron bars by the 1730s. By 1760, there were numerous coke furnaces, all emphasising the dependence of iron on coal. This iron came soon to be produced in oblong 'pigs', ready for use in wheels, hammer heads and everything else (65).

The process known as 'coking' made England overnight the major iron manufacturer in the world. Her leading manufacturers established a dominance over this critical trade that few merchants had ever had before. Coking freed the manufacturers of iron from reliance on charcoal. The two wars of 1756–63 and 1774–83 also greatly stimulated the English demand for iron, and made fortunes for a new breed of English iron masters. The great innovations in iron in England were, meantime, continued by: the first hydraulic cylinders, which, in 1761, gave to John Roebuck's iron works at Carron (near the Forth) an unprecedentedly strong blast of air (these cylinders, devised by John Smeaton were 4 inch pumps 21 feet long and 1½ feet in diameter, and had a piston worked by a waterwheel); rolling mills for flattening out the iron instead of hammering it, at Henry Cort's mills at Gosport in 1781; a 20 pound steam hammer, built by James Watt in 1783, at John Wilkinson's Broseley iron works in the Coalbrookdale works, which could strike 150 blows a minute; machines for cutting and drilling iron, turning screws, and metal boring lathes, the main credit for all these going to Henry Maudslay of London; and machines for forging nails, the achievement in 1790 of Thomas Clifford. These inventions not only expedited work and saved labour, but helped to give that uniformity of shape to products, which, once merely desirable, was becoming essential (66). Probably the most important of these inventions subsequent to that of Darby was, however, the discovery in 1784 by Henry Cort, an iron master who was the son of a mason from Lancashire, and who had a mill at Fontley near Fareham (Hampshire), of the process of 'puddling'. That meant a stirring and raking of the molten iron in the furnace,

* See above, p. 264.

giving it air, and enabling a far purer iron. This was beneficial, allowing, for example, Richard Crawshay, the iron 'king' of Cyfarthfa to increase his production of bar iron from 10 tons to 200 tons a week (67). Coal, instead of charcoal, also began to be used for the manufacture of wrought iron, the market in which remained for architectural and artistic reasons. Indeed, wrought iron made in coal furnaces provided the roof trusses for innumerable railway stations (for example, Euston, in 1839); for the inspiring Reading Room of the British Museum, finished in 1857; for the Menier chocolate works at Noissel-sur-Marne, finished in 1872; and, some years later, for the Eiffel Tower, intended to mark the centenary of the French Revolution of 1789, which was constructed from 12,000 pre-fabricated parts. Wrought iron was thus the material for many of the greatest buildings of the Victorian age (68).

TABLE OF IRON ORE PRODUCTION (million metric tons)

country	1880	1913	1938	1969 for comparison
Britain	18*	16	12	12
France	3	22	33	55
Germany	5	29	11	7
Russia		9	27	186
USA	7	62	72	46

*Note: 1880 was the year of the highest production of iron ore in Britain.

Probably the greatest figure of the first generation of iron masters was John Wilkinson, son of an enterprising Cumberland farmer, who, to begin with, used a blast furnace for wrought iron. Wilkinson built five or six blast furnaces at Broseley, obtained coal from mines which he himself owned, bought tin mines in Cornwall, and constructed landing stages on the Thames, while his brother William established an iron works at Indret, near Nantes, and subsequently built modernised furnaces for the French iron town of Le Creusot. John Wilkinson made iron chairs, iron pipes, iron vats for brewers, iron bridges at Coalbrookdale in 1770, Sunderland in 1796 and across the Severn in 1779. His London Bridge of 700 feet of 1801 was deemed by the great sculptor, Canova, to be worth a journey to England from Italy to see. Wilkinson launched an iron barge on the Severn in 1787 (to carry coal and other iron), innumerable parts of innumerable machines, and even forty miles of cast iron pipes for Paris. His machine for boring metal (originally for military purposes) made possible the cylinders in Watt's first steam engine. He made a steam threshing machine on his own farm and even issued his own currency, which had a wide circulation in Staffordshire and Shropshire. Much of the artillery used by Britain to win the Napoleonic wars was cast in one or other of Wilkinson's great furnaces (69).

Wilkinson was, however, only the most protean example of an astonishing generation of Englishmen. Superior to him, probably, in wealth, though not in invention, was Anthony Bacon, who realised as early as 1765 the critical importance of an interconnection between iron, coal and the vicinity of streams to supply power. All knew that South Wales had iron, but the bad roads had hitherto rendered it valueless. In 1765, Bacon, withdrawing at the right time from a lucrative career as chief supplier of food and equipment to the forces (70) — a commission evidently more valuable than any other at that time — gained, for £100 a year, a concession from the landowner, Lord Talbot, to exploit all the mines within forty miles of Merthyr. The subsequent building of the Glamorgan Canal made Bacon's fortune. He created Merthyr as the greatest centre of iron in the world and made Wales a furnace out of a pastoral land. In the war of American revolution, Bacon provided the Government with artillery. In 1782, he retired and sold off his works to a variety of entrepreneurs, whose names were all pioneers in iron-making for several generations (Hill, Lewis, Crawshay, Homfray and Guest).

Other great iron kings made their fortunes in the lowlands of Scotland, Sheffield, Newcastle and Rotherham. These men were, in every sense, the first 'captains of industry' who would seem later, to prejudiced eyes, the tyrants of a new age. In their own time, however, they appeared as innovators, philanthropists, winners of wars, men of vision, and, above all, the creators of work for a quickly growing population. During the early nineteenth century, these iron masters and their successors became the essential providers for English industry: in particular, serving the railways with iron rails and parts of engines. A vast export (over a quarter of output in 1848) was also possible, since both the USA and France laid down British rails on their railroads. In 1850, Guest's iron mill at Dowlais, then the leading iron works of Britain, just outside Merthyr, boasted eighteen blast furnaces .

Countries other than Britain had entered the new iron age long before the mid nineteenth century. In France, the royal foundry at Le Creusot, near Chalon-sur-Saône (founded in 1782 with the help of William Wilkinson and converted for the production of munitions by Napoleon) began using coke in 1810. It was anglicised (modernised) after Waterloo by English technicians, before passing to the family of Schneider, under whom it became great. But, until 1850, three-fifths of French pig iron was still coming from charcoal furnaces. The transition to modern furnaces only began during the Second Empire. Even then, the crisis of 1870—71 delayed growth, as well as cutting off the country from Alsace's iron deposits, whose size, however, was not then known. But from the 1890s onwards, France was beginning to compete with Britain and Germany. The ore came from Meurthe-et-Moselle, particularly the Briey-Longwy corner, later to be disputed by Germany. By 1914, France was already producing 22 million tons of iron ore, to Britain's 16 million and Germany's 29 million.

Germany had abundant metallurgical knowledge. Excellent ores had been mined for generations in the valley of the Sieg. But nothing much was done before 1860. In 1846, the furnaces of Germany were still worked by water-power and on a small scale. Iron-mining was a 'peasant by-industry' despite good railways* and the opening of the coalfield in the Ruhr. (An exception was the iron industry in Silesia; a characteristic of which was the iron bridge, in its capital, Breslau, built in 1800 (72)). In the 1860s, however, Germany began to industrialise and, after faltering again in the 1870s, due to the discovery of, and conversion of Britain and the US, to the Bessemer steel process,† Germany gained the lead in European ironmaking, overtaking Britain in 1906 (as she had done in the case of steel in 1893). The huge mines of Luxemburg and newly acquired Lorraine were the main power behind this. In the development of German iron, as in many other things, the Prussian state (through its educational enterprise) played an important part; Bessig, the first great German iron manufacturer was, for example, a prize pupil of the Gewerbe Institut of Berlin (72). The German iron-masters also constituted themselves in the 1870s as a powerful and successful nationalist pressure group against free trade (73).

Utterly different was the history of iron in the US. There, while pig iron was still usually smelted with charcoal, the American colonies, as they then were, were well-placed. They even exported (especially from Maryland) much pig iron to England (133,000 hundredweight in 1779) (74). Thereafter, however, the coming of coke, the invention of better machinery, and much reduced costs made iron more expensive in the US than it had been in England till the 1840s. Nor was the new USA particularly quick to take up new ideas in iron-making. Puddling, for example, was not done in the US till 1817. The first US railways were built with rails imported from England. Then the use of anthracite, used by blacksmiths in the Wyoming valley since about 1760, and a new hot air blast system of heating furnaces, transformed the position. Coke began to be widely used in the US about 1850. Thereafter, rails were usually made there too. Cast iron was substituted for the wooden parts of steam engines, as in the case of other heavy machinery. Sewing machines, stoves, and innumerable other domestic tools were soon con-structed from that metal. The American civil war, like all wars, ancient and modern, impelled a new demand for iron. The subsequent peace was even more demanding. In the 1880s, the completion of the American railway system took US production of iron beyond Britain's by 1890 (75).

The coming of steel on a large scale after Sir Henry Bessemer described his new process in 1856 transformed the history of iron.‡ The

---

* See below page 280.
† See below page 283.
‡ See below page 283.

production of iron ore still gives, however, a good indication of the relative economic strengths of Western industrial countries down to 1914, and perhaps even afterwards.

The role played by steel (iron containing only 0.5 to 1.5% of carbon) meant, however, that the production of iron continued to be a critical matter in politics. In the First World War, for example, the French Comité des Forges, the powerful French employers' association founded under Napoleon III (and as secretive as it was influential), became the main purchasing agency for buying iron for the war. Surviving, concentrated, free from nationalisation (perhaps by good luck), with many interests outside iron, far from united, and often eccentric, the iron masters of France have always seemed, and seem, to be characteristic captains of an essential industry (76).

Steam, coal, iron: the first consequence was 'the railway age', which itself had consequences of the first importance. For coal not only powered the early railways. The railways carried coal to innumerable destinations for further development.

The railway, as opposed to the railway engine, was born long before the nineteenth century. Some-time, among the German mines of the sixteenth century, perhaps about 1550, wooden rails were introduced to help the haulage of heavy trucks. These had flanged wheels before 1600, and were known also in English coal mines before that date (77). By the eighteenth century, the edges of these wooden rails, running from the pithead to the point where the coal could be embarked, were being protected, as ploughshares had been for generations, by iron. A cast-iron edged rail, on which the wheels of wagons were kept steady by flanges as if in modern lines, was to be seen at Loughborough in the eighteenth century. Thus railways were, to begin with, an accessory to coal. They began by being established in all industrial areas for that purpose (78). The use of canals enhanced these usages. Wholly cast iron rails were being made by Abraham Darby II at Coalbrookdale by 1767 (79).

The locomotive has a less ancient history than the rail. Even so, the French engineer Nicolas Joseph Cugnot constructed a steam carriage in 1769. William Murdock, the inspired foreman at Boulton's works at Soho, built a model locomotive, which travelled at 8 m.p.h. in 1785. In 1801, Richard Trevithick, son of the manager of a Cornish mine, designed a steam carriage for use in collieries (he was influenced by Murdock, who was then living at Redruth). Trevithick's carriage was a success. In 1803, he drove a steam carriage four miles in London, from Holborn to Paddington. In 1804, he devised an engine to pull seventy men and ten tons (of iron) at the Pen-y-Darran iron works near

Merthyr.* Then, in 1813, George Stephenson, an engine-wright at the Killingworth colliery in Durham, was given permission to build a travelling engine between his colliery and the pithead. The cost of fodder for the horses which previously had drawn the carts full of coal was rising. Stephenson had seen one of Trevithick's engines at work nearby at the Wylam colliery, eight miles from Newcastle, where his father had been a fireman. Stephenson's 'Blucher' (an appropriate name for an engine of that year) ran in 1814 from Killingworth to Tyneside. It was a success. Ten years afterwards, Stephenson built an engine for commercial use on a line which had been built between Stockton and Darlington, owned by a Quaker, Edward Pease, the son of a woollen manufacturer. The success of that first true railway journey (in 1825) caused a competition for an engine for the route between Manchester and Liverpool. Stephenson's *Rocket* won the competition. The line was opened in 1830. The permanent way between those two cities was finished before the question of the traction had been decided. Some thought that horses or cables, with a stationary engine, would be best (80). As much concern was spent on the character of the permanent way as on the engine, for the crossing of the bog known as Chat Moss necessitated the sinking of faggots of wood on to which huge loads of stone and earth had to be tipped. The early railway lines thus required almost as much care as the building of Venice. Subsequently, cuttings and embankments were dug, as well as special drainage works. A phenomenal amount of work had to be done by pick, shovel and wheelbarrow. Tunnelling in particular meant hard work in disagreeable circumstances. Still, even when the backbreaking labour by the workers is recognised, the drive, local patriotism, and conviction of engineers and local businessmen interested in the construction itself and the service which it would give to the community, should also be noted (81). Even many railway workers creating the railways were brought to 'love the locomotives', as a Spanish anarchist Angel Pestaña admitted (82).

Once these early problems had been resolved, country after country began to be criss-crossed by a network of railways, most undertaken by private enterprise, with nearly every nation transformed in the process even if the nation itself was not thereby built (83). Very early on, the possibility of an abuse of monopoly by railway companies was mentioned as a danger. Nationalisation was advocated in 1844. The law soon provided that the still private companies had to carry out certain defined functions (such as running at least once each way every day and stopping once a day at every station) (84). The great British constructors included Samuel Morton Peto (nephew and apprentice to the greatest British builder of the early nineteenth century and the constructor of the

* Trevithick went in 1816 to Peru in order to make his fortune by running the silver mines at Cerro de Pasco. He lost everything, returned, and died in poverty, his funeral being paid for by the workmen at John Hall's factory at Dartford (1833).

new Houses of Parliament) who, having started life as a bricklayer in his uncle's company, by the 1840s was employing an army of 14,000 men in building railways. He also built railways in Canada, Australia and elsewhere in the British Empire. A rival, Hudson, a gambler, was discredited in 1848. Isambard Brunel, engineer and universal man, builder of tunnels, ships and bridges as well as the Great Western Railway, symbolises that generation of great designers.

By 1850, Britain had 16,200 miles of railways. The problems of monopoly, rights of passage, and where the trains should stop, had everywhere become major questions of political business. The railways were carrying sixty million tons of freight and over 100 million passengers (85). An elaborate system of signals, based on the semaphore devised in 1792 by Claude Chappe (to help the French Revolution), had been introduced to serve this greater upheaval. In the 1850s, an electric telegraph* began to be used along most lines. Trains travelling at sixty miles an hour were by then common, but in the 1830s, some had thought it dangerous to health to contemplate travel faster than ten miles an hour. These engines burned mostly coke but, later, coal. On the continent, wood was more common (86). For the generation after 1830, British engines, British engineers, even British railway workers and British rails, were carried all over the world, taking the message of Stockton and Darlington to the continent, to the US, Russia, Canada, Egypt, South America, India and Australia.

Belgium, Britain's nearest and best client, was even more vigorous than her political protector (as Britain became, after Belgian independence in 1830) in organising a railway network. The Government there, in the first flush of its independence, decided on a national, planned network. By 1844, a system linking all the main Belgian cities had been made, all owned by the state. In France, a long discussion ensued as to whether the railway should be public or private. There were compromises. Thus though private companies did the work, the State assisted, by buying shares. The Government also insisted in laying down, in 1842, a national programme for railways, with lines radiating outwards from Paris. The Government offered to provide the land. Local authorities would be asked to finance the infrastructure (including bridges, tunnels and permanent way) while private enterprise would finance the superstructure (rails, rolling stock, and running costs). In the event, the local authorities dropped out of this finely conceived plan. Private companies were responsible for all the building.

The French network was finished during the Second Empire. Costs of transport became everywhere less and, by 1870, there had also been many amalgamations. Six large companies managed the great trunk lines (87). Napoleon III made all possible use of railways in 1849 during

---

* Discussed on page 333.

his intervention in Italy and, thereafter, rail, to supply and indeed make possible, a new epoch of armies a million strong, became the dominant factor in strategy (88).

Germany was ahead of France in realising the importance of the railway. An 'English coal road' had been in use in the Ruhr by 1800 (89). An experimental freight line was laid in Elberfeld in 1826. A passenger line between Nuremberg and Fürth was opened in 1836. The economist List soon proposed a national network of railways (he was aware of their potential military value). Though the different governments of Germany were well disposed to railways (and bought shares), private companies did the work (90). By 1848, 2,500 miles of rail were open in Germany (91). The German railways were dominated by the Prussian companies, and von Moltke in 1866 (recalling Peto in the Crimea) made the fullest use of the five railways at his disposal in taking troops to the front. The railway had, in Germany as in many other countries (including England), by then compensated for the poor roads which, in the past, had hindered both commerce and war (92).

The railway helped to unite Gemany. It played no part in the achievement of Italian unity. The Italian railways in 1859 were still organised within local frontiers, save for the line from Turin to Genoa of 1854 (one of Cavour's favourite projects, reducing the journey between the two cities to a day) (93). The role of railways, on the other hand, in creating a modern nation out of both the USA and Russia was fundamental.

The first railway in the US was built in 1830 in Baltimore, though horsepower and bizarre land sails were at first used as the source of power. Only in 1832 was steam decided upon as being better. In the 1830s, US lines were radiating out only from the few big towns. Wooden rails only were made locally, while English engines were imported. Difficulties derived from the vested interests of canal and turnpike companies. In New York, the Erie Canal had become a state enterprise. Competition was not desired by the legislators. Until 1851, New York State even forbade the carriage of freight on railways (94). In addition, railways were considered by many to be undemocratic. They seemed monopolistic by implication. The 'open road' seemed the right transport for a nation of free men.

Railways had, however, one obvious contribution to make to America. Roads and canals had followed the natural line of the country. That meant travel was usually from north to south. But many Americans, particularly pioneers, wanted to move from east to west. Railways enabled them to do so. By rail, they could soon also travel more cheaply than by other means, as could their freight (95). That enabled the colonisation of the previously empty West of North America. The US, by 1870, had a network of 53,000 miles of rail as compared with 50,000 in all continental Europe (96). A great part in this development was played by the individual states. From 1835 onwards, the states gave help by subscriptions to stock, loans, guarantees of railroad securities and so on. Federal aid enabled the completion of the railroad to the Pacific in 1869. Faced by a choice of what appeared to be the three evils of private monopoly, public monopoly or public regulation, the US chose private monopoly, perhaps thereby enabling alternative forms of transport to make a competitive challenge earlier than anywhere else (97). In return, the states gave grants of land to the railway companies of a size never equalled before in the history of landholding, surpassing by far, for example, the grants made by Spanish kings to conquistadors in Peru or knightly orders in Castile: for instance, the Northern Pacific Company received no less than 39 million acres (98).

The early railways were distinguished by magnificent station terminals, vast arched roofs of iron, of a spaciousness unknown among buildings since the cathedrals or, as some said, the pyramids, enabling the separation of passengers from freight. Though the most grandiose of these (such as St Pancras in London, or Milan) were of a later date, railway stations were already, by 1870, the largest of industrial buildings. Yet the self-confident railway engine symbolised to some a continent out of control: in 1908 the German Impressionist poet Detlev von Liliencron wrote 'Der Blitzzug' about a train which raced across Europe to end in a disaster. 'Is it going to arrive late in heaven's station?' asked the poet, and, like Pilate, he did not stay for an answer (99).

The second and more hectic half of the railway age was, however, made possible by an old material, namely steel, which, after 1856, began to be much cheaper and more reliable than it had ever been before.

28

The Age of Steel

Where iron played a great but perhaps not dominant part in the first part of the industrial revolution, the second part of that upheaval has been characterised more by steel than by anything else; though it is a mark of our time that nothing can be so sharply defined as it used to be.

Ordinary iron cannot give a sharp edge to an object. Steel can. It began to be made by the Chalybes of Asia Minor, a sub-tribe of the Hittites, about 1400 BC. Iron bars were hammered when in direct contact with heat and charcoal, and then thrown hot into water (hot iron becomes tougher when so tempered, unlike copper and bronze, which become weaker). Throughout the ancient world and the Middle Ages, this early 'wrought' steel continued to be made in small forges. The best known steel in Rome was a popular iron of South India, made in round cakes a few inches big (1). Makers of steel were, for a long time, a special sub-division of iron masters. They concentrated on the manufacture of knives and swords. Almost every country had its centres where such objects were made best: Sheffield or Toledo. Steel was used in literature as a metaphor for hardness: 'The friends thou hast,' Polonius said to Laertes, 'Grapple them to thy soul with hoops of steel.' Steel seemed almost a precious stone, man-made though it was. Then, about 1740—50, (the date is not clear), a Quaker clock-maker of Doncaster, Benjamin Huntsman, smelted cast steel for the first time. He used a very high temperature indeed, because he was dissatisfied with the quality of his steel instruments. He ultimately set up a factory at Attercliffe (a village near Sheffield). He began to be prosperous about 1770, making edged tools and parts for clocks. Many of them were exported to France (2).

The cutlers of Sheffield were, to begin with, hostile to Huntsman's process. They thought his steel *too* hard. But Huntsman's trademark became famous (3). Though the inventor tried to keep his process secret, it was betrayed (4). Even so, steel remained a minor side of the industrial revolution for a hundred years after this first smelting. The steel of those days was not, in fact, faultless. Even in 1849, when Krupps were testing their first big steel gun, they found that the steel which they made could not stand the pressure of the explosion. About that time, however, William Kelly of Kentucky, a manufacturer of sugar kettles, in a very small way, for the sugar industry in Louisiana, observed that an air blast on molten pig iron caused more heat than ever when the iron was not covered with charcoal. This led him to the conclusion that the carbon in pig iron could be blown out merely by air. The carbon itself would act as a kind of fuel. Kelly tried to develop this idea, but went bankrupt. He made over his claims to an English genius of Huguenot origin, Sir Henry Bessemer. Bessemer had already invented a perforated die stamp, a method of making imitation Utrecht velvet, and a machine for setting type quickly. Inspired by the need to create a stronger steel than that used in the guns of the Crimean War, Bessemer read a paper on the subject of 'how to make steel without fuel' at a meeting at Cheltenham of the British Association in 1856. After a few years of experiment, the 'Bessemer process' was soon in use — above all at Sheffield, in the inventor's own factory, using steel without phosphorus, though he was too late for the American Civil War (5). Subsequently, Friedrich Siemens, one of three brilliant scientific brothers from Hanover, with help from Sidney Thomas of Canonbury and his cousin Percy Gilchrist, developed the 'open hearth method', which enabled steel to be made straight from the ore; particularly the highly phosphoric ore of Germany. These two systems transformed the manufacture of steel in all the industrialised countries.

Britain, the old leader of the industrial revolution in its iron and cotton days, was rather slow to see the benefits of the new steel. The British even delayed twenty years till they introduced steel into guns. Only in 1877 did the British Board of Trade permit the use of steel in bridge-building (John Wilkinson had not *needed* such permission for his iron bridge a century before). Though the Forth Bridge was built of steel (1882–89), the USA took the lead in steel manufacture from 1886 (6). All the later railways of the US were built from steel, and there the age of steel indeed begat a new generation of financiers and captains of industry (such as Carnegie and Frick) who caused their European contemporaries to seem men of modest stature. Steel was also used by 1900 for buildings (above all, skyscrapers in New York and Chicago, where sites were so expensive that it was economic to build upwards), for bridges, for wire, and for offices – and then, after 1909, for cars. In 1909, there were 654 iron and steel works in the US employing 278,000 people, and already worth a capital of $1,500 million (7). They produced 21 million tons of steel. In comparison, Britain was producing 8 million tons, Germany 13, France 3 — and Russia already 3 (8).

Russia was thus becoming a major industrial power for the first time. Her output in 1913, of 5 million tons, was already greater than France's.

Her increase in production since 1870 was some 500 times faster than that of any other country. It was also faster than under Communism after 1917 (9). Meantime, by the First World War, Thomas's and Gilchrist's 'open hearth' method of steel making had taken over from the Bessemer one (20 million tons of steel were made in the US by the 'open hearth' method in 1913 against 10 by the Bessemer one). That subsequently became the normal method.

After 1918, US pre-eminence in steel manufacture was more pronounced than ever, being led by the boom of the 1920s in which Europe did not greatly share and which was specially characterised by the production of motor cars. In 1929, the USA was producing half the world's steel (56 million tons out of 128). It served new rolling mills for the automobile industry, and made use for the first time of new ferrous alloys, by which very tough, but light springy steel could be produced (10). Even when, during the depression of 1929–33, US steel production fell to 13 million tons (below her production of any year since 1901), she was still producing more than France and Germany combined. Subsequently, the US revived, being back to the level of 1929 by the 1940s. She had doubled that level of production in the 1960s. After that date, steel ceased to be the dominant manufacture that it had been since 1900. Steel works were running down, seeming overmanned and too large. The world since 1960 has been one of plastics, concrete and glass. By 1971, the US had even been overtaken as a manufacturer of steel by Russia (109 million tons to 121) and was being approached by Japan, a new contender, with nearly 100 million tons (11).

In the second half of the nineteenth century, the first benefit of steel was to improve the railway system. Steel rails turned out to be between ten and fifteen times more durable than iron ones. Steel bridges were tougher than iron ones. The huge compound engines of the late nineteenth century were also more powerful than their predecessors. That meant both further investment in lines and cuts in costs. In 1868, wheat per bushel carried in the US cost 42.6 cents. In 1910 it cost 9.6 cents (12). The US added 70,000 new miles of rail between 1880 and 1890 alone. Britain also more than doubled its length of rail between 1860 and 1913. France quadrupled hers. Germany increased her railways almost six times. Italy also completed her railway system after her unification in 1870. She trebled her mileage between that date and 1913, and linked herself internationally to France and Switzerland by the Fréjus and St Gotthard tunnels opened respectively in 1871 and 1882 (13). Spain, late into the railway age, had a mere 625 miles of line open in 1860, but had over 9,000 in 1913 (14). Russia, as late as Spain in embarking on this adventure, had only 125 miles open in 1860. In 1913, Russia had over 40,000 miles, a system of communications which, single track though the trans-Siberian railway was, enabled the Tsarist authoritarian state to be consolidated, east to the Pacific and south to the mountains of inner

Asia, laying a foundation for the totalitarian tyranny that was to follow (15).

Long before that, railways were to be found outside Europe and North America. India began to create a huge railway system, following the recommendation of the then Governor-General, Lord Dalhousie, in 1853.* Numerous South American countries had them too. Cuba, the rich, last colony of Spain, began to build private railways for the sugar industry in 1837 and the network was completed for the length of the island after 1900 (16). A line between Cairo and Alexandria was opened in 1856, and one from Cairo to Suez in 1857 (17).

Electric railways began in the US in the 1880s, with elevated city services inside New York and Chicago. After an overhead trolley railway was tried out in Kansas City (1895), inter-urban electric railways began in the US as a competitor to steam. The lack of a large steam locomotive cut costs, and the absence of steam made less dirt, while frequent stops were easier (18). Another innovation was the underground railway which was begun in 1863, with the Metropolitan line in London which passed through central London in built-over cuttings, just under street level. The first 'tube' train was the City and South London under the Thames of 1890. Subways with traction were also tried out, for example, in Glasgow, but not pursued. By 1900, most large modern capitals had underground railways. But Moscow did not have one till the 1930s. Yet another change, assisting the ease of long distance travel, was the introduction of the dining car, sleeping car and lavatories on the train, which began first in the US where distances were so great. They were soon copied in Europe, particularly in Russia, where the train which crossed Siberia had a chapel added as well. Electric lighting in the train, by dynamo under the carriage, was introduced during the 1890s.

This second great railway age created fortunes everywhere. In France, the railway companies became gilt-edged investments, but also bogey-men for the socialist opposition (19). Rails made riches, above all, in the US (20). Combined with the great increase in the size of ships, the railway also made possible the vast emigrations of the nineteenth century from Europe to the Americas.

In the end, however, this chief production of nineteenth century civilisation, became, as Norman Stone put it, 'the chief agent in its destruction' (21). Admittedly, Kitchener used railways to defeat the Mahdi at Omdurman in 1894. But Britain failed to carry through the

---

* Dalhousie, as President of the Board of Trade in London, had even for Britain 'recommended the control of the government, *directly but not vexatiously exercised*' for the development of railways, which he subsequently advocated in India. The definition of that concept has never been adequately achieved.

railway from the 'Cape [of Good Hope] to Cairo', which might have preserved for her a third empire in Africa, after India had rebelled successfully. The Russo-Japanese war of 1904 was a war *against* the railway. For the Japanese attacked when they did because they thought that they had to act before the trans-Siberian rail was completed. While there was a gap in the line at Lake Baikal, they believed that the reinforcements of Russian troops would be slow (22). In 1914, the trains, however, provided the warring nations with essential logistical support. For Germany, all depended on the country's capacity to use the rail service to carry its army to victory 'by timetable' in three weeks, as A. J. P. Taylor put it (23). In Russia, the far from backward industry of the country failed to organise adequate supplies for the front because, Norman Stone tells us, the main trans-Siberian railway could only take 280 wagons, of which 100 were reserved for railway material and 140 for government stores (24). That admirable historian of the Russian front adds: 'It was not trains but timetables which offered problems. Trains chased grain, not the other way about . . . The government watched grain, train and fuel competing, and each falling into chaos' (25). The trouble was that the horses at the front (essential to overcome the problem of local transport) needed a large daily supply of fodder. For his Bessarabian offensive, for example, General Ivanov needed 667 wagons for men, 1,385 for horses (over half the grain harvest of Russia was needed for horses at the front) (26).

In both Britain and France, governmental control of the railways during the First World War offered a foretaste of nationalisation, providing a good example of that cold, ideologyless but, in the end stifling, socialism which war in the industrial age brought even to capitalist countries. During the war itself, Victoria Station and the Gare de l'Est (which Guillaume Apollinaire described as having '*mangé nos fils*') seemed to be gateways to Death. Furthermore, when the Great War came to an end, the 130 railway companies in England of 1913 had been reduced to four (27), and French railways were already a public service (28).

At the end of the war, the chaos in Russia gave for a time authority to the railway union, remarked Adam Ulam, 'perhaps greater than that held by the army or the state itself' (29). Russia before the war had seemed a nation built on railways. How many train journeys occur in late nineteenth century Russian novels! The most famous heroine in Russian literature, Anna Karenina, threw herself before a train which was to take her lover, Vronsky, to the war in the Balkans in 1878. Anna's creator, Tolstoy, also died at a railway station. How appropriate, therefore, that the last of the old Tsars, Nicholas II, should have ended his days as autocrat of the Russians, shuffling from station to station in the royal train, seeking a place to come to a weary halt before his abdication (30). In 1918, the Bolshevik revolution was kept from collapse because of the Bolsheviks' control of railways* (31). Trotsky controlled the Red Army from an armoured train which exerted a powerful (if misleading) effect over the imagination of revolutionaries for a generation. In France, Theodore Zeldin says, the century from 1840 to 1940 'could be written round the railway', life centring round the station more than round the church or town hall, cheap fares keeping family life together. Proust's *petit train* to Cabourg was characteristic of a part of French life so complete that no one could remember what had happened before (32); and for Proust himself even Time had '*des trains express et spéciaux*' (33), as he put it in one of his final metaphors.

The First World War, however, brought the age of railways close to an end, even though the mileage of railways continued to grow in the US till 1924, in France till 1935, and in Russia to the 1960s (34). With the coming of the automobile the railways ceased, even in the USA, to be primarily private enterprises. The combination of automobile and aeroplane rapidly reduced the railway mileage in the US after 1939, so that except on the East coast the train became a memory: a disappearance which Americans will regret in the 1980s.

The Second World War was a conflict primarily of air and road traffic. Nevertheless, the railways which led to, and stopped, at Auschwitz (built by the Austrians when that town was a part of the Austro-Hungarian empire) carried more millions to their death than did even the southern line in Britain, or the eastern one in France, during the First World War (36). Before and afterwards, the trains of Russia have also formed the 'slave caravans' of the 'Gulag archipelago', in the phrase of Solzhenitsyn. In red cattle-cars, millions of peasants were transported to cities of the north in 1929–31. That is also how the Volga German Republic was physically removed to Kazakhstan in 1941, and how millions of Russians were sent back in 1945 from the free countries of the West (37).

Railways produced politically forceful unions. Here, as in other ways, their history in France is characteristic. The French railway union numbered 44,000 in 1854, and 310,000 by 1914 (38). They had ensured by then a twelve-hour day for drivers. Only a fifth of railwaymen were members of the union. To begin with, they had been organised in order to expel English train drivers. Later, they had become bourgeois in outlook, despite occasional strikes. Later still, the French railway union became dominated by Communists. They used their power conservatively, keeping down fares, the railway staff living like civil servants (39), proud, for example, of their skilled organisation which enabled so many special trains to travel so punctually at the beginning of the annual holidays. Others complained that, though railways had made it

* 'Though a minority,' said an eye witness, M. Philips Price, 'they [the committee of the poorer peasants supported by the Bolsheviks] possessed a central apparatus and controlled the railway system' (35).

possible to transport cheap wine all over France, this caused wine to lose its regional qualities (40).

The railway was for several generations the decisive unit of modernised transport. Along the tracks came the food and the coal which enabled the modern city to survive, or even to be constructed. Though in retreat in the 1970s, it seems likely that, if coal becomes again the major source of energy, as has been suggested is likely, the railway will be revived in many countries, at least as a carrier of freight. The 'permanent way' will thus deserve its adjective, after all, even if the actual means of locomotion may be transformed.

29

Cotton as King

Despite steam, coal, iron and railways, the first part of the industrial revolution remained primarily the history of cotton. In all modern countries between 1800 and 1860, the manufacture of cloth and clothes from cotton was the most important industry.

A few more technical innovations completed the picture as it was left by Arkwright. First, came a combination of the Spinning Jenny and Arkwright's water frame. That was the 'mule' devised about 1779 by Samuel Crompton, a violinist at the Bolton theatre. It gave a thread as tough as Arkwright's but as fine as that of the jenny. Crompton, an independent and philanthropic man of courage, did no better himself than most other inventors, even though his machine was soon used in hundreds of English factories. There were, thereafter, few major developments in spinning. Weaving, however, was a different matter. A great change there was brought about by Edmund Cartwright's power loom, a device distantly related to the old ribbon looms of France and of Danzig. Cartwright, a country vicar and scholar, placed a bet that he could produce a weaving machine to make more rapid use of the new quantity of thread now available as a result of the spinning machines. He was successful and set up a factory at Doncaster with a steam engine in 1789. Though he was a bad manager, his invention was successful. It was soon realised that two steam-powered looms tended by an unskilled man were three times as productive as one old loom looked after by a skilled man (1).

Other improvements in the textile industry included a copper cylinder, with a revolving press, which would impress a pattern automatically (1783); and Claude Berthollet's discovery in France in 1785 of the bleaching capacity of chlorine — a device taken up in particular at the St Rollox factory founded by Charles Tennant, a bleacher of Glasgow. The old sight of great quantities of stuffs, spread out in the open air to be bleached by the sun, which had previously marked weaving villages, vanished.

By the end of the Napoleonic wars, all stages of the manufacture of textiles were able to be carried out by machine — shearing the nap of cloth with revolving knives, printing the calico with revolving rollers, pressing, and even packing. Watermills were beginning to give way to steam engines. The first steam-powered loom in Manchester dated from 1806. All horse-driven machinery in the cotton industry had vanished by 1830. Hand spinning was almost dead in England by then, though the steam-powered looms for weaving still employed only about 20,000 to 30,000 people. Looms were still worked by hand by perhaps half a million outworkers in the 1820s (2).

Long before then, the world's cotton economy had itself been transformed. Until the late eighteenth century, most raw cotton came to Europe from the West Indies or the Levant. In 1786, Sea Island or long staple cotton was introduced to the US, but till then it could only be grown well near the sea (3). In 1793, Eli Whitney, a farmer's son from Massachusetts, invented the cotton gin in Georgia. Whitney's device was a fan and brush, which shook the seeds from the cotton boll so successfully that even short staple cotton (the old Eastern type, which could be grown inland in the USA) repaid cultivation. This invention transformed the economy of the US South. Slavery had been in decline there, as elsewhere in the US. Now the number of slaves fell short of demand. Cotton quickly became the South's main export. A single cotton gin could clean 300 pounds of cotton a day, instead of the one pound (of short staple cotton) which had been done by each man by hand (4). The demand for raw cotton (soon in US cotton mills as well as in Europe) was enormous. Eli Whitney enabled it to be satisfied. By 1860, cotton produced in the US had risen from 1½ million pounds a year in 1790 to 2,300 million pounds. The US slave plantations were producing five-sixths of the world's cotton, of which Britain was using 1000 million pounds, the European continent 700 million, and the US itself 350 million. The cost of a slave in the prime of life (a prime field hand) had also risen from $250 in 1815 to nearly $2000 in 1860 while, in 1860, there were four million slaves in place of 700,000 in 1790. Nor was production of cotton confined to the New World: one event indicating a re-awakening of Islam was the birth of the cultivation of cotton in Egypt under Muhammad Ali (5).

The availability of this easily worked and cheap raw material completed the transformation of the clothing of the world. The West Indies had played, by the production of sugar and coffee, a considerable part in the economy of the eighteenth century. Indeed, it was not till 1818 that cotton accounted for a larger sum in value than sugar in the English tables of imports (6). Sugar (and slaves) had assisted the accumulation of capital. But cotton provided the first occasion when a pastoral country made, at the same time, a substantial contribution to Europe's industries and also began to transform its own economy thereby.* In

---

* That was an indication that it is perfectly possible to be a major supplier of Europe and, at the same time, benefit absolutely: a proposition sometimes doubted in the twentieth century.

those days, cotton manufactures represented half of Britain's exports — the largest single such export from 1814 till 1938. In the mid-nineteenth century, English cotton mills employed between 200,000 and 250,000 people, while another force of the same number was employed at hand looms. Probably a majority of the total was made up by women and girls (7). Most mills were still small, employing 150 to 200. Most English cotton workers, hand or factory workers, lived in Lancashire (312,000 out of 527,000 in 1851) (8). US manufacturing was never far behind Britain's. In 1800, there were eight US cotton mills; in 1810, 269; in 1860, 1,091, employing 122,028 (9). But in this, as in all matters, a sense of proportion is needed. In this critical trade of the nineteenth century, there were still, in 1830, some 50% fewer people engaged than there were as servants, at a time when one third of all households in England had living-in servants (10).

The raw material for this industry continued to be grown (as opposed to being cleaned) by primitive methods. The cultivators of the US South used few fertilisers, had little idea of rotation of crops and used slaves (who were employed all the year). This system needed unlimited quantities of land: hence the steady movement westwards of cotton culture (11). The economy of large scale always apparently offset the inefficiency of slavery. The numbers of slaves grew: from 700,000 slaves in 1790, the US had nearly 4 million in 1860 (12), mostly by natural increase, with perhaps some stimulated breeding, and a few imports largely from Cuba.

The manufacture of cotton goods by machine was by then no longer an Anglo-Saxon preserve. Alsace, and Mulhouse in particular, had become as important to France as Lancashire was to England. The first steam engine was established for spinning cotton there in 1812. By 1860, the hand loom had vanished more completely in Mulhouse than it had in Lancashire (though other parts of France retained it for many years, especially Rouen and Lille). A thriving cotton industry also began in Catalonia. There, there was the advantage both of colonial imports of raw cotton from the West Indies, and of the South American market. There, as in England, cotton merchants were not organised in guilds, unlike the wool merchants, with their old customs. There, too, there had been a helpful ban, early in the eighteenth century, on the import of Asian cloths (1718). The government also encouraged cotton manufacture through tax concessions. By the 1790s, there were in Catalonia over 100 cotton factories, employing 80,000 workers (mostly women, as usual), with 3,000 looms. At least fourteen spinning machines had been imported, from England. No French city had a comparable cotton industry. Equally, there was no comparable industry to that of the cotton one of Catalonia in Spain (13). It was in this industry that, after years of ruin, brought about by the Napoleonic wars (and the failure to re-equip afterwards), labour unrest first occurred in Spain. At the same time, how appropriate it was that the most successful reforming prime minister of Britain of the first part of the nineteenth century should have been Sir Robert Peel, son of the Lancashire cotton millionaire who had entered parliament partly to introduce the first factory legislation!

Wool (much less linen) production did not share in all these changes. Till the late eighteenth century, wool was, in England, a local industry, concentrated in Yorkshire. There was a long fight by the half-organised labour movements of the day against factories. In 1803, only one sixth of the cloth woven in the West Riding was produced in large factories such as that run by Benjamin Gott, a Yorkshire spinner, who sought to introduce into the worsted wool trade the mechanical changes which had transformed the cotton industry. But with woollen cloths other than worsted, the thread was, for a long time, too fragile to allow a shuttle to move faster than it could in a hand loom. It was only when the power loom was at a more advanced stage that it was widely used. Among silk weavers, though, power was even used in cottage industries; for example, in Coventry (14).

The first stage of the industrial revolution, characterised by cotton and other articles of clothing, was, appropriately, completed by events in the US. At the Great Exhibition in London in 1851, much attention was paid to the new US mechanical reaper, made by McCormick,* a tardy reminder that mechanisation could affect agriculture as much as anything else. But the sewing machine was also shown in 1851, having been devised the previous year by Isaac Singer, an inventor from New York (15), ready to become both the pioneer of hire purchase and 'the real hero of the American Civil War', when the demand for uniforms and boots would give a great opportunity to machine-stitching. Machinery had also begun to affect shoe-making in the 1840s. Though a machine for sewing soles was only introduced into America in the last year of the Civil War, 1864, the mechanisation of leather-made shoes was soon completed, driving out wooden clogs and bare feet at least from the floors of the richer world. Modern man could, in the 1870s, first in the USA, then in Europe, dress himself from head to toe in cheap, manufactured goods. Could people have lived in the modern city without the machine-made shoe? It is hard to believe. Thus, just when the famous Russian radical, Chernyshevsky, was telling his readers that a pair of boots was more important than the plays of Shakespeare, their price began to fall. Within a few years, machine-made footwear came within the reach even of Russians. Boots play a great part in the books of later Russian novelists.

The wars of 1861—4 in the US and of 1864, 1866, and 1870—1 in Europe spelled the end of the age of cotton. The first of these wars was inspired by the spread of slavery on the cotton fields. The last of those

* See below, page 359.

wars ruined the French cotton industry, for the time being at least, since the country lost Alsace, including Mulhouse. During the war of 1864 in Holstein, Britain's inaction in the face of German determination had convinced Bismarck that Britain was pacific and would pose no difficulties. Cotton, of course, continued to be of importance. The US soon recovered her cotton industry, developed new steam gins, and used cotton seeds for oil and fertilisers, while a new kind of loom automatically caused the machine to stop should the thread break (a single weaver could now attend eighty four looms in place of eight). Until 1945, cotton was still the largest item of US merchandise (16). But, capital invested in cotton in the US after the Civil War was always less than it was in iron and steel and, particularly, food products (17). Similarly in France, though cotton recovered after the loss of Alsace (many cotton families moving away from there), those who controlled the cotton trade came, in Theodore Zeldin's words, 'to be the archetype of the conservative family business' (18), with their sung graces before Sunday lunch, secrecy, prudent economy, hard work and self reliance. As for England, the cotton trade declined rapidly after 1918, leaving Lancashire a shadow of its past splendour. After 1945, the number of cotton spindles and the output of cotton yarn produced in England even fell below that of most large European countries (19). Russia which, in the 1930s, still produced less cotton goods than Britain, produced ten times Britain's output in the 1970s (20). In 1980, cotton no longer plays such a decisive part. Though some cotton goods have had revivals, for example jeans,* the greatly increased population of the world dresses itself in artificial textiles made from oil or pine trees, and 'King Cotton' has gone the way of most other monarchies.

---

* The word derives from Gênes, Genoa, where twilled cotton of this sort was traded.

30

Industrialisation and Modernisation

By the time of the American Civil War in the 1860s, and the Italian and German wars of unification, which extended from 1859 till 1871, a new stage of industrialisation was beginning. At first sight, this seemed a mere change in the relative importance of the producing countries. Many countries other than England had begun to mechanise their industries and had done so both more cheaply and more quickly than had Britain. In 1800, the United States had seemed to be a group of agricultural republics which chanced to be able to produce a lot of cotton, a sought-after raw material. But the US had become a unified state – because the merchants needed a central government to protect their interests (1). In 1860, the US was the nation most concerned to introduce important innovations. An American seemed already more likely than an Englishman to ensure that tiresome and expensive manufacturing was done by machinery. Richard Cobden wrote, in the *Economist*, in 1851: 'The superiority of the United States to England is ultimately as certain as the next eclipse' (2). De Tocqueville had said much the same in the 1830s, coupling the US, with even greater prescience, with Russia.* The sewing machine and the mechanised reaper of 1850 symbolised a new era in which US inventiveness would be greater than that of the old world. Americans had already, by 1860, been forerunners in the use of chloroform for anaesthetics and had first made use of the Scottish engineer James Nasmyth's steam hammer patented in 1842 and the cylinder printing-press patented in 1847. In the beginning, capital to market such inventions had been hard to come by in the US. Foreign investments were not much found there before 1830. The capital which launched the age of industry in the US mostly derived from savings, helped by local savings banks and insurance companies, rising steadily and, in comparison with all European countries, except for England, fast. From a total of $50 million invested in the US manufacturing industry in 1820, the figure had reached $1,000 million in 1860 (3). By 1870, foreign investment in the US had probably risen to £300 million, most of it British (4).

* The prophecy is cited on page 504.

294

Once industrialisation had begun in the US, the advantages of working in a new country seemed great. There were few vested interests, either of landowning capital or of labour, to resist innovators, no frame-breaking rioters, as there had been in Arkwright's mills: instead, planters stole Whitney's cotton gin in order to use it more quickly. There was always a shortage of labour. The availability of land kept wages high since, had they been low, the wage earners would have left and gone west. The early operatives of US cotton mills usually stayed, indeed, for a short time only. Only during the age of mass immigration, after 1845, were conditions in the US cotton plants comparable to those in the English 'dark satanic mills' (5). By the 1840s, US factories were spreading fast. They were using power-driven machines, so that, by the time of the Civil War, that system already dominated many industries, including firearms, agricultural tools, watches, sewing machines and interchangeable parts of machines. The economies achieved by substitution were sometimes as great as 50 to 1. Thus the US was already, in 1850, on the way to becoming the greatest industrial power in the world. True, in the 1880s, agriculture was still the main source of wealth; but, by 1900, the US was predominantly industrial. In 1894, she outstripped Britain in volume of manufactured goods. By 1914, she produced as much as Britain, Germany and France combined.

What were the reasons? After all, not every rich pastoral country has made wise use of resources. Was it due to new methods of salesmanship and advertising? Vastly greater demand from a vastly greater population? The availability of capital? The special genius of the US in devising a system of interchangeable parts? The tariff? The patent law? The cheap transport? Or, perhaps, the free constitution, its enthusiastic acceptance by the waves of emigrants from tyrannies and the free life that it made possible? Surely it was the last factor that really counted. That at least is the clear implication of the argument in, for example, Gunner Myrdal's account of surviving poverty in Asia in the twentieth century.

Looking ahead still further, the inventiveness, willingness to take every opportunity, confidence in the 'system', and ruthlessness enabled the US to continue to dominate the world technically throughout most of the twentieth century. Only in the 1970s, after a brief experience of world power had brought excessive intervention by the central authority in the economy, would the technological and commercial lead of the US begin to falter.

On the continent of Europe, too, the British example had been followed. Indeed, industry often developed under British guidance. The role of British commerce has been noticed. But that of British workmen and entrepreneurs was also important. Many British skilled workers were to be found, in the early nineteenth century, near Calais, in the lace trade in Vienna, in cotton mills in Rouen, and in Alsace (6). Even

Napoleon set up a model weaving shed at Passy in the 1800s to teach weavers from the south how to work a flying shuttle, under the supervision of a Scots wool merchant named Douglas. By the late nineteenth century, say 1870, Britain also had about £800 million invested abroad: France £500 million (7).

German industrialisation was, if anything, faster than that of any other country. Her unification was, certainly, assisted by the fact that the settlement of 1815 enabled Prussia to dominate the commerce of other German states. Hence the Zollverein which, by 1834, embraced three quarters of Germany. In one generation, between 1840 and 1875, the Germans passed from the Middle Ages to modern times. Some individuals (the bootmakers of the Palatinate were an example) even experienced three stages of industrial life — industrial handicraft, outwork, and the factory system — as some peoples in the second half of the twentieth century did also (8). Railways, the end of restrictions on the mobility of labour, a modern financial system and the customs union all occurred in Germany in a single lifetime, accompanied by a swift growth of population. Then, in the next generation, came the great steel innovations, electricity, political expansion, national union and what Fritz Fischer would call the 'grab for world power'.* Still, for Germany, the critical years were the 1840s, the years when the machine-makers were gathering in Borsig's works in Berlin or the Ruhrort engineering works, forerunners of Krupp's cast-steel works at Essen: the first large scale private economic enterprises in a country accustomed to the operations of the state. But always the state played a far larger part in German industrialisation than in Britain, France, or the US: the Gewerbe Institut, founded in Berlin in 1821 to spread knowledge of new industry, had no precedent elsewhere. German science was not only financed by the state but anticipated enterprise: whereas in England, the first industrial research laboratory was established only in the 1870s, when the greatest age of industrial advance was past there (9).

It is not possible to neglect Russia in this discussion. Russia was already, by 1914, among the great industrial countries, even if industry there began even more under the shadow of government than was the case in Germany. Old Russia had had a few, simple domestic industries, such as iron, salt and coarse cloth. Under the Viking lords who, long before, established the Slav kingdoms and principates, Russia had indeed had a mercantile past. The first grand duchy of Kiev resembled the East India or the South Africa Companies. They were commercial enterprises which sought property. All that was long ago forgotten. Russia was gradually united around the leadership of the Sultanate of Moscow, a state which grew up as the tax farmer for the

---

* Fritz Fischer's *Griff nach der Weltmacht* (1961) was inexplicably translated into English as 'Germany's Aims in the First World War'.

Khans of the Golden Horde. Moscow's commercial ties were always with the East, not the West and, till the eighteenth century, Moscow's trade was primarily oriental. Many Russian words to do with money are Mongolian. The Khans insisted on being paid tribute in silver: hence the Muscovites' oriental business ethics. There was no sense of property, industry or individual enterprise (10). Later, when the Golden Horde had been driven off, Russian attitudes to commerce remained rather oriental. Only foreigners, tightly controlled and unable to play any part in politics, could be merchants on a grand scale. Still, Dutch and German businessmen set up foundries, Swedes produced paper, and the Dutch established wool mills. Subsequently, a few Russian merchants were permitted to establish industrial monopolies on the understanding that they would give the Tsar a share. Then came the age of Peter the Great, architect, anatomist, surgeon, expert soldier and consummate economist, as Frederick the Great described him in a letter to Voltaire (11). Peter sought to create a huge standing army. He needed weapons and uniforms exceeding Russia's manufacturing capacity. Those things could not be imported, since the Tsar had no money which would be accepted internationally. Nor did Peter wish to rely on foreigners. Hence, industry was created, under the Tsar's orders and, unusually in the history of manufacturing, specifically for war. Mines and cotton mills, foundries and fortresses, were founded on the basis of slave, or 'temporarily exiled', labour. Whole villages of State peasants were shipped to do the manual work. This State-directed system continued mostly unchanged till the nineteenth century. Catherine the Great tried to bring many mines in the Urals, and several metallurgical industries, under the control of rich landed families able to direct labour of their own. In the late eighteenth century, the abolition of internal tolls and tariffs, the opening of many State monopolies to general commerce, and the permission to peasants to enter the grain market (by the revocation of the decree by which merchants could buy serfs as labourers) created the beginnings of a commercial economy. But the State continued to dominate most manufacturing. A great German merchant, Ludwig Knoop, was permitted in 1839 to found cotton mills. When he died in 1894, Knoop had become the richest industrialist in Russia, but neither he nor his fellow foreigners were able to establish themselves as public men in Russia as Huguenot or German citizens did in other nations. The Russian railways were largely promoted by Germans, the chemical, oil and later electrical industries were developed by Belgians and Germans. The only specifically Russian enterprise was the agglomeration of textile mills, served by serf entrepreneurs (thus ensuring that industrialism could be combined with serfdom and bondage) (12).

Although, in the nineteenth century, the character of Russian industrialisation seemed barbarous, and certain to be less successful than that undertaken in freer countries, the Tsarist pattern of state direction has been carried on under the name of Communism' by Russia in the twentieth century. It has also been emulated by other nations incapable of ensuring enterprise in freedom. In Russia, three national plans (1928–32, 1933–37, and 1938–41 — interrupted by war) were devised, which sought to carry forwards the industrialisation begun under the Tsars at a breakneck pace, with an eye, as always in Russia, on military considerations. The methods used were, as well as state direction, a compulsory and brutal agricultural revolution; and propaganda appeals and great publicity given to those who, like the 'heroic' Stakhanov allegedly cut in one day 100 tons of coal (the average was 6). Rewards and comforts were graded in relation to contribution made, 'outstanding' workers being benefitted to the detriment of the average. Not surprisingly, there were instances, Leonard Schapiro tells us, of Stakhanovites murdered by their fellow workers (13). Similar things may have happened under Peter the Great. At all events, Russian industrial modernisation occurred in a way that anyone who knows anything of Russian history would have expected; fast, violently, closely connected with military preconceptions, wrapped up in extraordinary rumours, and in the tradition of oriental despotism.

To return, however, to our general survey of the world observed from about 1860. The characteristic of the time was not simply an alteration in the relative position, industrially, of one country or another which indicated the change in the character of the industrial revolution after 1860. It was change in what was being produced. Thus the age of cotton was giving way already to that of iron and steel before 1860. Whereas cotton primarily caused a change in dress, iron and steel caused changes in a vast variety of other things, from war to means of communication. The age of iron and steel saw the beginnings of the age of electricity as a substitute for steam and of oil as an alternative to coal; and, as factories grew ever larger in size, organised labour began to play as big a part in politics as in economics.*

But doubtless a much simpler question will be lurking in the minds of some readers: were 'things really getting better'?

Hitherto this book has not much discussed the question of prices and incomes which doubtless, to the modern mind, is the determining one in this matter. There are excellent reasons for that neglect. First, statistics may have been respected in Babylon and in Rome for fiscal purposes, but no serious figures were collected before the Renaissance. Second, and far more important, the standards of living of most people could not be expressed in the age of agriculture in terms of the prices available for goods in the remote and unrepresentative capitals. Services, food and labour were not susceptible of being generally priced.

---

* Discussed briefly in Chapter 50.

Of course, artisans were paid. Statistics of payment make amusing but, as a rule, meaningless paragraphs in the biographies of great artists. Cardinal Mazarin, we are told, offered Bernini 12,000 crowns a year to go to Paris (14). Brunelleschi received 100 florins down and 100 florins a year for his work on the Duomo in Florence, but Michelangelo declined fees for St Peter's (15). But all these grand enterprises were naturally uncharacteristic. Further, the impossibility of making accurate conversions into either contemporary foreign, or modern, money presents an impossible barrier to understanding. How can we even reckon the approximate meaning of Piedmontese *scudi*, Neapolitan ducats, papal *pasti* and *bajocchi* and Florentine sequins which were used as cash in Italy during the eighteenth century, much less say what they were worth in comparison with the equally bewildering differences of exchange in contemporary Germany? Finally, mass production has altered everything: a spoon in 1700 was almost as rare as a calculating machine in 1960; in 1800 it was an essential adjunct to a European's daily diet. Sugar was a luxury in 1650, and easily available by 1750.

Several general points should, however, be made.

The first is that, during the age of agriculture, the rich communities of the time had some experience of inflation. Very often the reason was the same as that of inflation today. The wars and building activities of Nebuchadrezzar, for example, meant that prices rose by 50% between 560 and 550 BC (16). Rome experienced a fierce inflation (deriving from debasement of money) in the second century AD and Diocletian even inflicted a death penalty for any infringement of the fixed prices which he introduced in 302 AD (17). A serious inflation of the Middle Ages caused China to desist from using paper money. European prices in the early seventeenth century were four times what they were between 1525 and 1550. That first great inflation of the modern world affected every country. The prices of food in France, as accounted by P. Coupère, suggest that another rise of 100% occurred in the seventeenth century (18). However, despite these experiences, it does not seem as if any country ever suffered, before the 1920s, the fate of Germany where the currency, stable in 1920—21 at fourteen times the level of 1914, was 1,475 times that level in late 1922 and, in November 1923, was no less than 1,422,900,000,000 times the level of 1914. Austria suffered almost as badly (19). Nor, previously, had countries experienced the prolonged high inflation which characterised South America in the 1950s and 1960s and Europe in the 1970s. These experiences are partly the consequence of a largely money economy, of interaction of one economy on another and, above all, of the appearance on the political scene, in that money economy, of spendthrift governments. Still, these experiences are not wholly new ones: 'Today,' complained a Spanish aristocrat in 1513, 'a pound of mutton costs as much as a whole sheep used to, a loaf as much as a *fanega* of wheat' (20).

Then it must be obvious that the difference between the incomes of well-placed men and peasants was often extreme. Peter Brown has calculated that a senator's income in Constantinople in 350 AD was 120,000 gold pieces, a peasant's 5 (21). The senator's income was thus at first sight 24,000 times the peasant's. In 1900, the Duke of Bedford's income was 'perhaps' £100,000 and a farm labourer's £50 (22). The Duke was, therefore, undoubtedly 2,000 times better off than the labourer, In 1940, twenty-nine people in the US had an income of over a million dollars, while half the families lived on $1,160 a year (23). But the chances are that all precise figures in the past misunderstand the true state of affairs: did not Peter Brown's peasant gain much of his income from his own back garden? Professor Klein, the historian of the great sheep transport of Spain, the Mesta, claims that the president of that body gained 8,000 to 14,000 reales in income, and 5,000 in expenses, whilst herdsmen were paid as a rule in bushels of grain, lambs, cheese, sheep and so on (24). Still, these differences in income in the past were by no means inevitable: in 408 BC, in Athens, a day labourer hired for the day received a drachma a day, but so did an architect: an equivalence which contrasted with an architect's four drachmas to a labourer's one in Delos, in 180 BC (25). No statistics of this sort take into account the role of apprenticeship, nor the predominant role of bread in most food in Western Europe before 1800 (two-thirds of the average food in England in the eighteenth century, according to Sir Jack Drummond) (26).

The final point is that, despite occasional scandals and panics, European prices were remarkably steady for those commodities which can be measured at all during the early years of the industrial revolutions. Wars usually increased prices, prices fluctuated often but at a steady level (27). The *Economist* has recently estimated that, between 1661 and 1913, prices in Britain declined by 10% over all (28). True, the growth of population after 1750 in most European countries led to a rise of agricultural prices because of the increased demands of an itself increasing non-agricultural population (29). But the overall price index scarcely reflected that, since there was such a general fall in the prices of manufactured goods, of potatoes,* and of imported commodities (particularly sugar, tea, coffee and afterwards meat). Still, the rises in agricultural prices were enough to cause riots everywhere in the late eighteenth century. Even in England, rioters often took over town markets and sold off goods cheap. But those changes did not occur in the nineteenth century. Prices may have fallen a trifle, Sir John Clapham tells us, between 1850 and 1887 (30) and, between 1896 and 1913, very gently risen, perhaps by 3%.

Of course, there were variations from country to country. Spanish

---

* The prices of potatoes were 10d a pound in 1607 and 2d a pound in 1701 (32).

prices, for example, dropped between 1710 and 1720, remained stable till the 1750s and then rose gradually till about 1790 when they were, say, 35% higher than they were in 1750 — partly caused by a new Mexican silver rush (31).

Given at least a stability in prices, it certainly seems as if, therefore, the steady increase in wages in the nineteenth century must have represented a steady increase in standards of living for the working people as a whole (32). Sir John Clapham believed that a man's real wage in 1900 was about 50% better than that of someone doing the same job in 1850 (33). In the US, wages in 1900 were probably twice as high as they were in England but they too had gone up by the same sort of percentage (34). These figures do not take into account that hours of work were constantly falling in the nineteenth century, nor that the population was rising. Thus, by any standard accepted in the twentieth century as giving appropriate indices of levels of income, the workers in the countries becoming industrialised were regularly and, except in the first twenty or thirty years, steadily becoming better off. Marx's theories of 'immiseration', therefore, seem as misleading for his own day as for now. There are, however, three qualifications to this judgment. The first is that, in the last years of the age of agriculture, a vast number of people gained what was, in effect, extra income — on top of the average of 7/6d a week in England in the mid-eighteenth century — by, for example, growing their own vegetables, poaching, shooting, occasional pilfering, as well as spinning. Those unmeasurable benefits largely disappeared if a man suddenly moved to a slum in Manchester, even if he earned more wages, as he usually did.* Secondly, the uprooting of an old rural family to what was undoubtedly a primitive urban society without traditions and, for some generations, lacking a real culture of its own, created a definite spiritual impoverishment. In the end, socialism, nationalism, and, finally, humane capitalism', with the car and the television set, posed solutions to these difficulties. In the twentieth century in France and Italy, communism offered its answer, just as Islam and rabid nationalism, 'Castroism' and 'Maoism' do elsewhere.

By the late twentieth century, meantime, in most rich countries, the new hazard of taxation for the factory worker had appeared and is being met, to a great extent, by innumerable varieties of 'informal, unofficial, illicit sources of reward't comparable to the benefits obtained by gleaning or poaching in the past (36).

Thirdly, all tests of income ignore the unemployed worker, the underemployed worker and the need of innumerable people to support

---

* Day labourers in the 1770s earned 5s to 6s a week in winter, 7s to 9s in summer, and 12s in harvest time. Cotton weavers in factories earned 7s to 10s a week all the year round, cloth weavers 8s, Wilton carpet makers 11s. By 1800, agricultural wages were the same as in 1770, industrial wages up to 16s (35).
† In the formulation of the Outer Circle Policy Unit, of London.

unemployed relations or friends. Lord Ernle, the best-known historian of English agriculture, believed, incidentally, that, in the mid-fifteenth century in England, the average labourer lived as well as he did in the mid-eighteenth (37), and other students have gone further to suggest that the 'equivalent of wage rates in terms of consumable foods was higher between 1380 and 1510 than at any time till the late nineteenth century' (38).

Yet even so, when every possible qualification is made, it should be evident that, measured by the simple, practical and generally recognised criterion of purchasing power, the opportunities of most working people in most industrial countries grew steadily during the industrial revolution. French figures are perhaps even more conclusive than English or American. The French sociologist, Alfred Sauvy, calculated that between 1810 and 1900 the purchasing power of the average worker increased by 82%, that by 1939 it had increased 255% over 1810 and, by 1965, 338% (these last two figures not taking into account the social security generally available in France since 1919). The reckoning which enabled Monsieur Sauvy to construct this table was based on primary goods, so that, if bicycles, railways, and so on, are taken into account, the rise would have been even faster still (39). Nor does his table take into account such matters as shorter hours, nor the provision of holidays with pay. These figures seem to be incontrovertible and decisively to rebut the argument that industrialisation under capitalism brought to most peoples pain and misery. They should be borne in mind when considering the second half of the industrial and scientific revolution, that which has elapsed since 1870.

31

New Sources of Energy

During this time, the sources of the world's energy had been transformed. Coal was not the only means of powering enterprises in 1900. Gas was discovered by William Murdock, son of a millwright of Ayr. Murdock gained employment in Boulton's factory in Soho, Birmingham, in 1777. It was said that he was offered his job because he went to see Boulton wearing a wooden hat which he had turned on a lathe of his own making. He was sent to Cornwall to supervise the steam pumps being used in mines there which had been provided by Boulton.* About 1792, Murdock began making experiments in the illuminating properties of gases emanating from coal and wood and, a few years later, was lighting his house in Redruth by gas. On his return to Birmingham, in 1800, he continued to experiment. He ensured that the Peace of Amiens of 1802 could be celebrated in Birmingham by extensive gas illuminations. In 1803, part of the foundry at Soho began to be lit by gas. In 1804, the firm of Phillips and Lee, cotton spinners of Manchester, decided to light their mill with gas. From then on, gas light became generally popular. Work similar to Murdock's had been done in Paris by Philippe Le Bon and the idea caught on there even faster than it did in England (1). That essential assistance to hard work in modern times, artificial light, spread soon thereafter, through factories, hospitals, barracks, and later, streets and houses. Huge gas tanks were distributed at random, often leading to 'gas house districts' polluting the air foully, symbolising very well, as Lewis Mumford put it, the 'ambiguous face' that progress has sometimes seemed to give to the world (2).

Gas, however, never did much more than light houses, buildings and streets. Paris was particularly proud of her 65,000 gas burners in 1844, mostly outdoor (3). The new illumination in cities made reading infinitely easier. It was probably as responsible for the growth of literacy as education was, but that is about the extent of the success of gas. A more effective new challenge as a means of securing energy was electricity. In 1881, the President of the British Institute of Mechanical Engineers said,

* As briefly mentioned earlier on page 256.

'It is possible and even probable that one of the great uses to which electric power will be applied *eventually* will be the simple conveyance of power by . . . . large wires.' During the very next ten years, that prophecy was fulfilled.

The history of electricity is long. The first philosopher, Thales of Miletus, discovered that amber, when rubbed, attracted light substances such as cork, pith or parchment. It is from the Greek word for amber (*elektron*) that this energy derives its internationally used name. (Electra, the 'bright one', was a daughter of Agamemnon, whom she avenged, with the help of her brother Orestes). Between Thales, in 580 BC and William Gilbert in England in the seventeenth century AD in England, progress, as in so many things, was petty, though the prince of early naturalists, Theophrastus, discovered that some minerals (tourmaline, for example) became electrified when heated. It was also noted that some fish gave out numbing powers, and, of course that the glowworm had possibilities.* William Gilbert, a scientist from an old Suffolk family, however, in his study of magnetism, *De Magnete*, first used the word *'electrica'* for these reactions. A hundred years later, Robert Boyle showed that the attraction between the body and the object which it attracts is mutual. Otto von Guericke, in Magdeburg, then built an electrical machine about the same time, with a revolving ball of sulphur, while Isaac Newton, in Cambridge, substituted glass for sulphur in his version of the same machine. Many others noticed that electricity could be made by, for example, subjecting silk, hair or wool to movement. Charles François de Fay in France established that electricity is of two kinds, repelling and attracting, negative and positive. In 1745, E. G. von Kleist and Musschenbroek in Pomerania and Holland independently discovered the 'Leyden jar'. That object was less elegant than it sounds, but it was a work of art, all the same, like most early inventions. A thin flask was partly filled with water, and corked up. A metallic nail was then pushed through the cork until it touched the water. With the bottle held in the hand, the nail was presented to an electric machine. A release of energy followed. Then a scientist from London, Sir William Watson (who also discovered that 'holly was polygamous'), found that a chain and iron or mercury could be substituted for the hand and the water respectively. Subsequently Benjamin Franklin, the first great scientist to be born in the US, made his famous identification of lightning with electricity (the first major scientific discovery of any sort made in the New World) by sending a silk kite into the sky during a thunderstorm. He rightly argued that electricity was not created by friction, but was merely collected from its diffused state through other matter, by which it was attracted. A glass globe, he said, when rubbed, attracted electricity and took it from the person who rubbed. The same globe was

* Theophrastus died in 288 BC, aged 106, regretting that life is short.

able to give out its electricity to anything or any person which had less. Franklin also proved that, in all electrical undertakings, as much electricity is added on one side as is subtracted on the other. A little later, Alessandro Volta, professor of physics at Pavia, discovered that, when a pile of copper or silver disks is divided from zinc disks by a wet cloth, they cause electricity, provided the least large one of each group is connected to a conductor. He thus invented the new word 'volt', which continues to be used in electrical jargon and, in effect, produced the first electrical current battery. Volta also realised that all metals could be placed in a series so that each one could become positive when coming into contact with the one next below it in the series. In 1807, Sir Humphry Davy, a genius from Cornwall, announced his discovery of the electrical decomposition of the alkalis, potash and soda, so obtaining two new metals, potassium and sodium. The Royal Society in London gave him 2,000 pairs of electric plates with which he produced the first electric arc light — the first practical use of electricity, it would seem. Next, Hans Christian Oersted, a professor of chemistry in Copenhagen, established in 1819 that, when a wire joining the last plates of one of Volta's piles is held near a pivoted magnet, or the needle of a compass, the latter is deflected to stand more or less transversely to the wire. That indicated a magnetic field around the conductor. A year later, a French physicist, François Arago, who came from French Catalonia, and Humphry Davy, both independently discovered the power of an electric current to magnetise iron or steel. Another Frenchman, André-Marie Ampère, professor of mathematics in Paris, who came from the neighbourhood of Lyons and whose father was executed in the Revolution for standing out against revolutionary excesses, in 1820 told the French Academy of Sciences of his discovery of the dynamic interaction between conductors conveying electrical currents.

The early discovery of electricity was, thus, more than any other such new departure an international, largely European, enterprise. Governments played little part. Both characteristics continued throughout the nineteenth century. Among numerous great men of ideas, the figure of Michael Faraday is outstanding. He was the son of a blacksmith in Surrey. Apprenticed to a bookbinder, Faraday went in 1812 to lectures by Davy, to whom he then became assistant. In 1822, Faraday caused a wire carrying an electric current to rotate round a magnetic pole. In 1831, he established that electricity could be generated by rotating a copper disk between the poles of a magnet. He also caused a wire carrying an electric current to circle a fixed magnet.

These discoveries led ultimately to the creation of a whole new industry. They are a good example (rare in the early years of the industrial revolution) of science influencing technology, rather than the other way round. As a rule, theorists worked out the principles of an invention after the inventor had finished his work. Faraday's rotating copper disk, meantime, became the parent of innumerable machines. Two years later, at Göttingen, Karl Friedrich Gauss, director of the observatory, with Wilhelm Weber, his assistant, sent electric signals to the house next door by means of a wire set on the Johannes Kirke in the city. The development in the 1840s of the telegraph* was the first major practical use of this new power.

Between 1832 and 1870, all the sciences dependent on Faraday's discoveries began to take shape: William Thomson (later Lord Kelvin) was working from 1842 on electromagnetics, Werner von Siemens on the dynamo, and James Clerk Maxwell on experimental physics. In 1870, the dynamo had been achieved by the Belgian, Zénobe T. Gramme.

These developments enabled the widespread introduction of machinery powered by electricity. The application of electricity to the manufacture of machine tools was demonstrated at the Vienna exhibition of 1873. Soon, electricity began to replace steam power for driving the overhead belts which were then already becoming common in large factories.

The earliest practical uses of electricity were for illumination. In 1858, the lighthouse at Dungeness on the south coast of England used electricity for its lamps (created by Faraday, with an assistant, Holmes). Other filaments were tried out during the 1860s. The Gare du Nord in Paris and the Menier chocolate factory (ever in the van of technology) at Noisiel-sur-Marne were lit by electricity in 1875. In 1878, Joseph Swan, a chemist from Sunderland, made the first satisfactory filament lamp, but Thomas Edison, a poor boy from Ohio, who had begun life as a newsboy on the Grand Trunk Railway, and one of the greatest geniuses of industrial society, developed another type, which he propagated with determination. Swan and Edison wisely merged their undertakings in 1883. The lighting by electricity of Boston and then of other US cities followed fast. Edison had already established a station for the supply of electricity in New York in 1881. The same year, a similar one was built in Milan (4). Debates in the House of Commons in England were lit by electricity in 1881 too. House-to-house installation followed. By 1900, the supremacy of incandescent electric light over gas and all rivals was established. Safer and more reliable than gas, it was also cleaner.

All these inventions had commercial consequences. Thus, in Germany, an engineer, Emile Rathenau, bought the German rights of Edison's invention and, between 1883 and 1903, his A.E.G. (Allgemeine Elektrizitäts-Gesellschaft) transformed Germany, filling the country with more electrical appliances, not just light, than any other in Europe so far (5). The distributors and manufacturers of electricity organised themselves into a formidable *kartel* (6) or vertical collaboration between

---

* See below, page 333.

the different elements within the enterprise.

The use of electricity for industry came more slowly than for light, since generators could only supply the maximum capacity of electricity for a short period during each day. Large-scale use, therefore, seemed too difficult. But those problems involved were resolved by the 1890s. Electricity was particularly important in new industries: electro-chemical firms were established producing aluminium and calcium soda. Even in a then comparatively backward country such as Italy, installation of electricity for industry was beginning in 1892 (7). Here, England was somewhat laggardly, behind the US and Germany, for it was only between 1903 and 1905 that large power stations began to provide energy in bulk rather than in each locality. A decline in the comparative rate of adoption of new technology in Britain was thereafter evident (8).

The use of electricity for industry was assisted by the growth of hydroelectricity after 1890. Ever since 1829, it had been known that water wheels could be fitted with a turbine (a discovery of Benoit Fourneyron). One of the earliest machines so developed operated at 2,300 volts per minute, under a 350 foot waterfall. But there are not very many such waterfalls in Europe. The first large successful hydroelectric installation was not set up till the one at Niagara, in 1886. Subsequently, the great water resources of the southern Appalachians were used extensively in the US, while Barcelona's electricity came from the hydroelectric plants in the Pyrenees. The use of turbines generally in electricity began soon after, though the greatest achievement in the use of that method of producing energy was to be seen in the steam turbines which were introduced into ships by Charles Parsons after 1884 and came to be generally employed in the then technically very advanced British Navy after 1897.

By then too, electricity had come to be used in a number of other undertakings. First in importance after the telegraph, no doubt, was the telephone devised in 1876, but there was also the microphone, invented about the same time*. From 1902, electric railways, in deep tunnels, were being introduced into many large cities. From 1904, many main-line railways began to try out electricity in place of steam. In the course of the next few generations, electricity also came to be the main method of providing energy in numerous other ways. Lighting, cooking, and heating by electricity all caused the average inhabitant of rich countries to depend upon centralised springs of power in a way wholly new. Subsequently, new sources of diversion and education such as radio and television also depended on electricity. Similarly, the relative consumption of electric power gives as good an indication of the relative wealth of nations as anything else. Unions running electricity works

---

* For these benefits, see below page 335.

were early aware of their power: Pataud, the leader of the French electricians during *la belle époque* plunged Paris into darkness by a strike in 1908 and, on another occasion, secured a strike at the Opéra, during a royal visit. The increase of wages demanded came within minutes of negotiation (9). Electricity workers have never forgotten the lesson implicit. Nor have politicians.

INSTALLED ELECTRICITY (10).
1976

		million kilowatt
1.	US	550·369
2.	Russia	228·307
3.	Japan	116·871
4.	W. Germany	81·631
5.	Britain	78·597
6.	Canada	65·566
7.	France	50·266
8.	India	23·689
9.	E. Germany	16·735
10.	Haiti (for comparison).	·089

Electricity has brought ease and comfort to the vast majority of those who have been able to use it. But the contributions made have not been wholly beneficial, since the use of electricity for war, and even for torture, have in the twentieth century given a new dimension to brutality. Lenin rather curiously said that 'socialism is the dictatorship of the proletariat plus the widest introduction of the most modern electrical machinery' (11). General Franco might have paid the same tribute to electricity when justifying his own system.

Long before 1900, too, there was not only a new method, electricity, of using energy to take the place of steam so as to power the industrial revolution, but a new source of energy to obtain steam and electricity: namely oil, which in the 1970s has been the main source of energy in industrial countries.

The use of petroleum for energy actually antedated both gas and coal. There are innumerable places between the Nile and the Indus where oil appears on the surface of the earth, mostly in Iraq. There, mysterious 'naphtha', as it was called, came out of the rocks to perplex the Babylonnians. Mixtures of the oxygenated hydrocarbon known as bitumen were used to caulk ships and to waterproof floors in the ancient world. It was continuously an object of commerce after 3000 BC, and was used as a basis in the middle ages for 'Greek fire'. Oil was used again in the Rennaissance to caulk ships, while the Aztecs used bitumen as a chewing gum, and the lake of asphalt, which is a form of bitumen, in Trinidad was prized from the sixteenth century onwards for many purposes. All this oil was on, or very near, the surface and had to be little more than scooped up.

In 1848, James Young, a chemist from Glasgow of humble origins (like the majority of great innovating geniuses), used a spring of oil which reached the surface at Alfreton, in Derbyshire, as a means of lubrication. Subsequently, by dry distillation of coal he made paraffin. This he sold as 'paraffin lubricating oil' and made a fortune which he used partly to finance David Livingstone's journeys. A variety of this, made from the oil from asphalt, was soon marketed in the US as 'kerosene'. A good deal of sporadic drilling in the deserts of the world, meantime, was going on at that time. The search was for water or salt. This method of drilling deep bore-holes was probably Chinese in origin since there were instances of it in Szechwan dating back to the first century BC. Some of these drills met oil instead. George Bissell, of New Hampshire in the US, wondered whether to embark on drilling for oil alone. He consulted Professor Sillman of Yale, who advised him to do so. Crude oil, said the professor, while being heated, might produce paraffin wax, illuminating gas, or lubricants. Bissell, thereupon, sought oil in Pennsylvania. He found it seventy feet down. Within fifteen years, Pennsylvania was producing 10 million barrels of oil, each holding 360 pounds. The US soon began to make lamps for kerosene, as well as kerosene in large quantities. Much was exported. Then an engine based on the use of oil was made in Vienna in 1870. Another such machine was made in New York in 1873.

There was, thereafter, heavy drilling elsewhere. Wells in Galicia (Poland) had been opened in 1863, others in Roumania in 1857, and in Russia, near the Caspian Sea, in 1860 (12), the last of these being the inspiration of Ludwig and Robert Nobel, two great Swedish entrepreneurs. By 1900, Russia was producing 10 million tons of oil a year, or about half the oil in the world. Baku, in 1800 merely the fortress city of a minor Turkish Khan, was incorporated into the Russian Empire in 1806. It had 46,000 inhabitants in 1886, and 108,000 in 1896. Huge reserves were also discovered in 1870 in Venezuela and in 1901 in Texas. Most of this oil was found in small places in porous rock, usually under some form of pressure which was (and is) released by the well.*

All these adventures implied a large infrastructure of commerce: oil was first carried in wooden barrels, then in tin cans, then in iron or steel drums, and finally in steam tankers (earliest in use on the Caspian in 1879). Long pipelines of steel were also built in both Russia and the USA in the 1870s, (13) and subsequently elsewhere.

The paraffin or kerosene lamp had a long history and it survives. But the most striking development based on oil was, of course, the motor

---

*Subsequently a good deal of oil has been recovered by artificially increasing the pressure on the deposit of oil by pumping water or gas into the reservoir.

car, the private means of travel which, with the truck,* in the twentieth
century, dethroned the railway from its dominant position.† Various
experiments in the 1880s ensured the success of an engine based on
internal combustion and so also ensured a continuing market for oil.
Unlike the shipment of coal, that of oil needed, from the start, a
business with great capital. From the 1880s onwards, it was plain that
huge profits would be gained by those who could control the distribution of oil. John D. Rockefeller was the first to realise that idea, with his
Standard Oil Company. Others followed. In the course of the twentieth
century, the oil companies of the world became among the largest
private enterprises, if not the largest of all, in the main industrial democracies. Some of those companies had budgets larger than those of
independent states. The world of oil came soon to be dominated by
these companies, each of which formed fleets which were also larger
than those of most states. Some of them signed treaties (such as that of
1902 between Shell, Royal Dutch and Caucasian interests) of greater
importance than many formal international pacts. This was not an
entirely new occurrence: Italian bankers in the Renaissance, the two
East India Companies in the seventeenth century, were forerunners.
There was sometimes state intervention. Thus, a large Anglo-Persian oil
company was set up in 1909 to exploit a concession previously granted
to a prospector from New Zealand, William d'Arcy. The British government became a majority shareholder of that company in 1914, after
Winston Churchill, an ebullient First Lord of the Admiralty in Britain,
had taken the decision, in 1911, to fuel the British fleet, then the largest
in the world, with oil (14).

Thereafter, oil played an increasingly important part in international
politics. World production of petroleum, about 20 million tons in 1900,
rose to 34 million by 1910 and more than doubled between 1910 and
1920 (to 100 million). It doubled yet again between 1920 and 1930. Even
the years of the depression of 1930 to 1940 saw an increase in oil production by another 50% (15). During and after the second World War, the
further increase was enormous, the production reaching over 2800
million tons before the 'economic crisis' of 1973. (16)

The political significance of this immensely convenient form of energy
scarcely recognised as such a hundred years ago has been considerable.
Ludendorff attributed the defeat of Germany in 1918 to a shortage of oil
and Lord Curzon, agreeing, put it more ceremoniously when he said,
'Victory came to us floating on waves of petrol'. The US tanks, which in
1918 eventually determined the outcome of the First World War, on the

---

* Known in England as the 'lorry', a curious word and one of the few instances of an
English original being *worse* than the American innovation. It is not an old word, despite
The Daily News of September 2 1881 speaking of 'the time honoured lorry, indigenous to
Liverpool'.
† See below, page 321.

Western Front were, of course, oil-powered. After 1918, ships, submarines, aeroplanes, not to speak of motor cars and trucks, all began to use oil on a huge scale. The assistance of the Texas Oil Company to General Franco in the Spanish Civil War was of critical importance to the nationalist victory in that conflict (17). Much of the Second World War can be explained as a battle for oil, one of the few raw materials in which Germany had not made herself self-sufficient. Hence the necessity for Germany to capture Roumania's ample oil wells. Hence too her unsuccessful drives towards the Middle East fields and to Baku, by then the main oil port of Russia's huge oil industry. War in the Far East also began in 1941 when the US sought to restrain Japan from building a mainland empire on the (apparent) ruins of the Chinese one by cutting her off from oil in Java (18). The inadequate supplies of oil of the countries of the Axis was their main weakness. The decisive weapons of the 1940s, aircraft and tanks, depended absolutely on petroleum, as did the car and the half-track vehicle. In the end, Germany's use of oil from Roumania and Japan's use of oil from Java continued till late in 1944 and 1945. On the other hand, the huge oil resources at home in both the US and in Russia (as well as the former's access to the wells of Mexico and of Venezuela) were of critical importance in the long war which the Germans succeeded in imposing on the world. Since 1945, the two most powerful countries in the world have been precisely the two largest oil producers, the USA and Russia – and the diplomacy of oil has been infinitely complicated. The Suez crisis largely derived from European anxiety over a safe supply of oil, and the crux in the history of the breach between the USA and Cuba occurred in 1960, when the major US oil companies refused to refine, in their Cuban installations, oil imported from Russia.

Meantime, the new organisation of countries which exported oil (OPEC), devised in 1960 by the Venezuelan Minister of Mines, Juan Pablo Pérez Alfonso, failed to reach any agreement within itself till 1973. Then, following the war between Israel and the Arabs, the Arabs forced a sudden rise in prices with the intention initially of persuading the democratic industrial countries to require Israel to withdraw from certain territories which she had occupied in 1967 after Egyptian threats. Subsequently, the Arabs brought equal influence to bear on all the industrial countries, which had taken cheap oil for granted for such a long time.

The world has since seemed to be suffering from a crisis in supplies of energy. Certainly, the need to import oil from a remote source has made the European industrial nations nervous. But as earlier suggested, there is a lot of coal in the world, and new sources of energy seem likely to make up for the shortages of oil. There is nuclear power and there are new oil fields, such as those discovered off Mexico. Tidal and solar energy have evident possibilities. Some natural growth (such as sugar) may play a part. The 'energy crisis', at the time of writing, seems really to be due to a rise in prices of oil at a time before other sources of energy have been adequately prepared. Even so, the dependence on oil from the Middle East by the industrial democracies and the chances that Russia will become an oil-importing country make the danger of international war occurring over these matters quite severe.

During the first part of the twentieth century, it was established that the essential chemical elements in the world were about one hundred. Could these be broken down? And with what consequences? In January 1939, Otto Hahn and Lise Meitner, two German physicists, after many years of research by Rutherford in Cambridge and others, showed that the atom could indeed be split, so causing a formidable release of energy. Subsequently, a group of central European émigré scientists in the US, afraid that the Germans (instead of themselves) would put this discovery to destructive purposes, devised the first use of nuclear energy, the atom bomb. It was tested in July 1945 and dropped on Hiroshima in Japan in August 1945. Another such bomb was dropped on Nagasaki. The two bombs helped to bring the war to a swift end. Since then, this energy has given rise to a range of weapons which have altered international relations.* Nuclear energy was the first example of a major source of power being first put to effect for the purpose of war: water-power, wind-power, coal and oil had all been used first for peace. It was also the first major scientific development which owed its character to state-sponsored research. The implications are, unmistakeable. Since 1955, nuclear energy for peaceful purposes has also become possible. In 1975, it was responsible for about 5% of the world's sources of energy, 9% in the US (19).

Nuclear energy will be an important source of power in the future. But the dangers of loss, or misuse, of the raw material are considerable. Bombs could be made easily out of stolen uranium or plutonium (the man-made element which powers hydrogen bombs). Even a small loss of the material could be fatal to anyone who came into contact with it. Accidents already have apparently occurred of unparalleled destructiveness, for example, in the closed community of Russia. The problem of what to do with nuclear material which has once been used is also formidable, and as yet unsatisfactorily resolved. But there is a good hope that this difficulty will be disentangled by storing such material in deep geological formations (20). Nuclear power is so baffling to the layman that he has largely ceased to reflect on it. Even so, and despite the understandable anxiety, it seems certain that much of the energy needed by man in the next century will be the consequence of this power.

---

* These are discussed a little later in the chapter on the Cold War.

32

New Communications

The nineteenth century may primarily have seemed the age of the railways but, in ports, the railways also made possible a growth in the quantity of shipping, and a rapid change in its character. Between 1750 and 1900 the changes in the character of ships were so great as to suggest that it was a quite new method of transport. 'No man will be a sailor who has contrivance enough to get himself into a jail,' said Dr Johnson, 'for being in a ship is being in jail, with the chance of getting drowned' (1). Those who reclined in the spacious state rooms of the Cunard or Pacific and Orient lines a hundred years later would have smiled condescendingly at that comment. The character of the development of shipping can best be observed, first, in the quantity of British shipping which totalled a million tons (about 12,500 ships) in 1788; in 1861, 5 million tons (27,000 ships); and 12 million tons in 1913 (only 18,570 ships) (2). British figures give here a good general impression, since, in the late nineteenth century, Britain was responsible for 60% of the world steam tonnage, so that the country then had a greater share of high seas traffic than at any other time (3). Sir William Petty thought that there were 2 million tons of ships in the world in 1666 (4). There may have been 4 million in 1800, 20 million in 1900 but over 300 million in the 1970s: statistics which should caution all who believe that the ship has had its day.

Behind these statistics, however, lies an irregular story. In the eighteenth century, and despite British naval victories, French marine engineers were ahead of their British counterparts in resource and capacity. But the sailing ship then seemed incapable of further development. The only recent innovation had been the introduction, during the American revolution, of copper bottoms, which were of great importance for their resistance to the destructive ship-worm found in tropical harbours (5).

Almost before Watt's steam engine was on the market, attempts were made to power ships by steam. In 1775, an abortive attempt was made to put a boat powered by an eight-inch steam cylinder on the Seine. In 1783, Jouffroy d'Abbans made his way up the Saône near Lyons in an 182-paddle wheel steamer, the *Pyroscaphe*. The same year, Oliver Evans, who had been apprenticed to a wheel-wright and had become a miller at Newport in the US, began experiments on steam boats. Others tried to power ships by drawing in water at the bows and driving it out by steam at the stern: an early example of jet propulsion. In 1807, Robert Fulton, a Pennsylvanian engineer of poor Irish ancestry – he had been apprenticed to a jeweller – returned to the US after years in Europe. A man of diverse talents, he had gone to England first with the painter Benjamin West, since he aspired to be a landscape artist. In England, he met James Watt and the Duke of Bridgewater and worked for a time on improving the locks on canals. In France, he constructed a submarine and a torpedo, but failed to interest the artillery-conscious Napoleon I. Fulton also experimented with steam-power and built a boat in Paris based on that use of energy. He first employed it satisfactorily when he despatched the steamboat, the *Clermont*, between New York and Albany, on the Hudson River (6). Thereafter, many such vessels were promoted on US internal waterways, particularly on the Great Lakes and, after 1817, on the Mississippi. The great days of the Mississippi steamboat were well depicted by Mark Twain. That was a momentous development making possible the organisation of viable settlements to the west of that river. Meantime, in Europe, the Clyde had a steamboat in 1812, as did the Seine, in 1822 (7). In 1825, there was a service on the Rhine, and also one on the Swiss lakes. A steam packet boat across the English Channel opened in 1821. Another service was soon arranged between St Petersburg and Stockholm.

Nevertheless, the use of these steamers on the open sea was delayed. Naval architects were convinced of the superiority of sailing ships for war. In England, the Board of Admiralty found it 'their bounden duty to discourage, to the best of their ability the employment of steam vessels as they considered that the introduction of steam was calculated to strike a fatal blow at the naval supremacy of the Empire' (8). So the great age of mercantile marine rivalry was dominated by the sailing clipper, which derived from the eighteenth century American two-masted schooner. Clippers designed to carry the vast numbers of European emigrants to the USA in the nineteenth century were specially built for driving through the worst seas, crossing the Atlantic in twelve to fourteen days, and achieving 400 miles a day (9). The smaller clippers which raced to bring back the first of the new tea crop from China could get from China to London in ninety days. The finest of these ships were built by Americans for British owners, as were the best ships in the trade with Australia. When Flaubert caused his hero in *L'Education Sentimentale* (published 1869) to reflect on the *'mélancolie des paquebots'*, they were, however, still short-distance or river boats (10).

The delay in turning over to steam for ocean-going ships was primarily caused by the difficulty of arranging for sufficient fuel. Early attempts at steam-powered ships (for example, Isambard Brunel's *Great*

Western) under-estimated the amount of coal needed. In the end, this difficulty was resolved by the establishment of regular coaling stations. Thereafter, the arrangements for 'bunkering' coal on board became adequate. Steam began steadily to take over from sail, though, until the early 1870s, more tonnage was registered under sail than steam, even in Britain. It was not till 1904 that Britain launched more steam than sailing ships (11).

A second development of the mid-nineteenth century was the shift from wood, first to iron, then to steel, as the basic material of shipping. Iron barges and canal boats led the way. Aaron Manby launched the first iron steamer in 1822 on the Seine. But, in 1850, iron ships were still rare. In 1858, the French, having learned several lessons from the early months of the Crimean war,* began to encase their frigates in iron. The British followed. The idea then caught on generally. But the age of the 'iron-clad' was short. Steel ships were already being constructed by the South in the American Civil War and, in 1877, the British navy began to go over to steel — a method which saved them one fifth in the thickness of the metal. By the end of the century, new battleships were all being built of steel, as were many other ships, from the Cunard passenger liners, such as the *Lucania*, to cold storage liners or oil tankers, which in the 1870s and 1880s began to exercise a domination over shipping which has lasted to this day.

Alongside these nautical alterations came improvements in the quality and number of lighthouses and the construction of huge new harbours, including some entirely artificial, such as that begun by the French at Cherbourg, in 1780. New docks, such as the West India Dock, transformed commerce. Floating docks were also devised, able to be towed to wherever a dry dock was needed, in whatever part of the world (12).

One aspect of the world's shipping was transformed by a single industry. The invention of refrigerated ships in the late 1860s made it possible to carry raw meat long distances as a major item in commerce (so much so, indeed, that, in 1895, imports of meat into England exceeded raw cotton and, between 1919 and 1939, became Britain's most valuable import) (13). Even before the coming of these iced meat ships, however, refrigerated fishing fleets enabled trawling to take over fishing, following Sam Hewett's use of ice for the first time in his Yarmouth fleet about 1855 (14). Thus were foreshadowed the huge Atlantic fishing fleets of the 1970s, with their vast 'mother' storage vessels, their huge fish catches and unprecedented reach.

Britain's dominance in shipping was still obvious in the late nineteenth century, when the merchant fleets of her commercial rivals were backward in comparison. The US was more than ever reliant on

* See below, page 316.

Britain's merchant vessels (and the protection of her fleet) during the years when she was, in other ways, overtaking Britain's economic prowess. Germany, it is true, made headway in the Wilhelmine era, starting from an initially very small tonnage. In 1880, German steam tonnage stood at 216,000 tons, rather less than that of Spain, but it had risen to over 2 million by 1914 (15). Similar headway was made by Italy, largely as a result of subsidies by the State to certain companies (such as Florio of Palermo or Rubattino of Genoa) (16).

During the nineteenth and twentieth centuries, this European thalassocracy was completed by a large investment in fleets for war. The wooden walls which gave Britain her victories in the Napoleonic wars were worthless after the development of the shell gun in 1832 – a fact made evident even to an already rather complacent Britain after the battle of Sinope in 1853, when a squadron of wooden Turkish frigates was blown to bits by Russian shells. Hence indeed Napoleon III's invention of the ironclad, hence, subsequently, the steel fleets and the 'dreadnoughts'. In 1914, Winston Churchill looked on the British fleet which he had mobilised as the living symbol of imperial might: 'We may now picture this great fleet, with its flotillas and cruisers, steaming slowly out of Portland Harbour, squadron by squadron, scores of gigantic castles of steel winding their way across the misty shining sea, like giants bowed in anxious thought' (17).

'Giants' certainly, but clumsy giants, for these great fleets of 1914, on which so much time, energy and money had been spent, and rivalry between which undoubtedly exacerbated international hatreds, and competition, played a modest part in the actual combats of the twentieth century. The great Lord Salisbury, British prime minister in the 1890s, observing the troubles ahead in the world after the death of Bismarck, used an appropriately maritime metaphor: 'This is the crossing of the bar: I can see the sea covered with white horses' (18). But the only way in which fleets played a decisive part in the First World War was in providing convoys for food ships. Submarines also nearly won both the world wars for Germany. The age of great ships and naval battles was actually over. But, even so, during the twentieth century, the US, previously rather unimportant as a mercantile power, twice saved Europe from German conquest (and from starvation) by a vast shipping programme. In 1914–20, the US launched ships totalling 3 million tons and, in 1943, over 10 million tons, creating a 'bridge of ships', to supply US forces abroad or allies with material and also to carry the troops themselves. In 1945, the USA had a total fleet of 30 million tons registered, in comparison with 12 million in 1939, while the once proud rulers of the waves, the British, had a total tonnage of a mere 10 million (19).*

* Direct comparison of tonnage in the 1970s is misleading because of the artificially high figures for Panama, Greece, Liberia etc.

Tankers for oil accounted in the 1970s for over a third of total tonnage in the world (115 million tons against 290 million tons in 1973) (20). Indeed, oil tankers alone far exceeded the total tonnage in the world's maritime commercial fleets of 1913. Even so, the increase in carriage of goods, as well as of passengers, by air, has grown even faster than the increase in shipping, and the twentieth century has seen few innovations of importance in the nature of shipping comparable to the extraordinary occurrences on land and in the air.

The earliest stages of industrialisation in all major European countries and the USA were, however, marked by a continuation of that great improvement in roads which had already begun in the late eighteenth century. Thus good French road-making continued under Napoleon. Napoleon desired to establish fourteen highways radiating from Paris to assist his movement of troops. This affected all the countries adjacent to France, in particular that region of West Germany which was a part of Napoleon's empire. Those roads were actually of great help to the new Prussia in the days after 1815, since they remained the best roads in Germany, a country which had not benefited from the network of Roman roads in the rest of Western Europe (21).

Equally, in the USA, the era of 1790 to 1820 was a time of improvements. Numerous 'turnpike' companies were formed. The cost of roads was met by the tolls levied on those who used them. States and the federal government, however, gave some assistance from the beginning. The federal government, for example, was entirely responsible for the 'Cumberland road' built between Maryland and St Louis and finished in 1836 (22). In England, at much the same time, John Macadam, a Scotsman who had been brought up in America and made a fortune there as 'agent for the sale of prizes', introduced, after 1827, his well-known method of surfacing roads with small granite lumps on top of a well-drained soil surface.

But these changes did not greatly alter the costs of carrying goods. It was still in 1830 more expensive to carry these on land than on water for almost every country under the sun. It cost $10 a ton, for example, to carry goods from Philadelphia to Europe but $100 a ton from Philadelphia to Pittsburg (23).

Two great achievements of the railway-builders were the construction of the tunnels and the bridges which they took over from road-builders. There were few tunnels before the nineteenth century, except those built in the previous fifty years for canals. Those had, on the whole, been carried through rocks by old-fashioned mining methods. From 1830, the railway builders began a new generation of such constructions. There were the Liverpool tunnel of 1830, the Rotherhithe tunnel of 1843 and the great Alpine tunnels: the Mont Cenis (eight miles, opened in 1870); St Gotthard (nine miles, opened in 1882); and, finally the Simplon tunnel (twelve miles, opened in 1906). Though plans for a tunnel beneath the English Channel were foolishly never carried through, comparable tunnels were soon being constructed in the US. All these were built by the use of large iron shields, pushed forward and pre-constructed, on the inspiration of Marc Brunel, a Norman émigré who fled from France to England during the Revolution.

The bridges of the railway age were equally spectacular. The decisive innovation was the suspension bridge. Now this was one of the many ideas first put into use by the Chinese – in this respect, apparently, as early as the sixth century AD (24). The Chinese origin was apparently not appreciated by its western initiator, James Finley in Pennsylvania, in 1800. Suspension bridges were most useful. They could be made off the site which they were to serve. They enabled engineers to dispense with pillars of masonry in rough rivers, or even seas, (for example, over the Menai Straits). There were several fine bridges of this sort built in the 1830s and 1840s. The climax came later, with Isambard Brunel's bridge at Clifton, opened in 1862; the grand Trunk bridge, at Niagara, in 1858; the Brooklyn bridge, of 1883; and the Forth railway bridge, of 1890. All these transformed local communications, and showed how technology could alter the old presuppositions of geography.

The effect of the railway age was, initially, to bring a decline to both roads and canals. Coaches and posting houses were less important. Turnpike trusts in all rich countries were hard hit. Even so, innovations on the roads themselves were continuous everywhere following Macadam's achievements in the 1820s. Most European cities were paved in the early nineteenth century. Paved raised footpaths ('pavements'), first seen in London in 1765, came into general use. Asphalt began to be used in France after 1835. 'Tarmac' was first seen in Nottingham in the 1830s. A steam roller to crush this mixture was invented in France in 1859. The first machine for crushing stones was introduced in Central Park in New York after 1858. That was a device needed more in the US (where labour was always expensive) than in Europe, where the breaking of stones by hand at the roadside continued until, in some places (Spain for example), the 1960s. Indian roads were not paved before 1900, and few streets in Indian cities were paved before 1914.

The railway, though it primarily affected long-distance travel, also increased the number of short journeys within cities: a factor shown by the growth of an army of taxis in most centres of the industrial world – 15,000 in London in 1881 – and by the creation in Paris in the 1820s of the omnibus, an idea and a word carried to London in 1829 by George Shillibeer, a retired midshipman who really began his career in Paris. It was not, however, till the 1850s that 'buses' became a prominent method of travel inside English cities. They were challenged by short-distance city trams devised in New York in 1832. A tramway car with thirty seats ran that year in the Bowery in New York, along four flanged wheels. It was unsuccessful, but was revived in the same city in 1852, by a French engineer, Loubat. A better system was introduced into Philadelphia in the 1860s. All these new forms of travel within cities, including trams, were drawn by horses, to begin with, but they never went faster than six or seven miles an hour. Steam cars soon began to be used in France, dirty and noisy though they were, as were cable cars. The first cable tramway was built, at San Francisco, in 1873. The tram came into its own, however, with the introduction of electricity after 1884, and the beginning of the overhead trolley car system in the US. The era of the tram then lasted for twenty-five years: from 1890 to 1914.

The decline of roads, therefore, during the railway age was relative. The decline in the use of canals and rivers was in some countries (the US, Britain) absolute, and everywhere noticeable, even on the continent of Western Europe, where waterways continued to be used for commerce. Throughout the US and Britain, nevertheless, a nation-wide canal system had been completed by the 1820s. The quantity of coal carried along those canals (and improved rivers) was enormous. A good example of a waterway which transformed the economy of a country was the Erie canal. It was opened in 1825 and not only brought grain from the region of the Great Lakes down to New York City (which was then growing very fast), but also established that city as the commercial metropolis of the nation. Much work too was done in the early nineteenth century on the improvement of rivers such as the Danube, Rhine, Guadalquivir, Mississippi and St Lawrence (25). Those works coincided with legal discussions about the status of international waterways such as the Rhine; for in the early nineteenth century, a cargo boat paid toll fourteen times on the Elbe between Hamburg and Magdeburg (26). Finally, at the very end of the age of canals, their three most striking examples were constructed: the Suez Canal, the Kiel Canal and the Panama Canal, opened in 1869, 1895 and 1914 respectively. The first of these confirmed the critical position of Egypt on the way between Europe and the East, restoring indeed Egypt to a position of importance in the world's communications that she had lost when the Portuguese circumnavigated Africa. Both the second and third of these canals had strategic significance from the beginning. Further large canals were constructed by forced labour in Russia under Stalin: for example, the canal linking the White Sea with the Baltic which probably cost more lives than the digging of the Suez Canal or the Pharaoh Necos's (27).

Still, the achievements of the new age of communication were in the end dominated by wholly new methods. The two great developments were the car on the ground and the aeroplane in the air. They were preceded by a more modest, but persistent, contribution: the bicycle.

There were some ideas for bicycles in the early nineteenth century. Thus Baron Drais von Sauerbronn, director-general of rivers and forests at Baden, devised his two-wheel 'draisine' in 1818. It was almost more a piece of gymnastic equipment than a means of locomotion. Then, Gavin Dalzell, of Lesmahagow, put cranks on to a hobby horse, in 1836 (28). The idea of treadles and a brake were thought of in the 1840s, while Pierre Michaux placed pedals directly on to the front wheel and formed a company in France to sell 'velocipedes' in 1861. By 1865, he and his brother Ernest were making 400 'velos' a year.

The idea was taken up in Coventry in England and also in the US, whither one of the Michaux's mechanics emigrated. By 1885, 3,000 men were making bicycles at Coventry. There were soon innumerable varieties on the English market, including a tricycle. Most were penny-farthings in style to begin with, though the 'safety bicycle' was created in 1885 (29). In 1881, John Boyd Dunlop, a Scottish vet living in Belfast, patented the pneumatic rubber tyre (30). The 'bicycle craze' then began. 'Every morning,' wrote a survivor, Amy Strachey, 'from eleven to lunch time, everyone who was idle enough to take two hours off and rich enough . . . went to Battersea Park . . . on Sundays, we went further afield . . . I have a little picture [in my mind] of Mrs [Beatrice] Webb, who rode extremely well, scudding before us down Lupus Street with both hands behind her back, steering by her pedals. She was a graceful and intrepid rider' (31).

Though this first fine careless rapture of a sporting craze died with the advent of cars, the numbers of bicycles in use steadily rose in, for example, France (981,000 in 1900, 8·7 million in 1938) (32). Only the coming of the cheap car after 1945 in Europe led to a real decline of the bicycle as a means of transport, but in the 'energy crisis' of the 1970s it experienced a revival. In Holland, there are over twice as many bicycles as there are cars: 7 million bicycles to 14 million people (33). Bicycling also remains a popular sport. In France, in particular, bicycle manufacturers worked hard in order to ensure that. The press have helped to turn bicycling champions in France and elsewhere into public heroes (34).

The bicycle was followed by the motor bicycle, a high speed petrol engine devised by Gottlieb Daimler, an engineer from Württemberg. Werner Frères of Paris marketed a machine of this type for the first time. But the motor bicycle did not become popular till the First World War, in which it played a considerable part, usually serving despatch riders — of particular value since it could travel along much worse roads and tracks than cars could and, of course, it travelled faster than any horse. Motor bicycles subsequently have served a small but fairly consistent public; there were 50,000 in France in 1920 and over half a million in 1935 (35).

Nevertheless, it was the motor car which altered the pace of transport in the years after 1890. Its contribution to life in the West during the twentieth century, for good or evil, is second to none.

The preparation for this was long drawn out. Thus Trevithick, the inventor of the locomotive, built, in 1800, a steam road carriage which would carry several people. Oliver Evans, the pioneer of steamboats, did the same in Philadelphia in 1804. Sir Goldsworthy Gurney, a Cornish surgeon, devised a steam road carriage which travelled from Bath to London in 1829. It ran for hire for three months regularly between Gloucester and Cheltenham, at about nine miles an hour. But Gurney was then prevented from continuing his work by a legal ban on steam vehicles on the road. In the mid nineteenth century, there were other attempts to use steam for road travel but, apart from the steam roller of 1857 and steam plough of 1850, and a few unsuccessful creations by an Austrian, Siegfried Markus in Vienna in the 1860s, nothing was done till the 1870s.

In 1876, Dr Nikolaus August Otto, a German engineer, made a stationary gas-powered engine, of which some 50,000 were sold for different purposes. But it became clear that oil-powered engines had a greater future, at least for undertakings which would try to ensure movement, for oil is easily transported and stored. It also yields more heat per unit of weight than coal does. From the 1870s, petrol was available to meet a demand for this type of fuel. In 1885, Gottlieb Daimler, who had previously worked with Otto, applied a single cylinder and an air-cooled vertical machine to a carriage. These engines then began to be used not only for carriages, but also for boats and stationary machines. In 1887, Daimler created his first 'four wheeled, wooden built light wagonette' powered by petrol. The same year, René Panhard and Emile Levassor gained French patents for road carriages. Karl Benz of Mannheim then built an engine specifically intended for motor cars, leading to the four-wheelers of 1893.

In 1894, *Le Petit Journal* in France gave impetus to the new invention by organising a trial run of motor cars from Paris to Rouen. In 1895, a race was organised, from Paris to Bordeaux. The winner averaged fifteen miles an hour. During the 1890s, the French led the world in production of cars (36). In 1896, automobiles took part in French army manoeuvres (37) and, in England, they were allowed to travel on roads at fourteen miles an hour. Henry Ford in the US began making cars in 1896, particularly his twin-cylinder water-cooled engine, which travelled at 25 miles an hour. In 1899, the first tactical motor vehicle, a four-wheeled bicycle with a Maxim gun* on top, was exhibited in England and, the following year, the politician Arthur Balfour, dismissed twenty years later by Maynard Keynes as 'perhaps the most extraordinary *objet d'art* that our society has produced', intelligently predicted in the House of Commons that the future might well see 'great highways for rapid motor traffic'. By that year, all the fundamen-

* See below, page 453.

tal technical problems of the automobile had been solved and, though, until then, all cars were 'custom' built to order, the market was ready for mass production (38).

In 1908, Henry Ford, a farmer's boy from Michigan with little education, after careful examination of the Sears Roebuck factory, began mass production of his Model T car, which sold in the next twenty years to fifteen million people (39). The benefit of this mass-produced machine was that it was cheap, which had been one of Ford's aims. The consequence was that, in 1913, there were already over a million automobiles on the US roads (40) as opposed to 200,000 in Britain, 90,000 in France and a mere 70,000 in Germany (41). France, leading the world in the early days of automobile manufacture, was still concentrating on hand-made vehicles (42).

So began the age of the car. In all cities of Europe and North America provisioning and travel generally depended on the horse till 1914. When the rich countries made peace again in 1918, the horse belonged to the past. The endless stables, blacksmiths, provenders of barley, hay and straw, gave way quickly to the garages and petrol stations which symbolise our times more than anything else. Ford's company produced a million cars in the single year 1920. Paradoxically, the innovator of this era, Ford, detested modernity, hated the cities which his invention ultimately ensnared and thought that the only Americans worthy of the name were those on farms in the Mid West. He had no understanding of history, politics or literature and, though he was a pronounced pacifist, he believed in the spurious Jewish conspiracy to capture the world known as the 'Protocols of the Elders of Zion' (43).

The automobile industry has now become the largest enterprise in all the richer countries. Cars were not mentioned in the census of US business in 1900 but, by 1929, their makers were at the top of the list. They have stayed there. There were 26 million cars in the US in 1929. The industry had become the centre of a host of connected industries which, even by 1939 were consuming, in one way or another, 90% of the oil products of the US, 80% of the rubber, 75% of the plate glass, 68% of the leather and even 51% of the malleable iron.

Already, by 1939, the manufacture of cars in the US was concentrated in three companies, Ford, General Motors and Chrysler, which were together responsible for 90% of production. Of these, Ford's was still owned largely by one family and directed by it. That family had organised, as it were, a vertical combination, since it owned, within the car industry, everything from the iron mines to make the chassis to selling agencies. Ford's had, long before that, carried standardisation to the limit. General Motors was more decentralised. Its separate units also retained an independent identity (44). Similar concentrations later came to characterise all the rich and free countries, and, by the 1970s, the size, anonymity, and tedium of automobile factories made them battlefields for industrial war more sharply contested than any other.

The demand for cars led to a vast improvement in the standard, and number, of paved roads. In 1916, the federal government, in the USA revived grants of aid for building roads, which they had abandoned for two generations. In 1913, there were 250,000 miles of surfaced roads in the US. By 1940, there were over a million and a half. In Nazi Germany, the new roads were an economic achievement, a metaphor and a symbol: 'the new road of Adolf Hitler, the *autobahn*, is in keeping with the essence of national socialism . . . we wish to fix our goal far ahead of us . . . we create for ourselves a road that leads only forward' (45). Though Nazi Germany was defeated, most other countries have since copied, with 'motorways', the *autobahns* which were the Nazis' proudest achievement.

The swiftness of cars, and the recklessness with which they were often driven, gave rise to a new major source of death. In a rich country such as the US, 40,000 deaths a year in the 1970s were attributed to accidents on the road and thousands of injuries on top of that. Restrictions on speed and other measures have, however, maintained these numbers steady since the 1930s when there were far fewer cars.

In the 1970s, the 125 million cars and light trucks on the roads of the US use up 16% of the energy consumed by the US and a third of the liquid fuel used (46). But, in the future, new low standards of use of petrol will be set, even if it may be some time, perhaps, before the car using one gallon for 1,000 miles is on the market: but a machine which did that won a prize in the US in 1976 (47). Otherwise, the evolution of the car has continued by a series of predictable, gradual steps. An increasing use of road services for freight has characterised the more recent years of all these developments so that, in the 1970s, about a fifth of the world's vehicles were used for commercial services (57 million out of 270 million) (48).

The manufacture of cars has come to symbolise the character of labour in an advanced country. A third of a car worker's day is probably spent in dull work in a factory, another third is spent in sleep and another third is free for 'leisure'. In no other job is the debilitating distinction between work and play so well indicated.

In the USA, the automobile came within reach of the average wage earner in the 1920s. It did not do so in Europe till the 1950s. Thereafter, the ownership of cars seemed for a time almost an index of development, thus:

CARS IN USE (49)

	France	Britain	USA
1923	91,000	209,000	1,253,000
1929	930,000	1,409,000	26,704,825
1938	1,818,000	2,527,000	49,161,000
1950	2,150,000	3,290,000	49,143,275
1970	16,000,000	12,000,000	107,000,000

The increase of prices for oil, meantime, led to unseemly panic and nervousness in North America in 1979. The extent of American society's dependence on the internal combustion engine became more evident than ever before. So did the fragility of that civilisation.

Most innovations in transport or mechanisation have, like railways and aviation, steam and oil, had decisive effects on war. But, apart from taking soldiers to the war and carrying infantry in blitz attacks, the motor car has had a modest role in military affairs. Its troubles have been those of peaceable people. Many have died because of it; few in battle. Russia, the country which in the late twentieth century devotes more of its research to war than any other, has little to spare for the private car. Nor curiously (*pace* Evelyn Waugh, Vladimir Nabokov, Scott Fitzgerald, Kenneth Grahame) does the motor car play much part in literature.

The history of motor cars has been mainly the history of a private possession. That of aircraft has been one of public considerations.

Human beings began to dream of flight as soon as they began to watch birds. The ancient Chinese flew kites and enabled men to be lifted by them. The Greeks and the Romans speculated on the matter. Leonardo did the same. In 1716, Emmanuel Swedenborg, a Swedish philosopher of innumerable interests, drew a detailed plan for a flying machine; he added: 'There are sufficient proofs and examples from nature that such flights can take place without danger'. Still, no successful ascents into the air were made within sixty years of that remark. When they were, they were made not in machines but in balloons, mostly in France. The first such was made by the brothers Montgolfier, in a paper balloon, in 1783, lifted by hot air. In 1785, Jean Pierre Blanchard and John Jeffries, an American physician who had sided with the British in the War of Independence, crossed the English Channel in a balloon. A balloon was used for observation by the French at the battle of Fleurus in 1794. After that, for a hundred years, balloons were mostly to be seen at fairs and carnivals, though some were employed in the American Civil War in the 1860s and in the siege of Paris of 1871. Then, in 1884, a balloon was fitted with a petrol engine by Renard and Krebs at the French Military Aeronautical Department. It was driven five miles, at fourteen miles an hour. One of these new balloons was used by the US in 1898 in their war against Spain, for reconnaissance at San Juan hill (50). A German engineer, Otto Lilienthal, carried out heavier-than-air flights with a glider. He was killed in 1896, when a gust of wind caused his machine to crash (51). In the 1890s, both the French and Germans experimented with numerous airships which worked by pressure. In 1900, General Count Ferdinand von Zeppelin, an aristocrat from Baden, who had fought in both the American and the German wars of the 1860s, launched the first of his military airships. It stayed in the air for twenty minutes, but was wrecked when it landed. But, hoping for war, he persevered.

The first mechanised flight, however, was in 1903, when, after years of experimenting with gliders, two American makers of bicycles from Indiana, Orville and his brother Wilbur Wright, sons of a bishop of the United Brethren in Christ, flew a home-built, petrol-engined, heavier-than-air machine equal to twelve horse power on sand dunes at Kitty Hawk, in North Carolina. For a few years, however, the idea was neglected. Then once again the French, so adventurous both in their early ballooning and motoring, began to appreciate the possibilities of such flying machines. In 1908, Wilbur Wright flew fifty-six miles across France. In 1909, Louis Blériot flew from Etampes to Orléans and then from Calais to Dover, across the English Channel. The Comte de Lambert next flew from Juvisy round the Eiffel Tower and back: the first flight over a town. In 1910, Chavez flew over the Alps and, in 1911, the aeroplane was first tried out in war: Hamilton, an American pilot, carried out a flight over Ciudad Juárez in the early days of the Mexican revolution. The Italians also used aircraft for reconaissance in the Italo-Turkish war, which ensured them the colony of Libya, while the Spaniards were soon dropping explosive devices, the forerunners of bombs, from aircraft against the Riffs in Morocco. By 1912, both the British and French governments were also convinced of the promising possibilities of aviation for war. Until 1914, however, aviation was a brilliant sport for the daring, with some military possibilities. It played almost no part in commerce or transport, though an airmail flight had been carried out in Australia, from Melbourne to Sydney (52).

The First World War transformed this state of affairs. To begin with, aeroplanes were used, as balloons had been used at Fleurus, for reconnaissance. Fighters were needed to protect such 'spotter' aircraft. Both functions were filled by two-seater aeroplanes, with engines of 150 horse-power, which flew at most at 80 miles an hour. Anti-aircraft guns forced these aeroplanes to fly high, up to 15,000 feet, while night flying began regularly. Bombing, photo reconaissance patrols in formation, signals by coloured lights, the escorting of slow planes by faster ones, and sensational air combats between individuals who became recognised as almost the last 'heroes', were among the early innovations of the Great War. Large, twin-engined flying boats were used against submarines. Aircraft had 400 horsepower, and the height at which they could fly came to be limited more by the endurance of the pilot with oxygen, than by the possible ceiling of the new machine. Brilliant 'aerobatics' gave the war in the air the reputation of reviving the old tradition of the single combat. During its course, a phenomenal number of aircraft was built. In 1914, Britain had 272 aircraft; in 1918 over 22,000. In the US, in 1913, only 43 aeroplanes were produced. In 1918, there were 14,000, nearly all military (53).

Innovatory though it was, and important though the war was for its future, aviation did not play a decisive part in the battles of 1918. Bombing was then a fairly minor activity. Tanks, gas, and propaganda were more important. But the First World War prepared aeroplanes for a new role in transport. There were also soon new achievements. In 1919, John Alcock, son of a Manchester horsedealer, and Lieutenant Arthur Brown, a young Glaswegian electrical engineer before 1914, flew across the Atlantic in a Vickers Vimy bomber. Passenger services soon began, though Imperial Airways started its career in Britain with a grant by the government and with directors appointed by the government: a contrast from the independence and financial success of railways at their beginning. The same happened in France: three quarters of the income of the early airlines in France came from the state. Among countries which early interested themselves in commercial flying, only the companies in the US made profits; and there those who travelled did so more cheaply. But, even in the US, there were still only 358 aircraft in service by 1940 (54). It was only after governments in the Second World War gave the manufacture of aircraft such an enormous priority that civil aviation came to be commercially viable throughout the world – even though most of the world's airlines have had often large state subsidies, hidden or explicit; for modern States regard airlines as a source of prestige.

The innovations of the next generation of aircraft were primarily connected with war. In the 1930s, a doctrine that the 'bomber will always get through' (Baldwin's words, which reflected the thoughts of the Italian general, Douhet) inspired widespread fears. Much bombing of civilians (in the Italian war in Abyssinia; in the Spanish civil war; in the Sino-Japanese war, which Russia joined; in Britain, Germany, Japan, and later, Vietnam) has, however, always failed to break morale. In the first of the fire-storm raids by the British and Americans on Hamburg in 1943, for example, 243,000 people were apparently killed or injured out of a population of 1·5 million. Even so, thanks to a well organised civil defence all the usual services in that city were functioning normally soon afterwards, and historians of the Second World War doubt whether the bombing weakened the German will to resist in any way, any more than similar ones did over Vietnam in the 1960s. The bombing of Hiroshima and Nagasaki by nuclear weapons in 1945 did help to cause the end of the war in the Far East, but that was, as it were, a *coup de grâce*, following innumerable other raids which had destroyed Japan's capacity to feed herself by eliminating her merchant fleet.

Some precision bombing in the course of the Second World War, such as the American and British raids on Germany's installations for oil in Roumania, was also effective, but only at the end of that conflict. In 1944, German production for war had not been seriously damaged. Characteristic of military attitudes by then was the approach of most governments to innovations. Frank Whittle, then a test pilot, applied for his first patent for a 'jet' engine in 1930 and submitted the idea to the British Air Ministry, (who thought the 'practical difficulties' were too great). He only flew a jet propelled engine for the first time in 1941.

More important than bombing in all wars since the development of aviation has been the use of aircraft as a means of supplementing, or substituting for, artillery. An air force able to destroy an enemy's similar force on the ground (as Israel did with the Egyptians in 1967) is able to establish an air superiority over the zone of battle which allows him to use his aircraft as firepower, attacking men, tanks, lorries, lines of communication and other land-based weapons with impunity. The vast number of Yak fighters which Russia was able to throw into the battle was the decisive element in the Second World War between 1943 and 1945. It was comparable to the use of 'jet' propelled fighters built in Germany at the same time.

After 1945, military aircraft played for the next fifteen years the decisive part in the potential carriage of nuclear weapons which provided the guarantee of the cold war. Types of fighters and bombers continue, indeed, to succeed one another, often without ever having been tested in a major battle. Innumerable fighters in several countries regularly travel faster than the speed of sound (in 1977, the USA had about 3,400 combat aircraft, Russia about 4,600) (55). Since 1957, aircraft have come to be supplemented by rockets and even substituted by them. Some of them admittedly were fired from aircraft. But mostly, they came from the ground or from submarines. Thus the age of military aircraft seems to be near its end. Yet there are many small wars in which conventional aircraft continue to play a great part, carrying troops, destroying communications on the ground, attacking infantry from heights and photographing land more effectively than spies could ever 'sketch' it. Those small wars will no doubt continue indefinitely.

Civil aircraft also play a determining role in inter-national, and, in the case of a few countries, internal, travel. The decisive change here was the development of Whittle's jet aircraft for civil purposes, after the middle of the 1950s. In the early 1970s, aircraft suddenly trebled in size, while, from 1975, a commercial aeroplane, the Concorde, faster than sound, was flown on a few routes. The easiest indication of the importance of these changes can be seen in the following table:

CIVIL AVIATION. (Thousand passenger miles) (56)

	France	Britain	United States Domestic	International
1938	45.6	53.75	299	33.1
1953	1,543.75	1,442.5	9,230.6	2,115.6
1972	10,972.5	15,199.3	153,291.8	29,251.6

People can now travel round the world in the same time (say forty-eight hours) as it once took to get by rail and boat from London to

Berlin. Before the age of railways, it would have been difficult to have travelled further in forty-eight hours from London than to York. Vast numbers of people, therefore, now travel fast to remote places on business or for pleasure. But, the shortness of the journey makes it impossible for most people to inform themselves fully on the significance of the country to which they are travelling. Then, the ease with which distant travel can be accomplished has led to, or at least been accompanied by, an increase in the restrictions enabling entry into countries. The 'jumbo jet' airliner enables emigration from Asia to Europe or America on a scale which would make that of the nineteenth century seem modest. But no advanced countries, particularly not the USA and Australia, open their doors to unrestricted immigration. Indeed, the age of easy travel has coincided with a period in which the possibilities of removal from one country to another has been as a result rendered more difficult than it has ever been. Vast regions of the world also remain as much out of bounds to the traveller as they did in the last century (to some extent, they are more so, for a nineteenth century traveller would have found it easier to travel, if he had money, to any part of the region which now constitutes the communist world, than today).

The beauty of flight, to begin with, inspired numerous artists. The futurists of 1910 looked to 'the pilots of the purple twilight', as an early film put it, as a means of purifying mankind. Gabriele d'Annunzio praised the aeroplane in *Forse che si, forse che no* in 1911. The crazed poet Marinetti dedicated his play *Poupées Electriques* to Wilbur Wright, who 'knew how to raise our migrant hearts higher than the captivating mouth of a woman' (57). Antoine de Saint Exupéry and André Malraux also had fine lines about flight, particularly the former, while the latter, in the Spanish Civil War, organised a brigade of fliers in order to give himself the raw material for a novel (*L'Espoir*). But since 1939, the facts of aviation have been so harsh that there is as little good writing about aeroplanes as about cars. Illustrative films and memoirs, of course, there have been without number. Aviation also remains for a few the sport that it first was during the heroic days. But it is hard to make the crowded airliners of the 1970s a fit subject for art, apart from the miracle of flight itself. W. B. Yeats's *An Irish airman foresees his death*, was, however, to some people his best poem:

> I know that I shall meet my fate
> Somewhere among the clouds above. . . .
> Nor law nor duty bade me fight
> Nor public men, nor cheering crowds,
> A lonely impulse of delight
> Drove to this tumult in the clouds. . . .

The reconstruction of communications since the early nineteenth century has enabled pre-eminently a level of commerce unbelievable at any previous age. Total world trade stood at something like $800,000 million dollars in 1972, the bulk of this in the democratic capitalist nations ($600,000 million) (58). Internal commerce in the US meanwhile, was approximately $220,000 million (59). The vast increase in these figures since even 1938, is, despite changes in the value of money, what must strike the casual observer: for the total then amounted to about $47,000 million (60). Even allowing for an unparalleled inflation since 1938, that increase must have been eight-fold, a growth far larger than that of population and one utterly unprecedented in the history of commerce: a change which naturally has accounted for some upheavals.

One further type of physical communication should be mentioned at this point; the series of actions made possible by the development of rockets, which has as yet had no commercial benefits directly.

The idea of a rocket was apparently first worked out for diversion by the Chinese in the twelfth century AD. Taken to Europe, rockets were sporadically used as fireworks and as missiles in war from then on, usually the former. Elaborate festivals of fireworks were given in all European countries from the time of the Renaissance onwards. Fireworks were frequent at ceremonies of triumph or thanksgiving. Indians, however, used rockets in combat against English troops, and English troops subsequently used an artillery rocket both in India and against Napoleon.

All these rockets were propelled by various types of gunpowder. Some of them were used during the First World War in order to try to destroy observation balloons, but rather ineffectively. It then became known that the use of liquid fuel would make possible more impressive performances. Robert Goddard, an American engineer, shot up a rocket with liquid fuel for the first time in 1926 at Auburn, Massachusetts. No one took much notice. Similar work was carried on in Germany. There, such activities were regarded less sceptically than they were in the US. The German army took over the ideas of the Society for Space Travel at Peenemünde, on the Baltic coast. This led, during the Second World War, to the V.1 and the V.2 long range rockets, and many other smaller guided missiles, of which 2,000 crossed the English coast in 1944–5, travelling at 360 miles an hour, and each with a ton of explosive. The British and US also began some less ambitious experiments during the Second World War, among them the bazooka or the anti-tank missile. German scientists in 1944 were already considering intercontinental missiles which would travel at 800 miles an hour.

After the Second World War, research on these rockets continued, partly concerned with space travel, partly with the idea that guided missiles might replace manned aircraft for carrying weapons, including nuclear ones. The first artificial satellite, the sputnik, was launched by

Russia in 1957 with the help of captured German scientists. Soon after, the US, also with the help of specialists born in Germany, began to launch such objects. By the late 1970s, there were already about 4,600 such artificial satellites circling the Earth, contributing to meteorology, communications of many sorts, espionage and preparations for war. Space journeys by men even began to be undertaken by both Russia (in April 1961) and the US (in May 1961). (Actually, two Russian dogs were the first living creatures lifted into, and then brought back from, space, in 1960). In 1967, the Russians landed a collection of instruments on the planet Venus, while in 1970, two Americans, Neil Armstrong and Edwin Aldrin, landed on the moon. Satellites were subsequently launched into the air by the Chinese and the French. Curiously, the names of the early heroes of space failed to establish themselves strongly in the public memory. Was it that the modern public realised that they were in no sense men who had achieved things on their own, but were merely cogs in a state's machine?

A far more sinister use of rockets, however, also began during the 1950s. Subsequently, these assumed major importance. These were continuations of the programme for rockets undertaken by Germany in the Second World War. Both the USA and Russia had, by the late 1970s, several thousand rockets of various ranges. Many were equipped with nuclear weapons. Peace between these states and, hence, in the world, seems to depend on the maintenance of the 'balance of terror' established between them. None of these rockets, so far as can be seen, has any future as a method of peaceful travel, though the satellites have evidently transformed telecommunications and meteorology.

In 1820, an Austrian official, asked by a student who wished to return home by a different route to that by which he had set out, angrily retorted: 'Do you think the Empire is a dovecote where everyone can fly around as he pleases?' Since 1945, the world has become that dovecote, but the spirit of Austrian officialdom is far from dead.

33

The Revolution in Information

Most 'revolutions' are deceptive. Not only are they almost always held to have been betrayed by someone but, often, radical political changes seem to historians to have been introduced to withstand, rather than implement, economic change. The French Revolutionaries, though they sought to create an unbridgeable gulf between themselves and the past, turned out, in the words of de Tocqueville, to be 'almost a natural outcome of the very social order which they made haste to destroy' (1). But there has been one real revolution in the world and that was the revolution in communications. That revolution goes far to explain the crises of the twentieth century. What this meant was well put by Carmelo Lisón-Tolosana, a social historian from Spain: 'In the decades before the advent of the Republic [in Spain, 1931] life in the community in [Aragon] followed its daily rhythm in a monotonous but peaceful way. The cultivation of the land kept the residents occupied. There were no radios to put the people in contact with the outside world, and, normally, no newspapers were received. Life was generally poor and hard, since fields were generally cultivated with the Roman plough, and the use of fertilisers and selection of seed . . . unknown. The community as such enjoyed tranquility, and unity, and order; there were no signs of internal hostility . . . months [only] before the rise of the Republic, one of the men who was to become leader of a political faction in the town organised an excursion in which everyone who wanted to could take part independent of . . . political differences [which], in fact, hardly existed . . . Such a community excursion . . . would have been inconceivable just one year later' (2), when radio, newspapers and political pamphleteering all brought a complete transformation in the town.

The first part of the revolution in communications, however, affected a very old form of contact between people, namely the post.

Some kind of postal service had existed fitfully from the days of the Persian Empire and in China since the Han dynasty. The more stable the empire, probably, the more repressive the empire even, the better the system of posts. All early posts were state monopolies, organised for the benefit of the government. In the Caliphate, the postmaster-general

331

was often at the same time chief of intelligence (3). Private persons, if they wished to communicate with others who lived at a distance, organised their own couriers, or persuaded (or bribed) governmental messengers to do the work. In mediaeval Europe, private merchants, such as the Medici family, organised their own postal services. As noticed earlier, princely families, such as the Thurn und Taxis family in Germany, later arranged a public service. They opened the letters and read what was in them. Thus they were able to run an espionage service and a news agency as well. In most European languages the word for 'post' recalls the Roman postal service along routes clearly designated by wooden posts. The Spaniards with their *correo* are an exception. Their word recalls the use of runners.

The history of posts in France before the age of industry is characteristic of European developments. The University of Paris had an internal post during the Middle Ages. A postal service for private letters was publicly organised by Louis XI. It was gradually developed during the centuries between then and the French Revolution. The right to collect income from it was (as usual in old France) farmed out. Parcel post existed by the time of Richelieu. There was even a French book post in the eighteenth century: the parcels were to be left open at both ends. A penny postal service was introduced by the English in the late eighteenth century, and a similar cheap service for Paris was also created.

By about 1820, most European countries and many others (for example, in South America) had well established postal services. Some stretched back, like those in Venice, to the Renaissance. Austria introduced a postcard in 1869, Sardinia a stamped postal paper in 1818, Britain a postage stamp in 1839 (and a new version of the penny post), and the postage stamp was copied by other countries.

The critical change in the history of the post derived, however, from the use of railways, to carry the letters so stamped. The greater availability and cheapness of paper, and the growth of literacy also assisted the establishment of good posts. True, the creation of post office savings banks (in England, from 1862), the creation of a money order department (in France from 1627), the system of postal orders (in England from 1881) and the rather unfortunate marriage of post offices with telegraph and telephone services certainly stimulated this service. But it was, however, the mail trains which really made possible a golden age of letter-writing (say from 1850 till 1939), whose character is, as a result, better documented than any era before — or since, for the letter gave way, after 1945, to the telephone as the best means of communication between people in the same country. The decline in letter writing is however, not, as it happens, borne out by statistics of postal services, because of the increase of commercial mail.

This history of the telegraph had a much shorter life than that of the letter, and its decay, as a result of the telephone (and telex, since about

1960) seems more absolute. But visual signalling is very old. Torches, bonfires and smoke signals were used from the days of the black sails which Theseus hoisted and which caused the death of his father. Naval signalling, however, began to be rendered coherent by two English admirals, Richard Kempenfelt, a man of Swedish origin (who sank in 1782 with his flagship, the *Royal George*, in a famous English maritime accident), and by Richard, Earl Howe, a man known to be 'undaunted as a rock and as taciturn', in Horace Walpole's words. In 1790, Claude Chappe devised semaphore by using movable shutters and wooden arms like railway signals, in order to assist communications between Paris and the French revolutionary army. The first message to be sent that way was despatched in August 1794, during the French invasion of Belgium. A message so sent could travel at 150 miles an hour. The English copied Chappe's system, speeding it up so that a message could soon be sent from London to Deal in a minute. Berlin could soon get an answer from Coblentz in four hours and from St Petersburg in fifty. But semaphore depended on good weather and, in all countries, governments reserved the system for themselves. Pigeon post, on the other hand, began to be used by private general traders, and it was from that that the new developments derived in the end. Chappe, meantime, killed himself in 1805 out of melancholia because the originality of his idea had been questioned.

The idea of an electric telegraph had already been suggested, soon after the discovery of the Leyden jar, by a surgeon of Greenock, Charles Morrison, who wrote of it in the *Scots Magazine* in 1753. Various other people worked on the same idea in the eighteenth century. Madrid was linked by wire with the royal summer palace of Aranjuez as a result of the efforts of a Spanish engineer, Francisco Salvá, in 1795; (4) an indication of the high level of technical achievement in Spain in the eighteenth century. Then, as seen earlier,* in 1833, Karl Friedrich Gauss, with Wilhelm Weber, sent his famous message by electricity from the observatory to the spire of the Johannes Kirke. At much the same time in the USA, Samuel Morse, the son of a Massachusetts congregational minister, who had begun life as a painter, reflected (on board the packet boat *Sully*): 'I see no reason why intelligence may not be transmitted by electricity.' In 1837, Morse made a circuit of 1,700 feet of copper wire. He later successfully sent a message on it by means of the code which he had devised. The scheme was soon commercially exploited, though not immediately to Morse's benefit. In 1844, a telegraph line using Morse's ideas was laid between Baltimore and Washington. Within four years, most of the USA east of the Mississippi was linked up. In England, a telegraph line was laid from Paddington to Slough in 1843, and then the company of Cooke and Wheatstone established 4,000 miles of telegraph

* See above page 306.

in Britain within four years. A Prussian state telegraph service followed in 1849. The success of these innovations led to the use of the new system throughout Europe. By then, the telegraph had ceased to be confined in its use to railways. Money orders by telegraph could be sent from 1850 in Britain and the laying of a cable between Dover and Calais, after 1851, meant that the stock exchanges of the two capitals could compare prices on the same day. A cable was laid successfully across the Atlantic in 1865 and, the same year, one from Europe to India. In 1873, Australia was in direct cable communication with Europe.

The subsequent story of the telegraph is best told in figures:

TELEGRAPHS SENT (5)

	Franc	Britain
1850	464,000 *(1858)*	not available
1860	720,000	not available
1870	5,664,000	11.8 M
1913	52,217,000 *(1914)*	87.1 M
1938	36,444,000	58 M
1969	27,332,000	29 M

On the continent of Europe, most telegraph services were from the beginning owned by the State. In the USA, and in other American countries, control passed into the hands of private monopolies. In Britain, a series of well-intentioned public servants demonstrated in endless memorials that only the State could provide an efficient, cheap telegraph service. The private companies were bought by the Post Office in 1869. It looks as if that body may abandon telegraphs altogether in the 1980s.

The early significance of the telegraph is to be seen in the career of Julius Reuter, born into a Jewish commercial family as Israel Beer Josaphat. A clerk in his uncle's bank at Göttingen, he chanced to meet Professor Gauss at Cassel. In 1840, he began to work for a French agency, headed by Charles Havas, a Portuguese entrepreneur from Oporto. A few years before, Havas had bought up the *Correspondance Garnier*, an office which translated foreign newspapers into French. Reuter managed to turn Havas into an agency for collecting information by pigeon-post between London, Paris and Brussels. Reuter began on his own just after the general acceptance of the telegram and, for a time, made money by providing a link (again by pigeon) between two telegraph services, the Berlin – Aachen line and the Paris – Brussels one. Reuter moved to London in 1850 when Paris became telegraphically linked to that capital, and began an agency for news by providing English clients with the closing prices of stocks and shares in Paris and *vice versa*. Then he extended his activities to other capitals. Newspapers, to begin with sceptical, started to take Reuter's despatches after *The Times* had promptly published a speech by Napoleon III which had been sent to them by Reuter's man in Paris in 1855. Offices in New York and Bombay were soon established (6).

Though it was the first news agency, Reuter's was not the only one. Havas in Paris copied their ex-employee and Wolff created a similar enterprise in Germany. The three exchanged news so as to make it possible to share the world's market between them. Associated Press of New York later joined these three, and another American agency, United Press, came on to the scene in 1907. These agencies seemed almost to be departments of government. Havas, in particular, had close relations with the French government from whom it later received a subsidy, in 1938. Associated Press, led by an indefatigable individualist, Kent Cooper, challenged the old agencies and, by 1934, had the right to sell news everywhere throughout the world on an equal footing with Reuter's.

For ordinary people, the telegram was for a few generations the most usual means of communicating a victory or a tragedy. The arrival of the 'telegraph boy' filled people of all classes between 1850 and 1950 with a mixture of dread and excitement. A scholarship? A proposal of marriage? Death in action? To historians, the world of the telegram has been the world of the diplomatic message, despatched at what the taxpayers would regard as inordinate length, but, even so, not always communicating the full meaning of the sender. The telegram sent from Ems by King Wilhelm I of Prussia in 1870 was construed, or revised, by Bismarck to justify the Franco-Prussian war. The exchanges of telegrams between diplomats and generals representing the European powers in July 1914 put the greatest strain until then experienced on the European telegraphic services. There was confusion, even on such an important matter as to whether Germany did, or did not, wish her ally, Austria Hungary, to mobilise: '*Ich habe es nicht gewollt*' said Emperor Franz Josef ruefully, after the war had begun. (7). Later, the breaking of the cyphers in which enemy military messages were hidden gave the British one of the greatest of their great technological triumphs (8).

In the 1970s, such important exchanges might have been over the telephone, one of the inventions of the nineteenth century which the twentieth is still using increasingly every year. In 1972, for example, the world's telephones numbered nearly fifty per cent more than they had only five years before (9). By that time too, in the USA, there were over 60 telephones per 100 inhabitants against a world average of 8·2.

This instrument derives from the telegraph. Several inventors, such as Dr C. G. Page in Massachusetts, Charles Bourseul in Paris and Philip Reis in Frankfurt came close to devising a telephone between 1835 and 1865. Alexander Graham Bell, a Scotsman from Edinburgh living in Boston, Massachusetts, was, however, the first person to create, in

1875, an electric current whose strength varied at every instant according to the vibrations caused by the human voice. (Bell was primarily concerned, as a professor of vocal philology, with work for the deaf.)

The first telephoned message was transmitted in 1876. A conversation between Boston and New York was held in 1877. Soon after, Thomas Edison, subsequently the pioneer of electricity, devised another type of telephone on which the first Telephone Exchange in New York was based. By 1880, the United States had 54,000 receiving telephones in operation, in 1900 nearly two million (more than India had in the 1970s) and, in 1912, 8·7 million (10). A line from New York to Chicago was opened in 1892, one from New York to San Francisco in 1915. This swift development was mostly carried out by a private company which, after 1918, effectively established a near-monopoly, the American Telephone and Telegraph Company (subsequently, International T & T). In Europe, Germany led the way, as in all electrical industries, so that she had, by 1912, four times as many installations as had France, and her people talked on the telephone four times as often as did the French. Britain was slow to develop the telephone. That, however, was partly due to the argument put forward by the Postmaster General that the telephone was an implement covered by the Acts relating to the telegram, giving him a monopoly. After the idea of municipal management had also been abortively tried out, a national telephone company, under state management, was founded within the Post Office and, in the 1890s, installation was going ahead fast. In 1912, Englishmen were making 833 million telephone calls a year in comparison with 396 million calls in France and, apparently, 2327 million in Germany (11).

The field telephone played a large part in the First World War. In the Spanish Civil War, many critical incidents revolved round the use of the telephone, or the capture of the telephone exchanges, correctly estimated to be as important in modern life as town halls. As early as 1909, a Spanish civil governor, in order to keep the millions in Barcelona from communicating with Madrid, lighted on the idea of banning long-distance calls (12). In the 1920s, the landlords of Andalusia were critical of the idea of establishing a telephone service, for they feared that it would enable their anarchist enemies to consort too easily (13). In the 1940s and 1950s, the use of the telephone assisted General Franco's government, like many other such military regimes, to pursue its enemies more effectively. The tapping of the telephone soon became a recourse of governments (and spies). Mussolini was believed to spend more time reading reports of such tappings than on public business (14). Mussolini's ministers indeed believed that the quickest way of getting information to their leader was to work it somehow into a telephone call which they knew would be tapped. In Russia after 1945, Solzhenitsyn symbolically made the work of certain privileged prisoners to identify a voice from an intercepted telephone the main theme of his greatest novel, *The First Circle*. There can be no doubt whatever that the telephone has been to centralisation of government what the loud-speaker has been to the mass orator. Yet one of the most successful statesmen of our time, Charles de Gaulle, is believed never to have used the telephone. Recorded telephoned dialogues (and that goes for many private conversations as well as ones of public importance) reveal a naïvety, ignorance and opaqueness among politicians rarely encoun-tered in ordinary life (15). The world was mildly comforted by the estab-lishment of a direct telephone line between the leaders of the US and Russia after the Cuban crisis which in 1963 nearly led to war between them. Relations have not subsequently much improved. Still, perhaps these rather gloomy conclusions will be confounded by the new system of telephone by light wave which the Bell Telephone Company plans to introduce into regular service by 1980, or at least some form of electronic telephone which is long overdue.

Some notice, finally, in a discussion of methods of communication should be paid to the typewriter, which came to be used extensively for the first time in the 1880s. A printer in Marseilles in the 1830s had devised what he called a *'machine cryptographique'* which, he argued, could write as fast as a pen. It was the first machine to have each character printed on a separate bar. Later, Christopher Sholes, a journa-list of Pennsylvania, worked out the idea of the inked ribbon and solved the question of where best to put the letters: letters used often next to one another should be apart. Sholes sold his patent to Remington and Co, famous arms manufacturers: Eliphabet Remington had received a large armaments contract from the Federal Government during the Civil War. Philo Remington put a typewriter on the market in 1873. The main impact of that was to increase the number of copies of documents, many of which were, however, unnecessary. The greater level of business correspondence (also much of it unnecessary) finally began the addition in the number of secretaries and assistants which, in the twentieth century, mark businesses, universities, armies, police forces and government departments alike (16). The typewriter has also widened the gulf between scholars and writers. Most of the former refused to type. Most of the latter have to. Nietzsche was apparently the first famous writer to use a typewriter: *absit omen*.

Forty years before the typewriter, photography had begun to trans-form visual memory. The result has probably been to affect adversely the memory of the mind's eye. The idea had been thought of often before. For example, the fact that a pinhole admitting light into a dark room projected an inverted image of objects outside, was known to Euclid (c. 300 BC) as to Alhazen (who died in 1038 AD), the best known mediaeval Arabic writer on optics. In the eighteenth century, the sun's light was observed to darken silver salts when they were exposed to it, just as sunlight caused sunburn. A few interesting experiments were conducted by Humphry Davy and Thomas Wedgwood, a celebrated chemist and son of the potter. Indeed, Wedgwood can dispute with the French pioneers the distinction of having made the first real photograph. At all events, Nicéphore de Niepce, who had retired from the French army because of failing sight, obtained images on a bituminous film and, in 1813, began collaborating with Louis Daguerre, a scene painter at the Opéra who had once been an inland revenue collector. They were successful, in the end, and Niepce took a photograph of his home town in Burgundy of Chalon-sur-Saône. The exposure, however, took eight hours. There could be only one copy of the print, and the result was not sharp. Daguerre soon improved on that achievement. In 1839, he showed his first collection of 'daguerrotypes' at the French Academy of Sciences. 'From today, painting is dead,' exclaimed Paul Delaroche, an artist who previously had made Romanticism acceptable. Actually, the effect was to make realistic painting fashionable. Meantime, W. H. Fox Talbot, an English mathematician and landowner, evolved a form of photography which is more clearly the ancestor of the modern type. His experiments, achieved independently of Daguerre's, make him the co-founder of this art. Wrangles over patents, however, disfigured those early days. The invention, in 1851, of a 'collodion' (a solution of gun-cotton in ether) glass plate leading to the first practical application of photography for those other than scientists, was an English sculptor of no great talent, Frederick Scott Archer. Even then, it was only in the 1880s, with the invention of the first ready-made dry plate, that photography as a hobby came within reach of the ordinary amateur. Mass-produced 'cameras' were soon available. The Kodak box camera was invented in 1888, the celluloid film in 1890, while the first newspaper pictures began to appear in the 1890s; for example, in the *New York Daily Graphic*. The next thirty years were as well commemorated in photographs as they were in letters. The portrait painters of the era immediately after mass photography, such as Sargent and Whistler, were as careful in depicting features as any cameraman. People desired painters to be as accurate as photographers and many painted portraits from photographs (Manet so painted the *Execution of Maximilian*). Ingres, Corot, Meissonier and Degas were also influenced by photography. Subsequently, photography has become a popular hobby of millions, with pictures dominating newspapers and, after the second half of the twentieth century, sometimes even dominating 'books'. But photography was a popular art of the nineteenth as well as of the twentieth century. Thus, in Paris, already in 1847, half a million photographic plates were sold and, in the 1850s and 1860s, the photograph in the shape of a postcard brought this invention within reach of all. Many early photographers indeed were ex-painters. Colour photography, however, was not possible before the 1930s and was not popular before the 1960s, save in advertising.

The emergence of the popular press and much cheaper printing and distribution costs is the next part of the 'revolution in communications' to which attention should be paid. In England, *The Spectator* in London was already selling about 2,000 copies a day in 1711, the *Gentleman's Magazine* 10,000 in 1739. Other countries copied these successes. Thus in Germany there was a *Litteratur Zeitung* which was 'read by everyone' (and sold 2,000 copies) (17). Most cities in Europe and North America had some journals of comment, mostly of a polemical kind, by 1750. Freedom to write with no censorship in newspapers began its history in Holland in the seventeenth century. In England, a system of licensing existed, but that was abolished in 1695, probably because it had by then begun to be impossible to control illegal pamphleteering (18). Between 1700 and 1760, a hundred and thirty provincial newspapers had made at least a temporary appearance. In 1753, seven million newspapers were already being sold every year in England, 20,000 a day, a figure far in advance of any other country at that time. Large sums were often paid out of public funds to editors who supported governments and, as a rule, newspapers had to pay taxes. Neither they nor periodicals were free from persecution. Yet they were established as a 'fourth estate' before 1789 in England. Newspapers in the US were also well established before the revolution of the 1770s. Indeed, the *Boston Evening Post* contributed to that revolution. In comparison, French periodicals and newspapers before 1789 were feeble. The State controlled and licensed all publications and so the most celebrated literary works were published abroad. The *Mercure de France* was believed, however, particularly by its contributors, to have played a great part in the coming of the French Revolution. Manuscript newspapers were theoretically forbidden, but they flourished in eighteenth century Paris. No publisher could then print anything in Spain, either a book or a newspaper, without a licence and no licence was given for a publication until a report had been made by a careful judge (19).

The nineteenth century transformation was caused by technical changes making possible the creation of mass distributed newspapers, by growing literacy and political awareness, and by the telegraph.

In 1800, Charles, Earl Stanhope, a radical English peer interested in science, and the brother-in-law of William Pitt, employed iron rather than wood to produce a printing press which would produce wood engravings and heavy type. In 1810, the *Annual Register* and, as noticed earlier, in 1814, *The Times* in London began to use its steam press.* Other newspapers copied them, for it worked four times faster than a hand-operated press. The intellectual, social and economic upheavals caused by the industrial revolution, and which threatened violence after 1815 in many countries, particularly England, were marked by, perhaps

---

* See above page 261.

really caused by, the greatest outpouring of books, satires, pamphlets, and political poems ever known till then. Working-class papers made their first real appearance. The prints of Gillray, Rowlandson and Cruik-shank circulated too. The novels of Scott, the poems of Byron and indeed of Scott also sold in formidable numbers: it seems that the latter's poem *Marmion*, for instance, seized hold of the public 'like a kind of madness; the lines not only clung to the memory but they would not keep off the tongue: people could not help spouting them in solitary places and muttering them as they walked about the streets.' In the 1820s and 1840s, railways began to make possible national presses, though in most countries, newspapers outside the capital remained important. In the 1840s, the invention of the telegraph* allowed the creation of efficient news agencies, and the commissioning of regular foreign correspondents. Newspaper taxes were finally removed in Britain in 1855. In the late 1840s, Richard Hoe of New York, son of an English-born printer, designed the rotary press; a stop cylinder press; and the web press. These made possible the modern newspaper. The rotary press could produce 20,000 impressions an hour. From 1865, a continuous roll of paper could be introduced into any of these machines, instead of having to be fed at different levels by twenty-five people. Meantime, a large new reading public, in almost every country, sought both serenity and excitement in the vast number of novels, poems, and political works which the nineteenth century, the first mechanised age but one before mass communication, as that phrase is usually understood, made available.

That, the increase in newspapers, and the concurrent increase too in the number of letters exchanged, stimulated, naturally, a demand for paper which defeated the old way of making it from cotton, linen and straw scraps. The solution reached (without which the paper revolution of the twentieth century certainly would be unimaginable) was to employ wood pulp. After 1874, a chemical method of using that was devised which enabled the paper manufacturers to meet a huge new demand.

Finally, lino-type machines were devised in the USA in the 1880s. They were introduced into Europe ten years later. The US also led the way in machine-setting of books with the monotype machine in the 1890s, even though most books were set by hand until 1914.

The first consequence of these developments was a vast increase in the sale of newspapers and books, at least in countries where there was no censorship. A typical development was that in the United States. (See table on facing page).

The second consequence was the realisation that, in democracies in which an increasing proportion of adults had the vote, it became recog-

* See above page 333.

nised, as expressly stated in the Rights of Man of 1791, or as put by de Tocqueville in 1835, 'the independence of the press is the chief and . . . constitutive element of liberty. A nation that is determined to remain free is, therefore, right in demanding at any price the exercise of this independence' (21). The importance of this was appreciated by tyrants of the old sort as by those of a new: Napoleon I suppressed sixty out of seventy-three newspapers when he conquered Italy and handed over the censorship to the police (22). He remarked, à propos of France: 'People complain we have no literature: it is the fault of the Minister of the Interior' (23). Napoleon III controlled the press as rigidly as any government had before 1789 (24). After 1815, in Piedmont, everyone who wanted to read a foreign newspaper had to obtain a permit for so doing.

U.S. NEWSPAPERS

	Number of daily papers	Circulation (daily) (20)
1850	254	758,000
1880	971	3,556,000
1900	2,226	15,102,000
1914	2,580	28,777,000
1956	6,315	78,090,000

The problem of censorship became more and more difficult as literacy gradually increased in the nineteenth century. Thus there was no official censorship in Russia before 1790, when Catherine the Great banned Radischev's account of his journey from St Petersburg to Moscow. Before that, few Russians could read and, anyway, the Government or the Church owned the printing presses. For Russia, the age of censorship began in 1826, after the Decembrists' revolt, with a literate population which could not have numbered 10% of adults. A code was introduced insisting that all publications had to meet the Government's approval and also to make a positive contribution to public morals (25). With alternating times of repression and tolerance, and different definitions, that system has continued in Russia.

A third consequence was the heightened importance of newspapers in political life. In the late 1890s, the Hungarian-born proprietor, Joseph Pulitzer, and the Californian, William Hearst, in the US, Alfred Harmsworth in Britain, and Charles Dupuy in France, created mass journalism. Moïsé Millaud in France had sown the seed in the 1860s with *Le Petit Journal*, which sold 582,000 copies in 1880 — four times that of its nearest rival (26). In every advanced nation, the world of the Press gave a new dimension to both literature and politics, establishing a new world half way between entertainment and education. Alongside the national and provincial daily press, every country also began to publish numerous specialised newspapers and journals dealing with medicine, music, sport, children and religion — everything under the sun. France was in the *avant garde* of this new 'mass culture'. *Le Petit Parisien*, for example, belonging to Charles Dupuy, son of a well-to-do shopkeeper, achieved, in 1916, the largest sale hitherto reached in any country — 2,183,000 copies. The enthusiastic or illiterate peasant in Andalusia meantime bought his paper and gave it to his companion to read (27).

Since the late nineteenth century, politicians have enjoyed, in democracies, close, and often unhealthy friendships with the Press, sometimes flattering newspapers as essential to liberty, often denouncing them as squalid merchants in intrigue. They have often been both, as have politicians. When, at the end of the First World War, President Woodrow Wilson promised a new era of 'open covenants openly arrived at' in place of secret diplomacy (such as, as he implied, had led to the war) he meant no more, in effect, than that editors of newspapers should learn of governments' decisions sooner than they had done before 1914. But the events of 1918—19 showed that the voice of 'public opinion' (and, even more, 'international opinion') was no sure guarantee of serene policy-making. Public opinion wanted to 'hang the Kaiser'. Public men prevented that from happening. Manipulation of the Press by Governments, and the playing by public men on the emotions of peoples through the medium of the Press (often by use of the calculated indiscretion to the carefully selected journalist), has subsequently characterised, sometimes even dominated, public life, sometimes to the public benefit.

The history of the Press has been most instructive in France, where the Revolution spawned hundreds of papers. Almost every political group between 1789 and 1794 founded its own paper. The same thing happened in other revolutions in France in 1830 and 1848. In the nineteenth century, journalists, like Balzac's Lucien de Rubempré, arrived in Paris determined to seek 'the bubble reputation'. Others, like Emile de Girardin, presented themselves as pioneers of mass education and, with such cheap papers as *La Presse* (which he wrote as well as published), inaugurated the popular newspaper (28). (Immensely successful as a proprietor, Girardin failed, like many others afterwards, to convert that success into the political power which he coveted.) Successful journalists soon began to make large incomes. Newspapers, on the other hand, began making money from advertisements as early as the 1840s (though, in France, that was never so great an element in their financing as it became in Britain or the US). They also soon started to receive bribes to put over a certain point of view from all sorts of quarters: from novelists, wanting their books well reviewed, or foreign governments. Russia, for example, distributed 2 million francs in France a year to enable her to raise loans after 1905. 'A large number of highly respectable journalists accepted, even solicited, bribes,' wrote Theodore Zeldin 'as a condition of writing articles in favour of Russia' (29) — among them the secretary of the journalists' union. Some French papers even received bribes from Germany during the First World War. The French government even now contributes almost half the income of the press, by means of special favours on railways, postal charges and raw materials. All the great French *'affaires'* of the Third Republic, such as the Dreyfus case, were newspaper scandals *par excellence* — and were, indeed, often created by the Press.

The golden age of the Press was short: from the Franco-Prussian War till the end of the Second World War. In 1871, the telegraph had linked Europe with America to enable the telegram to give immediacy to the news. The appetite for knowledge of remote places was great. Foreign correspondents, if sometimes absurdly, were among the heroes of the day (the young Winston Churchill in South Africa; Hearst in Cuba). But, by 1945, the radio had already cast its shadow over newspapers, which were already beginning to close in the face of the challenge by a usually government-sponsored news service. Television, a mass medium in the United States from the 1940s, and in Europe from the 1950s, transformed the old status of the Press. In the 1970s, labour troubles threatened the Press's future in most democratic countries in ways which would have seemed extraordinary to those who had struggled for a free press in the eighteenth century.*

Still, the circulation of newspapers is huge in comparison with anything which prevailed before the 1870s: 293 per thousand people in the US, 443 per thousand in Britain, 220 in France, even 536 in Sweden (31). Russia also claims high figures for circulation of its papers but, in a closed society, such boasts mean little.

---

* 'Today,' remarked Luigi Barzini, 'the Italian press is free in the sense that there is no censorship. But if you read our papers, you at once realize that eight out of ten newspapers have already succumbed to the temptation of pre-emptive capitulation . . . they are trimming their sails to what they think will be the wishes of their next masters, the communist party . . . the "workers' committee" which includes the printers . . . have the final say in what gets printed and what does not. Editors, journalists and writers, realising that these censorships exist, very seldom risk their jobs by challenging the powers that be' (30). Similar remarks can be made almost as truthfully about other European countries.

33

Part 2

Twentieth Century Mass Communications

Three new means of communication have come to dominate the mass democracies of the twentieth century: radio, cinema, and television. They are beginning to affect peoples who live under totalitarian governments, as they do those under democracies or more old-fashioned or traditional tyrannies. The origins of these three technical innovations of the twentieth century are rather easier to indicate than their consequences.

First, consider the radio. Faraday's experiments in electromagnetism began it. The Scottish professor James Clerk Maxwell proved that radio waves existed, in 1879. But he did nothing practical about his discovery. In the 1880s, Heinrich Hertz in Berlin established by experiments that light and radio waves were similar. In 1895, Ernest Rutherford, a young New Zealand physicist who had only recently come to Cambridge, carried those ideas further by transmitting messages three-quarters of a mile. Four years later, Guglielmo Marconi, a scientist from Bologna (with an Irish mother), sent radio waves between two cruisers during British naval manoeuvres and, subsequently, between France and Britain. In 1901, he despatched a similar message from Cornwall to Newfoundland. Sustained by obstinacy, resolution and a private fortune, Marconi carried on to establish wireless telegraphy between the Americas and England. These events made Marconi famous but, until the First World War, wireless radio communication was only used by ships. Most vessels were, however, fitted with radio in modern navies by 1914. It was realised how useful it might be in the pursuit of crime when the murderer Dr Crippen was apprehended, in 1910, after crossing the Atlantic, by means of a radio message sent from London. In America, Marconi, meantime, formed a company for the commercial transmission of radio. Little progress had been made before 1914. Large firms concerned with electrical communication showed scant interest in the 'dazzling possibilities' of communication without wires (32). 'Wireless' was regarded primarily as a new kind of telephone. No one before 1914 foresaw the value of wireless communication for the broadcasting of public programmes of music or speech.

The First World War transformed the world's radio services. Large transmitters were built which could send messages between the ground and aircraft on reconnaissance. The companies concerned in the installations were subsequently able to influence governments to permit peacetime broadcasting. In March 1919, a wireless telephone transmitter was built by the Marconi Company in England. Telephonic transmission to the United States followed. The singing on the wireless by the Australian opera singer, Melba, in 1920 was a turning point in this art. A broadcasting corporation sponsored by the government was soon established in England, in 1922. Similar institutions were established on the continent of Europe. Little hostility to this State interference was expressed. That curious monopolistic development was the effect of the First World War, which had accustomed people to an apparently benevolent state dominating its affairs. The British Post Office also feared that broadcasting would interfere with their work unless it was State-controlled (33).

In the US, where the first broadcasting station was opened in 1920, 'radio' remained in private hands, even though most wave lengths were soon controlled by three large companies. The US government merely established a Federal commission to license stations, assign wave lengths and establish standards of conduct. Since radio competed with the press, newspaper companies also began to buy radio stations. Established in 1920 in Pittsburg for the first time as a means of communication (or entertainment), radio in the US grew as an industry even faster than the manufacture of automobiles in the succeeding twenty years. By 1938, 26 million families had radio sets in the US, but, by the 1970s, the US had 350 million radios or the extraordinary figure of 1695 per 1,000 inhabitants. The 'fireside chats' of President Roosevelt, the judicious commentaries of Raymond Gram Swing, and the demagoguery of Father Coughlin were all, in the 1930s, brought to millions of Americans, completing the process of the making of a modern nation which railways had begun. Though the influence of radio subsequently declined because of the growth of television, it continues to play a great part in all countries, rich and poor alike.

Radio was well enough established in Europe for it to be of political importance by the 1930s. On Britain's 3 million radio sets in 1930, the voice of King George could be heard counselling national unity. On its 9 million sets of 1940, the British heard Churchill use his Augustan prose to preach resistance to Nazism. Listening to the BBC was a capital offence in the Nazis' 'new order', but it was a frequent crime. On the 300,000 radios of Spain during the Civil War, General Queipo de Llano introduced war propaganda on the radio while, on the 3½ to 4½ million sets of Germany after 1933, the Germans heard the increasingly irresistible voices of Hitler and his propaganda minister, Josef Goebbels. The radio had scarcely been used in political campaigning in Germany before 1933 but, once the Nazis were in power, the Ministry of Propaganda encouraged the production of cheap radio sets, so that all Germans could afford one. By 1936 thirty million people could be reached by radio, not including the public loudspeakers. In 1938, there were already nearly ten million German radios. On these, the voices of Goebbels and other propagandists fumed venomously. Some of the morale that Germany managed to sustain until 1944 was undoubtedly due to the radio, as it was in the other belligerent countries. The attention paid by the Nazis to the number of sets available has been followed by communist countries, in this, as in some other ways, successors to fascism rather than its opposite. Russia's figure of 404 sets per 1,000 inhabitants in the 1970s was one of the few indices of consumer standards which, if true, places that country nearly on a level with the West (compare Britain, 762; France, 372) (34).

An essential adjunct to the radio in the twentieth century has been the gramophone. As with radio, an early pioneer (in this case, Leon Scott) developed the thoretical possibilities, without considering practical ones. Scott demonstrated a 'phonautograph' to the British Association in Britain in 1859. That showed, for the first time, that sound was a form of energy. In 1877, Thomas Edison, a man intimately concerned with all the late nineteenth century developments in relation to electricity, devised in New York a method of cutting a permanent imprint of sound waves so that, by reversing the process, the 'record' thus formed could be 'played back'. Edison cut his 'record' on tinfoil. Later, that was replaced by wax. Then, in 1897, Emile Berliner, a German immigrant living in Washington, began to duplicate and to market gramophone records. Valdemar Poulsen of Denmark invented magnetic recording the next year. The age of the 'Gramophone' (originally a trade name, in which the rights were held by the His Master's Voice Company) had begun. More recently, tape recorders have, in the 1970s, already begun to dethrone the gramophone, though gramophone records are still with us. Sometimes they have been used for political purposes too.

The essential contribution of the gramophone was to increase the amount of music available, though, like the radio, it probably helped to reduce the numbers of those able to teach or practise music. Famous 'artistes' reached an immense audience, while the obscure village pianist or the daughter of the household could not compete. The sale of pianos fell in proportion to the rise in the sale of records. Still, the number of people able to appreciate music has probably increased, even if all discerning people are driven half-mad by the piped 'musak' of the 1970s. Pianos have ceased to be the 'symbols of bourgeois respectability', as Theodore Zeldin thought them (35), while guitars and wind instruments have become infinitely more popular.

Finally, there has been the cinema. Who can picture the twentieth century without it? Vast numbers have preferred films to books. Even intellectuals have delighted in the cinema's naivety: 'I like straight-forward films where people kill each other and make love,' remarked Louis Aragon (36).

The film can be given a long history. Ptolemy, for example, knew in 130 AD of the illusion known as 'persistence of vision'. The idea of a magic lantern was thought of by Fr Athanasius Kircher, a German Jesuit, who taught mathematics in the Collegio Romano in Rome in 1645. Still, nothing much transpired between his day and the 1820s. Then, in 1826, Dr John Paris, a physician from Cambridge, devised the Thaumatrope, a cardboard disk which had on it two separate images. When spun, the first was superimposed upon the other. A Belgian physicist, Joseph Antoine Plateau, who had gone blind looking at the sun too long, in 1833 carried this idea further and made a 'phenakisti-scope', which produced a moving image. In 1834, William George Horner, a schoolmaster of Bath, produced the Zoetrope, or 'wheel of life', a hollow cylinder, with vertical slots round the sides at regular intervals. Pictures on strips were put inside, spun round and viewed through the slits. Then in 1877, Raynaud produced his 'Praxinoscope' which adapted this scheme to drawn images.

The development of the photograph then transformed the situation: for, in 1872, Eadweard Muybridge, a British-born photographer living in California (born Edward Muggeridge, and son of a corn chandler) proved, by gathering a large battery of cameras together, that there are moments when all four legs of a horse are off the ground when it gallops: a fact never previously known for sure by painters or sculptors. Muybridge put his images of horses and other animals on a 'Zoopraxi-scope', first used to show horse races. Next, in 1880, George Eastman of New York began to sell celluloid film for use in his Kodak cameras. That gave experimenters in the cinema an essential raw material which they had previously not had. In 1890, Etienne Jules Marey, professor of physiology in Paris, achieved his first filmed series of photographs. Thomas Edison perfected his 'Kentoscope' which resembled a modern cinema in every respect save that it could be seen by only one person at a time.

All over Europe and the US, great efforts were then made to be the first to put a moving picture on to a screen. The competition was won by Louis Lumière and his brother Auguste, two French photographers who first showed two two-minute newsreels, at the Grand Café, in the Boulevard des Capucines, Paris, at the end of 1895. They exhibited their 'cinématographe' at the Empire Theatre, London, in early 1896. Edison then devised a 35-millimetre film; and, in 1898, a film cameraman accompanied General Kitchener to the battle of Omdurman. In 1900, 'moving pictures' were a side show at all places of entertainment.

The commercial cinema then finally got under way, a little slowly perhaps, for it took ten years for serious artists to agree to appear in films. Early films ('shakies') were too spasmodic in movement to tempt great actors. Still, Réjane appeared in *Madame sans gêne*, in 1911, and Sarah Bernhardt in *Queen Elizabeth,* in 1912. By then, 'stars' were being consciously created by US film companies, seeking publicity in a commercial war. The first of these was Mary Pickford, 'America's sweetheart' and D.W. Griffith's best money maker. Religious films were also popular till the Pope banned them. Detective tales and idiotic comedies soon followed, particularly the Keystone comedies, in which Charlie Chaplin first appeared, copying the behaviour of the French professional fool, Max Linder. Cinema receipts in France in 1914 reached 16 million francs a year and films were already a large commodity in international trade (37).

The war of 1914 confirmed both the promise of films and the US lead in their making. US producers shot their films out of doors. They built cinemas faster than Europeans did. While Europeans found it hard to sell films in the US, US films were immediately sellable in Europe. During the war, too, resources in Europe had to be directed away from films (38), while that was the time when Chaplin made his name as 'king of the silver screen.'

After 1918, the film industry, like the radio one, grew fast in all the rich countries. Film stars achieved unprecedented fame, setting fashions and commanding huge fees. Hollywood attracted European actresses and actors in large numbers. Films of epic dimension were built, rather than made, in enormous studios. The communists in Russia were quick to see the value of the cinema for propaganda, and that aspect of the matter was always at the back of the minds of even the greatest of Russian film makers, such as Pudovkin or Eisenstein. The 'sound track', introduced in 1927 (earlier there had only been the 'cinema organ'), transformed the industry. Many of the earliest 'stars' gave way to a new generation who mostly came from the stage. Film versions of nineteenth century novels enjoyed a long vogue. By the end of the 1930s, the 'motion picture business' was the fourteenth most important one in volume in the US, while some 75 million persons (58% of the population) visited the 'movies' every week (39). Large cinemas were built all over the US and Europe. Their huge auditoria were also used for the great public political meetings which had a brief heyday in the 1920s and 1930s. The Spanish Fascist Party, the Falange, was launched in the Cinema Monumental in Madrid, for example, while many theatres of the past were transformed into cinemas. The cinema queue, curling away into the distance, seemed the most characteristic sight in rich countries of the 1930s and 1940s.

The intellectual dominance of the US was shown in the 1920s for the first time by this new medium. It was a foretaste of the hold that the US had over intellectual life in all the West after 1945. No matter that the US refused to join the League of Nations and to take part in any organised reaction, to begin with, to communism and fascism. The cinema gave to the US a taste of world power. The early hopes for a new great British industry, meantime, faded. Americans bought up European cinemas. The leaders of the industry, even in France, thought that there was more money to be made distributing American films than making French ones (40). A few brave people, however, particularly Germans, continued to regard the cinema as potentially an art. Inexpensive films, with aesthetic aims, were shown in small cinemas, particularly in Paris: 'Studio Vingt Huit — high up a winding street of Montmartre in the full blasphemy of a freezing Sunday; taxis arriving, friends greeting each other, an excitable afternoon audience. In the hall stands a surrealist bookstall . . . a gramophone plays disturbing sardanas . . .' (41).

Once Hitler was in power, the German cinema was used for propaganda as much as it had been in Russia. A Reich chamber of films was set up by Goebbels to control every phase of the making of films and their distribution. Films were made of Hitler's rise to power, to illustrate the Nazi view of history and even to record the Nazis' own behaviour for immediate, and posthumous, observation. The annual rallies of the Nazi party at Nuremberg were filmed for domestic and international propaganda. (Hitler himself, it seems, saw a film a day when in power) (42). The rallies of the Nuremberg conference of 1934 were designed so that Leni Riefensthal could make her film, *The Triumph of Will* (43). Every phase of the Nazi era (even its atrocities) indeed was filmed in detail, both to influence people living and, if possible, to falsify history.

In the Second World War, films cheered spirits, it must be said, on all sides. Churchill saw films as often as Hitler did. Afterwards, the industry experienced a decline because of the arrival of television. By the 1970s, films had ceased in themselves to be a major method of influencing opinion. Cinemas were concerned either to show works of art, pornography, or spectacular films deliberately created for a worldwide audience. In 1959, the average Englishman went to the cinema nearly every week, in 1978 twice a year.

Television had made its bow in the 1920s, a direct if initially impoverished offspring of radio and of photography. There had been continuous experiment between the 1880s and 1920s as to how to transmit a picture, and, among the forefathers of the genre must be ranked Paul von Nipkov, a German who in 1886 devised a rotating disc; Ferdinand Braun, who produced a cathode ray in 1897; and Alan Campbell Swinton, an inspired inventor of innumerable mechanisms, who wished, in 1911, to use Braun's invention to scan an image. But the first actual transmission of a pictorial image was that effected by Logie Baird in 1924.

Baird was the fourth son of a Scottish clergyman. He suffered in early life from continuous bad health. He retired to Hastings in 1922 and, in an attic there, brought together a makeshift television apparatus on a washstand. The essential elements of his invention were: a tea-chest, a biscuit tin to house the projection lamp, scanning discs cut from cardboard, and four cycle lenses, held together by scrapwood, darning needles and sealing wax. By this means, he sent the dim image of a Maltese cross across the dingy room. Eighteen months later, he gave an exhibition of television in an upper room in Soho in London to fifty people. In 1927, Baird sent an image from London to Glasgow. He then formed a television company and, in 1928, sent a picture across the Atlantic to New York, also giving demonstrations of television in colour and stereoscopic television. Baird demonstrated television on a big screen in 1930 and he televised the Derby in 1931. The next year, the British Broadcasting Corporation, previously concerned only with radio, felt driven by the collectivist spirit of the time to interest itself in television as well as sound broadcasting, and bought Baird's company (44). In the US, meantime, a Russian émigré, Vladimir Zworykin, invented the iconoscope in 1928 which sent pictures by television more quickly.

This new idea, however, took a little time to become established.

Most people had bought their radios in the 1920s and had become accustomed to go regularly to the cinema. In the 1930s, because of the economic crisis, there was also little money available for new purchases of luxuries. Broadcasting of television only began in England in 1936. It did not do so in the US till 1941. There was no television elsewhere before the second world war, in which television, unlike radio, played no part. After 1945, however, first the US, then Europe, and then the rest of the world developed television for the mass market, so that, by the 1970s, the world's television services (many of them in colour) looked something like this (45):

TELEVISION RECEIVERS (1974)

	Number of Receivers	Number Per 1,000 Inhabitants
US	99 million	571
Britain	17 million	315
France	12 million	235
Japan	24 million	233
Russia	40 million	208
Haiti (a characteristic poor country)	12 thousand	2.9
India	49 thousand	0.4

Television began to be politically important in the US elections of 1952. Senator Joseph MacCarthy, about that time, was the first demagogue to create a national reputation on television. In Europe, television hardly reached mass audiences enough to tip the balance in the politics of any country till the 1960s. The first decisive impact of television on international affairs was in 1950 when the US were persuaded to resist the communist invasion of South Korea largely because of the television showing of debates in the UN. In 1960, Cuba had more sets of television per head than some European countries such as Belgium or Holland, and these were used to devastating effect by Fidel Castro (46). Capitalism in Cuba was thus defeated by one of capitalism's own most successful creations.

Subsequently, television has played a considerable if ambiguous part in democratic politics. The constant illustration of the war in Vietnam on television caused a mass revulsion in the US against that conflict, though it is not evident that the people of the US were made much the wiser what the war was about. In the 1970s, television seemed in most countries to be more a substitute for the circus of the later Roman Empire. It satisfied a craving in human nature to supplement with fantasy the mundane activities of ordinary life – a desire which, in the past, was satisfied by popular opera, church music, and the Sunday afternoon band in the rose garden (47). It also offered most central governments the temptation of increased power and, even in democracies, statesmen (such as Charles de Gaulle) have not scrupled to manipulate it for their own purposes. Though a 'medium' as influential as newspapers, it is infinitely more difficult for private persons to approach it than they can the press. It creates a caste of managers whose professional ethics hover uneasily between their desires to preach, educate and entertain. In tyrannies of the future, it will clearly play a decisive part in ensuring the subservience of the masses. It is already decisively affecting education: in the US, it is said, most children spend, before they are eighteen years old, between 10,000 and 15,000 hours watching television (between 14 and 22 months in all) (48).

The impact of the 'media' on politics and society is much discussed, but usually as if it were something which affects only the immediate present and the future rather than the past. But the subject already has a long history for, in the years since the 1890s, first the popular press, then the cinema, then, after 1919, the radio and television and, more recently, the transistor and the cassette have already exerted decisive influence in many societies, not only transforming taste but, on occasion, opening the way to demagoguery and the distortion of society into new ways. The Fascist and the Nazi captures of power in the 1920s and 1930s owed a good deal to the way those movements used the Press, Castro's revolution owed much, as earlier said, to television. It is said that the overthrow of the Shah of Iran in 1979 was due to the clever manipulation of crowds by messages and exhortations contained on cassettes. The growth of nationalism since 1945 owed a great deal to the radios which can be placed in public places very effectively – the equivalent to the circulation of millions of pamphlets before 1914. Radio can influence the illiterate and both radio and television can wholly dispense with rational argument if the manipulators concerned so desire. Of course, as Raymond Aron put it when discussing the French students' 'revolution' of 1968, 'the fire would not have spread if it had not reached inflammable material' (49). Even so, it is perfectly permissible to doubt whether the 'inflammable material' represents the best in a community. The inflammable might, for example, be the most brittle. The point is of some importance since the whole history of modern nationalism is inextricably implicated in the history of communications.

Why precisely is it that, in the nineteenth and twentieth centuries, people of diverse ethnic origins developed an increasingly intense devotion not only to their locality, or their region, or their family or their ethnic group, but to a huge tract of territory which they began to think of as *the nation*? This has been the chief consequence of the 'revolution in communications' since the nineteenth century. Songs, dances, poems and religion fanned the flames. Wars were not only caused by but stimulated the process further. So, in the end, did sport. A process which began with a stirring speech was continued with schools of historical philosophy and school text books used in mass education.

The two critical implements in modern politics are the loudspeaker and the television screen. The first has transformed electioneering and indeed all large meetings. It has virtually destroyed the constructive heckler. Today, only a few old men, the last survivors of their generation, can still remember what it was like to wear out their voices by speaking night after night in crowded halls, during elections. The television screen is, fortunately, not a medium for great rhetoric. But it also poses great attractions to the artful despot.

34

Agricultural Mechanisation

The world of agriculture was, perhaps more than anything else, transformed by a series of changes in agriculture itself. Some of these were merely refinements on what had been long practised in imaginative societies. Thus, in many of the old European open fields, beans, peas, barley, oats, vetches, hemp and clover had increasingly been grown in the spring corn field, sometimes to provide the winter feeding for livestock. There was also barley, for beer. The old three-course rotation of crops (winter corn, spring corn, fallow) had been challenged even in the early Middle Ages. Holland, in the fifteenth century, devised variations from the rotation of three crops. These included a complicated cycle of nine years, the soil increasingly being invigorated by fertilisers (lime, pigeons' dung, ox blood, soot and bones). The Dutch even preferred to import their corn, and sell, in exchange, vegetables, fruits, bulbs, and also hops, and, even in the seventeenth century, tobacco. Their agriculture depended on the minutely careful husbandry of a small portion of the soil. It included ideas for the reclamation of land from the sea by the use of dykes and of mills for drainage, driven by the wind. By 1650, the Netherlands' experiments had been so successful as to enable them, for the first time in Western agriculture, virtually to abandon the year's fallow — an achievement from which much else flowed.* One alternative to fallow was the progressive use of clover, brought from Italy. Clover both improved the supplies of winter fodder and also turned out to have chemical powers of attracting atmospheric nitrogen. That restored the fertility of the soil almost miraculously (1). Sainfoin, lucerne and turnips played their part too. A great merit of the last-named was the indirect one that it necessitated hoeing. The arable land was thus cleansed, as if it had become a branch of horticulture. Garden methods took over from tillage. Digging became easier after the iron, three-pronged fork was invented in the fifteenth century (3). Netherlands farmers also started laying down their arable fields from time to time for

---

* Fallow cannot be altogether abolished. In certain soils, and certain seasons, fallowing will always be advisable, to clean the fields, or unavoidable, due to weather (2).

pasture, instead of fallow: another source of invigoration. Stock-breeding then improved because of better food.

All these ideas soon spread — to England, where the Flanders 'Seven Course' became the 'Norfolk Four Course' (wheat, turnips, barley, clover), to Prussia, and to the Plain of Lombardy. Flanders soon had something like an eleven course rotation: wheat, and, after it, turnips in the same year, oats, clover, wheat, hemp, wheat flax, coleseed, wheat, beans, wheat (4). Thus, in the seventeenth century, there was a European revolution in agriculture, Flemish in origin, but first put into practice on a large scale in England, whose landowners in the eighteenth century, interested in ideas, free from feudal restrictions and increasingly able to rely on contract labour rather than labour provided by custom or status, became pre-occupied by innovation (5). The nub of this revolution was the spread of flexible ideas of crop rotation, so improving fodder, which enabled the land to bear more stock, which, in turn, could enrich the land by more manure (6). These ideas did not spread fast to nations such as France, where the ghosts of feudalism were still at large: many agricultural methods there of the mid-nineteenth century would have seemed orthodox to a visitor from the thirteenth (7) — though it is fair to add that the system practised at that same time in the American mid-West would have appeared barbaric even to a mediaeval European: a one-crop system (wheat) without fertilisation or rotation of crops (8).

In addition to these improvements in methods of growing crops, there were several changes in technology. The most important was Jethro Tull's horse-drawn drill to plant seed in rows, devised about 1730. That was superior both to the old idea of broadcasting seed indiscriminately and to the method of dropping seeds into holes prepared, one by one, by a dibble. Tull, a lawyer from Berkshire, who farmed land which he had inherited, arranged that the horse which pulled the drill should drag a bush harrow to cover the seed behind. About the same time, a light swing plough was devised in Holland, with a curved iron mouldboard, needing few animals. Some forty years later, Robert Ransome, a brassfounder of Norwich of Quaker ancestry, developed his self-sharpening, cast-iron ploughshares* and, in 1789, the first all-iron plough. A machine flail to separate grain from straw was devised in 1784 in Scotland by Andrew Meikle, an elderly millwright from Dunbar.

These and other innovations depended on inventions in other commodities. For example, mass-produced farm forks and spades had as big an influence as any, just as mass-produced knives and forks had. All depended upon cheaper, more easily smelted iron, to which attention

---

* The under side of the ploughshare was chilled by casting it on an iron mould, the upper part of the mould being of sand. The under side of the share was thereby made harder than steel while the upper part remained tough and soft. The upper part wore away faster than the lower and thereby sharpened itself.

will be paid later. There were, also, as it were, 'institutional' changes which assisted agricultural transformation permanently.

There were, however, also critical changes in landholding. In England the country which (for reasons which will be explored later) was the first in the field in industry, these changes were associated particularly with the word 'enclosure'. To this subject, Karl Marx devoted some of his most affecting paragraphs* but they were rather prejudiced.

The movement called 'enclosure' meant the final end to collective farming based on tradition and mutual obligations, and the establishment of an individualist system. It also meant the end of, and the distribution of, common or open fields, meadows, pastures and wastelands as it did of the old village. Many of these changes occurred by common agreement, stimulated by sheep farmers in the Middle Ages. By the early eighteenth century, only about half the arable land in England remained in open fields. That was concentrated in the Midlands and the central south of the country (9). In the eighteenth century, enclosures became more frequent. Many landowners had recourse to private Acts of Parliament to confirm what they wanted, since, though expensive, they provided legal certainty. They enabled the rest of the English common and waste land to be divided up. Enclosure was popular among landowners, for it allowed the conversion of land for new and more profitable uses. It expanded the area under arable. It improved the health of cattle.

Now it was once argued that the commissioners appointed to carry out the reallocation of land acted only in the interests of the great, and indeed might be nominated by them. That was Karl Marx's view, it was the great French historian Paul Mantoux's view, and it was the view of the eloquent economic historians, the Hammonds. Enclosure entailed 'massive violence exercised by the upper classes against the lower', wrote Barrington Moore Junior as late as the 1960s. But the same writer conceded that enclosure meant that 'modernisation could proceed in England without the huge reservoir of reactionary forces that existed . . . . in Germany and Japan, and removed the possibilities of peasant revolts' (10). That qualification points the way to a more realistic interpretation of what happened. Many modern historians have also been impressed by the fairness of the commissioners in what was usually a complex affair (11). The occasions when acts of enclosure were deliberately framed against small farmers appear to have been few (12). Not all poor farmers were against enclosure, nor were all rich landlords in favour. Many farmers with very few acres found that the concentration of their land in homogeneous parcels made it worth more after enclosure than before. Owners of small plots were increasing in numbers

* Chapter XXVII of Volume I of *Das Kapital.*

precisely in the years (1760—80, 1793—1815) when enclosure was at its height. The end of various types of mediaeval lease was also an encouragement to many small farmers. The farms of England were anyway increasing in size for reasons other than enclosure. New hedgerows created shade, birdsong, and shelter for animals. The health of herds improved and there was a drop in cattle diseases which could be transferred to men (13). Finally, though poverty probably did increase in the English countryside in the early nineteenth century, it seems to have been no more marked in places where enclosure was new than where there had been enclosure for a long time. The reason for the increase in poverty was probably first and foremost the rise in population which was the fundamental cause of the greater availability of labour, rather than the expropriation of small farms. Indeed, agricultural employment seems to have been improved, not damaged, as a result of enclosure. There were more families employed on the land in England in 1831 than there were in 1801 (761,348 to 697,353) (14).

This process of enclosure occurred elsewhere in Europe but only in Denmark, Southern Sweden and some parts of Germany was it possible, as it were, for a well disposed state to encourage the idea. Marat toyed with it in France. But, though the revolutionaries in theory disliked all feudal survivals, they did not do more than condemn compulsory rotation and proclaim liberty of enclosure. In the end, the Third Republic adopted a compromise whereby all feudal obligations were abolished in principle but each municipality had the right to ask for their continuance. Actually, some parts of France had had enclosure from the sixteenth century 'at an almost English pace' (for example, in Normandy). Elsewhere, the old system was sometimes dented a bit: for example, lords began to try to secure some means of exempting the meadows from collective grazing or postponing the entry of the common herd until the second crop of hay (aftermath) had been cut. Gradually, forage crops (clover, sainfoin, lucerne, turnips) began to make for that victory of horticulture over tillage which potatoes and sugar beet completed in many of the fields of northern France (16).*

Of course, there were some demerits or unfairness in enclosure in England, as elsewhere. The abolition of waste and of collective grazing had definite disadvantages for small farmers, even though the poorest gained something from the division of common land. Squatters, it is true, usually suffered. Those with access to the common by custom, not right, were not always recognised by the commissioners. But the

---

* Subsequently, in the nineteenth century, French peasants did much exchanging and rounding off of their holdings. But never was there any governmental policy of consolidation. In Germany, the end of open fields was promoted by governments, but modestly. A Prussian law of 1872 provided that an open field or part of it could be re-arranged, provided a majority of owners desired it (17). But manorial courts continued in Prussia till 1892.

common rights in the past had never belonged to all. They had belonged to those who had holdings on the common field. Sometimes, widows lost the rights which they had held under the old system to their husband's plot: hence, according to some, the increase in 'witches' in England after the sixteenth century.*

As important in transforming agriculture was an increase in the yield, or the number of times that a seed takes to reproduce itself. Typical yields throughout most of the agricultural era were 1 to 3, an annual doubling of the sown seed since, of course, every year one grain of every one harvested had to be set aside for seed. Sometimes 1 to 4 might be gained. Much higher yields were gained in exceptional circumstances. Many parts of the world do no better than 1 to 3 in the twentieth century. Most did no better in the nineteenth. Russian yields averaged 1 to 3, for example, between the fifteenth and twentieth centuries, as Richard Pipes tells us. Such a ratio, he says, is enough to support life but little more. In Europe, agricultural yields reached 1 to 5 in the thirteenth century and 1 to 6 or 1 to 7 in the sixteenth and eighteenth (19). That meant a surplus growing at a geometric rate. It enabled urban and commercial life. Below a yield of 1 to 5, the farmer has in truth no surplus. He and his colleagues, therefore, cannot support a population with interests other than farming (20).

The changes in agriculture between the Renaissance and the eighteenth century were thus numerous. But its essential character remained unaltered. In every country, even in England, in 1750 it employed the vast majority. Those people too mostly used much the same methods that they had used since the dawn of time. The sickle, the ox, the horse and the earthen threshing place, were all the dominant instruments or scenes of action. Indeed, they would thus remain for another hundred years or so, even in advanced nations. But everywhere in the old world all established agrarian undertakings felt the pressure of population growth in the eighteenth century. The pressure of population caused particular social unrest where it had never before existed in places where there were minifundia, handkerchief-sized plots, next to latifundia (21). The consequence was the foundation of legends about the old rural pasts of countries. The Chartist rebels in the 1840s in England said that they wished to 'live to see the restoration of old English times, old English fare, old English holidays and old English justice, and every man live by the sweat of his brow . . . when the weaver worked at his own loom and stretched his limbs in his own field.' As E. P. Thompson puts it, 'the myth of the lost paternalist community became a force in its own right – perhaps as powerful a force as the utopian projections of Owen and the Socialists' (22). (E. P. Thompson is not a friend of indus-

---

* 'Witches are usually such as one destitute of friends, bowed down with years, laden with infirmities,' wrote a contemporary (18).

trialisation; but his honesty as a historian compels him to draw attention in his history of the working class in England to many of the sufferings of agricultural people even in the old days).

The countries which prospered in the early generations of enlightenment were those which succeeded, by hook or by crook, in resolving such mediaeval or feudal patterns of landholding. One place which did not do so was Galicia in North West Spain. The history of landowning there has a claim to be characteristic of the mixture of innumerable legal and technical problems which adversely affected agriculture in the past in Europe and do so still in the underdeveloped world, and which would have been better off had there been enclosure.

In Galicia, the land had once been owned by the Church and was let off by hereditary lease. The tenant paid a quit rent of 2% of the capital value of the holding. He had to maintain the house and buildings in repair. He and his family could not be removed during three lives. This system was introduced in the twelfth and thirteenth century by, in particular, the Cistercian order, in order to induce free men to settle on moors and wasteland. The three-generation clause was usually exceeded and forgotten. In the seventeenth century, the Church and other landowners tried to draw in the leases. The tenants had a long struggle against them. By then, many of them had sub-let many of their original holdings. Legal disputes lasted from 1629 to 1759, when the Crown intervened to secure the tenants' victory. By then, tenants and sub-tenants were also in dispute with one another. Sub-tenants were usually poor. Many had only one acre farms, adequate to keep one family at bare subsistence. A cow did the ploughing and provided the family with cheese and milk. A little rye and maize was produced too and perhaps some cloth. None of these crops could, by the nature of things, be sold. The only way a farmer in Galicia could find any cash would be to sell a calf or go somewhere else to work for the harvest. Yet all sub-tenants had to find money for rent. Lawyers in the towns fomented arguments about that while the sub-tenants sank deeper into debt. These disputes dominated everything in Galicia until the twentieth century. Even in the eighteenth century, many tillers of the soil found themselves paying rent not to one man but to three or four. The original plots had been endlessly subdivided: hence the continuous emigration of peasants — to America, to Portugal, to Madrid (23).

Mechanisation began to have an effect on agriculture only in the second third of the nineteenth century. That began to occur in, above all, the US, a country where labour was always short and where, therefore, inventions were always popular. The US was also in the fortunate position of beginning her career as a nation with no traditional landowning habits to destroy and (apart from the Indians), no entrenched or backward classes; and agriculture remained there the main source of wealth till the 1880s (24).

The decisive years were those between 1830 and 1860. Until then, US agriculture seemed traditional. All work on farms was done by hand, save for ploughing and drawing loads, accomplished, as everywhere else, by oxen or by horses, though Jethro Tull's seeding methods with a drill were in use. Then, first and foremost, came the iron plough. It had been suggested ineffectively by Charles Newbould in New Jersey in 1797, but Jethro Wood made one like that in 1814 out of several castings, and tried it out on his farm at Poplar Creek in Cayuga county, New York State. That plough began to be used generally in the east of the US about 1830. Improvements were suggested. John Lane in Chicago introduced a steel mouldboard to which soil did not stick. Even before that, a 'cradle scythe' had been invented (about 1830) which replaced the sickle, and ended the stooping imposed by the traditional way of reaping. The cradle acted as a gathering rake too, for every swing laid the cut corn in even piles, easily gathered up. Then, in the mid-1830s, Obed Hussey in Cincinnati and Cyrus McCormick in West Virginia separately invented a mechanised reaper. (McCormick's father had unsuccessfully tried to do this for years.) Though Hussey was the first to register a patent, it was McCormick who began manufacture of this device which, to begin with, cut hay as well as corn. McCormick set up a factory in Chicago in 1847 and introduced the reaper to a delighted and admiring world at the Great Exhibition in England — a country which had just seen the success of a very effective lobby on food matters, 'the most effective political machine the country had known — the Anti Corn Law League' as Norman Gash put it (25). By then, threshing, which had traditionally been done in the US, as everywhere else, by a wooden flail on an earthen floor, had also been transformed by a machine devised in 1837 by Hiram Pitts of Maine. He too moved to Chicago and built a factory to market his invention, which made its first appearance internationally at the Paris Exhibition of 1855 (simple threshing machines worked by mule or horse had actually been devised in France in the 1820s) and threshed 740 litres of wheat in one hour, instead of the 36 which six men could do in the same time (26).

A host of other inventions followed: a cable plough in 1850 and a steam one devised by John Fowler, in 1858; a horse-drawn rake and a revolving hay rake; hand binding harvesters, wire binders and twine binders were all put on the market by McCormick (who was among the first businessmen to use field trials, guarantees, benefits for cash, and deferred payments).

There was, thereafter, no practical limit to production through an inability to harvest crops. The most important part of the farmers' difficulties was thus removed — or removable. A large crop could be harvested immediately it was ripe (unless the reaper went wrong) and the losses would not be great. Cheap and swift transport by railway or good roads reduced the importance of distance, enabling meat, in particular, to be carried much farther. The telegraph carried news of the markets. William Seward, Secretary of State in Lincoln's Cabinet, praised McCormick's invention as something which enabled 'the line of civilisation to move westward thirty miles a year'.* In the 1840s, machines were introduced to make clay pipes, so rendering the drainage of dry land easier. Naturally, those developments all favoured the creation of large farms. On smaller ones, farmers continued old methods or, perhaps, agreed to hire a machine for a few days — never a satisfactory alternative, since the days arranged might coincide with bad weather.

Equally important for mid-Victorian agriculture in the long run, however, was the scientific work of Julius von Liebig, professor of chemistry at the small town of Giessen, son of a dry-salter and dealer in dyes from Darmstadt, who laid the foundation for the chemical study of soils and manures. In 1840, von Liebig proved that plants did not derive their organic sustenance from the soil, as was previously believed. They did so from the inexhaustible supply of carbon dioxide in the atmosphere. Von Liebig also confirmed the importance of lime in regulating the acidity of the soils. His ideas were put into practice by an English landowner, John Lawes of Rothamsted, who had been working on similar schemes on his own. (Maintaining Rothamsted as the first real agricultural research station, Lawes ran a commercial factory for making superphosphates at Deptford.) Another consequence of von Liebig's discoveries was the increase in the quantity of guano traded as manure: Britain, for example, imported 2,000 tons in 1841, 300,000 in 1847 (27). Sodium nitrates, similarly beneficial for agriculture, were imported on a large scale from Chile by all agriculturally adventurous countries. The discovery of micro-organisms by the great French chemist, Louis Pasteur,† further transformed agricultural research. It was very hard to look at soil in quite the same way as before when it was realised that a saltspoonful of dry garden soil contained twice as many bacteria as there are people on earth (28).

Early reapers had merely cut grain. People were still needed to rake it into sheaves others still to gather and bind it. After 1860, there were experiments with a 'self-raking reaper' and a 'self binder', a twine binder and, in 1885, the combined harvester-thresher, made possible by the substitution of oil for steam and horsepower. In use by 1900 too were agricultural elevators, for transferring and storing grain. 'Cakes' made from cotton seeds or linseeds for winter feeding made it far easier to keep cattle alive during the winter (29). Finally, cheap wire after 1860,

---

* Seward was the Secretary of State who wisely bought Alaska from Russia for $7·2 million against the wishes of public opinion, which dubbed the new territory Seward's 'ice box'.
† See below, page 392.

and then barbed wire, were far from being the least of inventions; to fence forty acres with wooden rails in 1839 cost between $200 and $300. Stone was prohibitively expensive in the US plains, while hedges took too long to grow in a country where ownership was essential to define. All such demarcations were too expensive till the coming of cheap wire.

The mechanisation of agriculture spread. Thus France, the country of northern Europe which longest retained its ancient rural characteristics, became decisively mechanised between 1890 and 1910. French governments considered their most important task to be to keep France self-sufficient in bread (30). The country was already using much chemical manure after her conquest of Tunis, with its sources of phosphates, in 1880 (31). Some indication of what happened after 1890 can be seen in the figures from the Haute Garonne, a department neither specially full of large holdings nor full of specialist products. In 1892, there were, in the province, 450 mechanical mowers of hay, 180 reapers and 60 reaper binders. In 1908, these figures read 15,000, 25,000 and 1200 respectively (32). That meant the beginning of the end of subsistence agriculture, and the end too of a remarkably self-contained way of life. The agricultural way of life survived in some ways a generation or so longer in France, until the 1950s, and longer in some parts of Spain. But already, by 1910, the signs of change were everywhere visible.

Still in Spain, the old world survived. Even in the 1950s, a calendar like this, as recorded by Gerald Brenan, could be found: 'The year begins with olive picking [by women], then vine and fruit pruning, then the planting of garlic and onions [two cash crops] and the hoeing of cornfields. In early May, the harvest might begin on the coast, first barley, then wheat. The harvest would spread up the mountainside, 300 feet making a difference of 4 days, and the high mountain farms not being ready till September. The crop would be cut by the old short sickle and would be done at night if there were a moon. In August, the corn would be spread about on the threshing floors, two mules would haul the primitive, iron-teethed threshing machine [the region's only concession to mechanisation] which had taken over at last from the flail. At night, there would be winnowing, or tossing up of the ears of corn with forks of ash' (33).

The use of fertilisers completed the liberation of farmers from fallow. They no longer relied on cattle to provide manure, thereby breaking the age-old association between corn and cattle. That, in turn, freed farmers from their concern with forage, the cultivation of which had been essential since the beginning of agriculture (34).

Agriculture soon also began to be international as well as mechanised. This development was assisted by artificial ice, first devised by Sir John Leslie, professor of philosophy at Edinburgh, in a laboratory in 1810. But, though Sir Robert Peel in the 1840s was known to his critics as 'the refrigerator' (35), and though fish was taken to London in ice by

George Dempster in 1830, artificial ice was only generally available from 1850. In that year, James Harrison in Australia designed an ice-making machine, based on the idea of the evaporation of ether which produces a fall in the temperature, the liquid being regenerated by compression. Carré, a French engineer, found a better method, by using ammonia gas. A plant capable of holding 8,000 pounds of ice at one time was built in Sydney. By 1869, refrigerator cars were being built for US railways. A huge impetus was thus given to the meat packing and the slaughtering industries. By 1914, from accounting in the US for a mere $29 million in 1860 those two trades had grown to $34 million, and become the nation's largest industry (36). Long before then, both Australia and Argentina had begun sending meat to Europe by ice ship (37). The first successful trans-oceanic refrigerated ship was the French engineer Charles Jellier's *SS Frigorifique*, which sailed from Buenos Aires to Rouen in 1877 (38). Australia followed, in 1879 (39). Ice-making machines on steam trawlers enabled huge new banks to be swept for fish. Railways enabled large quantities of fish to be carried inland. That permitted a welcome decline of salted and pickled herrings, which for so long had been the only fish known away from the coast (40). The salted herring had made the merchants of the Hanse rich in the fourteenth century. Ice made those of Norway and Hull rich in the nineteenth. Fresh fish had never before been a big business except for a few river fishermen selling carp, or tench, or trout, caught in artificial ponds. Ice too became a commodity to be exported and carried immense distances. In New York, in the 1870s, jugs of iced water had also begun to appear on dining tables as a matter of course.

At the same time, tea (from India and Ceylon as well as China), coffee (from the East Indies or Brazil) and chocolate (taken from the Americas to Ghana and Nigeria) were added to sugar (still coming from the West Indies, though European beet was by then a serious competitor), among the exotic crops about to become normal ones at the European or American breakfast table. Grain from Russia came in on the new great railways from the East.

These exchanges greatly benefited the Western city. The transoceanic suppliers enabled Britain, for example, to feed her own population far better than was possible from British farms alone. Many farmers in the US, Russia, Australia and Argentina made fortunes. But the farmers of Europe did not prosper. Despite the fertilisers, machinery, new seeds and livestock breeding, European farming in the late nineteenth century went into a decline.

Mechanisation, after all, had no powers against bad weather, nor against the liver rot in sheep, and foot and mouth disease among cattle, which marked European farming in those days. The cheapness of imported wheat caused the growing area of Britain to drop from 8·2 to 5·8 million acres. Only dairy farmers did well.

The twentieth century saw the completion of the mechanisation of agriculture through the development of the tractor. This idea, which followed in the wake of the car, began in the 1880s, when some British engineers designed steam engines for heavy work on farms. In the US, the idea was launched of a mechanised plough powered by internal combustion*. The Burger oil-powered tractor soon appeared in the mid-West in 1889. Though heavy, it, or versions of it, soon replaced the steam tractors used previously. By 1913 there were already 8,000 tractors in the US.

The demand for food in the middle of the First World War increased the attention paid to this new machine. For the British government instructed its Ministry of Munitions to develop a utility 'tank'.† As a lightweight tractor, that was copied in the US. In 1919, the US had over 160,000 tractors. In 1939, they had a million and a half; and 4½ million in 1972. That meant the beginning of the end of the long-established part played in agriculture by the horse and the ox. It also meant substantial drops in the agricultural labour force of countries equipped with tractors, and huge increases in output (41).

Other innovations followed, with equally important consequences. For example, a mechanised cane cutter was used in sugar harvesting in Australia from the beginning of the twentieth century, though, because of the character of the crop or opposition by labour, it took a long time for it to be generally introduced among other cane growing countries (42). The well-organised labour union in the Cuban sugar industry prevented entrepreneurs using these machines as late as the 1950s. (The Cuban revolutionary government of 1959, after it had destroyed the free unions, began to use cane cutters in the late 1960s.) A machine to pick cotton was developed in 1889. The insecticide, DDT, began to be used in 1939 against destructive insects. Artificial insemination to improve livestock was introduced about the same time. After 1950, production in the mass of chickens and turkeys in concentration camps began. In the 1960s, too, a new method of growing wheat began to be tried out first in Mexico and then elsewhere in tropical zones.

For a long time, it had been noticed that, when plants are heavily fertilised in the tropics they shoot up excessively, and then collapse. If they are grown close enough to one another to avoid that, one plant shields another. In Mexico, a thickly-sown, short-stemmed grain planted on well-irrigated and fertilised soil was found to give high yields (43). That gave rise to a new 'green revolution' affecting many plants, not simply wheat. 'Miracle strains' of the main food crops were devised. The use of large quantities of fertiliser were found to give disproportionately impressive results. It was, for a time, believed that

* See above, page 321.
† See below, page 472.

all the world's fears of future food shortages with a high population were needless. Thus a huge rise began in the quantity of tomatoes produced, combined with a decline of land planted. That was possible because of an increase of yield per acre from, say 13·5 tons an acre to 51·5 tons in California (44).

The most obvious effect of all these changes in technology and science directed to agriculture was to bring a far greater amount of land under the plough than ever before and to increase greatly the food available. In the mid-1960s about 88% of the total cultivable land in Europe was being worked, 83% of the cultivable land in Asia, excluding Russia, and 64% of the cultivable land in Russia. Even in some of the less well-populated continents, there had been huge increases. The appropriate figures for North America (including Mexico and Central America), Africa, South America and Australia are 51%, 22%, 11% and 10% (45). Much land remains to be cultivated, it is true, but the transformation achieved by the tractor, the combine harvester and the fertilisers has been the most remarkable development in the history of agriculture. An idea of the changes caused can be seen in the increase of the production of grain in the US, which rose a million times, from 378 million bushels in 1839, before the impact of McCormick's invention had begun to be seen, to 3,422,000 million bushels in 1957 (46). The increase in Russia was from 254 million bushels in 1870 to 150 million metric tons in 1969 (47).

Yet the increase in agricultural efficiency has not by any means solved all the problems of the world's food. First of all, the benefits of the 1960s have been followed by disappointments.

For example, after a certain level of miraculous growth, arable yields cease to rise in proportion to fertiliser per acre. By concentrating certain strains of crop with high yields, there is a genetic danger. It is dangerous to depend too much on a single strain. That may be attacked by a disease which destroys it. Weedless fields are easier prey to infections which, in the past, might have been stayed by diversity of strain. Reliance on fertilisers from chemicals also greatly increases dependence on international trade.

The traditional connection between revolution and grain failures has also continued in the twentieth century. The failure to deliver the requisite number of poods of grain to Petrograd in early 1917 was the spark firing the Russian Revolution. In the next few months, peasants preferred to use grain for their own consumption (48). The consequences for them, as for the cities of Russia, were disastrous. The grain failures of Ethiopia in the early 1970s led to the overthrow of the traditional régime there, too, in 1974.

In addition, prehistoric men and women enjoyed a more varied diet than people do now, since they ate several thousand species of plant and several hundred thousand types of living creature. But only a tiny percentage of these were ever domesticated. Modern shops have accelerated a trend towards specialisation which began in the earliest days of agriculture. The food of the rich countries has become cheaper relative to wages. It is speedily distributed in supermarkets. But the choice annually becomes less and less great (49). Even individual foods themselves become more standardised. We live now in a world of the carrot specially blunted in order to avoid making a hole in a bag, and the tomato grown to meet a demand for a standard weight of eighteen tomatoes to a kilo (50). Siri von Reisaltschul asks: 'Only the three major cereals and perhaps ten other widely cultivated species stand between famine and survival for the world's human population and a handful of drug plants has served Western civilisation for several thousand years. A rather obvious question arises: are we missing something?' (51). After all, there are 800,000 species of plant on earth.

But there have also been more difficult developments in modern agriculture, partly related to technological change but also partly related to a set of illusions about the needs of ownership and management of land.

The increase in the amount of food available in the nineteenth and twentieth centuries has occurred in places where the number of farmers has been greatly reduced. The success of modern agriculture has been related not only to its mechanisation but to the concurrent decline in the numbers of those working in it. Thus, in Britain, a little over a quarter of the grown men were linked with agriculture in 1850 (52) but, in 1911, the number was down to less than 1 in 20. In 1961, the agricultural labour force in Britain was 874,000, less than those engaged in manufacturing, building, commerce, transport and a whole range of services. Comparable figures were to be found, or would soon be so, in most other European countries. This major social change, from which so much else flows, was first marked in Britain, and was followed by the US (there were more non-agricultural workers than farmers there in the 1870s) and Germany (in the 1880s). By 1970, agriculture, in almost all European countries, was less important as an employer than both manufacturing and also services or transport. It is true, too, of many nations of South America. The paradox is that the food supplies of Asia and Africa will only be assured when the same is able to be said of those continents.

There are several other paradoxes in the history of modern agriculture. The first is that the increase of the food available has helped – probably more than medical advances – to increase the world's population. That, in turn, has increased the pressure of population on food supplies.

This has led to the second paradox. Traditional agriculture assumed that a district's food would be supplied by its neighbourhood. In the Mediterranean world, that system was beginning to be overthrown by 500 BC. The Athenians bought their grain from the Ukraine, the

Romans bought theirs from Africa. Such commerce broke down in the Dark Ages, to be successfully revived, with other classical habits, during the Crusades. Then, and during antiquity, however, only rich coastal towns or towns on navigable rivers were able to resort to these imports.

During the nineteenth century, the railways and improvements in shipping made possible the beginning of a new international commerce in food. Some of these developments have been noticed in consideration of shipping. By 1913, most regions in the world expected to grow some grain and certain other foods. Europe alone imported such staffs of life. That international commerce continued till 1939. But now, with the huge increase of consumption of food in the poorer parts of the world as a result of increased population, and the relative failure of political experiments such as Communism, in agriculture particularly, the three large English-speaking ex-imperial nations of the USA, Australia and Canada supply most of the grain which is exported. 'It almost seems as if the less developed regions of the world are losing the capacity to feed themselves', wrote Dr Lester Brown (53). The alteration since 1939 is expressed best in the accompanying table.

Of course, the problems of food have been observed by governments, and many of them have sought to alleviate them. Two policies can be distinguished. The first one is that which, roughly, has characterised the two great nations of North America, Western Europe, and some other enlightened parts of the world, which have examined their methods in the light of what has been known of successful farming: namely, that the best farms are those which are medium-sized, mechanised, and in private hands, with as few legal restrictions as possible limiting the farmer's capacity to make his own decisions. Many European farmers would agree that this has been the character of their governments' policy towards them, but it has been the usual frame of mind determining policies, despite regulations. In fact, in the world's now most successful farming country, the US, the farms are not really very large. About 62% of US farmers farm and own their own land, nearly 30% are part owners, and only about 11% are tenants. The average sized farm is 393 acres. A great deal of land is in the hands of companies (not large landowners) but, still, only 6·7% of the agricultural land in the US is in farms of over 1,000 acres and agriculture there does not depend on the wreckage or survival of immensely complicated leases and semi-feudal arrangements such as are to be found in the old world, nor, even more important, on state enterprises (54).

The origins of these American farms were unusual from the point of view of the old world. From 1860 till 1935, the Federal government gave away land for farms up to 160 acres, on demand. It gave away more to those who would undertake to plant trees or to raise stock. This was a deliberate action designed to create a land-owning and farm-owning

THE WORLD GRAIN TRADE

NET GRAIN TRADE (MILLIONS OF METRIC TONS)

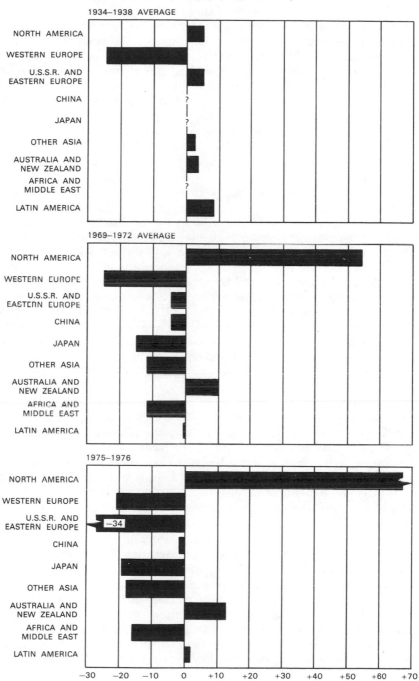

Source: *Scientific American*, September 1976

class of independent farmers – a division such as has been vainly dreamed of by anarchists in old Europe. Though many took excessive advantage of the system, and established big holdings through dummy householders, the plan worked, As a result, 190 million acres were added to the cultivable land of the US. Big increases in the numbers of cattle occurred too: Nebraska in 1880 had thirty times more than it had in 1870. Many US farms were also founded by squatters, who afterwards secured rights. Even then, out of 270 million acres settled between 1841 and 1860, only 69 million were sold. The rest were given away. Only at the beginning of the history of the US was much land sold — at between $1 and $2 an acre between 1784 and 1820. In the days of English domination, an effort had been made to establish a manorial system or even a feudal one of a sort, in New England (55). But it was not successful, and such systems have been everywhere in decline since then, even in Europe.

The attitude to landholding prevalent during the French Revolution and afterwards under Napoleon affected not only France but the rest of Europe and the European dominions beyond the sea. Clerical land and 'national land' were sold off in 1790 in conditions which placed poorer peasants at a disadvantage and which emphasised the essentially 'bourgeois social character' of the Revolution in a way more striking than any other. The Revolution destroyed the feudal legal structure of France, Albert Soboul pointed out, it damaged the aristocracy but it assisted the landowning peasantry and middle class (56). Much the same happened in Spain in the course of the nineteenth century. Thus the Conde de Campomanes, the liberal reformer of Spain, argued in the 1780s that he would like to see every Spanish peasant owning a house and garden, a yoke of mules and fifty acres (57). But how could that be arranged by the state? The liberal Cortes of Cádiz, in 1812, began to sell common lands on the open market in order to pay the national debt. Spanish liberals, in the 1830s, resumed the practice. A few years later, Church property, amounting to 12 million acres, began to be sold (58). But the consequence of these and other state-inspired sales was not encouraging. The peasantry hated being deprived of grazing and gleaning rights. An increasing population on the land found itself at the mercy of a new class of legally-minded, doctrinaire liberals, who were interested in producing food for the market. Hence the formulation of a series of illusions about the desirability of a different agrarian reform which, unlike that inspired by the French Revolution, would, in the minds of the reformers, benefit the population as a whole. Such ideas failed to take into account the fact that, in old nations such as those found in Europe or Asia, there is only one effective method of agrarian reform which increases agricultural production: that is, the method which occurred in the Mediterranean countries after 1945, inspired by the desire of the peasants themselves to leave the land for the city, where they would themselves help to make, among other things, the machines which would modernise the farming in the fields which they had abandoned.

The agrarian reforms introduced by Communist countries have been various. First of all there was the Russian reform. In 1913, most of Russia's 20 million peasant families lived in either formal or informal communes from which they gained, for a specific number of years, a certain number of strips of land. When their children grew up, they too would demand a strip (59). The Russian peasant of the days before 1914 was thus in practice more a self-employed individual than a co-operativist (60). Only a tenth of the land sown in Russia in 1914 belonged to great estates. To begin with, the Communist government after 1921 treated its agricultural problems with some subtlety. In the course of their civil war, the Russian leaders had observed the ineffectiveness of certain apparently idealistic programmes for agriculture designed to benefit the whole community. So they formed co-operatives on the large estates of Russia and other confiscated land and, on the rest of the territory – at least three-quarters of Russian farms – permitted private farmers to survive much as they had done before 1914 (61). But this compromise did not work very well. On the co-operatives, the land was state-owned, but the farmers were regarded as owners of the livestock, buildings and tools. All received a payment in cash and an allocation of the produce, after charges for state seed and other services had been deducted. The centres of these farms were, however, the Machine and Tractor Stations (MTS) managed by politically appointed bosses. (Russia made early on a big investment in tractors. They totalled 280,000 in 1934, compared to the USA's 1 million in that year (62).) Each peasant household was also allowed a plot of ground varying from half an acre to an acre and, in some places, as much as two acres, on which they could hold a few cows and sheep, and an unlimited number of chickens and rabbits. These private plots created many problems. The certainty of making a profit out of them caused peasants to put their heart into them, rather than into the collective farms.

At the same time, the surviving peasants were recalcitrant. Perhaps because the Russian government, particularly after Lenin's death, was increasingly managed by men who had been peasants or the sons of peasants, it used its political power with a bluntness which made the rule of the Tsar seem in retrospect a Utopia. Peasants were only supposed to sell their crop to state boards on which the characteristic bureaucracy of the old Russia was merged with the brutality of the new commissar. In most villages, too, the old 'elders' seemed an obvious focus of opposition to the communist party, in whom the government placed responsibility and trust. Thus the food production of Russia seemed to be in unsure hands and many peasants, without the chance of making money in the old way, simply refused to sell grain. In all items of production, Russian agriculture in 1928 was well below the level obtained in 1913, even taking into account the loss of territory caused by the substantial defeat in 1918. Meantime, the Russian government was anxious to press on with a programme of further industrialisation, linked, like that of Peter the Great, to preparations for war.

The consequence was the brutal revolution of 1929–33, whose aim was to force the bulk of the Russian rural population into the towns and establish state direction on the land. This was, in effect, the real Russian revolution, more important and more destructive than the events of 1917—21 (63). It was a subjugation ruthless, chaotic and swift. Communists from the towns came out, backed by the secret police (GPU), and, often fortified by brandy, forcibly took over land, grain and stock, and expelled or killed the peasants. A 'saturnalia of arrests' as Roy Medvedev put it, followed. Tens of thousands died of starvation, and millions were deported or fled to the cities. Thousands were shot for burying or even consuming grain which they had grown themselves. 'Dizzy with success,' Stalin described himself in 1930; but he later implied, in conversation with Winston Churchill, that ten million people had died during this time which was, in effect, a civil war fought against the whole peasantry (64).

This revolution was justified as enabling Russia 'to skip the capitalist stage of development altogether'. Actually, it established state feudalism in which workers, though no longer serfs, were more bondsmen than they had ever been. Although some attention was given later to various modifications of the idea of the co-operative, most Russian farms have become converted to state farms, where the workers are, as it were, day labourers on a large estate in which they are just as 'alienated' or remote from their masters and more so than those on a great estate of the past. This lack of concern with agriculture derives from Marx's sense of the 'idiocy of rural life', a notion which doubtless could have been justified in nineteenth century Russia, had he ever visited it.

Communist agriculture has admittedly had some successes. Thus the area under wheat in Russia seems to have doubled, from about 80 million acres to about 170 million, between 1913 and the 1970s. But then the Russian population has nearly doubled too*. Russia is now the largest sugar producer in the world. Russian livestock has apparently trebled since 1913 (32 million to 96 million in 1969). She produces infinitely more potatoes than any other nation. Russia seems also, since 1917, to have used a large female labour force in agriculture – in 1959, half as many again as men. Output of wheat has gone up 3½ times (in aggregate, not per head) from 28 million metric tons, in 1913, to something over 100 million tons in the 1970s† (65). But, still, Russian harvests continue

---

* The Russian population has increased since 1913 from about 150 million to 257 million.
† The following figures should all be regarded as uncertain, since Russian statistics are often published with a political, rather than a true, purpose. Black marketeering may account for an error of underestimation of 20%.

to be most unreliable. Instead of being a major exporter of wheat, as she was during the generation between 1870 and the First World War, Russia has had to stoop to importing grain from the capitalist USA. Communism has thus had the effect of diminishing the grain available for the rest of the world. Furthermore, such statistics as are available suggest that the ruins of private farming continue to be more productive than state farming. Even in 1938, men who worked on collective farms are believed to have owned, on their small private plots (3·3% of the cultivated land), 55·7% of all the cows in the country and 40% of the sheep. The previous year, production of peasants on the tiny plots was said to be 21·5% of the total agricultural output (66). The old failures of harvest also, of course, continue to dog modern Russia, Communist or no. Russia is a formidable agricultural nation, and the Government has absorbed many lessons from Western practice. But, even so, both there and in East Europe, agriculture has been an immensely discouraging aspect of the Communist régimes measured both in terms of production and of social integration.

The second major Communist experiment on the land was in China where, in 1949, a Communist party, at that time much influenced by Russia, gained control. The Communists were led by the son of a peasant, Mao Tse-tung, who himself worked on the land between the ages of thirteen and eighteen. In his early life as a founding member of the Communist party in China, Mao was a specialist in peasants' affairs. In 1927, he was chairman of the All China Peasants' Union. When he and his friends came to power in 1949, their first measure was to make freeholders of all peasants who previously had rented land. The redistributed land was given to the new owners as freehold. That move endeared the régime, to begin with, to peasants who were not very well informed of what had happened earlier in Russia. After about six or seven years, the communists embarked on a programme of inducing all farmers to pool their undertakings in a co-operative. This idea was offered both to new owners and to old freeholders. Boundaries between plots were eliminated. The whole village worked the land as a large farm under the direction of a committee elected by the co-operative: 'The great power of the propaganda machine,' wrote C. P. Fitzgerald, 'the constant exhortation of party cadres at meetings, an incessant campaign to convince the peasants that these measures would secure them against the risk of famine . . . all combined to persuade the peasant, albeit with some misgivings, that the 'Higher Stage of Co-operation' was a blessing . . . it did, indeed, bring much land into cultivation and make possible the rationalisation of irrigation and water conservancy' (67). Perhaps that description fails to evoke the reality of events in China in the country in those years. It is impossible as yet to know quite how that 'stage' of the agrarian revolution happened. It may have been as severe as the comparable one in Russia.

The era of the co-operative, however, did not mark the end of the agrarian changes in China. In 1958, the government in Peking decided to merge the co-operatives into larger units, to be known as 'Communes'. The same Australian historian of China, C. P. Fitzgerald, calls that decision 'rash, unwarranted and disastrous' (68). Severe droughts adversely affected the experiment in the early days. So did various theoretical ideas of 'scientific agriculture'. The continuing pressure of population on the land was exacerbated by a unique period of political stability. All that can be said of the Chinese agricultural experiment is that, though rationing has been continuous, famine seems to have been usually averted. The government has successfully established hoards of rice and grain adequate to feed even overgrown cities such as Shanghai. It seems probable that China, which has remained self-sufficient, has managed in agriculture to devise a system which was an improvement on the chaotic past during the age of 'warlords'. But that, of course, was an era of civil war. Meantime the water buffalo, the rice and the irrigation works continue remarkably unchanged.

The history of agriculture in both Russia and China, which together comprise a quarter of the world's population, illustrates two points; first, the immense capacity for destroying settled ways of producing crops now possessed by powerful governments; and, second, the ease with which such governments can conceal absolutely, for many years, the magnitude of disasters in their territories. It seems, actually, more likely that in future, human nature will be saved from famine by fish than by land reform.

35

The Transformation of Food

The Spanish conquests in America in the fifteenth century began the transformation of the world's food in a way already briefly noticed.* This transformation can be best illustrated by the story of two foods in particular: sugar and potatoes; and by that of a few crops which depend on sugar, or have been held to do so.

Sugar cane is one of the most interesting of crops. It is indigenous to the South Seas, being part of a large family of canes, bamboos, and grasses which have often been used for fibre or for thatch. Carried to south-east Asia and to India, it was crushed, in one way or another, to provide juice, from very early on. The boiling of the juice to make solid sugar was probably begun in India about 300—400 AD or perhaps Persia about 600 AD (1). It was taken to the Mediterranean from India and flourished in the late Roman world in Egypt, Sicily and Andalusia. The prophet Isaiah includes a reference to sweet cane (2). Both Ezekiel and Jeremiah speak of it too, but presumably no sugar in our modern sense was then made from it. In the region near Canton in China, sugar cane was known by the third century AD, but again that does not seem to have been commuted into sugar proper. There, as in the European Middle Ages, honey provided the best sweetening available. Cane was unpopular among early farmers, since it prevents the growing of other crops by rotation (a cane plant lasts seven years) (3). It cannot be grown north of the line where frost is a possibility. Cane figured, however, in the pharmacopoeia of the School of Salerno in the tenth century. Islam carried it anew to Spain at that time, also to Madeira and the Canaries. The crusaders grew it seriously on Cyprus, and made loaves of sugar from it almost in conditions of a plantation. So, later, did the Spaniards on the Canary Isles. In mediaeval England, some loaf sugar was imported via Venice or Germany principally to make marzipans or

* See above, page 234.

373

sweetmeats, costing 1s to 2s a pound in the thirteenth and fourteenth centuries, dropping to 10d in the fifteenth century, because of the new and successful exploitation of the Canaries (4).

From the Renaissance onwards, sugar has been grown continuously in, first, the West Indies, and then on the South American mainland. Cane was carried to the Americas by Columbus on his second voyage. The first sugar mill in the New World was established in 1508 in Santo Domingo (5). The main crop of Cortes' huge estate in Oaxaca was sugar cane (6). Very soon, fiscal advantages were given in the Spanish empire to those who founded sugar mills. Already, by 1520, cattle were exported from Spain and slaves from Africa, to the Indies, specially in order to power the mills and to cut cane. Cane, unknown to the Americas before Columbus, was firmly established.

Subsequently, as has earlier been indicated, an extraordinary undertaking was carried out in the West Indies by the Europeans. Ships set out from Europe for West Africa with cargoes of European manufactured goods, to be exchanged on arrival for slaves who were in turn carried across the Atlantic to the West Indies. Later, many slaves were also sold in North America for other purposes, but probably most slaves sold in the four centuries from 1500 to 1880 were to work on sugar plantations (7). At first these plantations were Spanish but afterwards they were English, French and Dutch - in Brazil. All these countries save Spain made money both from slaves and sugar. The iniquity of the business of dealing in slaves has most impressed later historians. Iniquitous it undoubtedly was, and an explicit contrast with standards of behaviour which had come to be accepted. It can hardly fail to cast a lurid light over the history of European business in the West Indies particularly and over African monarchs who connived at it for so long.

Sugar stimulated the use of coffee, tea and chocolate, above all the first two. Coffee, native to Ethiopia and not exported for drinking before 1500, was known in Constantinople by 1600 and was first sold in a Paris café in 1672. Coffee houses were open in London by 1652 (8). Most of this early coffee came from Mocha (Arabia). The plant was soon established in Java and then it followed sugar cane to the Americas. It was known in Cayenne in 1722, Martinique in 1723, and Jamaica in 1730 (9). Curiously enough, however, the demand for coffee only grew fast when the general availability of sugar began to make it less bitter to an increasingly self indulgent public. From the eighteenth century, sugar was indeed increasingly accessible, at least in Britain, France, Holland and, to a lesser extent, in Spain and Italy. Each Caribbean island grew some but, in the end, the largest producer was Brazil after the 1880s. Though some countries of Europe were persuaded, by imperial connections, to drink more tea than coffee, the world's trade in coffee was, by 1900, one of the most lucrative, persistent, and sensitive in the world (10).

Tea, meantime, had been used for many generations in China. First of all, the Chinese merely chewed the leaf, which grows wild in Manchuria. It was being cultivated there about 2000 BC. The leaves were later allowed to dry either by artificial heat ('green' tea) or by the sun (the tea leaves would then be fermented and become 'black' tea). Both types of leaf were rolled by hand. By the time that trade with Europe had opened up again, tea was being shipped in lead chests to the buyers. It was not, however, taken to India before the Europeans reached the Far East.

In 1609, the Dutch East India Company brought back several cargoes of tea from China to Europe. The British obtained some from the same source ten years later. A trade in tea leaves began. The crop itself was unable to bear European winters (it will not stand frost and suffers from drought). An increase in the consumption of sugar also coincided with the subsequent boom in tea, which affected all the European countries save for France, since she remained mistress of the coffee and chocolate islands in the West Indies (11).

The increase in consumption in England was specially striking; England imported about 20,000 pounds of tea a year in 1700, and 15 million in 1789. In the latter year, the average English citizen already consumed 1.16 pounds of tea a year. In 1938, it was 9 pounds (12). In 1797, an English worker might already spend 5% of his income, £2 a year, on tea (13). It sometimes indeed seemed as if strong tea were the sole food of poor people in manufacturing England (14). Later, tea became a replacement of beer, when taxes and temperance men insisted on taxes on malt, and many, including William Cobbett, rightly regarded this change as a disastrous deterioration in diet. Such doubts did not prevent the English from taking tea for propagation to India (from 1860) and to Ceylon (from 1877). The inability of the urban Englishman to brew beer in vast urban conglomerations was the beginning of a change in the national character (15).

Russians, meantime, had liked tea from about 1620 when a Khan of Mongolia had presented a case of it to an ambassador of the Tsar. But it was not much drunk till the nineteenth century, when Chinese ports were opened to Russia. Then, too, came more effective means of communication through the Suez canal and much later the Trans-Siberian railway line. Those changes made tea cheap enough to become the popular Russian drink in all classes which it seems to have been in the great days of Russian literature.

Of course, sugar was used for puposes other than simply to sweeten drinks. The pudding, for example, was inspired by the fall in sugar prices in the late seventeenth century. After the 1880s, manufactured jam appeared (it was immediately popular, though many jams contained little of the fruit from which they theoretically came, since, to begin with, they were mostly concoctions of the cheapest fruits or even vegetables available and then coloured or sweetened according to taste) (16).

The import of sugar, the most valuable import into a rich country such as England every year without exception from 1703 till 1814 (17), was, however, an index of general prosperity. The wealth made in the West Indies by Dutch, English, French, and finally Spaniards and North Americans (after 1870) contributed to some of the largest fortunes of those days. All the islands of the West Indies themselves underwent at least a generation or two of prosperity, though since the sugar was all taken back to Europe, and few European families settled there, the money concerned seemed even more like faery gold than most swiftly made and swiftly lost fortunes in the days of expansion. The exception to this rule was Cuba. That island remained the largest producer, and far the largest exporter of sugar from the 1830s until the 1960s. From the late eighteenth century till about 1930, every industrial innovation from the steam engine to the railway which could benefit the sugar trade was introduced early into Cuba. In the nineteenth century, Cuba thus became the richest colony on earth. In the twentieth it was the richest country in the tropics. Sugar was also the commodity which saw in the early twentieth century the most pronounced trend towards industrial integration: large consumers sought to secure their own supplies (18). The unreliability of the world sugar prices, however, made the economy of any country which relied on sugar seem like a lottery (19): 'diversification of agriculture,' a World Bank report on Cuba argued in 1950, was 'almost beyond capitalist laws'. It turned out to be beyond socialist ones too, though the frustration caused resulted in the nationalist revolution of 1959, which became a communist one within a year.

Long before then in Cuba, the manufacture of sugar had become mechanised. The old ox carts used for generations to carry the cut cane to the factory were beginning to be replaced by motor lorries. Tractors were available for ploughing. A considerable part of the sugar area of the country had been fertilised. But many difficulties were being encountered by underemployed wage earners who, in the past, had usually managed to find various jobs on a big sugar estate, even outside the harvest time (20).

Similar difficulties existed in most countries where sugar cane was being grown. Almost everywhere too, sugar has inspired the leaders of political disturbances. The sugar workers of the Mexican state of Morelos were the leaders of those who supported Zapata in the revolution of 1912 (21). On the other side of the political battle, the sugar beet companies of Ferrara in 1921 gave heavy financial assistance to the fascist movement (22).

A new dimension had by then been given to the history of sugar by the realisation that a beetroot indigenous to Europe (which had been used as a source of fodder) could, just as well as cane, be treated to produce sugar. This realisation came in 1747 to the son, later assistant, of the chief apothecary of the court of Prussia, Andreas Marggraf. Young Marggraf proved his point by showing that there were sugar crystals in the roots of beet. But nothing was done until Franz Karl Achard, another Prussian chemist, began, after 1789, to produce loaf sugar from beet on an estate in Silesia belonging to the King of Prussia. Napoleon became specially interested in the idea of sugar beet since he thought that it would help France to beat the British blockade. Like many ideas of Napoleon, the pursuit of sugar beet became gradually popular after his defeat. All northern European countries took up this method of making sugar. By the 1880s, more sugar was being made from beet than from cane. Germany became, for a time, a larger overall producer of sugar than was Cuba. This European lead subsequently vanished when the beet farmers went to war in 1914. In the 1970s, only 40% of the world's sugar comes from Marggraf's discovery, Russia being pre-eminent in production (23).

Beet was a typical development of the industrial age. It could not have been cultivated before the nineteenth century, for it requires deep ploughing and the seed has to be drilled if the crop is to be successful. It is a crop which thus needs the best tools (24) and it is, therefore, several times more expensive to gain sugar from beet than it is from sugar cane, though the final sugar is identical. Nevertheless, all countries which can grow beet do so. They desire to have a stand-by in case a war cuts them off from tropical producers. The coming of the nuclear age has not affected that preconception.

WORLD SUGAR PRODUCTION

	World Total
1843	1 million tons
1864	2 million tons
1873	3 million tons
1890	6 million tons
1927	27 million tons
1960	52 million tons
1972	76 million tons

These figures make plain that, however else the modern world is judged, we live in sweeter times than ever before. The consequences have not been beneficial. Decay of teeth has been stimulated by sugar since the early nineteenth century. Over-sugary diets lead to fat in the blood and hence to disease of the heart.

Though a major international crop, sugar in no way competes with the old great crops producing grain or rice upon which civilisation was built. Such a role has, however, been played by the potato, now the fourth most important crop in the world.*

* After wheat, rice and maize. See World Crops 1976.

The potato is an American contribution to the world's food, indeed, a South American one, for it was only taken even to Mexico by the Spaniards. Before 1500, the potato was grown only in the Andes. There, neither manioc nor maize could be raised successfully. The first 'Indian' immigrants there found the wild 'potato' their best chance of a stable food. They already knew potatoes in South America as 'papas', which is still the Spanish word for them. The potato was represented on Peruvian pottery as early as 200 AD. It can be stored as well as dried, but loses a third of its strength after three months.

The Spaniards reached Cuzco in 1533. Three years later, the first reference was made to a European eating potatoes: Gonzalo Jiménez de Quesada and his men entered the houses of Peruvians, who fled at their approach and found, as they supposed them to be, truffles in the village of Socotra, not far from Vélez, high in the Colombian mountains (25). Soon, the potato was taken to Spain. The first reference to it being eaten in Europe, however, was in the Sangre hospital in Seville in 1573 (26). A potato was found in Gerard's well-documented garden in Holborn by 1596. Shakespeare refers to the potato, twice, both times apparently as if it were considered an aphrodisiac. Thus Falstaff: 'Let the sky rain potatoes . . . hail kissing comforts' (27).

Potatoes took a long time to become popular ouside the Andes. No edible plant in the old world had been grown from tubers rather than from seed. No other plant previously had such mysterious, white, or flesh-coloured, nodules. The tubers seemed to people, at first, to be deformed, like the feet of lepers. Many, indeed, thought that the potato caused leprosy. When that disease vanished, scrofula was attributed to it too. The coincidence of the coming of the potato to Russia with the major cholera epidemic of the 1830s set back cultivation there a generation (28). 'The things have neither smell nor taste. Not even the dogs will eat them, so what use are they to us?' said the men of Kolberg in Prussia, to Frederick the Great in 1774, when that monarch was trying to encourage the cultivation of potatoes (29). Others disliked eating a plant not mentioned in the Bible. Tomatoes, it may be remembered, had similar problems to begin with.*

Ireland, a country already devastated and impoverished, with all old traditions breaking down with the coming of the Anglo-Saxons, was the first European country to grow these plants seriously. Irish farmers in the seventeenth century were the first to realise that a quarter acre of land would yield twenty hundredweight of potatoes — which, along with a few pigs, could keep a family infinitely better than any other crop on so small an area (30).† The potato was first noted in Ireland at Youghal in 1623. During the next forty years, it established itself. Else-

---

* See above, page 235.
† Grain has been held to need, in primitive circumstances, at least 1 1/3acres to feed a man.

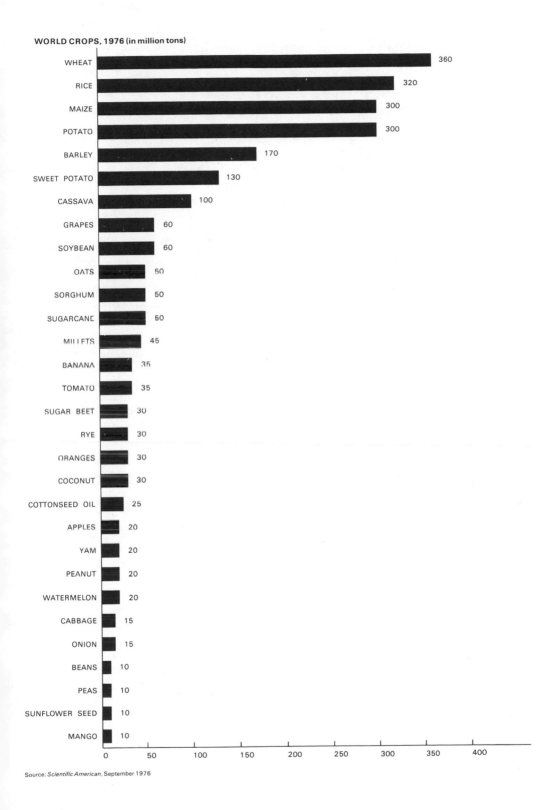

WORLD CROPS, 1976 (in million tons)

WHEAT	360
RICE	320
MAIZE	300
POTATO	300
BARLEY	170
SWEET POTATO	130
CASSAVA	100
GRAPES	60
SOYBEAN	60
OATS	50
SORGHUM	50
SUGARCANE	50
MILLETS	45
BANANA	35
TOMATO	35
SUGAR BEET	30
RYE	30
ORANGES	30
COCONUT	30
COTTONSEED OIL	25
APPLES	20
YAM	20
PEANUT	20
WATERMELON	20
CABBAGE	15
ONION	15
BEANS	10
PEAS	10
SUNFLOWER SEED	10
MANGO	10

Source: *Scientific American*, September 1976

where, progress was slow. In France, the jerusalem (girasole) artichoke (another American product, brought back about 1607) experienced a vogue. It was cultivated more for a time than the potato. Though it has less energy to offer, it is less subject to disease and is nearly as heavy in yield (31). In Burgundy, potatoes continued to be thought of as a kind of truffle till 1789. Occasional notes suggest a patchy but widespread cultivation on the continent, till the late eighteenth century, yet grown almost everywhere. 'Widely cultivated in Tuscany, especially at Vallambrosa', in the late sixteenth century (32) though it may have been, it was still 'not quite respectable' in southern England in 1815. Balkan peasants in the nineteenth century would not eat 'that cursed food hidden in the earth' (33). Even in the twentieth century, there were educated people who regarded the potato as 'sheer poison' (34).

Still, from the late eighteenth century, a good deal of propaganda was lavished by enlightened governments in an attempt to encourage the propagation of this plant. The reformer, Turgot, had it served ostentatiously at his table when first minister of France. Frederick the Great was successful in the end in persuading his subjects to grow it substantially. The enlightened Duke of Parma also cultivated it in 1765. It was the characteristic crop of the Enlightenment: when Voltaire describes Candide retiring to cultivate his garden, it would surely have been potatoes which he would have dug. In England, the potato was then widely cultivated north of the 'coal line' (35). Adam Smith predicted that potatoes might well replace wheat as the mainstay of the poor. He thought that 'the strongest men and the most beautiful women' of Britain (that is, the Irish) all lived on that root (36). It is indeed possible that the subsequent widespread cultivation of the plant 'saved mankind from starvation' in the late eighteenth century. Peasants became impressed since it thrived when the wheat harvest failed. Potatoes also contributed a good deal both to cattle and to industrial alcohol during the nineteenth century (37). Gradually, prejudice was overcome.

Still, there were setbacks: first, there was the famous and destructive blight which affected the potatoes of all Europe in 1845. Several times before, the potato harvest had failed. This blight, however, attacked plants without warning. It destroyed tubers as well as leaves. It originally came from America. Repeated in 1846, the loss of the harvest led to starvation, scurvy, dysentery, cholera and typhus. It struck particularly hard in Ireland, where the potato had been grown longer than anywhere else, and where the country lived, as it were, around the potato (38).

The effect was harsh. The Irish population, too poor to buy wheat, dropped sharply. Anyone who could afford to do so left for America. (Three and a half million Irish people left Ireland for America between 1851 and 1946). Subsequently, the Irish saw that their old notion of a small potato plot being able to support a family was no longer valid. The area under potatoes fell. Cattle increased. Fragmentation of holdings (which had gone on for generations) went no further. Irishmen became used to marrying late if at all (33.5% of the Irish male population are still unmarried between forty-five and fifty-four years (39). The Irish population is the only one in Europe to be less, much less, in the 1970s (4,367,000) than it was in 1840 (8,175,000) (40).*

The second setback to the potato was caused by the Colorado beetle. It was first observed in the Wild West about 1824 happily feeding on deadly nightshade. But Colorado remained almost uninhabited till 1858. Then the gold rush brought the potato there as well as 'pioneers'. The beetles soon found that this new member of the *solanum* family (the potato is related to nightshade) was a most succulent plant. The beetles went east, crossing the Mississippi by 1865, reaching Ohio by 1869, but were held back there by early arsenic sprays. There was alarm in Europe. American potatoes were banned. Nevertheless, in 1901, the beetle was found in Tilbury, and also on the Elbe. In the course of the First World War, US troops brought it to France. The French were negligent. Within a few months, the beetle had spead all over western Europe. In England, it was held off. Then one beetle was brought back from France in the Second World War, perhaps in one of the Lysander aircraft used for carrying secret agents to work against the Nazis. But chemical sprays defeated it, at least for a time. At the moment it seems a dormant threat (41). But the experience, both of it and of the blight, in the nineteenth century (as of the phylloxera which hit vines in the 1870s and the elm disease which hit Europe in the 1970s) is a reminder that if great killer diseases are a thing of the past for human beings, they may not be so for plants.

Despite its heavy protein, the potato is the main source of food able to ensure that the northern hemisphere has something in reserve if a grain crop fails. Russia is the largest producer, followed by Poland (which produces more potatoes than the whole of Asia), the US and West Germany. It looks, however, as if recent warnings over excessive diet have caused potatoes to reach their peak production in rich countries.

The histories of sugar and potatoes could scarcely be more contrasting for the one is primarily a matter of commerce, and the other is largely grown for the home market. The first is a manufactured product. The second is eaten untouched. The first has inspired innumerable wars; the eighteenth century wars in the West Indies were wars for the supply of sugar. The second has merely, on occasion, provided battlefields. Both, however, have altered the diet of rich countries, for good or evil.

Still, it is not the adaptation of these crops to the modern world that has made the greatest change to diets since the age of industry. Nor should the coming of the turkey and of the tomato (other American products) and the conversion of whale oil and other fats into margarine

* Both figures include Northern Ireland.

(by Mège Mouries, a French technologist working with the navy) (42) be regarded as of profound importance, interesting though they are. The transformation of a nation, such as Italy, from being one where working men might live on bread, ricòtta and water into one where nearly everyone is able to echo Johnson's remark that 'he who does not mind his belly will hardly mind anything else' may also appear to reflect a decisive change. Comparisons can be made between the diet of a Russian in 1900 and one in the 1970s, to prove, or disprove, the dietary benefits of the Revolution (Russian peasants in 1956 ate far more cereals and vegetable oil than they did in 1900, about the same amount of cabbage and fish, many more potatoes, eggs, cucumbers and sugar, and much more meat and butter). There were also, as has been indicated, fewer peasants. To those who place all their faith in the therapeutic powers of the tomato, the Revolution has proved a benefit, for there were none available under the Tsars (43). The same argument, however, would cause the Spanish Habsburgs to appear the great bene-factors of the Russian people, since it was they who first propagated that appetising fruit.

The four fundamental changes in the world's diet since 1750 have been scientific, technical, practical and political.

The first of these is probably the most important. Before the nine-teenth century, little was known of what needs men had in order to live. Then François Magendie in France, Lyon Playfair and Sir Astley Cooper in Britain, (surgeon to King George IV), and Gerard Mulder and, above all, Julius von Liebig in Germany,* embarked on a scientific study of food. Magendie, for example, demonstrated the passive role of the stomach in vomiting while Mulder in Utrecht, in 1838, suggested that there was one nitrogen component of all living matter, plant or animal, which he named 'protein', after the Greek for '1'. Von Liebig taught that all herbivorous animals built up tissues directly from the proteins of plant foods which were ultimately converted into those of muscles and other organs. Then, a generation later, Frederick Hiskins, working in a country (Britain) which, despite the fact that 70% of working, class and 45% of middle class, budgets went on food and drink (44), seemed in the preceding few generations to have experienced a serious reversal in nutrition, showed that all animals, including humans, decline in health when they lack certain factors of diet, even when they have enough protein. Dr Casimir Funk called this factor a *'vitamine'* (the final 'e' being dropped by Sir Jack Drummond). These developments are a good indication that, even in respect of food, ideas can rule the world.

The second, technical, factor in the modern history of food was the invention of the tin can. For centuries, food had been preserved in various ways, by drying, salting or, in the Andes and, among the Eskimoes, freezing. In 1807, an English scientist, Plowden, took out a

* See above, page 360.

patent for preserving meat by enveloping it in gravy. A little earlier, there had been a plan for evaporating soups, for use in ships. Then came the development of canning, of which the French scientist, Nicholas Appert, was the pioneer. About 1810, he worked out a method of bottling fruits and vegetables by subjecting the bottle to heat. This began to be used by the French navy under Napoleon for a variety of goods. Then in England in 1812, Bryan Donkin, a Northumberland-born engineer at the Dartford iron works, thought of using metal containers for Appert's method. Between then and about 1820, this idea was established for 'naval or explorers'' stores. One tin can closed in 1818 was not opened till 1938. The roast veal and vegetables inside were found still to be in good condition, save for a certain amount affected by part of the tin which had dissolved.

Canning factories were then built, but numerous scandals affecting the purity of the cans' contents prevented this method of keeping food from becoming of importance till the 1850s. Thereafter, the tin can has become reliable, cheap and easy. The use of cans, combined with that of refrigerator vans on railways, and refrigerated ships, for fish and meat, transformed, if they did not enrich, diets. Farewell to the days when the markets of great capitals might be crammed with thousands of oxen and even 30,000 live sheep, waiting for slaughter (45). Cattle need no longer be taken to Smithfield 'on the hoof', as they had been from time immemorial. The demand for tin soon exceeded that for silver. The tin can is perhaps more a typical object of the twentieth century than anything else, enabling armies, in particular, to live better than ever before. Tinned condensed milk was already one of the great successes of the American Civil War. Plastic began to play the same preservatory role after 1950.

Also in the 1860s came what for most cooks has been the third, decisive change: the kitchen stove. Until the nineteenth century, most cooking was done over an open fire or in a primitive brick oven, heated with coals. In 1795, the eccentric Count Rumford, an Anglo-American-born count of the Holy Roman Empire from Massachusetts, who went to Bavaria after siding with England in the American War of Independence, fed the poor of Munich by means of a stove which greatly economised on fuel. He later developed a range with a closed top which possessed all the heat of a small fire and could be adjusted. That heralded a real transformation in cooking. Until then, the finer sorts of cuisine could only be carried out by an army of chefs, whereas sautés, soufflés and sauces could thereafter all be done on small stoves and by one person (46).

For about fifty years, iron ranges such as Rumford had had in mind, were unusual. They only came into general use in northern Europe and the US in the 1860s. The iron stoves of that day used solid fuel. They provided the essential foundation for the great meals of the late Victorian era. No more would a Vatel have to contemplate suicide if he was unable to face the humiliation of not having two roast courses ready for a banquet! Even more precise adjustments of heat became possible with the gas stoves of the 1870s. Later, after 1890, electricity gave a clean alternative to gas, though it was not so popular as gas was till about 1920, since it gives too slow a heat (47). Gas fires, meantime, followed the principle of heating by gas and all sorts of other innovations followed in kitchens in rich countries. These included the mechanised domestic refrigerator, whose earliest version was that exhibited by Ferdinand Carré at the London exhibition of 1860; the 'dishwasher' (1946); the sink, with the built-in 'garbage disposer' (1935), and the planned modern kitchen with smaller mechanised tools, such as eggbeaters and potato cleaners — the culinary equivalent to such striking innovations in the rest of modern households as the carpet sweeper (1859), the machine for washing clothes (1869) and the electric 'iron' (1906), which succeeded the gas-heated one of 1850. The interesting aspect of these inventions is the relatively slow pace with which they came to be accepted or even sought after, in Europe. In the US, the kitchen was scientifically re-arranged by 1939. In Europe, many kitchens are still not so (48). The explanation that the 'servantless household' came quicker to the US is bad. French households are old-fashioned, whether there are servants or not. The food is better too.

The technology of eating was also transformed in the early days of industrialisation. Although in 1914 one could still find, in the Morvan in France, tables conveniently scooped out with regular hollows into which soup was poured, plates, cups, glasses, knives, forks and spoons had begun to be generally manufactured in large numbers in the late eighteenth century. In the nineteenth century, slums and palaces alike had their cutlery (49).

Equally important, the coming of railways made it possible for the first time to bring many interesting items of food up to the capital on a regular basis. Milk, in particular, became far more easily available. Then the studies of Pasteur showed that micro-organisms which cause disease, as well as fermentation, are destroyed when fluids are heated to 145° Fahrenheit. This 'pasteurisation' began in the 1890s to prolong the life of milk (50). Only in the late nineteenth century was it realised that milk could be ensured against infection by being boiled. By 1900, such familiar sights as the large steel-plate milk churn for use on railways and the milk bottle had also been introduced, while dried milk had been invented in 1855* (51). But it was not till 1922-25 that Dr Corry Mann argued that milk had some special value in the diet of children which could not be measured by estimating fats, proteins and calories (52) – a view now being challenged.

The history of milk was also affected by several changes in the way

* Other dehydrated foods have followed.

that infants were fed. Breast feeding declined in the nineteenth century. Women working in factories had too hard a life to feed babies. Both poor and rich alike used bottles instead. The wet nurse became a memory. But, at that time, the substitute for mother's milk was cows' milk and water. It was later skimmed milk, perhaps diluted with barley water, and later still the sickly-sweet condensed (canned) milk. That was enough to start any child off inauspiciously. Even worse, nothing was known of sterilisation. Many babies died, even after the invention of a rubber teat for the bottle (in 1856 by V. Scully and B. J. Heywood) (52). Meantime, gin was still often given to keep children quiet (53). Thus the interconnection between health and food can be said to begin at the mother's knee.

Finally, in the modern history of food, the fourth, and political, innovation was the system of rationing introduced in the First World War, designed to operate throughout the large industrial countries and subsequently practised during all times of conflict. Of course, in large cities, during sieges or famines, the grain and other food available has always been restricted. But the gradual shift of population to the towns in the nineteenth century, as well as their reliance on food from abroad, either as a raw material or in a form ready to eat, changed the position. In modern wars, whole nations can be besieged. This was a practice begun by Britain in her attempt to blockade Napoleon in the early nineteenth century. All the nations at war between 1914 and 1918 embarked on rationing, though Britain only did so, with misgiving, in early 1918. Attempts were, therefore, made by governments to draw up the precise amounts of proteins and calories needed by the population. By the summer of 1918, governments of most nations at war had taken over the shipments of food from private merchants, and made themselves responsible for its distribution. The same happened, even more effectively, during the Second World War. Many countries have even lived with rationing during years of nominal peace. Many communist countries have had rationing as a matter of course for many years: a failure in distribution as well as in agriculture.

Two remarkable changes in the history of diet in our times remain to be noted: the decline in the quantity of alcohol consumed and the change in the character of bread in rich countries.

It often seems as if Western civilisation is built upon the use of alcohol more than anything else. Yet, in nearly every rich country, the quantity of drink consumed per head has dropped. In the US during the 1830s, for example, most Americans drank seven gallons a head a year. In the 1970s, they drink 3 gallons. The use of spirits is a third of what it was in 1840 (54). This was the result of a powerful and well-organised temperance movement in both the US and Britain, making use of taxes to effect the change which they desired. Even in France, consumption of wine per head has gone down. What perhaps needs to be noticed to place this alteration in perspective is that the early nineteenth century, because of mechanisation, was an era of tremendous increase in the production of alcohol, as of everything else. In all countries, railways ensured that cheap drink could be carried far and also turned into an industrial product. In the early eighteenth century, wine was a luxury in France. In the mid-twentieth century, the average Frenchman – an admittedly difficult concept for the average non-Frenchman – drank 44 gallons of wine a year, and nearly a gallon of spirits (55).

The history of bread has other morals.

In the eighteenth century, white bread, made from wheat which had had most of its bran removed, was everywhere regarded as a token of distinction and privilege. Utterly ignorant of the scientific basis of such matters, the population of all Europe considered the brown loaf as 'coarse and coloured'. By 1800, the white loaf was almost everywhere available and was regarded as a symbol of egalitarianism, even if it was really a sign of the shrinking area of choice. Napoleon's armies took white bread with them wherever they went in Europe as a banner of liberation from old dull bran or rye breads. The proof that it was not a legacy of *la gloire* alone is shown by the fact that it had conquered England before then (56).

This 'universal taste' for white bread thus antedated the mechanisation of grinding by almost a century. All over Europe and North America in the early nineteenth century, bread continued to be ground in small water mills or windmills. Finer flours were made by adjusting the grinding stones. Even in the purest breads of that era, however, dirt, sweat and oil got into the bread. For that and other reasons, this new bread did not taste as fresh, nor remain as edible, as long as the previous ones. There were other difficulties. The demand for wheat was greater than ever, not only because of the manufacture of bread: hair powder, so popular about 1800, came from wheat, so did starch, to stiffen the spotless white shirts of Europe in the age of Victoria. Efforts were made in almost every European country to persuade the poor to return to bread made from barley and rye. But even the poorest claimed that they had already 'lost their rye teeth' (57). Other attempts were made to encourage the eating of rice. They failed. Panicky crises over the shortage of wheat characterised the early nineteenth century everywhere, particularly in Britain, where grain had already begun to be regularly imported from 1755 even if never on a large scale. Only in the late nineteenth century did this anxiety disappear almost completely. Then the fall in the cost of long-distance transport, by ship and rail, made possible large shipments of wheat to Europe from both the US and Russia. Those two political giants of the twentieth century were already the granaries of nineteenth century Europe – so that (as has been seen) grain land in England, for example, dropped by a quarter (58) and prices of wheat fell (59).

By that time, another ugly development had been begun: the introduction of metal rollers for grinding grain. This began in Austria-Hungary in the 1840s. It was almost the only major technological innovation of the Habsburg empire, and is not one of which the Habsburgs should be proud. These iron rollers (later made of steel) gave a much more constant quality to the flour. They produced flour far faster. The upkeep of steel rollers was easy. The white bread so made was even whiter than it had been before, since the very hot steel roller pushed the endosperm out of its coating. That left the germ as a minute flake, to be sieved off with the bran. Even the brown bread made by machine kept better since its germ too was killed. For many years, therefore, this flour was popular with bakers and customers. Manufacturers of biscuits also preferred a standard product.

But the killing of the wheat germ in the wheat destroyed what is, in fact, the real nutrient of the grain. As the iron and steel mills spread from central Europe, superseding the age-old process of stone grinding, the diets of the population of Europe fell in quality. Those who depended most on bread, the poor, suffered most (60).*

Ultimately, in the late twentieth century, a reaction has begun against these damaging artifical breads. But, even so, most modern types of bran meal bread are not, as a rule, the same as wholemeal bread of the past. Much European brown bread, for example, is made from ordinary white flour into which bran has been mixed or even molasses added for colour! (61). The chief consequence has been the collapse of bread as a 'staff of life' in most rich countries. Total cereal use in the US for example, has dropped from 300 pounds a person a year to about 130 (62). Modern men seek sweeter and fatter foods. Sugary drinks, fats, oils, an increase in meat-eating, and extraordinary manufactured beverages such as the mysterious coca cola, have begun to ruin the digestions of both rich peoples and poor, a change only mildly mitigated by the growth of the succulent tomato, which is today the most popular of US vegetables, whereas in 1900 it was rarely eaten, being still regarded as too close a relation to the deadly nightshade.

These fashions were not confined to the self-indulgent West. In the late nineteenth century, rice underwent the same experience as did wheat. White rice became as alluring to the East as white bread did to the West. To polish rice in order to remove its brown outer sheath became the obsession of the Orient. In the process, the rice germ went

---

* Major elements in stone-ground and roller-ground bread according to Sir Jack Drummond:

	STONE	STEEL	NEEDED PER DAY
Iron m.g.	13.0	7.0	11
Vitamin A i.u.	425.0	0.0	1,500
Vitamin B m.g	1.0	0.3	0.8
Nicotinic acid m.g.	5.4	3.8	8.0
Vitamin D	8.0	0	Not known

the way of the wheat germ. The effect on health can be explicitly seen in the disastrous rise in the incidence of beri-beri.

Some of these criticisms can equally be levied at those efforts of the 1960s to produce a rice which would grow more prolifically. A new cross-bred rice was being grown on millions of acres with a yield three times the traditional one. That great success of the International Rice Research Institute, in the Philippines, had, however, disadvantages: it needed a vast amount of water, it attracted the voracious stern-borer insect, and it demanded a great deal of fertiliser. It was also thought to be sticky and lumpy, and so could not easily be eaten with one's fingers. Have the 'miracle strains' of the 1970s avoided these difficulties and, if so, have they created new ones?

Every generation has seemed to imagine that food changes for the worse: 'Du temps de mon père on avait tous les jours la viande . . . on égouttait le vin comme si c'était de l'eau.' Thus the Sieur de Goubern-ville in the sixteenth century (63). One hears much the same in the late twentieth century. It would be easy to point to the lack of diversity in the food of our time, or to the artificial colourings or the dangerous preservatives as its chief characteristic. But more extraordinary still is the commercial significance of the humblest diet and the immensely complicated history behind the dullest breakfast. Here is a cup of tea, apparently an unexciting commodity. But the history of the 'China' cup necessitates an excursion into the industrial revolution, to mediaeval contact between old China and feudal Europe. The size and the capacity of the cup is a reminder of countless quaint measures in history, many of which are still fighting a stout battle against decimalisation and metri-cation. The tea has an equally diverse genealogy. If coffee is being drunk, the roots of our breakfast return, via the West Indies, to the Ottoman empire and the indigenous plant in Abyssinia, whose beans were not exported before the Renaissance. The salt on the table com-memorates one of the world's oldest trades, and the pepper is a reminder that it was in order to find another route to the spice islands that Columbus set off for America.* The history of bread, of milk, of eggs in modern industrial cities should not be too cursorily dismissed: was it only a hundred years ago that the dairies of London still had their cows on the premises, and no more than that since Pasteur discovered the roots of hygiene, and fermentation? In the history of such apparent banalities there is indeed, in microcosm, an entire universal history. Even the hours at which meals are eaten have their long chronicles, and the milk bottle its *histoire morale*: for, as Winston Churchill is believed to have said, 'Democracy means that if the door bell rings in the early hours, it is likely to be the milkman'.

* He himself was partly financed by salt merchants from Valencia.

36

The Great Medical Improvements

Industrialisation, of course, had profound, lasting and beneficial effects on health and medicine. In the nineteenth century, scientifically based medicine transformed health and the expectation of life in the population of rich countries, and subsequently began to do so in poor countries as well. But exactly at the time, and in exactly the places, that scientifically based medicine began to play a part in saving life, the birth rates began generally to slow down.

Two benefits derive from the eighteenth century. These were, first, the use of mercury, which began to have an appreciable effect on the consequences of syphilis. That disease, as has been earlier indicated, was unknown in Europe before 1492, when it was brought back from Cuba by Columbus, along with tobacco. (The first syphilitics of Europe were the Indian slaves exhibited by Columbus in 1492, in Barcelona.) The first epidemic of syphilis was in Naples the next year, and was taken there by a Spanish ship from Barcelona. Charles VIII's army was devastated by it when he reached Naples that year. So this American illness was, for a time, known as the 'French disease'. By 1498, syphilis had reached India, and China by 1505. Mercury was used in the sixteenth century against it, without decisive effect, so it was discarded. It only began to be used again beneficially in the eighteenth century.

The second benefit (and more important than mercury, since syphilis affected fewer people than is often supposed) was inoculation, and then vaccination, against smallpox: an innovation which led to the vast array of preventive injections which characterise modern medicine.

Smallpox is a variety of a mild disease of cattle which first appeared in Asia in late classical times. It does not seem to have made much impact in the West till the Renaissance. From then on, however, Europe was host to smallpox, a disease which caused ravages for two centuries. It hit the Americas very hard when there after 1492. The disease often affected remote Indian communities before the Europeans arrived.

The Chinese had inoculated themselves against smallpox with a mild dose of the disease since at least the eleventh century. Perhaps because of a discussion of the subject by the philosopher Li Shih-Chen in the sixteenth century, knowledge of the idea became known in the Middle East by the seventeenth century at least. (1). The idea was certainly brought back to England in 1721 by Lady Mary Wortley Montagu from Constantinople, where her husband was ambassador. Since inoculation was expensive and risky, it became fashionable. Catherine the Great had herself, and her court, inoculated in 1769. The French began to interest themselves in the technique after Louis XV died of smallpox in 1774. Frederick the Great instructed not only the court but country doctors to take it up. George Washington ordered his army to be inoculated in 1776. Without that order, he might not have won his great rebellion.

Twenty years later, the English Doctor Edward Jenner, in Gloucestershire, became interested in a local belief that milkmaids did not incur smallpox. That turned out to be so. They suffered a milder form, known as cowpox, which they caught from cows. After hesitation, Jenner inoculated a boy, James Phipps, with cowpox, which he contracted. When later exposed to smallpox, he did not get the disease. This use of cowpox marked a decisive change. The commander-in-chief of the British army, the Duke of York, shortly after asked Jenner to 'vaccinate' the entire 85th Regiment of Foot. The daring plan worked and the Duke of York deserves greater recognition for his farsightedness in that matter than his ill-fame as a commander in Holland has given him. The whole English army was next vaccinated. Napoleon did the same thing with his forces. The United States took up the idea with enthusiasm. By the middle of the nineteenth century, 'vaccination' for the entire people, not just those fortunate enough to be able to serve in the army, was compulsory in many countries. By the twentieth century, smallpox was almost eradicated. In 1976, it was reputed to be making its last stand in the southern deserts of Ethiopia (2), though occasional outbreaks occur in rich countries too.

These matters apart, the Enlightenment brought few immediate benefits to the health of nations. Great military surgeons such as Larrey, Napoleon's chief of the medical service, organised the first effective ambulance service in war, realised the importance of early treatment of wounds, and carefully noted the concept of traumatic gangrene. In 1819, René Laennec invented the stethoscope in order to listen to chests. He identified the sounds which he heard with certain diseases — making possible diagnoses more effective than before. Another Frenchman, Marie François Bichat, had earlier divided the materials of the body into membranes and tissues. He died young, as a result of excessive zeal in dissecting bodies.

The two great discoveries in medicine were those of anaesthesia and the antiseptic method in surgery. Both ideas, like most great ones, were simple and, theoretically, could have been discovered at any time. But only in the nineteenth century could the second, at least, have been adequately pursued, since it needed precision tools. Paré, in the six-teenth century might have found the antiseptic method, but he could not have ensured its effectiveness. Similarly, only in the nineteenth century were other methods of hygiene understood: for example, that decomposing matter is a danger to health. Sewers in London in 1820 were inferior to the system in Rome in 20 AD. When asked about drains in 1850, a London woman said: 'Thank God, we have none of those foul stinking things here' (3). But the growth of big cities made the disposal of sewage the most acute problem. It began to be resolved, as will be seen,* before antiseptic surgery.

The standards of private hygiene were actually higher in mediaeval Europe than during the Enlightenment. There were public baths in most European cities in the fifteenth century. These were abandoned in the late Renaissance. Even Jews gave up the ritual bath then, probably because of fear of catching syphilis, perhaps because of the rise in the price of firewood and hence of hot water (4).†

First, however, consider anaesthesia, the first important medical invention deriving from the US. Of course, efforts had long been made to diminish pain during operations. The Chinese had used acupuncture since very early times (5). The Arabs had tried mandragora, opium, and hyoscine, while the use of brandy had been common since the eleventh century. Later on, in the eighteenth century, Benjamin Bell in Scotland suggested that an iron clamp might with advantage compress the nerves during an operation. The apostle of electricity, Sir Humphry Davy, proposed that laughing gas might be used during operations. A Scottish surgeon, James Escrick, then successfully used mesmerism for operations in India, without pain. Returning to Scotland, he failed, the Scots seeming less appropriate patients than Hindus. Finally, William Clark, a student of chemistry in Rochester, USA, in 1842, took a tooth out of a woman painlessly with the use of ether.

So began the modern era in surgery. In 1846, William Morton used ether publicly, and successfully, for the excision of a tumour on the neck in Massachusetts General Hospital. Robert Liston, a Scottish surgeon of great dexterity, soon did the same at University College, London. The use of ether spread round the world fast. Sir James Simpson afterwards used chloroform for the same purpose. He and two assistants inhaled it in 1847 and fell simultaneously beneath the table (6). Henceforth, pain during surgery could be easily avoided (though the problems of using anaesthesia have not been wholly overcome). Speed was no longer the most important element in any operation. Thoroughness came to be the deciding question (7).

---

* See below, page 419.
† In the seventeenth century, baths were re-introduced as an Eastern luxury and became synonymous with a brothel (*bagnio*).

Major anaesthetics were one thing. Local ones were another. The Incas, for hundreds of years, had known of the anaesthetic character of coca trees. In the late nineteenth century, Austrians began to investigate the properties of leaves of coca, whose crystals they called cocaine. The later and various valuable uses of this drug came swiftly into being. Intravenous injections began in 1874.

Ordinary surgery, like medicine itself, had few successes before the early nineteenth century, though another French military surgeon, Ollier, introduced the principle of Rest, incurring the gratitude of innumerable soldiers: 'Absolute and permanent immobility of the wounded part is essential, in a fixed apparatus.' Sir Joseph Lister (together with Louis Pasteur), however, was the man of the decisive innovation.

In the mid nineteenth century, much suffering was caused by various forms of poisoning. Lister, the son of a Quaker microscopist from Essex, had been present as a student at Liston's first operation under ether. He became professor of surgery at Glasgow, and investigated inflammation. He decided 'that the essential cause of suppuration in wounds is decomposition, brought about by the influence of the atmosphere upon blood or serum retained within them and, in the case of contused wounds, upon . . . the tissue destroyed by the violence of the injury'. Making use of the discovery by Louis Pasteur,* that fermentation depended on the presence in the air of living germs, he resolved to use carbolic acid to kill the latter, knowing that the treatment of sewage in that manner at Carlisle had been successful. Lister made a satisfactory operation on a compound fracture in this way for the first time in 1865. He also later used catgut or other ligatures to be absorbed by the body to tie up internal wounds, so preventing the risks of further bleeding inevitable in opening the body up anew. Lister first thought too of lifting limbs upwards prior to an operation so as to render them bloodless before tying a tourniquet, and also of the tubes for drainage used subsequently in treatment of operations. The use of steam and boiling water, instead of carbolic acid, followed.

These innovations transformed surgery. The first kidney was taken out in 1876. The first operation on the brain was in 1879. The first appendix was removed in 1886. The first gastric ulcer was operated upon in 1892. A lung was removed in 1892. Among innumerable new developments of the twentieth century, successful operations on the heart seem the most daring.

Lister's work would have been impossible without that of Louis Pasteur, a French genius, the son of a tanner from Franche Comté. Pasteur believed in hard work, above all, and considered that a good educational system should be based on the cult of great men. Patriotic

* See below, page 393.

and authoritarian, he read and admired Samuel Smiles's famous pamphlet *Self-Help* when recovering from a cerebral haemorrhage at the age of forty-six (8). Pasteur explained the mystery of fermentation as being due to the presence of microbes known as 'ferments'. When those are removed, he argued, no fermentation occurs. Similarly, when no germs are present, no inflammation occurs in wounds. The whole world of the micro-organism was thus miraculously, as it seemed, laid bare. At first, these organisms could not be identified. Good microscopes soon showed some of them. Some were dots in shape. Others looked like rods. Bacteria were the most remarkable of these organisms. A quarter of a million of them can sit upon a printed full stop.

Something no doubt was learned by Lister from the Hungarian doctor, Ignaz Semmelweiss who, in the 1850s, reduced deaths from puerperal fever in the maternity departments of the general hospitals at Vienna and Pest from 16% of mothers to 1%, by merely insisting that the surgeons washed their hands. The intellectual climate of the Habsburg Empire prevented Semmelweiss from developing his theories further. Driven out of Vienna by the jealousy of his professor, Semmelweiss was consigned to a lunatic asylum, where he died of neglecting a dirty wound on his right hand.

The work of Lister, Pasteur and the American inventors of anaesthesia was crowned by the development of the first X-ray in 1897, when a student at Harvard medical school, Walter Bradford Cannon, showed that internal organs could be photographed. The X-ray itself had been discovered by Wilhelm Röntgen, Professor of Physics at Würzburg in 1895 (he called them X-rays because he did not know what they were).

Following Pasteur's discovery that without life, there is no ferment, Robert Koch, a German bacteriologist, began to designate innumerable bacilli, including that of tuberculosis, in 1882. By 1914, most microbes which harm man and beast had been identified, even though some diseases remained unexplained: for example, were the various skin diseases perhaps living organisms? (They turned out to be made by viruses so small as to be indistinguishable through microscopes.) Some old diseases were tracked down to their sources: yellow fever was correctly attributed to the mosquito in 1902* and beri-beri to bad diet in 1901. The lonely dreamer, Surgeon-Major Ronald Ross, identified the mosquito as the bearer of malaria, while working in the British army hospital at Begumpett, leading to a long international campaign, managed by others, against that agile carrier. It was ultimately successful only after the discovery of the cheap anti-germ, DDT, which has controlled, though not eradicated, that ancient killer of the tropics.†

---

* See above, page 62.
† It seems that, as in most colonial wars, the American army in Vietnam lost more dead from malaria than they did from bullets (9).

About twenty years ago, it was widely believed that the breeding grounds of malaria had begun to be destroyed forever. But some mosquitoes have defied DDT and to-day no one believes that the eradication of this ancient killer is practicable in the immediate future. But huge demographic, and practical, effects have already occurred in the countries which have been even partially cleared.

Medical practice had also been helped by some innovations much more simple than these great discoveries. Despite the ideas of Hero and Galileo (who both saw the uses of such a thing), the clinical thermometer did not exist before the 1850s. The most modern one then was ten inches long, 'like an umbrella'. It took twenty minutes to register. Thomas Albert of Leeds made the first short thermometer in 1866. Then, injections of substances through hollow tubes into veins had occurred since the sixteenth century. But a hypodermic syringe was first used by Alexander Wood in Edinburgh only in 1853. The professional training of nurses began in the 1860s, after following the example of Florence Nightingale in the Crimean War. The whole paraphernalia of modern arrangements of health – ministers, child welfare centres, free distribution of milk to children, and health visits, soon followed.

The medical innovations of the twentieth century have been numerous, beneficial and often startling. Consider two matters: the use of antibiotics; and a more serious attitude to madness.

Alexander Fleming, a Scottish professor of bacteriology in London, made many contributions to the treatment of wounds in the First World War. He still, however, found himself having to argue about the desirability of removing dead tissues from wounds: it was as if Paré had never lived. He also pointed out (and Larrey had realised it long before) that most infections then occurred to soldiers *after* they had been admitted to base hospitals. In 1928, he made the observation that microbes were destroyed when in contact with a contaminating mould. The subsequent elaboration of the medical use of this discovery by Sir Howard Florey and Ernest Chain began the age of antibiotics.

As to madness, Soranus and other Greek writers laid down the principles for a humanitarian attitude. But, under Christianity, the mad, for many hundreds of years, were looked upon as possessed by devils. Lunatics were not killed, it is true. Instead, they were held for public show in institutions such as the Bethlehem Hospital (founded in 1247). The great Catalan philosopher, Juan Vives, first suggested, in the sixteenth century, a humane treatment. Johann Wyer wrote, about 1550, that witches were often merely individuals suffering from mental sickness. Paracelsus, a German physician of acute observation,* had

---

* Paracelsus, born Theophrastus Bombast von Hohenheim, worked in the mines of the Tyrol owned by the Fuggers before travelling through Europe to observe the 'book of nature'. His lectures at Basle in 1527 broke new ground by the mere fact that they were in German and were more than mere commentaries on Galen.

meantime first distinguished mania in two sections: neuroses, the products of nature; and psychoses, disorders deriving from fantasies unrelated to life. In the eighteenth century, Friedrich Mesmer, an Austrian fraud, claimed that he could draw madness out of people by a magnet. He told his patients that a hidden force within him enabled him to dominate others: 'animal magnetism'. With this, he had for a time great success. Psychosomatic illnesses can often, it seems, be cured by charlatans. His contemporary, Philippe Puriel, made a real contribution when, while physician at the lunatic asylum at Bicêtre, Paris, he freed lunatics from their chains. William Tuke of York did the same. Later, while therapy by shock, drugs and electricity was beginning to be used for the mad, Sigmund Freud in Vienna argued that the mind could be divided into several zones – the Ego, the Id, and the Libido. The first represented awareness of self. The second stood for the unconscious. The third signified emotional energy. He considered that events which were unacceptable to the first of these were driven by the second into the third. Freud also believed that all such events had to be accurately recalled to ensure good health. But they could not be so without using Freud's own radical methods of encouraging the patient to talk endlessly. Freud, probably the most widely cultivated scientist of our times, was determined to give a complete explanation of human life. His disciple, Adler, thought that desire for superiority was the driving force. Another pupil, Jung, believed that the libido might be revealed as, or driven to become, indiscriminately either love or hate or ambition (10). These views had been previously discussed, equally vigorously, by novelists such as Balzac, also without scientific proof. What seems certain is that Freud ignored the varieties in behaviour among people and the changing behaviour of people in different civilisations. With him, as with other heroes of the twentieth century, a greater knowledge of history might have made for less dogmatic views.*

These ideas brought medicine to the centre of intellectual life more than at any time before. Among their effects was to cause it to be supposed that wrongdoing is a disease, not a crime.

In the 140 years or so following the first use of anaesthesia, medical developments transformed the character of life in the 'advanced' countries. The transformation is obvious, the effect on population less so. A decline in the death rate has never been so important in increasing population as a rise in the birth rate. The changes in medical practice noticed above began to affect the society of Western Europe after the 1870s, just when those countries' birth rates were dropping. Marked

---

* In an inspired passage, de Tocqueville anticipated Freud's view of the importance of childhood: . . . 'We must watch the infant in his mother's arms; we must see the first images which the external world casts upon the dark mirror of his mind . . . we must hear the first words which awaken the sleeping powers of thought . . . if we would understand the prejudices, the habits, and the passions which will rule his life' (11).

improvements even in infant mortality did not occur till after the First World War. The rates of infant mortality for pre-industrial Europe as a whole may have been over 200 per thousand. The figures for 1850 to 1900 did not show much improvement: for example, England's rate was 151 per thousand in 1839 and 163 in 1899 (12). Falls in overall death rates were also slow. Of course, there has been some striking general improvement over a long stretch of time: the world as a whole had a death rate of about 30 to 40 per 1,000 each year in 1750, while, today, no European country, apart from Albania, has a rate higher than 12.8 per 1,000. China, India and Indonesia have rates of allegedly 15, 17 and 20, which are close to Western Europe's rate in 1914 (13). Only Africa has countries with rates over 20 per thousand.

It would be complacent to suppose that the history of disease shows an irresistible forward progress. Man has continued to spread many infections, which were once locally controlled. Leaving aside the era of ignorance which followed the collapse of antiquity, the industrialisation of the eighteenth and nineteenth centuries caused tuberculosis to become rampant in the new and overcrowded towns. It was apparently much the commonest cause of death in the mid-nineteenth century in industrial cities. The imperial adventures of the nineteenth century had some destructive consequences. Take, for example, an instance in the Congo. In the Senliki valley, there had been grassland for many hundreds of years. About 1900, the Belgian administrators began to encourage cultivation and the flourishing pastoral population moved down to the valley, establishing contact with tsetse flies, which, at that time unknown to science, were the bearers of sleeping sickness. In consequence, by 1920, the whole population had either fled, was dead, or in hospital (14). This disease of sleeping sickness has been rampant in Africa since the remotest times. Perhaps it was that to which the prophet Isaiah referred when he said 'the Lord shall hiss for the fly that is in the uttermost parts of the rivers of Egypt' (15). Its debilitating drowsiness, high fever and swelling of lymphatic glands were among the main reasons for Africa's failure to advance faster in the past towards sophistication. Another example of evils following contact with civilisation occurs in Tasmania. There, out of seven thousand aborigines in 1804, when the English arrived, there were only 300 in 1830 (16). By 1888, the Tasmanian aborigine was extinct (17).

Similar catastrophes occurred in South America. In 1903, the 6,000- to 8,000-strong Cayapo tribe in Brazil accepted a missionary, who deliberately sought to safeguard that people from civilisation and its discontents. But, by 1918, there were only 500 Cayapo left, for the missionary had unwittingly carried with him several sicknesses of the cities. In 1950, the tribe had disappeared (18). That event, of course, reflects the devastating effect of the first Spanish conquerors in America, and many other contacts between the innocent and the experienced.

Nervous diseases are also on the increase in the twentieth century in advanced countries. The conventional view is: 'the great pressure at which modern commercial and intellectual life is carried on tends to exhaust the nervous system'. Heredity, accidents, syphilis, alcoholism, and diabetes also all play a part. It is, however, impossible to say how far these complaints have really increased. Though Hippocrates knew of the anatomy of the brain in the fifth century BC, and, though some of his immediate successors made interesting reflections on insanity, little was done in this matter till the Enlightenment. The raising of the expectation of life from thirty years to seventy has obviously also affected nervous diseases. Probably it has been the main single reason for the increase in such ills.

Advanced countries have also encountered troubles which they did not have before. Thus the population of Britain, then the richest country in the world, began to suffer seriously from cavities in the teeth during the nineteenth century. The coming of toothbrushes and toothpaste had little effect. The damage was done by worsening diet. Sugar and cheap tinned milk did the harm. The late nineteenth century thus saw a big demand for false teeth. Bad teeth were responsible for the rejection of two-fifths of those who presented themselves for service as volunteers in the South African war (19). In the late nineteenth century, the lamentable use of machine-made bread previously noted, also caused an increase in constipation, piles, and cancer of the bowel. The connection between health and eating habits had been forgotten. But in 1289, Arnau de Vilanova had pointed out, in a manual of social hygiene, the importance of fresh air, exercise, baths, rest and vegetables (20).

With the removal of older diseases, cancer has become a major cause of death. Since it kills people in their middle or later life, it was less prominent a threat before the twentieth century. But it is not a new disease: Ramón Lull, the thirteenth century Catalan man of all talents, suffered a shock, causing his apotheosis from the temporal to the spiritual world, when a lady to whom he was attached showed him, to cool his ardours, an ulcerated cancer in her breast (21). Influenza, too, has at times threatened to become 'the last great plague'. At least ten major epidemics of influenza have occurred since the early eighteenth century, above all, probably, the epidemic of 1918–19 which killed at least twenty million people. Probably influenza derives from diseases of domestic animals and migratory birds. Noticed by Hippocrates, the word 'influenza' was invented in Italy in the fifteenth century to describe a disease which was believed to be 'influenced' by stars. Its virus was first isolated in 1933, but no adequate defence against it has yet been found (22).

The twentieth century has also seen two major attempts at the distortion of medicine for political purposes, one by the Russian government, the other by the German.

After 1917, Lenin gave instructions that the health of the nation's leaders could not be considered an affair of state. Those Platonic instructions were soon used to his own discomfort: Lenin passed the last years of his life as a prisoner of politically directed doctors. He himself was unable to communicate, after his heart attack, with the outside world. His last strength was consumed by a 'conspiracy of secretaries' (23). He could not logically complain: earlier, he had written an order to 'the organisational bureau of the communist party': 'I ask that Comrade Krizhirzanovsky be compelled to go, with Krasin, to Riga, there to spend, in a sanatorium or a private apartment, one month of cure and rest.' There was no reference to a medical authority. After 1964, the Russian government began sending its enemies to lunatic asylums, an extraordinary misuse of medicine for which there is, however, some precedent before the Revolution.

The Germans under Hitler were less sanctimonious. They were even more brutal. Prisoners were used as experimental subjects for every sort of medical enquiry. Even before 1939, the courts set up as a result of the 'Hereditary Health Law' had the power to order compulsory sterilisation. (24). The misuse of trust by doctors in concentration camps between 1939 and 1945 was a betrayal of the Hippocratic Oath which again has really no precedent.

The two regimes, fascist and communist, which have so misused medicine demand special attention, however, not only because of these disgraceful acts of misconduct, but because their leaders seem, the more they are examined, to be themselves men who perhaps would have been classed as mad any time in the eighteenth century. The pathological loathing of Jews felt by Hitler, the extraordinary suspicions of Stalin, the mental debilities shared by so many of their lieutenants, from Himmler to Yezhov, make it possible that those systems will be looked upon as instances in which the lunatic asylum became the centre of government in half the world. The full implications of the capture of power in powerful totalitarian states by men who might in other circumstances have been classed as mad have, however, been ignored in a world too preoccupied by ideology to recognise illness.

37

Population out of Control

The recurring attribution given for historical phenomena to population requires a little more consideration of that subject even though the matter has been discussed before.

The world's population in the late 1970s was 4.2 billion (4,200 million)

The very high rate of growth of the years 1960—73 has somewhat declined. The latest estimate is that the world's growth rate per year is 1.9%. In 2000 AD, it seems, the world's population may be anything between 5.8 billion and 6.6 billion. The rich countries are now experiencing a decline in fertility, but still the diminution in the growth is modest: the growth of population in the seventeenth and early eighteenth century was only 0.013 a year, and the 'high growth rate' after 1740 was still only 0.456 (1). Even so it seems possible that certain countries will feel threatened in future by shortages, rather than excesses of population. The German population is already in decline. At least one major European political party, the Gaullists, has a conscious policy for encouraging population. Indeed, the French government has encouraged the growth of population for many years continously since 1870, under the Third, Fourth and Fifth Republics, a policy upon which, as upon some other things, De Gaulle and Pétain saw eye to eye (2). Michel Debré, a sometime prime minister of France, has proposed a family vote which would give parents an additional vote for each child under voting age. Many Eastern European countries have tried to increase their birth rates by financial incentives, as well as by rigid laws on abortion.

It is sometimes suggested that the population of such and such a country 'will be so and so by, say, the year 2000.' A popular and professional prophet, Hermann Kahn, has, however, suggested that the population of the world will 'stabilise' between 10 and 50 billion (3). At least as good a prediction of stability to come might, however, have been made about the world having 500 million people at any time between the birth of Christ and 1500 AD. A decrease may be possible, or an involuntary stabilisation may occur, before even the figure of 10 billion

399

is reached. The decline of the population of Germany, both West and East, and in Austria, suggests that political systems make less difference, so far as population is concerned, than do national disasters. It is ironic to recall that a generation ago Germany's anxiety about room to live, *lebensraum*, was once greater than similar ideas felt anywhere else, and had an influence on those disasters. The British population is now one of the most balanced in the world, with the number of deaths approximately the same as that of births (4). Most of the world's richer countries seem to be making their way towards that condition, for in them there has been a decline in the rate of births since about 1880, with exceptional eras such as the 'baby boom' immediately after the Second World War. The fundamental explanation of this change may have been a change in the economic value of children, from being a source of income in agricultural countries to an expense in industrial countries. The economic transformation of these countries has been accompanied apparently by a decline in religion, universal education, and an approach to equality of women – a change which has not been completed.

The first determining characteristic of the way we live now is that until the twentieth century, indeed until the 1970s in some countries, there was always a possibility of emigration. The era of colonisation and adventure-seeking which began in Europe in a small way in the sixteenth century, and came to a climax in the early twentieth century (in 1910 a quarter of the population of the USA had been born outside that country) seems now to have ended in the old sense of those words.

Until recently, the encouragement of emigration was the most effective, even the only, policy towards population. Greek colonisation in the fifth century BC, the German expansion east, beginning in the eleventh century AD; the settlement of Castile at the same time; those were responses to the pressure of population, even though some of the more famous emigrations derived from deliberate policies towards minorities; for example, the flight of 200,000 Jews from Spain in the fifteenth century (5). 300,000 Moors also left Spain in the sixteenth century (6) and 200,000 Huguenots France, in the seventeenth (7).

Emigration to the Americas stands apart from all others in scale. Though only 100,000 Spaniards went there in the sixteenth century (perhaps less than the number of Frenchmen who emigrated to Spain at that time) (8), and a mere 750,000 Europeans of all nations went to the Americas in the seventeenth and eighteenth centuries (9), nine million or more Africans arrived as slaves between 1492 and 1870 (10). The number of Europeans who emigrated in the nineteenth and twentieth centuries exceeds all precedents: 17 million left Britain between 1825 and 1920 (65% to the US, 15% to Canada, 11% to Australia, and 5% to South Africa). 9 million left Italy between 1875 and 1925 (though some returned about 1910 to revive the Italian South). 6 million Germans, 4 million Austro-Hungarians, 2½ million Russians, 4 million Spaniards, and over a million Portuguese all left Europe for new worlds. Only the French stayed at home, and themselves received immigrants, on a short-term basis mostly, including Belgians to work in sugar beet fields and 'child-rich' Poles to work in mines (11). Thus the New World and, even more completely, Australasia were won for the Europeans (12). So on the surface was Siberia, though the Russians who went there in the nineteenth century were far fewer in number than the Europeans who travelled to America.

During the 1920s, these places of refuge or opportunity vanished. A generation previously, the US had encouraged immigration. Up till 1900, there was always unappropriated land for whoever wanted it. Then, in the 1880s, came the first restrictions. There was initially a ban on Chinese immigration in 1882 and on contract labour in 1885. Then, with two laws, of 1921 and 1924, the US restricted all immigration thenceforth in proportion to the nations represented in the US since 1910 and then since 1890. The Japanese were banned, while the total immigration was restricted to 150,000 annually. Britain had a right to 43% and Poland to only 4% (13). The US laws derived from: fear of unemployment; criticism of those born in, or descended from those born in, Germany during the world war; and dread that the old US institutions would be ruined by too many Jews and central Europeans. These laws shattered the dynamism of old America, which had been built on the idea of ceaseless immigration and ceaseless expansion. Meantime, the old slave trade from Africa to the Americas had also come to an end, for reasons in which economic and moral calculation were nicely balanced.* Subsequent laws have altered the character of the immigration. 200,000 'displaced' persons (mostly Germans expelled from East Europe by Russia) were permitted entry to the US in 1948. A law of 1965 fixed the annual quota at 170,000, with no national subdivisions, and allowing specially qualified people beyond the limits (14). Major catastrophes, such as, in particular, the Cuban revolution of 1959 or the Hungarian revolution of 1956 caused other large immigrations. All in all, 16 million Germans were expelled from eastern Europe in 1945–48 (15), while the 500,000 Cubans who left home between 1959 and 1969 were more than those who emigrated there from Spain between 1511 and 1959.

The legal but large-scale emigration of unskilled and apolitical poor is now probably at an end for good, never to be repeated, unless, improbably, some new place really offers an attractive haven. Perhaps, though, artificial cities on the oceans or artificial moons should not be excluded.†

* The end of the East African slave trade to Asia was longer delayed. Its diminution, however, was assisted by British naval action. For example, the Sultan of Zanzibar closed the big slave market at Zanzibar in 1873 under threat of a naval bombardment. The internal slave trade in Africa continued.

† A mining colony on the moon has already been proposed. On the face of it, it is not an inviting prospect.

On the other hand, illegal immigration from poor to rich countries seems likely to be one of the major concerns of the future everywhere — particularly in the US, but also Venezuela, Italy, Britain, Germany: anywhere where there is a free economy, an easily learned language and a liberal political society. Finally, the chances are that the world's whole attitude to the problem of refugees from political oppression, or the threat of it, or simply from catastrophe, will be fundamentally altered by the vast upheavals caused by the collapse of traditional society in Indo-China: a tragedy too close to current politics to consider with serenity in this book, but one which will at least destroy any illusions that the days of mass movements of population are over.

The second extraneous fact limiting the growth of population has been the coming of birth control. The idea had, of course, been discussed before industrialisation. But first we should take notice of the Reverend Thomas Malthus. Son of a believer in the perfectibility of man who had been a correspondent of Rousseau's, Malthus became a fellow of Jesus College, Cambridge. He voted to have the poet Coleridge sent down for not paying his bills. In his *Essay on population*, published in 1798, Malthus argued that, while the supply of food increases in an arithmetical ratio, population does so in a geometric one. Population could only be checked, he believed, by vice or by misery. In a later edition of his book in 1803, he toned this judgement down, and recognised 'the prudential check' of self restraint.

This work was much read. When it was translated into German, a certain Professor Weinhold was so alarmed that he suggested a chastity belt should be forcibly applied to all unmarried males who did not have the means to support children. Another German, Robert Mohl, proposed that all states should repeal measures which encouraged early marriage, and the creation of propaganda on the subject of prudence. Malthus, meantime, was critical of contraception: 'I should always particularly reprobate any artificial and unnatural modes of checking the population, both on account of their immorality and their tendency to remove a necessary stimulus to industry' (16). But the industrious radical, Francis Place, a tailor with fifteen children, soon suggested that methods of control were necessary, since moral restraint seemed so inadequate. Nothing happened, however. So nineteenth-century Europe experienced the greatest increase in population that it has ever known.

The main argument in Malthus's book has, since that time, been disproved by events. 'There has only been one man too many on this earth,' said Proudhon, 'and that man was Malthus' (17). The conservative economist, Nassau Senior, pointed out in 1828 that 'food always increased faster than population. I admit the *abstract tendency* of population to increase so as to press on the means of subsistence. I deny the *habitual* tendency. I believe the tendency to be the reverse' (18). And so it has turned out: in the 1970s, food increased by 30 million tons a year. Of these, 22 million only are taken up by the growth of population (19). The 57 million inhabitants of Britain of 1979 are, on the whole, incomparably better fed than the 11 million of 1798. But there is serious doubt whether these conditions will continue.

Some claim to be influenced upon these matters by Karl Marx, whose views on population are, however, neither consistent nor interesting. At one point in *Capital* for example, he argued that 'misery produced population' (20). At another, he said 'population is stagnant when the working day is very long'. But the increase of population was specially marked in Marx's day − above all, in the two countries where he was born (Germany) and where he lived most of his life (England). Marx was born in 1818 and died in 1883. The population of Germany between those dates rose from about 25 million to about 60 million.

That of Britain increased between the same dates from 20 million to 40, without counting the many millions who, from both countries, emigrated in what David Glass called 'almost epidemic proportions'. (21)

In both those countries, as elsewhere, the rate of growth of population slowed as the working day became shorter: exactly the contrary to what Marx said. If industrialisation had been as bad as Marx implied, the demographic 'explosion' of the eighteenth and nineteenth centuries would scarcely have happened. Then, at the time of the Napoleonic wars, English cotton manufacturers employed only 2% of the labour force. The industrialised villages to which Marx paid such attention also showed a greater excess of births than did agricultural villages (22). It is thus understandable that countries whose fates are determined by Marx have no policies, and indeed no real attitudes at all, towards one of the obviously important matters of the present.

Against the muddled preaching by Marx and Malthus, Annie Besant, daughter of an Irish businessman and the separated wife of a clergyman, with Charles Bradlaugh, a republican and atheist, tried to redistribute one of the old pamphlets on birth control by Francis Place which had been banned fifty years before. They were charged with publishing obscene literature, tried, but found innocent. That verdict gave impetus to the idea of education about control of births. By the 1920s, there was a national movement under way in England under the inspiration of Marie Stopes, a lecturer in palaeo-botany at University College, London. By 1930, clinics had been set up for the planning of families. A role similar to that of Marie Stopes was played in the USA by Margaret Sanger, a midwife in New York, where her clients were trying incompetently to discover a means of spacing out their children. She travelled to France, gained there some understanding of such matters, and founded a clinic in New York for advice on the control of births, in 1916. She was persecuted but, in 1937, laws banning the sale of methods for the control of births were abrogated. Contraception began to be studied in medical schools. The vulcanisation of rubber soon made possible new methods of contraception. In the 1950s, Dr Gregory Pincus, a professor at Boston University, began to develop his pill which prevents ovulation and it came to be used on a mass scale in the 1960s.

The fact that, because of the 'pill' and other methods, people can now make love without fear of conception seems, along with the prevention of widespread outlets for legal emigration, to be one of the really decisive changes in the history of the twentieth century. Despite some anxieties about the medical effects of this 'pill', these facts mark out this century from all others, whether or no particular methods of contraception are effective. The technology of birth control is still imperfect but richer countries are fast approaching what Charles Westhoff rather optimistically terms 'the "perfect" contraceptive society in which there will be no unwanted births' (23). Meantime, probably as a result, the number of marriages has declined in richer countries and particularly of women who marry young. Partly this is a reflection of couples living together without (or before) marriage. In 1976, a million couples in the US or 2% of all couples, were believed to be unmarried, while in Sweden that percentage may be as high as 12%. A third factor bearing on population in the twentieth century is the increasing number of women in 'prime child-bearing years' who are working. The change here has been remarkable and recent: less than two fifths of women of that age were working in 1960 in the US. Three fifths were working in 1977. Other countries are far behind this proportion. Most women in rich countries earn about 60% as much as the average man earns. Plainly, the old purpose of marriage by which a woman offers her childbearing and domestic services in return for economic security is being transformed.

All these innovations in the control of birth were introduced, in the first place, as a result of private initiative, against the desires of governments. Plato would have regarded Annie Besant highly: Gladstone, who was educated on the classics, abhorred her. Since 1945, only Japan, after her defeat in 1945 (which showed that any further expansion of population would be very difficult), has, among free countries, successfully launched a government-sponsored eugenic programme. The discipline of the Japanese people, the hierarchic character of the society, the elevation of the idea of work above the idea of family, as well as the memory of defeat, and the existence of an already large market of 110 million people, have combined to make possible a successful and humane policy on the subject of population. In 1957, 80% of pregnancies in Japan were apparently aborted (24).

The brutal totalitarian states of the twentieth century also embarked upon policies of population: abortion, contraception, and easy divorce were the three impulses of early communist attitudes to population. The sexes were announced as equal in law. This careless rapture soon came to an end. In 1936, abortion and contraception were alike forbidden. In addition, the old Russian practice prohibiting emigration was reinforced. By 1944, the free association in Russia of men and women in common law marriages was no longer recognised. Divorce became much harder. Medals were given to mothers of twelve children while paternity summonses were forbidden because of the threat that such things might pose to the family. Since 1945, marriage has become as important a pillar of society in communist Russia as in any nineteenth century Russian provincial town and, in recent years, the East European communist countries have, in the interests of increasing population, increased the rigour of their rules against abortion (25).

These changes have been defended on the grounds that, in the 1920s, the priority seemed to be the need to destroy the bourgeois family, but that, since the 1930s, more people have been needed to man the frontiers of Russia against Fascism and 'imperialism'.

Both Fascist Italy and Nazi Germany had policies for controlling population. In Italy, Mussolini began with a ban on that emigration (except to the Italian colonies) which had previously relaxed the tensions of liberal Italy. The policy was copied from Russia and was carried out for reasons of prestige. The Russian ban itself was introduced at first to prevent the swelling of the size of the potentially conspiratorial emigrant colony. Actually, Mussolini's decision merely anticipated the decision taken in the US to limit the annual intake of immigrants. Despite that, Italian legislation was introduced to favour the large family and, in 1927, Mussolini launched a campaign for a high birth rate, recalling that the decline of the Roman Empire had been due to a fall in population: Italy's most precious possession, he said, was her 'demographic vitality' (26). Italy's imperial adventures and her conflicts with the Slavs in the Adriatic could thereby be underpinned by an increase in the numbers of Italians. Earlier, in direct contrast, Italian imperialism had been justified by the need to employ a large population: precursors of Fascism, such as Enrico Corradini, thought it desirable to try to find a 'national home' for all Italians who wanted to emigrate — and, in 1913, nearly a million Italians did indeed emigrate (27).

On paper, this programme of Mussolini's was successful. The population of Italy under twenty-two years of Fascism increased by 18%, while decadent France, static at about 38 million between 1861 and 1922, still stood at 39 million in 1945. On the other hand, the rise in the Italian population at this time was due not to an increase in the birth rate (it fell between 1922 and 1944 from 30.8 per thousand to 18.3 per thousand) but, unusually, to a fall in the death rate made possible by better medicine and, in particular, better care of babies.

Hitler's Germany learned from Italy, as Italy learned from Russia. The Germans also had, in the early twentieth century, a contradictory attitude towards what, on the one hand, they felt about the size of the population — too large and therefore, demanding *lebensraum* — and their actual policies on the subject: the Nazi regime in 1933 introduced decrees encouraging births, such as loans to young married couples, special allocations to families of five, and the repression of abortion. These latter policies were successful. Unlike what happened in Italy, the birth rate increased, from 14.7 per 1,000 in 1933 to 20.4 in 1939 (28): figures which Germany had exceeded regularly before 1914 and even, to begin with, during the despised years of Weimar, but would never approach again.

One other country under the direction of a determined tyrant has adopted a policy on the subject of population: China. To begin with, Mao Tse-tung admittedly followed what seemed to be Marxist ortho-doxy: that is, an inactive policy, supposing that an adequate social policy should be able to deal with any conceivable increase in popula-tion. In 1953, however, a movement towards the limitation of births was initiated. In 1957, contraception was allowed, but in 1958, the policy described as 'the great leap forward' in agriculture caused a return to demographic neglect, sanctioned by orthodoxy. Afterwards, a number of measures were adopted which were designed to limit the population of China. Marriage, for example, is only now officially sanctioned at the age of thirty. But the Chinese government has been reticent on these matters. No census has been published since 1953. Even then, it was said that the work of collecting statistics only occupied three weeks. Thus Chinese statistics seem less methodical in the twentieth century than they were under the Han dynasty (29).

The unprecedented growth in the world's population since the eight-eenth century has given rise to a widespread generalised anxiety that the world is over-populated. Thus the western world seems relieved when it hears of measures introduced to reduce the growth of popula-tion in China and Japan, or when it hears that German and Russian population rates of growth are falling, or even, as in the case of Germany, falling absolutely. But the fact is that, as Charles Westhoff put it, 'the record of population projections is not a happy one' (30). It seems very likely indeed that, by the year 2000 AD, though we may still feel alarmed about the overall growth of the world's population, Euro-peans, and perhaps North Americans and perhaps European Russians will have begun to be even more alarmed at the decline in their own fertility. Here the communist countries of Eastern Europe and Russia have already manipulated legislation to favour high birth rates — as yet with very limited success.

One solution to this problem might be a policy of encouraging further immigration, as most European countries did in the 1960s and early

1970s. But these immigrants have seemed to pose social and political problems. European countries worried about the future of their national identity, because of a shortage of births, are not likely to interest themselves in recruiting black or brown people to fill the gaps which they detect in their labour force. No country has ever yet chosen immigration for overtly demographic reasons, though it is possible that, in the twenty first century, with 'zero growth' they will do so.

Moralists worry more about divorce than they do about population. Here, as in so many matters, history has a few soothing lessons. At the time when statistics begin to have a basis at all, in the sixteenth and seventeenth centuries, early death meant that few marriages lasted more than about fifteen to twenty years. Today, even in the US or Sweden (where divorce affects perhaps half the marriages) most marriages last longer than that. In the past, as Lawrence Stone points out, marriages were shortened by death, whereas they are today by divorce. Only in the nineteenth century did a combination of a decline in mortality and a respect for the Church's teaching make possible marriages in Western Europe and North America longer-lasting on average than they have ever been before or since (31). In 1850, in France, the average marriage lasted twenty-four years and two months (32). Furthermore, after a brief period of fashionable hostility, in the 1920s, the family, though it has scarcely recovered quite its old cohesion, is still a powerful institution. Emancipation of women, the distinction of business from the family, compulsory education, the flight to often distant towns of grown-up children all contributed to what appeared to be the 'crisis of the family'. It became fashionable for couples to become engaged without even telling their parents. 'Free love' exerted a brief vogue. New constitutions, however, usually guarantee the 'rights of families'. The universal declaration of human rights of 1948 even asserted the family to be 'natural and fundamental'. Polygamy and concubinage are on the decrease even in Arab countries and in China. In socialist countries, no one has seriously suggested the expensive stratagem of replacing the mother by the State. Juvenile crime has been diagnosed, probably correctly, as deriving primarily from an unsettled family life. In countries which have experienced socialism and those which have not, parents still wish to leave their children their property. All recognise that the family has a part to play in education and 'family allowances' are well established. Despite experiments with communes and 'group living', the family, since 1945, has had a new lease of life, perhaps because both the television and the telephone, in different ways, keep families closer together, more probably because the state's covetous hands have extended over other institutions (33). De Tocqueville put it simply, 'as long as family feeling is kept alive, the opponent of oppression is never alone' (34).

As people live longer, curiously enough, there has been increasingly a cult of youth. Almost all the new radical movements, 'left' or 'right' of the nineteenth and twentieth centuries began, like 'young Italy', as revolts of youth. Mazzini and his friends, for example, considered men over forty to be too old to be regenerated, and too inclined to temporise. The futurists of pre-1914 Europe believed that parliament should be replaced by 'a committee of twenty specialists over thirty years old' (35). When the Nazis entered the Reichstag in 1932, the average age of that parliament dropped ten years. 82% of Nazi party members were under forty in 1934. The same emphasis on youth characterised communist movements in the 1920s and 1930s. One attraction of all these movements was that of an immediate revolution which gave students leaders and young unemployed, Nazi or Marxist, immediate access to power. But there is also that attraction of the fellowship of struggle, 'the compact columns . . . waving flags, eyes looking straight ahead, the beat of drums and the singing' which, in the words of George Mosse, constituted the appeal to the Hitler youth (36).

Finally, among political movements which have affected population, there has been the women's liberation movement. The movement has been led by high-minded and determined people. On the face of it, the changes have been less than once seemed promised. Women have done heavy work since time immemorial. Women, with children, played an absolutely decisive part in the cotton factories in the early days of the Industrial Revolution. Women workers in industry also set off the train of strikes which led to the revolution in Petrograd in 1917, in the estimate of Marc Ferro (37). In the upper class in the West women certainly had an inferior status in the past; but, Lawrence Stone reminds us, the state of affairs among artisans was less clear: women were part for many hundreds of years of a large economic unit comparable to the crew of a ship (38). Even in sixteenth century Spain women could be members of the Mesta if they owned sheep (39). No modern continent has found its politics so dominated by women as was Europe in the era of Catherine de' Medici, Elizabeth I and Mary Queen of Scots. Europe in the fifteenth century had many determined queens from Isabella in Spain to Margaret of Anjou in England (40). Furthermore, the modest preparations for allowing women more advantages in public and professional life in a few Western democratic countries have had no echo in two-thirds of the world. Nor have there yet been any female dictators in the west nor trade union leaders. Equal pay for equal work in rich countries seems difficult to ensure. Primogeniture still seems rootedly fixed in the imaginations of many Anglo-Saxon families: such a thing was unheard of in Rome, where a man carefully divided all he had between all his children, male and female.

Still, the women's movement so far has secured two benefits: the first is that educational opportunity for boys and girls is fairly equal in most countries; the second is that ambitious women can now seek their own fortunes in a limited number of Western countries without needing a powerful husband or father to help them. Let us ensure that the general opportunities for individual achievement are not allowed to close just as women have reached this much-to-be-desired position.

38

Urban Man

The age of industry transformed the place of living of the majority of the world's population. This was seen most evidently in the growth of citities. Half the population of England was urban in 1851: a predicament never before found in a great nation. By 1900, agriculture only occupied ten per cent of the English population.

The rise in population, rather than industrialisation, created modern life. Urbanisation is not the same thing as industrialisation. Egypt, for example, is now as urbanised as Switzerland, more so (on the basis of the percentage of the population living in cities of 100,000 or more) than France, but not nearly so industrialised (1).

The fact that people live in cities has often been regretted as if it were in itself a source of major decline in the quality of life. Of this, it is possible to be sceptical. Urban life makes for easier access to schools and to professions linked to literacy (2). In every country in the world where illiteracy exists, and where statistics are reliable, those who live in cities are more likely to be able to read and write than those who live in the country. Nor is it wise to feel nostalgic about lost rural serenity. The Elizabethan village was, says Lawrence Stone, as often as not a 'place filled by malice and hatred, the only unifying bond being the occasional outbreak of mass hysteria . . . to harry and persecute the local witch' (3). Village water was also often impure.

The Industrial Revolution found the world's population living in wood, mud, brick and stone. It is leaving it in cement, glass and steel. In the eighteenth century, there were places where living conditions were far worse than those which obtained in the days of Babylon. Even in England, in the early nineteenth century, there were many houses with mud floors, many turf houses with squatters (4). Some farm labourers lived in one-roomed hovels, sometimes below ground, usually damp. In Russia, many houses showed scarcely any improvement on the huts of hunters of the days before 10,000 BC (5). One of the first coherent observers of Russian life, Radischev, described a typical house between St Petersburg and Moscow in about 1770 thus: 'the upper half of the four walls and the whole ceiling were covered with soot; the floor was full of dust and covered with dirt at least two inches thick; the oven [was] without a chimney but their best protection against the cold; and smoke filled the hut every morning, winter and summer. Window holes . . . admitted a dim light at noon time; [there were also to be seen] two or three pots . . . a wooden bowl and round trenchers . . . a table, hewn with an axe, which they scrape clean on holidays . . . a trough to feed pigs and calves, if there are any . . . If they are lucky, a barrel of *kvass* [the drink made from fermented bread, much drunk by Russian peasants] that tastes like vinegar and, in the yard, a bath house* in which the cattle sleep if people are not steaming in it' (6). To those who lived in such places, the 'rough brick houses' of Babylon would have seemed a luxury. Yet, of course, those Russians had the countryside in which to breathe; and it is not clear beyond all doubt that they would have preferred to have lived in the London of the 1880s with what for Matthew Arnold seemed 'its unutterable external ugliness' (7). It also seems possible that half the population of Asia and Africa still live in conditions worse than those which pertained in eighteenth century England.

The first impact of the Industrial Revolution on cities and on building everywhere, was to increase the quantity of brick used. Unless the building was of exceptional importance, stone was only used in regions where it could easily be quarried. That ruled out much of England and the east of the US. Wood was also scarce because of the need for it in shipyards and in charcoal burning, or because the country concerned had already used up the forests. Subsequently, John Nash, a Welsh architect, popularised anew the ancient practice of covering inferior brickwork with the stucco which has subsequently marked so much of northern European architecture.

Nash was still at the height of his popularity when, in 1824, Portland cement was invented, (at Wakefield by a builder, Joshua Aspdin, and given that name since it was intended as a substitute for Portland stone). Cement came into general use after 1850, with big demands made for it for sewers in modern cities. Cast iron was also added to possible new building materials, first to support columns, then to replace wooden beams, later still to give large frames for large buildings, as in the new apartment blocks of New York. Reinforced concrete (cement with steel or iron rods embedded, with the strength of steel and stone combined) began to be introduced from the 1850s, after Edouard Coignet showed that such material could be laid under fifteen feet of earth, for sewers. Concrete bridges also began to be made (8). Subsequently, steel enabled large buildings, and bridges, to be prefabricated. The most striking consequence was the skyscraper, the demand for which derived from the rise of land values in New York and Chicago,

---

*Most Russian villages had a bath house, visited by most people once a week.

about 1880. Wrought iron skyscrapers could be built to the height of fourteen floors, but they had to have greater thickness at the base than at the top. The steel frame could be raised almost to any height without an increase in the size at the bottom. Thereafter, the function of walls was only to give privacy and shelter. The first steel skyscraper went up in Chicago in 1890, in New York in 1894. There were twenty-nine there by 1900. Europe, however, was restrained. It was only after 1945 that steel framed skyscrapers began to be built there. London was earlier saved from these developments by the theory, which turned out unfortunately to be an illusion, that the ground under it was soft.

Long before that, another invention had made the skyscraper a practical, as opposed to a theoretical, possibility: the hydraulic lift was devised in 1854 by Elisha Graves Otis, a Vermont inventor with many other achievements to his credit, such as a steam plough, a steam oven, and a turbine water wheel. Otis's elevator worked by steam and had safety appliances. The passengers were carried in a case with pawls which were forced by springs to engage in ratchets at the side should the rope fail. A hydraulic lift reached to the top of the Eiffel Tower. An electric version was soon introduced. The curious artistic sect who called themselves futurists later conceived of houses as being built with lifts and no stairs – an idea which palls now that futurists are men of the past.

By the time of the futurists, about 1910, prefabricated building of houses had indeed been started in, for instance, Chicago, where balloon frames, roofs, floors, walls were supplied in factories and put together by amateurs. Ready-made doors and windows were fitted into the prefabricated structures. This was the first concession to mechanisation in a business which had until then been resistant to it.

Then there was glass. Optical glass had been improving throughout the eighteenth century. Most glass made for windows, however, consisted of small round sheets, with bulls' eyes in the middle, constructed from a globe of glass attached by molten metal to an iron rod. But plate glass had been achieved in France in the days of Louis XIV (the Hall of Mirrors in Versailles was an early use of that). From the 1770s, plate glass could be made by steam power (9). That transformed the history of the window. In the nineteenth century, the demand for window glass in Europe, with so much new building, exceeded all expectations. 'Great windows open to the south' (in Yeats's formulation) could be easily and cheaply built while, in a self-confident and homogeneous society, robberies were relatively rare. Subsequently, the use of glass, with iron and steel, enabled engineers to make both roofs and walls transparent (10).

But it was not only technology which made the modern cities. As suggested earlier, those conglomerations could not have survived had their supplies not come from old methods of grinding corn, in local windmills or water mills, baking it at home, bringing meat on foot, and gaining milk from suburban cattle keepers (11). Railways, refrigeration and tins were needed to ensure the food of the new urban millions.

The modern city saw, too, changes in the commercial exploitation not only of these foods but of everything saleable. In the seventeenth century, some public markets and producers' shops dating from the Middle Ages were converted into specialised shops under continuous operation. Kromm invented the department store even before the revolution in Paris, with several thousand employees. Soon after 1815, the modern shop came into being, with fixed prices, low margins of profit, commissions on sales for the staff, sales at intervals and a social security system for the employees (12). This was developed in France with the Bon Marché, directed by Boucicaut, the Magasin du Louvre, managed by Chauchard, or the Samaritaine, and in Germany too after 1830 (13). Street lamps and lighted windows also caused a change in the mid-nineteenth century, as did the department store in the US, invented in 1862 in New York by Alexander Stewart, an Irish protestant in origin, but brought to its culmination by John Wanamaker of Philadelphia, who began life as an errand boy and first thought up the one-price system, the marked prices in clear figures, and the money-back guarantees, which characterise shopping in the twentieth century. Mail orders began in 1872 with Montgomery Ward in Chicago, and the chain store with Frank W. Woolworth's 'Five-and-Ten Cent' store at Utica, New York in 1879 (14).* These innovations led to the swift end of the old fairs as major commercial enterprises. Even in Germany, fairs were in decline after 1840 (15).

All capital cities grew at the expense of the rest of the country. Louis XIV tried to check the growth of Paris six times without success. Even before the Revolution, many provincial printing presses and other critical small businesses closed down in France (16). In the nineteenth century, similar efforts to cut the size of cities were even more unsuccessful. In democracies and tyrannies alike, all cities grew. Big cities grew faster than others. In the US in the nineteenth century, cities of over 8,000 inhabitants grew five times faster than the country as a whole (17). The reason was not so much the rise in population in the towns themselves, though that could not be ignored, as the influx from country-born workers. In 1851, out of 3,336,000 people aged twenty or over living in London, less than half had been born there (18). Much the same was true of New York, Chicago, Barcelona, Essen and Lyons, or other large English or Welsh towns, and soon would be of Moscow. Then, as the masses moved into the centre of the cities, the leaders of the society concerned moved out, living more and more in suburbs, often with separate municipal authorities, but linked with the city to

* When Woolworth died in 1919, he had 1,000 'five-and-ten cent stores' in the US and 75 in Britain.

which those same leaders began to 'commute', in order to work, travelling in daily, on horse or in coaches, before the railways, or the cars.

On the whole, the growth of the new industrial cities, particularly in Britain, denoted a major failure of imagination. In most such cities, there were, indeed in some cases there still are, long and dreary streets, street after street with the same formations, the same alleys filled with rubbish and the same lack of open spaces for children to play in. Little effort was made to plan the pattern of the streets according to sun and wind (19). The more respectable quarters, where 'artisans' or clerks lived, were almost as depressing as the straightforwardly shabby slums.

These cities were products of the managers of the railway, the factory and the coal mine. The slums served those institutions. They had, to begin with, no social heritage. All was subordinate to the factory concerned, including public services (police, fire services and water services, not to speak of hospitals, food inspection, education and church which came later). The early factory would usually be set on the best site, on the river, for it needed water for its boilers, for cooling and for dyeing, and it also provided the worst waste (thus ruining the bathing and fishing). The factory chimneys, magnificent though they were, polluted air and water. The railway was often driven into the centre of the town, severing such natural arteries as the place might once have had. Huge piles of waste metal stood untended for years. Workers' houses were built up against the 'works' and so were often bathed in dust. In many pioneering cities of the Industrial Revolution, back-to-back houses opened on to a yard and that meant that two rooms out of four had no direct daylight at all. Lavatories were inadequate. Manchester in 1845 had 33 per 1,000 inhabitants – a proportion which would now be thought bad in a prison. Rubbish was often thrown into the street. Cellars might sometimes house pigs, a sad reminder of happier rural days, but there was also a large human cellar population. Bedbugs, lice, fleas, rats and flies bred in the plaster walls. Plumbing was rotten, drains open, water bad. Even so, the building trades employed more men than any other profession. Reformers concentrated upon the need for good prisons and a state monopoly of sewage and failed to devote adequate attention to how people were housed. As Lewis Mumford points out, the nineteenth century was an age of rising nationhood, but the municipal councils did not rise to the occasion and built town halls only (20). London, for example, was ill managed in the mid-nineteenth century: some seventy-eight 'vestries' shared local power, their nomination varying from co-option to election, and they had control of everything, from drains to poverty. Only in 1888 was there a Local Government Act which created a London district council to cover the whole city (21).

Several things need to be said. First, the changes in the size of populations were unprecedented. Second, the worst conditions were to be found in the boom towns, then as now. Third, horrible though mid-nineteenth century London no doubt was, with its fog, tuberculosis and rickets, it began to be radically improved from the middle of the century and, for all its evils, the expectation of life was higher than it had been a century before. Fourth, the errors in planning showed a failure to think carefully enough what should be the role of the State. Victorian reformers in both the US and Britain, as well as elsewhere, insisted upon a role for the State in such things as the postal service which could have been well managed by private companies. They sometimes neglected to give a role to the State, or the community, in matters such as town planning where the commodity at stake was finite such as land. Fifth, when all is considered, many slum cities of the nineteenth century were able to achieve a greater humanity than has proved possible in the futuristic cities of the twentieth century.*

In comparison, cities in countries which were slow to industrialise seemed oases of peace. Vienna in 1848 still had walls and a moat. Green slopes lay between it and the suburbs. At night, the gates were closed. Even during the day, they were sometimes locked in the event of disturbances. The workers of Vienna lived outside the city, while students, nobility and middle classes lived inside (22). In general, cities which industrialised later had better services than those which did so early. Still, benefits in the form of better shops, department stores, internal city transport and vast numbers of salesmen followed industrialisation everywhere, and Vienna, like other such traditional cities was the battleground of class wars as much as more modern ones.

Modern cities of the poorer world, from South America to Africa, are also all surrounded by shanty towns so neglected as to make nineteenth century industrial cities seem prosperous. Africa, for example, has seen a more rapid industrialisation than anywhere in the world, specially confusing to those who live there since there is no real urban tradition on which to build. Instead, there is a juxtaposition of foreign investment with a population the majority of which are tribal people full of traditional fears, loyalties and prejudices. Usually populated by squatters, the urban areas of, say, Mexico, India, and Egypt, represent the most complicated of modern political problems. Still, the cities of Europe in the nineteenth century were marked by riots and, on the whole, are now at least politically tranquil and perhaps, when the pressure of population in Mexico City or Caracas has been alleviated, the intensity of their difficulties may diminish too. But will that happen?

It is hard to do other than compare unfavourably the lot of those who live in such new cities at present with those who lived, say, in Merthyr when it was the largest town of the British iron trade in 1820. Tough,

* As I put the final touches to this chapter, I notice, and cannot help recording, that an exhibition commemorating these 'satanic mill' towns is being organised by 'Save Britain's Heritage'.

rough, overworked though the life there must have been, its population, when its four iron works were the largest in the world, was still only 20,000. The city was in easy walking distance of green valleys. There has always been some safety in such relatively small numbers.

Though, in many modern cities, history seems forgotten or remote, the past often remains close in spirit. A comparison between the towns of France and of Britain makes that point clearly. Freed from the likelihood of invasion, England is a country whose towns have outgrown the need for walls long ago. Invaded four times since 1800, France held back her cities at the walls where she could. Thus, where London sprawled, Paris grew upwards. In Britain, only Edinburgh has a tradition of blocks five, six or ten stories high. Then, in nineteenth century politics on the continent, unlike the eighteenth, there were numerous internal troubles. Barricades were easier to put up in old cities. Most streets were only six to eight feet wide with tall buildings. The pattern of a mediaeval town life seemed to impose itself in Germany even during industrialisation. Under the Nazis, the mediaeval city of Nuremberg was a national symbol. The party rallies were deliberately held there in order to create a mood of national renaissance as well as one of nostalgia (23).

Another tendency in the life of cities was to begin with more marked in the US. In the 1950s, in all but one (Los Angeles) of the largest US cities, there was a decrease in population. Only in the South in what were, in effect, new cities (Dallas and Houston, in Texas, or Birmingham, in Alabama) did the urban population keep growing. Yet the countryside also continued to lose population. In place of both, the suburbs became, in the 1960s, the preferred living place of the successful family, first in the US, then elsewhere. The political consequences of this have been quite negative for cities.

In most countries, capital cities have become more and more important, as the pretensions of governments have grown. Networks of communication radiate from capitals often, as with airways, to serve the nation's bureaucrats, rather than the vital members of the society concerned. Hence the revival of nationalist or regional movements, though both the growth of the capital and of regionalism derive from the single cause of the increased power of the State.

No modern city, however, would be able to survive for a week if it were not for an elaborate system of hygiene beneath it. A modern city may be built of stone, steel, glass or brick. But it has to be built primarily upon water: which is needed against fire, for drinking, washing, sewage, and for most industrial processes.

At the beginning of modern times, the water supplies and the hygiene of cities alike had declined not only since *Roma antiqua*, but since the Middle Ages. The ancient Persians never polluted rivers, for they worshipped them, while the Egyptians bathed twice a day in cold water and washed their clothes often (24). But, even in a rich country such as England, there was, in 1800, rarely a distinction made between sewers and water mains. All rivers were contaminated by both domestic and industrial waste. Ditches in cities were everywhere used as latrines. Dead animals were left to rot where they lay. The decomposing bodies of the poor in common graves stank (25). Bed sheets were changed at most three times a year. Women wore quilted petticoats and stays of bone or leather which they never washed (26). The public baths of Rome, or Constantinople, the vast *cloaca maxima* and other Roman sewers copied from the Etruscans, the 1,352 public fountains which Rome had had in the fourth century, the dozen Roman aqueducts – all seemed inconceivable in England, much less in Rome, even in the time of Rome's greatest historian, Edward Gibbon. The hygienic arrangements of Babylon would have strained the imagination of an ordinary citizen of eighteenth century Paris, as they might that of many citizens of Mexico or Calcutta today. True, Muslims maintained the tradition of baths even more effectively than they did that of mathematics. They also had baths of hot air, *hammam* baths, most extensively. Steam baths were also widely used in Russia, following Muslim patterns.

A mediaeval town in Europe was also often in advance of the nineteenth century there, or the twentieth in some continents. Then, the provision of water was an established collective function, arranged by a spring or a public fountain, and sometimes still conveyed in old Roman lead pipes. The public fountain remained, until the present generation in many Mediterranean places, a centre of gregariousness (or gossip), a work of art in construction, an inspiration for poets. As García Lorca put it:

> A village without a public fountain
> Is closed, dark, every house is an isolated world

Or

> Who has shown you the road of the poets?
> The fountain, and the very old song of the stream. (27)

In fact, therefore, the most enviable people from the point of view of hygiene in the late eighteenth century seem, from the point of view of statistics, those who did not live in modern towns. Yet visitors to many old towns would have challenged that view. Goethe, in his famous journey in Italy, complained at the absence of a public cleansing service, of any sort, in Venice. Rubbish, including excrement, was pushed into corners, and irregularly carried away in flat-bottomed boats, as manure to the mainland, or thrown into the sea. Everywhere in Italy, Goethe found majestic colonnades which were simply 'made for people to relieve themselves whenever they felt the urge'. In an inn at Torbole, he found no lavatories: a valet pointed to the courtyard. 'Where?' 'Anywhere, wherever you like,' was the reply (28). But it was not simply the decadent south which seemed unhygienic. When Charles I's court was at Oxford, courtiers left behind excreta in every corner of every college (29). In Edinburgh, in 1760, there were no latrines, public or private: all emptied excreta into the street at 10 p.m. (30). When Mrs Pepys was seized with diarrhoea at the theatre, she had no option but to go to a corner of Lincoln's Inn Fields. Even 'on the marble staircases of the Louvre, the natural necessities were performed daily'.

Meantime, in Eastern countries, what little water there was afforded good chances of parasites spreading. The washing pools of Yemen's mosques were full of snails which carried all sorts of diseases. Cholera travelled along the pilgrims' routes in spite of a religion in which washing plays a great part (Muslims were instructed to wash frequently every day in running water). Actually, Muslim towns were often more hygienic than Christian ones, since they were built on hillsides in order to make the best use of water, from both streams and rain, to carry away rubbish (31).

There was also in the past no means of keeping water fresh. So, water carriers were essential. Even in the nineteenth century, most districts would count themselves fortunate if their population could go to a standpipe at the street corner once a day for an hour or so; though, by then, the rich were starting to be able to obtain running water in their basements.

A few other improvements began, however, in what seemed a dark time. Soap, for example, which started to be produced in France under Rome, continued to be made spasmodically during the Middle Ages and liquid soap, from potash, was used for laundry from the sixteenth century. Soap from palm oil was a possible alternative to the slave trade from Africa for many Liverpool merchants in the early nineteenth century. Sir John Harington, a Somerset squire who married an illegitimate daughter of Henry VIII, invented the water closet in 1596, but, for 300 years, there were few of them (32). Chamberpots continued to be emptied out of windows into the streets. Parisians went on relieving themselves in the Seine (33). Even the invention of an interior dry lavatory in the eighteenth century had no success. At Versailles, at the King's Court, there were little lavatories made as commodes on wheels (34). Mass-produced and, therefore, individual plates, knives and forks and cups, the decline of spitting, the custom of shaving heads under wigs (35), the fashion for changing underclothes every day (defined as elegance itself by Beau Brummell about 1820), all had certain good effects.

The problem of sewage became urgent in the nineteenth century, as towns grew yearly so big and so fast. The system of the 'privy bucket' meant endless emptying and removal of contents. Even so, where should it be emptied? The first solution found in London was the cesspool, of which there were about 250,000 in London by 1850 (36). But this had an adverse effect on water from wells, at a time when most water in capital cities came from those ancient sources.

Two changes came to rich cities in the nineteenth century and then were copied elsewhere. Both were based on the false assumption that dirt causes disease. In the nineteenth century in northern Europe, it was believed that cleanliness was next to godliness (37). Not for the first time, a wrong concept led to a revolution in habits (38). The pioneer in most of these changes was a German, Josef Franach, who first suggested, in the six volumes of his *Complete system of medical polity*, that ideally there should be a complete system of state management of hygiene.

The practical initiative in these matters was, as usual by then, taken in the US. New York was the first big city to arrange for its citizens an ample supply of pure water, by means of a system of reservoirs and aqueducts opened in 1842. By the twentieth century, New York was stretching out in its demands for water into the Catskill mountains a hundred miles away (39). In London, the two or three large private water companies were taken over by the municipal authorities in 1902. There is nothing to prove that free enterprise could not have performed these tasks adequately and cheaply; but they did not do so and, from the mid-nineteenth century, the provision of water in nearly every country came to be a national enterprise. Huge dams, aqueducts comparable to the Roman ones, fifty-mile-long pure water canals, and long tunnels were all soon built. Wild valleys in romantic countrysides found themselves placed under water to serve the need for water of some distant manufacturing town.

The appropriate treatment of sewage had a similar outcome. The career here of Edwin Chadwick, a many-sided reformer in England, is illuminating. He insisted in 1837 on the establishment of a sanitary commission. Appointed to head it in 1839, it became, in 1842, a general board of health. Chadwick then recommended that cesspools should be abolished and that sewers should cease to be merely bricked-over watercourses. His idea was that they should become established as great arteries in their own right to be cleaned by regular water supplies. Those arteries would carry all rubbish by long underground routes to be disposed of at places remote from the city (40). Hamburg was the first to build sewers of that sort (because of a big fire there) and Paris began sooner than London, whose problems were affected by a tangled web of local private and political interests (41). But the realisation that the cholera epidemic of 1850 was connected with pollution by excreta awoke the English to a serious appreciation of what should be done (the usual method of transmitting cholera is by water contaminated by discharges from the bowels of those suffering from the disease). Sir Joseph Bazalgette, a civil engineer of French origin, devised a system based on five huge sewers running parallel to the Thames which would be capable of dealing with all normal sewage and rain water. Only in stormy weather would it thereafter be necessary to use the old sewers connected with the rivers. The sewers discharged their vast quantities of refuse twelve miles from London Bridge at a place where it could be chemically clarified. Elsewhere, liquid sewage continued for a long time to be discharged into rivers or lakes. Various other methods of disposal developed: iron hydroxide, for example, and, in the twentieth century, chlorination. Here was an effective system of public works plainly superior to the negligent ways of the past.

At the same time, Europeans and North Americans, began to cease their fear of contact with water in other ways. Swimming began to seem again a practical part of education. Public baths began, from the 1840s, to be built again. Slowly, the idea of the private bath captured the imaginations of rich countries. The shower seems to have been devised in the 1880s. All these innovations, or revivals, depended not only upon running water attached to the houses – that immensely important innovation of the mid nineteenth century – but on the availability of heating it too – a possibility made easy after the gas heater of the 1860s and electricity a little later. Enamelled white baths began to be made about 1910 and to be mass-produced in the US and Britain by 1920. By 1939, the compact bathrooms of modern times (bath, basin, lavatory) were everywhere being constructed. The ideal of one such bathroom to every bedroom was beginning to be expressed as a goal by modern builders (42). These ideals were quickly passed on to a world which was anxious to copy US technology without copying their political ideals. The achievement of even the first of these aims was, however, far from complete even in rich countries before 1939 and, even in the 1970s, there are still many houses without baths – though all prejudice against them, like the old prejudice against tomatoes and potatoes, has vanished.

By the year 2000, a third of the world's population are expected to be living in cities of over 100,000 inhabitants in size. Tokyo with Yokohama, with about 17 million in 1980, may, by 2000, have 26 million. Cairo may have 16 million, Lagos 9·4 million, and Mexico, 31·6 million. São Paulo may rival Tokyo (43). The implications of these developments are enormous. We should recall that London only reached a million in 1800, and that Paris did not join her in that till 1850. Berlin and Vienna did not top a million till nearly 1880, and no Russian city except for St Petersburg reached a million before about 1870. Today, however, the cities of the world larger than one million number a hundred. Think of it, a hundred cities which are the size of Rome at her height, many of them larger!

One consequence of this extraordinary tendency has been, apparently, a vast increase of crime. From the evidence of primitive or hunting tribes surviving into historical memory, crime, as we know it, among those peoples, was both rare and severely punished. Still, the codes of law of ancient agrarian civilisations make clear that, in those early settled states, urban crime's long history had begun. In great cities such as Rome or Constantinople, or in Eastern cities, the growing semi-slave, rootless urban proletariat which did not accept, or even know, the customs of the dominant people, looked on robbery as part of their private war against the occupiers. Where peoples were insecure, or lived in a state of perpetual war, the distinction between crime and self-preservation was often ill marked. Of course, thefts and murders, rapes and minor acts of violence occurred often in the pre-industrial countryside. Figures recently analysed suggest that mediaeval Kent had a far worse record than anywhere in the US in the twentieth century. Two-thirds of all convictions in England in some years during the nineteenth century were under the game code (44). But crime in industrial society seems today more and more an urban problem: the Neapolitan *lazzaroni* of the eighteenth century are now to be found all over the world. The absence of rewarding work or stimulating play; the charmlessness of many modern dwellings – above all, alas, those provided by the community; the loose or non-existent scale of values in societies materially richer than those which existed in the past, and the conversion of many who live in cities to a mentality utterly opposed, or indifferent, to the community in which they have full rights as citizens, all contribute. In some cities of the US, murder has been said to have been the most common cause of death among male black people in their prime of life (45). In other ways too, sometimes, modern cities recall Juvenal's injunction: 'If you go out to dinner, first make your will' (46). That, of course, recalls the undoubted truth that all cities have been infested with crime since the earliest days. It is the increase in the cities which has offered greater opportunities.

The world of the future will be a world of cities. Older than nations and states, their history is as long as any other viable organisation of men. The errors of planning of the twentieth century have created worse asphalt jungles than the errors of neglect in the nineteenth. Communist cities, such as East Berlin or the new Moscow, do not suggest that there a new world functions better than capitalist ones.

39

Modern Capitalism

The early industrial changes in the eighteenth century were carried out by individuals, families, or groups of friends for whom the mediaeval name of company or *compagne* was entirely appropriate, for the associations formed by Watt and Boulton, Whitney and Wedgwood, would be hardly recognisable by the modern name of a corporation. These associations might be consolidated by common law, but the association brought unlimited liability for all partners, whatever the assets of their associates. The 'companies' of late eighteenth century England were less sophisticated enterprises than those of mediaeval Florence (they were as a rule less international, for a start). True, internationally competitive merchants, such as the slave dealers of Liverpool, might spread their risk among a large group (as a form of insurance) but most such individuals were both shareholders and company directors at the same time. Only a few large mercantile companies, such as the East India Company and the Hudson Bay Company (which were not pre-eminent in innovating), had a large body of investors and myriad activities in the way that we now conceive of as being typical of 'companies'. Those two English companies had some continental European equivalents, along with a few enterprises favoured by the State. The idea of a shareholder with no concern for the company other than what profit he might make from it was uncommon. Throughout Western Europe (indeed, in America too), the memory of the failure of the South Sea Company in England and of the Mississippi Company in France (in the 1720s) was persistent. (Those companies had offered to make fortunes for small savers but, instead, had ruined them.) Thus, until at least 1800, most savers thought that land, or a strong box, were the best means of saving. Prices were, after all, fairly stable in England in the eighteenth century, at least until 1789: a remarkable fact at a time of unprecedented economic growth.

Subsequently, there were four developments. First, limited liability, by which stockholders invested in a corporation with an artificial personality. When that personality's money ran out, its creditors could not claim what they thought they were owed by it from stockholders. This idea, in the end, stimulated commercial enterprise greatly but, in the short run, such limited companies were mostly used for banking, canals, and railways rather than for industry. Only after 1859 were limited companies anywhere of much importance in industry (2).

TABLE PRICE INDEX ENGLAND 1700—1789 (1)

	All Consumer goods	Consumer goods other than cereals	Producer goods
1701	100	100	100
1750	95	91	88
1780	117	108	107

Secondly, during the nineteenth century, companies became concerned with a great many different types of production. The most extreme example of this was to be seen in shipping but, to a lesser extent, the same happened in every industry, at every level, during the nineteenth century. In shipping, in particular, there was a realisation that 'either there must be an elaborate fitting together of the products of many specialised firms or single, many-sided firms must do most of the essential work themselves, as government dockyards had always done' (3). Indeed, government dockyards were the ancestors of these new undertakings in more ways than one. A firm which supplied plate had to know all about steel. Ideally, its managers should know all about marketing ships at home and abroad. A good example of what happened to large firms can be seen in the history of the engineering firm of Armstrong which, to begin with, was most renowned for its innovation in the use of hydraulic blast furnaces. William Armstrong, who was born in 1810, was an inspired industrialist who was, in his own right, an inventor. The inventor of the first hydraulic crane, the submarine mine (for use alongside Bessemer's guns in the Crimean War), and the three-pounder gun, he also founded the engineering works at Elswick, Newcastle (1847), and conceived the idea of using solar energy. He began to make ships in 1868 and bought a shipyard in 1882, in which year his firm launched the first iron-protected cruiser (the *Esmeralda*, for Chile). In 1885, Armstrong opened a branch in Naples to make guns for Italy. Twelve years later, he bought Sir Joseph Whitworth's famous gun-making firm and, in 1900, set up armoured-plate shops (4). Meanwhile, a Sheffield steel manufacturer, Vickers, a joint stock company of the 1860s, began making steel for almost every use, including armaments. In 1897, Vickers bought the Naval Construction and Armaments Company at Barrow and the Maxim-Nordenfelt Machine Gun Company at Erith. In 1902, they absorbed Robert Napier's famous shipbuilding firm at Govan (it had built the first ironclads) and bought themselves a share of William Beardmore's shipbuilding firm at Glasgow in 1902 (5). Then in 1924, after the First World War, when both firms became financially shaky, Armstrong-Whitworth was absorbed by Vickers, to form a firm which survived, with government subsidies even in 1924, in a much changed shape, into the 1970s (6). (Beardmores, having built a large number of ships during the First World War, also collapsed.) This history of what became one of Britain's largest firms is fairly characteristic of modern enterprise generally: an inspired founder, mergers, growth – and, in the end, a government subsidy when the firm has become so big as to be of national importance.

Companies got bigger, but their structure, when big, seemed increasingly disciplined, modelled almost on the armed forces. The enterprise might be run by managers of different grades, of different social rank from most of the others, and who (in England and America, anyway) often had been educated in the classics at remote schools for administrators. The workers could only rarely (for educational or social reasons) hope to rise to become managers.

In the United States, a steady increase in the development of the corporate form of organisation continued, particularly in the twentieth century. While 24% of business done was by corporations in 1900, the figure had risen to 52% in 1939. 94% of manufacturing was already being done by corporations by 1939, against 74% in 1904. The size of corporations increased too: in the 1930s, 600 or so corporations owning assets of $50 million owned over half the corporate wealth.

Another consequence was the improved development of the 'market', the heart of modern capitalism, a system illogical to those outside it, even cynical and immoral, but to those within it 'a delicate, experimental and easily abused credit mechanism . . . constructed without design . . . modified from year to year . . . without supervision save that of the unseen hand of self interest', primarily conceived to further the overseas trade of private firms and extend its control to internal commerce and to industrial development (7).

Corn exchanges and wool exchanges had been first founded and led to stock exchanges. In 1730, stockbrokers were considered barely respectable in England. An Act was even passed in 1733 to declare void all wagers relating to the present and future prices of stocks and securities. By 1760, even government stock could be dealt in by brokers. In 1762, towards the end of the most successful war ever fought by England, London's main dealers in stocks formed a 'stock exchange' in a coffee house. It survived the Napoleonic wars and, in 1815, French and other governmental loans were floated there. By 1820, the stock exchange had been formally recognised, and it moved to a building of its own. Soon, broking (dealing in anything) and jobbing (dealing in certain stocks) became differentiated. Cloth, coal and corn exchanges were similarly built, and chambers of commerce were established. All these developments were privately set up, without the help of the government, and usually despite the government's first inclination. All were copied in other capitals of the West. The Stock Exchange in London had 2,000 members in 1878. Speculative dealing in 'futures' had by then been greatly assisted by the telegraph.

The foundation of such permanent marketing centres for investment transformed commerce, and, with one or two setbacks, financed most of the industrial enterprise of the next hundred years. Money had always been pursued: what characterised capitalism is that it is not a series of individual enterprises but it is a *system* based on calculation of profit and free labour (8).

Parallel to the creation of the stock-market was the organisation of banking on a new international level. In 1789, the fabric of international banking was less intelligently organised than it had been during the Renaissance. But after 1815, a considerable amount of English capital was available, in comparison with the years before the wars. Much of it found an outlet in the loans to foreign states organised by such London-based banks as Barings' or Rothschilds'. Nathan Rothschild, a Jewish banker who had lived till 1784 in Frankfurt, arranged the subsidies which the British government gave to their continental allies during the Napoleonic wars. He insisted that the recipients paid their interest in pounds sterling (9). Later, the Dutch (who had led high finance in the seventeenth century but then been damaged by the wars), the Flemings and the French began to invest money abroad in a similar manner. France finished the Napoleonic wars with her economy in good shape, since Napoleon had financed his wars by living off tribute and foreign countries. During the wars also, the continent of Europe had benefited from being for a time almost one economic unit. Britain's opposition (and Napoleon's ambitions) prevented that state of affairs from leading to anything of any political significance. But in the years afterwards, British collaboration and investment again foreshadowed economic union, both Britain and the continent needing US cotton, and both were affected by the same economic diseases (10). This European economy became, however, in the nineteenth century, a world economy, a world *maritime* economy, of which Europe (particularly Britain) was the centre. Britain, France and Germany supplied over 60% of the world's exports. Britain then had 45% of all foreign investments, France 25%, Germany 13% and the US only 5%. A quarter of Britain's wealth was invested abroad. London was the world's uncontested financial centre, the pound sterling the nearest ever achieved to a world currency. In London or Paris, experts for all economic undertakings everywhere could be found. Most of the rest of the world save Japan and the US were subject to European states through a mixture of financial or direct military ties. If China and the Ottoman Empire remained unconquered, it was because the European states could not agree how to divide them (11). Joseph Conrad's wonderful novels, written between 1894 and 1924, well commemorate that open, expanding, increasingly unprejudiced and cosmopolitan world.

This episode of a European free economy lasted a hundred years between 1815 and 1914. During the last part of this time, travel became easier and quicker than ever before. Countries drew ever closer to one another so that, for example, the same critiques within those societies were internationally emulated: French and German socialists felt that they could use the same vocabulary when they criticised capitalism.

A change in the character of private enterprise came as a result of the increase in the nineteenth century of stock dealing and of foreign investment. At the beginning of the nineteenth century, China had a banking system but it made, and sought, no international impact. Britain alone had a national bank with a monopoly of state banking, which possessed the only serious reserve of gold in the country, and which looked after the reserves of other banks. It was then the central organisation for nearly 900 private banks. There was a great diversity of practice and some banks crashed every year. The banks in London were held together by the clearing houses which most banks supported in Lombard Street. They provided drawers into which clerks from other banks, twice a day, dropped bills or cheques payable by the owner of the drawer. The use of the cheque was already highly developed, and no London bank (of which there were then sixty) was in the habit of issuing its own notes, nor had it done so for fifty years, since cheques and Bank of England notes met all needs (12). Country banks in England did issue their own notes, though none smaller than for £5. Gradually, this system was modified so that, by 1914, no banks issued their own notes, and the number of banks had declined.

Gradually, too, a system very roughly comparable to this one was established in most industrial countries. The European continent took a long time to recover from the Napoleonic wars, however, and the size and diversity of the USA prevented it from spreading fast there. The idea of a US national bank for example, remained a controversial one for most of the early nineteenth century. On the other hand, France had a National Bank from 1800, with an exclusive right to issue notes, although cheques were unknown there till after 1848. The stagnation of French industry in the nineteenth century was partly due to the character of the Bank of France, a private monopoly with close relations with the government. It set itself a target of prudent management of the issuance of notes, and little else. The Imperial Bank of Germany, after 1871, served the same purpose as these other ones, monopolising the issue of notes. Though privately owned, it was managed by officials.

Equally gradually, too, this world banking system began to be supplemented by an expansion of the international organisation of trade in which firms were established whose entire business was the financing of one part or another of foreign trade. Similarly, this system began, during the nineteenth century, to be sustained by a single commodity, namely gold.

England had maintained a gold standard (that is, any citizen could exchange any Bank of England note for gold on demand) since 1718, when Sir Isaac Newton had established the price of gold at £3.17s.10½d. per ounce. That price prevailed, save for a short time after the Napoleonic wars (13). Gold was affirmed as the basis of the British currency by Sir Robert Peel's Act of 1819 (14). Silver and copper continued to be used but only as token money. The money in circulation did not increase very greatly: in 1789, £10 million was in circulation in England, £24 million in 1870 (15).

Elsewhere, at the beginning of the nineteenth century, the continent of Europe retained its ancient silver standard, disorganised though it was, while the US had made gold and silver interchangeable in 1792, at a ratio of 15 silver pieces to one of gold. (France had the same arrangement in theory. The silver franc was the real unit of exchange there while, in Germany, most states used silver thalers and numerous small coins). Most of the huge amount of new gold mined in California, Australia and the Urals, by new industrial processes, in the second half of the nineteenth century went into coinage. By 1870 gold was more abundant than silver was (16). Thus, during the 1870s, for the first time, a gold standard was internationally established. The new German Empire turned to gold in 1871. The US announced the gold dollar to be the sole unit of value in 1873. France, and the other European countries which had been using a franc, stopped coining silver in 1878. It was almost as if an international currency had been established. Indeed, a system of that sort was suggested in the 1860s, on the basis of £1 equals $5 equals 25 francs (17).

Between 1878 and 1914, this system prevailed. Since 1914, it has not been effectively revived, though, in democratic countries, where the free market has been able to survive, national currencies have, since 1945, revolved uneasily round the dollar.

Outside Europe, the Russian experience probably was characteristic: great fairs, for example, of a mediaeval type survived there till the end of the nineteenth century. Bills of exchange, letters of credit and joint stock companies played little part. Cash was short. Commercial banks were founded only in the 1860s (till then, Russia had only state-operated banks), and of the elaborate structure of international commerce, finance and speculation, Russia was ignorant (18). Equally, South America remained insulated from the *grande fête bourgeoise* of the nineteenth century, save in a few limited temporarily boom areas (for example, the rubber zone of Manaus on the Amazon). Spanish colonial rule did not as a rule encourage the growth of private enterprise or a modern middle class. South American independent states remained poor but were saddled with large governments and armies. In India, on the other hand, British rule did stimulate private ownership of agriculture, and Indian capitalism, which after a fashion had existed before the British conquest, led to the achievement of some degree of private prosperity (19).

Nothing shows more the new spirit of self help in the early days of the age of industry than the growth of insurance. Fire insurance was revived in Italy during the fourteenth century, having been known in Rome. It became common in Holland and England late in the seventeenth century. At first, this was done by individuals but big stock companies were founded in Liverpool and London in the eighteenth century. Goods travelling overland also began to be insured regularly. Most houses were insured in England by 1850, though they were less frequently so in countries where houses are made of stone. Equally, both marine and life insurance also had Renaissance origins. Underwriters who had first met at Edward Lloyd's coffee house in the seventeenth century benefited by the war against Napoleon to become a great international enterprise. Life insurance began too, after the accurate actuarial calculation of the current expectation of the insurer's life began in the early eighteenth century. By 1805, the value of goods insured in Britain was about £240 million (20).

Another consequence of industrialisation was to cause all societies within the richer world to become interdependent. In the age of agriculture, crop failures might be made up for by imports from other places. In the nineteenth and twentieth centuries, the availability of food and work in the rich communities increasingly depended not on rainfall but on the rise and fall of confidence in the international market. Increasing concentration, and increasing size, of businesses further augmented interconnections. There were many economic crises in the nineteenth and early twentieth centuries (for example, 1819, 1857, 1873, 1893 and 1907) when trade collapsed, unemployment of the workers drawn into factories increased, and prices dropped. Merchants found it hard to sell goods and factory owners found it hard to keep their plants open. Usually, however, agriculture was untouched by these crises. Some argued that the crisis was a useful purgative, curing high prices, inefficient management and over-production. Some crises of the nineteenth century, for example that in Cuba in the 1880s, were locally caused by some specific innovation such as the European cultivation of sugar beet on a large scale.

The worst such crisis was that of 1929 which followed ten years of speculation in the US, then the world's richest country. The consequence was a collapse in the stock market and the near end of the free market. In July 1932, the index of prices of industrial shares was an eighth of what it had been three years before. The US national product was down to half its real value of 1929 and unemployment accounted for 12 million people or about 25% of the labour force. This crisis was long-lasting: in 1940, unemployment still accounted in the US for 7 million people, in Britain for over a million (21). It was also worldwide. World trade collapsed. It became barely worthwhile picking coffee, mining copper or cutting sugar cane. In 1932, every country with a manufacturing industry had unemployment of over 10% (Belgium had 23%, Denmark 32%, Germany 30% and Britain 22.5%). The more 'advanced' the country, the more severe the crisis. Thus Germany had exported about a third of her total goods manufactured in the 1920s. When no foreign country had money to spend on imports, German workers naturally lost their jobs (22). The consequence was the wreckage of the world monetary system, already severely damaged by the First World War. All countries drew in on themselves. Many believed that free enterprise, and with it democracy, were doomed. Hence the attraction for extreme 'solutions': fascist or communist. Fascists believed that their leaders had some supremely effective medicine for the problems of their state.

Some supposed this crisis to be the 'final' one of capitalism. That, however, proved not to be the case. After the revival of the economies of the advanced nations in the late 1930s in the shadow of the Second World War (though Germany was the only advanced country to have cured its unemployment by 1939), capitalism went on to many victories in the 1950s and 1960s. The crisis of 1929–33 now appears to have been the result of great shifts in inter-state indebtedness, the excessive role played by the state in the economies during the war (23) and a sluggishness due to what Walt Rostow speaks of as 'the process of disengagement from the old leading sectors of the pre-1914 years' (24). In the early 1970s, competition was 'never so intense or so extreme' (25). That competition was probably the main reason for the steady improvement of the long term standard of living in the West. Western Europe embarked after 1945 on an age of high mass consumption, of plastics and cars, electronics and aeronautics. The number of enterprises in almost all capitalist countries grew fast. In the 1960s in the US there were a million separate operating enterprises, 400,000 of them being born every year, only about 350,000 dying (26). Enterprises have grown in size but so has the market. Large firms, such as the automobile ones, have gained publicity, and have established near monopolies, but the tendency to monopoly has not been consistent and manufacturing accounted in the 1970s for only a quarter of those in employment in the US (27). Furthermore, it became clear, about 1960, that, despite many illusions to the contrary, there was no evidence that large firms in the US were on the increase nor that big ones would soon replace small ones. Nearly a fifth of US citizens, too, are self-employed.

The number of stockholders also grew: in 1928 4.7 million people in the US had some kind of stock and in 1975 that figure had risen to 25 million (28). Until 1914, at least, nevertheless, the workshop and small establishment remained typical of much of even the industrial world.

By the nature of things, competitive capitalism does not lend itself very well to combination between different enterprises. Capitalists have common interests but large ones have few such interests which they share with small businesses or craftsmen. It is exceptionally difficult to make an adequate comparison between a large hierarchically organised firm in Japan and a bureaucratic public corporation in Europe. Differing rates of taxation have transformed the attitudes of companies to profit in one country or another. The role of the state in the economy differs everywhere, not only in its impact but in its form. Attitudes to fiscal morality differ. Thus it is almost impossible to speak in the late twentieth century as if capitalism has common characteristics the world over – though it was probably so in the nineteenth century and before. Some corporate officials have a sense of 'social responsibility' which goes beyond serving the interests of their stockholders and members; some do not, but think that they should. On the whole, combinations of employers have, unsurprisingly, been usually ineffective when working together. Employers in a single industry may combine in order to raise prices or even to carry out a project. But, except in time of war, political collaboration between great employers has been the exception, not the rule.

Perhaps it was for this reason that free enterprise was for a generation or so unpopular. Many who had been brought up on the study of classical literature felt that it was desirable to mount, in W. A. Robson's words, 'a great popular revolt against the ethics, the incentives and the results of capitalist enterprise' in the interests of 'higher moral values, superior moral incentives, and a wider conception of economic benefit' (29). Unwittingly, perhaps, such people who argued thus prepared the way for stagnation, for they had forgotten that, in criticising capitalist enterprise, they were complaining about the creative and dynamic force which had made Western civilisation what it is. Certainly, the alternatives as yet proposed, such as nationalisation, have not been more accountable to the public than private enterprise was (through share holders), have not introduced anything particularly new in the field of organisation, and have been at the mercy of political mismanagement and favour. Any student of the history of Colbert's industrial projects in late seventeenth-century France would have known that that was likely. There is, of course, as John Jewkes reminds us, no need to be rigidly doctrinaire. It has been commonly accepted, since the time of Adam Smith, that certain essential economic functions must be conducted by the state (30). But most economic activities are best performed by free enterprise. There remains in the world a vast amount of poverty and neglect. But uncomfortable though it may be for many students of political economy to admit it, the best way whereby those conditions can be relieved is by a flourishing system of competitive capitalism rather than by a managerial state. The role of states in providing this relief should primarily be concerned with laying down standards,* inspecting factories for safety and hygiene, ensuring payment of taxes and avoiding corruption. Those are not negligible roles.

* Including standards in education, and town planning.

40

The British Contribution

The enormous producing capacity and the great wealth of England are not the effect of national power and individual love of gain. The people's innate love of liberty and justice, the energy, the religious and moral character of the people have a share in it. The constitution of the country, its institutions, the wisdom and power of the aristocracy have a share in it . . . The geographical position . . . nay, even good luck has a share.

F. List

In the eighteenth century, the English, little given to speculation about general principles, were, for that reason, much more guided by strong opinions.
F. A. Hayek, *Law, Legislation and Liberty*, Vol. I

The question frequently arises, and must have ocurred to anyone reading the preceding narrative, as to why it should have been England, and Scotland, with their tiny population (7 million in 1750), which initiated the industrial era, rather than France (whose population was about 25 million in 1750) or Italy, with her intellectual pre-eminence in the Renaissance, or, indeed, one of many other states more or less well-placed to benefit from, or to achieve, the changes of the day.

The availability of cheap fuel (coal) was one reason for Britain's success. Coal certainly saved England from a fuel crisis when her supplies of timber, always more modest than those on the continent, became very short during the time of the Tudors (1). This is the traditional, rather carping, French explanation for English pre-eminence in the eighteenth century. But there is something to that view. Coal was Britain's main fuel by the end of the seventeenth century. That was already leading her to experiment with all sorts of new manufacturing. The existence of coal mines led, for example, to Newcomen's pumping machines. But that explanation ignores the important, and perhaps even more critical, social factor that the businessman, within the middle class, was regarded in France as inferior to the administrator while, in Britain, he was well-regarded — perhaps because a majority of English noblemen were *nouveaux riches*, in comparison with their continental peers.*

* However, even the French aristocracy renewed itself after the sixteenth century.

The availability in England of cheap labour (from people displaced by the enclosures) used also to be considered a reason for English industrial primacy, particularly by nineteenth-century moralists, such as Marx. That view has been discussed earlier. Others have argued that the natural growth of the population played the critical part. Yet growth of population was undoubted everywhere in Europe.

At the beginning of the twentieth century, religion, curiously enough, seemed to be everywhere in decline. But a religious explanation for England's early industrialisation was, paradoxically, fashionable. Max Weber, for example, and R. H. Tawney, after him, argued that 'Puritans encouraged work but discouraged display'. The consequence, they suggested, was the limitation of consumption, and the consequent release of acquisitive activity; hence, the accumulation of capital, through an ascetic compulsion to save (2). One of the leaders of what seems to have been, in most senses, Britain's second Protestant revolution, John Wesley, wrote in the eighteenth century: 'We ought not to prevent people from being diligent and frugal. We must exhort all Christians to gain all they can, to save all they can; that is, in effect to grow rich' (3). A century before, another more severe Protestant, the 'Leveller' Richard Baxter, had explained that 'waste of time is the first and in principle the deadliest of sins . . . Loss of time through sociability, idle talking, luxury, more sleep than is necessary for health (six or, at most, eight hours) is worthy of absolute moral condemnation. Every hour lost is lost to labour for God.' Baxter's creed consisted of continual and passionate preaching of the need for hard, continuous, bodily toil: 'Work hard in your calling.' The argument behind this interpretation of British industrial history receives some support from the evident truth that so many of the greatest early entrepreneurs of the industrial revolution in Britain (and in the US) were Quakers. The availability of the Bible in print, and in English after 1603, reminded men of the text of *Ecclesiastes* which told them, 'whatsoever thy hand findeth it to do, do it with thy might'. The vast outflow of Puritanical literature of the seventeenth century stimulated popular literacy. In the third quarter of the seventeenth century nearly forty per cent of the adult male population could read (4); and they read the Bible and *Pilgrim's Progress* above all.

An interpretation contrary to that of Weber and Tawney is, however, made by Lawrence Stone: 'At the root of all the significant changes in the late seventeenth and eighteenth centuries,' he argues, 'lies a progressive orientation of culture towards the pursuit of pleasure in this world rather than the postponement of gratification until the next.' There was a growing confidence, certainly, during those centuries, particularly the second of them, in man's capacity to master the environment, and a growth of indifference towards the authority of the clergy. Men and women began to choose their spouses more carefully. The idea spread that the selfish individual pursuit of happiness was desirable: 'the greatest good of the greatest number' was defined as an objective of the social order as early as 1725 (5). Britain in the eighteenth century, too, was also beginning to treat children as individuals rather than as objects slightly less valuable than animals, and less so than servants. Tolerance became generally evident: 'Let nothing be done to break his spirit,' Henry Fox instructed the preceptors of his brilliant son, Charles James Fox, 'the world will do that soon enough' (6).

Another perhaps even more important difference between Britain and other countries, where intellect and access to raw materials seemed also available, was that the British state, though respected, played no part, to speak of, in economic life. The few civil servants of England,* like George Selwyn, or the innumerable clerks, whose fortunes have been so lovingly described by Sir Lewis Namier, in his *England in the Age of the American Revolution*, knew, as Boswell did, that it was hard to live luxuriously on less than £2,000 a year (7). But they knew little more of economics. That was left to bankers, merchants, sea captains and a few writers. Perhaps indeed, the State in Britain was respected because the State did so little. At all events, the government took no interest in, but placed no obstacle before, for example, the building of canals. They even had no interest, to begin with, in how long, or how, children should work. The enlightened laws for work in factories were introduced into Parliament by independent philanthropists. The Government concerned itself with law, which touched industrialisation little more than through the upholding of patents. Tariffs interested governments of the eighteenth century in Britain, it is true. But otherwise government was conceived of as ensuring a benign neglect and preventing interference. When English statesmen in the eighteenth century thought of the word 'liberty' they saw in the concept the idea that the pursuit of wealth should be left to the individual. The free market, an invention of Italians and Dutchmen, between the fifteenth and seventeenth centuries, flourished in Britain successfully after 1688. Because it was established before industrialisation, it gave a decisive advantage to British manufacture. On the other hand, in France, a good idea, of an economic or technological nature, could only prosper if it had the support of the state. The same was true of most German states, with the exception of a few small, oligarchic cities. Some of those states were enlightened, such as the Duchy of Saxe-Weimar, which patronised Goethe; but they were, as we now say, *étatiste* .

Another signal point was that England was also a fairer society than any on the continent, since, as foreign visitors constantly marvelled, it was inspired by Law. That did not mean that punishments for crimes in England were specially mild. They were not. The forty-three executions

---

* They totalled 2,000, including placemen, in England in the late eighteenth century.

for robbery in London and Middlesex in 1785 prove that. It meant that there was a general acceptance that no one could be punished, or could lawfully be made to suffer, in body, in loss of goods, or even reputation, save for a distinct breach of the law established in a legal manner, before the law of the land (8). It also meant that all men, of whatever rank or condition, were subject to the ordinary law of the realm, and were amenable to ordinary tribunals. Law was independent of any private will in England, and was only rarely interfered with even by Parliament, and then only to tidy up doubtful points. On the European continent, in the seventeenth century, there were many governments which were far from oppressive, but there was not one where men were secure from arbitrary misuse of power. The singularity of England, A. V. Dicey pointed out, was not its leniency, nor its goodness, but its legality (9). When, in 1808, the English abolished the Atlantic slave trade, the rich slave merchants of Liverpool utterly changed the pattern of their commerce. In other European countries where the slave trade was abolished (in France in 1818, Spain in 1820, and so on) the traffic continued secretly. Of course, there were in England, as in most countries, distinctions between the legal code and the unwritten popular code. There were probably more acts of mob violence in England than there were elsewhere. Bread riots, cheese riots, meat riots were frequent, and organised. But even so, English law was not usually conceived of as the creation of a ruler, but as a barrier to power (10). The consequence was that England was more self-confident than her neighbours on the continent. That confidence was enhanced by the evident strategic fact that England was difficult for any State in the eighteenth century to invade. Her long coastline and her navigable rivers made her suitable for the commercial eminence whose arts she had learned from the Italians, Germans and Dutch. Her coinage might include a 'florin', deriving from Florence, and a pound 'sterling', a corruption of 'easterling' (the eastern, or Baltic, merchants in whose hands English trade rested for a long time). But the Navigation Act of 1651 had forced English merchants to do without Dutch carriers, one contribution to prosperity which the government can fairly be credited with. That obliged English traders to build a sea-going merchant fleet of their own, when, previously, only the coal trade from Newcastle to London had needed a regular marine (11).

One inspiration in the creation of the British merchant fleet was the East India Company which, like its Dutch equivalent, had received a grant of monopoly of trade with the East early in the seventeenth century. Its trade was tea, cotton and porcelain. But the decisive achievements, so far as English trade was concerned, were in the West, not the East, a particular benefit stemming from the increase of sugar imports from the West Indies. A little over 300,000 tons of shipping left English ports in 1700. In 1764, it was 658,000. During the next fifty years, particularly after the invention of the steam engine and the cotton gin, the tonnage trebled, nearly two million tons of shipping leaving English ports in 1801. The history of Liverpool is significant. A fishing village till the seventeenth century, Liverpool's population was 5,000 in 1700, 80,000 in 1773, and 376,000 in 1850. That growth primarily derived from the vast trade in slaves and sugar and subsequently cotton, which the merchants of Liverpool managed in the eighteenth and nineteenth centuries. The fortunes made in Liverpool assisted the transformation of the city into the great outlet for the first new cities of the Industrial Revolution, Birmingham and Manchester.

Despite much snobbery, violence and crudeness, Britain was also a robust nation in ways other than in commerce and industry. The modern novel was, in the eighteenth century, constructed by Henry Fielding and was subsequently given an international renown by Sir Walter Scott, in his great novels which began to appear in 1814. Moral history was being founded by Edward Gibbon. Modern philosophy was being reconstructed by David Hume, and economics invented by Adam Smith. James Watt's patent for a steam engine ran out in 1800, the year before Byron went to Harrow, having been extended the year before the birth of Constable, in 1776. Michael Faraday, the father of electricity, was born in 1791, the poet Shelley in 1792, and Sir Humphry Davy, the grandfather of electricity, in 1778. The year 1759 was an *annus mirabilis* for British arms: both Canada and India were conquered. In the 1770s, though America was lost, Australia began to be colonised. Today, when even 'the shade of that which once was great', as Wordsworth put it in respect of Venice, is not always easy to detect,* Britain between 1750 and 1815 seems to have lived a golden age, publicly crowned by the great victories at Trafalgar and Waterloo, and privately sustained by countless magnificent acts of private initiative. It was a tumultuous and aggressive country, full of hooligans, bigots and geniuses, radicals and political enthusiasts, possessed of a curious mixture of sensitivity, violence, moral persuasiveness and rapacity, rather well summed up in the unusual character of Nelson, the national hero.

In the mid-eighteenth century, Britain was also the only large country where anything like political freedom existed. Without it, the whole process of industrialisation would have been delayed. The countries which first copied Britain's example were also democracies: the Netherlands, Belgium, the USA, and then France. Only in the second half of the nineteenth century was there an alliance between an authoritarian government and innovatory industrialisation. Both Britain and the Netherlands had the wisdom to permit, or had lacked the strength to prevent, large private firms, such as the two East India companies, operating on a vast scale, with incomes larger than those of most states

---

* However, Wordsworth also thought England in his day a 'fen of stagnant waters'.

— 'multinational' companies of the following century — creating huge commercial enterprises, and benignly influencing public policy. In France and Spain, similar companies existed, but they were semi-official. Britain's merchants also controlled a high proportion of oceanic commerce. After the failure of the Jacobite movement, the relations between Scotland and England entered upon a generally fruitful era of partnership. Sir Walter Scott's heroes articulate that. The acute religious feuds of the seventeenth century had also helped to create a society where speculation and freedom of thought had become more generally accepted than they were on the continent. Thus the 'scientific revolution' could play a stimulating effect throughout society. Britain had, too, with its Anglo-Saxon colonies in the Americas, led the way to toleration in the West — the last witchcraft case had been in 1712 (11). The English had already a sense of the nation as a 'new Israel' in the seventeenth century and, on to images taken from the Authorised Version of the Old Testament or the Prayer Book of 1662, Bunyan's *Pilgrim's Progress* or Foxe's *Book of Martyrs*, there were imposed romantic views of Drake and Raleigh, or Elizabeth I and Alfred, with Nelson and Wellington as the modern representatives. The Whigs of the early nineteenth century noticed the slow growth of English institutions and thought, as J. H. Plumb put it, that that gave them a moral message to offer to mankind, as well as a political one (12). Such ideas were not, it must be realised, passed on by any system of public education. Britain in the eighteenth century, judged by the criterion of how many children were at school, was less well off than most of her neighbours on the continent. Charity schools existed but the numbers attending were a tiny percentage of the children of school age, and writing was omitted at some of those since, in the contemporary words of Bishop Viner, 'it may possibly turn the minds of children, or of their parents for them, to some other business than husbandry' (13).* Despite the lack of education, there seem to have been few demands for a more generous attention to the problem — though Boswell recalls Dr Johnson asking a boy whom he met, 'What would you give, my lad, to know about the Argonauts?' 'Sir,' said the boy, wisely, 'I would give all I had' (14).

England in the eighteenth century was a country where self reliance, a sense of local responsibility, successful dependence on voluntary action, and toleration of neighbours' differences all combined in the words of that acute modern observer of its affairs, F. A. Hayek, 'to give both respect for custom and tradition, but at the same time a healthy suspicion of power and authority' (15). In the late eighteenth century, Britain was, in short, a marvellous country, where the empirical discoveries of practical men could also have a greater effect on science than

* This point of view was not confined to England. As late as 1850, a Spanish minister told an education reformer that he would refuse to authorise a school for adults in Madrid, because 'here we do not need men who think, but oxen who work'.

science had on practice (16). The double success of Reformation and Revolution, in 1688, meant that, as Raymond Aron observed, the British intelligentsia 'never found itself in permanent conflict with Church and State . . . its polemics were closer to factual experience and less inclined to metaphysics than the intelligentsia of the continent' (17). By comparison, in France, the form of the State was never generally accepted after the fall of the monarchy: the debate between Revolution and Tradition was never resolved. At the same time, however, the pursuit of knowledge in England was lay. As in Greece in the fifth century BC, English scientific enquiry had ceased to be regarded as a matter of 'revelation', or to be handed down by priestly colleges, as under the clever Egyptians and Babylonians (18), and as was the case, to a modified extent, no doubt, with the clever Germans or Frenchmen of the eighteenth century.

Industrialisation, mechanisation, the factory age, the age of machines, however it is termed, could have happened anywhere in the eighteenth or nineteenth centuries in a number of countries. It was also natural that it should have occurred in what was then the richest country, had the largest share of oceanic commerce and was the most intellectually free. Britain in the mid-eighteenth century was probably about a quarter richer than France – if still perhaps poorer, measured in terms of income per person, than Holland (19).

The question is naturally often posed as to why China, at an earlier stage perhaps, did not make the decisive breakthrough into industrialisation. As has been shown, China knew the blast furnace and cast iron nearly 2,000 years before the West. She knew of paper and gunpowder in the early Middle Ages, while her irrigated agriculture was sophisticated long before the plough had reached much of Europe. Is the explanation that industrial development, in its first stages at least, needed the energy of thrusting entrepreneurs, rather than old dynasties of bureaucratic noblemen? Is the explanation to be sought in the culture of China, whose distinguishing feature was that no one can learn to read Chinese by himself: he has to be taught? (20) Did the changeless rhythm of a successful but necessarily disciplined society, based on the cultivation of rice, prevent any sustained enterprise? Did the low status of craftsmanship prevent a Chinese industrialisation in the sixteenth century? Or should we blame exclusively the palace revolution of 1432, which brought to power in China a group opposed to trade and to discovery? (21) Perhaps the critical point is that China, like most Eastern despotisms, was a bureaucratic empire turned towards the past. Families rendered tribute to ancestors who had successfully established stable village communities for intensive cultivation. A frequently hereditary class of artisans assured to those communities such manufactured goods as were necessary. Commerce was local where it was not based on the family. Muslim and European merchants traded with the monarchs, not the people, and kept to their ghettoes.

Within Europe, England's greatest opponent of an earlier day, Spain, also failed to inspire a spirit of innovation. After the unwise surrender to popular jealousy of the Jews and Moors, the King used the Mesta, the convoy which carried sheep up and down Spain, as a bureaucratic model as to how to manage trade with the New World. Trade was organised by civil servants, who ensured the Crown a revenue, but failed to serve the national economy. Even the trade to the Americas in slaves was farmed out to Genoese contractors (like many other despotisms, the Spanish Crown *preferred* foreign contractors, since they made for less political trouble and could not establish themselves as 'over mighty' subjects). Spain became dependent on them for investment in their mines and plantations. Later, French merchants dominated Seville. Most manufactured goods sold in the Spanish Indies were French in origin. The narrow character of Spanish trade to the Americas, the restriction of commerce to only one port for so long — Cadiz or Seville — the ban on American manufacture (except for sugar), the demand for precious metals (to the neglect of other products of the Americas) all this contributed to the ease with which Spain maintained control over her American empire. Stability and underdevelopment went hand-in-hand. Only in the late eighteenth century did Spain permit anything like an open trade with her colonies in the Americas. In Spain itself, theologians thought that business destroyed the mediaeval harmony of the spheres. Lack of roads, poor communications by river, and price-fixing also hampered enterprise (22). Then Spain did not, indeed refused to, create the naval power needed to protect her empire and failed to supply the cheap goods which the sophisticated in that empire desired. Nor did Spain have a staple. Exports of wool dropped after 1800 and only in iron, from the Basque country, did the nation find anything like a substitute for the Mexican silver upon which she had relied in the eighteenth century. So it was not surprising that while, between 1789 and 1832, the other countries of Europe grew commercially, after their different fashions, Spain's trade in 1829 was a mere third of what it had been in 1785 (23). In Spanish America, owners of capital had no inducement to invest in industry, in the absence of a strong and protected market. It was easier to allow English manufactures to flood in. English merchants, shippers, and bankers indeed filled the entrepreneurial gap left by Spain's withdrawal (24). In a well known passage, de Tocqueville explained that, in France, in the eighteenth century, many had differing views about the ideal state, but all wished to make use, beneficially or malevolently, of the central power as it stood. 'It never occurred to anyone,' he said, 'that any large enterprise could be put through successfully without the intervention of the state' (25). Spain, under the Bourbons, was, as it were, a dependency of France even more intellectually than militarily, and Spanish views on these matters were identical to those of the great French public servants. In England, one powerful reason for the success of the industrialisation in the generation between 1760 and 1780 was that the opposite could have been said.

BOOK V

Our Times II –
Political failures

Revolutions have so often taken the form of resurrections.
Lefebvre, introduction to Marc Bloch's *French Rural History*

One must make a little more revolution every day
Emiliano Iglesias, a Spanish Radical,
twirling his moustaches in the
Café Continental, Barcelona, about 1900

Life in the old Austria during the last decades of the Emperor Francis Joseph must
have been agreeable . . . tears come to the eyes of the old who lived through this
period when they see it sentimentally reflected on the screen. Why could it not last?
Why should the disaster which so profoundly changed Europe have started here, of
all places. . . ?
Golo Mann, *The history of Germany since 1789*

Fanelli [the Italian anarchist] managed to get together [in Madrid, 1868] in the house
of Rubau Donadeu, a few workers from the group of El Fomento de las Artes.
Fanelli did not speak Spanish and his hearers did not know a word of Italian and
very few of them could translate anything even mediocrely from French. . . Fanelli
began to speak in French and Italian indifferently. He spoke very vividly. *Cosa
horrible! Spaventosa!* when he spoke of the miseries of the workers. In a few minutes,
the audience was prisoner of a delicious enthusiasm . . . and those who heard went
out, as Don Quixote had gone out, ready to fight evil and to preach the good news.
J. Díaz del Moral, *Historia de las agitaciones campesinas: Andaluzas-Córdoba*

In all directions, our habitual courses of action seem to be losing efficaciousness,
credit and control, both with others and even with ourselves. Everywhere, we see
the beginnings of confusion and we want a clue to some sound order and authority.
Matthew Arnold, *Culture and Anarchy*

Two men quarrelled and then fought as to whether Ariosto or Tasso were the better poet. They mortally wounded each other and with their dying gasps confessed that they had never read either.
A Story as quoted by Francisco Cambó, in the Spanish Cortes, 20 November, 1918

About 1900, the assumption that life was improving was general. People lived longer than they had had ever done before. Women were beginning to be treated more equally. Education was being considered in most rich countries an essential charge on the State. The Rule of Law was increasingly respected. Large museums showed the masterpieces of painting to an ever more interested public. A few large, rich and open-minded States seemed to have tamed the world. The European conquests in Africa and Asia had largely been carried out without bloodshed. The Americans, it is true, had escaped from control of the European empires. But that the US and Latin America were European in origin and culture was evident. All the European Empires seemed to share views rather similar to one another. Their daily contacts seemed to grow closer, even if their Governments were divided by alliances and armaments programmes.

A belief in progress seemed justifiable to most leaders of opinion. Gibbon had said in the eighteenth century: 'We may, therefore, acquiesce in the pleasing conclusion that every age of the world has increased, and still increases, the real wealth, the happiness, the knowledge and perhaps the virtue of the human race' (1). Macaulay did not differ in the 1840s: the history of England at least seemed to him since 1700 or so 'the history of physical, of moral and of intellectual, improvement' (2). Lord Salisbury might have begged to differ: 'But whither are we going?' he asked in 1870, and found that no one answered satisfactorily (3). Thirty years later, in the early years of the twentieth century, it did seem that 'the peoples of Europe, save for a savage patch in the Balkans, had reached an unprecedented level of comfort and civilisation. Representative institutions, though in many parts of the continent ill rooted, ill practised, and ill understood, were universal. The belief that the world was moving towards unity seemed to be growing in strength. . . Recourse to arbitration for the settlement of international quarrels was becoming more frequent . . . it seemed as if statesmen had, at long last, learned the lesson that politics is the art of human happiness' (4) Thus the Oxford historian, Herbert Fisher.

Much the same point was made by Maynard Keynes, with his accustomed grace: 'What an extraordinary episode in the economic progress of man that age was which came to an end in 1914! The greater part of the population, it is true, worked hard and lived at a low standard of comfort, yet were, to all appearances, reasonably contented with this lot. But escape was possible for any man of capacity or character at all exceeding the average, into the upper and middle classes, for whom life offered, at a low cost and with the least trouble, conveniences, comforts and amenities beyond the compass of the richest and most powerful monarchs of other ages. The inhabitant of London could order by telephone, sipping his morning tea in bed, the various products of the whole earth, in such quantity as he might reasonably expect their early delivery upon his doorstep . . . he could secure forthwith . . . cheap and comfortable transit to any country or climate without passport . . . and would consider himself much aggrieved and much surprised at the least interference . . . he regarded this state of affairs as normal, certain and permanent, except in direction of improvement. . .

'The projects and politics of militarism and imperialism, of racial and cultural rivalries, of monopolies, restrictions and exclusion,' Keynes continued, 'which were to play the serpent to this paradise were little more than the amusements of his daily paper, and appeared to exercise almost no influence at all on the ordinary course of social and economic life, the internationalisation of which was nearly complete in practice' (5).

The twentieth century has certainly observed the continuance of many of the improvements of the nineteenth. This obvious truism has already been noticed. Even so, the 'savage patch' of which Fisher wrote was unfortunately not confined to the Balkans. It spread. In the end — though our evaluation need not be quite so gloomy as Berdyaev's ('man's historical experience has been one of steady failure . . . not one single project . . . has ever proved successful') (6), modern man has failed as yet to devise a successful alternative to the close-knit tribal organisation which characterised hunting tribes and the rule by landlords which characterised the age of agriculture. This is a result not of any 'general law of decay', as was supposed to obtain in Greece (at the least by Pericles (7)), but because of a political failure. The technological innovations noticed in the preceding chapters have quite simply not been complemented by political achievements of comparable ingenuity. Elie Halévy, the historian of the English nineteenth century, wrote in 1912, in the Preface to his great book that 'representative government bids fair to become part of the common inheritance of mankind'. That has seemed a premature judgement.

Several reasons suggest themselves: first, there has been a conversion of certain political movements into lay religions, so that, even in democracies, a number of political persons have ceased to accept the possibility that they may have made a wrong judgement.

Second, we have seen a growth of certain illusions such as that class and race are determing characteristics of human affairs. Third, the technological improvements have assisted despotisms at least as much as they have free societies; indeed, technological changes have caused upheavals within free societies. In particular, they have caused a disruption of the concept of neighbourhood, have destroyed many people's sense of belonging to a local community, have dislocated kinship. Until the eighteenth century, it can be argued, the roots of culture and personality lay in the neighbourhood as well as family and religion (8). But those ties which tied the individual to society in the past have recently been shaken. One consequence has been an enhancement of nation at the cost of all other associations. Even in so old a world as Western Europe, the nations of the twentieth century, democratic and with universal suffrage, are as unlike the old nations of the eighteenth century as an aeroplane is to an ox cart. The mass democracies are still in their infancy. But both they and despotic nations old and *new have been equally severely tested by what Isaiah Berlin has called the 'final breakdown of order known as war', which both enhanced and depressed Western Europeans' sense of nationhood (9).*

The consequent fractures of societies need to be mended very carefully. They have not been so yet. Perhaps pressure of population is the chief explanation. At all events, in the words of the Austrian, Hayek, 'We have seen great nations losing every shred of humour, all sense of honour, the very idea of decency and fair play' (10). How could it have happened? An English historian, J. H. Plumb, wrote, that one truth of history is that 'the condition of man has improved, materially alas more than morally, but nevertheless both have improved' (11). Has there been a moral improvement? It is hard to see. The country in the world with the best education for longest, the nation with the most serious national preoccupation with learning, the people with the highest rate of literacy in the world in the eighteenth century were the authors of Auschwitz.

Of course, there has been progress, by almost any usual definition of the word, in numerous fields, but there has, equally surely, been retrogression or stagnation in others. For example, the laws of Hammurabi in Babylon in 1800 BC were imperfect. But they probably guaranteed a more secure life than the code of laws which applies in Iraq today. In their earliest Sumerian society, women probably had a higher status than they have ever had since in that region. The use of torture for interrogation had almost disappeared from the practices of all-powerful states by 1800. The practice has been widely revived. Punishment of families for the alleged crimes of one of their members survives in half the world. Obviously, the qualities of intellectual vigour were more striking in the Renaissance in Italy than they have been there since the formation of the new Italian unified state. No one would use the word 'progress' in respect of art except in limited subjects such as the use of perspective or rhyme or counter point. It would be difficult to sustain an argument that people in the twentieth century are on better terms with minorities than they used to be. Many comparable instances suggest themselves. The very idea of Auschwitz and Vorkuta, or of the barrier which divides West from East Germany, would have been unthinkable in the eighteenth century. A weapon such as the nuclear weapon would have been rejected out of hand by most governments in the nineteenth century and, indeed, Lord Dundonald's far less destructive scheme for beating Russia was rejected in the 1850s. The dictatorships of the twentieth century, particularly, those established in the name of 'the people' are so harsh that they would have caused Voltaire and the philosophes, *had they known what might happen, to have hesitated before advocating the overthrow of the Bourbons. To read Boswell's* Life of Johnson *is also to become vaguely, incoherently, but unmistakably, aware of a world both more robust and more gentle, more individual, and more gregarious, more free but more coherent, more literary but closer to nature than is usual in our society today, formally considerate, liberal, indulgent and responsible though it may seem. The most 'violent' riot in English political history, at Peterloo, Manchester, in the tumultuous days of the first industrial revolution in the world, resulted in nineteen deaths in 1819 (12). There are few industrialising countries in the 1970s where at least that number are not killed for political reasons every year. The Book which follows discusses the occasions of these setbacks in human affairs. Meantime, by now, J. B. Bury's prediction in the 1920s, that a day would come when the idea of Progress would have to be judged as just one more star in the intellectual heaven, with its era of rise and of wane, seems to many to have arrived already (13).*

41

Modern Warfare

The modern state is an institution with many ancestors but its father is war. All states cherish as heroes the leaders in battle in the past, just as the armed services are the final sanction of the laws, and were the creators of the frontiers and the unity of the state. The 150 or so states of the world have mostly come into being as a result of conflict and the wise manipulation of military power. That may seem shocking to those with no knowledge of history. But history often shocks. Hence, there is a sense in which the historians of the last century were correct in concentrating so exclusively on the history of war. It is against the background of war and the fear of it that the history of our times also has been played out. Michael Howard, at the end of a survey of European history, recently also drew attention to one critical part of our affairs today which is sometimes overlooked: 'Nothing has occurred since 1945 to indicate that war or the threat of it could not still be an effective instrument of state policy. Indeed against people not prepared to arm themselves properly it could still be exceptionally effective'.

It is perhaps worth while pointing out something which should be obvious but is not always so. It is not only politics and war which have gone hand-in-hand: industry and technological change have done so also. In the eighteenth century, iron foundries became identified, above all, with the casting of cannon (2). Could the steam engine have been properly developed, had it not been for John Wilkinson's boring mill, which was also originally used for cannon? The 'American system of manufacture', that is, the interchangeability of identical parts, was first used in Paris in respect of muskets. The French desire for an assured supply of saltpetre to make gunpowder in the eighteenth century led ultimately to the discovery that the soil is inhabited by micro-organisms (3). Mechanised book-binding began probably because of the shortage of labour among binders during the Napoleonic wars, while the high cost of fodder for cattle used to haul coal from the pithead during the same conflict led to Stephenson's 'Rocket'. Tinning of food began to serve the French army during the Napoleonic wars, while dried milk was the response to a quartermaster's demand during the American

Civil War. The characteristic material of the age of industry since 1870, steel, has been mostly used for war; and, in the shadow of war, civilised life has continued since then, too – preparing for it, winning or losing it, recovering from it, and seeking means to avoid it. So it is desirable to consider the frame against which political life and religious life has been maintained very carefully. Of course, the history of the last two hundred years has also been the history of the novel, of the symphony, and of the tractor; but war has been its prime mover.

The modern history of war began with the fortress. In the eighteenth century, wars were marked by elaborate defence systems inspired by the French engineer, Sébastien Vauban. His main idea was a system of polygonal defence, stretched out beyond the city wall, using that wall as a platform for artillery. His fortresses required, it was said, as great an engineer as he himself was to demolish them (4). So, warfare on land mostly implied the slow assembly of siege batteries. The field gun began its career changing the character of battles on land and sea (5). Horse artillery was introduced by Frederick the Great (6). Meantime, the only guns used by infantry were muskets, with flintlocks which had an effective range of 100 yards at most. They were thus out-ranged by all artillery – particularly guns firing grapeshot (such as were used so famously by Napoleon at Toulon). Bayonet assaults, as devised by the French in the seventeenth century, for the most part kept infantrymen occupied. Rifles were still scarcely used, except for sport.

The field gun undid the fortress. The former could be accompanied by the telescope from the early seventeenth century. That improved the accuracy of artillery fire. Better mobility of supplies (by canals, improved roads, and an organised commissariat) gave an impetus in the mid-eighteenth century to a mobile army. Meantime, the improved professional armies could be turned, in the event of an economic crisis, to control a contrary populace.

Of this age of artillery, Napoleon, trained as an artillery officer, was the supreme beneficiary. He always had a large quantity of guns. Even more important, he had a lot of men. Unusually, he believed in detailed attention to their needs. 'A battalion commander should not rest,' he said, 'until he has become acquainted with every detail. After six months in command he should even know the names and the abilities of all the officers and men of his battalion.'

The largest army in the world in the eighteenth century, however, was that accumulated by Peter the Great: 200,000 regular troops and 100,000 militia (7). Peter thought of himself as first and foremost a soldier. When a son was born to him, he told the nation that God had blessed him with another recruit. But, when he came to the throne of Russia, his army was still an old-fashioned Muscovite horde. It was assembled in the spring – almost every spring – with all available weapons, massed together and let fly on the enemy at an appropriate signal, with scarcely any chain of command or officers trained to guide the men. Peter changed all that. But, though inspired in his organisation by Europeans, he still used Mongol custom to ensure him recruits. Thus, at a time when most European armies were manned by volunteers or foreign mercenaries, the new Russian government demanded that every twenty households annually should provide one soldier. Numerous exceptions cut down the numbers of men available, but this system remained much the same till the First World War. Built round two guards' regiments, Preobrazhenskii and Semenovskii (both composed of nobles), the Russian armies became a match, within a generation, for the professional armies of the Swedes and Turks. A regular navy was similarly established. With these two conscripted forces, the modern state of Russia was created by 1725 (8).* In particular, the Russians could prevent the massed hosts of Mongol cavalry sweeping into their country every summer from the Crimea in search of slaves, as they had done for 300 years.

Conscription was extended to Western Europe on a regular basis by the French Revolution, when the Convention decreed a *levée en masse*: 'From this moment until that in which our enemies shall have been driven from the territory of the republic, all Frenchmen are permanently requisitioned for service in the armies. The young men will fight; the married men will forge weapons and transport supplies; the women will make tents and clothes and serve in the hospitals; the children will make up old linen into lint; and the old men will have themselves carried into the public squares to rouse the courage of the fighting men.' (9). This characteristic development of the modern world was really a return to barbarism, even though the philosopher Condorcet thought infantry a first step towards political democracy. Primitive tribes had been armed hordes and, since all tribes engaged in war, warfare had then been total. Though that system was considered wasteful in the ancient world, it was revived in the Dark Ages in Europe. By the seventeenth century, however, all militarily successful states had come to depend on trained, professional standing armies. Spanish infantry in the sixteenth century had depended on conscripting one man in twelve, but he became a profesional and was well trained. No hereditary monarch of the eighteenth century would have dreamed of imposing mass conscription (10). In the mid nineteenth century, during the Crimean War, the manager of the Clay Cross works in Derbyshire told Matthew Arnold that, 'sooner than submit to a conscription, the population of that district would flee to the mines and live a sort of Robin Hood life underground' (11). By the time of the First World War, Ludendorff thought of mobilising the youth of both sexes in Germany the moment

* There were some instances of conscription before in Western Europe, but only periodically and in emergencies, e.g. in Spain in 1637, Sweden in the 1630s, in France in the war of the Spanish succession.

that they reached the age of sixteen. All would be sent to training camps. There would thus be left a society neither civilian nor military. Instead, a truly egalitarian society would emerge, a 'nationalist-aristocratic-corporativist-socialist consciousness', the whole nation in step (12): a prophecy of both communism and Nazism.

The innovation of conscription transformed war in a way almost more critical than gunpowder. For a few centuries before 1789, soldiers had been expensive. Battles were, therefore, avoided, unless inevitable. 'The object of the campaign,' wrote the historian of the British Army, Sir John Fortescue, 'was not necessarily to seek out an enemy and beat him. . . There were two alternatives. . . to fight at an advantage or to subsist comfortably . . . A campaign wherein an army lived on the enemy's country was . . . eminently successful' (13). After 1789, soldiers became cheap. Napoleon boasted to Metternich in 1813 that he cared 'little for the lives of a million men' (14). The losses could be made up from new acts of conscription.

A 'nation in arms' has to be fed on violent propaganda. The new means of communication, from newspapers to radio and television, have provided that. Peace thus became more difficult to establish. Peace treaties became more unreasonable than they had been in the eighteenth century. They were hence often more precarious (15). By then, too, nations not only conscripted their citizens when they were at war. They did so when they were at peace, on the assumption that a 'trained reserve' was essential.

These large armies of the nineteenth and twentieth centuries have played an important, even a predominant part, in politics, regardless of war, regardless even of the fact that an army successful in war can often inspire peace. Thus Spanish America, in her war of independence of the early nineteenth century, replaced the distant king over the Atlantic with armies whose size and cost were out of proportion to their function. European invaders were then improbable. Spain could not hope for reconquest. The army of the US in the 1830s numbered 6,000 (16). Yet the tiny state of Colombia, at that time, had an army of 25,000 to 30,000 (17). The military budget was three quarters of the budget of the country. (Admittedly, Peter the Great had gone further, for he regularly spent 80 to 85% of the revenue of the state on the army.) (18) Though justified as providing law and order, armies in Spanish America were usually the cause of anarchy. The government of colonial Spanish America had maintained itself with a minuscule military presence. There was no Spanish standing army in America at all till the 1760s. But the wars of independence created warriors, militarism and caudillos. Much the same thing occurred in Spain itself in the nineteenth century. There, a network of military forces was organised throughout the nation, which was divided into eight divisional commands, each with soldiers spread through the region concerned. That system was intended to give stability. Instead, it afforded opportunities for innumerable military interventions in politics between 1815 and 1936 on a scale and in a manner which had never occurred before 1789.

The Europeans had by now the largest armies. In 1813, at Leipzig, 539,000 fought. At Solferino, in 1859, the battle ranged over sixty square miles and almost 300,000 men were concerned. More people died there than at Waterloo (19). Fifteen years later, the new Italy, a country of no great military importance, already had 350,000 in its standing army and 350,000 reservists (20). Before 1861, the US army was still only 16,000 men strong. In the Civil War, both sides began with voluntary enlistment but, as war lengthened, conscription was resorted to, by the South in 1862, the North in 1863. The South called up 90% of all its men (perhaps 1,400,000) and the North 45% (2,900,000).

It is true that some small armies since the French Revolution have won victories. Even Napoleon I conquered the Po valley with 30,000 men, and Garibaldi in Naples had only 20,000 volunteers (21). Kitchener won the Sudan at Omdurman, losing 48 men killed against 11,000 opponents (22). The twentieth century also would see some examples of small numbers fighting successfully against larger ones. The Cubans in 1895 tied down 50,000 Spanish soldiers with about 6,000 guerillas (23). But, on the whole, the major engagements of the age of industry have been vast undertakings, with millions of men implicated

The technological inventions in wars of this age have been also continuous. Good examples of this can be seen in the history of the rifle. A regular rifle was in uspendence by American 'minute men' – picked marksmen with good eyes who could hit a target up to 1,000 yards away. But they were exceptions. Normally, rifles were used in the eighteenth century to cover a mere 100 yards. In 1784, Lieutenant Henry Shrapnel invented the 'spherical case' with which his name subsequently became associated and which was adopted by the Ordnance in 1803. That discovery began to make the rifle more useful. In 1807, the Reverend Alexander Forsyth, a Scottish minister from Aberdeenshire, devised percussion priming powder, which led to the percussion cap of steel and copper. Forsyth carried out his experiments in the Tower of London, and Lord Moira, then Master General of the Ordnance, provided a substitute for the discharge of the military inventor's pastoral duties. Napoleon offered Forsyth £20,000 for the secret of his invention. He patriotically refused, though the British government gave him nothing till he was on his deathbed (24). His system came into use after his death, in 1839, and was of great military benefit, because of the impermeability of this cap to wind and rain.

Not long afterwards, the bullet was redesigned by Captain John Norton in a cylindrical shape, with a hollow base, on the inspiration of lotus pith arrows which he had seen blown in India.

Again, the British Ordnance took a long time to put the idea into use.

The French developed it for Minié's rifle, which had a range of about 500 yards. That outdistanced accurate artillery fire and, along with the precision cap, transformed tactics of infantry (25).

By the mid 1860s, rifle-carrying infantrymen became the rule, not the exception. At the same time, the breechloading 'needle gun', which fired a paper cartridge, and was invented by J. M. Dreyse in the 1840s, adopted by the Prussians. It could soon be mass-produced: 400,000 needle-gun infantrymen were used by the Prussians at the battle of Königgrätz, which effectively, but, for the future tranquillity of Europe, fatally, weakened Austria (still reliant on muzzle-loaded weapons) from her historic role as a bastion of Europe against Russia.

The breech-loading rifle, as opposed to its muzzle-loading predecessor, increased the rapidity with which soldiers could fire and enabled them to do so when lying down or from behind cover. Field Marshal von Moltke was convinced that it made defence stronger than attack and that, therefore, battles would be won by envelopment (26). Meantime, the Americans were producing pistols in large numbers. After 1846, the revolver, in whose early production Samuel Colt was pre-eminent, turned out as very effective indeed in close fighting, particularly in the Mexican war. A mass demand for it followed among the gold seekers of California in 1849. All these US innovations were distinguished by a full interchange of parts, that essential modern contribution to manufacture.

The rifle, by methods of 'American manufacture', began to be produced also in the same way. It was copied in England by Sir Joseph Whitworth, the great Mancunian gunsmith, and the Royal small arms factory at Enfield was producing 1,000 rifles a week by the 1860s. Every rifle needed 700 separate parts, each being interchangeable. 'Form, riflemen form,' adjured the poet laureate, Tennyson, in a poem written in 1859, 'Ready, be ready, against the storm.' The new Enfield rifle used, to begin with, cartridges covered with grease which had to be bitten open before loading. The rumour spread in India, correctly, that the grease was made from beef or pork fat. For a caste Hindu to bite such fat was a serious sin. Many sepoys in the British Indian service were brahmins and, if they were to bite such fat, they believed that they would fall back in their next lives: they thought that it would take them many lifetimes to get back, through the cycle of reincarnation, to the summit which they believed that they had attained. Hence the Indian Mutiny in 1857.

The French were busy, too. Their *chassepôt*, introduced in 1866, and invented by an officer of that name, was in some ways superior to both the needle gun and the old musket, since it had an effective accuracy of 600 metres. Tougher than the needle gun, it could also fire 6 to 7 rounds a minute. But sustained heavy fire with the *chassepôt* caused trouble. It had to be well-maintained. When put to the test in the Franco-Prussian war, it was defeated by the needle gun (which the French generals assured their men would jam after it had fired a few rounds). The Second Empire fell (27).

During the rest of the century, the European powers competed to be the most effective producers of firepower, though really they had reached by 1871 an almost unimprovable standard of efficiency. Which was better, the French Lebel rifle or the Mauser, the Mannlicher or the 303 Lee-Metford? The Martini-Henry used metallic cartridges but Lebel's *poudre B* gave that an advantage. By 1900, all European states, anyway, had magazine rifles of roughly equal efficiency with calibres ranging from .315 to .256, all bolt-operated. All had smokeless powder and could be sighted to 2,000 yards. By then, machine guns which could massacre infantrymen had been devised too; for example, the ten-barrel revolving rifle fed by gravity and rotated by a handcrank, as invented by R. J. Gatling. The French *mitrailleuse* (with 25 barrels firing 125 rounds a minute) had been considered a secret weapon when begun in 1865. Excessive secrecy prevented its proper deployment in time for 1870. The machine gun was only finally successful after 1884, when Sir Hiram Maxim devised his recoil-operated gun to become the crucial weapon in both the last, African stage of European imperialism and in the trenches which were to destroy it. 2,000 rounds could be fired in three minutes.

Artillery had, however, its own critical developments in the nineteenth century. The gun shell, the now familiar device which causes a violent explosion on landing, was first used at the Siege of Gibraltar in 1780–83, being then known as 'Mercier's operative gun device'. It was not, however, in general use till after the Napoleonic Wars. But it became evident that it too could cause a revolution in war only in 1853 when Russian field guns destroyed the wooden warships of the Turks in Sinope Bay (so leading to the development of both iron-clad ships and floating batteries).* Nothing much happened, however, till the Crimea, when James Cowan tried to sell the British Army a boadicean device, consisting of a steam-driven land battery fitted with scythes to mow down infantry. Both that and a four-wheeled armoured vehicle full of guns were, however, rejected by Lord Palmerston as too brutal (28).

Before that, in 1846, a breech-loading 6.5"rifled gun had been invented by Major Cavalli in Sardinia. To begin with, no government felt able to pay for it. The Crimean War caused such hesitations to be swept away: many iron-cast, muzzle-loaded, smooth-bore 68-pounder and 8-inch guns were converted into rifled pieces. The rotation of the shell was achieved by the oval shape of the bore and then twisted (29).

This artillery contemporary of the 'rifled' air gun for infantry was used with effect by the French against the Austrians in 1860 (*Canons de 4*

---

* Iron has already been discussed. See page 270.

or *de 12)*. In 1870, the French had a new version of these: bronze, rifled muzzle loaders, with a range of 2,900 to 3,400 metres, of which each infantry divison had two or three six gun batteries. But the German 9-centimetre gun was three times as accurate as the *canon de 12* and had a higher rate of fire. The lethal nature of the German percussion fused shells (which exploded on impact) was also greater: here Napoleon III was personally responsible, for, ten years before, he had deliberately chosen a two-hole fuse, instead of the German weapon (30).

At the end of the century, with these changes, artillery was practically converted into rifle power. A bullet-proof shield protected the gun crew, and the gun itself, practically invisible, began to outrange rifles, and to be fired as fast.

The American Civil War had, meantime, constituted a positive laboratory of military invention. Armoured trains, explosive bullets, explosive booby traps and stink bombs all had their first use in that unexpected conflict. So, for the first time for a century or so, did terror used against civilians. Warfare at sea was transformed by the activities of the ironclads *Merrimac* and *Monitor*. Even a submarine (inspired by Fulton in the 1790s) was built. It sunk a battleship off Charleston. Sea-mines had first been used by Russians to protect their base at Kronstadt in 1853, while the self-propelled explosive torpedo* had finally been invented for the Austrians by a Lancashire inventor, Robert Whitehead, in 1864.

Propaganda in a modern sense began with the telegraph. But, once established for war-like purposes after the war of 1859 in Italy, it became an essential part of military communications. Telegraph wires also made it possible for events abroad to be reported in hours, not days or weeks (31). The telephone soon assisted that speed. The war reporter, the official communiqué, the special correspondent, the war photographer and the war artist thus entered battle. Legends have subsequently played as important a part in war as real news. Very often, what is believed to be the case is more influential on people's imaginations than what is the case: as, indeed, Shakespeare recognised when he began his series of plays about the civil wars of the fifteenth century with a speech by Rumour.

The preceding chapter has sought to analyse the technical and organisational preparations for war in the modern world. The wars which followed, in the twentieth century, were fought on a scale hitherto unknown. The causes of these great wars were various as were the causes of the so called 'cold war' which is, in many ways, a third world war in disguise. There were economic causes and there were, even in the century of mass movements, personal causes. Nevertheless, ideas were also at stake and, as the wars continued, these became more and more

* Having earlier been conceived by Robert Fulton, see above, page 314.

important. The most cynical politicians became aware that their peoples could only be persuaded to continue fighting and making munitions if they were doing so for an idea. The main idea at issue in the first world war, the 'Great War', as it was known for a generation afterwards, was that of government by personal rule of traditional monarchs. In the course of the conflict, four emperors were ruined: those of Germany, Russia, Austria-Hungary and Turkey. The next chapter discusses the modern history of monarchy and its relation with other forms of despotism.

42

Causes of War: Monarchy and Despotism

'I do not know how the lust for power is among other rulers,' said Catherine the Great, 'with me it is not very great.'
> quoted by Radischev *A Journey from St Petersburg to Moscow*

It is not mere imperfection, not corruption in low quarters, not occasional severity that I am about to describe, it is incessant, systematic, deliberate violation of the law by the power appointed to watch over and maintain it . . . it is the wholesale persecution of virtue when united with intelligence . . . operating on such a scale that entire classes may with truth be said to be its object so that the government is in bitter and cruel, as well as utterly illegal, hostility to whatever in the nation lives and moves . . . I have seen and heard the strong and too true expression used, '*E la negazione di Dio eretta a sistema di governo.*'
> W. E. Gladstone, *Two letters to the Earl of Aberdeen.*

In the 1750s, at the birth of the age of industry, almost the whole inhabited part of the globe was formally ruled by hereditary rulers, among whom succession passed by primogeniture. Several nomadic societies survived, and there monarchy, primogeniture, and a settled succession were less common, though the technologically advanced European monarchies encouraged a pale version of their own monarchical arrangements in remote places with which they came into contact. A few mercantile republics had also limited, or abolished, the authority of monarchs: Switzerland, and a few German and Italian cities. But monarchies seemed generally to be becoming stronger, not weaker. Italian cities were every year becoming less and less able to withstand the power of States. The rulers known as the 'enlightened despots', in Prussia, Naples, Tuscany, Spain, Austria and even Russia, were using their authority both more intelligently and more overbearingly. The new official known as the *Intendant* made government more efficient in France and Spain. For a time, there were some who thought that George III of England might also turn out to be more than a *roi fainéant* and be 'the common father of all his people' (1). These monarchs were everywhere trying their best to abolish privileges and remove inequalities within their territories, everywhere seeking to level out disparities of income, replacing members of the aristocracy with trained civil servants, and a diversity of powers with a strong, centralised government (2). They were usually successful. It was they really who created the modern States. Democracies later inherited them. Of these enlightened hereditary rulers, Napoleon I was the real, if bastardised, heir. No one believed more strongly than he in absolute monarchy and every feature of his innovations showed the characteristic marks of the old régime, from the prefect (the *intendant*, in a new guise) to the *Conseil d'état* (based on the old *Conseil du Roi*) (3). His rule in Italy, abolishing feudal law and laws against Jews, permitting civil marriage and introducing open trials, were those of an enlightened despot *par excellence*. So were the provisions in the *Code Napoléon* giving great power to husbands and fathers, and to masters against servants – in that respect, as in some others, being less liberal than the old régime had been (4).

Britain was the only exception to this picture of growing monarchical strength since, though her monarchs survived, they were ineffective. As with the Merovingian kings of France, in the sixth and seventh centuries, the power of the British monarch was exercised by a prime minister (or *maire du palais*), in this case chosen by the elected representative of a strong, enlightened aristocracy. Nor were the British ministers making any effort to create a strong and centralised government.

Naturally, the word 'monarchy' gives an inadequate picture of what constituted government in 1750. As suggested earlier*, monarchy was everywhere, even in Britain, the apex of a system in which the lower sections were run by landed aristocracy. The history of politics in the age of industrialisation is, as John Vincent put it, one of a search for a new system to replace government by those landowners (5), or alternatively, the history of how some of those men accepted loss of power gracefully or fought against it, sometimes successfully, usually not. When it came to the point, the monarchies mostly destroyed themselves by destroying first the structure of aristocracy which had hitherto supported and inspired them.

In the eighteenth century, the concept of monarchy was already being criticised: 'of the various forms of government which have prevailed,' wrote Gibbon, 'an hereditary monarchy seems to present the fairest scope for ridicule,' adding, 'In the cool shade of retirement we may easily devise imaginary forms of government in which the sceptre shall be constantly bestowed upon the most worthy by the free and incorrupt suffrage of the whole community. Experience overturns these airy fabrics' (6).

In 1750, in many established monarchies, the outlying parts of the rulers' dominions also had already many powers of self-rule: the British empire in North America, for example, or the cities of Spanish America, or the Mamluks who ruled Egypt on behalf of the Sultan of Turkey,

* See above, page 102.

were close to self-government in practice, even if, from time to time, law was invoked to remind the places concerned of their formal subservience. Meantime, within regions legally part of one monarchy or another, nomads (as in Spanish and Portuguese America) or tribal authorities (as in central Russia or the Ottoman Empire) maintained *de facto* supervision of a number of subjects only theoretically subordinate to the higher authority. In vast regions (most of Africa, western North America, Australasia, the South Seas) such nomadic or tribal authorities were still independent. In other places, such as the Far East, ancient monarchical despotisms, static and stable, fearful that the slightest change might cause the collapse of the edifice, survived, as they had for many generations, sometimes (as in India) making a humiliating obeisance to European or Arab powers, in hope of being left alone most of the time.

These circumstances remained much the same till the early twentieth century – till, indeed, 1917–1919. Three monarchs (Victor Emmanuel, Napoleon III and Franz Josef) personally fought in the war of 1859. True, there were several formal changes: the European colonies in the Americas broke away into independence, in a political revolution which began at Lexington in British North America in 1775 and ended at the battle of Ayacucho in Peru in 1824*; the Europeans reconstructed the Empires which they had thus lost in Africa instead – a different type of Empire from the one which they had controlled in the Americas since, in Africa, a much larger indigenous settled population existed and one which had shared in many technological changes, inspired by the innovations of the ancient Near East. In the British Empire, the indigenous monarchies remained where they were, kingdoms and chieftainships existing on sufferance beneath colonial rulers. The Europeans increased their hold over certain parts of East Asia and extended it to Australasia and the South Seas. Finally, several European states suffered upheavals, so that France, like the USA and Switzerland, became a republic, while a newly united Germany and Italy were, like Spain and most other European countries, monarchies, with some democratic control – less than that in England, but more than that in the still dynastically dominated empires of Austria, Turkey and Russia.

Many absolute monarchies made effective use of industrialisation to begin with, though most ultimately collapsed because of the inherent difficulty of maintaining such an institution in circumstances increasingly unlike those in which they were founded. Even Brazil boasted an emperor who survived until 1889. The last forty years of that new empire brought great prosperity. The Prussian, Russian and Japanese

* Of course some American colonies survived till 1898 (Cuba and Puerto Rico) and others till the 1950s. Indeed Europe still has a few Caribbean possessions (Guadeloupe and Martinique, Curaçao, etc).

monarchies made every adjustment that they could to take advantage of the new benefits which technology could bring to them. Speed and ease of communications made their kingdoms for several generations able to maintain, to expand and to take advantage of military opportunities. The Prussian monarchy, for example, became the focus for German unification in the nineteenth century, and the motor of the first of Germany's two 'grabs for world power' in the twentieth. Kaiser Wilhelm II considered his task 'as having been imposed on me from heaven' and sustained that absolutism by militarism. (7) So the monarchy became discredited after the defeat of 1918 and vanished, dragging down with it the surviving smaller monarchies of old Germany, but leaving behind certain hankerings for heroic leadership which played a part in the rise of the Nazis. The Italian monarchy had a roughly comparable history, becoming a symbol of Italian unity between 1848 and 1871, and being also dragged down by defeat, in 1943. The Austrian emperors ceased 'to think the throne an easy chair in which to sprawl', and became more repressive than previously (8) though the Emperor Karl failed, in the crisis of 1918, to maintain united the disparate parts of his multi-national domain. Though the Austrians 'in their white coats and shakos', in the words of Trevelyan, 'moved unceasingly in their fruitless, mechanical task of repression' (9) over Italy, they ultimately failed to maintain themselves there – doubtless because the method of working of Franz Josef had 'the narrow penetration of a gimlet' (10).

The Russian monarchy also devised new methods of repression, from the mid-nineteenth century onwards. It combined subsidies to industrialisation with a greater control over its fast growing population. That monarchy also collapsed during the First World War, not so much as a result of military defeat as because of the economic stress brought by the rapid wartime industrialisation. As with Germany, the monarch passed on a centralising repressive tradition, to be immediately revivified under the communist leaders since that time (Lenin, Stalin, Khrushchev and Brezhnev). The Japanese monarchy had a history similar to that of Germany, with a different outcome: clever enough to transform itself in the 1860s to become the focus for Japanese modernisation (unification had been achieved long before), the Japanese monarchy allowed itself to be used in the 1930s as the inspiration of the militarists seeking to establish the 'co-prosperity sphere'. Yet it survived defeat in 1945, as an institution, shorn of its magical qualities, to become a constitutional monarchy comparable to that of England, an indication of ceremony, not of power.

In the 1970s, a few traditional absolute monarchies still survive, in Morocco and Saudi Arabia, as in the Persian Gulf. Those kings are desirous of putting every modern source of energy at the service of their ancient, almost pre-agricultural, methods of rule. Whether they will survive is doubtful*. But, as late as 1975, a new King of Spain skilfully chose for himself the mission of providing a 'motor for democracy' in a country which did not see how to descend from the heights of tyranny to the valley of freedom (11).

On the whole, industrialisation wrecked traditional monarchy, chiefly because the incapacity of hereditary rulers for the tasks which they were undertaking became patent: Gian Gastone, the last Medicean Grand Duke of Tuscany, for example, 'out of mere indolence and sloth never dressed for the last thirteen years of his life and scarcely left his bed for another eight'. Surrounded by several hundred *ruspanti*† he invited these individuals to 'pander' as Harold Acton put it, 'in innumerable gross ways to his caprices' (12). On the other hand, those states in Western Europe which have retained constitutional monarchies have been able to offer to their peoples the ceremony and carnival which modern industrialised communities require as much as do agricultural ones. Their future looks secure; even in some republics, a certain 'democratic royalism', in Robert Nisbet's formulation, lingers (13), while the rationalist intellectuals who believed that the eclipse of monarchy would end people's desires for magical authority have been proved wrong.

Very few prophecies by historians have been worth the paper on which they are written. The great historian of the Renaissance, Jacob Burckhardt, however, made one prediction which was accurate − a good deal more so than any made by his contemporary, Karl Marx. For a long time, Burckhardt said, 'I have been aware that we are driving toward the alternative of complete democracy or absolute despotism. . . That despotic regime will not be practised any longer by dynasties. They are too soft-hearted. . . . The new tyrannies will be in the hands of military commanders who will call themselves Republican' (14). He was quite right.

While monarchy, in the old accepted sense of the word, has all but disappeared, monocracy, or government by a man who was not a monarch by birth but who gained supreme power by his own skill, strength or brutality, has played a larger part than it did in the past. Such monocrats did not play much of a part in the age of agriculture save in Italy during the Middle Ages and Renaissance. On the other hand, monocracy is a good name for what happened to the political system of Rome under the Empire and, during the more recent years of the age of industry, such tyrants, who have much in common with the mediaeval Italian despots or with Roman Emperors (except during the age of the Antonines), have been frequent. Often, these tyrants reached power through the army, as in Spain, Africa or South America. Some-

---

* Since this sentence was first written in draft, one major monarchy has fallen: Iran.
† A *ruspo* was a Florentine coin with which these persons were paid on Tuesdays and Saturdays.

times, as with the Nazis and Fascists, they did so through the skilful direction of mass movements. Sometimes, they have risen through a free political system, whose liberties they subsequently subverted. It is true that the leaders of Fascist or communist states are often considered as being specific emanations of specific ideologies. But their leaders have much in common, all the same, with traditional despots, even if they use apparently modern methods, to protect their egotism, and some superficially modern arguments, to persuade people to fawn upon them. The leader of communist Cuba, for example, and the Duce of Fascist Italy, both have much in common with ancient tyrants, while many modern despotisms of both 'left' and 'right' (particularly the new eastern communisms) have often presided over what Gribbon described as a 'long butchery of whatever was most noble or holy or innocent' (15).

It has been reserved to the self-made despots of the twentieth century to argue that such actions were not only beneficial to the people but actually desired by them. Some despots, it is true, even in the twentieth century, have been mild men. But modern despotism, in order to survive, has usually had to be brutal. Thus General Primo de Rivera in Spain established an easy-going dictatorship and had to resign after seven years, in 1930. The harsher rule of General Franco lasted from 1939 until 1975.

Sometimes, the actions of such rulers in the twentieth century directly recall their predecessors of antiquity. Compare, for example, a concert given by Nero to a public speech in the days of Stalin. 'No one was allowed to leave the theatre,' wrote Suetonius, 'during the emperor's recitals, however pressing the reason, and the gates were kept barred. We read of women in the audience giving birth and of men being so bored from the music and the applause that they shammed dead and were carried away for burial' (16). Solzhenitsyn tells of a speech made by Stalin at which all the hearers are afraid to be the first person to stop clapping.* All looked round despairingly and clapped on, sweat standing out on their foreheads, exhaustion stealing over them (17). Elie Halévy appropriately, writing in 1936, spoke of the twentieth century as the 'era of tyrannies' (18). He was right to do so.

In the late 1970s tyrannies exist throughout Africa save in Morocco (where there is a traditional monarchy)† and in South Africa, where democracy exists, but limited to those of white race. In Latin America, all the governments are tyrannies save those of Venezuela, Colombia,

---

* Compare also the modern Russian tyranny with remarks allegedly made by a remarkably precocious judge in Russia in the 1770s. He said that all men were equal. When he spoke thus 'everyone turned his eyes away . . . It looked as if terror had seized those who stood near . . . they withdrew from me as from one infected by the plague' (19).
† Since 1976, General Bokassa, in the Central African 'Empire', reigns however, as the Emperor Bokassa I.

Costa Rica and Mexico, and the government of the last has some tyrannical elements: the President always comes from the same well-named
institutional revolutionary party, his selection is secret and he has
absolute power for his seven years of office. There are no democracies in
Asia, save in India and Israel. The rest are tyrannies, with either communist or military colouring. In Thailand, a *roi fainéant* lives on the
sufferance of his generals. These tyrannies have, by and large, succeeded traditional monarchies within the last generation or so, though, in
South America, the Spanish and Portuguese monarchies collapsed in
the nineteenth century, and though some of these tyrannies, particularly in the Americas, have experienced eras of democracy.

Since 1789, there have often been suggestions that rule by a single
man is of great benefit to the state concerned since it makes it more
efficient. The best example of this was Napoleon, the first modern
tyrant, even though he made himself emperor. Napoleon was,
however, a man of exceptional quickness of brain, power of decision
and capacity for detail. That enabled him to codify the social reforms of
the Revolution as effectively as he could win battles. But the myth of
Bonapartism has not been of much help to the French. His spiritual
successor and nephew, Napoleon III, did not justify the illusion that a
single ruler can accomplish more than a parliament. Nor has it been
much help to others. The Nazis under Hitler made the myth of the
'hero' a keystone of their system. They would, in fact, have been served
better by the myth of the 'team'. Some communists have also envisaged
what would seem a contradiction in terms. Trotsky envisaged a species
of heroes: 'Man will become immeasurably stronger, wiser, and subtler,
his body will become . . . harmonised, his movements . . . rhythmic,
his voice more musical. The average human type will rise to the height
of an Aristotle, a Goethe, a Marx' (20). In Spain, Franco was a cruel but
accomplished ruler who, by skilful management of foreign affairs, was
able to keep Spain out of a world war. But, on the whole, the monocrats
have not fulfilled the hopes that have been placed in them. Mussolini,
for example, declared war against Britain and France in 1940 without
assuring himself of the whereabouts of his merchant fleet. The consequence was his loss of a third of it (21). Nasser, the tyrant of Egypt
between 1954 and 1970, gave his country a demagogic leadership, but
the officers in his wars were afraid to tell him the truth about their
defeats. Like Diocletian, according to Gibbon, he saw only 'with his
courtiers' eyes, he heard nothing but their misrepresentations' (22).
'Besides never hearing the truth about anything,' Ottoviano Fregoso
remarked of absolute rulers in Castiglione's *The Courtier*, they 'are intox-
icated by that license which dominion carries with it, and by the abundance of their enjoyments . . . always finding themselves obeyed and
almost adored with such reverence and praise . . . they are subject to
such boundless self-esteem that they take no advice from others' (23).

Tyrannies are thus hard to justify; can they be explained? Caudillismo prevails in almost all Hispano-Portuguese countries, wrote Américo Castro, because 'the will of a few to dominate and the desires of many to be dominated meet in a happy engagement to fill the void caused by the absence of a social culture based on a system of ideas' (24).

Then, in the twentieth century, a strange thing has occurred: many countries which are still agrarian have come to be ruled by military officers, engineers, lawyers, businessmen – above all, the first — who often know nothing of agriculture.*

In all these societies, which are dominated by despots, life is less stable than it often seems to temporary visitors since, underneath an artificial serenity, which is a work of art achieved by police, each man is haunted by the fear that he may come up against the regulations or arbitrary prejudices that govern the state. Yet the casual traveller does not see those fears. He only sees the bland smiles.

Few modern tyrants have managed to devise a system of government which ensured a peaceful transition to a like ruler after his death. One reason is that many tyrants begin life as friends of liberty; who would have detected in the friendly, progressive, country physician, François Duvalier, the ferocious despot, 'Papa-Doc', patron of the Ton-Ton Macoutes?† But even under Rome the problem of the succession was never resolved: the greatest Roman emperor, Diocletian, sought a mixture of heredity and adoption. But his successors sought pure heredity. *Coups d'état* destroyed Diocletian's settlement. The single year 307 AD saw seven emperors (26).

The novel features of despotism in the age of industry are, among those formally believed to be on the Right or the Left, close to what was foreshadowed by de Tocqueville in the 1830s, in a prediction as brilliant as Burckhardt's: 'An innumerable multitude of men and women, all equal and alike, incessantly endeavouring to procure the petty and paltry pleasures with which they glut their lives. Each of them living apart is a stranger to the fate of all the rest: his children and his private friends represent to him the whole of mankind. As for the rest of his fellow citizens, he is close to them; but he does not see them; he touches them, but he does not feel them; he exists only in himself and for himself alone, that is, [he is] an individual lost in the crowd. . . . [Above these men stands] an immense and tutelary power which takes upon itself alone to secure their gratification and watch over their fate . . . It would be like the authority of a parent if its object was to prepare man for manhood,' de Tocqueville continued, 'but it seeks, on the contrary,

---

* Compare Bloch's comment (following Arthur Young) that, after 1789, left to themselves, the country people in France would have gone back to communal practices in agriculture. But the 'men of the assemblies' were people of the educated and prosperous bourgeoisie, who believed in enlightenment and hated 'feudal barbarism' (25).

† Actually, Duvalier successfully passed on power to his son.

to keep them in perpetual childhood. For their happiness, such a government willingly labours, but it chooses to be the sole agent and the only arbiter of that happiness. It provides for their security, foresees and supplies their necessities . . . what remains but to spare them all the care of thinking and all the trouble of living? After having thus taken successively each member of the community in its powerful grasp, and fashioned him at will, the supreme power . . . covers the surface of society with a network of small complicated rules, uniform and minute, through which the most original minds, and the most energetic charac-ters, cannot penetrate to rise above the crowd. The will of man is not shattered but softened, bent and guided; men are seldom forced by it to act, but they are constantly restrained by it from acting.' (27)

The prophecy gave an accurate picture of some of the tyrannies of subsequent days which dominate 'not a people but simply a disciplined multitude of subjects' in Burckhardt's description of the age of Frederick II of Germany (28). From the Elbe to Shanghai, that is the characteristic way that most men live. Where de Tocqueville erred was in his assumption that such an 'absolute' and 'provident' society would be 'mild', and would 'not tyrannise but [merely] compass, enervate, ext-inguish and stupefy a people, till each nation is reduced to nothing better than a flock of timid and industrious animals, of which the government is the shepherd'. But, under the great tyrannies of our day, such supreme powers have often been, indeed usually have been, harsh. A benign tyranny would also be an unlikely successor to cur-rently ailing democracies of the West, for the likelihood is that, even there, the fall of freedom would be followed by harsh, authoritarian direction. De Tocqueville could not have imagined how modern tech-nology could devise means of propaganda which would, in totalitarian states, succeed, to a high degree, in making people think as their rulers want. Robert Ley explained that the Nazi Labour Front realised that 'people are like children . . . they have childish wishes. The State has to care for them and see to it that they get . . . presents if they are to be happy and apply themselves to their work' (29).

Another qualification to de Tocqueville's predictions is that many of these new tyrannies are more inefficient and more corrupt (morally and economically) than he supposed would be the case.

Aldous Huxley once remarked: 'The abject patience of the oppressed is perhaps the most inexplicable, as it is also the most important, fact in all history' (30). The continuing patience of many peoples nowadays has a simple explanation: the size of the police. The late Roman Empire, it is said, employed about 10,000 men with apparent police functions (31). It is a characteristic of modern times, obsessed though we are with figures, that it is difficult to find exact figures for such organisations as the KGB or the Gestapo. But it is said that the small Cuban despotism has 10,000 'state security troops' (32). Russia, then as now, the most police-conscious state in the world, had, in 1895, 100,000 police, a corps of gendarmes of 10,000 and a political police of under 1000 (33). The figures for the KGB are believed to be 500,000 (34). Of course, some such despotisms have brought the benefits of order in place of chaos. But most have relied for the technological means which preserve them on inventions far away from their own shores; and, as Bertrand Russell put it after his visit to Russia in 1920, 'if a more just economic system is only attainable by closing men's minds against free enquiry, the price is too high' (35).

43

The Great War

No one will ever agree exactly why the First World War broke out. The causes of great tragedies are bound to be many. The direct cause was undoubtedly, however, the result of miscalculation. This miscalculation was primarily a miscalculation among the monarchical despots who then directed the affairs of the strongest countries. Thus whatever else it did or did not do, the war of 1914 seemed to show that monarchical despotism was a bad form of government for modern times.

The war had been long expected. 'The Great European war begins,' wrote *The Times* on August 7, as if to allude to something much talked of, before that date (1). A disposition, after years of peace in Europe, to suppose that war had its benefits was then widely held, not only in the poems of romantics such as d'Annunzio, but in the speeches of politicians. Europe had had, for a generation, the smell of gunpowder in all its transactions. Even the art critic John Ruskin told an audience of cadets at Woolwich that no great art had ever yet risen on earth but among a nation of soldiers (2). The poetry of the generation of 1914 was heavy with premonition: in 1896, A. E. Housman wrote:

> On the idle hill of summer,
> Sleepy with the sound of streams,
> Far I hear the steady drummer
> Drumming like a noise in dreams.
>
> Far and near and low and louder
> On the roads of earth go by,
> Dear to friends and food for powder,
> Soldiers marching, all to die (3).

The chief characteristic of war in the age of industry has been its unchivalrous character. That has not prevented its directors, and sometimes its chroniclers, from speaking of it often in terms more appropriate to a tournament. Even during the worst fighting on the western front in the First World War, the special correspondents referred to the

466

battle as if they were at Agincourt, not Mons (4). Even today, in the nuclear age, war colleges are adorned with heraldic emblems and mottoes, such as 'Truth, Valour, Duty', 'Stalk and Kill' or *La Fortune sourit aux braves*' (5). There is, in all this, a certain ambivalence. Even in the most unpromising circumstances, people seek an historical continuity. Many, from fascists in Italy, during the First World War, to revolutionary socialists of the 1960s, have spoken of 'the educational value and the ethical aspect of war' (6). But similar phrases can be found in the works of the men who were, respectively, probably the most popular President of the US (Theodore Roosevelt), and certainly the best writer among the Prime Ministers of Britain (Winston Churchill). Roosevelt, for example, told cadets in 1897 at the Naval War College, 'Peace is a goddess only when she comes with a sword girt on thigh. . . . No triumph of peace is quite so great as the supreme triumphs of war' (7). Such romantic views were a contrast with the calculations of strategists, such as Clausewitz, who believed war to be diplomacy carried on by other means; or Bismarck who, when asked if he wanted war, replied, 'Of course not. I want victory' (8).

The First World War broke out because the heir to the Austro-Hungarian multi-national empire was assassinated by a Bosnian nationalist. The event symbolises the destructive face of nationalism. A multi-national Austria–Hungary in the middle years of the twentieth century would have saved the world much pain. But, unfortunately, the government in Vienna resolved to put an end to Bosnian nationalism by demanding humiliating concessions from Serbia, whose government had harboured the murderer. Russia was the protector of the Serbs. The Austrians found themselves engaged against that Empire also. The German Empire by then was to Austria what Russia was to Serbia. Military preoccupations were uppermost in the German imperial government, which had not tried unduly hard to work out a harmonious relation between civilian and military authority. Before 1914, no war council had ever been held in which the politicians had a chance to participate in discussions of military plans and preparations (9). The German master class, anyway, dreamed of world power at Russian expense. Russia, however, had an alliance with France, who thus also became implicated.

Germany was a country, or rather a group of states, which had, at the beginning been at a disadvantage in the age of commercial enterprise. No German emperor had been able to establish a common law. All was left to territorial princes, of whom there were nearly 300, ranging from kingdoms to bishoprics, countships to lay princes. The hereditary succession to the empire had been only vested in the Habsburg family after 1437, when the electoral princes had, in effect, whittled away all their power. Most German states had elaborate bureaucracies, but Prussia had the only efficient one. Most princes in old Germany regarded their job as a sinecure. For many years, there was no national German currency, no national literature and no national industry. A few French Protestant immigrants had brought some good commercial ideas to Prussia, a quarter of whose population in 1740 were immigrants from France. Kant believed that the one common characteristic of Germans was their 'pedantic inclination to classify themselves in relation to other citizens according to a system of rank and prerogatives' (10). From a background of diversity and hierarchy, a challenge was mounted which was in the end simplistic. A nation in which the centralised state was weak became the supreme advocate of state power. A society supremely conscious of hierarchy in Germany came to demand of the world the acceptance of a view that all Germans, from private to field marshal, were a superior people.

Five other important powers (the word is appropriate, for the European nations brought their empires into the conflict) also became engaged. Britain had had an understanding before 1914 with France which fell far short of an alliance. But British statesmen rightly considered that the German invasion of the small state of Belgium was evidence of a bid for world power. Italy had before 1914 an alliance with Germany and Austria. She allowed herself o be bought by the French and the British. The Ottoman Empire, whose army had been trained by Germany, became drawn into the conflict out of hatred of Russia and suspicion of both France and Britain. The USA entered the war since she rightly feared that a German victory might result in a European military dictatorship: Germany improvidently had also attacked US shipping on its way to provision Britain. Finally, Japan became an ally of Britain in order to seize German colonies. In the end, though, the war became a struggle against Germany more than, as it seemed to be at first, a war of Austro–Hungarian succession. Economic motives there were in the dislike of Germany, but all merchants of all nations had thought of themselves as the promoters of peace. They, like Norman Angell, knew war to be a 'great illusion'. The illusion that war was inspired by private manufacturers has taken a long time to die but, as Sir John Clapham reminded us, during the generations when private merchants were most powerful, the world was free from 'general war' for ninety-nine years; nor did anyone suggest that the wage earners accepted the war of 1914 primarily because of the high pay received during it (11).

In the summer of 1914, France made a feverish effort to finish the grain harvest. She then mobilised her 2,877,000 reservists. That caused much unemployment because of the number of managers and technicians who had gone to fight. By the end of August 1914, half the factories of France were closed. Germany conscripted 5 1/4 million men. There, too, there was a rise in unemployment for the same reasons as in France. Russia, far larger than Germany, also mobilised a little more than 5½ million men in 1914, among them 4 million peasants. Though Russian agriculture had suffered from under-employment before the war, the consequence there was similar to what happened in Germany and France. Production from land sown with grain dropped in 1915 to less than two-thirds of what it had been in 1914.

Britain in 1914 relied on volunteers, but otherwise she was no more farsighted than were her co-belligerents. One fifth of the miners and a quarter of those in chemical industries 'joined up', so damaging industry severely (12). The US mobilised, in 1917–18, 4·8 million men and women. The likelihood that more millions of Americans were fit, and of the right age, had decisive consequences on events. Even more important was US spending – which totalled $33 billion: twice the expenditure of the federal government during the first hundred years of its existence.

All the main contenders had several million men under arms until the end. Even in Russia, there were still 6·5 million fairly patriotic men at the front in November 1917 (13).

All the combatants expected a quick war. Politicians believed that no economy could stand a long conflict. Trade surely would be too greatly disrupted. The contenders had prepared stocks of armaments, not armament industries. They used their arms budgets to buy shells from manufacturers rather than to build factories. In addition, the officers concerned had been educated to believe that the spirit of attack would triumph.

These predictions proved false. In the past, governments under pressure of defeat made peace before their internal crises became too strong. In this first great war of the twentieth century, governments found the strength to carry on the fight longer than ever before, with hundreds of thousands of recruits available and a willingness to pay them with an endless supply of paper money (14). In the First World War, people wondered whether the war would ever end: 'I see no end to it . . . it is the suicide of nations,' a German doctor told Philip Gibbs, a British journalist (15). 'Artillery conquers the ground, infantry occupies it', was the slogan of Foch and repeated as if it were the formula for a great scientific discovery (17). In practice, it meant that, after throwing thousands of tons of shells and metal at the enemy (107,000 tons of explosive were deposited by the French and British on the first dawn of the third battle of Ypres (18)), masses of men were ordered forward in an attempt to exploit the enemy's shock by capturing their guns or their observation points and, in the end, above all, to break through their defences of barbed wire, sometimes three belts of thirty strands (19). (Barbed wire, the American agricultural invention of the nineteenth century, turned out to be the master defensive weapon of the twentieth, making it possible to convert the most unpromising fields into fortresses more resilient than long prepared stone edifices such as Kovno or

Antwerp, which played negative roles in the First World War (20)).

Of equal importance was the spade. After the first few weeks, it was found that the best defence against artillery was not stone but soil (21). Hence the vast network of tunnels and dugouts by which the war of 1914 is most remembered. 'Dugouts' with ceilings ten metres thick were found to be invulnerable even to heavy shells and, if reinforced by concrete, only three metres were needed (22). 'In the art of war, it is an axiom that he who remains in his trenches will be beaten,' Napoleon had said (23). That failed to take into account the character of soil's resilience against big guns. Prefabricated huts invented by Colonel Nissen also made possible the quartering of large numbers of men behind the trenches. So even if the 'front' was broken, it was easy to insulate the 'bulge' so formed.

What could be done against this stalemate? Cavalry? The early days of that war marked the apotheosis of the horse. Huge armies could be taken by rail to the front. But there was little available there to make them mobile, particularly once the land became muddy. Neither cars nor lorries were numerous. Neither were effective on rough territory (24). So horses were still essential. The generals used cars to get around, but the field commanders were not able to, though, as Marc Ferro pointed out rather sharply, the generals paid obeisance to a bygone era of chivalry by taking victory parades on horseback (25). Cavalry charges, on the other hand, could no more deal with barbed wire than huntsmen can jump it.

Aeroplanes seemed one possibility for breaking the deadlock. To begin with, these were used primarily for observation. Then came a short stage when there were great air duels between 'aces', such as Von Richthofen of Germany or René Fonck of France. These had little effect on the battles on the ground. There were also bombing raids, but on a modest scale. The worst raid of that war was a German raid by Zeppelins on London in June 1917, when 162 people were killed and 432 injured (26). These raids had no effect on industrial production and little on morale. At the end of the war, however, aircraft did begin to play a part on the battlefield. Squadrons of fighters flew low in support of infantry. The success of that tactic persuaded the warring countries to build huge numbers of aircraft. By November 1918, the US had 3,200 fighters, the British 22,000 altogether (in comparison with 272 in 1914) (27). These aircraft went fast: 140 miles an hour instead of 80 in 1914.

But even aviation failed to interrupt the monotony on the ground, useful though it turned out to be once a line had been broken.

Gas was also tried, though all the countries concerned had signed an international convention in 1907, forbidding its use. The Germans experimented in October 1915 with a type of tear gas which they allowed to drift to their enemies' lines (28). Everyone close to the front choked and panicked. The Germans, interested by that effect, used gas again and it enabled them to advance three miles. But it soon turned out that gas could be countered by masks, by specially treated cloth helmets, or by box respirators. The unpredictable behaviour of the wind could also blow the gas back in the users' faces. The weapon was made more effective by its use as a gas shell, which could be accurately despatched and, though small, could operate more powerful gases. These shells were used at Ypres in July 1917, causing 20,000 British casualties, of which the vast majority survived. The British responded by using chlorine gas. Hitler was poisoned by gas in this way. Perhaps that suggested to him that if 12,000 or 15,000 Jews 'had been put under poison gas, as hundreds of thousands of our very best workers from all walks of life had to endure . . . the sacrifice of millions . . . would not have been in vain' (29). Gas did not, however, turn the fortunes of the war, save on two occasions. In September 1917, General von Hutier was enabled to capture Riga easily by using gas; and, in May and June 1917, the Germans were enabled to occupy Armentières, with almost no losses. Gas was looked on as atrocious: actually, it was more humane than most modern weapons (30).

Economic warfare helped to defeat Germany. But it was not the main factor. Britain sought to stop supplies from entering Germany. But many British goods went to Germany through neutral countries, particularly Holland. Holland imported twelve times as much cocoa in 1914–18 as it did in 1910–14, while her exports to Germany rose by the same proportion. The celebrated block-houses of the German lines were made, too, from English cement – also bought via Holland (31). German goods, even shells, continued to be sold to Russia. Still, in 1915 the Germans declared that, in return for the British blockade, they would block the waters round Britain and Ireland with submarines. Among the ships which they sank was the passenger vessel, *Lusitania*. A few days later, the British declared all goods going to Germany to be contraband. They thereby established a full blockade. In January 1917, the Germans, in a delayed reply, announced an unrestricted submarine campaign. Between then and April, they seemed close to victory. They sank 540,000, 580,000 and 847,000 tons of shipping respectively in the first three months. England seemed to be cut off from her supplies from the USA. Even the entry of the US into the war as a result of that submarine campaign at first made no difference. Then innumerable mines were sown. 8,000 warships were brought in to escort the merchant fleets – the main use of navies in the twentieth century – and the sinkings declined (32).

Germany was, with her allies, seriously short of food. Only her occupation of the Ukraine, with its grain, and its occupation of Roumania, with its oil, prevented central Europe from starving. By 1918, the cattle in Austria–Hungary had dropped in number, from 17 million, in 1914, to about 3½ million, the number of pigs from 7½ million to about 200,000.

Lack of fertiliser reduced the German grain harvest by a third, and the decline of cotton imports caused a shortage of clothing worse than that of food. But even so that did not bring victory to the Allies. 800,000 non-combatants died of disease from malnutrition. The blockade continued until mid 1919, when the Germans signed the Treaty of Versailles. When the Germans complained, 'HUN FOOD SNIVEL' was the unedifying comment by the *Daily Mail*, the most sensational of London's papers. That and other comments were not forgotten by the Germans in the 1930s. They took care to make themselves self-sufficient in food as well as in armaments, so far as they could, before they embarked on their next grab for world power in 1939.

The weapon which destroyed the stalemate of the Great War of 1914 was the tank. The idea of it came to the British and the French at much the same time: both Winston Churchill and Colonel Estienne thought of developing an armoured engine which, by using caterpillar tracks, like the tractor, could move on all sorts of terrain and would, by its weight, destroy barbed wire as well as enemy machine gun nests, and so protect advancing infantry. Though considered by Kitchener a mere 'pretty, mechanical toy', its production by the British soon began. The secret was kept by the well-leaked rumour that the steel plates used in the production were for petrol tanks: hence the name 'tank'.

About 130 very primitively designed 21-ton tanks were used in September 1916 in an ill-fated Allied offensive, led by General Nivelle. Germany wrecked 60 tanks, and the crews inside boiled to death. The supporting infantry were massacred. The Germans were thus convinced that guns would always win such a battle (33). For a year, the Allies' tanks were used only in driblets, from place to place. Their first effective use in a concentrated manner was at Cambrai in November 1917. 378 light tanks led two infantry corps over the Hindenburg line. The Germans broke in panic. By the late afternoon, the British had conquered 10,000 yards – an incomparable day's work for the First World War. Only lack of reserves to exploit the gap in the offensive (and a German counterattack) made the victory less than complete.

Finally, in August 1918, the Allies combined 462 tanks with aircraft, at the battle of Amiens. Though the tanks could barely travel faster than one and a half miles an hour across the battlefield, they nevertheless inflicted a major defeat on Germany in one day. That persuaded Ludendorff to accept defeat (34) though, oddly enough, the name of that victory, and others in the great campaign of which it was part, is scarcely recalled today beside those of terrible stale-mates, such as Verdun or the Somme. The co-ordination of tanks and aircraft was made possible by field radios and telephones.

The difficulty was to make a real peace. Not only had between 10 and 13 million been killed and 20 million wounded — unheard of figures then — but, in order to cajole men to go to war and to stay there, and to persuade both men and women to work hard in ammunition factories, 'society', says Marc Ferro, 'had to be terrorised by propaganda into giving its last energies' (35). The legacy of this propaganda was as pervasive for the following generations as were the remains of gas attacks among those who had suffered. Old comrades and industrial workers alike were affected. The Allied propaganda was, if anything, more effective than that of the Germans: Ludendorff paid tribute to it: 'We were hypnotised by the enemy propaganda as is a rabbit by a snake' (36). Certainly British propaganda helped to draw the United States into the war, so there is something to that. Two distinguished US historians, Commager and Morrison, also point out that 'one of the appalling revelations of the war was the ease with which modern techniques and mass suggestion enables a government to make even a reasonably intelligent people, with individual backgrounds, believe anything it likes' (37). Characteristic of the time were the 'four minute men' in the US, whose task was to infiltrate every public gathering with four-minute celebrations of Wilson and war: 'the US's first plunge into near socialism or . . . near fascism' in Marwick's words (38). The story that the Germans were boiling down bodies of dead Allied soldiers for fat, was also alleged by *The Times* in April 1918 (39). The subsequent revelation that those stories were false may have been the reason why the stories of the extermination camps of Jews were disbelieved twenty odd years later.

Propaganda apart, war brought brutality. The Western front reflected some of the rules of war which all the belligerents nominally accepted. The Eastern front was different. For example, in 1917, General Brusilov's successful offensive into Austria led to the endless laying waste of estates, the killing of cattle, raping of women, a rehearsal, as Dr Stone comments, for the Russian agricultural atrocities of 1917–18.

The belligerents of 1914 all tried to stir up disaffected minorities within their opponents' territories. The Germans and Austrians endeavoured to awaken Russian minorities, preached a holy war against the French, and interfered, where they could, in Ireland and in other British, French and Italian possessions overseas. They proclaimed Polish independence, and encouraged Flemish nationalism. In the countries which eventually won, national unity was strengthened. But, in the states which lost, disintegration, partly caused by external interference, constituted a reason for defeat and a serious impediment to the peace. Myths were created in this war as much as they ever were in the Dark Ages. Thus in Arab history, as in *The Seven Pillars of Wisdom*, there is a legend that the Arabs, led by T. E. Lawrence, freed Damascus. Actually, it was the 3rd Australian Light Horse Brigade (40). Idealism of sorts caused the victors to see good reasons to speed the break-up of both the Austrian and Turkish multi-national empires. They failed to destroy German unity, however, while Russian unity was in the end preserved. Only Finland, the Baltic states and the Poles escaped from the huge fortress of modern Russia, along with Georgia and Armenia, for a short time.

The collapse of Austria and Turkey led to the creation of weak states, which also helped to destroy the chances of lasting peace. The war of 1914 had been in a sense the logical extension of the idea of the self-sufficient 'nation state'. The peace after it, though in theory appreciating that idea — Wilson's 'fourteen points'* specified an end to the 'great game of the balance of power' — served, through the principle of self determination, to create many more states. A war which had really broken out for similar reasons as those which had caused wars in the past (injured pride and the hope of making the best of an opportunity that might not recur) thus ended with the promulgation of idealistic war aims: 'No peace is possible until . . . the principle of nationality and of freedom of small states is recognised.'

The war left behind huge financial imbalances. All the defeated countries were bankrupt. That included Russia. But the victors were also half bankrupt. British trade had been in deficit every year since 1822: the gap had been made up by 'invisibles' — profits on insurance abroad, commerce abroad generally. Those 'invisibles' were lost (41). British markets in Asia went to Japan. The war ended the days when there was a balance of gold stocks between industrial countries. The international gold standard, achieved in 1870, never recovered.

At the peace, few were able to be thoughtful. Max Weber had written in Germany: 'This war, with all its ghastliness, is nevertheless grand and wonderful. It is worth experiencing' (42). Lloyd George in England was an exception for a time: 'We must not allow any sense of revenge, any spirit of greed, and grasping desire to overcome the fundamental spirit of righteousness,' he said on November 12, 1918. But he soon capitulated to an intolerant national mood famously expressed by a member of his cabinet, Sir Eric Geddes, when he said, at an electoral meeting in Cambridge, that, 'If I am returned, Germany is going to pay restitution, reparation and indemnity and I personally have no doubt that we will get everything that you can squeeze out of a lemon and a bit more' (43). Hence the harsh peace of Versailles which kept German tempers aflame for another generation.

The First World War had other legacies, one obvious, the other less so. One was the communist *coup d'état* in Moscow. 'We now face an enemy of a new type,' the last Habsburg emperor Karl wrote vainly but wisely to the Kaiser in 1917, 'more dangerous than the Entente . . . please look beyond its initial advantages to us. These threatening clouds can only be dispelled by immediately ending the war' (44). The second

* '*Quatorze commandements!*' exclaimed Clemenceau, '*c'est un peu raide! Le bon Dieu n'en avait que dix.*'

legacy was the precedent for a new form of half-socialist, half-nationalistic, 'statist' society which, since 1945, has made considerable headway even in peace time, even in the democratic states.

This latter political innovation was described by Pastor Naumann in Germany in 1915: 'Our self-knowledge is this: we Germans have slipped into this state of socialist or popular [*volkisch*] activity, in the strictest sense of the word . . . When we emerge from the war, we shall no longer be the same economic beings as before . . . upon the basis of wartime experiences, we will demand a regulated economy – regulation of production, from the point of view of the necessity of the state' (45). To a lesser extent, the same could have been said in every state at war. Germany (which was not for nothing dominated by Prussia) was, however, ahead, and realised what was happening more clearly than others did. The industrialist Rathenau, for example, coined the term 'state capitalism' to indicate the industrial reorganisation with which the government went ahead (46). German industries, he said, were doing the work (of providing the necessities of war) without having full liberty, serving the public interest by distributing neither profits nor dividends, their co-ordinating committees being intermediaries between capitalism and government. All this constituted 'an innovation that the future may take to' (47). Rationing was introduced into Germany from January 1915. Price controls came later in the same year. A subsequent regulation insisted that no worker could leave his employment without a licence. In 1916, all male Germans were supposed to be drafted for war service and a systematic effort was made to increase female labour. Admittedly, this programme was dismantled after 1918. But, when the Nazis came to power, and addressed themselves to national regeneration, they did little more than draw on these precedents.

These dangers were evident at the time to clear-headed observers. Maynard Keynes, in 1915, for example, saw that German economic writers were arguing for the permanent 'militarisation of industrial life'. 'A system of regulations must be set up, the object of which is not the greater happiness of the individual . . . but the strengthening of the organising unity of the state for the object of attaining the maximum degree of efficiency, the influence of which on individual advantage is only indirect. This hideous doctrine is hidden in a cloak of idealism . . . the peace will bring with it a strengthening of the idea of state action in industry . . . in the new Germany of the twentieth century, power without consideration of profit is to make an end of that system of capitalism which came over from England a hundred years ago' (48). Characteristic of the acceptance of this tendency in the war itself were three articles in *The Times* in July and August 1916 which suggested the need in England for a national plan – 'a development towards nationalisation, . . . a development not by the socialist's panacea of appropriation . . . but by amalgamation, by co-ordination and by bringing the state into partnership, and an increasing partnership, in the big businesses that result' (49). Supervision, self-regulation, import controls, rationing of import space in ships according only to the military value of the commodity, a state with an omnipresent role in agriculture, huge taxes, inflation of civil services – that was the accursed inheritance of the First World War. The depression and the New Deal, the challenge of Nazism and the Second World War, the establishment of immensely ambitious welfare systems – all this transformed the small-scale states of 1914 into huge 'cold monsters', engaged on a war footing without the stimulus of belligerency.

What gave this new *'étatisme'* its special effectiveness had been its liaison with humanitarianism and the consequent excuse that it has for entering into every detail of everyone's lives (50). Mr Justice Brandeis, however, gave a good warning when he said: 'Experience should teach us most to be on our guard when the government's purposes are beneficent' (51). But warnings went astray. The consequence was that, in every country at war, belligerency inspired elaborate new bureaucracies, censors of letters and of newspapers, secret services with far larger budgets than ever before. In England a Cabinet secretariat was invented. The 130 railways of Britain in 1914 became four in 1918 and the 43 banks also became four. In the United States, the government also temporarily took over the railways, and the Food Administration Board under Herbert Hoover bought food in bulk for the first time. Roosevelt's New Deal, with its large number of national enterprise boards, was a lineal descendant of the political arrangements of the war (52). The British Labour movement undertook to forego strikes for the duration of the war in 1915, and in 1917 strikes were actually prohibited, arbitration of wage disputes became compulsory, profits were limited and in certain war industries all trade union activities were suspended (53). Here was the modern corporate state of which some statesmen formally on the Right and on the Left have ever since dreamed.

After the failure of British, French, US and German supplies to help Russia adequately, a great internal economic thrust forward in 1916 resolved almost all Russia's problems of war supplies. She showed herself fully capable of substituting her own for imported machinery. The many mechanisms inside rifles were all being made by 1916 in Russia (54). By 1917, she had achieved by her own efforts a superiority of guns and supplies on the Eastern front. Where the Kaiser's economic programmes were a direct anticipation of Hitler's, and Wilson's of the New Deal's, the Russian war effort of 1915–16 became what Norman Stone provocatively describes as a 'first experiment in Stalinist tactics of modernisation'. So in the summer of 1917, 'most of Russia went on strike' (55).

That breakdown in Russia in 1917 was primarily caused by the great industrial effort of the previous years. It did not occur anywhere else in such a sharp form. But it nearly did so everywhere. To begin with, the war had usually been greeted with euphoria, even in Russia (56). Generally, the socialist and labour movements were soothed by greatly increased social benefits. Children were better fed than before. Hours of work were shortened. Women's 'right to serve' meant a breakthrough by women into professions dominated by males till then (it led directly to the women's vote in England and the US of 1918). In the US, the war also opened up many jobs to blacks in the North, and gave black service-men a glimpse of equality.

Most people in most countries believed in the rightness of their cause: the Germans thought that they were defending Europe against Russia, the Russians knew that Holy Russia had to be defended against Teutons. Longuet, Guesde and other French socialists wrote to the 2nd International to say: 'The workers have no thought of aggression, but are sure they are upholding their country's independence against German imperialism' (57). Euphoria lasted till the nations at war began to increase governmental power sharply. In Germany, Ludendorff after 1916 set up virtually a military dictatorship. A Kaiser *fainéant* only remained. In France, Marshal Joffre and the army almost took power in the state in 1914: 'The prefects are finished, the deputies don't matter, the generals can feed on human flesh.' The deputies did not meet between August and December 1914, and, though they reassembled then regularly, 1914 seemed an internal political *revanche* for which the professional army had been waiting since the days of Dreyfus and Bou-langer (58). Later, Clemenceau ruled in France in the last years of the war as a dictator in the strict Roman sense of the word. With the eclipse of Asquith in 1916, the age of the scholar-statesman was also over in England. Lloyd George, the successful British war leader, ceased to be leader of the House of Commons, and his parliamentary appearances became rare. Though Britain retained a real parliamentary life, opposi-tion to the war coalition was shaken by the splits which the war caused in all the parties, including the Labour one, and by the transformation of politics on class lines which the war, despite its nation-building role, increased. Even in the US, Woodrow Wilson, more cautious in his use of presidential power than Lincoln had been in the Civil War, asserted executive authority so much as to force Charles Evans Hughes in 1929 to wonder 'whether consitutional government as hitherto established in this Republic could survive another great war, even victoriously waged' (59). In Italy, the war strengthened all anti-parliamentary forces which dreamt of overthrowing the constitutional monarchy and installing a national revolutionary régime.

Such assertions of authority everywhere caused protests. In France, in 1917, there were many strikes, bread riots, even mutinies in the army, after the Nivelle offensive. They were partly inspired by Russia's example but principally caused by protests against inflation (prices rose 80% in France in the war) and shortages. That was no insurance against revolution, admittedly, for it had been bread riots which had led to revolution in Russia as well. At no time, however, was there 'privation' in Britain. 'Shortages' became apparent in 1917. 'Queues' for potatoes and bread occurred. There was some mild rationing — beginning with sugar (half a pound a week per head — too much for a healthy diet) (60).

One protest against the war seemed to come from the surrealists. But the Dada movement was a challenge to the old bourgeois life as much as to the war. There was also a 'Left opposition' to the war, organised by dissident, apparently internationalist, Russian socialists headed by Lenin in Zimmerwald and then at Kienthal. Lenin called for civil wars in order to end the national wars. That call for further confusion within the existing conflict did not strike an immediately appealing note.

The defeat of Russia and her replacement by the US among the Allied nations made it easier to suggest that the war had been fought and won for the principles of democracy. Wilson, from that point of view, made a better ally for the English and French than the Tsar did. 'Autocracy is dead, long live democracy and its immortal leader,' cabled Colonel House to Wilson on November 11, 1918, 'in this great hour, my pride goes out to you in admiration and love' (61). But the leaders of the democrats themselves shared the destructive passions of their peoples. William Archer in *The Great Analysis*, a book published in 1911, thought that 'some great catastrophe', such as the war of 1914, would usher in a happier world order. That optimism proved quite false (62). The First World War ushered in an era of international conflict which has continued ever since with only rather short intervals.

The war, in the short run, showed that, in the great world struggles of the twentieth century, there was little real chance of the US remaining isolated. All the same, the US decided, through the vote of her Senate, to try to play no part in the postwar world. Russia was divided by a civil war which masked the extent to which she had in 1916 successfully mounted an offensive against the Austrians. Nor did the Germans, temporarily defeated, play any part in the peace. The peacemaking thus enabled the enfeebled imperial powers, Britain and France, to try to freeze the movement of the world against further change.

The consequences of the 'Great War' were primarily four: First, the political experiments of collaboration between industry, labour and government went a long way to inspire that idea of a corporate state desired by Fascists, communists and some democratic politicians. Second, the bitterness and propaganda left hatred which meant that another war would probably follow soon. Third, the combined effects of war and peacemaking ruined the system of credit upon which the pre-war serenity had been built. The German currency was ruined. The stories of bank-notes being carried in wheelbarrows, of sandwiches costing 14,000 marks one day and 24,000 the next, and of demented people stating their ages on forms to be '150 million years' are well known. What is less evident is that the war initiated an era of widely fluctuating, and depreciating, currency which has never come to an end. The fourth change was that the power and influence in the democratic world shifted, irreversibly, it seems, to the US. That was reflected in the change of indebtedness more than anything else. In 1914, the US owed Europe $6,000 million. In 1918, the US was owed $16,000 million (63). Debts, inflation and fear of war have never ceased since then. Furthermore, in one way or another, the 'World Crisis', as Winston Churchill named his history of the war, has really never ceased. The collapse of monarchical despotism created the need for new forms of government. Those forms of government were, as will be seen, often nervous and aggressive partly because they were new and ill-established. The pattern, as in so many things, had been set after the French Revolution. The governments set up by the French Revolution were less stable than any of those which they overthrew. Yet, 'paradoxically, they were infinitely more powerful. . . . This new power was created by the Revolution or rather grew up almost automatically out of the havoc wrought by it'. In those words, De Tocqueville summed up very well what happened after 1918. President Woodrow Wilson, in a speech entitled 'the Four Ends' on July 4, 1918, said that the rulers of Prussia had 'aroused forces they knew little of'; but events were to show that they were forces of which a progressive liberal such as Wilson knew little also.

44

The Nazis' War

The Germans' second 'grab for world power' in 1939 was begun in, at first sight, circumstances more favourable to them. The Nazi movement rendered more solid many of the prejudices of the previous generation. Hitler was a real warlord, not a Kaiser *fainéant*. The Nazis had taken care first to silence, or to force into exile, potential critics (socialists, communists, liberals, Jews) before the war began. Possibly, the German nation was less united behind its government's quest for world power in 1939 than it had been in 1914. Still, by a clever use of diplomatic intimidation, Hitler secured the integration with Germany of the more valuable remains of the Austro-Hungarian Empire (Bohemia and Austria) and dominated the economies of the rest of south eastern Europe. The German economy in 1939 had recovered from the defeat of 1918 as from the world depression of 1929. In 1939, Germany also had Italy, Japan and Spain as likely allies, all transformed by Fascism or militarism into probable friends of what they referred to as a 'new order'. The Italian Fascist dictator wished his country to 'terrify the world for a change rather than charm it with its guitar', as he told his son-in-law, and anyway believed that war was 'to man as maternity is to woman' (1). As for Japan, the military rulers there had ambitious plans for a Co-Prosperity sphere in the Far East dominated by herself, comparable to Hitler's plans for a New German Order.

Germany before 1939 had made herself self-sufficient in food, as a result of a four-year plan introduced by Goering. Her investment in synthetic products and easy access to strategic raw materials from Spain, Sweden and Roumania enabled her leaders to be sceptical, at least to begin with, of the efficacy of another British blockade (2). The German armed forces had also been built up fast since 1933. Their commanders were mostly young, though experienced, survivors from the First World War. The Nazis also had a great appeal, even among people who, in reflective moments, would have thought better of giving such a brash enterprise the benefit of the doubt. The Nazi state had benefited from the socialists' unwitting preparation for it in the 1920s. In 1928, 53% of the German national income was in the hands of the central or local authority (3). The German government drew extensively on the economic and social innovations of the First World War and abolished strikes as well as limited dividends. Labour camps, freely available credit, road building, as well as repression, characterised the social and economic policies. Meantime, foreign opposition was slow to grow. The British and the French governments not unnaturally distrusted the Russian government under Stalin rather more than they distrusted the Germans, since most of the Russian governing class, including 65% of the generals, according to their military attaché (4), had been recently murdered by their own head of government, many on the charge that they had been working for British intelligence. That was an accusation which British intelligence, at least, knew to be unfortunately not true. Also there were numerous Frenchmen who wished to recreate a permanent version of Joffre's military dictatorship of 1914 under some semi-Fascist auspices.

Nazism had an intimidatory appeal beyond the frontiers of Germany. George Kennan put the nature of the challenge very well: 'it is hard to visualise the tremendous head of emotional and political steam which the Nazis had developed,' he wrote, 'Here was a great political movement on the march. We must not let our distaste for Hitler's methods blind us to the fact that this man was one of the greatest demagogues of whom history sears record and, in many ways, an able statesman . . . He was backed up by a party which had fantastic powers of organisation and was inspired by a fanatical stony determination to let nothing stand in its path. It was not easy in those days to know how far this political force was going to carry. Many . . . in Germany and Austria [and elsewhere in central Europe] who were at first sceptical were finally overwhelmed both by the emotional impetus of the movement and by the success which Hitler had in achieving, by relatively bloodless means, objectives which the Weimar Republic had not been able to achieve in many years.' (5)

The Second World War was really caused by a misreading of the reasons for Germany's defeat in 1919. During the nineteenth century, Germany had begun to regard herself as the likely dominant race of the future. Her swift industrialisation, her unification as a modern nation, her technological resourcefulness, and her brilliant creativity, certainly seemed to offer support for that view. Historians, good and bad, found justification for such ambitions in the recent, as in the mediaeval, past. The German quest for world power had begun before the First World War (6). Many Germans were anxious to be again on the road to world power after 1918, though their intelligence should have told them that, though they might succeed in war against the other European states, a conflict which involved them against new extra-European powers, Russia and the US, was likely to end in disaster. But the German victory over Russia in 1917 caused them to underestimate Russian strength (as

did many others). Even so, the Germans could perhaps have established their hegemony over Europe and the Mediterranean indefinitely, had they not been led by a leader, Hitler, who, for all his determination and willpower, had an untrained mind dominated by obsessions
(such as his fear of the Jews). Yet his daemonic personality made it
difficult to replace him by a more prudent and calculating person.

All went well for Germany at first. Hitler made an agreement with
Russia to divide Poland, and to re-establish the eastern frontiers of 1914,
on lines rather more favourable to Germany. The British and French
decision to treat the German invasion of Poland in 1939 as a justification
for war, though morally and politically right, was militarily calamitous.
They were not strong enough to do anything to help Poland against
either Russia or Germany. A British feint to establish themselves in
Scandinavia went awry. Germany found herself speedily in control of
Norway and Denmark. In May 1940, Germany turned against the Low
Countries and France. She again was completely successful.

These victories were won partly for tactical, partly for psychological
reasons. Hitler had resolved never again to fight 'long wars of fronts', as
he himself had experienced in 1914–18 (7). The German High
Command, from Hitler downwards, conceived of modern war as being
characterised by swift offensives which would not only surprise, but
overwhelm, the enemy at his weakest point. A breach in the enemy's
line could be made by tanks and aerial bombing as well as by a judicious
use of artillery as in 1914–18. Once the breach was made, all available
tanks would be flung in, and would drive as far as they could, striking
in all directions. Motorised infantry, paratroops, bicyclists would be
thrown in, too, to prevent, by 'methodical opportunism', the establishment of a regular front. These ideas had been worked out by several
military theorists between the wars, among them Basil Liddell Hart, in
England, and Charles de Gaulle, in France, but it was left to the German
General Hans Guderian (commander of the tank spearhead in 1940) to
bring them to perfection. This technique of 'lightning war' used all
modern technology, such as radio. The field commanders were also
instructed to be willing to experiment and not to stick to rules in old
order books: as Liddell Hart himself wrote, it was 'one of history's most
striking examples of the decisive effect of a new idea carried out by a
dynamic executant' (8).

In the early days of the war, the idea of a German world mission (not
a Nazi one) was shared by all ranks. A hostile witness, Djilas, commented on talks between the Yugoslavs and the Germans in 1942: 'What
surprised me more than anything else during these negotiations . . .
was how little of the Nazi ideology and mentality was evident in the
German army, which did not seem like an unthinking automated
machine. Officer-soldier relations seemed less disciplined and more
cordial than in other armies. The junior officers ate out of the soldiers'

kettle at least here on the battlefield' (9). Teilhard de Chardin even believed the Germans 'deserved to win because they had more spirit' (10). Pétain thought the Germans beat the French because the latter had had 'unpatriotic schoolmasters' (11). The great historian, Marc Bloch, thought that the German victory over France was 'essentially a triumph of intellect' (12).

Thus, in June 1941, Germany was at first sight in a stronger position than any European conqueror had ever been. Even Napoleon had been less successful. All continental Europe except Portugal was in German hands, or in those of her close allies. Even in France, many captured officers relied upon fair treatment after the peace (13). England, together with a few friends in remote mountains in the Balkans, was holding out with encouragement from the USA, but the British bombing of Germany was not effective. Russia had shown every sign of welcoming the German successes. The Nazis found the communists in Russia personally congenial*. The communist parties of Western Europe accepted Germany as the new paramount power. Russia was profitably trading with Germany. America was far away. Germany's Japanese ally was proceeding well with her plans for the 'co-prosperity sphere'. Within the German 'new order' in Europe, there was much support, willing or grudging, for the new state of affairs, notably from the traditional conservatives, who, despite the Russian alliance, saw fascism as offering protection against communism. Many workers even from France went to work for Germany without much reluctance. The German network of numerous and brutal concentration, or labour, camps was less large than the Russian one. The extermination camps for which the Nazis later became infamous had not yet been established.

The first reason for the defeat of this empire was that it sought to expand even further at the cost of Russia, a natural ally of Germany at that time more than a natural enemy, since two totalitarian régimes have more in common with each other than with liberal democracies. They were, in reality, two sides of the same coin. Had Hitler been able to see that, it is doubtful whether the old world could have been saved from permanent dictatorship.

The early days of the German invasion of Russia were nevertheless successful. It seemed as if the new German aims of establishing a colonial empire in west Russia might be attained. But the German High Command had underestimated the extent of Russian industrialisation which, under Stalin, had made several advances over the level reached in 1917. The Germans also underestimated the Russians' 'illimitable

* Ribbentrop, the Nazi foreign minister, thought 'that, talking with Stalin and the other Kremlin potentates, he had felt that he was among comrades barely distinguishable from his National Socialist acquaintances' (14).

capacity for obedience and subservience' in Liddell Hart's words, as they did the tenacity of Russian patriotism (15). Then the German army was not able to cope so easily with the terrain in Russia as they had been in France. The bad Russian roads helped the defence, as the French good roads had been in 1940 a friend to the invaders' motorised infantry. Germany was also far behind Russia in numbers of vehicles which could cross rough country. Germany thus became engaged in a long war with an enemy able to use the conflict as a means of national reconciliation.

Before Hitler launched the German army against Russia, he should either have negotiated with Britain or, if that were unsuccessful, he should have conquered her. For that he would have received every help from Russia, including the sale of strategic raw materials. (Russia would probably have taken advantage of a British defeat to occupy Persia.) But Hitler shied at a direct onslaught on Britain. He failed to destroy the British air force in 1940. For Hitler, what he took to be blood was thicker than ideology. Even in 1941, his admiration for Britain, and his hope for an eventual alliance with the British Empire, triumphed over his strategic sense (16). Thus he scarcely worked out a real plan for the invasion of Britain or a complete blockade by submarine.

The second reason for the defeat of the 'new order' was that Italy led Germany into difficulties in Africa, where the British and, ultimately, the Americans and French exiles were able to salvage their strategic positions. A rebellion in Italy drew its government out of the war in such a manner as to help Germany's enemies at the most sensitive moment. Rebellions occurred everywhere, even in Germany. In these actions by a 'resistance' against a Europe united by Hitler, the seeds were sown of a democratic Europe: of what the French historians of the movement described as 'a break with the mediocrity of the past, and rejection of conformism, injustice and degradation' (17). This 'secret war' of murder and ideology, with no rules or hierarchy, of the high quality radio receiver and of interrogation, of cutting telephone lines and defacement of notices, of a secret press (France had 1,200 papers selling a total of a million copies an issue), of 7,000 agents dropped by parachute or landed by submarine (18), had a great psychological effect on postwar politics (and on colonial politics); but the effect on the war itself was modest.

Finally, the Germans' other ally, Japan, miscalculated in their plans for the development of East Asia. The US considered that they had a role in Asia to prevent Japanese hegemony over China, and were looking for ways of thwarting them (partly by trying to prevent Japanese access to oil in Indonesia). The Japanese foolishly launched a surprise attack on both the US in Hawaii (as they had on the Russian fleet in 1904) and on the European possessions in the Far East. Once again, as in Germany's attack on Russia, indeed as usual in war, the aggressor won the first battles, and drove out the British, the US, the Dutch, and the French from their possessions in East Asia (including Burma, the road through which Britain could help China). But those actions brought the US to full mobilisation, against Germany as well as Japan. A counter attack began from some Pacific islands which the Japanese had failed to capture, from Australia (which inflicted the first defeat on Japan in New Guinea) (19), and from India, where the British had been for two centuries the paramount power. In the West, counter attacks could be mounted from Africa and Britain — and, of course, Russia.

The crowning error of the Germans was their quixotic declaration of war on the US immediately after Japan's attack.

The consequent war was of a more global nature than that of 1914, comparable in its international significance to the wars of the eighteenth century. In this contest, Germany and Japan, even if they were able to dominate much of Europe and East Asia by force, were in a weak position in comparison with the US and Russia, combined with Britain and a few remains of the British and other European empires. Germany and Japan were, for example, short of many of the basic products needed for a long war such as oil, whereas the US and Russia were the world's largest producers of that fuel. Nor did the Germans and Japanese even seek to play with any subtlety on the suspicions which most British and American people had of Russia and communism. Actually, Stalin was at least as much of a tyrant as Hitler was, and had already profited from the war to conquer Bessarabia, half Poland and the little Baltic states. The conflict could scarcely be held to be one of democracy against tyranny. But this discrepancy was never played upon successfully by the Germans. The Western democracies, mean-time, were induced to forget temporarily about Stalin's extraordinary crimes. Hitler, whose leadership had been one of the reasons for Germany's early successes, became less and less flexible in retreat, even though he continued personally to dominate the generals. His mind became overborne by irrelevant historical parallels, absurd obsessions and trivial details.

Hitler's, Mussolini's and Japan's empires were overthrown, though at a great cost. Once again, technology played a decisive part in the victory. Thus the German High Command in its wars on all fronts used radio-telephony. That led to a far swifter contact between headquarters and field commanders than ever before. The aid to navigation in the air was also incalculable. But the use of radio had some unexpected conse-quences. First, it enabled Hitler, as commander-in-chief, to be in daily contact with generals. Though Hitler's military sense was strong and often effective, it discouraged commanders from thinking for them-selves. Second, the use of radio meant that Allied code-breakers could intercept nearly all their communications. Thus, for the first time in any war, British and American commanders in the field were able to organise their battles with their enemies' plans all in front of them. It may well seem surprising, therefore, that they did not win the war quicker.

The German leadership had at their disposal a large labour force. They combed Europe to make it bigger. Perhaps because they had never had slave colonies in the New World or elsewhere, not even under Rome, they did not realise that people do not work well if they are treated badly. At all events, the slave labour camps of Nazi Germany were much less efficient than ordinary factories.

Germany, despite, or because of, her totalitarian leadership, also took a long time to awake to the necessity of organising her economy for war. In early 1942, the production of civilian goods was only 3% below peacetime levels (20). Germany was still making refrigerators for private buyers in 1942. Road and public building continued till then. There was little redeployment of labour (it was admittedly already controlled) and little use of women, whom the Nazis believed to be best employed at home. Speer's attempt at a national reorganisation for war, in 1943 and 1944, met many difficulties, from the Nazi party in particular (21). Then, despite some encouragement of local nationalism, the German régime never gave any sustained help to the Flemings, the Ukrainians, the Slovaks, and the Croats, all of whom had genuine complaints against the old order of things (22). Against this, the Allies developed a sound method of compiling statistics, which enabled them, unlike the Germans, to know exactly what they were producing, and what not. They, therefore, mobilised their resources better than did the Germans. Since their peoples were mainly behind them, in the 'war effort', the Allies did not have to take into account large margins of error, as has been the case with subsequent national statistics.

The Russian defeat of Germany in the East was primarily a triumph of that industrial power which Germany had avoided noticing. Russia had had 20,000 tanks (more than the rest of the world put together) in 1941 (23), and produced another 100,000 between then and June 1945. The import of many US lorries helped the Russians too, enabling their motorisation and a clever use of mobile land warfare. Western bombing tied down Germany's fighters which, otherwise, could have been used against Russia. The Russian production of thousands of fighters (137,000 according to Russian figures) was enough to give them, in the end, command of the war in the air. The building of new industries in the Ural mountains removed the centre of Russian industry away from the battle. Even more important, in 1945, over half the industrial workers in Russian factories were women. Meantime, the most strict forms of state control in collective farms diminished. Anti-religious and Marxist slogans declined (24).

The US organisation for war was even more impressive. While the

Russians lost millions, the US lost under 400,000 dead. 14½ million people were, however, successfully mobilised. The US was never touched directly by war, save for the occupation of her dependency, the Philippines, and the bombing of Hawaii. The cost ($330 billion) admittedly necessitated a new structure of taxes which drew most US citizens into becoming tax-payers for the first time. But, in return, unemployment, high in 1941, was cut by the establishment of new governmental agencies. Industry boomed. A new synthetic rubber industry was created. 300,000 aircraft were produced by 1945. Not only businessmen but scientists and professors were brought into a new collaboration with the government and the military. An espionage service in the US was founded (there had scarcely been such a thing before 1942). Half the national income was devoted to military expenditure from 1942 (25). The constitution remained, however, untarnished and, though the President's power was increased, elections and normal congressional work continued. The leaders of the American trade unions accepted an agreement not to strike in return for an agreement by employers to ban lockouts (26) — the perfect compromise dreamed of by young Fascists in the early 1930s. The US entered the war in 1941 politically parochial, and ended it in 1945 the dominant world power. Few wars have ever been so successful for any nation.

The tank and the aircraft were the distinguishing weapons of the Second World War, both being used as they had begun to be used at the end of the First. All developments in the course of the Second World War were to some extent a response to them. For example, anti-aircraft guns were put on lorries to guard convoys and the motorisation of artillery. Tanks got bigger but, afterwards, they declined in importance, as first Russia, then Germany invested in mines on the ground. In 1944, the US developed the Sherman tank, with a mine detector in front of it. In the second half of the war, names of aircraft replaced those of battleships as emotive marks of military strength — Spitfire, Blenheim, Wellington — mostly harking back to a lost era of limited war (27). The most significant aircraft was, however, the US's Flying Fortress, which could carry 20,000 pounds of incendiary bombs, flying at 300 miles an hour, with 13 machine guns protecting it on all sides. Raids by these fleets of bombers, accompanied by fighters, began, from 1944 (though not before, because of inadequate results achieved before photo reconnaissance) to have a devastating effect on German industry, and precision bombing of communications and oil plants in the end was effective (28).

Then in June 1944, at the invasion of Normandy, the British and Americans had 6,000 aircraft to face 900 German, and were able to use these weapons continuously as a substitute for artillery. The Western use of paratroops too (in Sicily and in France) was as effective as the earlier German use of such troops had been.

The war in the Far East was won by air power, itself a consequence of the superior industrial system in the US. Aviation was the foundation of General Macarthur's 'Island Campaign' which began in 1943 and which enabled the setting up of bases for the heavy bombing of Japan, from 1944 onwards (from the Mariana islands, then Okinawa). The consequent raids were few but effective. General Le May's raid on Tokyo of March 1945 with nearly 300 B29 bombers each carrying 6 to 8 tons of explosive burned about 16 square miles of land and caused 185,000 killed or wounded. By August 1945, 60% of Japanese merchant shipping was lost and, although she still had most of her overseas conquests, she could not count on getting to them, nor on supplying herself. The atom bombs dropped in August 1945 were extensions of this policy, and were probably instrumental in persuading the Japanese government to make peace, so enabling the US to avoid what would undoubtedly have been a bloody invasion of Japan.

Thirty years after the Second World War, some of the aims of the vanquished have come about, though not as they would have liked them. Thus Germany, though divided, certainly has no problem of living space, since its population is static. It is the richest nation in Europe. Japan is the most powerful country in the Far East. Economically, it is now the most successful power in the world. Even the corporate state, fitfully and ineffectively put forward by Mussolini, seems increasingly to characterise the economies of many nominally free nations. Similarly, the concept of National Socialism is one which has attracted innumerable African and Asian states. The leaders of these societies would not recognise any link with Nazism. Nor is there any direct one. Yet Socialist Nationalism turns out, unsurprisingly, to be very like National Socialism. So far from being defeated in 1945, a version of what would have certainly seemed before 1939 to be Fascism – vulgar Fascism, no doubt, bastard Fascism perhaps – is with us, unrecognised everywhere, the strongest political movement of the century. Several democracies which the Fascists regarded as decadent in the 1930s also seem almost to be so. Nor has the world been shocked by the triviality and cruelty of what happened in the war into new ways of settling disputes. Several extraordinary heroes of the Left, such as 'Che' Guevara, have again elevated violence to a moral virtue. It now seems as if 1945 indeed was, so far from being the end of an era of war, a mere halt on the route in the major multi-national conflict which has never ceased since 1914. Still, before considering the continuance of that conflict since 1945, it is interesting to notice the extent to which the Second World War was inspired by, and to some extent lost by, the Germans' obsession with the question of race.

45

Causes of War: Racialism

We got into the Reichstag in order to acquire the weapons of democracy from its arsenal.
We become Reichstag deputies in order to paralyse the Weimar democracy with its own
assistance.

Goebbels, in *Der Angriff* (1930)

However the Second World War is explained, justified or commemorated, it lives as primarily the conflict in which the dictatorship in
Germany made use of its absolute power to destroy the Jews. This
memory perhaps diverts the attention of the student of history from its
significance as a final attempt by the Germans to unite Europe by force
(resulting in the division of both Germany and Europe into two), but the
problem of racial prejudice needs to be examined.

There are five branches of the human species. They are known to
anthropologists by the unhelpful names of Caucasoid, Mongoloid,
Australoid, Congoloid and Capoid. The Caucasoid group includes
Europeans and White Americans, Middle East whites, Arabs and Jews,
Persians, Indians and the Ainus of Japan. The Mongoloids are the
Chinese, most East Asiatics, Polynesians, Eskimoes, the Indians in the
Americas, and Indonesians. The Congoloids are held to include the
blacks of both Africa and America, as well as the pygmies. The Austra-
loids include the Aborigines of Australia, some Indian tribes of India,
and the Negritos of South Asia, while the Capoids are represented by
the San (bushmen) and Hottentot tribes of South Africa (1).

The main question outstanding about these species is, did they
branch off a single stem 'recently ' (say a million years ago) or did they
separate earlier, when long extinct groups, such as ape men, were still
alive? (2). Some time, a definite resolution of this uncertainty may be
found. If the second explanation turns out to be true (as it well may,
considering the number of diverse languages), the existing races of men
will have been shown to have been separately evolving over tens of
thousands of years. Such a discovery may inspire some superficial
reflections on the nature of racial differences, but a moment's thought
would remind the most prejudiced person that the real dislikes between

peoples have been those within sub-species: French and Germans; Russians, Germans and Jews; Moslems and Hindus; Arabs and Jews; and Chinese and Vietnamese. 'The less we differ the more we hate', George Canning's cynical comment on the history of the British and the Dutch has been the best judgement on the relations between peoples who have quarrelled. Kings and nations alike have gone to war because their interests seemed the same, not because they were poles apart.

The evidence of anthropology and history suggests that there are no pure races. This point was made in the 1930s by the Italian professor, Orestano, to Alfred Rosenberg (the theorist of race), when the latter was lecturing in Rome. Every nation was a hybrid, Orestano pointed out, including the Chinese and especially the Germans (3); especially the Prussians, he might have added, since they are half Slav and registered themselves as a Slav monarchy at the Congress of Vienna (4). Every Slav, too, probably has a dose of some blood from his conquerors between the fifth and thirteenth centuries: Huns, Avars, Bulgars, Magyars, Pechenegs, and Mongols. India has assimilated Greeks, Scythians, Turks, Mongols, Parthians, and Huns. From the earliest times, England has imported Flemish wool weavers, Italian financers, Germans, Sephardic jews, Venetians, and Huguenots. From the days of Alexander onwards, every great empire has embraced populations of mixed origin, above all Rome, where, from 212 AD, all free citizens were Roman citizens. All old distinctions between Romans and provincials vanished, in respect of both opportunities and punishments (5).

A wholly isolated group of 400 people can perpetuate themselves, if they are closely grouped on an island, in a valley or ghetto. But anything wider than this makes dispersal inevitable. There have been many instances of minor groups being absorbed without trace in a dominant population, within a few generations. The black population of England in the eighteenth century numbered 20,000 in London alone, many becoming beggars and known as Saint Giles's blackbirds (6). There was a similar, but larger, Arab population in China in the eleventh century. That also has been absorbed (7).

Almost always, it is true, when two peoples come into contact, one tends to dominate in the end. Had it not been for that, the world would already be khaki in colour since, over the last half million years, the tramp of peoples backwards and forwards has been ceaseless (8). The Germans were held by Tacitus to have 'never been tainted by intermarriage': hence their 'wild blue eyes, reddish hair and huge frames' (9). But perhaps the 'red hair' came from a different breed from the one which caused the blue eyes. Cuba is one of the few countries to have a population roughly equal between black or mulatto and white. In the 1940s, the pure negro was increasing at a slower rate than the native white, and slower than the mulatto. Essentially, the whites were winning that encounter. The blacks had higher death and lower birth rates in cities than whites (10), and the black proportion of the population in Cuba dropped continuously between the mid-nineteenth century and 1959 (11).

Larger groups, on the other hand, can survive indefinitely if they are left alone to thrive, as, for example, the Basques have been or, more recently, the Germans of the Volga (left alone until Stalin deported them). Other nations have changed their colours imperceptibly. The ancient Egyptians may have been black and become lighter in colour (12).

Within various groups, indeed within the human race as a whole, certain combinations of factors (climate, religion, diet) have created great diversity of talent, custom and priorities. 'Adaptation' can take the form, as with the Alaskans, of developing large chests, lungs, hearts and so on (13). There are no distinct blood groups, save for the Rhesus factor (which is rare). But those facts invalidate the idea of segregation for natural selection. Nor would any balanced man deny now the influence of both heredity and environment in forming peoples' characters; though probably heredity, as Professor Sauvy says, has the 'edge' as a decisive influence (14).

Prejudice against half castes has been continuous in history but it is without foundation. The faults attributed to them all derive from environment. But can it really be true that Professor Sauvy is right to argue that 'the best way to avoid racial quarrels is to encourage mixed marriages'? (15). Some countries have mixed two peoples of different racial origin so much that the mulattoes constitute a majority of the population: but the large number of US citizens who are racially mixed (and would have been known by the almost forgotten words mulatto, quadroon or octaroon in censuses during the nineteenth century) are now classed as black. They also think of themselves as black, are happy to be treated as black, and contribute to a generally false impression of the extent to which the population of the US is characterised by African blood. But many even of the more prominent leaders of the US 'black' population have pigments which are more white than black. The position seems odd, and is only to be understood in relation to past attempts by slave owners to avoid a mixture of races by telling strange stories of blacks as sexual maniacs (16). Furthermore, the 'racial question' in countries where Caucasoids and Congoloids mix is not only a matter of colour; physiognomy plays a part. De Tocqueville, incidentally, thought in the 1830s that the prejudice of race appeared to be stronger in states of the US which had abolished slavery than in those where it still existed (17).

Equally important, many discussions which are considered as affecting race should really be considered, as they were in the past, matters of language or of religion (18). For example, in the early Middle Ages, the relations between Spaniards and Moors were without extremes of bigotry. The Castilian conquest forced on Spain a painful choice between race and religion (19).

Still, 'racial prejudice is an aspect of human nature' (20), as Professor Saggs, the historian of Babylon wrote, and, with religious and linguistic prejudices, it was part of the background of the swift judgments and coarse jokes of the eighteenth century. The only new element that has been introduced recently into the problem is the growth of new nationalism under the stress of better technology and mass sensationalism.

The changes in attitude to race over a few hundred years can best be seen from a comparison of the treatment in Spain of the Jewish population in 1492 and afterwards the German treatment of the Jews in the 1930s.

In the fifteenth century, the Jews of Spain were the real middle class of the Castilian state, the tax gatherers and also the tax payers, the favoured group upon whom successive monarchs of every part of the peninsula relied to carry on the business of the kingdom, including, indeed the formation of the kingdom. Subject to one terrible pogrom at least under the Visigoths, the Jews' condition had greatly improved under the Muslims, whom they assisted in their conquest of Spain. They mastered new customs. Many excelled in Arabic — indeed, the language of the greatest Spanish Jews of the Middle Ages was Arabic, if written in Hebrew characters (21). Many great Jews flourished under Islam: for example, Hasdai ibn Shabrut, physician and minister of finance of Abd al Rahman II; and a famous family of Jews were grand viziers to the Kings of Granada. The Arabs taught the Christians how useful Jews could be as judges, officials, translators, astronomers, and even bishops; the chief rabbi of Burgos in the 1380s was bishop there in 1415 (22). Jews even sang dirges at Christian funerals. Meantime, Portugal was, if anything, more 'judaized' than was Castile and a Majorcan Jew, Jaime Ferrer, taught the great Portuguese navigators their cartography. Spanish Jews largely escaped the continent-wide persecution of their race which marked the beginning of the First Crusade and which had led to the expulsion of Jews from England in 1292, pogroms in Naples and burnings and massacres in Germany at the time of the Black Death.

The trouble was that, by the fifteenth century, the Church and the peasantry in Spain had begun to see the Jews as rivals or even new masters (23). Many of the peasants were christianised Arabs, even if perhaps their remote ancestors had been arabised Christians. The Bible was read in Arabic in Seville for many generations. The public disliked the Jews' high rates of usury (24), while the Church looked on the rich synagogues and merchants' houses as valuable booty. Until the kings failed to force the Moors of the south into the Christian states, there was, however, little danger to the Jews, though there was a serious pogrom in 1391. In 1481, Ferdinand the Catholic reproved the Prior of the Archbishop of Saragossa for his persecution of the Jews of that city on the grounds that they are 'our treasure chests' (25). But, even so, the strange tales current about Jews' religious practices since the twelfth century in other parts of Europe had begun to spread in Spain. The alleged stories of ritual murders of Christian children, poisoning of wells, and torturing of the holy wafer (since Christ was supposed to be present in it) were all soon told in a country previously a byword for tolerance of all religions. Did the Jews really worship the Devil? So at least it was said in Seville, where men were known to have run through the streets demanding the 'extermination of the accursed race'. In vain, did the Conde de Niebla and the mayor try to stop them. They were pushed aside, while the populace attacked and destroyed the *barrio judio* in Seville. The wind of prejudice ran like an epidemic through Andalusia and many Jews and their families were murdered (26). (Some of these tales may be based on rumours of the activities of gypsies. It was said, for example, that, in 1910, a family of gypsies were still living in the Sierra de Gador in Andalusia, stealing babies and drinking the blood as it flowed from the skin: a *curandera* , or 'wise woman', had let it be known that that was a cure for consumption (27)).

The expulsion of the Jews in 1492 was the consequence of an outburst of demagoguery led by the Church, in direct opposition to the King who, like most Spanish noblemen, had Jewish blood.* But Ferdinand, as Américo Castro says, was a politician above all and not one to support lost causes (28). The great nineteenth century nationalist historian, Menéndez Pelayo, looked on the expulsion of the Jews as the 'principal cause of decadence for the peninsula' (29).

The 400,000 or so Jews of Spain in 1492 were given the choice of abandoning Judaism or leaving the country. The richer Jews, or about half the Jewish population, accepted the first alternative. Later, in the seventeenth century, efforts were made, where possible, to strip converted Jews of their disguises. State genealogists toured Spain in order to ensure that no *conversos* (or *marranos*, the pejorative word used) were still public officials. Many, like the families of Spain's most famous writers and artists of that time, successfully concealed their ancient faith, the families of Saint Teresa, Luis Vives, and Cervantes among them (30). 'I'm a mortal enemy to all Jews,' Sancho Panza was caused to remark by Cervantes, doubtless in self-defence (31). Others left for Hamburg, Amsterdam or Livorno, and Cromwell later enabled Jews to go to England for the first time since they had been expelled in 1292. This diaspora enriched (perhaps initiated) the commerce of those countries which received them and, as in the case of the Huguenots in

---

* Through his mother, Juana Enríquez, Ferdinand was a cousin of Fernando de Rojas, the Jewish author of *La Celestina*, the first European novel.

France, impoverished the persecutor. When the Venetians began to discuss expelling their Jews in 1571, Giovanni Soranzo, a Venetian diplomat, denounced the idea: 'Do you know what it may cost you in years to come? Who gave the Turk his strength, and where else would he have found the skilled craftsmen to make the cannon, bar, shot, swords, shields and bucklers . . . if not among the Jews expelled by the Kings of Spain?' (32). Nor did the Jews produce only works of war: the first book printed in the Ottoman Empire was the Pentateuch dating from 1547 in Constantinople, a publication which led to the preservation of *ladino* Spanish in Hebrew letters throughout the eastern Mediterranean (33).

There were qualifications to the orders expelling Jews from Spain. The *reconquista* of the country from the Muslims had been assisted by several military orders of chivalry which, by the fifteenth century, possessed large estates. Members of those orders, if they were Jewish or had Jewish blood, were excused the expulsion orders. That meant that the King himself, his cousins, the Enríquez family, the Hurtado de Mendozas, and many other noble families were able to survive (34). Another qualification was that, as elsewhere by the fifteenth century, the Jews in Spain were at least half Spanish. The Jews there had never lived cloistered lives, nor did they live in ghettos (a word taken, like 'arsenal', from Venice, where the *ghettare* was, in the past, the place where cannon were made (35)).

These diasporas were later followed by the expulsion of some 275,000 Moors (though Article 5 of the order expelling the Moors of Granada exempted 6% of that population who could, it was hoped, tend the sugar mills and systems of irrigation) (36).

This two-headed pusuit of purity of blood was the consequence of a determination by Philip II to ensure the success of the Counter Reformation. It coincided, curiously, with a substantial import of black slaves from Africa to both Portugal and Spain. In every Mediterranean town in the sixteenth century, there were also innumerable other immigrants: Corsicans, Berbers, Turks, Slavs, Albanians, Armenians and Greeks (37).

The more one enquires into these illiberal policies of Renaissance Spain, the more it seems that, despite certain excitable remarks, they were due, like the hatreds in India between Muslim and Hindu*, less to a search for purity of blood than to religious and cultural enmity. The Jews and the conquered Moors were expelled because they refused to change their dress, customs and types of houses (38). This judgement is confirmed by a consideration of the Spaniards' attitude to Indians in the Americas. The Indians were looked upon as free men, able to move about, to own property, to sue and be sued in the courts to which they

* Actually, in India, in, say, the fourteenth century, those two peoples were close to fusion, despite arguments to the contrary by polemicists of the twentieth.

had access and were free to change employers and to choose their work. But they were not free to practice a false religion, nor to be lazy.

The treatment of Jews in the twentieth century by Germans was a different matter. It derived from a theory of race which had no rational intellectual backing but was firmly believed in, by leaders and by the led: an illusion which led to a tyranny as brutal as the Communist one based on a false reading of the idea of class, even if it was less long-lived.

Anglo-Saxons in North America nearly destroyed the Red Indians by mistake. The British in Australia did much the same as the Spaniards in South America. The French in the nineteenth century talked of 'driving the natives back' in Algeria (39). In the late eighteenth century, Spaniards, such as the Conde de Peñaflorida, suddenly discovered that the French, whom they had admired for their enlightened ideas, really thought themselves to be superior to all other peoples. Louis XIV, like the encyclopaedist Masson (and Alexandre Dumas) believed Spain, for example, to be like Africa (40); and the eighteenth century had a contemptuous attitude to Africa. Gibbon wrote: 'The tedious enumeration of the unknown and uninteresting tribes of Africa may be reduced to the general remark that they were all of the swarthy race of the Moors' (41). 'The inaction of the negroes,' he said elsewhere, 'does not seem to be the effect either of their virtue or their pusillanimity . . . this rude ignorance has never invented any effectual methods of defence or of destruction; they appear incapable of forming any extensive plans of government or conquest; [and] the obvious inferiority of their mental faculties has been discovered and abused by the nations of the temperate zone' (42).

The eighteenth century thus inspired a new attitude to race in several ways. The French Revolution was a fiesta for absurd notions. Like everything else, race came into the discussion. Equally extraordinary illusions affected both 'left' and 'right'. In 1797, a French Jesuit, the Abbé Barmel, argued that the Revolution itself had been caused by the Knightly Order of the Templars,who had not been exterminated in 1314 (as was generally believed), but had survived in order to plot against monarchies and Popes and afterwards to found a world republic (43). The revolutionary, Louis-Michel Le Peletier,* president of the Constituent Assembly, proposed in 1792 the deliberate breeding of a 'race of revolutionaries'. During the nineteenth century, the idea of a good and, therefore (by implication), of a bad, race was on many lips. Another Frenchman, the Comte de Gobineau, devised a whole theory of history based on race. Violence and upheaval, he believed, were a consequence

---

* He proposed the abolition of the death penalty in 1789 but voted for the execution of the King in 1793. He was assassinated before the King died by a member of the Royal body-guard.

of intermixture of races (44). Even the benign James Stephen recommended in 1843 against allowing black labour to be taken to Australia, adding, 'We now regret the folly of our ancestors in colonising North America from Africa' (45). Sir Francis Galton, an Englishman more intelligent than Gobineau and more influential than Le Peletier, argued (with Aristotle) that intelligent people have fewer children than unintelligent ones. The intelligence of a people must, therefore, diminish over the centuries. Decay could only be staved off by organised breeding, or the establishment of a system of castes, such as prevailed in India, which forbids exogamy. Galton, a cousin of Charles Darwin's, invented the word 'eugenics' to describe the study of these matters, in 1884. (He also invented the word 'genius', a useful addition to our supply of meaningless superlative nouns.) A French contemporary, Vacher de Lepouge, wrote in the same year that 'in certain conditions a very small number of absolutely perfect males would be able to fertilise all the women deserving to propagate the race' (46).

None of these formulations were, in the first place, directed *against* any race, Jewish or other. The aim was to formulate a superior race (even though such an idea is almost Jewish in its exclusiveness). But then: 'It is no use mincing matters,' wrote the historian E.A. Freeman in 1877, 'but it will not do to have the policy of England, the welfare of Europe, sacrificed to Hebrew sentiment . . . we cannot sacrifice our people, the people of Aryan and Christian Europe, [even] to the most genuine belief in an Asian mystery' (47). The Anglo-Saxon conquerors of Australia and, later, immigrants including Labour politicians as well as Liberals, were by then determined to preserve a 'white Australia' by prohibiting the immigration of Asiatic and Pacific islanders, and deporting labourers on sugar estates. Australia was to be 'saved from the coloured curse . . . not to be a mongrel nation torn with racial dissension, blighted by industrial war. Australia was [to house] the only pure white race' (48).

A blatant if innocent sense of national superiority thus, in 1900, distinguished the white nations, who were astounded at their own technological achievements and the ease with which a few white Europeans seemed to be able to run the world. Kaiser Wilhelm wrote in 1900: 'You should give the name of Germany such cause to be remembered in China for a thousand years, so that no Chinaman, no matter whether his eyes be slit or not, will dare to look a German in the face' (49). Even Sir Mark Sykes, (who was probably a Zionist in order to rid England of the Jews), like many, could write of his hero, the proconsul, Lord Cromer, as a 'strong dominant figure dreaded by an inferior race, whom he knew and who knew not him' (50). That may not sound innocent, but innocent it was. It was still innocent when Kipling adjured the British to 'take up the White Man's burden', in a great poem of that name, and when the *Daily Mail* told English people in the First World

War to refuse to be served by an Austrian or German waiter: 'If your waiter says he is Swiss, ask to see his passport' (51).

Germany had, by 1914, developed a particularly strong sense of her own destiny, based on a romanticised view of the Middle Ages, and an absolutely justified view of her achievements in the late industrial revolution. Illusions were certainly as strong there as anywhere. Because the Germans were recently united, they felt more passionately than others the need to have an enemy, as well as a master, race. Paul de Lagarde in *Deutsche Schriften*, published in 1878, expressed disillusion with the united Germany which had just been achieved and demanded the higher unity of the German *volk* as it had once been in the Middle Ages. The Jews (recently freed from living in ghettoes) were meantime still pre-eminently town dwellers in Germany, and were naturally reformers, if mostly fully integrated into the old Germany and prosperous in the new. To de Lagarde, Jews seemed the incarnation of decay, modernity, separateness from the national soul. The evangelical pastor Stoecker and the historian Treitschke agreed, though their arguments were religious and nationalist, without racial animus (52). Wilhelm Marr invented the word 'anti-semitism', in 1873, and Treitschke gave some respectability to it by saying, in 1879, in an article, that 'Jews are our national misfortune' (53). An anti-semitic deputy was elected to the Reichstag in 1887 (54). Volkish racism soon became appealing to middle class university graduates and lecturers, though less so among peasants. These ideas spread to Austria. The *volk* there began to seem as if it were a mythical church, with its festivals at solstices, the sign of the swastika* being used first in Europe by Lanz von Liebenfels, an Austrian who desired to found a new religious order of the racially pure (and which inspired Himmler's SS). He believed that men were divided into Aryans and apemen (55). Von Liebenfels was an isolated individual with little following. But the mixture of arrogance and sentimentality, self-confidence and bitterness (particularly at having been patronised by France for so many generations), ignorance and hierarchical authoritarianism, was symptomatic of much of Germany at the turn of the nineteenth and twentieth centuries. The consequence was much dislike of Germany outside. Winston Churchill looked on Germans as 'carnivorous sheep'. Clemenceau believed Germans 'understand and can understand nothing but intimidation' (56).

The Germans also allowed themselves to develop a phobia about the allegedly small space in which they were living. Thus the word *lebensraum* began to be used as a clarion call to expansion. But the German population had, like others in Europe, ceased to grow very fast. That was observable in the figures for German emigration to the US. Between 1850 and 1894, large numbers of Germans went across the Atlantic: in

---

* It is Hindu in origin.

1854 alone, 250,000, and in the 1880s, 100,000 to 200,000 a year. But, after 1894, the figures became negligible. 'Germany had no longer men to spare,' commented Sir John Clapham (57). *Lebensraum* was thus an idea deriving from another set of illusions.

Antisemitic fantasies were, if anything, stronger in Russia than in Germany. Among Tartars, Kalmuks and Turks, the Jews, having no connections with land and being among the newest minorities, were specially vulnerable. They had been incorporated into Russia after the partition of Poland in the eighteenth century (58).

Much of the antisemitism of the men who subsequently became Nazis derived from the Baltic Germans active in forming the antisemitic 'Black Hundreds' in Russia before 1914, since *émigrés* from that region played a major part in inspiring National Socialism. Rosenberg, the Nazi racist ideologist, was born in Riga, along with Tsarist antisemitic professionals (59). Tsarist ex-officers played a decisive part in disseminating the forgery, *The Protocols of the Elders of Zion* (60). This derived from a novel published in 1868 called *Biarritz*, written by Herman Gaedsche under the pseudonym 'Sir John Retcliffe'.* In it, the Devil appears in the Jewish cemetery in Prague in order to ask representatives of the twelve tribes what they had done in the previous hundred years. They explain how they had begun to dominate stock exchanges, churches, army, artisans, and how, soon, they would take over the world. (The Jews were already linked by the Jesuits, in particular, to the idea of masonic conspiracies, particularly in countries where there were few Jews.) The *Protocols* described how world domination would be achieved and was first published in *Znamya* (in St Petersburg) in 1903. It became well known after 1917, being at first taken seriously even by *The Times* (May 8, 1921), which subsequently admitted its error. The forgery was carried out in Paris about 1897 at the height of the Dreyfus affair by Pyotr Rachovsky, then head of the Russian secret police (Okhrana) outside Russia, perhaps with the short-term intention of discrediting the Russian statesman, Witte (61).

Innumerable racist theories were thus current in Europe in the child-hood of the Nazis. They were no more extremely felt in Germany than elsewhere. There were indeed only 400,000 Jews in Germany in comparison with 700,000 in Hungary, 1,000,000 in Roumania, and 3,000,000 in Poland. Most Nazis were, however, brought up in an atmosphere of political uncertainty because of the growth of non-German populations, not only Jews, in central Europe, and were affected by the immigration of substantial numbers of Jews into central Europe as a result of the persecutions in Russia. The collapse of the German Empire in 1918 inspired the darkest thoughts in a nation which had accustomed itself to

---

* The following summary of the extraordinary history of the Protocols derives from Norman Cohn's brilliant work, *Warrant for Genocide*.

the idea of world power. It seemed a small step between the views of serious scientists such as Galton and those of zealots such as Hans Gunther, professor of 'racial science' at the University of Jena in 1930, even though the step was across a divide between genuine scientific enquiry and prejudiced demagoguery.

Hans Gunther himself took that step. His *Short Ethnology of the German people*, which sold 272,000 copies between 1929 and 1943 (62), set an explicit target. The Jews could not be seen as a race, he argued, for they constituted a nation of mixed races – the worst thing possible. Gunther and his friends were encouraged to set up an Institute of Racial Marriage, by whose agencies eugenically selected men and women were supposed to give birth to supreme beings, for whose upbringing the State would be responsible. Hence, too, the boycotts, the burnings of books, the discriminatory Nuremberg laws, the fines and levies on Jewish property and, in the end, the plans for the 'final solution' or the 'desired solution', of the Jewish problem, in order to make Germany 'Jew-free' – a scheme which, to begin with, until 1939, seemed merely to envisage resettlement (in Madagascar, perhaps) but which became murder on a grand scale after 1941. The ground for this was prepared by a cultural revolution, a real counter-renaissance, as it were, in which the idea of German racial superiority was inculcated into everything, from education to chamber music. The names of Handel's oratorios were aryanised: 'Judas Maccabaeus' became 'William of Nassau', 'Israel in Egypt' became 'Mongol Fury'. The appropriate note was sounded by *Neue Zeitschrift für Musik* of May 1933: 'Soon again German opera houses will give bread to German opera singers and become houses for the cultivation of German music . . . Freed from the alien past . . . German universities and German music schools will give refuge once more to the German scholars and German teachers who may be trusted to guide our German youth to the great German masters' (63). Mad though this may sound, it was only the obverse to Allied propaganda of the First World War: Marc Ferro quotes a French propagandist who wrote, 'It is now time to draw a veil over those works which recognisably express the spirit of our latter day Huns: the future is to the young hero who will have the courage to banish the works of Handel, Mendelssohn, Wagner, Brahms and Richard Strauss . . .' (64). It was also unwise. Antisemitism destroyed German intellectual pre-eminence in the 1930s and drove many Jews and Aryans into exile to work against Germany. Had Hitler used the Jews as the Kaiser did he might easily have won the war.

The murder of over three and a half million Jews in gas chambers in six main, mostly Polish, camps of extermination and of nearly a million and a half by execution in Russia is now one of the best documented as well as the most atrocious crimes of history. The murders derived from a cult of an illusion just as did the Russian labour camps. The men responsible were men of will-power possessed by demons though, once men join a savage crowd, they become part of it, as the spectators at a gladiatorial show sometimes admitted, even in Saint Angustine's recollection (65). Himmler believed that he was still doing right after he fainted at the sight of 100 Jewish women being shot at Minsk (66). 'To have seen 100 corpses piled up, or 500, or 1,000 . . . and remain decent . . . that has made a glorious unwritten page in our history' (67). Yet the carriage of nearly four million people by railway to Poland was a severe burden on the German war machine while, if the Germans had used even the Russian Jews intelligently, along with other nationalities, they could have won the war. Far more Jews were, of course, murdered then than have been killed in most wars.

Had the war been won by the Germans, others would have suffered similar fates. The central European gypsies were destroyed, as it was. 'Certain ethnographical tasks' had been begun in 1939 in Poland (68). Himmler had also conceived of 'consanguine fishing expeditions' to France in order to capture promising blond or blue-eyed men who might become leaders (69). Himmler in 1941 told a gathering of SS officials that the destruction of 30 million Slavs was an essential prerequisite for German planning in the East. Meantime, the German victories enabled 'various dingy figures, hitherto known only as editors or publishers of the Protocols . . . to be changed', says Norman Cohn, 'into important administrators' (70); for example, Darquier, commissioner-general for Jewish affairs under Laval, or Endre, who became Secretary of State in Hungary and sent 450,000 Jews to Auschwitz. Even the eminently mongrel Spaniards, whose country was not even occupied by the Germans, had brief bouts of very artificial hostility to Jews whom some of their propagandists discovered, in the absence of any Jews in the country since the sixteenth century, to be identical with Catalans (71). In France, laws in October 1940 excluded Jews, above all, from responsible positions in culture and also in the civil service, judiciary and army. Throughout Europe, the yellow star was a badge of persecution. All the half-submerged racial prejudices of central Europe and western Russia came to a head and gave the richest continent in the world a reminder that the crust of civilisation was extremely thin. There was some illogicality in the thought that Hitler, anxious to preserve the purity of blood, wanted to create a German empire. Imperialism, as Gobineau appreciated, renders a mixture of races inevitable. But perhaps, behind Hitler's desire for empire in that particular region of the world, was his recognition that he would, thereby, be able to destroy the 'bacteria', the 'abscess', the 'germ carriers' and the 'tropical parasites', in order to preserve the 'host nation' (72). Hitler compared his task to that of Pasteur and Koch (73). (Lenin also liked medical metaphors, for he spoke of his movement as an infection which would pass through any wall built against it (74).)

The illogicality of Nazi racist theories, however, has not prevented them from having an odd subsequent history. First, they introduced violent political considerations into all discussion of the differences of races. By poisoning the character of that discussion, they have prevented desirable enquiry. In particular, it has become impossible to discuss peoples' rational fears of the cultural consequences of intermingling of peoples without inviting the accusation of racism. Second, while the milder version of Nazi racial attitudes practised in South Africa has incurred universal execration (even though it has been, at least, accompanied by democracy among the ruling white tribe), Jews have continued to be persecuted without exciting a great outcry. Russian antisemitism, in abeyance for a short time after 1917, grumbles on, and the Jews of the Middle East and North Africa, including the 80,000 Jews of Baghdad, who had lived in that city for a thousand years before the Arabs conquered it, were expelled soon after the formation of the Jewish state. Meantime, most of the multinational empires of the past have vanished. Russia remains an exception, since its rulers have been prepared to be harsher to their subjects than the Habsburgs or the Ottoman Sultans ever were.

Racism was not the only spring of Fascism nor even, in the case of all countries other than Germany, its most powerful motive. (The early Italian Fascists included Alfredo Rocco, a Jew, who wrote the Labour Charter of 1927.) 'Those who have never experienced the downfall of their country can hardly realise the grief and suffering which all patriotic Austrians, and especially the young among us, endured when the Monarchy crumbled to dust,' wrote the founder of the Austrian Fascists, Rüdiger von Stahremberg, 'nor can they imagine the rage and bitterness felt by the young soldiers of an old and ever victorious army doomed . . . to a shameful surrender' (75). Some 'Fascists' formed vigilante groups to protect homes or churches from 'anarchist mischief makers' in 1918–1919. Some hankered after the peasant militias of the Napoleonic wars. Some, like W. B. Yeats, longed for what he called 'the despotic rule of the educated – the only end to our troubles' (76). In politics, Yeats wrote, 'I have but one passion and one thought, rancour against all who, except under the most dire necessity, disturb public order'. Others saw Fascism as a movement which would liberate them from the unworthy compromises of party politics or articulate the ethical idea of war, or provide a uniform, or make possible the historic role of the great man, who would enable the nation, above all the young, to live dangerously, and forget the mediocre life of the bourgeoisie (77). The religiosity of Fascism will be discussed later* but one should also remark upon the cult of physical fitness, and its glorification of an idealised past. In the incoherent anarchy of its ideas and actions,

* See below, Epilogue II.

its aspiration to a permanent revolution without limits ('Rebel against everybody: nobody, or almost nobody, is just'), Spanish radicalism, like some other radical movements of the early twentieth century, was an authentic precursor to Fascism, just as some socialist or communist movements have been its bastard sons (78). The mixed ancestry of this movement, however, needs to be noticed when, as a word, it has taken over, in modern politics, the role once occupied in theology by evil.

The ancestors of Fascism are as difficult to identify and to isolate as are its children. The Radicals' violence was one origin. So was Antonio Maura's (conservative) demand for a 'revolution from above'. George Sorel was the ancestor of both Fascist and anarchist violent politics. Among the forerunners of Fascism were the agitators of the Futurist movement in art: hitherto, 'literature has tended to exact thoughtful immobility, ecstasy, and sleep, whereas we are for aggressive movement, febrile insomnia, mortal leaps and blows with the fist . . . no masterpiece can be anything but aggressive' (79). Not even the state as a work of art.* Of all these elements, the demand for a national revolution rather than an international working-class one, as demanded by the socialists, was perhaps the strongest. But there was also the desire to avoid being left on the upper shelf of nations as felt by Italian Fascists — 'we don't want to be just a museum, a hotel, a . . . Prussian blue horizon where foreigners come for a honeymoon . . . we must put our stamp on the molten metal of the world'. Pétain's régime in France had the same mixture of regeneration and reverence for the past. The Marshal began his decrees as a monarch (*Nous, Philippe Pétain*) and placed a great effort upon his role as moral tutor to the nation. His followers believed that 'thanks to us, the France of camping, of sports, of dancing and of collective hiking will sweep away the France of the aperitifs, tobacco dens, party congresses and long digestions' (80).

Doubtless, there were some aspects of Fascism in France, in Italy, even in Germany, which may even be described as beneficial. Do we see in Pétain's regime, as argued by Robert Paxton, the beginnings of the efforts to reverse decay, the willingness to give technology a high place, larger factories and economic growth which characterised post-war France? (81) The long digestions and aperitifs have almost been swept away. Do we not see even in Nazism the beginning of that destruction of class, which, according to Ralf Dahrendorf, characterises modern Germany? (82). Did the necessities of war enforce the modification of the New Order so as to lay the ground for the future economic integra-

---

* Out of innumerable futurist *occasions*, let us single out the dinner in London organised by Wyndham Lewis and C.R.W. Nevinson. Marinetti, dressed in a futurist suit with dynamic buttons, recited a poem about the Siege of Adrianople, with various kinds of onomatopoeic noises and crashes in free verse, while, all the time, the band played 'You made me love you. I didn't want to do it'. Marinetti subsequently became secretary-general of the Italian Academy under Mussolini.

tion of Europe (83)? Then some characteristics of the appeal of Fascism will probably always be with us: above all, the nostalgia for 'action'. Croce wrote about the end of the Risorgimento in Italy: 'Every close of a period of history brings with it the death of something, however much the end may have been sought . . . however essential it may be to the work which was so clearly envisaged and brought to completion . . . no more youthful strivings and heartburnings after an ideal that was new, lofty and far removed from realisation . . . Men even went so far as to regret the dangers' (84). Fascism was born among those regrets. The role of a form of Fascism in other circumstances after 1945 has been discussed earlier. Its role in the post war economy will be discussed again. Its part in the development of the world crisis since 1914 as a whole has not always been appropriately measured. Racialism and Fascism are not inevitably allies. Indeed, it was only National Socialism in Germany which made that equation so insistent.

46

The 'Cold' War

The 'cold war' has been a struggle between the two powers which emerged victorious over Germany and Japan in 1945, the US and Russia. The appearance of these as the two dominating powers in the world had been foreshadowed, on economic grounds, by de Tocqueville a century before*. The difference between them is that, while the US has been constructed on the basis of individual colonisation, with the encouragement of a lax and open state, the Russian Empire in Asia has been constructed by a strong, determined, increasingly secretive and jealous central government. Racially both the US and Russia are mixtures, as Peter Struve pointed out in the early 1900s (1). The USA has usually been a defensive power, but has appeared aggressive. Russia has been expansionist, though afraid. The United States is the central power of a conglomeration of allies, most of whom retain many of the realities of independent sovereignty. Russia's allies retain little more than the trappings. Millions of citizens of the US are the descendants of Russian immigrants. The futures of the two nations seem interlocked. Also, in the formulation of Henri Bergson, one nation represents 'the open society', the other the 'closed society' (3). One inherits the traditions of the free cities of Babylon and of the Mediterranean, of Greece, the German and Anglo-Saxon habits of consultation and law; the other is the inheritor of an oriental tradition of despotism, command, regularity, secrecy, conformity and centralised power, and also of Byzantine courtly bureaucracy.

The first ground for contest between Russia and the USA was Europe, the main battlefield of the war of 1939. The new conflict began there before the old war ended. In the last year or two of that war, the great

* 'There are, at the present, two great nations, Russia and the US which . . . started from different points but which seem to tend towards the same end . . . the American struggles against the obstacles that nature opposes to him . . . the adversaries of the Russian are men. The former combats the wilderness . . . the latter, civilisations. The principal of the former is freedom, of the latter servitude. Yet each seems called by some secret design of providence one day to hold in its hands the destinies of half the world.' De Tocqueville, *Democracy in America* Volume I (1835) (2).

conferences were as much concerned with the future of the world as with the battles being fought. The Russians understood that better than Roosevelt, perhaps even than Churchill. The 'Marxist' despot, Stalin, realised that, at such conferences, great men can have a decisive effect on history. Churchill and Roosevelt, who knew history well, especially the history of great men, thought in terms of ideas. Roosevelt was for a time enthralled by Stalin: he once said of Stalin, 'I think, if I give him everything I possibly can, and ask him for nothing in return, *noblesse oblige*, he won't try to annex anything, and will work with us for a world of democracy and peace' (4). Churchill, though a political genius, also gave Stalin the benefit of the doubt for a long time, for he admired him as a war leader*. Roosevelt said of Hitler that 'a nation can have peace with the Nazis only at the price of total surrender'. Peace with the Russians was obtainable at a lower price, but a price all the same.

At all events, between 1945 and 1948, Russia was able to draw the line of her influence in Eastern Europe much as she wished, while the US and Britain were slow to see that the days of tactical wartime collaboration could be over so soon. But arguments about the right attitude to adopt were continuous. This led in the end to the creation of the North Atlantic Treaty, the Warsaw Pact, the acceptance of the permanent division of Germany and, after 1952 (when the Republican party had won a US election on an unconvincing programme of freeing the Russian 'satellites'), of a general acceptance of a division of Europe between US and Russian spheres of influence. The economic success of the US zone of Europe was made more complete by the formation of a European Economic Community. Efforts to turn that success into an alternative centre of power have, however, as yet proved fruitless.

After 1950, the centre of competition between the US and Russia became first the Far, and then the Middle, East†. A communist party captured power in China in 1949. Combined Chinese and Russian pressure led to the war in Korea, which ended divided, as Germany was. South Korea and Formosa remained, like Japan, part of the US Empire. The subsequent history of this competition has primarily been a struggle for influence over the oversea territories which European Empires were persuaded or forced to abandon.

After 1949, there were two large centres of authority in the communist world. Both remained closed countries till the end of the 1970s. The

---

* 'In these general discussions', Churchill wrote in the last volume of his memoirs, 'maps were not used and the distinction between the East and the Western Neisse did not emerge as clearly as it should have done' (5).
† Up till about 1945, Western writers spoke of three regions, the Far East, the Middle East and the Near East. Since then, the Near and the Middle have been merged as Middle, so far as contemporary politics are concerned. The Near East is confined to archaeology. Somewhat against my will, I have kept to this illogical change of vocabulary. Henceforth in this book 'Middle East' extends from Libya to Iran. The 'Far East' is China and Vietnam. The East is the Indian sub-continent.

French ex-colonies in Indo-China also eventually succumbed to various forms of communism. The French abandoned the fight in Indo-China in 1955, on the assumption that the already small state would be divided, as Germany and Korea had been. The southern, capitalist Vietnamese state, however, never established itself. The communists in the north mounted an elaborate programme of subversion. The US allowed themselves to become drawn into its defence in the 1960s. A major, though defensive, war then began, in which the US apparently dropped as many bombs as they had on Germany in 1941–5. It was however, to no avail. The US fought the war, as Dr Guenther Levy has suggested, more as an administrative bureaucracy, not as an army (7). They decided neither to use nuclear weapons nor to invade the north of Vietnam. The consequence was an ignominious withdrawal, in 1975. Since then, the frontiers of the Far East seem clearly drawn between communist and open societies. However, the disputes, nominally on doctrinal grounds, between China and Russia, disturbed the serenity of the Communist world in the 1960s. Outright warfare between Russia's protégé, Vietnam, and China's, the apparently most murderous Cambodia, showed once more that, in the words of Paul Levi, at the Livorno conference of the Italian socialist party, at which he was the representative of Germany, 'in the history of the proletariat, the time arrives when we must recognise that yesterday's brother is not today's brother, nor will he be tomorrow's' (8). Latterly, there have been even encouraging signs that may result in unprecedented political changes in China. They may in turn transform the world. Meantime, most of the ex-colonies of the Europeans in the Far East chose a form of independence which, like that of postwar Europe, attached themselves to the USA as a protector. Australasia, Indonesia, Singapore and Malaysia, and the Philippines (a direct US protectorate since 1898) drew, in the end, towards the US, though communism nearly triumphed in 1965 in Indonesia, and in the early 1950s in Malaysia. India and Pakistan, as well as Persia, made much the same choice, though India has toyed with a Russian alliance, while seeking to revive an Indian historical past of its own. The emblem of modern India was adopted from the capital of one of the ancient Emperor Ashoka's pillars. Indeed, Ashoka's version of Buddhism, the policy of *Karma*, which might be roughly translated as a neutral but vague attitude of social responsibility, has, under the influence of Mahatma Gandhi, purposely characterised the policies of most Indian governments since 1947 (9).

The Middle East became a centre of rivalry after 1955. In 1945, Britain was still the paramount power there, her influence maintained by a small number of tactically well-placed troops, combined with friendly and traditional régimes. She had established this place after the First World War, though her interest in the region had been continuous since she began to use it as a road to her empire in India. Immediately after

1945, Jewish colonists and new settlers in Palestine re-established the state of Israel, in conditions of ambiguity, as a result of British negligence. Some Arabs fled, others were expelled, leaving refugees, whose frustrations fed and, in the end, were fed by Arab nationalism. Probably as many Jews fled from long-established sanctuaries in the Arab world.

The quarrels between the British and the French, on the one hand, and the Arabs, on the other, had begun before 1939. France was dominant throughout North Africa. The successful establishment of the state of Israel exacerbated the complication. In addition, the Middle East since 1945 had become the world's major source of exportable oil and, therefore, a commercially more important and explosive region than it had been since the Crusades. Russia began to interest herself in Egyptian nationalism after 1950. After the failure of an Anglo-French military expedition to keep the Suez Canal international in 1956, parts of the Middle East began to fall into the Russian sphere of influence. That ancient region, though, showed itself to be a snare for all outside powers. In the 1970s, Egypt expelled her Russian friends. The Kings of Saudi Arabia and Jordan and the tribal leaders in the Persian Gulf created a new grouping of countries concerned to protect pre-feudal monarchies by means of capitalism and modern weapons. Numerous wars between Israel and her Arab neighbours (one of them intertwined with the Anglo-French expedition to Suez) threatened to turn the cold war there into a world one. But on each occasion, the conflict was successfully contained, though the issues at stake seemed much like those which had led to the world war in 1914. Today rivalries in the Middle East still seem the most probable cause of major international war, partly because of the continuing dependence of the rich countries in the Western hemisphere and in Europe on oil from the region; partly because the Arabs have been caused to look on the Palestinian problem as more important than any other; partly because of the clash between American modernisation and Islamic traditionalism; and partly because of the region's close territorial proximity to Russia.

Between 1959 and 1968, the Caribbean and Latin America also became a region for the rivalry of Russia and the USA. But, though Cuba became Communist, the US, by a mixture of intervention, threats and defensive diplomacy, for a long time prevented any other country from succumbing. Skirmishing supported by Cuba (and Russia indirectly) threatened the peace of Venezuela, Guatemala, Bolivia and Peru, while Chile, Brazil and the Dominican republic experienced short periods when it seemed as if a group friendly to Russia might seize power. After 1968, however, Cuba abandoned her efforts to export her draconian revolution to that part of the world, while the US gave up any attempt to overthrow Castro in Cuba.

Tropical Africa only became touched by the cold war after the sudden disintegration of the European imperial system there following the independence of Ghana in 1957. Britain, Belgium and France then withdrew from Africa in the 1960s after about eighty years of direct power. The Belgian Congo, or as it became known, Zaire, had nothing in the way of a state established. For months, it was an issue for international rivalry. In the end, a sergeant-major was found to maintain Zaire as a united state. It subsequently became a matter of policy on the part of the new ex-imperial African states to keep the often arbitrary boundaries of colonial days. These had earlier been drawn without much consideration of tribal interests. But a general re-drawing was thought to be certain to promote a conflict equally general.

Three elements altered matters: first, the refusal of the minority of English settlers in Rhodesia to accept a transfer of power to the local black Africans, as the British government had engineered in other places; second, the determination of the much larger minority of originally Dutch settlers (with some descendants of Englishmen) to maintain a state based on the dominance in South Africa of their own number; and, thirdly, the unexpected revolution in Portugal of 1974, which led to the withdrawal of Portugal from her anciently established (if only recently co-ordinated) holdings in Mozambique and Angola.

South Africa was of great external interest because of its mines, which produced gold, diamonds and many other minerals. But the cause of opposition to the Dutch colonists (originally established there to serve the Dutch fleets on their way to the East) was one which could bring together the otherwise divided new despotisms in black Africa.* The withdrawal of Portugal from Africa opened a chance for Russia and her allies, principally East Germany and Cuba. A *coup de main* by 30,000 Cuban troops led to the establishment of a tyranny friendly to Russia in Angola. A rather similar régime was soon established in Mozambique. In 1978, a further Cuban expedition, with overt Russian and East German direction, confirmed another new communist régime in power in Ethiopia. It was the only territory in Africa which had withstood the European 'grab for Africa' in the nineteenth century, though Italy had held it between 1936 and 1941.

Meantime, South Africa has been the only African state to have carried through a real industrial revolution, though it has been one powered by black labour and managed by the whites. The 'Shanty towns' became a magnet for a black African working class comparable to the similar first generation urban work forces of the world.

The main theme of the cold war thus has been since about 1950 a battle between the US and Russia to control the 'Third World', a formulation coined by the French sociologist Alfred Sauvy in 1952, making a characteristically Gallic reference to the French Revolution ('for this Third World, ignored and exploited and despised exactly as the Third

* It is to Africa what Israel is to the Arabs.

Estate was before the Revolution, would also like to become something' (10)). Battle of economic systems? Of power? Begun by the US pre-emptively or aggressively? Really a consequence of Russian determination since 1917, or the result of a clever manipulation by Russian propaganda of the resentments and envies caused by the collapse of the old Empires? Or is there some rule whereby all states are aggressive when they industrialise, except perhaps for the US? That certainly seems to be true, though, since this is a conflict still under way (despite premature judgements to the contrary) it is hard to reach so simple a conclusion. A guilt on the part of certain Western nations has not been the least important element in the curious story.

This conflict has lasted for over thirty years. Its dimensions have had about them all the characteristics of old-fashioned struggles for influence, even if they are dressed up by modern language and given a new character by the uniquely destructive power of the weapons which the two large powers have at their disposal. The US monopoly of atomic power lasted only from 1945 to 1949, when Russia exploded her first such weapon in a test. The US then began to build a more powerful weapon still, the hydrogen bomb. She successfully tested that in 1952, but the Russians tested a similar one only a year later. Britain, France, China and India all then entered this perilous field, though none of their equipment has the strength of that held by the US and Russia.

Ater the competition in bombs came competition in means of delivery. Bombers gave way to rockets and submarines, and some of them are giving way to satellites circling the world. The US and perhaps Russia too have embarked upon paid assassinations such as characterised Italy during the Renaissance. It sometimes even seems that we have almost already reached the stage in which, as Burckhardt put it of Italy in the time of the Borgias, 'the death of any powerful man is seldom attributed to natural causes' (11). Meantime, large conventional armies (mostly carried by armed vehicles) are maintained by the two largest states and all their allies. Ground and air-to-ground missiles, helicopters, tanks faster and heavier than those in 1945, all make a 'conventional war' possible. Nations are still increasing their arms budgets and the international traffic in arms continues to grow. Apparently, about 6·3% of the gross output of the world is spent on arms: a total of about $380 billion in 1976* (12). It is beleived to compare with about $343 billion on public education and $157 billion spent on health.

Under the shadow of the nuclear weapon, innumerable 'small' wars have indeed already broken out: in the heart of Europe, there has even been a semi-civil war in Ireland, and that is a fair word to describe the incidents of terrorism in Spain, Italy and West Germany. In both Russia

---

* Half of it probably goes on wages.

and the US, the role of the military is greater than ever. As for their Allies, as with Athens after the Macedonian hegemony had been established, many of them, as Maurice Bowra put it, have 'no longer bothered to improve their institutions' (13). Both sides, too, know the critical importance of the battle of the ocean as well as the air and land.

There seem three possible outcomes of the cold war: first, the continuance *ad infinitum* of the present co-dominance of the world by Russia and the US; second, a resolution of their rivalry in favour of one or the other (either from defeat in war, or in 'peaceful competition', or from decay); or third, the appearance of new forces which may cast the old leaders of the cold war into another or an old, mould. What could these be? Anarchism? Regional terrorism? A revived, expansionist, but backward-looking Islam or perhaps some other, some new religion? A new co-prosperity sphere in the Far East, based on Sino-Japanese co-operation? A new Europe, in which the golden years of that embattled continent will indeed return?

The most likely of these alternatives looks as if it will be the appearance of new forces which cannot yet be quite foreseen. It is hard, however, to believe that, in an age of easily aroused nationalism, the Russian Empire will last indefinitely. The slightest serious slackening of repression in the Russian political system would surely cause a revolution among the nations which go to make it up (14). That long term chance of disintegration may make, probably is already making, for greater Russian adventurism in the short term. It needs also to be recalled that aggressors unfortunately prosper in the early stages of most wars, particularly when fighting democracies. The trouble is that nuclear wars could very well be finished very quickly. Equally, it is sometimes said that micro-electronics will give defence in the future an advantage over attack.

It is certainly hard to believe that the present era of stalemate and self-control based on the nuclear deterrent will last indefinitely. It may be that, in the short term, these weapons have guaranteed peace. But a successful Russian nuclear attack on the US, mounted by a mere five missiles, say, could launch 800 40-kiloton warheads and kill 37 million people. Similar US attacks on Russia could wreak the same havoc (15), or worse. A US Senator has recently suggested that half the population of the US could be killed within less time than it took to transmit a declaration of war in the Second World War (16). It is very difficult, indeed, to believe that a system of this sort can continue *ad infinitum*. It should be an aim of statesmanship to end it. For the present state of affairs to continue for ever, the world would have to be governed not only by good luck but by statesmen of willpower, magnanimity, courage and imagination in a way that, at the moment, does not seem to be a reasonable expectation. On the contrary, many political leaders seem even more ill-prepared, and, in some countries, as ill-disposed, as they have ever been in the past. Weapons of mass destruction can be applied at any point in less time than it normally takes for the police to respond to an emergency in a city. The whole globe is in closer mutual touch than a middle-sized European people were to their own capital fifty years ago. Yet unity without repressive conquest is as remote as it is undesired. The world state which H. G. Wells in his *Outline of History* regarded as inevitable and desirable seems rather further away than it seemed in his day.

The present international position is undoubtedly unique. Never before has power in the world been so extraordinarily concentrated. The origins of the two powers which dominate the world should perhaps be explored as a conclusion to the preceding summary of what has happened during the cold war since 1945.

Much has been mentioned already about Russia, the heir, under both Tsar and communist secretary general, of the Tartar Khanate. The ethnic European character of most of the population has been overlaid by a despotism whose centralised discipline is essential to ensure the survival of the communist party in power. This party, minority though it is, is one which has been able to compel admiration from the surprisingly large number of Russians who admire brutality, force and ruthlessness. Others support the Russian despotism, either directly or indirectly, out of fear or ambition. Even the more 'humane' communist leaders such as Bukharin believed that 'proletarian coercion in all its forms from execution to forced labour, is, paradoxical as it may sound, the best method of moulding communist humanity out of the human material of the capitalist period' (17). The modern Russians' attitude to truth can best be seen in a remark, cited by Leonard Schapiro, by Piatakov, an 'old Bolshevik' who, after siding with Trotsky in the 1920s, joined Stalin in 1928 and had a number of posts in the Russian government before being shot in 1937. Piatakov once told an acquaintance about 1930 in Paris that a true Bolshevik is one who has so submerged his personality in the 'collectivity' that 'he can make the necessary effort to break away from his own opinion and convictions . . . and be ready to say that black is white and white black if the party requires it' (18). Still, not everything can be attributed to Communism. From the time of the Decembrist plots of 1825, Russian institutions of repression have become steadily worse. In 1826, Tsar Nicholas I founded his Third Section of the imperial chancellery, theoretically to give protection to widows and orphans (hence the handkerchief adopted as its symbol), in practice to control the citizens. His successor, Alexander II, made an effort to curb this and other police forces, but his murder ended the hope of that. After 1882, the Tsarist police had the right to detain and to send into administrative exile even those who were merely suspected of political crimes. The police were exempt from any demand to hand over to the judiciary those whom they believed to have committed crimes (19). Only the approval of the Minister of the Interior or the Chief of the Gendarmes was needed to endorse such acts. This attitude to the police was to be found nowhere else in Europe. Thus was established a totalitarian state under the Tsars which the communists revived after the confusion of 1917, though the old régime (unlike the new) respected, as a rule, the families of its victims. Foreign travel was often possible in the past too (20). But there were chapters of the criminal code before 1917 'which are', as Richard Pipes put it, 'to totalitarianism what Magna Carta is to Liberty' (21). Even Lenin himself, in the end, accepted that the system which he had established was 'to a large extent the survival of the old one . . . repainted on the surface' (22).

Russia's evolution from city to world empire has something in common with that of Rome: the small city state of Moscow, numbering 9 to 10 million in 1550, expanded by conquest, absorbing more free nearby Slav city states and taking on much of the colouring of the central Asiatic despotism of the Tartars to which it was for a long time itself subject. For 240 years, the Russians paid tribute to the Tartar Khan, whose agents were established throughout Russia, checking on the correct payment of tribute: the slightest false step brought a summons to the Khan at Sarai: 'In this era', to quote Richard Pipes again, 'Russians learned that the state was arbitrary and violent, that it took what it could lay its hand on and gave nothing in return, and that one had to obey it because it was strong' (23).

The despotism in Russia has oriental characteristics. That in China is, of course, purely oriental, with some Western variations. Formally China is still Marxist, Leninist, even Stalinist (since Stalin's name has not been repudiated in China). Doubtless the existence of the vocabulary and argument associated with those names are a matter for confusion, perhaps a means of drawing some of Chinese thinking into Western ways. In the end, however, the Chinese despotism has more in common with the rule of a competent dynasty of absolute emperors. In China, we are more conscious than elsewhere of the wisdom of the Spanish philosopher Unamuno's prediction that communism may end up as a kind of religion, even if it does not seem to be Buddhist in character. In modern China, as in old, power is controlled by a single ruler advised by mandarins, themselves insulated from contact with ordinary people (despite a show of manual labour *pour encourager les autres*). In communist China, there is, too, the same ambiguous attitude towards outsiders that there has always been: sometimes warm and welcoming, in the 1970s; sometimes cold and distant, as in the 1960s. The 'eternal wisdom' of the Chinese often impresses visitors, as they might have been equally impressed by a Benedictine monastery or a militant order in the Middle Ages. The brutality, evident roughness, and seething violence of Russia is not apparent. But the immense secrecy of modern Chinese life makes it absolutely unknown whether or not there are large slave labour camps. But there is no certain evidence on the matter – itself a surprising thing.* Meantime, unchanged and unchangeable since 2000 BC, the rhythm of the rice harvest, irrigated as in the past according to a remorseless routine, continues, the harvest drawn in by the invaluable water buffalo under Hua as it was under the Han.

For some generations now, communism has seemed to most of its enemies and, indeed, many of its friends, a radical means of achieving a new society. In practice, this has not been quite what has happened. Communism in power, and out of it, looks more like a system of political management which enables certain countries and people to withstand the modernising innovations and challenges of free enterprise and technological change. Communism offers to many, as Luigi Barzini has put it, 'a return to the feudal order', to the security of the man who had his place in society established at birth and could neither regress nor progress from it; it could not be discussed and he could not be promoted by evaluations of merit, or cast down for other reasons (24). For those who do not have independent thoughts, who like to be told what to do, who wish their lives to be planned and who have no moral objections to the corruption and drabness associated with all dominant bureaucracies, it is likely to continue to have a certain attraction.

The US, on the other hand, since 1945, has incarnated the Western ideals of an open society with a law independent of the government, with substantial devolution of power to localities and with an appropriate emphasis laid on the uniqueness of the individual. Only in the US, among even the democracies, is the belief now general as it was in Britain in the eighteenth century that if a thing is done by private action it is liable to be better done that if it is done by the state or the community. The US view of politics and the economy is thus based on an optimistic view of human nature.

Five points in the history of the US are worth recalling: first, its steady expansion for its first hundred years. In 1776, it constituted 400,000 square miles. This doubled when the peace at the end of the War of Independence allocated to the thirteen colonies the 492,000 square miles of the Indian Reserve, between the Allegheny mountains and the Mississippi. These 892,000 square miles were then almost doubled by the 'Louisiana purchase' of 1803, a transaction with Napoleon I, for a mere $15 million. Napoleon knew that he could not hold that territory, save

---

* Some part of this story is now beginning to be told (1979).

by a long colonial war for which he was unprepared. At that time, the whole of the Mississippi region was unmapped, though explorers, such as Meriwether Lewis and William Clark, soon set off for St Louis and reached the Pacific, via North Dakota. Florida was bought from Spain in 1819 for $6·5 million – another 72,000 square miles. In the course of the nineteenth century, there followed the admission of Texas, which had been independent and, before that, a part of Mexico – another 389,000 square miles (1845); the purchase of California, Arizona, Nevada, Utah, and parts of Wyoming and Colorado from Mexico for another derisory $15 million – 529,189 square miles. Oregon and Washington state were negotiated with Canada along the 49th parallel, at no cost, for 286,500 square miles; and finally Alaska in 1867, Hawaii in 1895 and Puerto Rico in 1899 for respectively $7·2 million, $4 million and without payment. These added another 586,400, 6,400 and 3,400 square miles to the US. Subsequent acquisitions, such as Guam, Samoa and the Virgin Islands, caused the land area of the USA to exceed 3·7 million square miles, the extra 3·3 million square miles since 1776 having been bought for a mere $136 million in all. No other country has ever grown so fast, so cheaply and with such relatively little fighting (25).

The second element has been the increase in the population of the US. In 1700, the population totalled a mere 250,000; in 1750, still only 1,170,000. One can thus understand the reluctance of Britain to take seriously the revolt against her which had the support of so few. The US population in the late eighteenth century grew wonderfully, however, partly because of the great challenge of empty spaces, such plentiful land, the demand for labour, the early marriages (men commonly in their mid-20s, women at 20), the longevity and the small proportion of landless men (20% only of the rural population of New England in 1750). Partly by natural increase, and partly by massive immigration from Europe, the US population increased between 1780 and 1860 from 2·78 million to 3·1 million; between 1860 and 1910 to 92 million; and, between 1910 and 1979, to 217 million (26).

The third element was the transformation of rural America into urban America. In 1800, 94% of the population was rural. 85% was still rural in 1850. From that figure, the proportion decreased to 60% by 1900, 35% by 1950, and must now be only 20% (27).

The fourth characteristic has been the manufacturing success. Some of the detail of this has been indicated earlier. The manufacturing section of society was greatly stimulated during the Revolutionary war. The tariffs of 1791 and 1804 were successful against England. More important, the early Americans, working alone in a lonely continent, had the moral compulsion of a disciplined community which, as Richard Hofstadter put it, looked on work as having 'a quasi-religious merit' (28). The fortunate accident of possession of a territory which controlled 70% of the world's oil production, 80% of the sulphur, 51% of the copper, 60% of the aluminium, 50% of the zinc and over 95% of the natural gas against only 6% of the population and 7% of the total land area is rather important too (29)* – although as this book has repeatedly sought to emphasise, the possession of natural resources has never been the decisive element in political power.

Finally, the US successfully adapted a beautifully written constitution, completed in the 1790s, to the evolving population, territory, complexities and responsibilities of a large nation of mixed origin. The US began as an aristocratic democracy in which the landed aristocracy had been abolished. De Tocqueville rightly emphasised the part played by good laws in ensuring America's successes. Old laws, based on English practice, were modified by the rebellion of the 1770s, and by the civil war of the 1860s. The latter was a war between two different economic systems, which stimulated industrialisation in the north by causing labour-saving machinery to be sought after (265,000 mechanical reapers saved the north as much as Sherman's guns did) (30).

The consequence was that, in the twentieth century, the US had become both the main 'innovative and creative society in the world' and the main disruptive influence. Already, by the 1920s, after her commercial and military victory in Europe, the US had become the focus of global attention, envy, emulation, admiration, and animosity. By 1945, the eclipse of Europe, the declining confidence in the European empires, the political and economic failure in Russia, had combined to make of the US the only successful and self-confident democracy. The modern US has since become a world of its own, one of statistical analysis, technology, and electronics, great emphasis on education and on innovation, scientific investigation without shortage of money, huge car-ownership and radio-ownership, and instantaneous telephones – the 'world's social laboratory', says Zbigniew Brzezinski, from which the rest of the world learns what may be in store for it (31). The communism which patriotic Americans used to see as the main cause of unrest in the world itself capitalises on the thwarting of aspirations whose main source is the American impact on the rest of the world. The self-confidence of this society has been impaired in the last few years but, in 1945 when the cold war was beginning, there were still many who would have echoed President Wilson's boast: 'My vision is that as the years go on, and the world knows more and more of America' – he was speaking in 1914 – 'It also will drink at these fountains of youth and renewal . . . If there will ever be a declaration of independence and of grievances for mankind . . . it will be drawn up in the spirit of the American Declaration of Independence' (32).

Nearly seventy years later, so much rhetoric, stale and rotten language and lies, have splashed down the river of civilisation since

* These figures are for 1940, the year just before events made the US into a world power.

then that it may at first sight be hard to recognise that statement for the clear truth that it ought to be.

The US has constructed its wealth, its nation, and its way of life on the basis of free enterprise, free commerce and the free exchange of ideas. Russia began its industrialisation under the manipulation of the despotic power of the Tsar, adopted a millenarian creed, converted its old bureaucratic caste, the *dvoriáne*, into a communist party and expanded its army and its police. The US has pursued its goals internationally by limitation and scepticism. Russia has done so by zeal and ruthlessness. In the US, it is still possible to see behind a thin veil of scientific assimilation, the shade of Pericles. In Russia, the shadow is that of Darius the Persian.

47

Causes of the 'Cold' War:
Class Consciousness

If the Revolution came before the bourgeois revolution, it could result in a political monstrosity similar to the ancient Chinese or Peruvian empire, or, in other words, in a renovated Tsarist despotism, with a communist lining.

Plekhanov

I'm a Marxist, not a dogmatic one but still a Marxist. I've always believed men were instruments or interpreters of history and that great historical movements were uninfluenced by the charades involved in democratic politics. But after what I've witnessed for a year in Portugal, I'm beginning to believe in Cleopatra's nose. Man counts. He really does.

Mario Soares, Socialist Prime Minister of Portugal (1975) (*New York Review* , 1975)

We must finish once and for all with the neutrality of chess. We must condemn once and for all the formula 'chess for the sake of chess' . . . we must organise shock brigades of chess players and the immediate realisation of the 5-year chess plan.

The State Prosecutor of Russia, N.V. Krylenko, c.1931

The cold war has many causes. But the main cause is that one of the world's greatest nations, Russia, has imposed upon its population and the population of its allies an illusory belief that the determining factor in human history is conflict between classes. It is an illusion which gives the ideology, or even the religion, to about a quarter of the world's population and to it the loyalty of several millions more.

The question of a man's birth was a critical one in agricultural communities. Where agriculture did not exist, as among nomads, or in a time of troubles and breakdown, less rigid demarcations existed. Most 'class' systems probably depended on the imposition of a military aristocracy upon a conquered people, such as that which the Celts imposed on the original inhabitants of Spain and elsewhere (1), the Normans on the Saxons, the Spaniards on the Aztecs and so on.

The most rigid system of differentiation of people within a nation, at least in a large nation, was, and is, that which has, for 2,000 years, divided Indians into castes. That system partly derived from conquest

517

by the Aryans. and was also partly at least based on attitudes of colour: indeed, the Sanskrit word for caste, *varna*, signified colour (2). The Aryans treated the slightly darker Dasas whom they conquered as inferior and those who descended from mixed Dasa and Aryan as very inferior. The Aryans themselves, meantime, divided into three: warriors or aristocrats; priests; and common people. Though, when the Aryans reached India, those divisions were not yet castes (since there were no rules limiting marriage or social contact between them), they became so. The priests (brahmins) steadily arranged a system in which heredity within professions became normal too. New ethnic groups which occasionally developed were given the status of sub-castes. Elaborate rules as to who one might eat with, or marry, were soon made. By about the second or third centuries BC, the functions and limitations of the four castes dominated social activity. The only way to escape from the bondage of caste was to associate with foreigners, and that was far from easy (3). In India, caste and profession soon became intertwined, so that even sensitive foreign observers confused the two.

Nowhere else probably was so rigid a system of classes established as it was in India — though perhaps ancient Egypt approached it with a similar system also probably deriving from earlier conquest and later from professional distinctions. Certainly, no such rigidly observed system of castes prevailed in feudal Europe and in European agricultural society. For example, in Anglo-Saxon England the word 'thegn' (for which 'lord' is an approximate translation) designated a relation between two people: a thegn was somebody's thegn. A King's thegn was his free servant but also his companion. All the dominant families of Carolingian Europe were men of recent riches, decendants of peasants, ostlers or men-at-arms at the court of Louis the Pious or later (4). The nobility of Castile, at the same time, was divided into *ricos hombres*, who acted as governors of royal lands; and *infanzones*, or minor nobility who lived on their estates. There was antagonism between the two, though both swore fealty to the king whom they recognised as overlord (5). French society in the eleventh century could, according to Marc Bloch, best 'be conceived of as an essentially vertical structure consisting of innumerable small groups, clustered round superiors, dependent in their turn on others higher in scale' (6). It was, then, hard to see a class society as such existing. In the twelfth century, Marc Bloch added 'human blocks tended to become distributed in horizontal layers'. But was there ever a real division between, simply, nobility, bourgeoisie and working people? It seems improbable. The bourgeoisie were always urban. They as a rule co-existed with, married into, collaborated with, and both preceded and outlived what is conventionally known as feudalism. What really was the 'class-structure', if such a thing ever exists, of Renaissance Italy? Scarcely comparable to that of Renaissance Russia — again if such a thing can be imagined. Within the feudal system, there were great differences between stewards, labourers with or without livestock, and so on, who differed because of their status, not their class. Many historians employ the words 'middle class' when talking of some aspect or other of the Roman Empire, but those people seem to have been men far from absolutely differentiated from the poor: rich merchants, for example, were held to be middle class, poor ones plebeian, because of their wealth, not their birth. The traditional 'middle class' of republican days, had, it is true, made themselves as rich as the patricians by tax-farming and some other activities (7). But the history of the Roman Empire is more the story of constant struggles by new waves of humble men seeking power to establish themselves and their families than a rigid system of classes. Those waves were led by men who were able to seek their fortunes with the same determination as Napoleon's marshals did (8). Very nearly all the old patrician families died out. The 'golden age' of Rome was directed by Spaniards of comparatively humble origin, such as Trajan and Hadrian, and the revival of the third century by Illyrians of equally humble origin, such as Aurelian and Diocletian (9). Gibbon gave a vivid picture of the Roman nobility during the fourth century AD, walking through the streets, their long robes floating in the wind, followed by a train of fifty servants, walking up the pavements with 'the same impetuous speed as if they travelled with posthorses' (10). But the grandfathers of those splendid noblemen were probably slaves, or at least poor men. All those imposing adjectives as *clarissimus, eminentissimus, perfectissimus, egregius*, which prefixed the names of senators, prefects and officials in Diocletian's reign, and whose remote shadows can be seen in our modern 'excellencies' and 'highnesses', cloaked a society open to talent, not one bound by brahminical castes (11). Nor was Byzantium a monarchy primarily with an aristocracy. Earlier, before Rome had been corrupted, as it were, by ideas of conquest, there was even then a far from hard-and-fast all-embracing system of classes. The elementary group in society was the family. The aggregation of families formed the *gens* or the House. The aggregation of Houses made the Tribe. The aggregation of Tribes made the Republic. All ancient peoples, rightly or wrongly, regarded themselves not as being part of a 'class' but as having proceeded from one original stock, and, in Sir Henry Maine's words, 'even laboured under an incapacity for comprehending any reason save this for their holding together in political union' (12). People believed in kinship, not class, as is the case in, for example, Saudi Arabia to-day.

If there are difficulties about any categorisation of society based on the idea of class in western Europe before industrialisation, how much more difficult it is to see such a society elsewhere. Africa continued largely tribal. The Aztec and Inca monarchies were served by bureaucrats, not classes. Whether it was appropriate to consider the thousands of bureaucrats employed by the Chinese emperors members of an upper 'class' would, however, seem as doubtful as the question whether Egyptian priests can be so 'classified'. The 'class divisions' within the Abbasid caliphate were plainly an example of different races and religions intertwined. It took some time for Muslim people who were not racially from Arabia to become accepted as Arabs, but they did so in the end, though a distinction remained. The large number of non-Muslim inhabitants of the first Arab empire, Christians, Armenians, Jews, Druses, Copts, Nestorians and so on, were thought of primarily as people of a certain religion different to the paramount one. They were second class citizens all right, but they were employed by the state, could make money, be admitted to guilds and fight. Their 'class', such as it was, depended on belief (13).

The changes in agriculture discussed earlier began to break old feudal ties in Europe, and class distinctions more based on blood than status came to characterise several richer Western European countries from the late Middle Ages and the Renaissance onwards. Perhaps something close to a class system existed more nearly in Europe between the collapse of feudalism and the coming of industrialism than at any other time, though Europe as a whole did not, as has been supposed by some, see a triumph then of the bourgeoisie: 'If any social group bettered its position . . . in those centuries,' says Professor Elton, 'it was the landed nobility' (14). 'By keeping close to the practical things,' said Marc Bloch, 'which give real power over men, and by avoiding the paralysis which overtakes social classes which are too sharply defined and too dependent on birth, the English aristocracy acquired the dominant position which it retained for centuries' (15). Italy was another exception: Florence had a social system in which the aristocracy of the early Middle Ages lost their wealth, and rich and poor had an identity of interests by dint of belonging to one of the city's guilds (16). Thus, if a system of classes or castes existed in some parts of mediaeval Europe, it certainly did not do so everywhere. From the sixteenth century, it was usually possible for the rich and successful merchant to buy a title or otherwise make his way into the aristocracy (particularly in England), the intelligent poor man to make his way upwards via the Church, or a peer's brother to make money in a warehouse.*

In 1750, an extremely incoherent series of divisions, cross-sections and radiating systems of prejudice existed almost everywhere. Had it been possible to plot them on a map, they would have resembled an open field in the days of the high Middle Ages. In some countries such

---

* In Austria-Hungary, Dr Bruford points out, 'it was always possible to buy titles'. Under Joseph II, it cost 20,000 gelden to be a count, 6,000 to be a baron and 386 to be a 'von' (*adliger*). Louis XIV in France abolished all titles conferred during the previous 92 years but allowed their owners to retain them on paying a further sum. In England, Defoe wrote, 'Antiquity and birth are needless here! 'Tis impudence and money makes a peer'. (19).

as Britain, the aristocracy was financed regularly by good marriages with merchants. In Germany the peasants, burghers and gentlemen even had their own laws: nobles could not buy peasant land, nor could peasants buy ground rents (17). Nearly everywhere, in contrast, wrote Jacob Burckhardt of Italy during the Renaissance, even those who might be disposed to pride themselves on their birth could not maintain any superiority in the face of culture and wealth (18). The Russian nobility were more bureaucrats than aristocrats and so had a different position vis-à-vis their sovereigns. Russian society was also complicated by the great number of foreigners among the top civil servants. Racial divisions were continuously complicating issues: 'the lowest, least educated and uncultivated European believes himself superior to the white born in the New World,' wrote the great traveller in South America, Humboldt. Poor whites and free negroes were everywhere in close touch, and collision, in Spanish America in the eighteenth century (18). At all times, and in every type of agricultural society (except, as a rule, the Indian), it was possible, to a greater or lesser extent, for gifted children to escape from the bondage to which their birth might otherwise have condemned them. Confusion in social status derived from confusion over landholding. City dwellers had, in the Middle Ages, a series of divisions of their own, based on profession, even if people remained as a rule in the professions of their fathers. Even in France, under the old regime, there was plainly, within the world of agriculture, as Sir John Clapham put it, 'perpetual movement from class to class' (20).

At first sight, the industrial revolution seemed likely to simplify the matter radically. Into Lancashire and Tyneside, South Wales and the west Midlands; into Glasgow and Belfast, into Lille, Rouen and Saint Etienne, into the Ruhr, Pittsburgh and Chicago, vast numbers of men and women were drawn by the prospect of regular wages paid in cash and by the absence of work on the land for the rapidly growing population. Those and other foci of industrial growth seemed to be creating a new class, the industrial workers, who began, even at the start, a trifle invidiously, to be called, and call themselves *'the* proletariat', *die Arbeiter*, as if to suggest that agricultural workers, farmers' boys, domestic servants and soldiers were somehow different from factory workers. It seemed to some that the multifarious distinctions of feudal or agricultural society would vanish, and give way to a harsher simplicity based on two or three classes.

Between about 1850 and 1914, a coherent culture based on the professional occupation of those who worked with their hands in mines, factories and attendant services such as railways or merchant navies, seemed to take shape in Europe, North America, parts of Latin America, Russia and some other parts of the world. This culture always excluded more people than it included, even among the great majority who worked for their living, even in England, even in Germany, even in the US.

The conditions of these workers, in the early days of industrialism, were harsh. Their working conditions have, to some extent, been discussed.* The living conditions of the workers were also often appalling†. The slum cities constructed cheaply to house the workers became hotbeds of hatred. The thought, or sight, of others living in luxury aroused in some a bitter wrath against society, even if in others it inspired a desire to rise and enjoy similar benefits themselves. Perhaps the fact that ironmasters and cotton kings were new men stimulated in workers an extra resentment. Large factories generated the possibility of large scale outbreaks of protest and so justified, or at least explained, despotic management. This in turn led to more political preparations in protest. In mining villages, for example, where nearly all the heads of families worked for mining companies, the combination of residence and place of work, the danger and the importance of the work, the often evil conditions, gave the persons concerned a high morale, often antagonistic to the existing industrial order which the coal produced by them powered.

As the nineteenth century continued, factories and mines drew in more and more craftsmen, who previously might have employed several people on their own. That naturally seemed a decay in status and assisted the way that many workers, bound together by common grievances, began to organise an opposition which was partly political, partly social and perhaps primarily cultural. Meantime, on the other side of the towns concerned, newly rich families, Forsytes or Buddenbrooks, lived in an ample and cossetted, luxury often expressed by a cult of music and long novels ideally suited to the splendid leisure which new and largely untaxed wealth made possible.

Thus, in the richer, more adventurous, countries of the nineteenth century, a period of acute resentments between the different sections of society followed. Of course, this was not the first clash between employees and employed, for disputes on the land, and slave revolts, had sporadically disorganised agriculture since the dawn of time. The *jacqueries* of the fourteenth century in the countryside of Western Europe had echoes in the developing cities. The lowest-paid clothworkers in Florence, the *Ciompi*, led to a violent withdrawal of labour, almost a rebellion, against the merchants. Similar upheavals occurred among weavers in Ghent. The religious quarrels of the sixteenth century caused these protests to be largely forgotten. In some countries, absolutism buried them till the eighteenth century or later but still, in Britain and France, beneath the religious disputes, under a veneer of theology, lay a core of social protest, which never disintegrated.

Nor was the dispute between classes of the nineteenth century

* See above, page 250.
† See above, page 410.

confined to factory, mine and railway shed. It had repercussions on the land where, in some countries, in certain specially tense conditions – for example, Spain – the battle assumed the character, as Gerald Brenan put it, of a steady competition between landowner and labourer, the first to see how little he could pay, the second to see how little he could work (21). Still, severe agricultural disruption was always limited by the fact that a serious strike could only be mounted during the harvest and the idea of such a thing seemed so immensely risky and against the long-term interests of everybody that it happened only rarely. Nor were labour unions very well organised.

From the very beginning of the modern era, these problems gave rise to misconceptions. First, those who wrote about class during the nineteenth century seem to have known more about antiquity than they did about their own times. They remembered the three classes of Lacadaemon – the free inhabitants of the land; the helots, or serfs; and the Spartans who lived in the cities (22). Had not Plato written: 'God has put gold into those who are capable of ruling; silver into the auxiliaries; and copper into the peasants, and other producing classes' (23)? They knew also that Rome, in its republican days, was divided into three 'classes' (it was then, after all, that the word began its fateful career), the patricians, equestrians and plebeians.

These divisions of society actually ceased to apply to Rome during the Empire, when there were as many classes, in fact as opposed to theory, as there are in modern Europe. But economists, social scientists and a few historians often wrote of the nineteenth and twentieth centuries as having social divisions as strictly delineated as a classical building. In 1869, Matthew Arnold mockingly spoke of the 'Barbarians, Philistines and populace' as being 'the three great classes into which our society is divided' (24). Arnold's contemporary, Karl Marx, was not only influenced by such tertiary divisions, even more important than the divisions between peoples; but, being a romantic as much as a revolutionary, he supposed that the working class were a chosen class, a substitute for a more orthodox Jew's belief in a chosen race. To Marx, the workers were a class with 'radical claims, a class in bourgeois society which is not *of* bourgeois society', though he was thinking of the factory workers who were, when he wrote, as has been seen*, a minority even of the workers in England.

As suggested later, something very close to a new religion has been based upon this view. Some were attracted to Marxism out of guilt, some out of a desire for discipline. Some merely desired a complete explanation of human life, but believed that Montesquieu was wrong in attributing it to climate. Some coveted an opportunity to lead a sect, however small. Some were attracted by the accuracy of some of Marx's

* See page 244.

prophecies – for example, about the inexorable march of industrialisation – to accept his general prognosis. Then the need to belong to a particular group is, as the German philosopher of history, Herder, was the first to point out, an elementary need almost as basic as the need for food. At all events, political life has been transformed by Marx, or at least by Marx's concepts.

But even if these concepts had validity, in many countries what Marx would consider the middle class has only recently taken power. In Germany before 1914, Army, diplomacy, administrators, politicians – all these professions were dominated by people whom it would be usual to consider as noblemen. The same could be said of other European countries. Everywhere, save in the US, an old nobility was entrenched until well into the beginning of the twentieth century. That made contempt for the 'bourgeoisie' and 'middle class values' rather premature.

The only country where in Europe a bourgeois revolution seemed, indeed, to have occurred in the nineteenth century was France. Yet France had the most conservative of all European societies. The French bourgeoisie were possessed of a sense of family, thrift, and hard work. But they combined those things with the prudence and unimaginativeness traditionally possessed by the peasant. The French bourgeoisie had a peasant soul, but an aristocratic sense of harmony and permanence, combined with, as Theodore Zeldin put it, scepticism about machines. The 'bourgeois revolution' was thus a myth too (25).

A prominent historian of America, Richard Hofstadter, argued that all American society was middle class in the eighteenth century (26). What he meant, no doubt, was that the essential characteristic of the US was that, while its policies were directed by rich men, there was no court, nobility, hierarchy, nor great estates manned by serfs, nor even (until the high days of Victorian industrialism), extravagance in styles of life. Anglo-Saxon America was a middle-class rural world, with no lords of the manor. That classlessness characterises the country to this day. If the class structure exists anywhere, it would be necessary to forget about it in considering the US, at least since the eighteenth century, for it has been a nation throbbing with energy and one still open to the adventurous and talented. The same has been true of other countries created by Anglo-Saxon colonists, such as Australia and Canada. Those societies, too, were less warlike than most which had preceded them, though the crowding in cities which was caused, or permitted, 'suggested violent solutions to violent minds'. But the individual selfishness to which they gave scope was probably less threatening to the peace of the world, said Sir John Clapham, than 'the centralised, impersonal, property-controlling and property-owning state-selfishness which shows signs of succeeding it' (27). At the same time, capitalism did not create a coherent social class either. Between the captain of industry in his mock Gothic castle and the village shopkeeper, there was little in common save in their appreciation of the profit motive. The two were never able to act in common, and certainly not so much as to drench the world in blood in the way that Marx considered likely.

Sometimes errors of a different sort have been made. Some socialists in Spain in the early twentieth century, for example, argued that there was no middle class there before 1917. They thus, to their very great disadvantage, ignored the large numbers of shopkeepers, small businessmen, farmers, and even poor men who rejected both collectivism and the radical socialist and liberal movement throughout the 1930s, and fought for Franco enthusiastically in 1936. But, even in Spain, where the poor have always been held by observers to have been 'uninterested in the position and the money of the rich', there were in the cities as a rule an immense array of difficult grades within society. For example, at what stage does the skilled worker cease to belong to the 'proletariat'? Is the manual worker, in the public services, a proletarian – even though he receives wages from the state, rather than from a private employer? Are wage workers in commerce in the same group as wage earners in industry (28)? A sense of alienation cannot be the only definition of a membership of the working class. For there are many others apart from industrial workers who feel 'alienated': conscripts, homosexuals, criminals, and Jews have felt 'alienated' from a national culture, while some workers at a conveyer belt do not feel so.

Some attempts have been made to argue that class distinctions can be measured by money. It has been claimed that, before 1914 in England, the three-quarters of wage earners who were paid by the week, plus the 1.2 million salaried people who earned less than £160 a year, were the working class. The middle class were held to be the 400,000 salaried men earning over £160 a year, the professional men numbering 330,000 and some of the 580,000 farmers. The 620,000 employers and, presumably, the 60,000 people of 'independent means' were the upper class (29). But if class be determined by income, a higher income can presumably make people of a higher class. In that case, why should not the divisions be spoken of as being of wealth, not of class? If that were so. it would presumably be best to follow Tom Paine's advice and make available capital subventions to everyone at the age of twenty-one, to be provided by a graduated tax on inheritance rather than to seek the capture of power of a particular class (30). Class can certainly be measured better than anything else by money; even in the seventeenth century in Aragon, burial in the common grave, in the cemetery, in the church, and in a monastery was held to correspond to four categories of people, distinguished essentially according to whether their families could pay anything or 100, 300 or 400 *sueldos*.

Then, conditions in factories have greatly improved, and wages have risen in relation to the cost of living, partly as a result of conscience on

the part of the employers, or their realisation that a contented worker is
likely to produce more efficiently than a discontented one; and partly as
a result of activities by trade unions. Some members of the so-called
'working class' have now begun to earn higher incomes than those of
the 'middle class'. Conditions and work even in mines have also ceased
to be as back-breaking and demoralising, while some workers at desks,
in government departments as in companies, have a more unhealthy
and more boring day of work than some manual workers. In every
country in Western Europe and the USA, factory workers' conditions of
life in the 1970s approximate to those traditionally regarded as 'middle
class', whereas middle class lives have become less attractive. Factory
workers of the 1870s working sixty-three hours a week and protected
neither by trade unions nor by social legislation might have seemed
'departicularised' by misfortune (31). But that is not the case with the
worker in 1979 in Detroit, Coventry or Billancourt. Not surprisingly, the
old working class culture of the nineteenth and early twentieth century
has declined. The libraries formed, for instance, in Welsh mining
villages have vanished. With his colour television set and his car, his
holiday in the Mediterranean and often his materialism, the well paid
worker of the late twentieth century would seem to Marx to be the
epitome of – bourgeous life! Indeed, it now seems that the working
class culture of the early stages of the industrial revolution was as brief a
stage in human history as the middle class one which it was supposed
to succeed. Indeed, 'working class culture' never really recovered from
the blows it suffered in the wars of the twentieth century. Swept along
by mass communications and by patriotism into ultra-nationalism, the
European working-class showed in 1914 that patriotism was more usual
than Marx had believed it to be in the 1860s and 1870s. True, the two
world wars left the populations of the combatant countries unen-
thusiastic for a repetition of such displays. But it also left them nationalistic, a tendency which mass education (which has usually emphasised a *national* past) and mass media (emphasising the *national* language
and *national* issues) exacerbate. Thus education and entertainment,
combined with fewer differences between incomes, encourage a
national culture which is both all-pervading and not very patriotic. Any
illusion that classes of the same category within one country collaborate
naturally with those of the same status within another (upper or lower)
was shattered by the events of 1914. Nor is nationalism evident only in
time of war, not even in relation to other countries. For example, an
historian usually regarded as Marxist has argued that 'Catalanism' (the
subject of his particular interest) was not exclusively a representation of
bourgeois interests: 'in 1927, the frontiers between peasants, merchants, small business and working class were blurred,' he wrote (32),
and '*à la fin de la dictature [de Primo de Rivera], toutes les classes en Cata-
logne unissent leur griefs et s'affirment minorité nationale*' (35). What

seemed on the surface a matter of class has also often turned out to be a matter of national prejudice or resentment (36).

All advanced societies (all societies which have industrialised since 1750) have always had far more subdivisions than a mere three or four. No theory of class has been of sufficient subtlety to do justice to the differences within the middle class of Europe or the US in the nineteenth century (37): '*Entre ouvriers, il y a des catégories et un classement aristocratique. Les imprimeurs prennent la tête; les chiffoniers . . . les égoutiers ferment la marche*' (38). Instead of a class society, in the eighteenth century, wrote Dr Laslett, 'we should think of a group of some 300,000 families, very various in character . . . which several million families were busy imitating unsuccessfully, because they had not enough money to do it well' (39). That might be a better picture of a later time than Marx's over simple one.

How small too the enterprises were in the nineteenth century when theories of class were being formulated! Large factories of 2,000 strong were exceptional then and only came into being when those very theories were being displaced. In most cities of Spain, for example, in 1850, employers outnumbered employees (40). The small artisan lived on throughout the nineteenth century and only vanished even in the USA after 1945. Yet, only in factories with a labour force of 2,000 or so, do conditions provide any suggestion of the mass phobia and 'alienation' which was deplored by Marx.

Some of these illogicalities were evident at the beginning. Yet one of the prophets of class consciousness, Engels, could not believe them and complained about the English working class that: 'the most repulsive thing in this country is the bourgeois respectability which has invaded the very blood and bone of the workers. The organisation of society into firmly established hierarchical gradations in which each one has his proper pride . . . is taken so much as a matter of course, [and] is so ancient . . . that it is comparatively easy for the bourgeois to play his part of seducer' (41).

One explanation for these curious illusions is that the leaders of the so-called working classes have very often been rich people of easy circumstances, perhaps acting in the interests of realising certain fantasies that the bourgeoisie have entertained of the poor. In 1914, for example, out of 110 social democratic deputies working in the Reichstag, only two were ex-workers. Even that symbolic representation was lacking then among the French socialists (42). The French revolutionary leaders were of relatively privileged origin, as were such precursors of 'socialism' as Saint Simon, Fourier, Owen, Blanc, Blanqui, Lassalle, Marx, Bakunin, Engels and Lenin. A law might be devised which proves that the more to the 'left' a political leader is, the more well born he is likely to be. Yet in politics no laws of this sort are really valid. The variety of origin of early fascists and early Nazis anyway puts paid to any serious analysis of politics based on class. For example, in 1932, out of 250 Nazi deputies, 43 were in industry of some sort, 55 were employees, 12 were teachers, 29 were party officials, 20 civil servants, 9 were ex-officers and 50 were farmers (43).

Fascism has, however, a connection with class consciousness at least in that, in the years after 1919, many poorly paid European workers who found the internationalism of contemporary socialism inadequate, along with ex-cavalrymen, clerks, businessmen and landowners, turned towards a mass movement which made a deliberate appeal to nationalism.

Considerations of class continue to persuade many of us to maintain our foolish reliance on the vocabulary of the French Revolution to designate differences. In the French National Assembly of 1789, the nobles took the position (of honour) on the President's 'right', and the Third Estate took the 'left'. What began as ceremony ended as ideology. The usage was for a time restricted to legislatures whose shape (as on the continent) was in the form of a hemicycle but, in the twentieth century, it has been extended to the English parliament. Words have lives long after the death of the ideas which gave them birth. Even more, perhaps, where Marx is concerned, many of the prophet's followers wrote far less vividly than he and left to future generations a damnable inheritance of abuse and propaganda from which even the enemies of Marx have suffered. The 'purification' of language, as Leonard Schapiro puts it, is one of the most important tasks facing Western civilisation in its struggle to remain afloat on unfavourable seas as (42).

47

Part 2

Class in Power

In the twentieth century, the ideas of Karl Marx have been the justification of communist governments in Russia, China and several other countries whose common factor is not that they are undeveloped or new but that their old social structure has failed to make a successful transition to industrial life. The governments concerned have been set up on the basis of a false reading of the roots of industrialisation. Marx would certainly have been shocked to know that his plans for abolishing the state had led to the establishment of the strongest state the world has yet seen; nor would he have been assuaged to learn that this strong state represents the stage which he knew as the 'dictatorship of the proletariat' — that is, after the destruction of the middle class, but before the realisation of full communism. Marx invented that concept, it is true, but devoted little attention to it (save in the *Critique of the Gotha programme*) and believed it would be 'less violent' than eighteenth century changes in society and 'of shorter duration' (43).

'Imagination to power', the students of 1968 wrote on the walls of the Sorbonne, not realising that, in one sense, imagination or at least illusion was already in power. The illusion that *all* history is the history of class struggles characterises régimes which have usually gained power by ruthlessness, guile and force. Though denouncing class, the managers of these new societies have assisted the creation of nations at least as much dominated by class than any other which they purport beneficially to have superseded. In communist societies, at the top, there are managers and party members, neither capitalist nor proletarian, though, in the Russian case, probably the grandchildren of peasants, who reflect, at one remove, the *dvoriáne* or upper class of old Russia, being bureaucrats; men who have embarked on a career as formal as that of ancient Egypt, with access to special shops, transport, cars, clothes and some travel on certain conditions (44). These party members, perhaps no more than 1% of the population on average, are, as it were, locked into collaboration with the State, since they know perfectly well the vengeance which would be wreaked upon them if the party ever lost the controlling power (45).

Beneath them are the ordinary citizens of the country concerned, factory workers or agricultural workers, whose lives can never flourish unless they join the élite.

Below them again are the third class of prisoners or slaves, 'zeks' in camps who have made major economic contributions in the country concerned but whose lives would have made those of helots in Sparta seem Arcadian. They at least know the meaning of the word 'class'. 'Secure the Soviet Republic against its class enemies,' Lenin instructed his followers in September 1918, 'by isolating them in concentration camps' (46). Those few individuals who have managed to establish their heroic individuality within this slave class will be remembered, let us hope, long after the White Sea Canal or other labours of Hercules in Russia, China, Cuba or Cambodia which they undertook have been forgotten.

The illusion that the determining factor in human society is class has, at all events, formed the basis for a most powerful and ruthless despotism of a kind which had not been seen before. No one can tell how many people died during the worst period of the Marxist dictatorship in Russia, nor would everyone even agree that that is the best question to ask. One can well compare with advantage the 170,000 or so killed throughout the French Revolutionary Terror (47). During the worst part of the tyranny of Stalin, 'every region and every national republic [in Russia] had to have its own crop of enemies so as not to fall behind the others', wrote Evgenia Ginsburg, 'for all the world as if people were deliveries of grain or milk' (48).

Now Marx had originally written his prophecies for advanced societies such as England, whence his statistics mostly derived. 'Marxism' was conceived of as a theory for highly industrialised societies. 'No social order' he wrote, 'ever perishes before all the productive forces for which there is room in it have developed.' He regarded Russia with contempt for much of his life. Indeed, he expressed forcibly most historians' commentaries on the role of the Mongols or Tartars: 'the bloody mire of Mongol slavery, not the rude glory of the Norman epoch, forms the cradle of Muscovy, and modern Russia is but a metamorphosis of Muscovy. Kalita's whole system may be expressed by the machiavellianism of the usurping slave' (49). (Kalita was Tsar Ivan III, 'the tax collector', who founded the post-Mongol Russian state.) But, after the failure of the Paris Commune in 1870, Marx changed his mind. Thereafter, Russia seemed revolutionary to him: when Vera Zasulich, in 1881, wrote asking whether the village commune might not be transformed directly into a socialist commune or whether they, the Russian Marxists, should concentrate on turning Russia into a bourgeois society, Marx replied that the historic inevitability of capitalism was limited to the West, while the village commune was 'the fulcrum of Russia's social regeneration' (50). Engels had a similar view of Russia, for a slightly different reason: he believed that it was 'one of those exceptional cases when a handful of people can . . . bring down a whole system' (51). The Populist revolutionaries were, therefore, able to ally themselves, if not see eye to eye, with Marx. As Tibor Szamuely put it, Lenin was the inheritor of both traditions: that which stood for Marxist 'social democracy' and that which represented a Russian millenarian violence, in which individual will could perform wonders.

The class structure of Russia, however, was inappropriate for Marx's ideas. For example, as Pushkin had openly regretted, Russia never experienced feudalism, much less normal capitalism. Though, before the Tartars came, the nobles (*boyars*) had some independence of the princes of Russia, they were not linked with them as their own tenants by the intimate interlocking relationship known as vassalage. Afterwards, the Grand Dukes of Muscovy articulated their status as supreme tax farmers to the Tartar Khan and adopted the Khan's way of looking at politics. The early Tsars considered Russia as their own property and saw no distinction between their private property as human beings and the property of the State. These rulers also took over such institutions of the Mongols as the posts and intelligence services (52), and tried to turn their nobility into a ruling class without territorial roots (unlike the Western nobility). All who served the state had a right to land but the nobles never held their estates by freehold. Indeed, they could be made into 'non persons' overnight, in the nineteenth as well as the twentieth centuries, and frequently were. In 1857, this upper class numbered about 1 million. A third of these were non-hereditary officials, and held no serfs at all. Between 45,000 and 60,000 landowners held serfs in Russia, of which 18,500 had over 100 and 1,000 had over 1,000 (53). The 'bourgeoisie' in Russia was, meantime, largely non-Russian – mostly German – and, therefore, debarred from playing any combative role. The working class, as defined as those working in factories – numbered 679,000 in 1879, 2 million or so in 1900 (54). 150 million Russians in 1914 lived on the land, only 27 million in cities.

Furthermore, the industrialisation which occurred in Russia between 1860 and 1914 was not inspired by a national bourgeoisie of restless capitalists anxious for profit. Russian industrialisation had always been sponsored by the State. It was usually carried out by foreigners. As a rule it had been put into effect with an eye to military considerations. Russia's industrialisation was thus in keeping with its Mongol past and its old absolutism, but had little to do with the capitalism as practised in the countries which Marx had studied most carefully. This industrial process had its curiosities: Russian factories in 1900 averaged 90 men per plant – or larger than the contemporary US average; and it had its successes: the standard of living increased by a third, foreign investment grew, iron ore produced increased from 1.7 million tons to 9.5

million between 1890 and 1913 (55). But all this was no more a capitalist success than the economic achievements of Russia under Stalin can be credited to capitalism. Was Marx simply deceived into supposing a capitalist class existed by the foundries in the Urals in Russia which, in the eighteenth century, smelted more iron than anywhere in Europe? By the cotton spinners who, in 1850 produced more yarn than Germany did? By the bustling cottage industries? If so, he was wrong: all industrialists in Russia knew that the path to wealth lay not in fighting the authorities but in collaborating with them; that any product which became successful risked becoming a state monopoly, and that, as in ancient China and ancient Egypt, the safest way of becoming rich was to be a foreigner.

In addition, the touching attachment which Marx had after 1870 to the village community was odd, to say the least since, though the commune had given peasants a certain identity and a certain sense of primitive democracy, it was really no more than the basic unit of administration in Russia and had been set up in the seventeenth century to be so – above all, to ensure an orderly payment of taxes (which it had done), as well as to assign people land commensurate with their needs and periodically reallocating it (56). Nor did Marx apparently know that Russia, like the USA, was a nation which still had much virgin land even after his own death in 1883. The history of a country which was still colonising itself as Russia was in the 1880s was very different from that of places in Europe with which Marx was familiar – or that he admired!

Nor did Marx seem to know that the main political problem of Russia was already one of nationalities. In 1900, Russia was a state of about 120 million people, in which some 56 million 'Greater Russians' dominated 22 million Ukrainians, and a lesser or greater number of White Russians, Poles, Jews, Tartars, Lithuanians, Letts, Germans, Armenians, Estonians, Finns, Bashkirs, Georgians and Circassians. This 'prison house of nationalities', to use Lenin's phrase about Tsarist-Russia, has increased by over 100%, with the minority races even more proportionally numerous now than they were then. Events in 1917–18, when Russian state power was temporarily at an end, suggest that any 'thaw' in Russia, either of Tsarism or of Communism, will lead to a revolt of nationalities.

The first explanation for Marx's success posthumously in Russia was simply that the Tsar had gone. A new upper class was also needed to run the absolute state and to strengthen it. Lenin offered himself as the 'little father' in the Tsar's place and the Communist party instead of the *dvoriáne*. To begin with largely composed of Jewish intellectuals, the Communist leadership imposed a dictatorship, since anarchy and disintegration was the alternative. The old upper class was dead, cowed, in gaol or in exile. The peasants, who formed the overwhelming majority of the population, probably preferred absolutism to everything except anarchy, and anarchy they could not obtain. Then the system of soviets, through which the centralising powers of the Communist party in Moscow were managed, ensured that the local party organisations would dominate state institutions (57). The Tsar's power was now vested in the secretary general of the party, advised by the political bureau of the central committee — the latter being something like a nominated parliament. The federal constitution also looked at first sight like that right to devolution which Stalin had thought desirable in 1914. Marx gave to Russia a theory, justifying an indefinite and nationalistic dictatorship of some members of the old rural proletariat over everyone else (58). Many of Marx's real doctrines have been abandoned by his followers perhaps because they did not understand him. Many who call themselves Marxists merely do so since they consider history to be motivated by greed. Marx himself saw history as determined by the unwanted consequences of actions by those who are caught as puppets by historical forces over which they have no control.

The explanation of what happened in Russia is probably that the situation on the land between 1860 and 1917 had become most unstable. Serfs became legal persons in 1861, though they had some dues to pay to the government for their land and had to ask permission to be away from the commune. But freedom meant new difficulties: the landlords after emancipation held on where they could to the bulk of the meadow and the forest which previously serfs had shared. The cultivation within the communes by joint families which had characterised Russia declined. A large increase of population between 1858 and 1897 from 58 million to 120 million bedevilled everything. Even large-scale emigration to the US could not cope with it. The mood was, therefore, ugly, and the huge numbers of half-literate peasants were ready for an upheaval: war or revolution or urbanisation. They got all three, war particularly. In 1917, the millions of peasants in uniform who constituted the Russian army were willing to believe Trotsky's rhetoric and Lenin's comforting assurances. In St Petersburg, a majority of those who rioted against bread queues in the snow were probably recent immigrants from the land drawn to the capital to work in new factories. By 1930, the sons of peasants constituted a new urban bureaucracy, the Communist party, ready to destroy those relations of theirs, who had remained on the land, in the agricultural revolution.

Communists have never gained power in a free election. In the only election ever held in Russia, in November 1918, the Communists gained 9.02 million votes (25%), the Social Revolutionaries 20.9 (58%), the Kadets 4.62 (13 %) and others 4 % (59). The Communists in Russia established their despotism by means of a victory in civil war and never again put their popularity to a test. The Chinese, Cuban*, Vietnamese,

* The complexity of the Cuban revolution may seem too curious to sum up thus, but the régime certainly sprang out of a civil war.

Cambodian and Yugoslav communists were also victors in civil wars. Every other Communist régime has been established either by a *coup d'état* or by the manipulation of a volatile system of politics, as in East Europe between 1945 and 1949. The highest vote a Communist party has ever gained in a free election was the 38% obtained in Czechoslovakia in 1946. That led to a Communist capture of power within two years. Thus Lenin's triumph, like Tito's or Mao's, was a military one, in which the Communist leaders showed greater military skill than their opponents. In the first major victory of 'dialectical materialism', leadership was the decisive factor. Patriotism also counted. By clever use of both, Trotsky transformed a 'flabby panicky mob' of Red guards into an efficient fighting force (60). Military victory too was the explanation for Communist control in Georgia where, in February 1919, the Mensheviks won 105 out of 130 seats in a national assembly (61). The 'kingdom of necessity' might have left Georgia free.

The two types of tyranny imposed on the world in the name of racial purity and the superiority of a supposed working class can with advantage be compared. They were once for a brief and natural period between 1939 and 1941 allied. Nazism appears to be dead in name at least, communism is still with us. The first looked backward to a heroic past, the second forward to a heroic, if very ill defined, future. The first made a deliberate cult of the individual leader a feature of its programme before it came to power, the second introduced that cult of its director once it was in power. To explain Russian despotism, some consideration of Tsarism is necessary and also some discussion of the (negative) role in Russia of the Orthodox Church since, between 1550 and 1917, the Church in Russia believed, without hesitation, as Richard Pipes says that 'the absolute monarchy was best for religion and for the Church' (62).

To explain national socialism it is necessary also to explore the by-paths of German romanticism and the long centuries of French cultural domination of central Europe.

In judging Russia, it is usual to recall the comment of the Marquis de Custine in 1839 ('It is a country in which the government says what it pleases because it alone has the right to speak') together with André Gide's in 1936 ('What is wanted is compliance, conformity. What is desired and demanded is approval of all that is done . . . the smallest protest, the slightest criticism, is liable to the severest penalties') (63). 'Has not everything been done under constraint?' asked Peter the Great.

Behind all this, many detect the mark of the Tartars. The Tartars had a fine military organisation bequeathed them by Genghis Khan. Peter the Great copied it. The Tartars aspired to achieve a world empire by war in which 'the price for the security of mankind would be permanent service to the state on the part of each and all'. Ivan the Terrible set the tone for subsequent Tsardoms by razing the once mildly liberal city of Novgorod to the ground because of its doubtful loyalty and made himself quite popular (as popular as Stalin perhaps) by murdering the ancient noble families (as Stalin killed the old Bolsheviks).The 'police mentality' of Russia was too great for a reasonably humane ruler like Catherine II (or Khrushchev) to eradicate it. The simple ruthlessness of Stalin is attested by a thousand anecdotes. For example, according to Djilas, he regarded Tito's reluctance to have the King of Yugoslavia back in 1945 as a tactical error. 'You don't have to take him back for ever,' he remarked. 'Just temporarily and then, at the right moment – a knife in the back' (64).

In judging Hitler and the Nazis, a long history of violent despotism cannot be invoked as a justification. Instead, however, there was the hierarchical German family, the long history of ranks and grades, the division of the nation for so long into principalities, upon which unity had in the end been ruthlessly imposed in one generation. The Soviet system was more tenacious in its pursuit of control over the entire economy, the Nazi system was more successful in reviving its economy by exhortation and intimidation. The Russian system sent millions of Russians to concentration camps before the war, the Germans sent their own people only in hundreds of thousands but sent millions of others, including Jews in particular, to camps once the war had begun. In communist camps many died from overwork, cold and indiscriminate brutality. In Nazi camps millions died by direct plan, by timetable. On the whole, unless one were a Jew, one would have been more likely to die a violent death at the hands of the state in the 1930s and 1940s if one were a Russian than a German; while life under Italian Fascism was mildness itself compared to life under Stalin.

Yet the similarities between the systems are what strike the sceptical observer. Both systems gained the sympathy of people who might have been supposed to have been democrats: 'Under Fascism, Italians no longer spit in public,' said Lord Howard of Penrith, a British diplomat, in 1923 (65). Julian Huxley gave an affecting picture of a volunteer gang of workers who, on being told that an urgent job needed doing, came down to the railway lines to work after their own work was over without extra pay. . . . 'One is told that Stalin himself sometimes came down to the Moscow goods siding', added the famous scientist (66). Both systems controlled labour, in both systems law did not protect individuals, and culture, history, art and private behaviour were all expected to conform to rules established by the government concerned. In both states, the police became a kind of super-caste, able to behave without fear of reproval or dismissal whatever they did.

Furthermore, even the offshoots of these systems have much more in

common than not. Thus Italian Fascism gives many interesting lessons
on how power can be won by an unrepresentative but ruthless minority. In May 1921, the Italian Fascists had only thirty-five deputies
elected. They were helped to power afterwards by the *squadristi*, armed
bands of unemployed or recently demobilised thugs enrolled by landowners or factory managers to resist socialist or communist take-overs.
Such groups would set off in lorries from large towns singing the beguiling song 'Giovenezza', bent on punitive expeditions to Tuscan villages
and determined to humiliate or beat their opponents. The government
and the police, the magistrates and even constitutionally minded landowners turned a blind eye. They did not want to stop the Fascists for
fear of opening the way to revolution by the Left. Officials who
ventured to protest were threatened and were easily intimidated to abet
crimes in the name of order. The Fascists simply took over municipal
councils, by bullying, first in the country, then in the smaller towns and
finally, in 1922, in the large ones.* Fascist propaganda in Italy played on
the unreality of Rome as a capital (as unreal as Mussolini's 'March on
Rome' itself), the artifically centralised state imposed on a regional
country, the disillusion since 1870 with the great ideals of the Risorgimento, the lack of a Verdi, the thwarted imperialism of the 1890s, and
the political failure of the constitutional monarchy (67). But the morals
are international ones and, indeed, have been consciously or unconsciously drawn upon to enable captures of power by other ideologies.
To take a recent example, Castro's campaign against Batista between
1956 and 1958 and his own seizure of power in Cuba have very many
parallels with Mussolini's victory in 1922. True, Castro probably had a
majority behind him in his 'march on Havana' but he consciously used
propaganda, public relations, intimidation by television, thuggery, and
intervention in the normal process of law to ensure the overthrow of a
social order which was rotten, corrupt and neglectful even if it scarcely
deserved the visitation that Castro's version of national communism
brought to it.

The effects of despotism are also usually much the same on the
persons who suffer from it.

An established despotism naturally causes all but the strongest to
consort with it and hence accept it, perhaps finding a good reason to
suppose that with it, as with other systems, all change is necessarily
likely to be evil — depending indeed on a caution of spirit as unheroic as
it is comprehensible. Modern despotisms have managed, by making
illusions, such as have been discussed earlier, the foundation stones of
their philosophy, to devise whole languages with which to ensnare
populations: who can be resilient if 'revolutionary defeatism' is

---

* 'In 48 hours of systematic, warlike violence we won what we would never have won in 48
years of preaching,' the Fascists said after they had captured Bologna.

demanded of him, who can show enterprise if he is shown to be living in 'the opportunistic rut'?

Now, the continued existence of so many tyrannies, their increased strength, achieved by technology, the obeisance and acceptance which they are able to extort, is the first reason for the ill health of the world in the late twentieth century. Technology is politically neutral. It can be turned indifferently to good or bad effect. In the hands of tyrannies, television and radio, armaments and communications, can become overwhelming instruments for ill-doing.

The existence of so many ruthless régimes is the chief reason for the wars and rumours of wars which exist internationally. The First and Second World Wars were both caused by the attempts of a German tyranny, first monarchical and military, subsequently Nazi and personal, to make a 'grab for world power'. The cold war derives from the challenge posed to the world by the despotism based in Russia. Were that despotism, and those which it supports, to disappear, it would be an illusion to suppose that all evils would vanish too. Illusions of class and race survive, even in tolerant Western communities. Even so, a country which develops strong forces of repression to keep down its own citizens is likely to be a danger beyond its frontiers. No tyranny, therefore, is an island. Democratic leaders should recall that wars between democratic states have not been seen in the twentieth century. Indeed, wearied and demoralised though modern man's democracies have sometimes been, there is no instance at all of any of them being bellicose against each other: an elementary truth which their leaders should take a little trouble to point out to their critics.

48

Causes of the 'Cold' War:
Notions of Imperialism

The illusion that class is the determining factor in history is the heart of the communist challenge to the open society. But in the last few years, a further illusion has caught the imagination of half the world and has been skilfully used as a supporting argument, by those who claim to believe in that interpretation, for use in countries where classes either obviously do not exist or plainly do not constitute serious problems. This is the illusion associated with the word 'imperialism'.

This word does not have a very long history in English. 'Imperialists' there were, however, from an early time. They were supporters of the Holy Roman Emperor or of Napoleon I or III. 'Imperialism' was a concept which began to be used in the mid-nineteenth century to designate the idea behind ancient Roman expansionism and, by easy stages, the French Empire of the two Napoleons. It seems, to begin with, to have begun by being used in a pejorative sense but, in the 1890s, was being employed by those who advocated empires for all the European countries as well as by those who disliked or feared them.

By that time, the small group of nations which inhabited Europe and which had dominated intellectual life since the Renaissance, had conquered most of the globe. Admittedly, the European empires in the Americas had largely foundered and were in the hands of colonists, or their descendants and other immigrants. But there, in Spanish and Portuguese America, in the south, and Anglo-Saxon America, in the north, European traditions of the homeland survived under a thin guise of American assimilation and alongside a gathering of indigenous tribes and African slaves or their descendants. The main countries which remained exceptions to the European imperial system were the Chinese and Ottoman empires; and the monarchies of Japan, Ethiopia and Thailand. The first two of these had, by the 1890s, already accepted substantial penetration by Europeans and North Americans. Ethiopia, though unconquered, slumbered in ignorance and oblivion. Thailand, though picturesque, could not have resisted any determined European onslaught. Only Japan had resolved to modernise its industry and remain both isolated and in complete control, so far as was possible, of its own fate. Persia (or Iran) also maintained a limited independence under the Kajar dynasty, as did Afghanistan under the Barakzai, and Nepal under Chandra Shamsher.

To this picture, four qualifications must be made. First, the expansion of the always ambiguous state of Russia eastwards to embrace most of central Asia had altered the Russian personality. The Slavs had been living in Europe long before most Germans, Franks or Anglo-Saxons. But their early divisions, and their ceaseless wars against the Mongols and other Asiatic opponents, had caused them to become, in many of their reactions, more comparable to an oriental despotism than to a European empire.

Second, all these empires, and that included the Russian one, were, as it were, overlords embracing a vast number of petty princes, cities, mayors, sheikhs, sultans, emirs, kings and even in Annam (central Vietnam), emperors. It was as if, as it would now be said, the imperial powers had laid in India, in Central Africa, in the Maghreb, an 'extra layer of government' over indigenous and historic systems which they sought, as a rule, to maintain, trade with, protect from invasion, render less corrupt, enrich and improve. Of course, there were some regions of the world such as South Africa, Algeria or Australia where substantial numbers of colonists had become established and sought and obtained privileges, but most European emigrants preferred to go to settle in the already free states of the Americas.

Third, the astonishing technological inventions of the nineteenth century gave the Europeans a sense of superiority to the backward African and Asiatic countries which was certainly justified in the short run. It enabled them to establish what Elie Halévy described as a 'great international commercial republic' (1). Whether that would have been maintained had it not been for a revival of the wars which had characterised the eighteenth century between the European states but in a harsher and more profound way, is unclear. Whether the empires were really of benefit to the home countries commercially is equally unclear. Britain, though she expanded her imperial interests in the early twentieth century, had already passed her economic peak in the 1890s when the idea of 'imperialism' was at its height. Germany, with scarcely any colonies of substance, was about to become Europe's richest power. The US, with even fewer colonial possessions, was already even richer. Even were it to be proven that the pursuit of empire was a compensation for declining markets in rich countries — an improbable eventuality — it would still be difficult to sustain the argument that even economic imperialism was the fountain of 'capitalist revival', as is sometimes done.*

* By, for example, J. A. Hobson and, following him, Lenin.

Fourth, already a striking imbalance had been established in the achievements of Spanish-American and Anglo-Saxon American countries. Argentina, it is true, had an income per head comparable to that of rich countries in Western Europe, and was the focus, therefore, of substantial immigration from Europe, particularly from Italy. There were some other rich regions. Whites from Europe were, on the whole, the managers of South American politics, just as the USA was a continuation of European politics. Nevertheless, certain fatal flaws in the Spanish legacy to Latin America had become evident. The rich were speculating in land, the young, ambitious men were studying law, and intellectuals such as José Martí, the Cuban martyr of independence, were beginning to blame the US for all their troubles: Spain and Portugal were no longer influential in themselves, and so could not be accused of 'imperialism'. Indeed, Latin American intellectuals were all ready by 1900 to embark on that career of seeking scapegoats abroad for their own irresolution which has unfortunately affected much of their history in the twentieth century (2).

These European empires had been founded for a variety of economic, religious and other reasons. The usual pattern was that commercial considerations began a European nation's interest in a particular region, and afterwards that European nation occupied it, either to safeguard the commerce or to prevent other Europeans gaining control. The African empires, for example, were achieved between, say, 1875 and 1900 as a result of rivalry between Europeans who thought that, unless they acted, their rivals would obtain a decisive advantage over them. This 'scramble for Africa' was begun by King Leopold of the Belgians in the Congo in the 1870s and pressed further by the Germans: though neither of those two countries had previously been much concerned in Africa. These African empires were quickly consolidated as administrative structures and then the administrators began to reflect why they were there. 'We don't want to stay in your country forever,' wrote Lord Milner of Egypt, 'We don't despair of leaving you to manage your own affairs. [But] if we were to go away tomorrow, you would not succeed in doing so, because you have not shaken off the old tradition. You still require a good deal of training in a better school' (3). Innumerable French, Belgian, and Dutch proconsuls said much the same: 'We fought these colonial wars with a clear conscience,' wrote General André Beaufre, 'sure that we were bringing with us civilisation and progress, certain that we would help these people from their backward state' (4). The idea was developed that the colonial powers were where they were as 'a sacred trust for civilisation'.

This idea was not the hypocritical front for exploitation that it has been depicted. The main economic goal of every colonial governor was to achieve a self-sufficient economy. But the Europeans had too little time at their disposal. All the colonial powers soon sought to educate their new subjects — or at least a quarter or so of the most intelligent ones (5). But the first generation of those so educated became the leaders of local nationalism. Nor did the imperialists in the different European nations see eye to eye. The British expected the Africans, in the end, to mature into independent nations; the French looked forward to assimilation with the home country. Contact between the different colonial powers was modest, and not encouraged. Essentially, the Europeans succeeded in Africa in destroying much of the influence of many old monarchies and tribal despotisms which, however brutal, might, in the end, have given continuity and a focus to future political evolution. Instead, nearly all the colonies were divided by differing tribal attitudes towards the occupying forces: for all colonial empires needed their sepoys, *regulares*, or other native troops, under European officers. The consequent feuds, the memory of which was to many the most humiliating experience of occupation, made innumerable people educated in the European empires begin to look on them with hatred and to aspire to independence on a basis different from that which the Europeans desired for them. In the formulation of those feelings, most nationalists overlooked that the Europeans had created the basis, at least, of states which they could try and capture. That was particularly so in French North Africa (Morocco, Tunisia, and Algeria) but it was also so elsewhere.

These hatreds were enhanced by the high expectations which Europeans had of their empires, in the first half of the twentieth century. Cecil Rhodes's almost religious enthusiasm for the British Empire was widely shared. In a poem of 1911, D'Annunzio wrote: 'Africa is the whetstone on which we Italians shall sharpen our sword for a supreme conquest in the unknown future' (6). He was, no doubt, merely echoing English or French imperialists in spirit; but that sort of sentiment led to the collapse of Europe all the same, and the transformation, not the conquest, of Africa: though, as late as 1939, a Polish government was announcing that it, too, needed its share of Africa (7).

These political considerations now overshadow the social and economic changes which, with all their complexities, have started these ex-colonial or ex-imperial countries on their way to an industrial history. The long list of benefits which they received ranged from railways to the control of malaria, innumerable agricultural techniques and mining, and many plantation crops. Many European colonies received large grants-in-aid for specific projects, or subsidies, if, as a rule, not so great as that of Mussolini's supplies to his Italian empire before 1941, when between a half and three-quarters of the budget depended on such investments (8).

Vietnamese, Cambodians, Indians and Africans lost land, it is true, in places where there was substantial European immigration, or where the state or large companies elected to invest. But these places were not a substantial proportion of the total areas concerned. On the other hand, a great many Africans were entrusted to carry out what was, in effect, compulsory labour service, at the behest of their chiefs, no doubt, but to do the work of the Europeans. Elsewhere, there was, for the first time, a demand for labour for wages, and hence the beginning of modern economies.

The era of European imperialism was a relatively short one. It will be a long time before it will be fairly judged. A consideration of it from the angle of 1980 certainly shows it to have been a time when the European nations were more openly cosmopolitan than they are to-day. Herman Merivale, a professor at Oxford, summed up the British attitudes in the 1830s, before the real age of imperialism had begun: 'The destiny of our name and nation is not here in this narrow island: it lives in our language, our commerce, our industry, in all those channels of inter-communication by which we embrace and connect the vast multitudes of states, both civilised and uncivilised, throughout the world' (9). It was true; and it is true now, however much we seek, vainly, to cultivate our garden.

The impact of those empires upon the countries which they ruled was so great that it is naturally difficult for either the rulers or the ruled to make fair assessments. The impact on continents differed, the impact of different European countries differed, and, of course, different groups within the different countries thought differently. Everywhere, the actual experience of administration from European capitals, in the nine-teenth and twentieth centuries, was, at the end of several centuries of commercial experience, of varying significance. Essentially, Europe brought the countries which it ruled within grasp of modern technol-ogy, education, and mercantile enterprise. In doing so, strains and social upheavals followed. To blame 'imperialism' or 'neo-imperialism' for all the troubles and economic crises of those countries is an ex-tremely convenient propaganda weapon in the armoury of the enemies of the free society. But to call the commercial activities of large American or European businesses by the name of 'imperialism' is a sad, if occas-ionally deliberate, misunderstanding. The USA, South Africa, Austra-lia, and Canada all benefited from foreign investment when they were pastoral nations. So do the still poor countries of the world. Japan did not receive much foreign investment, it is true, but the pattern of Japan's military, monarchical and nationalist industrialisation is scarcely one to emulate – nor is it easy to do so. In the endless disputes over the nature of the 'Third World', or the 'underdeveloped world' or the 'developing world' – each few years produces a new euphemism – three things are usually forgotten: first, bad politics cause poverty more often than bad business; second, the rich world was once a poor one and the resources, population and geographical position of many countries now poor are such as could enable them also to become prosperous; and third, 'economic imperialism' means, as Jean François Revel has put it, no more than 'economic activity itself, the distribution of capital, goods and innovations' (10).

The concept of imperialism has been allowed to play strange tricks in many places — none more so than in Latin America where, paradoxically, the main imperialists, Spain and Portugal, were obliged to abandon most of their dominions in 1822 and 1825, respectively, though the former maintained Cuba and Puerto Rico till 1898, and Britain, France and the Netherlands all maintained footholds in the Guyanas till 1966. In the early nineteenth century, many of these countries were at least as advanced in the sense of producing as much as the US. In the early twentieth century Cuba and Argentina were better off than many European states. But a combination of nationalism, over-population, romanticism, inertia, class consciousness, bad management, a desire to blame others (as admirably described by Carlos Rangel in his brilliant book *Du bon sauvage à bon révolutionnaire**), caused Latin America to fall behind the rest of the world's more advanced peoples and even to cause some countries, such as Argentina, to return to becoming underdeveloped again. Latin American intellectuals blame the North Americans and call their businessmen, health inspectors, advisers on education, and other philanthropists by the name of 'imperialists'. They do this in order to find scapegoats, not real explanations, of their historic failures over the last few generations to work out for themselves viable and just political systems. With a few shining exceptions, democrats in Latin America have lacked both moral and physical courage. The surrender in 1952 of President Prío of Cuba to the *coup d'état* of General Batista without doing anything in his own defence, or of the political system of which he was the custodian, was all too characteristic of a political tradition which has perhaps been more at the mercy of illusions than any other.

---

* Foolishly translated into English as *The Latin Americans.*

49

The Democratic Alternative

I claim complete exemption because I have a conscientious objection to surrendering my liberty of judgement on so vital a question as undertaking military service . . . I am not prepared on such an issue as this to surrender my right of decision as to what is or is not my duty to any other person, and I think it morally wrong to do so.

Keynes to the Tribunal on conscientious
objection, February 2 1916

The frequent recurrence to fundamental principles is absolutely necessary to preserve the blessings of Liberty.

Constitution of North Carolina

The urgent consideration of the public safety may undoubtedly authorise the violation of every positive law. How far that or any other consideration may operate to dissolve the natural obligations of humanity and justice is a doctrine of which I still desire to remain ignorant.

Gibbon, The Decline and Fall of the Roman Empire Vol. III,

We must plan for freedom and not only for security, if for no other reason than that only freedom can make security secure.

Karl Popper, The Open Society and its enemies

As far as the leaders of bourgeois origins in the working class parties are concerned it may be said that they have adhered to the cause of the proletariat either on moral grounds, or from enthusiasm, or from scientific conviction. They crossed the Rubicon when they were still young students, still full of optimism and juvenile ardour. Having gone over to the other side of the barricade to lead the enemies of the class from which they sprang, they have fought and worked. . . Youth has [now] fled. Their best years have been passed in the service of the party or of the ideal. They are ageing . . . and their ideals have also passed, dispersed by the contrarities of daily struggles, often, too, expelled by newly acquired experiences which conflict with old beliefs. Thus . . . many of the leaders are inwardly estranged from the essential conflict of socialism. Some of them carry on a difficult internal scepticism; others have returned . . to the ideals of their pre-socialist youth. Yet . . . no backward path is open. They are enchained by their own past. . . They have a family . . . Regard for their good name makes them feel it essential to persevere in the old round. They thus remain openly faithful to the cause to which they have sacrificed the best years of their life. But renouncing idealism, they have become opportunists. These former believers, these some time altruists whose fervent hearts aspired only to give themselves freely, have been transformed into sceptics and egoists whose only actions are guided solely by cold calculation.

Michels, Political Parties (English Translation), 1915

I now accept that the settled and just management of society by a progressive oligarchy is probably the best we can hope for.

R. H. S. Crossman, *Diaries* 1967

On one side in the cold war, it has been argued, are the forces of despotism with its long roots. On the other, there is democracy, with its myriad heads. After two centuries of industrial endeavour, there are now in the world about thirty such democracies. Nearly all are mass democracies, in the sense that, in nearly all of them, there is universal suffrage of all adults and freedom to organise meetings, distribute literature, claim the protection of the law against both the state and other citizens. None of these democracies is perfectly managed and no doubt some will collapse, as democracies have collapsed in the past. This number of democracies though small enough, is relatively new.

In 1750, England, some German and Italian cities, the Swiss, and a few English colonies were the only places to possess the shadow of even oligarchic democracy. The roots of these enterprises owed something to the memory of ancient Mediterranean achievements, something to a formalisation of Germanic habits of consultation dating from the era of tribalism: 'The most civilised nations of modern Europe issued from the woods of Germany, Gibbon wrote', and, in the rude institutions of those barbarians, we may still distinguish the original principles of our present laws and manners' (1).

Alongside Liberty, there was also Law: and both the ancient Greeks and mediaeval Europeans believed that Law should rule the world – indeed that was, in the Greeks' view, what distinguished them from barbarians.

The political systems of the world in 1750 would not have suggested that the most likely future method of managing a country in most rich nations would be democratic. Indeed, except for the recent and apparently exceptional events in England, democracies seemed in decline. Local freedoms were everywhere being replaced by efficient absolutisms. The eclipse of the oligarchic democracies of Italy, and the substitution of short-term elected men by grand dukes and kings, is a well chronicled, if gloomy, tale. Then, in early mediaeval Germany, there was an attempt at creating free clan assemblies, and elective monarchies. By the eighteenth century, only Württemberg among German territorial states (along with Hungary in the Austrian Habsburg dominions) had an assembly with any real influence and that assembly consisted of a group of burghers whose ancestors had established themselves during a time of anarchy, while a certain Duke Ulrich had been nominally reigning (2). In mediaeval Catalonia, all social ranks had been represented in a Cortes which met once a year, and no law could be passed without the consent of the representatives of a majority of the three estates (3). The crown of Aragon also once had a Cortes which limited the power of monarchs in dramatic ways (4), while the interlocking relations between kings and vassals in mediaeval Castile obliged the latter, in certain circumstances, to rise against the king: 'If ye swear falsely, may it please God that a vassal slay ye as the traitor Veludo Adolfo slew King Sancho.' The king, it is said, turned pale when the Cid uttered this momentous statement (5). Even when the Crusaders conquered Byzantium in 1204, power to choose a new emperor of the East was given to an electoral college of twelve, six from Venice, six from the Franks (6). For a time in the Middle Ages, some thought that kings should be elected as abbots were (7). But by 1789, the Spanish Cortes, drawn from the whole united country, was far feebler. They met for two months in secret. They approved without discussion the son of the king as the heir. They discussed, but did not challenge, royal plans to limit entail and to permit the enclosure of orchards. There was some passive opposition to the enlightened reforms advocated by the prescient minister, Floridablanca, but the most animated discussion concerned the question of how the deputies could obtain seats at a forthcoming bullfight (8). The assemblies of Castilian cities did not meet after 1665. Similarly, the French had lost their right to elect municipal councils in 1692 (the King wished to supervise such assemblies in order to raise cash, not to control the people more) (9). In no country, indeed, did the eighteenth century seem to compare so badly with mediaeval practice as France: 'I have found much evidence in support of the view that, during the Middle Ages, the inhabitants of each village formed a community independent, in many ways, of the seigneurs,' wrote de Tocqueville (10). Assemblies of clergy, nobility and commons had been common in France in many provinces. At the end of the eighteenth century they existed only in Brittany and Languedoc (11). (This decay was as the result of boredom more than anything else: people preferred to stay at home rather than vote in free elections – just as many people in the twentieth century do not bother to vote in elections in trade unions.) Rudimentary elective institutions of the Kievan Rus had lingered on into the sixteenth century in Russia. But Ivan the Terrible centralised the structure of the state and deprived it of all genuine content (12). Such bodies as the Zemstvo Sober became simply conferences between a government and its own agents. The Duma, or Tsar's council, merely ratified decisions taken by the Tsar though, in Viking days, it had, in an earlier form, at least a consultative status. Novgorod had a democracy of all male citizens until it was closed peremptorily in 1477 by the Tsar of Moscow (13).* Poland had been obliged by conquest to abandon its elective monarchy, while the Austrian Diets had only recently ceased to have a decisive voice in taxation and the drafting of soldiers. Similarly,

---

* In practice, in the eighteenth century, Russian rulers were often chosen by the officers of the guard and by senior officers. They favoured women, who might give them presents of large estates.

the slightest knowledge of Indian history suggests that village autonomy in the eighteenth century was much less alive than it had been, say, in the eighth. A precisely similar statement, in relation to custom if not law, could have been made among many ancient peoples during the early days of agriculture, though there were few Asiatic countries, or others, which had anything like the self-administration (of villages) to which to look back on that India had, when thinking of village autonomy under the Chola dynasty before 1300 AD (14). The town councils of the Spanish empire in the Americas had also once been occasionally elected by all citizens. By the eighteenth century, they had become self-perpetuating and venal oligarchies, if not necessarily incompetent, as John Parry adds, depending for their income on rents from municipal property, not from taxation (15).

The new history of democracy during the age of industrialisation begins, like industrialisation itself, with the Anglo-Saxons. The management of the English government was then firmly in the hands of a group of landowners who had reduced the power of the monarchs, while allowing them to retain the ceremonial function which the monarchy continued to offer. Few thought of reviving a strong kingship. The suffrage, however, was tiny, being restricted to freeholders in a limited number of cities and counties. No women played any part either as voters or as politicians (save sometimes through influencing their husbands or friends). Electoral activity had been sporadic. Between 1700 and 1715, there were eight general elections, more, J. H. Plumb tells us, than any ever held since within a similar span of time, elections in boroughs being especially difficult for governments to manage. But, afterwards, both borough and county elections become passive affairs, with the democratic system seeming to have given control to 'a self-gratifying oligarchy that held power for its own profit' (16).

Despite this, foreigners looked at the English system with envy. This was not because they admired the electoral process, nor because they knew that the last time an English government had formally ordered torture, or had burned a witch, was in 1641 and 1684 respectively, but because they admired the way that Britain kept the Rule of Law.* Voltaire and other visitors to England in the eighteenth century realised that, in England, sentences were often harsh, but the three essentials of the Rule of Law (in the formulation of A. V. Dicey) were observed: first, that there was nobody so grand as to be able to claim to be above the law (Voltaire was impressed when Lord Ferrers in 1760 was hanged for murdering his steward, after a trial by the House of Lords. Such a fate would not have occurred to a nobleman in France); second, people could not suffer loss or injury save by breach of the law as established in a properly constituted court — a man might be punished for a breach of the law but for nothing else; and, third, King and parliament were the

* Some of these points have been developed earlier, in Chapter 40.

source of a law which ran throughout the land (17).

At that time, there was no country except England where men were secure from arbitrary power. Law had been considered so important there that, even in the middle of the Civil War, the twelve justices of England continued to make their bi-annual circuits. By comparison, there were several countries on the continent where there was an absolute failure to distinguish between political and judicial decisions, while the neglect of many states to interest themselves in affronts by one man against another were at their worst in Russia where, until 1864, Russian laws did not even have to be made public for them to be put into effect: even afterwards, laws were often promulgated as confidential memoranda known only to officials (18).

England was thus an inspiration in the late eighteenth century and for a long time afterwards, though foreign admirers often failed to take into account one essential element of the English experience: namely, that the general principles of the constitution (for example, the rights of personal liberty or the right to hold public meetings) derived from judicial decisions determining the right of private persons brought before courts in particular cases. Parliament in England had begun not as a legislature to make laws but as a court concerned to interpret laws. Even the Habeas Corpus Acts, as Dicey put it, declared no principles and defined no rights.

Montesquieu considered that the strength of the English constitution derived from the separation of the legislative, executive and the judiciary powers. Those powers were, and are, not divided thus, but Montesquieu's interpretation of them had some effect on the constitution of the United States when they broke away from Britain in the late eighteenth century. That American revolution itself helped to inspire the French Revolution, though the contribution of that breakdown to the achievement of anything which might be called democracy was modest. In 1815, after the battle of Waterloo, there was still only one major inspiration of democratic practice: the one deriving from the Anglo-Saxons, by then in the US as well as in Europe. The lesson of the French Revolution seemed to be that pure democracy would lead in modern Europe, as in ancient Greece, first to demagoguery and then to tyranny. For over a hundred years, however, the echoes of events between 1789 and 1801 were regularly detected in other countries and even other continents, Girondins being detected in Spain, an eighteenth Brumaire in Russia: historical parallels falsely evoked on a hundred occasions to deceive.

The French Revolution also had in much of Western Europe one major negative consequence: it destroyed the organic life of the peoples where its ideas were taken. The great Catalan conservative, Francisco Cambó, put the matter very well: 'All those organic divisions in political life separating one group from another which had been created over the centuries were cut off from us by the hurricane of the revolution . . . there only remained left the omnipresent state and the solitary individual without resources' (19). Burke would have applauded him.

The French Revolution excited everyone: 'even the whores ask you about Robespierre' (20), Fr Pedro Estala wrote from Paris in 1795. But its message was unclear. As Alexander Pope said of Blenheim Palace, ' 'tis very fine. But where d'ye sleep and where d'ye dine?' Napoleon appreciated the emptiness: while *la grande armée* passed him en route for Moscow, he remarked, '*Tout cela ne vaut pas des institutions*' (21); and, on another occasion, reflected, 'Well, the future will show whether it would have been better for the repose of the world if neither I nor Rousseau had existed' (22).

The French Revolution had, undoubtedly, many consequences which seemed to be liberating at the time even if they look a little ambiguous now. It introduced a vast body of rational legislation affecting everything from weights and measures to marriage. It overthrew landlords who would not, because of their long dependence on the Crown, have turned their estates into innovating market concerns, as their English colleagues had done. Noble as well as royal absolutism was destroyed and a new alliance was created between urban merchants and old nobility (23). The irresistible combination of nationalism and radicalism has survived ever since in one form or another. But the real friends of liberty in France and abroad could not stomach Robespierre, while Napoleon, with his interest in hereditary monarchy and a new nobility, was worse still in their estimation.

The success of the US experiment in democracy, meantime, made a great impression, perhaps greater than that of England in the nineteenth century. Most continental Europeans believed, after all, that the British monarchs continued to exert some influence on events (a correct assumption until 1885 at least)* and the British leadership of the opposition to Napoleon had given her conservative governments some strange bedfellows. Indeed, in the years after 1815, Britain hardly seemed a good advertisement for democracy, being beset by labour troubles, riots, and fears of revolution which were met by a government more autocratic than democratic. The United States, however, had an elected president, a representative legislature (even if the representatives were elected by a minority of men till 1918) and strong devolved powers to the states. Its Declaration of Independence spoke of Equality as well as Freedom. Knowledge of US legal procedure was communicated because of the unrestricted entry which the USA allowed to the adventurous, the protesters, and the repressed minorities of Europe. The impact of the US constitution was greater in Latin America than anywhere else,

* The choice of Lord Salisbury as Prime Minister by Queen Victoria (instead of Sir Stafford Northcote) seems to have been the last major intervention in politics of the English monarch.

even if little durable came of it. Meantime, as a result of the revolutions of 1830 and 1848, and the military defeat of France in 1870, several new democracies were established, pre-eminently in France, but also, under the patronage of monarchies, in Spain, Italy, Scandinavia, and the Low Countries. The Anglo-Saxon dominions of Canada and Australia (with New Zealand) also established democracies in the late nineteenth century; and some political manifestations of it were to be seen in Germany and central Europe, though the wars of the twentieth century would show them to be modest. Still, in 1910, the three richest states (Britain, the US and France) were democracies.

Observers such as de Tocqueville in America particularly noticed the extent to which national self-government genuinely grew from local self-government. Thus, he remarked, taxes were voted by the state but they were levied and collected by townships. The establishment of a school was obligatory but each town itself built, paid for and superintended it. In France, the state collector received the local imports, in the US the town collector received the taxes of the state. The township, it seemed, was organized before the county, the county before the state, the state before the union. The independence of the township was the nucleus which gave scope to the activity of 'a political life thoroughly democratic and republican' (24).

At the time, those mid-nineteenth century régimes did not call themselves democracies, and still feared the idea. Disraeli, a skilful practitioner of parliamentary democracy, hoped in 1867 that 'it will never be the fate of this country to live under a democracy' (25). Most educated Englishmen feared that to give the vote to the masses would risk revolution. Though two new reforms of the suffrage, in 1867 and 1884, increased the numbers voting in England to about 4.6 million, the large quantity of servants, bachelors living with their families, all who had no fixed address, and all women, were still excluded from participation in English democracy before 1914. A few new democracies such as Italy and Spain had, in the 1880s, more generous laws on voting than England. But they were unsteady, and the free votes there hid many inequities. The first European régime to introduce universal male suffrage, France in 1848, was overthrown within three years.

All these free states, save the US, had, by 1911, gained large territories by conquest overseas, linked with them as empires in which political control was directly exercised by proconsuls. These empires had been originally established for commercial reasons, or, in some cases, for religious ones. By 1914, though 'there were good reasons for believing that parliamentary institutions would supply the sovereign

* For example, in Russia, the Zemstvo had come into being in 1864. Its members had limited powers of levying taxes and of using the money so raised. Alexander II in 1881 was about to convoke several elected committees (which could have led to a states general) when he was murdered (27).

formula for the coming age' wrote H. A. L. Fisher, 'no country in the world claiming to be civilised — not even Russia* — had been able altogether to withstand the public pressure in favour of responsible cabinets, representative assemblies and democratic electorates' (26). Most imperial countries believed that their mission was to prepare the peoples whose government they had assumed for self-government on their own model.

This optimism was upset by the two world wars. True, most of the world's thirty or so democracies are now mass democracies and, therefore, formally at least, more perfect than any of those which existed at the beginning of the century. True, the old proconsulships have mostly gone, and European democracies have now no need to reproach themselves that they are democratic at home and authoritarian abroad in their empires (though they were not able to achieve the establishment of democracies, except in new nations where Europeans dominated). But all democracies have met difficulties. States which were once briefly democratic, such as Cuba or Czechoslovakia, Chile and Brazil, have ceased to be so. Western democracy has failed to make headway in Asia save in India. Senegal and Kenya seem the only democracies in Africa. Old arguments that certain countries (Argentina, Chile) were more likely to become democracies than others (Peru, Mexico) because, in the former, there were no 'alien masses' have been shown to be meaningless (28). It is still difficult to avoid concluding that the anxieties of conservatives in nineteenth century England at the prospect of mass democracy might not after all have had some basis: they argued that it would lead to extravagant expenditure, discontent in meeting it, rash wars, insecurity of property and of liberty: culminating in despotism (29). All democracies too have been subject to strains, as the old oligarchic democracy gave way to mass democracy, with universal suffrage, male and female, for all over the age of eighteen. Mass circulation newspapers, posters, radio, cinema, gramophone records (of songs and speeches), symbols, television, polls of public opinion and agencies of public relations imperceptibly affected the working of the system, never perhaps more than during the German elections of 1932, when the 'black magic of slogans' cast such a spell over the populace.

There are also a number of problems in modern democracy which it would be idle not to notice.

First, the necessity of keeping the rule of law as a principle of equal importance for the maintenance of democracy as that of the free vote has occasionally been forgotten. Minority groups, for example, have failed to heed Bertrand Russell's advice (on his return from Russia in 1920): 'Once the principle of respecting majorities as expressed at the ballot box is abandoned, there is no reason to suppose that victory will be seized by the particular minority to which one happens to belong. . . All groups, communist and others,' he believed, 'ought to have the patience to set about the task of winning by propaganda (not force) . . . we take it for granted that most people will be law-abiding and we hardly realise what centuries of effort have gone to make that possible' (30). This truth was known in Greece and in the Renaissance: the Catalan humanist, Vives, in 1526 wrote: 'It is no liberty to refuse respect and obedience to the public magistrates, rather it is an incitement to savagery and an occasion for license' (31). Old truth though it may be, it has not always in our day been properly appreciated.*

Corrupt judges have also sometimes made nonsense of the ordinary process of law. The movement westwards of the US railroads in the nineteenth century, for example, was attended by a staggering series of scandals (32), and make some of de Tocqueville's high-minded comments on the US constitution seem starry-eyed.

Second, some otherwise good-hearted democrats have forgotten not only that democracy and liberty assisted the beginning of industrialism but also that a critical part has always been played by commerce and free enterprise in maintaining democracy. A good presentation of such a point of view was that made by John Stuart Mill in his essay *On Liberty*: 'If the roads, the railways, the banks, the insurance offices, the great joint stock companies, the universities, and the public charities, were all of them branches of the government; if, in addition, the municipal corporations and local boards with all that now devolves on them became departments of the central administration, if the employees of all these enterprises are appointed and paid by the government, and look to the government for every rise in life; not all the freedom of the press and popular constitution of the legislature would make this or any other country free otherwise than in name' (34).

From the early days of Greece onwards, free enterprise and democracy have gone hand in hand, with the first usually preparing the way for the latter, even if (as in Nazi Germany and, for a time, in the communist régimes) sometimes surviving it.

The neglect of some democrats to measure the importance of a flourishing system of private commerce has led, in several countries, to wholesale intervention by the state in the working of the market. The latter may survive since it is resilient, but the universal opinion in the best universities of the West has, for some generations, been that service to the state is a superior undertaking to that of private commerce and manufacture. The spirit of bureaucratic Rome seems to have overtaken that of sceptical Greece, that of Bourbon France seems to have con-

---

* In *Democracy in Crisis* Harold Laski once described how parliamentary democracy should not be allowed to form an obstacle to the realisation of 'socialism'; and Aneurin Bevan, a politician who later became a committed democrat, wrote in 1929, 'There still remains *unfortunately* [My italics] a degree of law-abiding conduct amounting to a broken spirit among the miners of the district' (33).

quered Hanoverian England. Sometimes, it has been suggested that people who work in the public service must be more civic-spirited than those in private enterprise. Not surprisingly, in some democracies (Britain among them) the spirit of innovation among many entrepreneurs has consequently declined. Exhausted by problems of labour, hampered by taxation, tempted by increasingly corrupt practices, or at least tax evasion, modern entrepreneurs sometimes seem like their equivalents in the last years of Roman civilisation: ignorant, timid, backward-looking and more likely to appease than to lead.

Third, many modern democrats seem to forget that the strongest free systems have been based on a view of ethics in which natural rights exist. The founders of the Constitution of the US, for instance, not only reflected the concept of the separation of powers, but argued that all men had, from God, the right to life, liberty and the pursuit of happiness. It is not always evident that all democratic politicians accept the existence of those 'rights of man', even though they may be doing much for what they believe to be the good of the people of the country concerned.

This partly derives from a difficulty pointed out by A. V. Dicey: 'We have all learned from Blackstone, and writers of the same class, to make such constant use of expressions which we know not to be strictly true to fact that we cannot say for certain what is the exact relation between the facts of constitutional government and the more or less artificial phraseology under which they are concealed' (35). Much of modern life also reflects what Marc Bloch described as the condition of the Middle Ages: 'Although men were not fully aware of the change, old names which were still on everyone's lips . . . slowly acquired connotations far removed from their original meaning' (36).

Fourth, despite a network of local governmental organisations, many complain that for many there is no real participation in politics. The Cubans, in their democratic period, told an American sociologist, Lowry Nelson, 'The government does not remember there are inhabitants living in this town except during elections' (37). Very often, democracies have failed to work out an adequate inter-relation between national and local politics. Local government often does not constitute the school of political training which it should (38), and it is no use telling somebody who wishes to influence, say, educational policy that he should stand for his local council. He knows that that policy, in almost every nation except the US, is centrally decided and financed.

Fifthly, there is no doubt but that the concept of one man and one woman each having a single vote often awakens, and fosters, a passion for equality which can never be satisfied, nor even properly defined, for, as, the Victorian Prime Minister, Lord Salisbury, was quite correct, to say, 'Political equality is not merely a folly — it is a chimera' (39), despite its generous citation in the American Declaration of Independence.

Then enormous public meetings commonly carry resolutions by acclamation or by general assent, whilst these same assemblies, as Robert Michels reminds us, 'if divided into small sections of fifty would be much more guarded' (40). The age of huge public meetings in democracies has declined, but congresses of parties and trade unions, 'demonstrations' and marches, sometimes allow crowd psychology to dictate policy; yet, as Lord Halifax put it in the late seventeenth century, the 'angry buzz of a multitude is one of the bloodiest noises in the world' (41). It was because of this that representative democracy is so superior to direct democracy.

Next, it is essential to notice that democratic legislatures, especially if they have only one chamber, can, in the heat of passion, constitute themselves a serious threat to liberty. 'The tyranny of the legislature is really the danger most to be feared,' wrote de Tocqueville (42), recalling the dictatorship which the National Convention had exercised in the French Revolution between 1792 and 1795, particularly when its powers were concentrated in the twelve members of the 'committee of public safety'. (When the constitution of 1795 was introduced in order to reestablish a semblance of predictable conduct, the most important change was that the legislature should have two chambers.)

Democracies have also given inadequate consideration to the fact that majorities can often exercise a tyranny over the minority: whereas the great object of all constitutional restrictions should plainly be to ensure that that does not happen (43). 'If the free institutions of America are destroyed,' wrote de Tocqueville again, 'that event may be attributed to the omnipotence of the majority, which may at some future time urge the minorities to defeatism' (43). The will of the greatest number is not as a rule the real, even if it is the legal, interpreter of all the people (44).

Doubtless Karl Popper was right to argue that it is 'wrong to blame democracy for the political shortcomings of a democratic state. We should rather blame ourselves' (45). But it plainly is equally correct that democracies have a tendency to be militarily weak. It is not easy for example, to persuade peace-loving people that such-and-such constitutes a threat to their liberty. This is one of the serious weaknesses of mass democracy as of limited democracy (46).

But the most important weakness of democracy is that its practitioners take it too much for granted, forgetting how recently democracy in any form has become current; how often democracies have been overthrown even in this century; and how the nervous representative democracy of the present mass society has a different pattern of behaviour both from that of the limited types of direct democracy practised in Greece, and from the oligarchic system of eighteenth century England, both of which inspire, by language and memory, present day systems.

Democracy has failed recently, for numerous reasons. Sometimes, the democratic politicians have been too inexperienced for, or even afraid of, command. Such was the provisional government in Russia in 1917 (47). Fatalism, optimism or diffidence characterised the democratic politicians in Spain in 1936. France and other Western European democracies collapsed in defeat in 1940. The fledgling democracies of Eastern Europe of 1945 were crushed because, in the course of the Second World War, Communism came to be regarded as a liberator from Germany, and no honest anti-Communist movement had time to emerge. Italy in 1922, and Germany in 1933, accepted Fascism and Nazism for fear of communist revolution; as well as in the hope of a national regeneration. Democracies in Latin America have usually been overthrown because their leaders have behaved extravagantly (such as President Goulart in Brazil) or invited parties to share power whose loyalty to democracy was, at least in the long run, doubtful (Chile in 1973; Guatemala in 1954). The overthrow of democracies has sometimes been the work of armies which have regarded themselves as somewhere between a safeguard for traditional values, and a focus for regeneration. Occasionally, though, democratic life has been successfully subverted by radical, revolutionary, or Communist parties, though most instances of that occurring have been in the shadow of prolonged wars, much as occurred after 1917 in Russia, or 1945 in Eastern Europe.

The process whereby democracy gives way to dictatorship has sometimes, in modern times, been as legal as it was in, say, 46–44 BC when Caesar established the empire in Rome. Caesar took over the government in Rome as leader of the democrats against conservative senators who, intimidated, gave him all the honours and offices he wanted – Dictator for Life, Imperator, the right to have a statue to himself named Demigod, the right to have coins in his name and so on (48). Equally, Hitler was asked to be Chancellor as leader of the largest party, and his Enabling Act, which gave him dictatorial powers, was passed by the Reichstag.

In the twentieth century, a certain part in the overthrow of democracies as of other régimes has been played by the conspiracies of other states. Thus the Bolsheviks in Russia received substantial money from Germany in the course of 1917 before mounting their *coup d'état* against the weak democracy established in March 1917: 'It wasn't until the Bolsheviks received from us a steady flow of funds through various channels that they were able to build up their propaganda effort,' wrote the senior diplomat, Kuhlmann, to the Kaiser (49). That method of conducting war by conspiracy has continued, but more often than not the covert use of international intervention has been a kind of scapegoat for inadequacy. Innumerable small states have to face the fact, though, that the decisive springs of their politics lie outside their own frontiers (50). Though they may claim to be independent and legally are so, modern weapons, technology, economics and communications make small states more dependent on large ones than ever before.

The failure of states to evolve any source of power beyond their own authority has been the chief cause of war. Nothing was more striking in 1914 than the contrast between the intelligent organisation of states within their borders and their failure beyond it. A few treaties on the conduct of war, or the treatment of prisoners, did not constitute an organisation. After 1919 and 1945, the League of Nations and United Nations were set up, as committees of victors in the preceding war. This idea was conceived in the Middle Ages by the Majorcan mystic, Ramon Lull: in *Blanquera*, written in 1280, he planned an organisation in which 'once a year, each power should come to a safe place whither all other powers should come likewise and there, after the manner of a chapter, they should hold discussion in all friendship and make correction each of the other . . . they that refused to abide by the decisions of the chapter should be fined' (51). The United Nations is a parliament of the world, with an unequal representation and no authority. It unfortunately now represents the collective sanctimoniousness of the world, not its piety. A few other international organisations collect statistics usefully. Since 1919, statesmen have met very often in private conferences. Whether those meetings have served any benefit seems doubtful. Nor is it clear how the organisation known as the European Economic Community will develop. At the moment, despite much generosity of thought, it recalls the Peace of Lodi (1454) between the Italian states. That treaty gave 'an appearance of confederation . . . but it failed as a general league of peace (52). Still, European institutions have been for the first time founded, weak though they still are; Europe to-day is less demoralised than the US is; a loose European union may well be achieved by the year 2000.

From time to time, pessimists predict the end of democracy once more, as if to suggest that the mass, or representative, democracy which many Western countries have been fortunate enough to experience during the last few generations is something comparable to the oligarchic democracies of Italy in the Middle Ages or the early ones of the classical age. But there is a very wide range of type. A presidential system, such as exists in the US, is a different matter from the parliamentary one of Britain and even the presidential system of the US differs, because of the role of the head of government in France, from the French system. What must strike the relaxed observer of such systems most, however, is the relative paucity of the variety of the undertakings concerned. The Eastern Mediterranean alone, for example, must have had, in the sixth century BC, more than the present thirty or so different democratic systems. They differed, too, substantially. No modern system experiments with those limitations on periods of power to, say, a year or even the weeks that marked mediaeval Italian states: and, indeed, to suggest that we might have anything to learn from such experiments is to invite ridicule. There are no two-headed systems, despite the increasing equality which the wife has with the husband in determining the business of the family in Western countries. Yet Rome had two annual consulships and even Sparta had two kings.

The life of politics has also increasingly become the life of political parties, now often seeming great new palaces of stone which often over-shadow the labyrinthine ways of the constitution which they were initiated to serve.

All this makes modern politics different from what it was in, say, the eighteenth century in England where, despite some suggestions to the contrary by nineteenth-century historians, who craved and indeed found intellectual lineage, there were only groups of friends united by common sentiment and the recollection of past loyalties. There were then neither in the Americas nor in Europe, large institutionalised parties as we know them.

In many respects, the struggle of parties has actually seemed at its most creative when actual representation was not at its fairest but, when, as in late nineteenth-century England, in the words of John Vincent, 'the ceremonies, processions, banners, posters, music, bands of "lambs" and supporters, colours, favours, and seating arrangements at the hustings, were much more a drama enacted about the life of the town . . . . than a means of expressing individual opinions about the matters of the day to which candidates confined themselves. . . . Elections were for the England of 1860 what drama, sport and literature have been for earlier and later times' (53).

Democracy thus became, more than any minor despotism achieved during the Italian Renaissance, a work of art: Burckhardt's phrase about Italian despotisms applies equally strongly to our modern systems, since modern democracies were conceived in most countries as 'a calculated conscious creation . . . . a work of art' (54).

Some of this spirit remains, particularly in the USA, sometimes in England, perhaps even in some new democracies such as Venezuela,* but much less in Europe now that ideological parties have become so well-established. In the US, politics remain much as they were in nineteenth-century England, if more flamboyant. The two parties of the USA since the Civil War have no clear ideological position. From being the party which lost the Civil War, the Democratic Party, founded by

---

* A brilliant creation of the 1960s, Venezuelan democracy has about it some elements of plutocracy, but it is a great achievement none the less, causing its architects, among them Rómulo Betancourt and Rafael Caldera, to merit their names carved in gold.

Jefferson, has matured to become a party more inclined towards collectivism, if led by rich men. The Republicans, who held the Union together in the 1860s, matured to become distrustful of the extension of the power of central government and, at the moment, more inclined towards a decisive international attitude. Essentially, though, both are powerful interest groups unrelated to doctrine, each of them being primarily organisations in which those who wish to play a part in public life can realise those ambitions, rather than serve as a method whereby a certain ideology can be put into practice.

Within most mass democracies, more ideological parties have taken shape. They have been primarily dedicated to the realisation of an idea. Most parties have allowed themselves to be influenced by the foolish nomenclature of Left and Right. Some believe that their long-term designs must be to enthrone a class, others to preserve a Church. The three most important of these groups are the Christian Democrats, socialists and communists. The first derived from a determination to ensure the role of the Christian religion in lay schools, and the role of the Church in a variety of ways (a corps of military chaplains being considered important in one country, a crucifix in state schools in others), but broadened to imply a general recognition of the Church's teaching: the life of the individual soul. Their organisation dates from before the Second World War, during which young Catholic laymen played an important part in the Resistance in France, Belgium and, to a lesser extent, Italy. Since then, these parties have played a decisive part in the political lives of Germany, Italy, France, Belgium, Chile and Venezuela, along with several other smaller countries. Unfortunately, in Italy, they have been corrupt.

The socialist movement is as widely represented. Its roots are partly in the nineteenth century's dream of a new society organised on a communal basis, partly reformist and progressive, partly, in England, non-conformist. Unresolved dilemmas remain: do socialists believe that, in the end, private enterprise should be abolished entirely, only differing, therefore, with Communists about the way that that ideal society is to be realised? Or do they hope for a society in which capitalism and state enterprise go hand in hand? Most socialist parties veer backwards and forwards, unsteadily but regularly, towards class consciousness and then back towards democratic politics. Nearly all now have a very superficial sense of international brotherhood, in practice in least, if not in theory. Few socialists, for example, seriously propose the equal distribution of all the wealth in the world. Instead, they seek to approach wealth on a national basis. The consequence of carrying out that recipe would be to create a series of rival monolithic states competing for the world's resources in a way which would make the competition of capitalists resemble an elegant minuet.

The decision of working class leaders in England, about 1895–1900, to think in terms of an independent party rather than to act through an existing one, either Liberal or Conservative, was a fateful step which altered the spirit of old English politics. The actual decision may have derived from a failure by the Conservatives 'to do anything about old age pensions,' as Robert Blake put it, but essentially the Labour leaders were then men who hoped to capture, not to destroy, the State as it then functioned and to cause it to work for the interests of the working class. Thus they could have no real collaboration with liberals, for whom the State seemed not the only, nor the best, institution for improving society. The growth of the English Labour movement can be compared with that of the Socialist party in the US, which failed to make any mark whatever on the old system. The chief reason for this is that, in the 1890s, the US was still a thrusting nation alive with opportunity and, as cynics would say, American politics, then as now, required a lot of money.

Before 1914, Socialists made little impact upon governments, though, in New Zealand, a Liberal-Labour government had been formed in 1890, and a French socialist (Alexandre Millerand) joined a coalition government in 1899. A 'Labour' government was also formed in Australia in 1904. The other Socialist parties busied themselves with discussions as to how far they should or should not take part in the existing political institutions, which, for a long time, they had despised. Most Socialist parties supported the First World War, all were divided by the Russian Revolution, and most split in consequence, between Communists who joined Lenin's Third Communist International, and 'Socialists' who, though in theory dedicated to the same long term cause, wished to achieve it by democratic politics. The experience of the latter effected changes in most socialist parties and, in the 1970s, the Socialist parties of Spain, France, Germany (and Britain), with similar groups in smaller democracies, all declare that they represent a collective approach to be determined by democratic methods.* The connection which all of them have with trade unions is a complication which, despite appearances, seems unlikely to be to their benefit in the long run. Some democratic socialist leaders become, in the end, as hostile to change as formerly they were in favour of it, 'coming to regard the functions which they exercise,' said Robert Michels 'as theirs by inalienable right' (55).

Communists are well organised in several democracies, particularly in Italy, France, Spain and Portugal. In some other democracies, they have more the character of conspiracies within the trade union organisations than of political parties. All these parties were founded in the

---

* The question whether this form of humane socialism is a mirage is now a critical one in almost all democracies. On balance, it seems that either the humanity or the socialism will have to be modified. The difficulty about modifying the socialism is that such a modification always seems, or can be made to seem, a betrayal of principle.

months following the Russian Communists' *coup d'état* in 1917 and have paid the Russian government a subservience only comparable to the Russians' attitude to the Tartars. Apparently 'moderate' policies and competence in managing municipal councils have, however, enabled Italian Communists to appear as an equivalent of the Democratic party in the US, or of the English Liberal party in the nineteenth century. But the communists everywhere still seem slaves to one part of Marx's and Lenin's ideology, if not to its totality; as Oliver Goldsmith wondered: why should we believe that men who are themselves slaves to a theory 'would preserve our freedoms if they should chance to conquer us?' (56). The idea of democratic communism anyway seems as improbable as roast icicles (Solzhenitsyn's phrase) and, even though we live in an age of absurdities, and the unexpected has almost always happened, no guarantee exists that modern communists would act democratically (or be able to) should they gain a position of authority in Europe.

The oldest organised political party is the Conservative party in England. Though its present structure, with branches and committees, dates only from the 1830s (57), and though some even suggest, ascetically, that 1846 should mark its real beginning (58), a genealogy of this association can be traced to Pitt the Younger and Burke, at the time of the French Revolution, if not to Dr Johnson, Bolingbroke and before. The constitutional principle which Burke evolved, and which later both Benjamin Disraeli and Lord Salisbury echoed, was to recognise that change was inevitable (and, therefore, no ideal state could be achieved) but that the test of a good policy was how far the change concerned could be articulated within an accepted series of rules or a constitutional frame. Lord Salisbury put it thus: referring to crusades such as Communism, he said that all such 'rest on the false assumption that there is a final and ideal state of affairs in politics which can be aimed at and then fixed. There is not. The spirit of innovation must always exist' (59). For Raymond Aron, conservatism is intended 'to prevent the decomposition of eternal moral values' (60). For others, it is to revive them; for others still it is to-day again what it was in the days of Sir Robert Peel: to free industry and society generally from the shackles which have grown up round it during an age of war, crisis and ignorant 'planning'.*

It is easy to contrast this party with a more anti-constitutional view more prevalent on the continent of Europe where the peaceful transition from landowners' rule to democracy was more difficult: no English (or US) conservative, however extreme, would ever have gained applause (as a German conservative did) if he announced firmly, 'The King of Prussia . . . must always be in a position where he can say to any lieutenant: "Take ten men and shoot the parliament" ' (61).

* 'Only if the state's role in our society is kept to modest dimensions, will respect for it be combined with respect for the large number of private associations which contribute so much to the stability and richness of a society,' said the present leader of the British conservative party in 1978 (62).

50

Democracy: Internal Anxieties, I

Two further troubles affect the working of democracies. The first is the power of 'overmighty' institutions or associations which have arrogated to themselves corporate power and anyway seem to have the attributes of a state within a state. One good example of this is the power gained by trade unions. These organisations are very much in the forefront of debate in politics in some countries, but the immediacy of the problems which they seem to pose should not prevent a historical meditation.

Different gatherings of workers are among the oldest form of civil organisation. For example, in India under the Maurya empire, in the third century BC, most artisans worked in guilds, such organisations being to avoid the expense of working alone. As the centuries passed, in a static community dominated by castes, guilds in India assumed many habits which were comparable to modern trade unions. They not only fixed rules of work, quality and prices but arranged professional education. The behaviour of members was controlled through guild courts, customary usage had the force of law, while, since children almost always followed their father's professions, guilds could be sure of new blood. Guilds, were not, it seems, very political but they patronised artists, they had property, they acted as bankers and trustees in a modest way (1). In different ways, and, perhaps in emulation of Indian methods, guilds were found later in nearly every mercantile city, under Rome and in mediaeval Europe. In Rome, for example, there were trade associations of every sort – bakers, tally clerks, stevedores, firefighters, bargees, carters, masons, lime burners (2).

Guilds operated, to a great extent, as friendly societies, often taking responsibility for the cost of burying their members or recompensing their losses by fire. They established 'rules of the game' in unpromising circumstances, insisted upon honourable conduct, sought fair conditions, and established codes for apprentices – as a rule providing that no one should enter a trade without several years' apprenticeship, that stage to be followed by one as a 'journeyman' in search of work. By the eighteenth century most guilds — and this seems to have been so throughout the world — were like those in Spain, in Richard Herr's words, 'closed monopolies of master craftsmen, hampering the introduction of new methods and of self made men, and insisting on the minute specification of the nature of processes and products' (3)*. As seen earlier, the guild in the English wool trade had been both particularly strong and particularly hostile to innovation. Hence the technological changes of the eighteenth century affected cotton before they affected wool. One reason for the relatively late date of the industrial revolution in Germany, was, no doubt, the power of the guilds there (4).

The political transformations of the years between 1780 and 1832 damaged guilds in most of Europe beyond repair. Populations moved to cities such as Manchester where there were no civic traditions. Apprenticeships collapsed. Some old skilled crafts tried to keep certain rules for admission but, except among a very few (naval engineers and cabinet makers, for example), these attempts were usually defeated by mechanisation (5). By 1900, only builders, stone masons and printers even maintained a semblance of apprenticeship, chiefly for the benefit of their sons. At much the same time, serfdom was also finally abolished throughout Europe. Thus a unique situation prevailed. For the first time almost in history, the richest continent had both a swiftly growing population and almost no restrictions on its use for labour either of a feudal or any other form. Sir John Clapham pointed out that, in France as elsewhere on the continent of Europe, the revolutionary legislators had 'one common and keen desire for industry: to rid those who directed it from the surviving mediaeval restrictions and excesses of official control. They abolished the half decayed guilds and cut down state interference.' But, he added, 'problems of the wage contract' hardly interested them (6). In addition, the efforts to regulate wages previously made by governments, since the Black Death at least, had largely been discontinued.

However, there were already in being various organisations or clubs of journeymen which had been founded partly for social reasons, partly for mutual insurance. These 'friendly societies' flourished in the eighteenth century, and were specifically protected by governments. Already, in the eighteenth century, the verb 'to strike' work (as in striking or bringing down, a sail) had begun to be used, while the historian of the English trade union movement, Henry Pelling, detects a combination to raise wages among the journeymen feltmakers in the 1690s, in the woolcombers of Tiverton around 1700, the knitters of London in 1710, the journeyman tailors in the 1720s, and the weavers of Somerset at much the same time (7). These were held to be illegal but, as in almost every law on the subject until this day, that had little effect in

* Most guilds in Spain were founded after 1530.

preventing them. There were strikes by silkweavers in 1763, and by colliers and miners in Newcastle several times about that time (8). Vast numbers of small clubs were founded, often linked with similar ones in other forms. Thus, in the mid-eighteenth century, the 'Union Society of Journeyman Brushmakers' had a network of clubs up and down the country, undertaking to give hospitality for a day to any member 'on the tramp', that is an unemployed labourer who had set off on foot to seek work. All these clubs were, however, normally limited to those who had served their apprenticeship though there were exceptions made for sons of members. Most of them were in a skilled craft. Though it is hard to find any equivalent for these bodies on anything like the English scale elsewhere, there were also similar undertakings in the US, even during colonial days, particularly in Philadelphia and New York among, as usual, printers and shoemakers. Such activity was modest because of the slaves and the large number of indentured servants – according to Richard Hofstadter, probably half the white immigrants in the US till 1750 were such – who worked for four or five years in bondage on several hard tasks, such as clearing land. These men, from Germany and Holland as well as Britain, travelled to, and worked in, conditions barely better or, as some thought, worse, than those of slaves (9).

The history of these associations was transformed by, first, the coming of the factory and, second, the French Revolution. The factories, as has been seen, demanded disciplined work. Both work and meals were begun by bells. Foremen and managers ruled their new and, in the beginning, young labour force with iron discipline. Many workers hated the new conditions, regretting the days when they worked at home or in the manufacturer's house (10). From the beginning of factory life, the larger numbers made possible more violent clashes in times of dispute – as, indeed, had been the case in sugar mills in the West Indies. Thus, as early as 1787, the manufacturers of muslin in Glasgow tried to take advantage of a temporary glut of labour by cutting wages. The workers combined and refused to work for less than a minimum sum. Employers who refused were boycotted. Many organisations to maintain wages in succeeding years were founded all over Europe and small manufacturers – iron workers, knife grinders, papermakers, hatters – also formed combinations because they were afraid of mechanisation. Similar movements were founded in the US, though, since most early cotton factory workers were women and children, those were largely outside the factory system. They were directed against merchants more than employers. Merchants seemed in the US to be reducing both master and journeyman to a single, common level (11).

The coincidence of the French Revolution with these events was an accident, but its outbreak had an electrifying effect in an England already beset by early labour troubles and awakening political resentments of every sort. Frightened that labour troubles might turn into revolution, the British government, for example, in 1799 passed an Act forbidding workers to combine to gain higher wages or shorter hours, with William Wilberforce, the friend of the slaves in the West Indies, taking a prominent part in support. The aim was essentially to make the Royal Proclamation on the subject earlier in the century more effective. The Act was followed by another marking the beginning of new arrangements 'to settle disputes which arise between masters and workmen engaged in cotton manufacture' (12). Neither of these Acts was fully applied. Thousands of combinations survived. Plans were made to form general unions of workers, particularly in Lancashire. Trade and labour clubs were formed which, their organisers claimed, were not specifically combinations to raise wages. Sentences under the Combination Acts were generally mild: three months' gaol or two months' hard labour (13). No one knew how the government should respond to these new movements. In 1812, the law officers were asked to advise about the proposed congress of the illegal woolcombers' union. 'These combinations are mischievous and dangerous,' they said, 'but it is very difficult to know how to deal with them.' So nothing was done (14). In 1824, the Tory government of the day repealed all the old legislation and permitted free combinations in the name of the free market: Sir Robert Peel said 'Men who have . . . no property except their manual skill and strength ought to be allowed to confer together . . . for the purpose of determining at what rate they will sell their labour' (15). The following year, magistrates were permitted to appoint mixed panels of masters and men from which parties would choose referees to decide on the fair wage. If there were no settlement, the magistrates themselves would give an award.

This series of interacting laws, with subsequent modifications, provided the basis for the British trade union system, though few existing unions trace their history to any body of that day. Endless devices were introduced in the course of the nineteenth century to fix wages, usually locally. In Wolverhampton, for instance, in the 1860s, there were permanent arbitration agreements and acceptance of arbitration was part of the wage contract. Sometimes, as in Durham, in the late 1870s, sliding scales were introduced to keep wages indexed to prices (16).

These details of labour problems in the early industrial age remind the reader that the labour problems of the late twentieth century do not represent much of a novelty. Nearly all the difficulties of our day were faced by our great-grandfathers, with the major differences, however, that far fewer people were implicated, that the differences between rich and poor were far greater, and that the majority of the populations concerned were poor.

In countries other than Britain much the same pattern developed, always a little differently, and usually later. The early labour demands in the US were more political than those in Europe in that they included a demand for free schools, the end of gaol for debt, and less expensive courts. The clearcut distinction between employer and employee only returned gradually in the US since, in the colonial era, most articles were produced at home. In those circumstances, there were no arguments over prices. But in the US as elsewhere, printers played an important part early on and, indeed, formed the first national union (17). In France, in 1848, the individual worker still had not become a factory hand. He still had an excellent chance of becoming a master craftsman. Until 1868, the *Code Civil* established by Napoleon stipulated that the master's word should be decisive in courts of law when a question arose over wages. The *Code Penal* equally forbade both combinations and picketing. Indeed, a law of 1803 instituted a pass book *(livret)*, in which a workman had to have his employer's name inscribed. No one could be hired unless the history included therein was satisfactory. Napoleon wished to restore old apprenticeships too, since they were so plainly good for political control but, though he did not legislate for that, the old *compagnonnages* of trained artisans continued till half way through the century, when the idea of those peripatetic brotherhoods was ruined by railways (18). But printers in Paris organised friendly societies and, by the Second Empire, there were already the bases for a trade union movement, despite the power of the *patronat*. In Germany, by 1848, journeymen were beginning to call themselves *arbeiter* (workmen), and to make demands, for, for example, a twelve hour day, a minimum wage, and the right to travel where they wanted through Germany. Collective bargaining was particularly slow to be adopted in Germany since employers were reluctant to abandon the old relationship between master and man (19). Spanish union organisations were much delayed too, despite much political agitation from 1808 onwards. But the protests of the 1830s against, for instance, an increase in the size of cloth pieces, because the workers were paid by the piece, were more a recollection of mediaeval protests in the cloth trade than a foretaste of modern industrial disputes (20).

A few co-operative associations began, however, to be founded: for example, the society for the mutual protection of cotton workers, founded in 1840. In 1855, Spain had its first modern strike, over a demand for a legal right of association and, in 1861, a number of Andalusian workers demanded the division of the large estates. Rafael Pérez del Alamo, a vet from Loja, took direct action in a way characteristic of later Spanish working-class endeavours and conquered the valley of Iznájar and established a 'republic of the poor' there for a few weeks. By 1864, the workers were tacitly permitted to organise at least in the then only important industrial region, Catalonia, and a large number of friendly societies were soon founded (21).

These early years of trade union movements usually had some kind of political colouring, particularly on the continent of Europe, simply because they were illegal. But they were not primarily political movements. They were, on one level, ahe workers themselves, in the absence of either a feudal system or a modern state, to establish a countervailing power to the force which they found industrial capitalism to represent. But, they represented also a desire for professional organisation to replace the guilds in a state of affairs where, in Britain, the US and much of Europe, people could, by the 1860s, for the first time in history, follow whatever trade they desired (22).

The history of trade unions since the 1860s can be briefly summarised. First, in free countries, they have increased in numbers so as to represent in the 1970s something between 20%* and 50%† of the work force, and their good organisation in key industries and discipline generally places them at an advantage over an unorganised multitude of individuals. Thus France may have only 25% of its members of the labour force in unions in the 1970s, but those unions are still exceptionally powerful. Both world wars, incidentally, of the twentieth century, stimulated union membership almost everywhere: in the First World War, the American Federation of Labour doubled its membership and, in the Second, union membership increased from 9 to 15 millions (25). Meantime, almost everywhere, the old functions of unions as 'friendly societies' concerned with funerals, sick pay, compensation for injury, superannuation, have vanished as those activities have been taken over by the state.

The tactics of trade unions have changed. Though the phrase to be 'in union', had for a time a half-sacred meaning to those who used it of themselves, from about 1880, the chief means of protest of labour unions has been the 'strike'. The 1880s and 1890s saw in all industrialised countries a tidal wave of violent and harsh withdrawals of labour. There were the great British dock strike of 1880, the first big miners' strike in Britain of 1892, and the strike of the British Post Office clerks of 1891. There were the rail strike in the US of 1877, the US steel workers' strike of 1892, the Pullman car strike of 1894, and the US anthracite coal strike of 1902; and strikes of the vineyard workers in France and in the harvest followed (26). There were great dock strikes in Australia. Even in Russia, there was a general strike in the port of Odessa in 1903, and others in that year in Baku and Rostov-on-Don. Railwaymen in Russia – as noticed earlier – struck during the early stages of the revolution of 1905 (27). In the years before 1914, throughout Europe and the US, says Sir John Clapham, 'loss of work through industrial warfare became normal': miners, transport workers, railwaymen, woodmen, champagne vineyard workers (in France), mushroom pickers, became

*In the US (23).
† In Britain (24).

engaged in a series of long and often brutal battles in which States as a rule, in difficult moments, sought to hold open 'essential services' and so really sided with employers (at that time, most essential services were in private hands) (28). The First World War brought this era to an end, trade unionists as a whole fought the national enemy with much greater ferocity than they had fought employers, while their leaders, as socialists, joined cabinets. After 1918, strikes resumed. The strikes in Italy in 1919 to 1920 helped to bring the Fascists to power: a socialist paper, indeed, blamed the 'devaluation of the mighty weapon of the strike' and the 'stupid and ruinous ranting of the irresponsible', for the conditions which led to the march on Rome (29). Very violent strikes and inter-union warfare helped to lead to the *coup d'état* of Primo de Rivera in Spain in 1923. In England, the miners' strike of 1926 (leading to a general strike), the US steel strike of September 1919 and the US General Motors strike of 1937 were formidable challenges (30).

These struggles were particularly violent when, as was almost always the case before 1914, unions had limited reserves, and no charitable assistance was given by the State to strikers or their families. That meant that, to be successful, a strike had to be short, sharp, intimidatory and damaging. Those conditions changed after the Second World War. In many countries, unions became richer and invested cleverly and heavily in shares. In most free countries, unions abandoned any thought of being instruments of revolution and became permanently concerned with better benefits.* In other states, the state's munificence extended to strikers and their families a measure of financial support to prevent return to work out of misery and starvation. The deliberate advocacy of a general strike to paralyse society and ensure of all means of production to the workers, such as advocated by Eugene Debs in the US or anarcho-syndicalists in Spain, was always the tactic of a minority: it is today the policy of a fraction within the minority, though often a well-organised one.

Thirdly, there has been a movement towards centralisation of the labour unions. A British trades union congress was formed in 1870, to which most large unions soon affiliated. Large unions, as a rule, such as, in England the Amalgamated Society of Engineers (founded in 1851), the boilermakers (which though founded in the 1830s, expanded greatly in the 1870s) or the coalminers (whose union developed greatly in the 1860s), became larger and larger, and sought to absorb smaller associations. Just as the First World War increased combinations in banks and railways and large companies, so too it increased combinations among unions (31). As a rule, all these developments were a

---

* The true significance of the wave of strikes in the winter of 1978–79 in Britain against the background of which this book has been concluded is surely that the British unions have abandoned any desire even for a privileged moral position in the nation and have joined the American unions in revelling in their place as a powerful pressure group.

response to what had happened among companies, but they were none the less critical. The American Federation of Labour was one of the real victors of the First World War and, though their numbers temporarily declined afterwards, they remained the dominant voice in American labour. Despite those changes, making for concentration, in many countries the old patterns of rivalries and interactions, between those who were, or regarded themselves as, superior within a particular industry, which became evident in the nineteenth century, remained to dog the twentieth.

While unions became bigger, the role of those who ran branches became more and more important. Hence, for example, the conversion in England of shop stewards from being minor officials into major spokesmen of rank and file (32).

While these tendencies to concentration have occurred in all countries, every country except perhaps Germany (where the movement was refounded from the bottom after the war) has experienced innumerable anomalies in the method of organising their unions, some countries having primarily craft unions (as in Britain), unions which have taken in all skills (for example, the Knights of Labour in the US), unions which seek to organise all workers in a given industry, or politically motivated ones. These anomalies have given rise to some of the worst disputes. In the USA, for instance, there is no logical reason why persons should be members of one or other of the large trade union movements of the US. The CIO, the Congress of Industrial Organisations, broke away from the A F of L in 1935 because it wished to organise workers on an individual basis in mass-production factories, but it would be very difficult to make such a precise definition of the differences today.

Fourth, there has been a steady growth in trade union law. Lord Randolph Churchill saw the shape of things to come when he asserted: 'Our land laws were framed by the landed interest for the advantage of the landed interest. . . . We are now come . . . to a time when labour laws will be made by the labour interest for the advantage of labour' (33).

Thus, after some years of argument, a bill was introduced in 1906 by a British Liberal government which declared that 'an action against a trade union, either of workmen or masters, in respect of any tortious act alleged to have been committed on behalf of the trade union shall not be entertained by any court'. The bill in effect placed the trade unions in a privileged position at law. A 'scandal to the lawyers', as the great French historian Elie Halévy put it, it became law without serious opposition (34). The consequences began to seem anomalous or wrong, however, when the unions grew in strength and wealth (35). Equally, that same Trades Disputes Act of 1906 confirmed that people could seek 'peacefully to persuade any person from working' – a provision which has subsequently led to acrimony.*

These changes have been limited to Britain. In no other country is there a legal insulation for trade unions in this manner. For example, courts of law in the US have annulled many labour laws there as infringements of the constitution. Till about 1900, US courts even held that laws which specified fixed hours of work were unconstitutional. The US courts refused to uphold legislation banning 'yellow dog' contracts — by which workers agreed not to join a union while in the employment of the company concerned. Subsequently, a great deal of discussion has continued in the US (and elsewhere) on the subject of the so-called 'closed shop', an aim of unions in the US since the mid nineteenth century though declared illegal. The Supreme Court in the US declared that no worker can be compelled to join a particular union and to obey its rules. But there are instances, nevertheless, of 'union shops' in which all employed people are automatically members of unions and have to pay fees even if they do not have to accept the union's instructions (36). Meantime, both in the US and elsewhere, certain trade unions have arrogated to themselves the right on occasion to set up special courts from which there is no satisfactory appeal. Those 'kangaroo' courts are a breach of the 'Rule of Law' but they have nevertheless lasted a long time and reflect some similar managerial practices.

The legal position of unions is one of the most acute problems of the late twentieth century. The problem which these labour organisations pose within democracies is a severe one, since the organisers of unions first arrogate to themselves a role as the first, private protector of as many members of the labour force as they can, as a replacement of the Church, or lord in the age of agriculture; and, secondly, increasingly seek to influence both policy within the industry concerned and legislation within the State. Such actions may have benefits for workers, though that is far from certain. But it is difficult to see that such syndicalism can be combined with representative democracy. Whatever happens, unions pose a threat to that concept. Either the unions will take over the State; or the State, in having to assert itself against the unions, may have to risk a form of authoritarian direction – for example by using an army to guarantee essential services on a permanent basis.

Unions have also had a long history of opposition to innovations in technology, particularly in the printing industry, but also elsewhere. Since 1945, when unions have had more power than ever, and automation has opened innumerable possibilities of changes in methods of work, this too has become one of the most complicated of questions. Very often, the unions have seemed less the revolutionaries which the

---

* The Act owed its origin to a strike of railwaymen in the Taff Vale, in the Glamorgan coalfields. The strike was carried out in opposition to the wishes of the railwaymen's leaders. The colliery then sued the union for damages, and won, had the judgement reversed on appeal, but reaffirmed in the House of Lords.

words they use sometimes proclaim them still to be than the arch-
enemies of change. They are also rather disinclined as a rule to give a
substantial place to women. No female labour leader seems yet to have
arisen anywhere, and unions have never put equal pay between men
and women for equal work very high on their list of priorities.

Then, as the pattern of employment has changed, so has the character
of trade unions to include not only simple men in heavy industry but
also those in trade and clerical work, and even professional and public
service. In the US in 1900, clerical or office workers numbered 15% of all
workers. In 1970, they numbered 40% and the percentage is growing.
That is a trend also becoming evident elsewhere (37). Senior diplomats
even have a union in Britain – an astonishing misuse of the original
purpose of trade unions.

The achievements of unions are, perhaps, a little hard to chart firmly.
Certainly wages have risen, hours of work have fallen, conditions of
work have improved and, in some countries such as the US, as has been
noticed, the labour unions have exerted effective pressure on governments and councils to introduce free education. Even so, wages among
workers who have never been in unions (such as, for example, the
special case of domestic servants) have also grown (and the hours of
work also fallen) and most successful employers realised long ago that
good conditions are an incentive to work and to keeping good
workmen. Wages also grew in the nineteenth century before unions
were properly organised. They have undoubtedly risen in countries
such as Spain or Russia, between 1945 and 1975, which did not have
free trade unions; and wages have grown as fast in the US with its low
proportion of workers in unions as in any other country. One of the
main problems of the industrial age has been chronic unemployment. It
is not at all evident that unions have made much of a contribution there.

Most people who have joined unions have, of course, done so in
order to benefit, as they suppose, from the system based upon wages
and free enterprise rather than to destroy it. Unions which have been
opposed to the wage system have failed particularly absolutely in the
US, where the American Federation of Labour (AF of L), founded about
1886, by Sam Gompers, has now been, for nearly a hundred years, in a
dominant but politically aseptic place (38).

The part of unions in the poorer, or less advanced, world has as a
rule, been as much the history of collaboration with, as of challenges to,
the often unrepresentative régimes in power. The Cuban case is instructive. In the 1880s, when Cuba was still a Spanish colony, numerous
friendly societies were formed. By 1900, many of these had been converted into semi-anarchist clubs in touch with Spain. The anarchist connection continued till the 1920s and rendered those unions ineffective,
though there were some very serious strikes. In the late 1920s, the

Communists captured most of the more powerful unions, led them in a revolution in 1933 and, in the late 1930s, secured their legalisation. For ten years, between 1938 and 1948, in a country in which probably nearly 25% of its working population was in one union or another, the Communists secured a large number of social benefits such as reduced hours of work, government arbitration in the workers' favour in wages disputes, holidays with pay, and so on. But as a result, probably, of the cold war, the Cuban unions were split in 1948 into two, and the larger non-communist union movement not only dominated labour for ten more years but became associated with the corrupt and, latterly, tyrannical régime. When Castro came to power, the unions were easily taken over by the government and subsequently, as in all communist régimes, were, in effect, a ministry of labour conceived to put into effect governmental policies rather than represent the employed population. Many other less politically advanced countries now have unions of the same model that Cuba had after 1948: powerful, sectarian, corrupt.

Politics has, of course, affected unions in advanced countries too. 'Socialism' was a word apparently coined about 1830 and used, to begin with, by French intellectuals. Between then and 1848, there were innumerable schemes for ideal forms of reorganising society in the interests of workers. Some of those ideas had roots in the French Revolution, the English Revolution of the seventeenth century or mediaeval dreams of social regeneration. But there was a difference in the mid-nineteenth century in that a great many intellectuals were anxious to persuade workers' movements, or to organise them, to take up such concepts and to abandon humdrum efforts to improve living standards. Similar ideas were contributed in Spain, Germany, in Britain and in the United States, though usually with little reference to each other. In the United States, indeed, Robert Owen and others had tried unsuccessfully to establish socialist colonies in Indiana and Massachusetts. In 1848, socialists played a definite, if modest, part in the revolutions of that year and, in 1864, an attempt was made to bring these ideas together in London at a discussion, after which the 'First International' association of working men was founded. That fledgling organisation was specifically a revolutionary one.

At subsequent meetings in various cities of Europe, representatives from more and more countries gathered to discuss both tactics and aims. Should land after the revolution be divided up or farmed by the community? How would industrial collectivism work? Did terrorism have a part to play? And so on. The organiser of these gatherings was Karl Marx, the German polemicist who then lived in London.

During the course of these discussions two distinct trends of thought developed: first, that which led to the formation of the anarchist movement and dominated the early stages of trade unions in Spain and South America; and second, that which led to 'social democracy' which in turn later divided into the movements known as Socialism and Communism. The first broad stream of thought believed that it was desirable and possible to destroy the state as it then existed at an early date and proceed to establish a millenarian society organised on a temporary and amateur basis by the good, with the support of a benign public opinion. The second school argued that that was over-idealistic and that, anyway in the early stages of setting up an ideal socialist state, it would be necessary to maintain a powerful, even a dictatorial, bureaucracy. The first school was led by the Russian anarchist Mikhail Bakunin, a dreamer of genius of aristocratic family, and the second by Marx. Personal rivalry, as usual in politics, heightened and sharpened the ideological differences between the two. In the end, the International collapsed. Anarchists have been quarrelling bitterly with the subsequently more powerful socialists and communists ever since.

Within a generation or so, these idealistiv views had been solidified into institutions which had a hold over most labour movements. In Spain, the largest such organisation was anarchist in its inspiration and that vision of tactics and goal was shared by the few trade unionists of Latin America. Elsewhere, anarchists were few and far between, though their conversion to violence – by the 'propaganda of the deed' – had made their presence known everywhere after their murder of President McKinley in the US, the Empress Elizabeth of Austria, and several Spanish prime ministers and Russian archdukes. Their plan was to destroy the apparatus of the state and to establish a world of self-supporting communes possibly linked by a statistical apparatus. In theory, they agreed on this matter with Marx and with the socialists or the communists, but the anarchists did not believe that the revolution should aim at 'a bourgeois revolution' (as the communists in theory did) and did not think it desirable to maintain a strong state until the real communist world could be introduced. The anarchist movement rejected politics as 'leading to nothing good' (39). 'The political idea,' said a Spanish anarchist, Anselmo Lorenzo, in Barcelona in 1869, 'whatever the party may be which professes it, is born out of the sphere of privilege' (40). 'To be governed,' wrote the French revolutionary, Proudhon, who inspired many anarchists, 'is to be watched, inspected, spied upon, directed, law-driven, numbered, regulated, enrolled, indoctrinated, preached at, controlled, checked, estimated, valued, censured, commanded by creatures who have neither the right nor the wisdom nor the virtue to do so . . .' (41). Such ideas would now find an echo among *poujadist* shopkeepers, tax rebels in California and Denmark, and perhaps businessmen and others who would prefer the state's role to be the minimal one 'limited to the narrow functions of protection against force, theft, fraud, and enforcement of contracts' (42), but anarchists disputed the need even for those things. Finally, anarchists hearkened back, like many early socialists, to the self-sufficiency of the mediaeval village, in which, as happened in England as else-where, 'the people control their own affairs, and the daily incidents of their work, by a scheme of voluntary administration, maintained by public opinion, without recourse to the law of the land, and without the expenditure of a single penny . . . whereas latter-day villagers could do no more than cast a vote' (43). Most trade unionists in Spain about 1914 maintained views of this sort, especially in the industrially advanced region of Catalonia and the politically restless and poor agricultural region of Andalusia. But they were always a minority of the labour force (if a very vocal and militant one) and a small socialist movement also existed.

Elsewhere in Europe, social democrats, as the Marxists called them-selves at that time, were dominant. Large and well-organised labour movements on those lines had been founded almost everywhere, always powerful in large and cohesive industries, such as mines and railways, but always somewhat divided as to whether or no to take an active political part in the usually rather oligarchic democratic system and whether or not to negotiate on wages, conditions, hours and so on with employers: for such negotiations would naturally mean parleying with the 'class enemy'. In the end, most of these movements did take part in politics and did negotiate, where they could. In 1914, the German Social Democratic party was the largest one in the German Empire, even if the structure of that system prevented it from gaining any power. French socialists had already been in the government. An Austrian socialist was mayor of Vienna. Several Spanish socialists (as opposed to anarchists) were members of Parliament. The Russian social democrats, divided though they were between Bolsheviks and Menshe-viks, were members of the Duma. Through all these parties, there were rifts and arguments, as to how far it was possible to revise the ideas of Marx in the light of changing circumstances; and, in some of them a new kind of political culture, already a sort of 'counter community', in the phrase of Annie Kriegel, already existed as a challenge to 'bour-geois' society (44) – or, as some thought, a utopia so well cushioned against change that nobody felt any need for a Revolution.

A little to one side in this movement were the British, the British imperial and the United States' labour organisations. Except for the, by 1914, declining Knights of Labour in the US, and a few enthusiasts in Britain, labour movements in those countries were primarily concerned with improving conditions within an existing constitutional system, not revolution. In the US, a small socialist party was making no headway at all, thanks, according to Werner Sombart, the German student of labour movements, to the already existing concept that the people were already in power, that the USA was already egalitarian, that the Ameri-can's chances of rising from his class were greater than they were else-where, and that the US standard of living was already high: 'all socialist utopias came to nothing on roast beef and apple pie' (45).

Though no one could say that Edwardian England was egalitarian, there is a sense in which England was also more homogeneous, proud of its constitutional evolution and less bitter than continental Europe. At all events, the Labour Representation Committee founded in 1901 had become, by 1914, very much like a third parliamentary party, democratic in habit and outlook, even if its constitutional position as the 'parliamentary wing of the trade union movement' made it a little anomalous.

The history of labour movements in the world wars and as political parties has been touched upon elsewhere. In both conflicts, on both sides, the advanced countries became used to the idea that, in certain circumstances, normal union activities could be suspended along with other 'basic rights and privileges'. The attraction of a fully regulated society has since then never ceased to interest reformers, particularly when faced by the new and unforeseen problem of how to adjust wages and salaries in nationalised industries and services. But no such regulated society has yet been achieved, save in war, in free societies. Indeed, the idea is a contradiction in terms: a fully regulated society is the negation of freedom. Today, there are roughly three forms of union: those such as dominate the US and Germany and exist almost everywhere in the free society and are primarily still concerned with material improvements; secondly, those which also occur almost everywhere and dominate the unions in France, Spain and Italy and which are primarily concerned, at least in the long run, to establish a communist society, perhaps already positing some prefigurement of that in the way that they run railways and municipal councils (46); and third, those which exist in Sweden, Israel, perhaps in Britain and also have some followers more or less everywhere and would like to see the union organisation itself as a kind of pre-enactment of or precursor of a new, syndicalist and collectivist society.

This attitude of mind has itself had a long history by now. In the 1830s, in England there were those who were already claiming that 'the unions themselves could solve the problem of political power' and that 'a parliament of the industrious classes could be formed delegated directly from workshops and mills' (47). But this last school of thought, though it has been endlessly embroidered, is not one which, as a rule, seems likely to lead to innovation or enterprise. Schemes for workers' participation in industry as a rule propose a series of measures which tend to institutionalise private firms, not rejuvenate them. One child of 'Guild socialism' was Fascism. Some hoped, in the 1860s, that limited liability might lead to a new type of company, in which worker and capitalist might start to share both profits and risks. Some co-operative mills were established. But the wage earners who were also shareholders unfortunately ceased to look upon themselves as wage earners as soon as they could. Others who stayed where they were put shares into banks, building societies, and other enterprises in order to spread their risks (48).

Yet workers' co-operatives such as those founded in the 1950s at Mondragón in the Basque country still do offer a good chance of a new form of industrial life, providing, however, that they stand on their own feet; do not expect assistance or favours from the state; and offer the opportunity of turning workers into capitalists. The trouble with existing unions is that such laudable aims often seem heretical to them*.

It would, of course, be wrong to suppose that the organisations described in the preceding chapter are characteristic of the labour arrangements in all countries in the twentieth century. Thus, in a large number of countries with strong governments, fascist and communist alike, trade union systems have been devised which bear a slight similarity to free democratic ones, in name and style, but are, in fact, merely departments within the ministry of labour. Their fine-sounding names, and their attempts to be accepted on their own evaluation by trade unions in free countries, are good examples of hypocrisy paying tribute to what it itself knows to be a juster, if more disorderly organisation. England has evolved a trade union structure which is 'the merest chaos', in the words of G. D. H. Cole (50) but it is one which is at least technically susceptible of reform. Equally, those strong governments which seem, at the time of writing, to be in no immediate danger of collapse, have also drawn on huge numbers of their citizens to work as prisoners on one large project after another. Pious discussions of working conditions, hours of work and even payment are quite out of place in considering such systems. They are referred to sometimes as 'slave labour' camps but the conditions of work in sugar mills of the eighteenth century in the West Indies or on cotton plantations of the nineteenth in the US would doubtless seem paradisaical to those whose job was to build the White Sea Canal. If, in the future, liberal historians survive to write about the labour conditions of the twentieth century, they will concentrate upon these Russian waterworks as Gibbon emphasised the evil rule of the Byzantine emperor Constantine V or the Roman Domitian.

Meanwhile, in the West, the question of conditions in early industrial

* The experiment known by the name of Mondragón is a network of industries, agricultural projects and marketing businesses in which all the workers hold a stake. They have received no governmental assistance; there are no trade unionists; and there are no strikes. Within 20 years, they have established factories which are among the leaders in Spanish exports of machine tools, washing machines and other domestic objects. Every worker invests the equivalent of £1,000 in the enterprise and expects to take out ten times that on retirement. All plans are carefully managed by the co-operative's bank. It seems likely that associations of this productive nature are a more promising pointer to the future than the systems of collective enterprise sketched out by trade unions (49).

life continues to be highly argued. On the one hand, there are Sir John Clapham's and Professor Ashton's soothing words in favour of improvement, and Eric Hobsbawm's and E. P. Thompson's passionate words on the other side. J. S. Mill wrote in *Principles of Political Economy* (51) published in 1848, 'Hitherto, it is questionable if all the mechanical inventions yet made have lightened the day's trial to any human being. They *have* enabled [author's italics] a greater proportion to live the same old life of drudgery and imprisonment'. But even then there can be no reasonable doubt that, over all, the conditions in England had improved, measured by all the indices now used for underdeveloped countries. What statistics did not take into account, and do not now, is that in certain trades, such as mining and, say, lower grade hand-loom weaving, conditions in the mid-nineteenth century were much worse than they had been in those professions a century before. Some jobs too were infinitely more demanding than anything known in the agricultural age: working at a blast furnace, for example; or mining coal, with foul air and inadequate safety conditions; while signalmen and engine drivers plainly have responsibilities heavier than almost any known before.

These are not, however, problems of democracy. They are, or were, problems of industrialisation. The changing character of modern industrial life obviously needs different legislation on working conditions from those considered desirable or necessary before 1750; and that would have been the case whether or not there were a democracy in the country concerned. The essential task of governments in modern industrial democracies is to ensure humane laws governing the way that work is carried on; not to carry on the work itself. Most prosperous countries where the standard of living has risen so far as to abolish poverty are, on the whole, ones where this limited role of government has been accepted.

The industrial regions of the world still remain small in territorial extent in relation to the social changes they have brought. In 1938, for example, the factory workers in the world did not exceed 100 million, or 6% of the population of working age. In 1938, two thirds of the world's manufacturing output was still, as in 1870, to be found in the US, Germany and Britain The position has changed a great deal since then, and Russia, France, Japan and most recently some other small Eastern countries have industrialised fast. Even so, it still seems improbable that as many as 10% of the world's workers are employed in factories. The percentage is even falling because of the increase in the number of persons concerned with services, from transport to entertainment. Workers in factories, after a few generations, have become the aristocrats of workers.

In the late nineteenth century too, the question of what attitude a state should have towards 'those out of work, able to work and looking for a job', that is, the employable unemployed (as defined by the US in the 1930s) began to be looked at in a new way.

In ancient Rome for example, a third to a half of the population is said to have lived on free grain at public expense. All settled communities had, from the earliest days, a policy of assisting the poor, out of self interest and self protection. When Rome collapsed, those arrangements collapsed too. Unemployment and poverty, along with famine and disease, marked all cities in the Dark Ages of Europe. Even in the Enlightenment, unemployment was avoided only by a huge domestic service. In Venice, in 1760, the servants numbered 13,000 or 10% of the population. 'Stamp your foot on the Paris cobblestones and you can conjure up an army of clerks, runners, secretaries and public writers. Look for one, and a hundred will spring up;' wrote one eighteenth century traveller. Where there were still unemployed, male and young, those concerned often joined armies. Where they were girls, they became prostitutes. Where they were old, they became beggars, or witches, or 'pilgrims'. In the late eighteenth century, Madrid convents were giving out 30,000 bowls of soup a day. By that time, with capitals growing, the existence of a large class of semi-beggars in so many cities had begun to seem a political, as well as a social, problem: in Madrid, for example, there were numerous riots by 'mobs' in the late eighteenth century, culminating in the riots, 'heroic' according to patriotic history, of 1808. In London at that time, out of a total population of less than a million, 115,000 were believed by one observer to be 'criminals', though the figure included 50,000 prostitutes. Vast numbers of peasants were 'unemployed' in the age of agriculture during the winters, as vast numbers still are in agricultural countries today.

Among tribes, no doubt, a rough and ready concern for the sick and old marked most peoples. In settled communities, an essential part was the role played by the lord. A typical feudal provision was that of the Prussian code of 1795: the lord had to see to it that poor peasants were given education, that a livelihood for such of his vassals as had no land must be provided and, if they were reduced to poverty, he had to come to their aid. Where lords' powers, or other traditional methods, had disintegrated, most European communities began to consider laws like those 'Poor Laws' of England set up by a succession of Tudor monarchs. These laws appointed 'overseers' of the poor charged with levying a local tax, the poor rate, and making provision for the poor concerned. These laws destroyed the old system of mutual charity. For the law even allowed local authorities to ban alms at the door. Henceforth, the moral duties of householders were ambiguous. These laws were criticised by continental Catholics, who believed them to be inferior to individual or monastic charity. Nor were continental critics impressed by the provision that workhouses were later added to the equipment of parishes, so that relief could be directly tied to labour, nor by the melancholy houses of correction (such as Bridewell). These laws underline some of the resentments which still deface English society. Even so, the English rules in the eighteenth and nineteenth centuries provide an interesting general indication of the world's main preoccupations. In 1782, a special Act empowered parishes to give 'out-relief', that is, relief in the form of money given at home, to the able-bodied but deserving poor. Workhouses could, thereafter, be reserved for the old, the crippled and children. Parish officers were enabled to seek work on behalf of the poor in farms and, if wages offered were inadequate, to supplement them. In 1795, another English Act limited expulsions to those who were without means. The same year, a famous meeting was held by the magistrates of Berkshire at the Pelican Inn, Speenhamland, to discuss what should be done to combat the increasing pauperism, the consequence of the rising prices of food, itself caused by the rise of population. The magistrates were afraid of revolution in the French style. They decided to help the poor in proportion to bread prices: 'When the gallon loaf of flour . . . cost 1 shilling, every poor and industrious man will have three shillings supplementary weekly and one shilling and sixpence for each of his family'. These rules were put into effect almost everywhere, though they seemed humiliating. The high poor rates to be paid also fell heavily on small farmers without subsidised labourers. One should not, however, exaggerate: in 1834, only 300,000 able-bodied labourers and dependents were in receipt of aid.

That year, a new Poor Law established that, in every specially prescribed district there should be one workhouse each for children, men, women, and the aged. The aim was to make public charity so disagreeable a deterrent that any self-respecting person would prefer the meanest independent labour. Still in 1850, about a million people in England were on relief of one sort or another. All trades were subject to recurrent unemployment or lesser employment, though, of the larger trades, only hand-loom weaving had a large and permanently redundant labour force over many years. Was this a 'reserve army of labour' to be used to batter down the pay of the regular troops? Sir John Clapham gives a moderate answer: there is an element of truth in this interpretation that the reserve was never strong enough to do all the evils credited to it; even in weaving the 'reserve army' did not prevent the steady, if slow, rise, in the power-loom weavers' wages.

At that time, there were numerous schemes for 'self-help' in most countries. Again, England provides good examples. In the eighteenth century, innumerable friendly societies were established. Many derived from guilds, and provided for relief of sickness and old age. In 1786, John Acland devised a National Friendly Society, which proposed a contributory age pension scheme. Nothing came of that. By 1815, there were over 7,000 such clubs, with nearly a million members (60). In Germany, Bismarck, after the unification of the country, introduced regulations in 1883–5 providing insurance against sickness and accidents. Laws to insure against old age followed in 1889. Employers, workpeople and state all contributed by a series of intricate provisions (including the subsequently general use of stamps and cards). These ensured a modest average pension in old age to all except casual labourers and wilfully unemployed. Bismarck knew that insurance against unemployment would be the form of social insurance which German wage earners would like best. But he did not do anything to that end (61). In England, there was much discussion on this matter: Joseph Chamberlain believed in similar legislation, but his opponents, the Liberals, took the appropriate initiative. From 1908, in England every person not a criminal, or one who had failed to work 'according to his ability or opportunity, or need,' would receive a small pension at seventy-nine if his income were not above a certain amount (62). Improvements were subsequently introduced. Bismarck's methods were imported for the payment of these pensions (contributions by three parties; cards; and stamps). Similar schemes for accident, illness and even unemployment were introduced in 1911, a chain of labour exchanges being established throughout the nation in order to administer the arrangements (63). These plans worried even some reformers: thus Beatrice and Sidney Webb wrote, 'The fact that the sick and unemployed . . were entitled to money incomes without any corresponding obligation to get well and keep well, or to seek and keep employment, seemed to us as likely to encourage malingering and a disinclination to work' (64). Despite such authoritative scepticism, these acts, subsequently to be even more liberal, have hence constituted the basis of legislation on welfare in all countries.

During the course of the twentieth century, in Europe and the advanced industrial countries, poverty has changed radically. About 1900 a careful investigator in York found that 28% of the population were living on incomes insufficient to obtain the minimum food necessary for the maintenance of mere physical efficiency (65). In 1936, in the same place, he went back and thought that 31% of the population were still in poverty. Using what he considered a better method of analysis, he believed his figure for 1900 should have been 43%. But, in 1961, another investigation showed that 3% only of the population of York were destitute. Even if that is an underestimate for Britain as a whole, that is an appropriate measure of the changes which have characterised a typical advanced country. In 1900, the poor were so because they were paid low wages. In 1936, they were so because they were unemployed. In 1961, the explanation was their age. In the past, riches seemed a scandal in the face of poverty. Now poverty seems a scandal in the face of riches (66).

Some other changes during the twentieth century in respect of poverty were as follows: first, paupers in 1900 were as short-lived as the entire population had been in 1688 – an average age of 30 (67) – and all working people, even if themselves above the poverty line, had seen poverty close. Second, there have often been occasions when popular leaders have reinforced their appeal by saying that they could provide work for millions unemployed because of the closure of factories or the collapse of exports. Hitler and Roosevelt in Germany and the US respectively were good examples of this approach. In particular, the Nazis' labour front, with their scheme of '*Strength through Joy*', holiday camps and cheap cruises, made the régime quite popular despite the control of labour that it necessitated (68). Equally, between 1934 and 1939, huge sums ($14,000 million) were spent on unemployment relief in the US (69). The third change has been the effect on the character of employment caused by trade unions and the state. Unions in numerous countries have often ensured that dismissals are difficult, even impossible. Protection against competition in the labour market has created a gulf between those who, either in private enterprise or in public, hold an employment of some kind and those who, either through age or bad luck, have none (70). Fourth, almost all countries outside Europe and North America are the victims of seasonal fluctuation in employment at least as great as in the age of agriculture. For example, Cuba in the mid 1950s might have an average unemployment of 20·7% from August to October. It would drop to 9% during the sugar harvest (71). It must be realised that where people have been unemployed for a long time, all initiative dries up and they succumb to an inertia in habits which is both debilitating and hard to break away from (72). 'Job creation' has, however, in the last few years been a preoccupation of all democratic governments. So have endless secondary benefits to anyone in any form of employment. The car company, Fiat, in Italy, for example, estimates that every worker who takes home $73 a month costs Fiat $305 in social facilities and arrangements at the factory (73).

The character of work in rich countries in the twentieth century is utterly different, of course, from that which still pertains in primarily agricultural countries and which used to pertain in all countries before industrialisation. Yet probably the received view of what work means in, say, the US today is false. Thus one expert recently wrote: 'of all people who work in the course of a year almost 45% are employed less than full time . . . 55% only fit the stereotype of the conventional worker and 30% of all work is performed by those who are not full time workers' (74). Willy-nilly, the US is likely to dictate the pattern of behaviour elsewhere.

There is, however, a tragedy in modern times relating to the character of work. In the world of modern work, there are two quite separate worlds: those who gain satisfaction from what they are doing and those who are simply in their factories or offices for want of anything better. This surely is the real source of labour troubles.

51

Democracy: Internal Anxieties, II

> The role of the state can never be spelled out once and for all in terms of specific functions . . . because each day brings new opportunities and circumstances. Government may enable us at times to accomplish jointly what we would find it more difficult to accomplish severally but any such use of government is fraught with danger.
>
> Milton Friedman, *Capitalism and Freedom*

The second malaise in democratic politics derives from a reluctance of many practitioners of politics to think carefully as to what should be the role of the State. 'The State is the nation in its collective and corporative character,' wrote Matthew Arnold, 'entrusted with stringent powers for the general advantage, and controlling individual wills in the name of an interest wider than that of the sum of individuals' (1). 'General advantage': are we sure of it? And what is that mysterious interest 'wider than the sum of individuals'? Does not that need very precise definition? 'Society is a garden . . . in continuous need of being tended by wise gardeners lest it be overrun by weeds and pests,' wrote a nineteenth century Tory Radical, Richard Oastler (2). But what is a weed, socially speaking? This and similar questions are specially important to answer intelligently now, when, through the capacity of technology, a state can make itself artificially far more powerful than any of its predecessors. In 1978, the proposal for a 'national data centre', linking together the 11,000 computers working in the US government, was rejected in the name of liberty (3). We cannot be certain that all countries will do the same if they have the chance.

The relation between nation and state is elusive. If the state seeks to absorb, or become co-terminous with, the nation, the nation recedes, becomes elusive, and even hides its identity. An over-active state loses the respect of the nation. That occurred in the later Roman empire when the state, before it fell, became the largest landed proprietor, the greatest industrialist, and the biggest owner of mines and quarries (4). But it had long ceased to be respected. In modern times, patriotism has also declined in inverse proportion to the growth of state power.

The character of a state can best be judged by an evaluation of how its civil servants behave. Three things mark the development of bureaucracies since the age of agriculture. First, they have increased in size: in Athens, in the fifth century BC, there were no permanent officials at all attached to their assemblies. Britain had barely 2000 men in the entire central government at the end of the eighteenth century, inclusive of sinecures (5). In 1978, it employs directly or indirectly in national government or local government, in education or health services, in the armed forces and in establishments making weapons or servicing them, 30% of the British labour force (6). One worker in four depends on the state in the US (7). Similar figures could doubtless be found for many other countries. Yet under the Roman Empire at its most flamboyant in the fourth century AD, the total civil service was never more than 40,000 at greatest (8). The increase of civil servants in Spain in the seventeenth century has been regarded by many historians as a cause of its decay: 'huge sectors were converted from activity to inactivity,' writes Vicens Vives, at the cost of productive work (9). But there were then only 150,000 government servants in the country.

Beyond most modern bureaucracies in the West, the shade of Rome can, of course, be plainly seen. Diocletian's hundred provinces, with their civil and military commands, their city councils and bureaucracies, their judges of first instance and of appeal, their prefects in charge of roads and of sewerage, their urban cohorts and their postal services, form the foundations of the way that our states are managed just as Athens gave the inspiration for our ideals. Equally, behind the vast bureaucracies of communist China, we see the ghost of the old imperial army of 40,000 higher civil servants, 1,200,000 clerks and over 500,000 runners (10).

Today, in almost every country, civil services appear to be vast, uncontrollable organisations without peers. In the past, the state was only one among a group of institutions to which individuals were loyal. Indeed, a man's loyalty to a great European household was, till the sixteenth or seventeenth century, far greater than it was to the state. That has been the case in many counties of Asia till recently and is doubtless still so in a few. Now bureaucracies give to secular states the kind of support which the Church gave the old system (11). Nearly all those states which, in the eighteenth century, had already the beginnings of a powerful civil service have descendants of them still despite intellectual *mésalliances* (Russia, the Spanish empire, China, France, Austria-Hungary), sometimes serving a communist régime, sometimes a democratic president, but all of them, as a rule, accustomed to intervene in the economic lives of their peoples, usually confidently, often arrogantly and sometimes even instinctively.

The exception to this is Germany, whose old system, based on loyalty to the Prussian state, was broken in 1945, and whose subsequent history, in Western Europe, at least, has come to be constructed on the basis of hostility to hierarchy. In the past, a greater part of the civil life of

Germany was organised from the top than was the case in other countries.* That was doubtless one of the reasons for Germany's 'grab for world power', in the phrase of Fritz Fischer. The failure of that 'adventure' led to a strict reversal, at least in West Germany, of the nation's hierarchical arrangements: the only occasion that such a thing has occurred recently.

Bureaucracy admittedly exercises such charm over people in search of a competence as to raise a question about their loyalty to ideologies. Could it be that Professor Are of Pisa is correct in suggesting that even the Italian communist party is interested less in Marx than in letting its friends have a share over the proceeds of bureaucracy (12)? Is it perhaps possible that the communists have no desire whatever to dismantle the system of economic patronage and political interference built up by the Christian Democrats? In South America, caudillos have behaved primarily as distributors of patronage and benefactions. Independence there inspired the birth of a growth of bureaucrats whom even Bolívar regarded as parasites before the revolution which he planned was complete (13). 'I can still hear Sidney Webb explaining to me,' wrote Elie Halévy, 'that the future belonged to the great administrative nations, where the officials govern, and the police keep order' (14). Max Weber reflected: 'It is horrible to think that the world could one day be filled with nothing but those little cogs, little men clinging to little jobs', for that would spell a 'bureaucratisation of the spirit' without precedent (15).

The growth of centralisation has been the second characteristic of the history of bureaucracy. Despite the realisation that centralisation was slow death in such an empire as the Ottoman (16), it has everywhere increased. Wars, revolution and conquests have all promoted it. Centralisation of administration enervates as much as centralisation of government fortifies, a fact forgotten or confused by people as various as Machiavelli, Bentham, Hobbes, Rousseau, even Marx, who all believed that progress meant an escape from localism.

For many people, the state and the bureaucracy signify regulations, first and foremost. Actually, they are not new. Any mediaeval code contains a formidable number of royal decrees whereby manufacturers, for example, were constrained. In the eighteenth century, innumerable forms circulated in France, with blanks to be filled in by individuals, about the nature of the soil, the means of its cultivation, the livestock and the crops: 'We find the state constantly coming already to the rescue of individuals, in difficulties . . . lavish of promises and subsidies . . . and, as there was no danger of publicity, no one felt any qualms about informing it about his personal troubles' (17). Nevertheless, there was a time, in the nineteenth century, when rules seemed to be, and probably were, becoming fewer. In 1791, for example, every French

* In Saxony, under Augustus the Strong, there were ninety-three grades of rank.

cultivator was allowed to store grain exactly as he wished for the first time (18). Jeremy Bentham, the reformer who inspired much institutional change in nineteenth-century Europe, believed all government to be one vast evil (19). He advocated handing over the poor law to a national charity company. He assumed that powerful governments would inevitably be corrupt and inefficient, and suggested that civil servants should tender against each other for those few jobs which even he admitted that they should carry out, so that the state would find out which of them would do the work cheapest. Bentham looked quizzically at laws on apprenticeships, on how things should be measured or made, on sizes and weights, even on those fixing the weight of a loaf of bread in relation to the price of grain, as at the, by then, mostly evaded usury laws. Even in Germany, there were some signs of criticism of the state: 'No other state has ever been administered so much like a factory as Prussia since the death of Frederick William,' complained the poet Novalis, in 1798 (20). Wilhelm von Humboldt, who secured the control of education for the state, wrote, in his *Limits of State Action*, that the operation of government ought to be severely limited to what directly and immediately relates to the security of person and property (21). Ernest Renan believed liberty to be definable as non-intervention by the state, while admitting that 'the very means to remove that idea to an indefinite distance would be precisely that state's withdrawing its action too soon' (22). But since the middle of the nineteenth century, the tendency has been for states to have larger pretensions. But on what principle? Once it is admitted that the state has a role in the economy, it is impossible to decide where that role should end. 'On what principle shall railway rates be controlled? Is the traveller, or sender of goods and messages, to be served at the expense of the same public as the tax payer? Shall one form of transport in the hands of the state subsidise another? In the absence of the vulgar book-keeping test of profit, how shall the utility and efficiency of government enterprises be decided?' (23). All those questions put by Sir John Clapham in the 1930s are as inadequately resolved now as they were in 1878. Russia in 1906, for example, was able to persuade herself that 'years of government railway construction began to pay off'. Her strategic railway in 1914 could send a hundred divisions to war within eighteen days (24). But that simply meant that one, military, view of what the state should be doing had triumphed, and others (that the state should collect money to provide schools, or that the state should collect less money) had not been successfully put. The problems which might follow from nationalisation were appreciated by some socialists before 1914. Thus a trade union congress in England, in 1913, expressed 'the opinion that the nationalisation of public services such as the Post Office is not necessarily advantageous to the employees and the working class, unless accompanied by a steadily increasing democratic control' (25).

It seems likely that, if democracy is to be preserved, the values of localism and regionalism, the habits of decentralisation, and voluntary, rather than state sponsored, association, all small-scale operations and commercial endeavour need to be revived.

On these matters, Burke and Kropotkin, Proudhon and de Tocqueville, as well as other nineteenth-century political critics of the new state such as Coleridge and Bakunin, conservatives and anarchists, see eye to eye (26), though the error of Bakunin – as indeed of Marx – was to suppose that, in ideal circumstances, the power of the state would 'wither away': a clear indication that those prophets never 'grasped the paradox of freedom', as Karl Popper put it, namely 'that state power is the guarantee of freedom' (27), and that only in law can liberty be obtained.*

In the eighteenth century, all sovereign states already had elaborate fiscal systems, some taxes stretching back for hundreds of years. A typical tax was that levied on sheep. When once the idea of wandering herds of sheep escorted by herdsmen had become accepted, the fiscal possibilities seemed alluring, both for localities and for national governments. Towns assessed the damage caused by these sheep, and the subsequent fines became taxes. Such taxes were paid in Southern Italy in the time of Caesar and, in the pastoral hinterlands of Morocco and Tunis, local chieftains and municipalities in the twentieth century still exact from migrating flocks a toll of one sheep for every hundred (29). The eighteenth century also had well developed the idea of taxes on sales, on heads of families, and, above all, tolls and customs. Monarchies still also had endless recourse to loans, including forced loans to pay for wars (a wealth tax of 3% of entailed capital was raised in this way by the crown of Spain in 1795). The diversity of ways in which governments raised money in the past was almost as ingenious as it is in the present. In 1798, for example, all municipalities which rented Spanish buildings to private individuals were ordered to be sold to the individuals concerned. The proceeds were to go to the Crown. There were innumerable intimidatory requests for gifts, sales of titles, offices, and taxes on servants, horses and carriages, shops and inns, windows and sales. Sometimes, such taxes were designed to favour domestic industries. Usually, they were specific recourses to raise money to serve the state undertakings of which war and the servicing of debts were the most important.† Collection of taxes by tax farming continued and,

---

* Thus Goethe: 'In vain do undisciplined spirits seek to achieve perfection. . . For the master first reveals himself in limitation and only law can give us liberty' (28).
† The total expenditure of Britain in 1828 was £56M of which £16M went to the army and navy; £7M went to the civil list, bounties and occasional expenditure; £29M went to collection of revenue. The revenue derived from £36M customs and excise; £13M other taxes; and £7M probate registry.

indeed, continued to be essential in days of bad communications. Most governments had property of their own: saltbeds, mines, tunny fisheries, farms, vineyards, and most monarchs depended on those very considerably.

In the course of the nineteenth century, these taxes were almost everywhere formalised, 'modernised' and simplified. There was in most countries a movement towards tax on incomes and death duties as the simplest methods of collecting what was needed.

Income tax, it would seem, was invented in Tuscany in the early fifteenth century (30). It was not regularly used until after the beginning of the nineteenth century. During the Napoleonic wars, income tax was introduced in England but subsequently abandoned. Sir Robert Peel appealed for 7d in the £ on all incomes over £150 for three years, in 1845, and from then on a modest tax on incomes constituted the basis of finances in England till 1914. Gladstone tried to use the abolition of income tax as a vote winner in 1874 but he failed, though in 1887 he was still denouncing income tax as 'the most demoralising of all taxes', and 'an engine of public extravagance'. John Stuart Mill had thought income tax unworkable because of the low state of public morality but, from the end of the nineteenth century, it has never ceased to grow. The First World War, in taxation, as in other matters, ended the old era; people were cajoled by patriotism into paying in England (and, equivalently, in other countries) an income tax of 6s in the £ and a supertax too. England's best economic historian wrote: 'Seldom had there been such tax-paying, or more smoothly working machinery, for the transfer of wealth from the purposes of peace to those of war; and, when the war was over, from class to class' (31). Since then, a vast variety of taxes has been constructed in most democratic states, causing the highly diverse world of the ancient régime to seem a model of simplicity. Taxation has also ceased to be simply a source of revenue and become, instead, an instrument of social justice, welfare, and economic management: which is not its proper function.

The part played by excessive taxation in causing the fall of Rome has been already discussed. The English civil war of the seventeenth century broke out over the government's demand for 'ship money', from which the King hoped to restore the Navy. The first two great upheavals of the industrial age, the Revolution in the US in the 1770s and that in France in 1789, were both directly inspired by complaints about taxes: the Stamp Act passed in London in 1765 was the prologue to the American Revolution as surely as the Finance Minister, Jacques Necker's, attempt to regularise the French system was the same to the Revolution in 1789. The American Revolution was a tax revolt before it became a war of independence, for the colonists were not simply against taxation without representation; they did not really want to pay taxes at all (32). In the years since 1945, other tax revolts have spluttered. It seems certain that reductions in taxes will be a way of limiting the excessive bureaucracies of Western democracies. Perhaps 'proposition 13', adopted in the US in California in 1978, will point the way to a new liberalism. Meantime, most democracies are managing their fiscal affairs rather badly. When taxes are too high, most peoples devise a dishonest means of evading them. It is said that in Russia, for example, in the late 1970s, the 'parallel economy' may account for 20% of the national income. Some have suggested that the British figure may be approaching that (33). No wonder governments find it hard to devise effective policies on incomes.

Four things need to be said, in conclusion, about the modern State: first, history suggests that the reason for national decline is, as a rule, that the State in the nation concerned has sought to do too much, not too little; that applies as much to the Roman Empire as to the Spanish; second, that though the state should provide security, it must not stifle the desire for opportunity and responsibility; third, that centres of power and influence, both public and private, should be diffused so far as is possible throughout the community; fourth, planners and reformers need to bear in mind that the concentration of power in the state places an ever increasing power of patronage in the hands of those people who manage it. Those people are human beings of a perfectly ordinary sort, even if they are likely to have some special gift, either of good luck or tenacity or eloquence or even goodness to have travelled so far. But consciously or unconsciously the wisest president will make mistakes, or have to choose between appointing people whom he knows to be loyal and those whom he knows to be able. Sometimes the two qualities are united. Often they are not. The responsibility on the shoulders of all the leaders of the rich countries, above all the President of the US, is too great. The only appropriate way to change these arrangements for the better must be to seek to dismantle the State's overweighty pretensions and powers. The State can call on the loyalty of free individuals often more easily than it can on its own servants. Local leaders of local communities will flourish in direct proportion to the extent that they are free of national supervision and interference. The French historian, Gabriel Hanotaux, in a life of Richelieu, praised that statesman as a 'precursor of democracy', since he abolished 'the intermediate powers which imposed themselves dangerously between king and people'. We should now prefer de Tocqueville's insistence that those same 'intermediate' authorities, however ancient and apparently illogical, very often constitute the sort of authorities which people respect. They are, therefore, the real foundations of freedom.

The essence of the argument put forward in the two last Books, which are both entitled "Our Times", is that the five or six generations since 1750 saw a wonderful series of technical innovations and inventions. For a time, there seemed a reasonable chance that these opportunities would be wisely and humanely used. About 1900, there was a general sense of optimism. As has been recalled, a widespread expectation was that representative democracy would become the characteristic form of government in much of the world, within the forseeable future. But the technical opportunities, though certainly helping to liberate mankind in many ways, exacerbated some of the world's ancient troubles, and scientific achievements have scarcely been matched by political ones. In the late 1970s, it seemed possible that Western civilisation might collapse before the end of the century, either from the onslaught of irrationality without or the failure of nerve within. The Epilogue seeks to illumine this crepuscular vision.

Epilogue

What the next hundred years will bring I cannot predict; but I fear we shall not have repose . . . the great are not such that there will be no abuse of power; the masses are not such that, in hope of gradual improvements, they will be contented with a moderate condition.

Goethe, *Conversations with Eckermann* (about 1825)

Nothing is more remarkable – though to believers in nationality and ordered progress nothing is more natural – than the stability of the Italian kingdom. The oscillations of the structure that Cavour reared in the earthquake of 1860 went on for some forty years. But the vibration is now ceased and the building is now as safe as any in Europe. Today, politics in Italy would be more criticised for their stagnation than for any dangerous tendency towards revolution and reaction. The foundations of human liberty and the foundations of the order exist on a firm basis.

G M Trevelyan, *Garibaldi and the Roman Republic* (written in 1911)

We shall have the means (and, therefore, the temptation) to manipulate behaviour and the intellectual functioning of all people through environmental manipulation of the brain.

De Carlo, *Towards the Year 2018* (about 1970)

A historian . . . cannot make any generalisations about the past the basis for predictions of future actions and events; he cannot do so not only because he has insufficient knowledge of the complete causes of the past, but because he cannot predict which one of the many tendencies and forces which determine actions may have a dominant place . . . Only one historian . . . Jacob Burckhardt was able to foretell the . . . tyrannies of the twentieth century . . . And no one predicted the nightmare which emanated from the Marxist dreams of heaven on earth.

Niebuhr, *The self and dramas of history*

The physiocrats attacked not only specific forms of privilege but any kind of diversity whatsoever: to their thinking, all men should be equal, even if equality spelled servitude. For contractual engagements they had no respect and no concern for private rights. Indeed, private rights were in their eyes negligible. Only the public interest mattered. Though most of them were amiable, well-meaning persons . . . such was their enthusiasm for the cause they sponsored that they carried their theories to fanatical lengths.

Alexis de Tocqueville, *French Revolution*

In the French Revolution, both religious institutions and the whole system of government were thrown into the melting pot with the result that men's minds were in a state of utter confusion . . . Revolutionaries of a hitherto unknown breed came on the scene: men who carried audacity to the point of sheer insanity; who balked at no innovation and were unchecked by any restraint . . . who acted with an unprecedented ruthlessness . . . They are still with us.

The same

Thou waitest for the spark from heaven! and we,
   Light half-believers of our casual creeds,
     Who never deeply felt, nor clearly will'd,

Whose insight never has borne fruit in deeds,
  Whose vague resolves never have been fulfill'd;
  For whom each year we see
Breeds new beginnings, disappointments new;
  Who hesitate and falter life away,
  And lose tomorrow the ground won today —
Ah! do not we, wanderer! await it too?

Matthew Arnold, *The Scholar Gipsy*

I

At first sight, the most curious innovation is that much of the world in the twentieth century apparently lives and dies without religion. This seems, at first sight, to be a unique condition. Even imperial Rome had its formal deities.

But, on examination, this concept of a lay world needs several qualifications. First, putting the matter at its simplest, the last two hundred years have been characterised by revival as well as by disintegration, by innumerable new kinds of religious enthusiasm from messianic preaching to mystical healing. Sceptics in the eighteenth century, such as Gibbon, would have been astonished to find that, two hundred years later, religious conflicts such as those in Ireland, the Middle East, Iran, India, the Philippines and the Sudan were both more numerous and more violent than they were in his day. 'Barbarism and religion', whose triumph, during the fifth century AD, Gibbon claimed to be commemorating, have continued hand-in-hand in the twentieth (1). The overthrow of the Shah of Persia in 1979, for example, was, on the surface at least, the result of a traditional revolt led by conservative holy men in protest against modernisation – an identification of religion with reaction similar to the popular alliance in Spain in 1808 against Napoleon.

The illusion that religion has declined absolutely derived from the creation of large societies of persons in towns with different outlooks from those held in old villages or settlements. The very metaphors of the Christian Church seemed inappropriate in industrial life; and, in many industrial towns, those who went to church and took communion, excluded, in the first generation or two of industrialisation, the factory workers. Professor Pevsner believes that no church designed after 1750 has been in the first rank among leading examples of architecture (2). But, taking the word in its broadest sense, religion has since fought a very good defensive battle. Methodism, for example, was, in an astonishing degree, able to attract the loyalties of both factory owners and factory workers in much of England, acting as an invaluable source of discipline for work (3). Catholicism, on the other hand, has become 'a refuge from the pressures of mass civilisation', as well as the inspiration of an international political movement of the first importance, while the century of anticlericalism which began with the French

Revolution inspired almost as many articulate defenders of the Church as did the Counter Reformation. Just as industrialism was beginning in Europe, the Protestants also embarked on a world-wide crusade of missionary activities. Catholic countries also redoubled their missionary efforts. By the 1870s, missions had been set up, for example, everywhere in Africa, reflecting almost every sect of Christianity, and that greatly assisted the discovery and charting of that previously unknown continent. It was not a soldier nor a business man nor an agronomist but a missionary, David Livingstone, who first crossed the continent in the 1850s. In the twentieth century, the churches have, if anything, been more active in politics than ever before, even if some of their activities seem extraordinarily questionable on both theological and political grounds. True, the Orthodox Church made no serious defence of itself against communism after 1917, and exchanged its loyalty to the Tsar for an almost equally uncritical one to the Secretary-General of the communist party – though there is a sense now in which religion today forms a real opposition to communism in Russia. The Protestant churches had many martyrs as well as time-servers in Nazi Germany.

Meantime, beliefs in charms, spiritualism, ghosts, demons and other mysteries have contrived to exercise a fitful attraction even among educated people. Astrology's followers are increasing. Odd numbers, magpies, four-leafed clovers, black cats, spilled salt, dropped teaspoons, still exert modest despotisms over rational people. The most learned Englishman of the eighteenth century, Dr Johnson, insisted on knocking every post as he walked along Henrietta Street. Burckhardt believed that the religion of the nineteenth century was 'rationalism for the few and magic for the many', while a modern writer, Geoffrey Grigson, estimates that today, in Britain, 'about a quarter of the population . . . holds a view of the universe which can most properly be designated as magical' (4).

There have also been some instances in the world since 1750 when a sense of religion has been consciously heightened by a state. A good example of this was what happened to Shintoism in Japan. Industrialisation initiated not only the beginning of Japan's rise to industrial strength but the cult of the emperor as a descendant of the sun.

Every traditional religion has also had, since 1750, heresies, splits or re-interpretations which, in the end, have probably strengthened the appeal of those faiths. The eighteenth century, for example, saw a series of innovations in Protestantism, such as the Methodism previously noticed which amounted, particularly in the US, to a second reformation, whose emphasis was on popular styles of worship. Partly this was the consequence of inspired sermons by, for example, men such as George Whitefield who could make, it is said, congregations weep merely by pronouncing the word 'Mesopotamia' (5). Churches, on the whole in Western countries, have now ceased to be great landowners and have also lost their freedom from taxation and other exemptions, though disputes about these questions were at the heart of many problems of the nineteenth and early twentieth centuries. For example, the role of the Catholic Church in education and culture generally was a determining point of argument before the civil war in Spain, in the kulturkampf in Germany, and in the Dreyfus case in France. The peculiar position of the Church in Italy was only resolved by Mussolini. Judaism has also divided, while the collapse of the Ottoman Empire and the Arab awakening caused a 'revolt of Islam' very different from that envisaged by Shelley. True, Islam was expanding in Africa in the nineteenth century. Had it not been for European colonisation in that continent, Islam might have consolidated its position in East Africa and the Congo as well as throughout the Sudan. Even where foreign Arab rulers were unable to establish themselves, many local institutions might have become 'islamised'.

The world wars of the twentieth century placed a strain on religion for two reasons. First, churches in belligerent countries became more explicitly than ever instruments of state. Preachers and priests assumed the roles of recruiting sergeants. One Minister of St Giles's Cathedral, Edinburgh, declared in 1917 that anyone who talked of initiating peace negotiations with the rulers of Germany was 'a moral and spiritual leper' (6).

But at the same time many were so distressed by the suffering which modern war imposed as to contemplate abandoning religion altogether. An English Liberal politician, a strong Anglican, C. F. G. Masterman, wrote, in March 1918, 'God is a devil who rejoices in human suffering. He may be. There's no evidence to show he isn't' (7). Winston Churchill in his last speech as prime minister in the House of Commons, in March 1955, wondered openly whether God had 'wearied of mankind', after the coming of the atom bomb (8).

In addition, a strange nationalisation has overcome many religious attitudes. In the nineteenth century, men were still often primarily distinguished in the world by their religions. In Jerusalem, a man was a Druse, a Muslim, a Christian or a Jew. In the twentieth century, a man's ethnic or national loyalties seem stronger. People appreciated the change as it was happening: 'Yesterday we were an ecclesiastical community,' proclaimed an Armenian nationalist in 1872, 'tomorrow, we will be a nation of workers and thinkers' (9). Yet the revival of Islam is beginning to raise the question anew as to whether the future may not after all be a new age of religion rather than of nationalism. The churches are awake as well as the mosques. Class-war may be a thing of the past. But there is nothing to suggest that religious war is. This is not an age of toleration, except in Europe and north America. On all previous occasions when there has been widespread fear of, or uncertainty about, the future, holy men have stretched forth their hands. The chances must be that that will happen again. Already there are indications that churchmen are ready once again to offer political leadership in a world where too many politicians have become pre-occupied with vote-seeking.

II

The most curious aspect of the evolution of society since 1750, has, however, been the steady substitute of a lay religion for a real one, a lay religion which promises that happiness will (one day) be achieved in this world rather than the next. This suggests that human nature will never abandon its desire for some general explanation, some general scheme which places the day-to-day business of ordinary life in a grand frame.

Rousseau was probably the first to suggest, in the eighteenth century, that even in an atheistic state, an organised religion was necessary, though he thought it could not be Christianity, since this divided men from the state. He perhaps did not know much about the orthodox version of Christianity. He at all events proposed a civil profession of faith, the articles of which the sovereign people would determine 'not exactly as dogmas of religion, but as sentiments of sociability, without which,' he argued, 'it was impossible to be a good citizen' (10).

Once the Revolution had got under way in France after 1789, these ideas began to be put into effect. There were civic festivals organised, in particular, by the painter David. A movement towards 'dechristianisation' got under way. The Catholic religion in France was replaced, however, not by humanism, or scepticism, but by the worship of Reason. All churches of Paris were consecrated to Reason. Martyrs to that cause soon began also to be worshipped. Reason herself was depicted with the outward characteristics of a chorus girl. She was soon replaced by a *Culte décadent*, based on the simple belief in Republican citizenship and morality. Later still, the worship of the Supreme Being was propagated by Robespierre. That sought to place republican doctrine on metaphysical foundations. Robespierre, educated at a Catholic college, believed in God and the immortality of the soul, and the decrees which he introduced reflected that. Under him, four republican festivals were instituted as days of homage to the revolutionary *journées*, each consecrated to one civic virtue or another. This new religion was introduced by Robespierre himself at the Festival of the Supreme Being in 1794. The ceremony made a great impression on those who were present, but it infuriated the ardent 'dechristianisers', those who thought the state should be merely secular, and also the Christians. After Robespierre's overthrow, liberty of worship was introduced. Christianity, therefore, returned, first of all in private but, subsequently, as Napoleon's state religion (11). Napoleon believed that religion was the vaccine of the imagination:* *'elle la préserve de toutes les croyances dangereuses et absurdes'* (12). So 'the people must have a religion and that religion must be in the hands of the government' (13).

Actually he believed, rightly, that even Western Catholicism could be turned into the servant of the kind of state which he wished to build. Subsequently, Auguste Comte, troubled by what he considered the perennial Western malady, the revolt of the individual against the species (14), formulated more clearly than anyone else the difficulty of rationalism: theology and metaphysics were, he believed, incompatible with positive knowledge. He believed in the application of scientific canons of explanation in all fields: indeed, in a cosmic order established by science. But only in Brazil did this idea catch the imagination.

Meantime, de Tocqueville had observed that the belief of many living during the French Revolution turned very early 'into a species of religion . . . which, like Islam, has over-run the whole world with . . . apostles, militants, martyrs'. 'The French Revolution, though ostensibly political in origin, functioned on the lines of, and assumed many of the aspects of, a religious revolution. Not only did it have repercussions far beyond French territory, but, like all religious movements, it resorted to propaganda and broadcast a gospel' (15). The great French historian, Jules Michelet, wrote: 'The Revolution did not adopt a church. Why? Because it was a church itself' (16). 'It is with an armed doctrine that we are at war,' Burke had written earlier, in words copied by his political leader William Pitt (17). A generation later, nationalism took on all the attributes of a lay religion. Was Garibaldi a politician or a preacher? Who cared when he was actually speaking to a crowd with 'that beautiful voice of his which was part of his fascination. . . . "Make arms of every scythe and axe," he would say, "Come! He who stays at home is a coward. I promise you weariness, hardship and battles. But we will conquer or die." They were never joyful words but, when they were heard, the enthusiasm rose to its highest. It was a delirium. The crowd broke up, deeply moved' (18). Germany followed Italy into this trough of deception, in spite of her fine educational system, to articulate strange follies and hatreds such as those expressed in the historical writing of Treitschke.† For Cecil Rhodes and imperialists of his generation, the idea of Empire also almost took upon itself the attributes of a religion. At least Rhodes said that that was so (19).

For a time anticlericalism, brought on by hatred or fear of the Church's economic or cultural dominance, did the same. For a generation in France, democracy and Catholicism seemed to many incompa-

---

* The metaphor was doubtless on his mind since smallpox vaccine had just been introduced. It was echoed by Marx when he said religion was the 'opium of the masses'.
† Compare a similar comment about Russia. 'Russia cannot be fathomed by the mind or measured by a common yardstick,' said Tyutchev, 'She has a stature all her own. Russia *cannot but be believed in'* (20).

tible. This anticlericalism had its consummation in the most Catholic of all countries, Spain, in the twentieth centufotwo or three generations of overweening importance elsewhere, too.

But, in most senses, Communism was Nationalism's real successor. The Spanish philosopher, Miguel de Unamuno, wrote in 1920: 'Lenin is like a prophet of Israel, and what he preaches is a lay religion. Materialistic, if you like . . . but a religion. Atheistic, undoubtedly, but a religion. And a religion which will end up in a type of Buddhism. An Asiatic religion in any case' (21). Maynard Keynes said much the same when, in 1924, on return from Russia he wrote, 'I feel confident of one conclusion, that if communism achieves a certain success, it will achieve it not as an improved economic theory but as a religion' (22).

This lay religion had its most extreme manifestation in the cult of Stalinism. Consider Alexis Tolstoy's poem addressed to Stalin:

> Thou bright sun of the nations
> The unsinking sun of our times,
> And more than the sun, for the sun has no wisdom.

Thus the twentieth century has seen a revival of idolatry, which the worship of power always turns out to be. It may be a 'relic of the time of the cave, of human servitude' (23), but our times have shown, in both great and old countries, such as Germany or Russia, and small and modern ones, such as Cuba, Uganda or the central African 'empire', that rulers still wish to be worshipped, at least as much as they ever have done in the past.

The translator of Nietzsche, Oscar Levy, argued that, in spite of its atheism, Communism was actually a Christian heresy, since it had an international and cosmopolitan faith, and it looked back to a garden of Eden in which strife was non-existent, and in which property was held in common. The Marxist movement in Europe at all events became something very like, as Karl Popper put it, a 'great religious movement . . . a movement of workers to educate themselves . . . to emancipate themselves, raise the standards of their interests and passions, to substitute mountaineering for alcohol, classical music . . . serious books' (24). An observer* of events in 1917 in Russia wrote, even before the Bolshevik *coup*, that 'the first of May was celebrated in 1917 in Petrograd throughout the length and breadth of Russia *as a great religious festival* [my italics] in which the whole human race was invited to participate and to commemorate the brotherhood of man' (25). A year later, the same observer wrote: 'My mind went back to 1793, the 20th day of Brumaire, when the great convention did homage to the goddess of Reason in Notre Dame. Today, no formal deity was set up on high and

---

* The English journalist, Philips Price.

honoured. There were no signs of deism in this carnival of November 8th, 1918. But the new God was everywhere. He resided in the heart of every one who took part in the ceremonies of that day and who was inspired by the great impulse to struggle for a new social order. His symbol was seen in the great banner that hung from the House of the Soviets . . . where the gigantic figure of a half naked workman was wielding a sword to defeat the Republic's enemies. Another of his symbols was a great red axe which, in Red Square, lay embedded in a gigantic white block labelled "White Guards" . . . Everywhere his symbols were seen that day denoting struggle, the essence of life, the worship of the "world spirit" . . .' (26).

In the USA, even, communists of the 1930s were characterised by 'an impassioned longing to believe' (27) in a collectivist creed which repudiated most of modern American history, which has liberated the individual: according to Berdyaev, 'escape from self and a search for a new communion, a new congregation and a semblance of church' (28), but one which also involved a repudiation of the world of the spirit. In Marx, Karl Popper concluded, 'the religious element is unmistakeable' (29).

In Spain, the anarchist movement also had all the characteristics of a secular religion: 'When will the great day arrive?' an anarchist worker asked a Spanish Senator in 1903. 'What great day could that be?' asked the Senator. 'The day when all will be equal and the land is divided among everyone,' was the reply (30). The pursuit of this millenarian belief excited, and still excites, the fascination of many imaginative travellers. In Spain, the belief in the absolute goodness of the anarchist 'Idea', and the absolute evil of those who did not partake of it, led to a cult of terrorism which helped to cause both a military dictatorship and then a civil war. 'I fear,' wrote a prominent anarchist, Angel Pestaña, 'that when the critical history of the terrorist days and the establishment of the dictatorship of General Primo de Rivera comes to be written . . . we will appear as the efficient cause of it' (31). The judgment applies to other ideas sought with religious enthusiasm and ungodly methods.

A similar, conscious and, for a time, successful policy to replace religious emotions with ideological ones approached in a religious manner marked Nazism (though not Fascism in Italy, even though Mussolini fatuously called his movement a 'church of all the heresies'). Great importance in Nazi Germany was, first of all, attributed to ritual. Hitler thought that the mass meeting was desirable not only because of the ideas transmitted but because it enabled the ordinary man to 'step out of his workshop' (32). The figure of Hitler, his words, and the sound of his voice were blended with startling visual effects, in order to mesmerise the masses of one of the most intelligent peoples into accepting a religious frenzy of patriotism (33). This patriotism was organised at the 'congress city' of Nuremberg, the Rome of a new paganism, where huge flags flew from tall wooden towers. Eagles and loudspeakers, spot-lights, electric organs and neon tube lighting (invented in 1935), granite podiums for the speakers, huge avenues for the parades, all were brought together to support a cult which was as religious in intent as it was political in effect. One Nazi 'prayer' ran:

> Führer my Führer,
> Thou hast rescued Germany from deepest distress
> I thank thee for my daily bread
> Abide thou long with me, forsake me not
> Führer my Führer, my faith and my light (34).

A friend of the great poet Yeats, who was interested in Fascism, thought that 'what looked like coming out of Yeats's reflections' in the 1930s was 'Fascism modified by religion' (35), but Fascism turned out to be more like communism; a religion for those who accepted it. We have not seen the end of these religious illusions in political life. The fathers of both Fascism and communism both feared or looked forward to some terr-ible, or some glorious, catastrophe, a Day of the Lord, in which all evil would cease. In the thousand-year Reich, as in the communist society, immobility would be the rule. It is astonishing that such illusions as have been mentioned survive the failure of prophecies to be fulfilled. But so it has been throughout history with prophets.

III

It has, sometimes, seemed in the nineteenth or twentieth centuries, as if art has been a substitute for God. Modern Christian industrial society devotes its biggest resources in architecture to opera houses, art gal-leries, perhaps libraries, rarely churches. What the cathedral was to the Middle Ages, complains Professor Pevsner, the symphony was to the nineteenth century (36). The regular visits to concerts paid by, for example, the agnostic Jewish merchants of Germany were actions purely religious in implication, if not in fact. So were the visits to operas of Italians, even if men went to the opera in the nineteenth century in Italy in order to talk politics; and Verdi obligingly included in many of his operas a chorus about 'La Patria' (37). Yet much of art existed in the age of industry in a curious no-man's-land. Great aesthetic achieve-ments have, of course, been carried out but often 'torn out of the common ground of life' (38). The fact that, in the nineteenth century, easel painting flourished at the expense of wall painting suggests an imbalance between architecture and painting which contrasts badly with the golden days of the Renaissance. Perhaps music too began to lose its way when it became a purely individual performance instead of being related to the carnivals or rituals of society. Dancing did. But Shelley thought 'Poetry is capable of saving us' (39). He may have been right.

IV

Thus the chief characteristic of modern life is not really that it is one without religion after all. Where we do seem to differ from our ancestors, so far as the world of ideas is concerned, is the extraordinary attention paid to formal education. Here, surely, is a revolution worthy of the word. Yet, on examination, there are some indications that there is a little less novelty in our educational attitudes, as opposed to our institutions and achievements than seems to be the case at first sight. History should teach us to guard against any spurious sense of our uniqueness. For, in the agricultural age, children were educated as adequately as was necessary to carry out the rhythmic tasks which would await the vast majority, just as, in our times, children are educated for the service of industries and factories. The real difference is the increase of literacy, not of education as such.

In the late eighteenth century, the majority of the adult population of the world was illiterate, even in the richer countries. Then as now, a large number lived on the frontiers of literacy and illiteracy, including those who could read but not write, and those who could scarcely write anything, save their name. The incidence of illiteracy is perhaps testified to by such statistics as that, in East Yorkshire, in the 1750s, two-thirds of bridegrooms could sign their name, only a third of brides (40). In Britain, at that time, there were only 2000 schools in the country, all maintained by private charity, one for every fifth parish, and very few with more than one teacher attached to it (41). The few 'public schools' of England catered for a tiny minority of sons of aristocrats and of a few merchants. Some rich families educated their children at home, however, where they learned more classics and literature than they did at the boarding schools which were often (particularly after 1770) turned upside down by open battles between the impoverished, and usually inefficient, schoolmasters and the high spirited, and often acute, upper class boys (42). France was probably equally illiterate and schools were equally few and far between. A few schools were maintained by the king, and a few more by the Church or lords of manors. The status of teacher was not high. In south east France, for example, teachers could be hired at fairs. A man willing to teach reading would wear one feather in his hat. One who could teach writing as well wore two feathers. One who could teach arithmetic wore three feathers (43). As a rule, the pupils themselves paid the teachers, though a few town councils of the ancient régime provided the buildings in which the *maître d'école* would live and teach. Most countries were much the same. The Chinese and

Indians had had for a long time schools at which the children of their noblemen-bureaucrats were taught, as indeed Romans, Egyptians and Sumerians had been and as the Russians had copied after Peter the Great's reforms for those who were between ten and fifteen years old (at fifteen, sons of this service-aristocracy entered the army) (44).

The only nation in the world which, in the eighteenth century, had a policy for education was Germany, though there was no German state. The view that everyone should receive some education was held most strongly by Gotha, whose duke, Ernest the Pious, in 1642 ordered that all children should go to school at five years old; and by Prussia, whose king, Frederick the Great, in the eighteenth century decreed that attendance at school should be compulsory between the ages of five and thirteen for six hours. These rules were not kept. Most teachers were unqualified, and ill-paid. The school buildings were in bad repair. The curriculum was narrow, attendance was irregular, and very few children went to school at all in the summer (45). Nevertheless it seems that most peasants in Prussia, at least, and perhaps elsewhere in Germany could read. Merchants and noblemen sent their children to school too and many to universities. But Germany was very solitary in the world in this respect.

Anyone who knew anything of the history of education must have found this a surprising state of affairs six thousand years after the invention of writing, and about three hundred after the birth of printing. True, most ancient societies, such as those of Iraq, Egypt, China and Rome, had restricted literacy and education to a few, but most Greeks in the fifth and fourth centuries BC were apparently literate. The average Athenian's education was admittedly limited. It did not include the learning of a foreign language*, there was little science, history or geography, and no economics (46), but most Athenians seem to have been able to read and write and they also learned both poetry and music. Euripides, for example, assumed that his audience could read. (Probably the Ionic Greek alphabet, with each symbol having a different sound and a distinct, simple, shape, was an especial aid to literacy and, after all there are, in Greek, only twenty-four simply drawn letters) (47). Schools flourished. Homer was known as 'the schoolmaster of Greece'. The gymnasia, where wrestling and music were taught, were financed by the state (as a preparation for military training).

Equally, late mediaeval Italy was a much more educated society than was eighteenth century Italy. Professor Cipolla estimates that 40% of children went to school in Florence in 1338 (48) – an exceptional educational achievement at that time. In the sixteenth century, the historian Guicciardini thought, after a journey northwards, that 'the greatest part

---

* Maurice Bowra tells us that the Greeks believed foreign languages were like the 'twittering of swallows'.

of the people of the Low Countries master the rudiments of grammar and almost all, even peasants, know how to read and write' (49).

Surely, given these achievements in the past, it would have been possible to have expected a higher rate of literacy than say 30% at most in Europe in 1750*?

Such an attitude would, however, be anachronistic. What is education for save to prepare people for the life which they are going to live? Athenians needed literacy because, on the one hand, as has been earlier indicated, they had grasped the crucial part played in society by law: on the other, there was no professional class of lawyers. Hence, literacy was essential for the day-to-day business of living. Rhetoric, scepticism and arithmetic were all also required for survival within and the management of, that precocious society of ancient Athens (50). Subsequently, the Hellenic system of education based on Alexandria was primarily concerned to ensure that the clever had access to the right materials: hence the great library — and hence education between seven years and fourteen was a public charge (51). Roman education, like that of Athens, was concerned with the law: 'We learned the law of the twelve tables in our boyhood as a required formula,' wrote Cicero, adding, with a familiarly nostalgic comment, 'though no one learns it nowadays' (52). Other parts of Roman education dealt with obligations to gods, parents and benefactors, but all schools were privately financed. During the Roman Empire, literacy was insisted upon for the middle class throughout the Roman world, and the large number of clerks and civil servants led to the gradual increase of educational opportunities, though almost all were the work of Greeks. Even Latin literature was taught in Greek. Roman legionaries were also often literate. Roman writing was, after all, easy enough and the wax tablet with the metal or wooden *stylus* was simple to use, too (53). Children of the rulers and civil servants, like the rich, went from a primary school to a grammar school in order to study literature and rhetoric (54), usually under a Greek. Except for that, the Roman arrangements were more comparable to the modern European ones, which they inspired. Equally, rather as occurred in modern European civilisation, fairly late in the day, under Vespasian, the State began to concern itself seriously with education by subsidising teaching from public funds. By the days of Constantine, in the full decline of the Empire, many schools flourished at the expense of cities, though those rather empty and bureaucratic institutions were too formal to have any effect on the speed with which the political system continued to decline: another parallel perhaps with modern times. The Emperor Valentinian drew near to the idea of universities: every metropolis of every province was supposed to

---

* Say 50% in England, 10% in Italy and Spain, 40% in France, 60–70% in Germany and Holland and 40% in Austria–Hungary.

have a school of grammar and rhetoric in Greek and Latin: 'the studious youth were prohibited from wasting their time in feasts,' wrote Gibbon (55). Whether the invaders would have been restrained, and the Roman and Byzantine Empire preserved, even by compulsory universal education, seems, however, improbable. The Byzantine Levant, for example, was conquered by Arabs, whose education for anything other than prayer and war was evidently modest.

Thus, look where we will in the past, there is no sense whatever that the average peasant or working man had a right to or a desire for any education other than what was necessary for his work. Even in the eighteenth century most people did not send their children to schools, even if they could have afforded it and even if there were any schools, since they needed them to work at home. Children were always needed at harvest time and could be employed from their earliest years. Only in the winter did they have time on their hands. Many were afraid that schools offered hazards to health. The age of agriculture educated its children for their appropriate functions. The peasants who constituted the vast majority of the population taught their children at home what they needed to know. Those who managed small farms before the age of universal taxation did not need to read, or even to count, to carry on their main work, even if large farms, as John Chadwick, the historian of Mycænae, reminds us, need elaborate accounting (56). Those who lived in cities and sought to sell or exchange commodities had had to read and write for thousands of years – since, indeed, the days of ancient Iraq where, by 3000 BC at the latest, there were schools, mostly in private houses, to enable the children of priests and some soldiers to learn cuneiform and add, as well as speak (57); or ancient Egypt, where surviving tablets make it evident that the mathematical problems of 2000 BC were much the same as those set in schools today ('What equal areas should be taken from five fields, each of one setat, if the sum of these areas is to be three setats?') (58). Equally, those who sought to pass on knowledge of the governance of their state to their descendants always had them educated. Mediaeval education in a few royal or noble families was sometimes admirable. Such, doubtless, was the basis of all education till the eighteenth century, though a few exceptional peoples such as the Jews, after their captivity in Babylonia, attributed greater importance to it for reasons of religion: indeed, the synagogue began as a place for teaching and the instruction of adults and continued as one for boys over sixteen (59). The modest general educational system of the Middle Ages – the cathedral schools began to teach children intended for the priesthood and then in private institutions – was, equally, designed for the needs of a society in which the Church had, for a long time, a monopoly of literacy and education; and where even great rulers such as William I, Hugh Capet (probably), Otto the Great (perhaps), and Charlemagne, certainly, could not write – though the last named

could talk Latin (60). It also suited the Church to propagate a general
view that the truth was 'something which had been once known but
was now lost' (61). Priests, of course, did their work better if they were
literate. So did monks if they were able to read the scriptures – which
they had not universally been before 800 (62). Chivalry required horsemanship, swordsmanship and skill with the lance. The guilds needed
technical learning, and subsequently in later centuries, municipal
councils began to found lay schools for the sons of burghers – the first
since antiquity, though anyone who wanted anything more advanced
than the abacus and arithmetic had to go to clerical schools (63). Girls'
education, meanwhile, was minimal. Only if she wished to become a
nun was there much chance of a girl learning to read. Otherwise, even
in Italy, the most enlightened European country in the late Middle
Ages, girls were never taught more than household tasks – to weave,
embroider and so on, so that 'when you give her in marriage, men say
not that "she cometh out of the wilds" ' (64).

It may seem perhaps that these arguments place the order of priorities
erroneously; that, for instance, the educational achievements of
Tuscany in the fourteenth century were the consequence of Tuscan
learning and artistic vitality. This seems not to have been the case. A
country's morals may be decided by its education, but a decision to have
a good educational system is something which an already
educationally-minded country has to take itself. There seems, interestingly, no direct connection as a rule between riches and education.
Scotland and Switzerland, both poor until recently, have been for many
generations more highly literate than their richer neighbours.

Actually, in the eighteenth century, there were to be some serious
doubts as to the benefits to society of mass education. The attorney-
general of King Louis XV wrote in 1766: 'every man who sees further
than his dull daily round will never follow it out bravely and patiently',
while the President of the Royal Society in England in 1807 opposed the
prospect of 'giving education to the labouring class, for it would teach
them to despise their lot' (65), just as, in the sixteenth century, the
missionary Gregorio López had found it 'damnably dangerous' to teach
Indians in Mexico to read and write (66).

These views were, in the end, swept aside. The industrial age was
plainly served better by literate and educated people than by illiterate
ones. 'In most artisan trades,' wrote E. P. Thompson, 'the journeymen
and petty masters found some reading and work with figures an occu-
pational necessity' (67). Germany's education service improved to
become a genuinely universal system by 1815, and Holland and Switzerland followed to introduce universal, free and compulsory education.
Europe was probably half literate by 1850, with Italy* and Spain rather

* 73% of Italian men could not vote because they were illiterate, in 1871.

behind the average, and Germany ahead — indeed, Protestants were everywhere ahead (68). But most schools still had only one teacher, one room, and England, like Italy, only introduced compulsory education in the 1870s. Professor Cipolla speaks harshly of the English attitude: 'Part of the price England paid for being the first country to industrialise,' he says, 'was that the rapidly growing urban population had no access to schools.' But, by the time that the industrial revolution reached most countries apart from England, there were laws which channelled wealth to the education of children (69). The same was true of the US: only 10% of the white population of the US was illiterate in 1850, perhaps due to the high level of intelligence among immigrants, and perhaps also due to the demands of labour unions, as suggested before, for free schools (70).

Since that time, in the last three or four generations, education in all rich countries has become universal, free, compulsory, and, as a rule, co-educational. No greater change has ever occurred in human history. Some qualifications are required. First, there are some countries where the law's provision has never been carried out, however good the system seems to be on the surface. Second, there remains in some countries, such as Britain, a widespread incoherence in the methods of administering education dating from the nineteenth century and only comprehensible because of it. Third, though an industrial society benefits from an educated population, not every country has decided what sort of education that should be. Obviously, it should be more than simply knowing well a series of national classics, such as *The Pilgrims' Progress* or *Foxe's Book of Martyrs*, which was believed to be all that was needed in the few English schools of the eighteenth century. Managers of industries in the nineteenth century in much of Europe, recalled J. H. Plumb, had learned to speak 'of Job or Odysseus, of Catiline or Cicero as if they had lived but yesterday' (71). Generation after generation throughout the Western world studied one aspect or another of classical civilisation. That approach to education has now been rejected. In its place, there is more science, perhaps a badly taught foreign language: but a clear vision is often lacking of Western education in the 1970s, perhaps because some teachers are unclear what Western civilisation is. The most recent generation in the West has reacted strongly against Aristotle's concept of a liberal education ('a gentleman must never take too much interest in any occupation, art, or science') (72), as it has against formal education. Now a reaction against that reaction is beginning. But many societies, caught between two worlds, the world of a very good education for a few and that of a mass education, seem powerless to decide on their aims. In the communist world, a more resolute attitude to education is detectable. It is based however, on traditional methods, such as competition, selection, vocational training and nationalism. Probably, however, the muffled sense of Western education is only a short-term interlude, a halt on the journey. A return to a traditional, disciplined education now seems inevitable.

Fourthly, the history of education since the late nineteenth century has become inextricably concerned with the history of school and the 'education system'. This is an extraordinary change from the old method of learning in small villages or colleges, where the teachers carried out themselves the small amount of discipline needed. The modern educational system is the reverse of this desirable parochiality and insulation from politics. The conversion of education into one more major political issue in democracies is a challenge to the mood of serenity in which true education should be carried out. However, it is hard to point to a beginning for this. Thus, there is no doubt that education, like the development of the Press and the rebirth of sport, assisted at the birth of nationalism. The versions of history taught in European schools of the 1880s and onwards pressed a knowledge of the national past of peoples into the imaginations of schoolchildren that rarely emphasised the 'international republic of letters', nor of commerce. Germans learned anti-Slavism, Frenchmen anti-Germanism (73). A new consciousness of national literature and history added fuel to aspirations and resentments. The symbolic revival in the nineteenth century in Germany of old Nuremberg, so long neglected, as the centre of the new German culture in place of frenchified cities, such as Berlin, was largely the work of nationalist historians.

Thus there is no need to follow Schopenhauer's denunciation of Hegel as a fool and a charlatan to realise that a bad education is worse than no education. Gibbon rightly pointed to this when he described the Emperor Valentinian, who so nearly founded the university in the Roman world, as being 'unenlightened, but uncorrupted, by study' (74). One of the first tasks of real education is to ensure that empty verbiage is not mistaken for learning. Yet Western experience shows that teachers, including even teachers at universities, have shown themselves, in the age of mass education, to be as inclined to subservience to intimidation as any other group of people. A majority of dons of German universities, for example, survived the Nazi capture of power without dismissal or resignation, and a Nazi salute, at the beginning or end of lectures, as required, seemed a small price to have to pay for tenure. A good picture, admittedly, of what German education meant was given by a speech in 1870 of Emil du Bois-Raymond, the most famous German physiologist and Rector of the University of Berlin: 'We, the University of Berlin, quartered opposite the royal palace, are, by the deed of our foundation, the intellectual bodyguard of the House of Hohenzollern' (75). It was thus not surprising that sixty years later, Hans Schemm, the first Nazi minister of culture in Bavaria, could say 'We are not objective, we are German.'

Stalin criticised the calm study of history more violently. In a journal of the central committee of the communist party of the Soviet Union devoted to history, he criticised editors for allowing the publication of an article which had tried to examine with objectivity the attitude of the Bolsheviks to the German social democrats in 1914. He pointed out that the day had passed when 'archive rats' could 'prefer objective facts to history which suited the current policy of the party' (77). The actual education in the Hitler youth may very well have been complete and strenuous even if the boys were in an army reserve, but the emphasis on German history, 'racial biology' and physical education was a distortion of truth, and the aim to destroy the liberal heritage of Germany was overweening.

Education was in the Middle Ages in Europe carried out, if at all, with a view to enhancing the power of the Church. In the twentieth century, in the same continent it has almost replaced religion as a prime preoccupation. The library is more important than the chapel in most modern universities. Though education is not the good life itself, and though no quantity of grants, subsidies and scholarships make up for lack of clear thought as to what the good life should be, education certainly can point the way to the good life as nothing else can: its universal acceptance is one of the few unquestionable benefits of the last generation.

V

It may be said that this book, with its multitude of odd and banal facts, arranged so cavalierly, as in a bazaar, has forgotten some of the critical parts of human life which now, as always, interest the majority. It has been the history, after all, of people's working hours. But where is the appropriate mention of Callimachus who carried off the prize in the horse race? (78) Where is the special kettledrum set up at Sumer in the temple courtyard? Where is the waltz, first danced at a court ball in 1794? (79) Did not Amasis I, King of Egypt, when reproached for having spent the whole day hunting, reply: 'Bowmen bend their bows when they wish to shoot; unbrace them when the shooting is over . . . so with men. If they give themselves continuously to serious work . . . they lose their senses and become mad, or moody, (80)? Games anticipated agriculture. During the long years of famine which drove the Etruscans from Lydia, they devised games of dice in order to spend one day out of two gambling to distract themselves from hunger (81), while Buzing, the Persian, imported chess from India long before the Renaissance (82).

Games, indeed, are more than they seem. That inspired historian of the subject, the Dutch professor Huizinga, pointed out that, according to ancient Chinese lore, 'the purpose of music and the dance is to keep the world in its right course', so as to force Nature into benevolence towards man: the year's prosperity in ancient China was held to depend on the right performance of sacred contests (83). The Greeks' attachment to games, particularly victory in games, was a mark of their appreciation of beauty, their desire to celebrate health, and grace, which played such a critical part in their entire attitude to life (84). In the earliest days of Sumer, games, music, dancing and religion were indeed part of the same ritual, and the ball games of Crete and Mycenae tell as much about the life of that civilisation as the staircases, the pottery and the estimated figures for the export of wool (85). The Romans' passion for gambling, for varieties of backgammon and draughts, began the era, it would seem, of real games, but 'the Games', the great chariot races and gladiatorial combats, at their appropriate and fixed times each year in fixed places, reflect, in their prefigurement of modern Mediterranean *fiestas* and *feste*, an historical continuity as strong probably as the more obvious ones of law or architecture. Modern Italy's *'ferragosto'* is a direct memory of the Romans' *feriae augusti*. Under Claudius in Rome, there were, in the first century AD, apparently 159 days of holidays in the year, of which ninety-three were devoted to games at the public expense (86). The modern tourist with his camera and guidebook stumbles admiringly over the ruins of amphitheatres, where ferocious battles were fought between buffaloes and elephants, or Saxon prisoners and Christians, probably condemning the practices whose institutions nevertheless survive, and no doubt ignoring that one effect of such shows was to purge the Mediterranean world of wild beasts, and perhaps failing to calculate that the 150,000 or so spectators at chariot races in Rome would have exhausted the capacity of all but the largest modern arenas: such temples of entertainment of the twentieth century as the Opera at Paris seat a mere 2,156. Sometimes, of course, games in the past got out of hand, and the rivalries induced by games between the 'blues' and 'greens' at Constantinople led to the civil wars and the death of thousands at the hands of what Gibbon described the 'blue livery of disorder' (87). 'A happy variation of the natatorial contest,' wrote Huizinga, 'is to be found in *Beowulf*, where the aim is to hold your opponent under water till he is drowned' (88). Some games such as the tournaments which were the pastime of the European landowners between about the twelfth and the seventeenth century plainly acted as a substitute for manoeuvres for war, and indeed war, for many hundreds of years, was little more than hunting carried on by other means. The insistence upon the Book of Sports which Kings James I and Charles I in England made into law and commanded to be read from pulpits, was a definite attempt to counter the 'anti-authoritarian ascetic tendency of Puritanism', in Max Weber's phrase (89). Certain morals too can be drawn from the character of those charming German courts of the eighteenth century where the household of the palace concerned might sally out, to tinkling bells, in long curved processions of sledges, to masquerades on the ice, or to skating, while, at the same time, in Italy, the friends of such ancient games of football as *calcio* or *ponte* fought their own civil against the advocates of *basset, faro, bimbi* and *minchiate:* or were such things in Italy anyway of small account, in comparison with the *conversazioni* and the *saloni?*

The great ball games of the twentieth century which are the mass entertainments *par excellence* of the industrial age have also their curious histories. Their origins are to be sought, like so much of the second half of the twentieth century, in England in the Victorian age, in the unusual structure of English social life, in the existence of a village green, perhaps in the absence of compulsory military training and the spirit of local self-government — even if afterwards they became much regimented, made scientific, disciplined, and certainly cut off, as games of the past were not, from the ancient as well as the modern culture of the people (90). The histories of baseball, pelota, tennis, bicycling, polo, golf, even croquet and cockfighting and bowls, clamour for attention. Where did they all begin, and why, and when?

Then there is gambling. That may have been the main reason for the downfall of old Cuba in 1959. An American sociologist in the 1940s wrote: 'Whether or not they plan in advance for other expenses, there is no doubt that many people on small incomes regularly devote a specified portion of their earnings to lottery tickets. It is useless to argue with them that the same amount placed in a savings account would, in time, provide a competence for old age or for a possible emergency. The lottery is the most potent enemy of any program designed to promote thrift. It encourages a . . . speculative mania, where everyone lives in a bubble which for most investors bursts every Saturday evening' (91). Perhaps too a history of when a people has holidays tells more than it seems about that people, whether it is the ancient Sumerians who had no weekly holidays but eleven to fifteen days at the New Year's feast (92), or whether it is the modern 'holidays with pay' desired by workers in factories.

Yet there is perhaps a more didactic point to be made. Earlier, it was tentatively suggested that the best form of democracy might have occurred when the system concerned was far from perfect from the point of view of voting but when elections were, in the words of John Vincent, 'much more a drama about the life of the town' and when the essential preoccupation of politicians was the frame within which the programmes and policies were written; the rules and forms were realised as being of prime importance. Perhaps there has been some decline since then. De Tocqueville rather gloomily wrote that men living in democratic times 'do not readily comprehend the utility of forms . . . Their chief merit, however, is to serve as a barrier between the strong and the weak, the ruler and the people, to retard the one and give the other time to look about' (93). Even so, most people concerned to establish or preserve free institutions today appreciate the point or can be made to do so. Keynes, writing after the First World War had shocked all civilised spirits, pointed out that his generation had suddenly become aware that Western civilisation was 'a thin and precarious crust erected by the personality and the will of a very few and only maintained by rules and conventions skilfully put across and guilefully preserved' (94) – a democrat, that is, is one who keeps the rules of the game. That is what Plato meant surely when he said that 'life must be live as play' (95). If the rules are kept, policies can be changed. The rules are, therefore, more important than the policies. 'No scepticism is possible where the rules of a game are concerned, for the principle underlying them,' wrote Paul Valéry, 'is an unshakable truth' (96).

Though it is easy to see that sport may turn out in the end to be as much a cause of international disputes as a substitute or emollient for them, it is more important to appreciate that constitutions have, indeed, much in common with games for they prescribe rules, knowing that, without rules, the barbarians will always win.* The conversion of thousand of adult people into followers of one or other football team can only, in the end, be a political lesson of great benefit. The chief danger to sport is the nationalisation of the talents and ambitions of the players.

VI

There seem to be precedents for many of our manifestations – even the fears which we believe to be uniquely ours. Even the fear of the destruction of the world as a result of a nuclear war which characterises our world as we approach the year 2000 can be compared without extravagance to the anxiety which the Christian world felt as it approached the year 1000. The difference, no doubt, is that there is, today, a more real chance of disaster than in, say, the year 980. It is perhaps surprising that some churchmen indeed have not seen, in the history of the twentieth century, the mark of Antichrist, whose dreadful empire, it was supposed, in the Middle Ages in Europe, would precede the coming of the

---

* The constitution of mediaeval Florence: all candidates to the 24-member Priorate had to be enrolled in a guild to prove that they were not aristocrats – a very important point to establish. Nobody leaving office could be re-elected to it within 2 years, and the prior held his office for 2 months. Nobody could canvas or ask or intrigue for office, but none could refuse it. Priors had to live altogether in one house where they lived and ate in common, not accepting invitations or giving private audiences. They received nothing beyond 10 solidi a day – a token sum. The Gonfalonier of Justice was chosen every 2 months from a different section of the city. He was, in effect, the chief of the priorate. His electors were the incoming priors, the captains and guild masters and two men from every section. When in office he lived with the priors (97).

kingdom of God (98). The perilous world of struggling nation states seems rather similar, too, to the condition of the eastern Mediterranean in the time of Plato and Aristotle, though transposed to the entire globe. Then, as now, there were a multitude of states of varying sizes and constitutions, each squabbling amongst each other, with a few large empires in the wings. The rest of the universe is to us what the sands of Africa, the tundra of Russia, or the seas beyond the Pillars of Hercules were to the Greeks. Then, as now, as Gilbert Murray put it, in respect of Greece, after the Peloponnesian war, the world was 'full of occult super-stitions, cults of the anti-rational, faith in chance, and huge audiences attracted by orators who promised all' (99).

But, all the same, it is desirable to notice several innovations. First, though the world seems more bitterly divided than at any time since the Renaissance at least, there is already something like a world society. At least in the non-communist world, news travels fast, rumours travel faster, fashions and moods cross and recross the Earth like waves of quicksilver. Behind the threat of world destruction, there is still the shadow of a world state, perhaps benevolent, or probably repressive, as it might turn out to be. A world with a population of over 4,200 million is an utterly different one from one with 500 million people, or 750 million people, the figures for 1500 AD and 1700 AD respectively.

Then, to ascend from the condition of masses to that of individuals, there can be no doubt whatever that women in the twentieth century have a different life from that which they were as a rule obliged to have in the past. Some of the technical innovations which have made this possible have been amply noticed earlier. But the critical change is surely that women have a far greater chance of achieving things in their own right, as opposed to the possibilities that might come to them from the accident of birth or marriage, than ever before. Women have always had a chance of power through their relation with certain rulers, as mothers, wives, widows or mistresses. It is possible that the day will be long delayed before women dominate the politics of western Europe as Elizabeth I and Catherine de' Medici did in the late sixteenth century. The great queens of antiquity look down at us from the towering height of twenty centuries of fame. But never have so many opportunities been open to so many women in so many parts of the world. Equal pay for equal work may not have been achieved in the rich countries, and the communist and Islamic countries are some way behind the democra-tic world in these as in many other matters. But the fact of change is evident here for all to see.

Then some parts of the political condition are new too. Gone are the nomadic tribes, gone the city states, gone the majority of the tribal monarchies which flourished still in 1750 throughout so much of the world. Gone too is the ambiguity as to whether such and such a terri-tory is part of the preserve of this people or that. The entire land surface of the Earth, and much indeed of the sea, is now divided up between some 150 or so states modelled institutionally at least approximately on the states which were already in being in Western Europe in the eighteenth and nineteenth centuries. The character of these states has absolutely changed too. About thirty or so of them are democratic. Another thirty are totalitarian*, where the state presumes to control the whole life of the people in the interests of what the administration argues must be the people's good. The rest are authoritarian, autocratic, or still monocratic, in which, though there are as a rule no peaceful means of changing the government, there are some sources of independent authority (such as churches, rich men, large companies, unions, aristocrats) within the polity. Both the democracies and the totalitarian states are really new since the age of industry began, the former being dependent upon mass education and the latter upon the artful use of technology. Before the coming of railways, the telegraph and the telephone, as Richard Pipes points out, bad roads and communications generally prevented the Tsars from imposing a repressive dictatorship in Russia on the scale made possible in the twentieth century (100). Technology has also placed many temptations towards centralisation and interference before both autocratic and democratic states and we can be sure that, if some autocratic (or even democratic) states become converted into totalitarian ones in future, as may be possible, it will be technology which will make that possible, even if ideology will have made it sought after.†

Fourthly, nearly all modern states now have written constitutions, comprising a large accumulation of written laws. Here is a striking difference from the condition of life in 1750, when no states at all had such documents. Their political arrangements depended then largely upon custom. The curious irony of this development is that, while the only important country in the world without a written constitution remains Britain, it is British laws and practices which have really inspired the writing of the constitution of the US, which itself has influenced, directly or indirectly, the constitutions of half the world — indeed has influenced the very idea that a written constitution is desirable.‡

Fifthly, the difficulty of making helpful comparisons between the rich industrial countries and the poor agricultural ones is probably greater

---

* The word 'totalitarian' was apparently invented by Mussolini to describe the state which he had founded. However, the survival of monarchy, *monsignori* and Mafia made Fascism in Italy less totalitarian than the Duce desired.

† Nor, incidentally, is there 'any automatic stabilising factor', as Henry Kissinger put it, which means that economic improvement makes for greater political stability or freedom (101).

‡ As the great Dicey put it, the US constitution represents a 'gigantic development of ideas which lie at the basis of the political and legal institutions of England' (103).

than it ever was. This is not only because, as the figures quoted earlier suggested, the poor agricultural countries are now importing grain from the rich industrial ones. For, while the rulers of rich countries are wondering how to prevent the 'secure, but aimless lower middle class or blue collar workers' of their cities (in Dr Brzezinski's formulation) (102) from taking up crime on a larger scale than they are at present, the poor countries are seeking to feed and employ millions of still hopeful agricultural poor who thrust their way into the already overcrowded cities. To both groups, in rich countries and poor ones, audiovisual mass communication presents visions of limitless opportunities but, at the same time, puts them at the mercy of magnetic leaders. Despite that apparent similarity between rich and poor, the preoccupations of the first are now of a quite different order from those of the second. It is not that there is such a thing as a developed world, with no problems to speak of, and an undeveloped one, which needs the help of the others. There is no such table arranged in any easy unilineal form of development and undevelopment. Perhaps it would be easier if there were. The pressing concerns of the rich countries seem trivial to those of the poor and those of the poor seem incomprehensible, even enviable sometimes, to the rich. How often have travellers arrived in remote regions to envy the rural simplicity of some undeserted sweet Auburn in upper Peru! The poor countries do not realise that the rich countries can be ruined by bad government or over-government as much as poor ones can be starved by neglect. Cuba, a country which now puts itself forward as a leader of the 'underdeveloped' world, is actually a good example of a rich country gone to seed and then to revolution, not of a poor one which has never had a chance.* Here, though, we are reminded of a continuing historical pattern: the French revolution executed Antoine Lavoisier, the father of French chemistry, who had been a farmer-general of taxes before 1789. When a petition reached the Tribunal appealing for his release, the President of that body rejected it and scrawled on it, '*La République n'a pas besoin de savants*' (104).

Another novelty of our time is the curious fact that most of the politicians who direct modern states are at a loss in the scientific and technical labyrinth which gives the states concerned their power and their opportunities. Hitler was probably the last would-be conqueror to insist on knowing the working of the weapons which he used.† These incapacities of politicians reflect well the bewilderment of their publics. Every year nowadays brings its new crop of miraculous tales and rumours. Could it be true that, were the sky to be filled at the same time by a relatively small number of supersonic aircraft, the envelope of the Earth

* Cuba had railways before most of Europe, a steam engine before the US and more televisions in 1958 than Italy did.
† It is said that he refused to countenance the construction of atomic weapons because he did not know how they worked (105).

would disintegrate?* Such stories abound. The layman is too badly educated scientifically as a rule to judge their truth. So it is as if the whole world were living under a kind of censorship in which a scandal is eagerly passed from person to person. Thus, we are told that the amount of carbon dioxide is increasing: that, indeed, it has increased, from 290 parts in a million to 330 parts per million. By the year 2020, it is said, the amount of carbon dioxide could approach 660 (106). The increase was once believed to be due to the burning of fossil fuels. Now it is said that it was because of the world-wide destruction of forests. The layman has always suspected that such things are likely. Where in England, he has wryly, but ineffectively, asked, for generations, are the great forests of Knaresborough, Charnwood, Sherwood, Cranborne Chase, Bere? All are gone, more completely than the great mediaeval noble families. The effect, it is said, will be to increase the heat and aridity in the world. Or so it seems. But each man chooses his own evil rumour to believe. This state of affairs differs from the rational nineteenth century, even if it recalls the Middle Ages and even if there is a rational basis to many such fears.

The critical developments of the last few years have, however, been achieved by a new science itself incomprehensible to the layman: namely, microelectronics. The small but reliable antennae devised as a result have enabled men to land on the moon, build the numerous satellites which circulate the earth, and create inter-continental ballistic missiles. Computers and calculators, communication satellites and digital watches, are now at the service of all rich societies, even if those societies are often incapable of maintaining their political sense and sense of continuity. All these developments derive, it seems, from the transistor, devised in 1947, and the computer, the first electronic version of which was built in the University of Pennsylvania in 1945. The prices of these and other such extraordinary systems of calculation, remembrance and analysis are falling steadily. Soon, a computer will be within the reach of an ordinary layman. Indeed, it already almost is so. To well-educated people in the arts subjects, it seems, to parody Voltaire, as if one incomprehensible machine after another succeeds each other on the banks of the Hudson River. Not far away, perhaps, are man-powered aeroplanes, or 'flying bicycles', the battery-operated car, the typewriter which will type as its master dictates, the cure for the slightest cold, and the cheap desalination plant. Further away, but perhaps within reach of man within the foreseeable future, is some way of assuring indefinitely the right atmospheric conditions for the Earth's survival by some force in the universe after the sun burns out. Human life itself is almost possible to invent – though that seems one of the

---

* I was assured that this was so by the editor of a Catholic weekly who claimed to have heard it from a grandson of Marconi. I have since ascertained that it is not true.

inventions least likely to be needed. States will need to consider these opportunities in the future with great care. All the more reason, therefore, why they should leave aside the many things that they now insist unnecessarily on financing and managing, in order to give their statesmen time to consider those more complicated matters of scientific opportunity with knowledge and wisdom.

The complement to these opportunities is, of course, the threat of nuclear war which has been often mentioned in this book. Here certainly is another novelty. This is a direct threat to most of the world, even if it touches some people more directly than others. If nuclear war occurs there plainly is a chance, remote no doubt but undeniable, that the consequence will be the destruction of the human species and perhaps of many other species as well. The world might at best return to somewhere close to that stage of evolution where it was after the destruction of the larger reptiles.

There are too, any number of possible setbacks less severe than one which would return the earth to the condition that it was in several hundred million years BC. That, in a sense, happened once before, after all, in Europe at the end of antiquity. The discoveries of the nature of anatomy, for example, which led to a proper awareness of the possibilities of surgery, had been made, or were on the brink of being made, before the birth of Christ. Almost every discovery necessary for the achievement of modern Western civilisation indeed had been made, or was nearly made, in ancient Alexandria before 200 AD. What was done to analyse and describe plants between Theophrastus, who was born in 370 BC and the Renaissance? Very little. Aristarchus, in 250 BC, said (in words summed up by Archimedes). 'The earth revolves round the sun in the circumference of a circle, the sun lying in the middle of the orbit' (107). During the Dark Ages, and Middle Ages, most of these and other comparable theories were forgotten. Matthew Arnold in *Culture and Anarchy* suggested that such discoveries were 'unsound at that particular moment of man's development', being 'premature'. He went on: 'The indispensable basis of conduct and self-control upon which alone the perfection aimed at by Greece can come into bloom was not to be reached by our own race so easily; centuries of probation and discipline were needed to bring us to it' (108). His own comments suggest that he did not think that his own generation was adequately prepared either. On the contrary, he described his countrymen during his own day as living in anarchy.*

---

* Arnold's comments on the working class in Victorian England were that: 'body upon body are beginning to assert, and put into practice, an Englishman's right to do as and what he likes . . . meet where he likes, enter where he likes, hoot as he likes, threaten as he likes, smash as he likes' (109). It is interesting to speculate what he would have said had he lived a hundred years later.

The trouble perhaps is that we are finding it harder than we expected to live in a world which cannot risk another major war. Our states were founded on wars, our national heroes who look down at us, from plinths and pillars, were all soldiers or admirals. Wars have, in the past, also been the stimulants of technological change, the lever of social change (more probably than considered programmes of socialism), and have also brought to countries a 'spiritual peace' otherwise rarely obtainable. War and golden ages have gone together (Athens in the fifth century was continually at war, Britain often so in the sixteenth and eighteenth centuries.) Even during the terrible wars of the twentieth century, the ties established between civilians and soldiers alike create a sense of community apparently unattainable in modern times during the piping days of peace. Bringing in the harvest used to be a possible alternative to war, but it is no longer. Could sport really be William James's 'moral equivalent' to war? It still seems possible. Or is it an illusion, considering what has been said in an earlier chapter, to suppose that we are indeed still at peace?*

VII

With the decline of the absolute authority once established by religion, appeals to History to justify actions have seemed to be on the increase. Hitler, at his trial after the failure of the putsch of 1923, said, 'You may pronounce us guilty a thousand times over, but the goddess of the eternal court of history will smile, and tear to pieces the brief of the prosecutor . . . For she acquits us' (110). Castro said much the same in 1953: 'Condemn me. History will absolve me' (111).

Modern industrial society sometimes seems free of its past. A modern family, living perhaps in a town without history, eats food unknown to its grandfathers whose names it often does not know, gains much of its knowledge of society from an invention, the television, undreamt of a hundred years ago, and perhaps uses constructions and words which would have been unrecognised by people nominally talking the same language in the eighteenth century. Nevertheless, history dominates political life: Russian harshness is explained by two hundred years of Tartar occupation (which itself ended five hundred years ago), and Russian suspicion of the West is justified by recalling the efforts at Allied intervention after the First World War.† People make use of words such as 'feudalism' to explain phenomena which would have been unrecognisable to the Cid. The understanding Westerner seeks lines of contact between rural China now and the same region under the Manchus. The Irish fight anew the Battle of the Boyne almost daily. The

* See above Chapter 46 about the Cold War.
† Or other invasions, from the Tartars onwards.

Arabs fight to recover territory that they lost in 1967 or 1948, the Jews to confirm their hold over what they lost in 70 AD, while their soldiers take their oaths of allegiance on the very site of the last stand, at Masada, of the old Jewish nation, in their fight against Rome. The Aztecs were lovingly recalled by Mexican revolutionaries of 1911–1919, the Incas by the urban revolutionaries (Tupamaros) of Uruguay. Mussolini remembered the Roman legions, and José Antonio Primo de Rivera, the Spanish Fascist leader, revived the symbols of Ferdinand and Isabella. Kwame Nkrumah, in rechristening the old Gold Coast colony of Britain by the name of Ghana, sought to revive a myth unknown to the grandfathers of modern Ghanaians, while the old controversies over the Atlantic slave trade are revived to stimulate, as well as to explain, racial hatred between black and white. Admittedly, an interest in history can often lead to false analogies. The number of times that Hitler recalled how Prussia had been saved in 1762 by the death of the Empress Elizabeth would suggest that here was a man who knew and loved history. But Hitler's knowledge of the past was selective, and injudicious. What was the point of recalling 1762 but forgetting what happened in 1918, the lessons of which (avoid a war with the USA, above all else) were most relevant to modern Germany?

Indeed, a case can be made for thinking that most modern tyrannies, even those which have wished to bring history as it were to an end by a perpetual despotism, have been driven onwards by a strong but misguided view of the past. Hitler sought an empire for Germany in the Ukraine, and dreamed of how the Germans of the future would holiday in the Crimea, driving there along great motorways, thus fulfilling the aspirations of the Germans of 1910, but without realising that the days of the European empires he wished to emulate were already drawing to an end and, on the other hand, that the Russian state had been always able, except during the revolutionary circumstances of 1917–18, to prevent such a transfer of territory. As has been seen, the whole drive of the Nazi movement derived from a false view of the past history of races, and of the German and Jewish races in particular. Lenin in 1917 used evidence about the state of Russia which bore some relation to the truth as it had been when he was young, in the 1890s, but which took no account of the transformation of the Russian economy between 1905 and 1917, particularly between 1914 and 1917. Again, as has been suggested earlier, the view of the future which dominates Marxism derives explicitly from a series of false comparisons between the behaviour of the world's working classes, merchants and landowners. Both Nazism and communism have also gone to great lengths to present a distorted view of the past histories of the countries in which they have established their rule.* They have appreciated that one of the best ways to

---

* See Stalin's comment about 'archive-rats' noticed above, page 605.

capture the mind of a people is to distort its historical imagination, confuse people with new legends and divert them with artificially constructed heroes. Sometimes, these deceiving visions of the past may be embarked upon fairly unconsciously. For example, in the preliminaries to the establishment of one of the most recent tyrannies, that of the communist regime in Cuba, Fidel Castro made many speeches denouncing most violently the allegedly overbearing behaviour of the government of the US. What he was saying bore some relation to the conduct of the US a generation or so earlier. It bore little relation to the prudent international posture of President Eisenhower in 1959.*

Free countries should learn their history well too. They should not allow a natural caution to cause them to forget the historic origins of their institutions and ideals. Of course, to all scholars of integrity, the past gives uncertain, confused and complicated answers as well as inspiration. The truth of the most straightforward occurrence is elusive. The great Marc Bloch wrote, in the concluding lines of his *Rural France*, 'In the continuum of human societies, the vibrations between molecule and molecule spread out over so great a span that the understanding of a single moment, no matter what its place in the chain of development, can never be attained merely by contemplation of its immediate predecessor' (112). Let us be cautious, certainly. Caution spells wisdom. Wisdom is rare. But let us not be over-modest. Free societies have achieved much. They are certainly the only ones where self-respecting historians can live and work in peace.

Free societies sometimes seem today to have lost their nerve. Lord Clark, at the end of his essay *Civilisation*, has apparently given up the cause for lost (113). Solzhenitsyn, in his lecture at Stockholm accepting the Nobel Prize for Literature, remarked that he found the civilised world to be 'frightened', with 'nothing better than concessions and smiles to offer to the assault of barbarism' (114). The eminent French historian of demography, Pierre Chaunu, has suggested that the West has 'ten years left to put its house in order' — an activity which he wisely believes to consist in returning to reflect upon, and reburnish, the ideals which sustained us in the past.

Certainly there is ground for misgiving. Half the population of the West itself seem sometimes to have lost faith in their own ideals. Many have forgotten, or never been told, what actually the West stands for; and they certainly do not feel that that 'very word is like a bell', as Keats put it of something else, or at least a reminder of antiquity's Zephyrus, who was supposed to produce flowers and fruit simply by the sweetness of his breath. De Tocqueville held strongly the view that 'when the

* Castro, for example, made a most virulent attack on the new ambassador of the US to Cuba, Philip Bonsal. He spoke of this able diplomat arriving in Havana as if he had been a proconsul of the old Roman Empire. He was really describing the way that Mr Bonsal's predecessor but ten, Sumner Welles, reached Havana in 1933.

religion of a people is destroyed, doubts get hold of the higher powers of the intellect and half paralyse all the others. Every man then accustoms himself to having only confused and changing notions on the subjects most interesting to his fellow creatures . . . His opinions are all defended and easily abandoned; and, in despair of ever solving by himself the hard problems respecting the destiny of man, he ignobly submits to think no more about them.' Such a condition, de Tocqueville believed, could not but 'enervate the soul, relax the springs of the will and prepare a people for servitude'. De Tocqueville indeed questioned whether man can ever support complete religious independence and entire political freedom: 'If faith be wanting in him he must be subject: and, if he be free, he must believe' (115). History since de Tocqueville's day has, however, shown many examples of nations and people who have been both believing and subject, and incredulous and free, as well as sustaining many faiths, not just a national one. The great French historian also seemed to imply that any religion would serve, true or false, to sustain intelligence. But the moral of that argument is correct. Only societies which have faith in themselves survive, and deserve to survive. That self-confidence must derive from the study of that society's past. Those who wish to revive the West cannot afford to forget that the freedom which we respect in the form of representative democracy has only flourished successfully as yet in societies which have been inspired at one time or another by the absolute value which Christianity gives to the soul (116). Capitalism may have warts, but they are minor disfigurements in comparison with the swelling tumours caused by collectivism. The history of industrial capitalism and European imperialism has black chapters but Europeans should look back in anger at neither. Capitalism generally has inspired peace, not war, prosperity, not poverty. 'Progress' and 'science' may seem to have led the world to the edge of destruction – from nuclear war or shortage of resources – but statesmen can still draw us back from that precipice. They should not forget Burckhardt's judgment that the concept which has most guided civilised Europeans since the Renaissance is the 'enigmatic mixture of conscience and egotism known as Honour' (117). They must remember Bertrand Russell's dictum, made on his return from Russia in 1920, that the idea of a society based on Law had only been achieved after many centuries of patient struggle and should not lightly be abandoned in the supposed interests of immediate economic benefit (118). They should also recall that the way that ideals are presented need naturally to be reconsidered anew by each generation if they are going to survive the fires of the particular time. They should take comfort from the fact that the vast majority of people to whom such a choice is ever put rationally and calmly usually prefer a country 'which is poor and weak and of no account than powerful, prosperous and enslaved', as Lord Acton formulated the dilemma in his sonorous manner (119). They should know that their actions, if they go ill, will certainly be examined, if historians survive at all, by some future personification of Lord Macaulay's New Zealander, who would surely be puzzled by the fall of a civilisation so rich and so intelligent.* They should notice surely that the first history to survive antiquity, that of Herodotus, written 'in the hope of preserving from decay the remembrance of what men have been', concerned a battle between free men and tyrants (120). They should also recognise that one of the benefits of a study of history is that it is always possible to reverse, as Plato put it, an apparently fatal tendency towards decay, however late the hour.

---

* Lord Macaulay's New Zealander appears in the Essay on Ranke's *History of the Popes*: he pictured the survival of the papacy even in some remote future when 'some traveller from New Zealand shall, in the midst of a vast solitude, take his stand on a broken arch of London Bridge to sketch the ruins of St Paul's' (121): were such a traveller now to appear he would have to go to the United States even to find an arch of London Bridge.

References

The notes here refer to books, pamphlets and articles listed in the following bibliography. Where there are two items by the same author in the latter, the item is distinguished here by a short title: e.g. Bloch, *Rural France*. Where there are two authors with the same surname, they are distinguished by initials.

BOOK I
Notes to pages 1–15

Chapter 1

1. Saggs, 454
2. Molnar
3. Hsü, 53
4. Coon, 44
5. Valentine, 115
6. Washburn, 150
7. Isaac, 106
8. Coon, 78
9. Coon, 659
10. Washburn, 156
11. Washburn, 158
12. Cohen, Marcel, *Language*
13. Coon, 80
14. G. Clark, 34
15. Sommerfelt in Singer etc, *History of Technology*, I, 101
16. Coon, 5
17. Arnold, *The Scholar Gipsy*
18. Mumford, *Transformations*, 7
19. Young, 380
20. Singer, 146

21. Jeans, 86
22. Jeans, 66–68
23. qu. M. Balfour, 13
24. de Tocqueville, *Democracy*, I 202
25. Malraux
26. Gibbon I, 209
27. Roederer, III, 461
28. Isaac, 102
29. *Scientific American*, August, 1978
30. Lewortin, 157

Chapter 2

1. Bogart, 283
2. Keeley, 108
3. G. Clark, 14–15
4. G. Clark, 55–56
5. Coon, 39
6. G. Clark, 45

7. Berenson, *Autobiography*
8. G. Clark, 61–2
9. Rousseau, 178
10. Berlin, *Vico*, 53
11. Jaurès
12. G. Martin

Chapter 3

1. Coon, 70
2. Clark, 74; Saggs, 4; Derry, 4
3. Herodotus I, 355
4. Saggs, 4
5. Coon, 101; Zeumer, 120
6. Clark, 70
8. Derry, 6
9. Tannahill, 37
10. G. Clark, 80
11. Montet, 81
12. Wrigley in Fage and Oliver 66
13. List, 35
14. Montet, 11
15. G. Clark, 203
16. Saggs, 259
17. Gibbon II
18. Chadwick, 4
19. Needham I, 81
20. Zeumer, 37
21. Thapar, 34
22. Thapar, 54
23. Pipes, 28
24. Wittfogel, 17
25. Needham, 1, 67
26. Bloch *Feudal Society* 225
27. Peck, 121
28. Bloch, *Feudal Society* 245

Chapter 4

1. Saggs, 17
2. G. Clark, 100
3. Jeans, 4
4. Derry, 78
5. Wainwright, 161
6. Needham T, 82
7. Parry, 80
8. Jeans

9. Derry, 80
10. Herodotus I, 84
11. Thapar, 41
12. Mumford, *The City*
13. Saggs, 6
14. Saggs, 10
15. Saggs, 13
16. Saggs, 180
17. Chadwick, 137
18. G. Clark
19. Briggs, 8
20. Wittfogel, 27
21. Montet, 16; Butzer,
22. Thapar, 76
23. Wittfogel 23
24. Wittfogel, 29
25. Childe, in Singer etc., *Hist. of Technology*, I, 130
26. Saggs, 451
27. Saggs, 450
28. Gardner, 22; Montet, 23
29. Jeans, 4
30. Jeans, 9
31. G. Clark, 287
32. Wheeler, 10
33. Schamndt-Besserat, 38–42
34. Derry, 209
35. qu. Plumb 30
36. Derry 215
37. G. Clark 230
38. *Scientific American* May, 1978
39. Chadwick, 182
40. Bowen I, 170

Chapter 5

1. Multhauf
2. Needham, I, 20
3. G. Clark, 112
4. Polyani
5. Needham, I, 93
6. Singer, and Underwood
7. G. Clark, 112
8. Montet, 100
9. Sutherland, 20
10. B. Cunliffe, in Singer and Holmyard, 271
11. Saggs, 278
12. Derry, 120

13. Gall
14. Derry, 122
15. Saggs, 254
16. Montet, 60
17. Needham I, 93
18. Saggs, 169
19. Montet, 191
20. Thapar, 126

Chapter 6

1. Wheeler, 65
2. Thapar, 19
3. Orwin, 70
4. Orwin
5. Gibbon III, 141
6. Orwin 26
7. Bogart, 283
8. Bogart, 284

9. Braudel, *Capitalism*, 18
10. McNeill, 91
11. Thapar, 21
12. Sánchez Albornoz, I, 88
13. Szamuely, 80
14. Pipes, 4–6, 16,
15. Needham I, 184
16. Carr, *Spain*
17. Utterstrom
18. Ladurie, *Times of Feast*
19. Rodgers, V
20. Strachey, 153
21. Ladurie, *Times of Feast*
22. Cipolla, III, 80
23. Ladurie, *Times of Feast*
24. Post
25. Huntington, 102
26. Braudel, *Capitalism*, 58
27. Bowra, 177
28. Sánchez Albornoz

BOOK II

Preparatory note

1. Clapham, IV, 205
2. E. Russell, 20

Chapter 7

1. Saggs, 4
2. J.Z. Young, 339
3. Cipolla, I
4. Deevey, 194
5. J.Z. Young, 340
6. Carr Saunders
7. Carr Saunders
8. Borah
9. U. N. *Annual Survey*
10. Braudel
11. Jones, *Decline*, 8
12. J.C. Russell
13. Braudel, *Mediterranean*, 6
14. Guillaume, 42 and 'Atlaseco.'
15. Frank; Brunt, 72
16. J.C. Russell

17. Braudel   *Mediterranean*,   410;
Cipolla in Glass and Eversley, 373
18. Guillaume, 42
19. Guillaume, 4
20. Mitchell & Deane 5
21. Glass 21
22. Bloch *Rural History* 37–8
23. Reference lost
24. Sauvy, 232
25. E. Anderson, 190
26. Qu. *Times*, April 6, 1977
27. *World Population*, 1975
28. Glass I, 95; Guillaume, 169
29. Mitchell, 86
30. U.N., *Annual Survey*
31. Lukacz, 73
32. Needham I, 92
33. Himes, 73–116
34. Glass, 10
35. Sauvy, 412
36. qu. Fabre Luce 93
37. Sauvy, 361
38. Elton, *Reform and Renewal*, 158
39. Mckeown & Brown in Glass and
Eversley II, 298

40. Chaunu, *l'histoire sociale*
41. Drummond, 70
42. qu. L. Stone, 432
45. Saggs, 213
46. Genesis I, 28
47. Plato, 457–61
48. Gibbon, I, 101
49. Carcopino, 70
50. Gibbon, IV. 38
51. Finlay, I, 160
52. Gibbon, IV, 38
53. qu. Fabre Luce, 103
54. Alberti, *Ten Books*
55. Montesquieu, *Lettres Persanes*
56. qu. Sauvy, 412
57. Thapar, 15
58. Burckhardt, *Civilisation*
59. Herodotus, 109
60. Bloch II, 142
61. Bloch II, 167
62. Glass II, 124
63. Laslett, 107

Chapter 8

1. Samuel, II, 24. V. 13
2. McNeil, 120
3. H. Thomas, 1522
4. Trueta, 36
5. Singer and Underwood, 215
6. Jones, 113
7. McNeill, 78
8. Boccaccio, 24–25
9. Nadal, 55–60
10. Medawar, 6
11. Braudel *Capitalism*, 45
12. Singer and Underwood, 216
13. Frank
14. Brunt
15. Homo, 82
16. Jones, 8
17. J.C. Russell
18. Braudel, *Mediterranean* 153
19. Mitchell, 76
20. Recollection of Dr E. Tejera, Caracas, 1976
21. Thapar, 27
22. Lambrecht in Fage and Oliver, 42
23. Singer and Underwood 223

24. Needham I, 204
25. Saggs, 474
26. Singer and Underwood 235
27. Jones, 235
28. Jones, 97
29. Southern I, 64
30. Tannahill, 179
31. Needham I 24
32. Thapar, 154
33. K.V. Thomas 220
34. K.V. Thomas, 249

Chapter 9

1. Sauvy, 518
2. Huizinga, 100
3. Glucksman qu. Laslett, 162
4. Fuller, 40
5. Sauvy, 521
6. Chadwick, 178
7. G. Clark, 160
8. Herodotus I, 41
9. Herodotus I, 54
10. Bury, 300
11. Oman 200
12. Wittfogel, 66
13. Herodotus II, 170
14. Thucydides 84
15. Bowra 83
16. Homo 94
17. Homo, 164
19. Trevor–Roper, 27
20. Tacitus II, 4
21. Homo 246
22. Gibbon I, 157
23. Gibbon III, 271
24. Gibbon II, 221

Chapter 10

1. Tannahill, 17
2. Chadwick, 120
3. Bowra, 126
4. Bowen, I, 74
5. Homo, 72
6. Herodotus, I, 219
7. Huntington, 60

8. Homo, 96
9. Brunt, 90
10. Gibbon, III, 417
11. Jones, Decline, 235
12. Braudel *Mediterranean*, 329
13. Drummond, 56
14. Braudel, *Mediterranean*, 245
15. Díaz del Moral, 128
16. Braudel, *Mediterranean*, 153
17. Guilbert
18. Sánchez Albornoz, 93
19. Braudel, *Capitalism*, 65
20. Tannahill
21. Derry and Williams, 66
22. Hémardiquer 93; Drummond 466
23. Fusell, 27
24. Vasari II, 182
25. Cervantes, 131
26. Cervantes, 20
27. Montaigne, 42
28. Thapar, 41
29. Genesis ix, 20–21
30. Montet, 84
31. Seltman 100; Tannahill, 79
32. Derry, 61
33. Southern, I, 40
34. Sánchez Albornoz, 90
35. *Chanson de Guillaume* qu. Bloch, II, 294
36. Bloch I, 23
37. Montet, 84
38. Tannahill
39. Parry, 70
40. Tannahill, 48
41. Zeumer, 437
42. Tannahill 250

Chapter 11

1. L. White, *Mediaeval Technology*. 90
2. Clapham IV, 171; Pipes, 10; Orwin
3. C.S. & C. S Orwin
4. Braudel *Capitalism*,241
5. Derry, and Williams, 52 6. C.S. & C.S. Orwin, 90
7. L. White, 53
8. Derry and Williams, 195–8
9. L. White, 27
10. Howard, *War*, 2

11. Gibbon VI, 172
12. Ménendez Pidal, 74
13. P. Anderson I
14. Bloch *Rural France* 54
15. L. White 30–8
16. Bloch *Feudal Society*, 313
17. Oman in *Camb. Med. History*, VIII, 656
18. Braudel, *Capitalism*, 255
19. Derry and Williams, 27
20. L. White
21. Braudel, *Capitalism*, 75
22. Derry and William, 70–1
22. Derry and Williams 69
23. Wainwright, 158
24. Thapar, 146
25. L. White, 85
26. Braudel *Capitalism*, 261–3
27. L. White, 89
28. Derry and Williams, 311
29. Mumford *The City* 258
30. Montet, 281
31. Hollington, 4
32. Carr
33. L. White

Chapter 12

1. Wittfogel, 69
2. Bloch *Rural France* 170
3. Lynch, 341
4 Sarmiento qu. Lynch 346
5. Thapar, 35
6. Jones *Decline*
7. Bloch, *Rural France* 75–77
8. Bloch, *Feudal Society*, 218
9. Wagner, 33
10. Pirenne, 81
11. Bloch *Rural France* 77
12. Bloch, *Feudal Society*, 170
13. Bloch *Feudal Society*,1
14. Lynch, 342
15. Clapham *France and Germany* 35–6
16. Blake, 142
17. Thapar, 242
18. Needham I, 91
19. Parry
20. Bloch *Rural France*, 100
21. Carr, 19

22. Glotz, 248
23. Maitland *Domesday Book.* 56
24. Wittfogel 100
25. Clapham *Britain,* 40
26. Bloch, *Rural France*
27. Bloch *Feudal Society,* 202
28. Bloch *Feudal Society,* 202
29. Maitland, *Domesday Book* 171
30. Bloch, *Rural France* 151; Thapar 242
31. Bloch I, *Rural France* 170
32. Maitland, *Domesday Book,* 152
33. Maitland, *Domesday Book,* 156
34. Bloch, *Rural France* 10
35. Burckhardt, 42
36. Needham I
37. Wittfogel, 84

Chapter 13

1. Bloch, *Rural France,* 8; *Origo,* 243
2. Clapham *France and Germany,* 15
3. Clapham, *France and Germany,* 161, 199
4. Bogart, 514
5. Brenan, 97
6. Campbell
7. Cobbett. qu. Clapham *Britain,* 22
8. C.S & C. S Orwin, X
9. Mantoux, 151
10. Clapham *France and Germany,* 31
11. Clapham *France and Germany,* 45
12. Pipes, 16
13. Wittfogel, 69
14. Thapar, 182
15. Pipes, 17
16. Thompson. E.A. 1–28
17. C.S. & C.S Orwin, 150
18. Bloch, *Rural France,* 26
19. Carr, 28
20. Bloch, *Rural France*
21. Thirsk, 326

Chapter 14

1. Chadwick,
2. Derry and Williams, 7
3. Finlay, *Ancient Society,* 36

4. Andrews, *Greek Society,* 135
5. Wittfogel
6. Derry and Williams, 200
7. Finlay, 76
8. Carcopino, 65
9. Jones, *Decline*
10. Carcopino, 61
11. Finlay, *Aspects,* 176
12. Carcopino, 184
13. Carcopino, 60
14. Gibbon I, 55
15. Jones, *Decline,* XXI
16. Bloch, *Feudal Society,* 265; Maitland, *Domesday Book,* 35
17. Maitland, *Domesday Book,* 56
18. Pipes, 2
19. Origo, 101
20. B. Lewis, 104
21. B. Lewis, 148
22. Thapar, 77
23. Bloch, *Feudal Society,* 265
24. D. B. Davis, 91
25. Bloch, *Feudal Society;* Maitland, 35
26. Pipes, 101
27. Szamuely, 42–6
28. Clapham, *France and Germany,* 39
29. De Tocqueville, *French Revolution,* 22
30. Herr, 98
31. B. Lewis
32. Clapham, *Britain,* III, 18
33. Díaz del Moral, 90

Chapter 15

1. Braudel, *Capitalism,* 230
2. Origo, 37
3. Chadwick, 129
4. Grimal, 4; Chadwick, 152
5. Pirenne, 155
6. Derry and Williams, 98
7. L. White, 119
8. Weber, 61; Bloch, *Rural France,* 91; Laslett, 18
9. Mantoux, 200
10. Origo, 74
11. Zeumer, 198
12. H. F. Pelham, *Essays*
13. Klein, 66

14. Macaulay, *Essay on Ranke*
15. Klein, 43
16. Klein, 60
17. Herr, 118
18. Klein, 338
19. Klein, 335
20. Gibbon IV, 312–13
21. Needham I, 185–6
22. Derry and Williams, 96
23. Thucydides, 5
24. Origo
25. Boswell II, 397
26. Candolle, 410
27. Thapar, 60
28. Derry and Williams, 98
29. Braudel, *Mediterranean*, 217
30. Parry, 217
31. Braudel, *Capitalism*, 230
32. Derry and Williams, 265
33. Schevill, 122
34. Parry, 288
35. Gibbon IV, 33
36. Candolle, 41

Chapter 16

1. Acton, 28
2. Saggs, 6
3. Saggs, 440
4. Herodotus, I, 102
5. Montet, 273
6. Montet, 194
7. Barry Cunliffe, 27
8. Chadwick, 185
9. Hood, I, 221
10. *Scientific American*, Nov. 1976
11. G. Clark, 316; Herodotus I, 315
12. G. Clark, 243
13. Herodotus I, 209
14. G. Clark, 218
15. Grimal, 182
16. Mumford, 21
17. qu. Grimal, 227
18. G. Clark, 98
19. Childe in *Hist of Tech*. I, 48
20. G. Clark, 286
21. Wittfogel, 95
22. Juvenal qu. Grant
23. Montet; G. Clark, 196

24. Chadwick, 180
25. Popper, I, 11
26. Bowra
27. Bowra, 126
28. Protagoras, qu. Bowra 182
29. Bowra, 117
30. Bowra, 226
31. Thapar 48–49
32. Dawson, 71; Gard, 106
33. Zaehner, 56
34. Gibbon I, 37
35. Trevor-Roper
36. Jones, 38
37. Gibbon II, 356
38. Gibbon III, 213
39. A. Castro, 468
40. Gibbon II, 9
41. Lecky, 19
42. Gibbon V, 421
43. Hobbes, *Leviathan*
44. Trevor-Roper, 84
45. Gibbon
46. B. Lewis, 48
47. B. Lewis, 58
48. Sánchez Albornoz, 163
49. Sánchez Albornoz, 289
50. Koran XVIII, 220; LVI, 347
51. Wittfogel, 86
52. Thapar, 291
53. Ullmann, 264
54. Bloch, *Feudal Society*, 80
55. Bloch, *Feudal Society*, 87
56. M. Pidal, 37
57. A. Castro
58. Southern, 189
59. Briggs, 75, 128
60. Southern, 130
61. Southern, 55
62. Pevsner, 111
63. Trevor-Roper, 160
64. Bloch II, 84
65. Burckhardt, 347
66. Pipes, X
67. K. V. Thomas, 323
68. Trevor-Roper, 150
69. Burckhardt, 112–3
70. K. V. Thomas, 614
71. K. V. Thomas, 28
72. Burckhardt, 321
73. Herodotus, I, 213
74. B. Lewis, 261

Chapter 17

1. Huizinga, 11–15
2. Herodotus, I
3. Saggs, 200
4. De Tocqueville I, 102
5. Herodotus
6. Bowra, 86
7. Thucydides, 122
8. Bowen, I, 90
9. Finlay, *Aspects*, 61
10. Popper, I, 58
11. Finlay, *Studies*, 24
12. Finlay, *Studies*, 24
13. Homo
14. Homo
15. Homo
16. Maine, 31
17. Jones, *Decline*
18. Jones, *Decline*
19. Jones, *Decline*, XIV
20. Gibbon, V, 33
21. Ullmann, 119
22. Gibbon, V, 33
23. Gibbon, V, 418
24. Homo
25. Jones, *Decline*
26. Carcopino, 191
27. Jones, *Decline*, Chapter XIII
28. Jones, *Decline*, 15
29. Jones, *Decline*, 211
30. Entwhistle, 242
31. Trevor-Roper, 142
32. Fage and Oliver, 47
33. Thapar, 37
34. Thapar, 57
35. Thapar, 60
36. B. Lewis
37. Wittfogel, 131
38. Jones, 21; Homo, 85
39. Bloch, *Rural France*, 81–2
40. Maitland, *Domesday Book*, 3–6
41. V. H. Galbraith, 175
42. Bloch, *Rural France*
43. Acton, 32
44. Holt, 292

BOOK III

Chapter 18

1. Needham, I, 4

2. Jeans, 57
3. Démangéon, 303
4. Bloch, *Feudal Society*, 52
5. Edwards, 86
6. Burckhardt, 183
7. Burckhardt, 84
8. Needham I, 264
9. L. White
10. Bloch, *Rural France*, 204
11. Needham I, 205
12. L. White, 128
13. Boccaccio, II, tale 1
14. Braudel, *Mediterranean*, 535
15. Bloch, *Feudal Society*, 141

Chapter 19

1. Braudel, *Mediterranean*, 295
2. Hourani, 101
3. Needham, I, 134
4. B. Lewis, 93
5. Bloch, *Rural France*
6. Needham, I, 164
7. Derry and Williams, 216
8. Trevor-Roper, 190
9. Boxer
10. Trevor-Roper, 129
11. Parry, 45
12. Herodotus I, 30
13. Pius II, *Encyclopedia Britannica* (1911)
14. Momigliano, 137

Chapter 20

1. Mantoux
2. Barbour
3. Adam Smith
4. Braudel, III, 340
5. Saggs, 298
6. Derry, 12
7. Derry, 128
8. Needham, I, 248
9. Herodotus, I, 290
10. Sutherland
11. Thucydides, 108
12. Sutherland
13. Pirenne, 17

14. Pirenne, 34
15. Maitland, *Domesday Book*, 195
16. Bloch, *Feudal Society*, 67
17. Sánchez Albornoz, 711
18. Needham, I, 178–80
19. Southern, 60
20. Pirenne
21. Origo
22. Braudel
23. Origo, 146
24. Schevil, 125
25. Hale, 33
26. Needham
27. Dawson
28. Thapar
29. Parry
30. Parry
31. Sutherland
32. Braudel, I, 100
33. E. Hamilton
34. Barbour, 43
35. Leonard, 26
36. Mantoux, 96
37. Burckhardt
38. Burckhardt
39. Braudel, I, 284
40. Barbour, 24
41. Barbour, 142
42. Barbour, 134

Chapter 21

1. Herodotus, I, 354
2. Saggs, 249
3. Herodotus, II, 252
4. Wittfogel, 57
5. Herodotus, II, 135
6. Jones, *Decline*, chapter xxiii
7. Chevalier
8. Jones, 341
9. Brown, 13
10. Trevor-Roper, 80
11. Wittfogel, 57
12. Polo, I, 329
13. Wittfogel, 58
14. L. White, 67
15. Bloch, *Rural France*, 63
16. Southern, 28
17. Bloch, *Feudal Society*, 70

18. Needham, I, 141
19. Braudel, *Mediterranean*, 284
20. Von Hagen, 149–50
21. Zeumer, 437
22. Braudel, *Capitalism*, 249
23. Parry, 75
24. Braudel, 250
25. de Tocqueville, *French Revolution*, 23
26. Pipes

Chapter 22

1. Carcopino, 202
2. Needham I, 216
3. Braudel, *Mediterranean*, 774
4. Steinberg
5. Burckhardt, 158
6. Parry
7. Braudel, *Capitalism*, 300
8. K. V. Thomas, 355
9. Mitchell & Deane
10. Plumb, *Man vs. society*, 12
11. Mumford, *The City*, 550
12. Leonard, 13
13. Needham I, 148
14. Berenson, *Italian Painters*
15. K. V. Thomas, 184
16. Boswell II, 262
17. Burckhardt, 118

Chapter 23

1. Burckhardt, 30
2. Jones, *Decline*, 50
3. Dante, *Inferno*
4. Hale, 16
5. Hale, 26
6. qu. Braudel, *Mediterranean*, 400
7. Mumford, *City*, 200
8. Pevsner, 86
9. Origo, 225
10. M. Pidal
11. Giedion, 297
12. Mumford, *City*, 286
13. Mumford, *City*, 384
14. Giedion, 268

15. Origo, 225
16. Mumford, *City*, 283
17. Sánchez Albornoz, 713
18. Alberti
19. Pipes
20. Pipes
21. Polo
22. Saggs
23. Saggs
24. Derry and Williams
25. Mumford, *City*, 24
26. Carcopino, 40
27. Derry and Williams, 19
28. Jones, *Decline*, 235
29. Jones, *Decline*, 233
30. Jones, *Decline*, 233
31. qu Mumford, *City*
32. K. V. Thomas, 629
33. Burckhardt, 47

Chapter 24

1. L. White, 103
2. Needham I, 142, fn(d)
3. L. White, 100
4. Cipolla, *Guns*, 39
5. Cipolla, *Guns*, 100
6. Derry and Williams, 149
7. Burckhardt, 59
8. Gibbon II, 319
9. L. White, 36
10. Howard, *War*, 11
11. Trevor-Roper, 27
12. Bloch, *Feudal Society*, 313
13. Oman, *Camb. Med. history*, VIII, 656
14. Cipolla, *Guns*, 38
15. L. White, 164
16. Origo, 36
17. Cipolla, *Guns*, 130
18. M. Weber qu. Galbraith I, 15
19. Braudel, *Mediterranean*, 1102
20. Laslett, 243
21. Parry, 234
22. Reinhard, 159
23. Fuller, 15
24. Mumford, *City*, 363
25. McNeill, 233
26. Burckhardt, 102

27. Barbour, 29
28. Barbour, 38
29. qu. Fuller, 42

Chapter 25

1. Morison, *Admiral*
2. Singer and Underwood, *Medicine*
3. Singer and Underwood, *Medicine*
4. Jeans
5. Casanova, ed Boyd, 7
6. Cellini, 178
7. K. V. Thomas, 231
8. Glass and Eversley, I, 79
9. Ibid
10. Mckeown and Brown in Glass and Eversley, 307
11. Mckeown & Brown in Glass and Eversley, 284
12. Sauvy, 26
13. Reinhard
14. J. Hajnal in Glass and Eversley, 30
15. Laslett, 81
16. Bloch, *Rural France*, 135
17. Hajnal, in Glass and Eversley
18. qu. L. Stone, *The Family*
19. Cellini, 3
20. Franklin
21. L. Stone, *The Family*, 6
22. M. Pidal, 395
23. Reinhard, 133
24. Aristotle, *Laws*
25. Carcopino, 83
26. Montet
27. Rick, *Sc. American*, Sept. 1976
28. qu. Trevelyan, 287
29. Drummond, 47
30. Drummond, 114
31. Drummond, 195
32. Franklin
33. Trueta, 63
34. Braudel, *Capitalism*, 171
35. Derry and Williams, 62
36. Needham I, 7
37. Pipes, 157
38. Pipes, 156
39. Drummond, 116
40. Drummond, 209
41. Mantoux

42. Carr, 22
43. Franklin, 231
44. Tannahill, 306
45. Curtin, 46
46. Fage and Oliver, 113
47. Curtin, 46
48. Hofstadter, 70

49. Klein, 36
50. Eric Williams
51. Anstey, 57
52. C. L. R. James
53. Oliver and Fage, 128
54. Howard, 40

BOOK IV

Introduction

1. Pipes, 155
2. L. Stone, 270
3. Arnold
4. Keynes, Collected writings, vol IX
5. Various figures in Clapham, Zeldin, Craig &c

Chapter 26

1. Mantoux
2. Clapham, *Britain I*, 146
3. D.N.B.: Kay
4. D.N.B.: Hargreaves
5. Mantoux
6. Mantoux, 197
7. Herr 134; Parry I, 132
8. Jones, 315
9. Mantoux
10. Herr, 128
11. Clapham, *Britain I*, 202
12. Clapham, *Britain*, II, 110
13. Bogart
14. Clapham, *France and Germany*, 288
15. Giedion, 77
16. Clapham, *Britain*, I, 252
17. Finlay, *Studies*, 27
18. E. P. Thompson, 554
19. Sauvy, 126
20. Sauvy, 126
21. Adam Smith
22. Sauvy, 117
23. Laslett, 29
24. Clapham, *Britain*, I, 565
25. Hofstadter, 97
26. Mantoux, 376

27. Laslett, 2
28. Clapham, *Britain*, I, 372
29. Bogart, 435
30. Bogart, 425
31. Bogart, 579
32. Clapham, *Britain*, I, 566
33. Szamuely, 407
34. Clapham, *Britain*, II, 405
35. Szamuely, 407
36. Bogart, 428; Balfour
37. Sauvy, 192

Chapter 27

1. Clapham, *Britain*, I, 85
2. Bogart, 386
3. Braudel, *Capitalism*, 274
4. Derry and Williams, 313
5. L. White, 92
6. Derry and Williams, 313
7. Mantoux, 314
8. Derry and Williams, 320; D.N.B.
9. Thomas, *Cuba*, 79
10. Carr, 32
11. Mantoux, 230
12. Bogart, 326
13. Clapham, *France and Germany*, 88
14. H. Thomas, *Cuba*, 138
15. Derry and Williams, 340; D.N.B., Parsons
16. Derry and Williams
17. Clapham, *Britain*, I, 132
18. Mantoux, 336
19. Mantoux
20. Derry and Williams, 592
21. Clapham, *Britain*, III, 157

22. Braudel, *Mediterranean*, 273
23. Gibbon
24. Herr, 194
25. Mitchell, 116
26. Bremner
27. Nef
28. Mitchell
29. Craig, 172
30. Clapham, *France and Germany*, IV, 232
31. Mitchell, 365
32. Clapham, *Britain*, III, 234
33. Mitchell *loc.* cit.
34. Source lost
35. Mack Smith II, 160
36. Churchill, *World Crisis*, I
37. Twining, 218
38. Griffith, 28
39. G. Clark, 237
40. Derry and Williams, 122
41. Genesis, IV, 22
42. Saggs, 288
43. Chadwick, 139
44. Saggs, 78
45. Grimal
46. G. Clark, 202
47. Wrigley in Fage, 73
48. Phillipson
49. G. Clark, 218
50. Braudel, *Capitalism*, 219
51. G. Clark, 231
52. Braudel, *Capitalism*, 275
53. Derry and Williams, 216
54. L. White, 41
55. Bloch, *Feudal Society*
56. Braudel, *Capitalism*, 275
57. Derry and Williams, 261
58. Cipolla, *Literacy*, 140
59. Herr, 28
60. Braudel, *Capitalism*, 283
61. Mitchell and Deane, 131
62. Cervantes, 85
63. Braudel, *Capitalism*, 275
64. U.N. Statistical Survey
65. Clapham *France and Germany*, 61
66. Clapham *France and Germany*
67. Mitchell 308
68. Derry and Williams 399
69. D.N.B.
70. Namier, *Journal of Business Studies*,
71. Clapham *Britain*

72. Clapham *France and Germany*, 63
73. Craig 86
74. *Historical Statistics*, 763
75. *Historical Statistics*, 366; Bogart 401
76. Zeldin I, 71
77. Nef.
78. Clapham I, 80
79. Mantoux
80. Clapham *Britain*
81. Clapham *Britain*
82. Pestaña qu. Meaker, 284
83. Clapham *Britain* 398
84. Clapham *Britain*, 429
85. Mitchell, 500
86. Derry and Williams, 335
87. Clapham *France and Germany* 154
88. Fuller, 90
89. Derry and Williams, 448
90. Clapham *France and Germany*, 158
91. Mitchell 581–3
92. Clapham *France and Germany* 156
93. Martin, 430
94. Bogart, 333
95. Bogart, 335
96. Clapham *Britain*, III.
97. Friedman, 28
98. Bogart 350
99. qu. Craig, 324

Chapter 28

1. Derry and Williams, 126
2. D.N.B.
3. Mantoux, 297
4. D.N.B.
5. Derry and Williams, 468
6. Mitchell, 399
7. Bogart 544
8. Bogart 720; *Historical statistics*, Mitchell 401
9. Mitchell 399.
10. Bogart 721
11. *Statistical Yearbook* of U.N.
12. Bogart, 724
13. Croce, 52
14. Mitchell 582.
15. Mitchell 584
16. Jenks 152
17. B. Lewis, 171

18. Bogart 616
19. Zeldin I 637
20. Josephson,
21. N. Stone, 43
22. Fuller 141
23. Taylor
24. N. Stone, 157
25. N. Stone, 291
26. N. Stone, 135
27. Marwick, I, 277
28. Zeldin II, 1050
29. Ulam, *Lenin and the Bolsheviks*
30. Katkov, 309
31. Philips Price 311

Chapter 29

1. Mantoux, 216
2. Clapham, *Britain,* I, 180
3. Bogart, 445
4. Bogart, 259
5. B. Lewis, 167
6. Mitchell, 289
7. Clapham, *Britain* I, 73
8. Clapham, *Britain* I, 7
9. Bogart, 404
10. L. Stone, 28
11. Bogart, 292
12. Bogart, 447
13. Herr, 414; Carr, 17; Parry, 314
14. Derry and Williams, 508
15. Clapham *Britain* II, 15
16. *Historical Statistics* 346; Bogart 548
17. *Historical Statistics,* 411
18. Zeldin I, 65
19. Mitchell, 435
20. Mitchell, 431

Chapter 30

1. J. Adams qu Bogart
2. qu. Clapham, *Britain,* II, 10
3. Bogart 388
4. Clapham, *Britain* III
5. Bogart 440
6. Clapham, *Britain* I, 491
7. Clapham *France and Germany,* 7

8. Clapham *France and Germany,* 301
9. Derry and Williams, 704
10. Pipes, 204
11. Voltaire, 55
12. Pipes 219
13. Schapiro
14. *Life of Bernini*
15. Briggs, 162
16. Saggs, 147
17. Jones, 33
18. Hémardiquer 249
19. J. K. Galbraith, 158
20. Braudel, *Mediterranean,* 519
21. P. Brown, 30
22. Laslett, 202
23. Bogart, 406
24. Klein, 55, 59
25. Briggs, 22
26. Drummond, 174
27. Clapham, *Britain* I 138
28. *Economist,* July 13, 1974
29. Chambers 117
30. Clapham, *Britain* III, 470
31. Herr, 89
32. Salaman, 485
33. Clapham, *Britain* III, 466
34. Bogart, 436, 536
35. Mantoux, 36
36. *Policing the hidden economy,* 3
37. Erne, 148
38. E. H. Phelphs Brown, *Economia,* Nov. 1956. qu Drummond, 403
39. Sauvy 560

Chapter 31

1. D.N.B.
2. Mumford, 47
3. Clapham, *France and Germany,* IV, 70
4. Croce, 15
5. *Cambridge economic History of Europe,* II
6. Clapham, *France and Germany,* IV 308
7. Croce, 26
8. Derry and Williams, 704
9. Zeldin I, 237
10. *U.N. Statistical Yearbook,* 351

11. qu. Popper II, 102
12. Mitchell 371
13. Seton-Watson, 658
14. Churchill, *World Crisis* I.
15. Cipolla I, 55, 86
16. *U.N. Statistical Yearbook*
17. H. Thomas, *Cuba*, 363
18. Liddell Hart, *Second World War*
19. *World Energy Supplies, 1971–75,* 190
20. B. Cohen, 21

Chapter 32

1. Boswell II, 22
2. Mitchell & Deane, 218
3. Clapham *Britain* I, 212
4. Petty
5. Derry
6. Bogart, 326
7. Derry and Williams, 331
8. Fuller 91
9. Derry and Williams, 370
10. Flaubert
11. Mitchell & Deane, 218
12. Derry and Williams, 466
13. Mitchell & Deane, 300
14. Clapham, *Britain* II, 74
15. Clapham *Britain* III 280
16. Croce, 280
17. Churchill I, 212
18. Balfour, 119
19. *Historical Statistics*, 446
20. *U.N. Statistical Yearbook*
21. Clapham *France and Germany* IV, 108
22. Bogart, 316
23. Bogart 316
24. Needham I, 231
25. Derry and Williams, 700
26. Clapham *Britain* III, 113
27. Solzhenitzyn, The *Gulag*, II
28. D.N.B.
29. ibid
30. D.N.B.
31. Strachey, 69
32. Zeldin II, 637
33. *Marie France*, August 1978
34. Zeldin II, 689

35. Zeldin II, 632
36. Zeldin II, 640
37. Fuller, 137
38. Derry, 607
39. Derry, 395
40. *Historical Statistics*, 462
41. Mitchell
42. Zeldin II, 649
43. Cohn, 164
44. Bogart, 725
45. qu. Mosse, 48
46. D. G. Wilson, 27
47. D. R. Blackmore and A. Thomas
48. *Statistical Yearbook*, 415
49. *Statistical Yearbook*, 1973, 415
50. Thomas, 393
50. M. Clark, 199
51. Hoover, 133
52. M. Clark, 199
53. *Historical Statistics*, 466
54. Bogart, 784
55. *Military Balance*, 1977
56. *U.N. Statistical survey*, 1973, 354; Mitchell
57. Joll, 163
58. *U.N. Statistical Yearbook*, 1973, 354
59. *U.S Annual Abstract of statistics*, 1976
60. P. L. Yates, 28

Chapter 33

1. De Tocqueville, *French Revolution*, x
2. Lisón Tolosano
3. Wittfogel, 52
4. Kieve
5. Mitchell
6. Storey
7. Joll, Intellectuals
8. B. Lewis
9. *U.N. Statistical Yearbook*
10. Ibid
11. Mitchell, 657
12. Ossorio y Gallardo
13. Observation by Philip Bonsal
14. Mack Smith, *Mussolini's Roman Empire* 70
15. Macmillan, 608
16. Zeldin, II, 70

17. Bruford
18. Dicey, 282
19. Herr, 208
20. *Historical Statistics*, 306
21. De Tocqueville, 146
22. Martin, 146
23. *Ibid*, 163
24. Dicey, 256
25. Pipes, 292
26. Zeldin, II, 528
27. Díaz del Moral, 291
28. Zeldin, II, 495
29. Zeldin, II, 523
30. *Encounter*, May 1978
31. *U.N. Statistical Yearbook*, 1976
32. Jewkes, 20
33. Jewkes, 21
34. *Statistical Yearbook* 816
35. Zeldin, II, 489
36. Clair, 26
37. Zeldin, II, 389
38. Marwick, *Deluge*, 143
39. Morison & Commager, II, 450
40. Graves, 140
41. Connolly, 117
42. Maser
43. Burden, 95
44. D.N.B.: Baird
45. *Statistical Yearbook*, 1976
46. *Basic facts & figures* (UNESCO 1962)
47. Barzini in *Encounter*, May 1978
48. *Scientific American*, Sept, 1978
49. Aron, *La Révolution introuvable* 167

Chapter 34

1. Chambers, 8
2. Clapham *Britain*, III, 176
3. Derry and Williams, 331
4. A. Young, cited Clapham, *France and Germany*, 10
5. Bloch, *Rural France*, 256
6. Chambers, 54
7. Leopold Deslile, cited Clapham, *France and Germany*, 6
8. Bogart, 286
9. Chambers
10. Moore, 20

11. W. E. Tate
12. Chambers, 86
13. McNeill, 248
14. Chambers, 99
15. Bloch, *Rural France*, 231
16. Clapham, *Britain* III, 164
17. Clapham, *Britain* III, 202
18. K. V. Thomas, 671
19. Braudel, *Mediterranean*, I, 81
20. Pipes 8
21. Carr, 15, 26
22. E. P. Thompson, 230
23. Herr, 99
24. Bogart
25. Gash in Butler, 95
26. Bogart
27. Chambers, 175
28. E. Russell, 81
29. Tannahill, 326; Drummond, 287
30. Clapham, *France and Germany*, 183
31. Ibid, 173
32. Ibid, 174
33. Brenan, *South*,
34. Bloch, 240
35. Gash in Butler
36. Bogart, 517
37. Giedion, 235
38. Drummond, 325
39. M. Clark, 160
40. Drummond, 309; Carr, 16
41. Bogart, 69
42. Thomas, 1144
43. Tannahill, 382
44. Chas Rich in *Scientific American*, August, 1978
45. *Scientific American*, Sept 1976
46. *Historical Statistics*
47. Mitchell
48. N. Stone
49. Tannahill, 324
50. Altschul 98
51. Altschul, 92
52. Clapham, *Britain*, II, 450–51; I, 66; Mitchell
53. Lester Brown, *Scientific American* Sept 1976
54. *Historical Statistics*
55. Hofstadter, 16
56. Soboul, 206–207; 556–557
57. Herr
58. Carr, 18

59. N. Stone, 295
60. Pipes, 169; 170
61. Schapiro, 439
62. Mitchell; *Historical Statistics*
63. Schapiro, *loc cit*
64. Medvedev
65. Mitchell
66. Schapiro, 438
67. Fitzgerald, 165
68. Fitzgerald, 168

Chapter 35

1. Deerr, II, 449
2. Isaiah, 13, 24; Candolle, 158
3. Candolle, 158
4. Drummond, 38
5. Ortiz
6. Parry, 104
7. Curtin
8. Drummond, 166
9. Braudel, *Capitalism*, 186
10. W. H. Akers, *All About coffee*
11. Hemardiquer, 299
12. Mitchell & Deane, 289
13. Drummond, 105
14. Drummond, 329
15. Braudel, *Capitalism* 182
16. Drummond, 332
17. Mitchell & Deane, 289
18. Jenks, 219
19. World Bank, *Report on Cuba*, 56
20. *Ibid*, 56
21. Womack
22. Corner, 125
23. H. Thomas, *Cuba* 1564
24. Clapham, *France and Germany*, 217
25. Salaman, 58
26. Salaman, 68, 143
27. Shakespeare, *Merry Wives*, Act V
28. Pipes, 143
29. Salaman, 118
30. Clapham, *Britain*, 124
31. E. Russell, 77
32. Salaman, 121
33. Hémardiquer, 292
34. The late Fred Swynnerton
35. Clapham, *Britain* I
36. Adam Smith, I, 199

37. Clapham, *Britain*, 111
38. Salaman, 344
39. Glass, I 33–4
40. Mitchell, 20
41. Salaman, 186
42. Drummond, 304
43. Hémardiquer
44. Blake, *The Conservative Party*, 150
45. Tannahill, 343
46. Giedion, 536
47. Tannahill 323; Derry
48. Giedion, 597
49. Hémardiquer, 167
50. Drummond, 310
51. Derry, 694
52. Drummond, 76
53. Drummond, 384
54. Drummond, 384
55. Sauvy, 481; Braudel *Capitalism*, 95
56. Letitia Brewster & Michael Jackson
57. Chambers, 115
58. Tannahill, 356
59. Cipolla in Glass, II, 584
60. Drummond, 297
61. Drummond, 406
62. Braudel, *Mediterranean* I, 19

Chapter 36

1. Needham, I, 147
2. *Scientific American*, March 1977
3. Tannahill, 320
4. Mumford, 294
5. Needham, I, 219
6. D.N.B.
7. Singer and Underwood, 340
8. Zeldin, II 582
9. I. B. Macgregor speech at British Associate Symposium on malaria, *Daily Telegraph*, September 7. 1976
10. Singer and Underwood
11. De Tocqueville, *Democracy*, I, 35
12. Mitchell, table B7
13. Guillaume, 13
14. Fage, 92
15. Isaiah, VII, 18–19
16. M. Clark, 62
17. M. Clark, 87
18. McNeill, 204

19. Drummond, 387
20. Trueta, 15
21. Trueta, 16
22. Kaplan & Webster, 91
23. Ulam, 562
24. Mosse, 90

Chapter 37

1. *Scientific American*, September, 1978
2. Medawar
3. Kahn 151
4. Charles Westoff, 'Marriage & Fertility in the Developed countries, *Scientific American*, Dec. 1978
5. Castro
6. Braudel, *Mediterranean* II, 793
7. Scoville 99
8. Braudel, *Capitalism*, 23
9. Guillaume, 106
10. Curtin, 268
11. Clapham *Britain* III, 168
12. Reinhard
13. Bogart, 744
14. Guillaume, 350
15. Zayas, 256
16. Glass, 42
17. Proudhon, 319
18. Glass, I, 6–7
19. L. R. Brown, qu. Goldsmith, 1
20. Marx, Capital, III
21. Glass, I 427
22. Glass, 88
23. Westoff loc. cit.
24. Guillaume, 358
25. *Scientific American*, January 1977
26. Lyttleton, 353
27. Lyttleton, 19
28. Mitchell, 116
29. Guillaume
30. Westoff *loc. cit*
31. L. Stone, 62
32. Guillaume, 174
33. Sauvy, 406–7
34. De Tocqueville, *Democracy*, I, 328
35. Joll, *Intellectuals*, 159
36. Mosse
37. Ferro, *Great War*, 35

38. Stone, 36
39. Klein, 37
40. Bowra, 27

Chapter 38

1. Herr, 49
2. Cipolla, *Economic History*, 75
3. L. Stone 98
4. Clapham, *France and Germany*
5. Clapham *Britain* I
6. Radischev, 220
7. Arnold, 20, quoting Cato
8. Derry and Williams, 410
9. Joll, *Intellectuals* 150
10. Pevsner, 212.
11. Derry and Williams, 411
12. Zeldin, I, 109
13. Clapham, *Britain* III, 1134
14. Bogart, 634
15. Clapham, *loc. cit*
16. De Tocqueville, *Ancien Regime*, 74
17. Bogart, 420–1
18. Mumford, *City*
19. Mumford, *City*
20. Mumford, *City*
21. Guillaume, 281
22. Martin 291
23. Burden, 3
24. Herodotus, I, 73
25. L. Stone, 487
26. L. Stone, 239
27. Auclair, 44
28. Goethe, 172
29. L. Stone, 27
30. L. Stone, 29
31. Braudel, *Britain* III, 437
32. D.N.B.
33. Braudel, *Mediterranean*, II, 240
34. Mumford, *City* 385
35. L. Stone, 258
36. Drummond, 310
37. Sermons, XVIII
38. Singer, and Underwood
39. Mumford, *City*
40. D.N.B.
41. Singer and Underwood
41. Giedion, 452
43. *Scientific American*, Sept 1975
44. Chambers, 140

45. *Daily Telegraph*, Sept 1977
46. Juvenal, quoted Grant

Chapter 39

1. Mitchell & Deane, 468
2. Clapham *Britain* III, 400
3. Clapham *Britain* I 263
4. D.N.B.
5. Clapham *Britain* I 263
6. Nicholls
7. Clapham *Britain* I 254
8. Weber, 35
9. D.N.B.
10. Clapham *Britain* I 136
11. Crouzet
12. Clapham, *Britain* I 284
13. Moggridge, 11
14. Clapham *Britain* I, 20
15. Mitchell & Deane, 444
16. Clapham, *Britain* II 340
17. Clapham, *Britain* III
18. Pipes, 209
19. Wittfogel, 432
20. Clapham, *Britain* I 782
21. J.K. Galbraith, 182
22. Child, 44
23. Bogart 675
24. Rostow, 10
25. Friedman 128
26. Friedman 62
27. Jewkes 178
28. Clapham *Britain*, II, 159

29. W.A. Robson *problems of Nationalised Industry* (1952)
30. Jewkes, 6

Chapter 40

1. Nef
2. Weber, 175
3. qu. Weber 176
4. K.V. Thomas, 778
5. L. Stone 235
6. G.O. Trevelyan
7. Quennell, *Four Portraits*
8. Dicey, 150
9. Dicey, 152
10. Hayek, *Law*, I, 85
11. Hofstadter, 189
12. Plumb 86
13. qu. Plumb
14. Boswell
15. Hayek, *Law*, I, 159
16. Derry and Williams 608
17. Aron, *Opium* 26
18. Jeans 15
19. Glass, 90
20. Plumb, *Man versus Society*: Braudel, *Capitalism*, 276
21. Manning Clark, 2
22. Vives in Cipolla, *Decline*, 147
23. Carr, 36
24. Lynch, 338
25. De Tocqueville, *French Revolution*, 69

BOOK V

Introduction

1. Gibbon, IV, 242
2. Macaulay, *History* I, 1
3. *Political Quarterly*, January, 1870
4. Fisher, 1114
5. Keynes, *Economic Consequences*, 9
6. Berdyaev, 198
7. Thucydides, 121
8. Ostrogorsky qu. Nisbet, 79
9. Berlin, *Fox and Hedghog*
10. Hayek, *Road to Serfdom*, 205

11. Plumb, *Death of the past*, 19
12. E.P. Thompson
13. Bury, 352

Chapter 41

1. Howard, *War*
2. Clapham, *Britain*, I, 140
3. E.J. Russell, 75
4. Mumford, *City*
5. Derry and Williams, 752

6. Howard, *War*, 8
7. Pipes, 126
8. Szamuely, 96; Pipes, 122
9. qu. Fuller, 32
10. Aron, *Opium* 18
11. Arnold, 37
12. qu. Ferro, *The Great War* 184
12. Fortescue, I, 353
14. Nicolson, 42
15. Fuller, 53
16. De Tocqueville, I 224
17. Pipes, 120
18. Lynch, 345; Parry, I, 371
19. G. Martin, 502
20. Croce, 49
21. Martin, 500
22. Derry and Williams 305
23. G. Maura, II, 236
24. D.N.B. Forsyth
25. Fuller, 86
26. Howard, *War*
27. Howard, *Franco Prussian War*
28. Liddell Hart, *The Tanks*, I, 13
29. Fuller, 89
30. Howard, *Franco Prussian War*
31. Martin, 194

Chapter 42

1. Boswell II, 259
2. De Tocqueville, *French Revolution*, 9
3. Dicey, 400
4. Martin, 155
5. Vincent, 10
6. Gibbon, I, 215
7. Craig, 229
8. Metternich qu Martin, 303
9. Trevelyan *Garibaldi*, III, 8
10. Martin, 392
11. *Cambio 16* (Madrid)
12. H. Acton
13. Nisbet, 261
14. Burckhardt
15. Gibbon, V 301
16. Grant, 426
17. Solzhenitsyn, *Nobel Lecture*
18. Halévy, *Era*
19. Radischev, 103

20. qu. Nozick 241
21. Mack Smith, *Italy*
22. Gibbon I, 463
23. Castiglione, 248
24. A. Castro, 650
25. Bloch, *Rural France* 235
26. Jones, *Decline*
27. De Tocqueville, *Democracy*
28. Burckhardt, 15
29. Mosse
30. Huxley, Source Lost
31. Jones, *Decline*
32. *Military Balance*, 1978
33. Pipes
34. H. Smith, 553
35. Russell, *Practice and Theory*

Chapter 43

1. *Times*, August 7, 1914
2. Ruskin
3. Housman, *Shropshire Lad*, xxv
4. Fusell
5. Personal observation of Royal Military College, Kingston, Ontario
6. Corner, 24
7. Address to Naval War College, 2 June 1896, in works ed. Morrison, XIV, 182
8. Bismarck
9. Craig, 317
10. u. Mayer
11. Clapham, *Britain*, III, 517
12. Marwick, I, 57
13. N. Stone, 36
14. N. Stone, 218
15. Fusell, 72
16. Fusell, 22
17. Ferro, *Great War*
18. Fuller, 171
19. N. Stone, 235
20. N. Stone, 186
21. Ferro, *Great War* 94
22. N. Stone 92
23. Fuller, 52
24. N. Stone, 50
24. N. Stone, 50
25. Ferro, 222
26. Marwick, *War and Social Change*
27. Ferro, *Great War*, 117

28. Fusell, 10
29. *Mein Kampf*, 772; Maser, 108
30. Liddell Hart, *First World War*, 196
31. Ferro, 130
32. Ferro, 111
33. Ferro, *Great War*, 96
34. Fuller, 176
35. Ferro, *Great War*, 145
36. Ludendorff, I, 358
37. Morrison and Commager, II, 479
38. Nisbet, 181
39. Marwick, *Deluge*, I
40. Kedourie, *England and the Middle East*, II, 121
41. Moggridge, 2
42. Weber, qu. Marwick, II, 26
43. *Times*, December 10, 1918
44. Ferro, *Great War*, 144
45. qu. Marwick, *Deluge*, 48
46. Ferro, *Great War*, 119
47. qu. Ferro, *Great War*, 119
48. Keynes, *Economic Journal* 1915
49. Marwick, *Deluge*, 176
50. Nisbet, 196
51. Nisbet, 196
52. Leuchtenberg
53. Marwick *Deluge*, 61
54. N. Stone, 154
55. N. Stone, 310
56. N. Stone, 219
57. Ferro, *Great War*, 159
58. Ferro, *Great War*, 147
59. Schlesinger, *Imperial Presidency*, 192
60. Marwick *Deluge*, 191
61. Bendiner, 56
62. Archer
63. Bogart, 810

Chapter 44

1. Ciano; Mack Smith, *Mussolini as a military leader*
2. B. Klein
3. Hayek, 45
4. Documents on German Foreign Policy, 2nd series, II, 306
5. Kennan, 32
6. Fischer
7. Rauschning, 27

8. Liddell Hart, *Second World War*
9. Djilas, 234
10. Paxton, 22
11. Bloch, *Etrange défaite*
12. Ibid
13. Fresnay, 19
14. Irving, 29
15. Liddell Hart, *Second World War*
16. Liddell Hart, *Second World War*; 66
17. Michel, 247
18. Michel, 128
19. M. Clark, 245
20. Milward
21. Marwick, *Deluge*
22. Michel, 171
23. Knightley, 253
24. Marwick, *War and Social Change*, 125
25. Bogart, 732
26. Marwick, *War and Social Change*
27. Crouzet
28. Liddell Hart, *Second World War*, 589–612

Chapter 45

1. Coon, 6–8
2. Clark, 14–15
3. Mack Smith, *Mussolini's Roman Empire* 45
4. Popper, II, 50
5. Jones, *Decline*, 23
6. E. Williams
7. Coon, 602
8. Coon, 612
9. Grant, *Readings*, 381
10. Nelson, 28
11. Ortiz, *Negros Esclavos*
12. Fage, 103
14. Sauvy
15. Sauvy, 513
16. Hofstadter, 108
17. De Tocqueville, I, 359
18. Sauvy, 573
19. Entwhistle, 117
20. Saggs, 49
21. Castro, 486
22. Castro, 313
23. Vilar 476–8
24. Sánchez Albornoz, 792

25. Castro, 528
26. Díaz del Moral, 34
27. Auclair
28. Castro, 61
29. qu. Castro, 509
30. Castro, 566
31. Cervantes, 516
32. Braudel, *Mediterranean*, 808
33. Entwhistle, 178
34. Castro, 560
35. Braudel, *Mediterranean*, 807
36. Lapeyre
37. Braudel, *Mediterranean*
38. Braudel, II 790
39. Sauvy
40. Herr
41. Gibbon, II, 119
42. Gibbon II, 119
43. Cohen
44. Gobineau
45. qu. M. Clark, 100
46. Sauvy, 510
47. Freeman qu Kedourie, *Britain and the Middle East*, 84
48. Manning Clark, 212
49. Balfour, 227
50. Kedourie, 68
51. Marwick, *Britain in the century*, 50
52. Craig, 154
53. Craig, 204
54. Bracher
55. Bracher, 274
56. Keynes, *Economic Consequences*
57. Clapham *France and Germany*, 209
58. Tobias, *The Jewish Bund*
59. Cohen, 120
60. Cohen, 103–105
62. Mosse, 57
63. Groves, *Dictionary of Music*
64. Ferro, 123
65. qu. Grant, *Roman Readings*, 454
66. Hillsberg, 219
67. Hillsberg, 219
68. Irving, 15
69. Bracher, 107
70. Cohen, 249
71. *Catalunya sota el regim de Franco*
72. Maser, 251
73. Tabletalk, 332
74. 6th Congress of Soviets, qu. Ulam
75. Starhemberg, 5

76. Tuohy, 204
77. Popper, II, 62
78. Pabón, I, 236
79. Joll, *Intellectuals in Politics*
80. Paxton, 33
81. Paxton, 231
82. Dahrendorf
83. Milward, *The New Order*, 179
84. Croce

Chapter 46

1. Seton–Watson 674
2. De Tocqueville, *Democracy*, I
3. Bergson
4. Fuller, 275
5. Fireside Chat, December 29, 1940
6. Churchill, V
7. Levy, reviewed by Kenneth Minogue *Daily Telegraph*, March 1979
8. Braunthal, II
9. Thapar
10. *L'Observateur* (Paris) 14. viii 1952
11. Burckhardt, 316
12. *Scientific American* October, 1978, 71
13. Bowra, 14
14. Todd
15. Brzezinski, 135
16. Collins and Cordesman, ix
17. qu. Berlin, *Four Essays*, 137
18. Schapiro, 381
19. Pipes, 302–16
20. Pipes, 294
21. Pipes, 57
22. Lenin, works, XXXIII, qu Wittfogel 400
23. Pipes
24. Barzini, *Encounter*, May 1978
25. Bogart, 232
26. European world Book 1978; *Historical Statistics*
27. Brzezinski
28. Hofstadter, 148
29. Bogart, 410
30. Bogart, 489
31. qu. Brzezinski, 31
32. Wilson, July 4, 1914 qu. Bendiner, 19

Chapter 47

1. Entwhistle
2. Thapar
3. Thapar
4. Maitland, 164
5. Menéndez Pidal 48
6. Bloch, *Rural France*, 104
7. Homo 85
8. P. Brown 28
9. P Anderson, I, 73
10. Gibbon, III, 410
11. Jones, chapter XX
12. Maine, 106
13. B. Lewis, 94
14. Elton *Practice*, 54
15. Bloch Feudal Society, 33
16. Origo, 62
17. Bruford,162
18. Burckhardt, 261
19. Bruford, 176
20. Clapham, *France and Germany*
21. Brenan, 121
22. Herodotus II, 79
23. qu. Popper I, 140
24. Arnold, 60
25. Zeldin
26. Hofstadter
27. Clapham, 518
28. Szamuely, 59
29. Szamuely, 99
30. Aron, 66
31. Reference lost
32. Glass, I, 13
33. Aron, 70
34. Vilar, I, 136
35. Vilar, I, 139
36. Ferro, 17
37. Niebuhr, 58
38. qu Michels, 290
39. Laslett, 218
40. Carr, 54
41. qu Michels, 313
42. Ferro, 5
43. Bracher
44. Leonard Schapiro, *New York Review of Books*, 13.11.'75
45. Tiersky, 290
46. Brzezinski, 169
47. Schapiro, 379
48. Solzhenitzyn, *Gulag*, II, 17
49. Medvedev
50. E. Ginsburg, 26
51. qu Szamuely, 19
52. Szamuely 377
53. Szamuely, 402
54. Szamuely, 200
55. Pipes, 160
56. Szamuely, 49
57. Mitchell, 388
58. Szamuely, 48
59. Schapiro, 258
60. Brzezinski
61. Abramovitch
62. Footman, 156
63. Schapiro, 224
64. Pipes, 294
65. Szamuely, 103
66. Djilas
67. Laquer, *Terrorism*
68. Caute, 65
69. Croce

Chapter 48

1. Halévy
2. Rangel
3. qu. Kedourie, 26
4. Beaufre, 31
5. Fage & Oliver
6. Mack Smith, *Mussolini's Roman Empire* 33
7. Ciano
8. Mack Smith, *Mussolini's Roman Empire*
9. qu Sidgwick
10. Revel in *Commentary*, January 1979

Chapter 49

1. Gibbon, I, 272; cf I, 322
2. Bruford
3. Trueta, 47
4. Vilar, I, 440
5. Menéndez Pidal
6. Gibbon
7. Bloch, *Rural France*
8. Herr, 242

9. De Tocqueville, *French Revolution*, 42

10. De Tocqueville, 45

11. De Tocqueville, 220

12. Szamuely, 361

13. Pipes, 31

14. Thapar, 203

15. Parry, 103

16. Plumb, 9

17. Dicey, 400

18. Pipes, 240

19. Palón I, 49

20. Herr, 325

21. Napoleon

22. J. H. Rose, *Life*, I, 21

23. Moore

24. De Tocqueville, I, 40

25. Southgate in Butler, 163

26. Fisher, 118

27. Pipes, 265

28. Entwhistle, 257

29. Cecil, I, 146

30. Russell, *Theory and Practice*

31. Trueta, 126

32. Bogart, 604

33. *Welsh Miner* 14. ii. 1929. qu. Francis, 96

34. *Essay on Liberty*, 165 (Everyman ed)

35. Dicey, 11

36. Bloch 90

37. Nelson, 215

38. Hayek, 175

39. Lady G. Cecil, I 159

40. Michels, 25

41. Halifax, 203

42. *Democracy in America*, I, 270

43. Lord Salisbury in Lady G. Cecil, 145

44. Bloch, II, 202

45. Popper, I, 127

46. De Tocqueville, I 229

47. Katkov, *passim*

48. Homo

49. Schapiro, 176

50. Moore

51. Trueta 26

52. Schevill 80

53. Vincent, 15

54. Burckhardt, 41

55. Michels, 208

56. Goldsmith

57. Gash in Butler

58. Blake 59

60. Aron, 100

61. qu. Moore, 49

62. Thatcher, 9

Chapter 50

1. Thapar, 78, 110

2. Jones, 235

3. Herr, 125–6

4. Clapham, *France and Germany*, 85

5. De Tocqueville (*Ancien Regime*) 227

6. Clapham, *France and Germany*, 2

7. Pelling, 26

8. Mantoux, 82

9. Hofstadter, 38

10. Mantoux, 376

11. Bogart, 136

12. Clapham, *Britain, II*, 176

13. Pelling, 28

14. Clapham *Britain*, I

15. qu Pelling 32

16. Clapham *Britain*, II, 176–7

17. Bogart, 427

18. Zeldin

19. Clapham, *France and Germany*, 84

20. Termes, 26

21. Termes, 26

22. Friedman, 137

23. *Daily Telegraph*, Feb 26, 1979

24. Trades Union Congress Information

25. Marwick, *Deluge*, 1096

26. Clapham *Britain*, II, 493; Bogart 576

27. Seton-Watson, 506

28. Clapham *France and Germany*, 192

29. qu. Corner, 142

30. Bogart, 754

31. Marwick *Deluge*, 278

32. Marwick *Deluge*, 70

33. Churchill, *Lord Randolph Churchill*

34. Halevy VI, 382

35. Clapham III, 494

36. Beloff, source lost

37. Bell

38. Bogart, 574
39. Termes
40. Lorenzo
41. Proudhon
42. Nozick
43. C. S & C. S Orwin
44. Kriegel, 122
45. Sombart, qu *N. Y Review* Feb 8, '79
46. Kriegel, ibid
47. E. P. Thompson
48. Clapham *Britain* II
49. Campbell
50. Cole

Chapter 51

1. Arnold, 96
2. Glass *Malthus*, 18
3. *Scientific American*, July 1978, p. 62
4. Oestel qu. Wittfogel, 211
5. Plumb
6. *Times*, 22 July 1978
7. *Scientific American*, Dec. 1976
8. Jones, 200
9. Cipolla, *Literacy*, 11
10. Wittfogel, 307
11. Nisbet, 70; L. Stone, 229; Ferro, 12
12. *Times*, Sept 9 1977
13. Lynch, 306
14. Halévy, *Era*, 193
15. Weber qu. Nisbet, 38
16. Kedourie, *Chatham House*
17. De Tocqueville, *Democracy* ix, 621
18. Bloch, *Rural France*
19. Clapham, *Britain* I, 360
20. qu. Hayek, *Road*, 30
21. Arnold, 37
22. Arnold, 88
23. Clapham, *Britain* II, 210
24. Stone, 48
25. Marwick, *War*, I, 154
26. Nisbet
27. Popper, II, 126
28. Goethe, works, II
29. Klein, 146
30. Schevill, 58
31. Clapham *Britain* III, 46
32. Bogart, 199
33. Kaiser, 317
34. Hanotaux

Epilogue

1. Gibbon
2. Pevsner
3. E. P. Thompson.
4. qu. Keith Thomas
5. Hofstadter
6. Oliver & Fage, 183
7. Marwick, *Deluge* I, 298
8. Hansard, March 1955 (CHECK)
9. Kedourie, *The Chatham House Version*, 300
10. Rousseau, *Social Contract*, IV, ch viii
11. Soboul, 397
12. qu. Maurice Baring, 197
13. Martin, 143
14. Aron, *opium* 279
15. de Tocqueville, *Democracy* I, 11–13
16. Michelet
17. Burke, *Letters on a Regicide Peace*,
18. Giovanni Conti Ventosa, qu. G. Martin, 501
19. Rhodes D. N. B.
20. qu. Szamuely, 60
21. qu. Meaker, 209
22. *Collected Writings*, IX
23. Aragon
24. Popper, II, 271
25. Philips Price, 21
26. Philips Price, 21
26. Philips Price 347
27. Lionel Trilling, 'Whitaker Chambers' Journey', New York Review of Books., April 5th 1975
28. Berdyaev, 12, 171
29. Popper, II, 198
30. Díaz del Moral, 207
31. Pestaña, 49
32. Bracher
33. Mosse
34. Mosse
35. Tuohy, 202
36. Pevsner, 146
37. Martin
38. Pevsner, loc. cit
39. Shelley, works
40. Laslett, 195
41. Laslett, 10
42. Keith Thomas, 11

43. Cipolla, *Literacy*, 30
44. Pipes, 126
45. Bruford, 146
46. Bowra, 141
47. Bowen I
48. Cipolla, *Literacy*, 46
49. Guiccardini qu. Cipolla, *Literacy*, 30
50. Bowen II, 116
51. Cicero *de Legibus*, II, XXII, 59
52. Bowen, 191
53. Jones, 231
54. Carcopino, 118
55. Gibbon II, 82
56. Chadwick, 191
57. Saggs, 189
58. Bowen 40–42
59. Roth
60. Bowen II, 8; Bloch II 75
61. Popper II 303
61. Popper II, 26
63. Pirenne, 237
64. Origo, 187
65. Cipolla *Literacy*
66. Parry, I, 42
67. E. P. Thompson, 717
68. Cipolla *Literacy*, 72
69. Cipolla, *Literacy*, 71–2
70. Bogart, 425
71. Plumb, 51
72. Popper I, 6
73. Ferro, 11
74. Gibbon III, 82
75. qu. Hayek, 142
76. Mosse, XXXI
77. Medvedev
78. Herodotus, II, 101
79. Bruford
80. Herodotus I, 205
81. Grimal, 5
82. Gibbon V, 141

83. Huizinga, *Homo Ludens*
84. Bowra 94–5
85. Chadwick, 62
86. Carcopino, 224
87. Gibbon IV 305
88. Huizinga, *Homo Ludens* 196
89. Weber, 160
90. Huizinga, *Homo Ludens* 201
91. Nelson
92. Saggs, 172
93. de Tocqueville, *Democracy*, I, 57
94. Keynes, qu. Vansittart, 223
95. Plato,Laws VII, 803
96. Halévy, qu. Huizinga
97. Villari
98. Bloch, *Feudal Society*
99. Gilbert Murray, source lost
100. Pipes, 21
101. Henry Kissinger in *Economist*, February 10, 1975
102. Burckhardt
103. Dicey
104. Lavoisier, *Encyclopedia Brittanica*
105. Jungk
106. *Scientfic American*, January 1977
107. Jeans
108. Arnold, 7
109. Arnold, 44
110. qu Bullock, 120
111. Thomas, *Cuba*, 851
112. Bloch, *Rural France*
113. K. Clark, *Civilisation*
114. Solzenitsyn, *Nobel prize*,10
115. De Tocqueville, *Democracy*
116. Aron, *Opium*
117. Burckhardt
118. Russell, *Theory and Practice*
119. Acton, *Freedom*
120. Herodotus I, 1
121. Macaulay, *Essays*, 548

Bibliography

The following, it is hoped, lists all the books, pamphlets and articles from which direct quotation is made in the text and to which reference is made in the notes.

ABRAMOVITCH, Raphael, *The Soviet Revolution* (London, 1962)
ACTON, Lord, *The History of Freedom and other Essays* (London, 1907)
ACTON, Harold, *The Last Medici* (London, 1932)
AESCHYLUS, *The Lyrical Dramas*, translated into English verse by John Stuart Blackie (London, 1922)
ALBERTI, Leone Battiste, *Ten Books on Architecture* (London, 1955)
ALTSCHUL, Siri von Reis, 'Exploring the Herbarium' (*Scientific American*, May 1977)
ANDERSON, Edgar, *Plants, Man and Life* (London, 1954)
ANDERSON, Perry, (1) *Passages from Antiquity to Feudalism* (London, 1974)
(2) *Lineages of the Absolutist State* (London, 1974)
ANDERSON, S., *The Sailing Ship* (New York, 1947)
ANSTEY, Roger, *The Atlantic Slave Trade and British Abolition 1760–1810* (London, 1975)
ARAGON, Louis, *A History of the USSR from Lenin to Khruschchev* (London, 1962)
ARBERRY, A. J. (editor), *The Legacy of Persia* (Oxford, 1953)
ARCHER, William, *The Great Analysis*. A plea for a rational order. With an introduction by Gilbert Murray (London, 1912)
ARISTOTLE, *The Politics of Aristotle.* Translated and edited by Ernest Barker (Oxford, 1946)
ARNOLD, Matthew, *Culture and Anarchy* (London, 1869)
ARNOLD, Sir Thomas (and Alfred Guillaume), *The Legacy of Islam* (London 1931)
ARON, Raymond (1) *La révolution introuvable* (Paris, 1968)
(2) *L'opium des Inteis* (Paris, 1955)
'ATLASECO', *Les cahiers du club nouvel observateur 1978* (Paris, 1978)
AUCLAIR, Marcelle, *Enfances et mort de García Lorca* (Paris, 1968)
BALFOUR, Michael, *The Kaiser and his times* (London, 1975)
BARBOUR, Violet, *Capitalism in Amsterdam in the 17th Century* (Ann Arbor, 1963)
BARING, Maurice, *Have you anything to declare?* (London, 1936)
BARZINI, Luigi, 'Can one still believe in European civilisation?' (*Encounter*, May 1978)

BEARD, Charles, *Economic Interpretation of the Constitution* (New York, 1913)
BEAUFRE, André, *1940 The fall of France.* Translated by Desmond Flower (London, 1967)
BELL, Daniel, *The End of ideology* (London, 1965)
BENDINER, Elmer, *A time for Angels. The tragicomical history of the League of Nations* (New York, 1975)
BERDYAEV, Nicholas, *The Meaning of History* (London, 1945)
BERENSON, Bernard (1) *Italian Painters of the Renaissance* (London, 1963)
(2) *Sketch for a self portrait* (London, 1949)
BERGSON, Henri Louis, *The two sources of morality and religion.* Translated by R. Ashley Audra and Cloudley Brereton (London, 1935)
BERLIN, Isaiah, (1) *Four essays on Liberty* (London, 1969)
(2) *Russian Thinkers* (London, 1978)
(3) *Historical Inevitability* (London, 1953)
(4) *Vico and Herder* (London, 1976)
BISMARCK, Otto, Prince, *Bismarck, the Man and the Statesman.* 2 vols (London, 1898)
BLACK, C. E. (Editor), *The Transformation of Russian Society* (Cambridge, 1960)
BLACKMORE, D. R., and A. THOMAS, *Fuel economy of the Gasoline Engine* (New York, 1978)
BLAKE, Robert, *The Conservative Party from Peel to Churchill* (London, 1972)
BLOCH, Marc, (1) *L'étrange defaite* (Paris, 1957)
(2) *Feudal Society* (London, 1961) (Tr.)
(3) *French Rural History: its essential characteristics*
(4) *Mélanges historiques* (Paris, 1963)
BOCCACCIO, Giovanni, *The Decameron.* Translated by J. M. Rigg. 2 vols (London, 1930)
BOGART, L., and D. L. KLEMMERER, *Economic History of the American People* (New York, 1946)
BORAH, Woodrow, *New Spain's century of depression* (Berkeley, 1951)
BOSWELL, James, *The Life of Samuel Johnson.* Ed. by Augustine Birrell. 6 vols (London, 1904)
BOWEN, James, *History of Education.* 2 vols (London 1972, 1975)
BOWRA, C. M., *The Greek Experience* (London, 1957)
BOXER, C. R., *The Dutch Seaborne Empire* (London, 1965)
BRACHER, Karl Dietrich, *The German Dictatorship* (London, 1971)
BRAUDEL, Fernand, (1) *Capitalism and Material Life.* Tr. (London, 1973)
(2) *The Mediterranean in the age of Philip II.* Tr. (New York, 1972)
BRAUNTHAL, Julius, *History of the International.* 2 vols (London, 1963, 1967)
BREMNER, David, *The Industries of Scotland* (Edinburgh, 1869)
BRENAN, Gerald, (1) *South from Granada* (London, 1957)
(2) *The Spanish Labyrinth* (Cambridge, 1943)
BREWSTER, Letitia, and Michael JACOBSON, *The Changing American Diet* Ph. D. Centre for Science in the Public Interest (Washington), 1978)
BRZEZINSKI, Zbigniew, *Between two ages* (New York, 1970)
BRIGGS, Asa, (1) *The Age of Improvement 1783–1867* (London, 1959)
(2) *The Nineteenth Century. Contradictions of Progress* (London, 1970)
(3) *Victorian Cities* (London, 1965)
BRIGGS, Martin, *The architect in history* (Oxford, 1927)
BROWN, Peter, *The World of late Antiquity* (Thames & Hudson, London 1971)

BRUFORD, W. H., *Germany in the eighteenth century* (Cambridge, 1965)

BRUNT, P. A., *Italian Manpower* (London, 1971)

BULLOCK, Alan, *Hitler, a study in tyranny* (Penguin Books, 1962)

BURCKHARDT, Jacob, *The civilisation of the Renaissance in Italy* (New York, 1961)

BURDEN, Hamilton T., *The Nuremberg party rallies: 1923–39* (London, 1967)

BURKE, Edmund, *The Works of the Right Hon. Edmund Burke*. 2 vols (London, 1842)

BURY, J. B., *The Idea of Progress* (London, 1921)

BUTLER, Lord (editor), *The Conservatives: a history from their origins to 1965* (contributions by Norman Gash, Donald Southgate, David Dilks and John Ramsden) (London, 1977)

BUTTERFIELD, Herbert, *Man on his Past* (Cambridge, 1955)

BUTZER, Karl W., *Early hydraulic civilisation in Egypt* (University of Chicago, 1976)

Cambio 16 (Madrid)

Cambridge Economic History

Cambridge Mediaeval History

CAMPBELL, Alistair (and others), *Worker Owners: the Mondragón achievement* (London, 1977)

CANDOLLE, Alphonse, *Origine des plantes cultivées* (Paris, 1883)

CARCOPINO, Jerome, *Daily Life in ancient Rome* (Tr.) (London, 1941)

CARR, Raymond, *Spain 1808–1939* (Oxford, 1966)

CARR SAUNDERS, A. M., *World Population* (Oxford, 1936)

CASANOVA, Giacomo, *The memoirs of Giacomo Casanova*. Edited by Madeline Boyd (New York, 1946)

CASTIGLIONE, Baldassare, *The Book of the Courtier* (New York, 1959)

CASTRO, Américo, *The structure of Spanish History* (Princeton, 1954)

CAUTE, David, *The fellow-travellers* (London, 1973)

CECIL, Lady Gwendolen, *Life of Robert, Marquis of Salisbury*. 4 vols (London, 1921)

CELLINI, Benvenuto, *The Life of Benvenuto Cellini*. Translated by J. A. Symonds. 2 vols (London, 1888)

CERVANTES, Miguel de, *The Adventures of Don Quixote*. Translated by J. M. Cohen (London, 1950)

CHADWICK, John, *The Mycenean World* (Cambridge, 1976)

CHANG, Kwang-Chih, *The Archaeology of Ancient China* (New Haven, 1978)

CHAMBERS, J. D. and G. E. MURGAY, *The Agricultural Revolution* (London, 1966)

CHAUNU, Pierre, (1) *La civilisation de l'Europe classique* (Paris, 1966)
(2) *Le Sursis* (Paris, 1979)

CHEVALIER, Raymond, *Roman Roads* (Tr.) (San Francisco, 1977)

CHILDE, V. Gordon, *The Dawn of European civilisation* (6th ed., revised) (London, 1973)

CHURCHILL, Winston S., (1) *Lord Randolph Churchill* (London, 1906)
(2) *The World Crisis 1911–1915* (London, 1923)

CIANO, Galeazzo, *Diaries, 1937–1938* (London, 1952)

CICERO, Marcus Tullius, *Letters of Cicero . . .* Selected by L. P. Wilkinson (London, 1959)

CIPOLLA, Carlo Maria, (1) *Guns and sails in the early phase of European expansionism 1400–1700* (London, 1965)
(2) *Literacy and development in the West* (London, 1969)

(3) *Money, Prices and Civilisation in the Mediterranean world* (Princeton, 1956)

(4) *The Economic History of World Population* (London, 1962)

CLAIR, Réné, *Réflexion faite: Notes pour servir à l'histoire de l'art cinématographique de 1920 à 1950* (Paris, 1951)

CLAPHAM, Sir John, (1) *An economic history of modern Britain*. 3 vols. (Cambridge, 1926–38)

(2) *The economic development of France and Germany 1815–1914* (4th ed.) (Cambridge, 1966)

CLARK, Colin, *Population growth and land use* (London, 1967)

CLARK, Grahame, *World pre-history* (Cambridge, 1969)

CLARK, Kenneth, (1) *Civilisation: A personal view* (London, 1969)

(2) *The Gothic Revival* (London, 1956)

CLARK, Manning, *A short history of Australia* (London, 1964)

COBB, Richard, *Paris and its provinces 1792–1802* (London, 1975)

COCHRANE, Thomas, *The Inner Revolution* (New York, 1964)

COHEN, Bernard, 'The disposal of radio-active wastes from Fission reactors' (*Scientific American*, June 1977)

COHEN, Marcel, *Language, its structure and evolution* (Tr.) (London, 1975)

COHN, Norman, *Warrant for Genocide* (London, 1967)

COLE, G. D. H., *British Trade Unionism Today* (London, 1939)

COLLINS, John M., and Anthony M. CORDESMAN, *Imbalance of Power* (London, 1978)

'Commentary' (New York)

CONNOLLY, Cyril, *The Unquiet Grave* (ed.) (London, 1951)

COON, Carleton S., *The Origin of Races* (London, 1968)

CORNER, Paul, *Fascism in Ferrara 1915–1925* (London, 1975)

CRAIG, Gordon A., *Germany 1866–1945* (Oxford, 1978)

CROCE, BENEDETTO, *Storia d'Italia dal 1871 al 1915* (Bari, 1928)

CROSSMAN, Richard, *The Diaries of a cabinet minister*. 3 vols. (London, 1975–77)

CROUZET, Maurice, *Histoire generale des civilisations*. Tome VII: 'L'époque contemporaine' (Paris, 1966)

CUNLIFFE, Barrington, *Iron Age communities in Britain* (London, 1974)

CURTIN, Philip D., *The Atlantic Slave Trade: A Census* (Madison (Wisconsin), 1969)

DAHRENDORF, Ralph, *Class and Conflict in Industrial Society* (London, 1959)

DANTE, *Inferno*

DARLINGTON, C. D., *The evolution of man and society* (London, 1969)

DAVIS, David Brion, *The Problem of slavery in western Culture* (Ithaca, New York, 1966)

DAWSON, Raymond, (1) *The Chinese exprience* (London, 1978)

(2) *The Legacy of China* (London, 1964)

DEERR, Nöel, *The history of Sugar*. 2 vols (London, 1949)

DE GAULLE, Charles, *Mémoires de Guerre: L'Appel 1940–42* (Paris, 1954)

DEMANGEON, Albert, *Le déclin de l'Europe* (Paris, 1920)

DERRY, T. K. and WILLIAMS, Trevor I., *A short history of technology* (Oxford, 1960)

DIÄZ DEL Moral, José, *Historia de las agitaciones campesinas andaluzas-Córdoba* (Madrid, 1929)

DICEY, A. V., *Introduction to the study of the Laws of the Constitution*, 10th ed., Introduction by E. C. S. Wade (London, 1959)

DJILAS, Milovan, *Wartime* (London, 1977)

D. N. B.: *Dictionary of National Biography*

DOCUMENTS ON GERMAN FOREIGN POLICY 2nd series

DONNAN, Elizabeth, *Documents illustrative of the History of the Slave Trade to America*. 4 vols (New York, 1965)

DRUCKER, Peter F., *The End of Economic Man: the origins of totalitarianism* (New York, 1969)

DRUMMOND, J. C., *The Englishman's Food* (London, 1957)

DUMONT, Réné, *False start in Africa* (London, 1966)

Economic History Review

EDWARDS, Harold M., 'Fermat's last theorem' (*Scientific American*, October 1975)

ELLIOTT, J. H., *The discovery of America and the discovery of Man* (London, 1972)

ELTON, G. R., (1) *England under the Tudors* (London, 1974)

  (2) *Reform and Renewal: Thomas Cromwell and the Common Weal* (Cambridge, 1973)

  (3) *The Practice of History* (London, 1969)

Encyclopaedia of the Social Sciences

ERNE, Lord (Rowland Prothero), *English farming, past and present*. 4th ed. (London, 1927)

ENTWHISTLE, William, *The Spanish Language* (London, 1965)

FABRE LUCE, Alfred, *Men or Insects?* Tr. by Robert Baldick (London, 1964)

FAGE, J. D. and R. A. OLIVER (ed.), *Papers in African prehistory* (Cambridge, 1970)

FAGE, J. D., *A history of Africa* (London, 1978)

FERRO, Marc, (1) *The Great War* (London, 1973)

  (2) *The Russian Revolution of 1917* (London, 1972)

FINLAY, Moses, (1) *Aspects of Antiquity* (London, 1967)

  (2) *The Greek Historians*

  (3) 'Myth, Memory and History' in *History and Theory*, 1964–5, iv

  (4) *Studies in ancient society* (London, 1974)

FISCHER, Fritz, *Germany's war aims in the first world war* (London, 1967)

FISHER, H. A. L., *A history of Europe* (London, 1936)

FITZGERALD, C. P., *The Birth of Communist China* (London, 1964)

FLAUBERT, Gustave, *L'education sentimentale* (Paris, 1869)

FOOTMAN, David, *Civil war in Russia* (London, 1962)

FORTESCUE, Sir John, *History of the British Army*. 13 vols (London, 1899–1930)

FRANCIS, Hywel, *South Wales in the Spanish Civil War* (Unpublished PH.D Swansea, 1977)

FRANK, Tenney, *An Economic Survey of Ancient Rome* 5 vols (Baltimore, 1938–1940)

FRANKLIN, Benjamin, *The Autobiography* (London, 1960)

FRESNAY, Pierre, *La Nuit finira* (Paris, 1973)

FREYRE, Gilberto, *The Masters and the slaves* (New York, 1970)

FRIEDMAN, Milton, *Capitalism and Freedom* (London, 1963)

FULLER, J. F. C., *The Conduct of War* (London, 1961)

FUSELL, Paul, *The Great World War and Modern Memory* (Oxford, 1975)

GALBRAITH, John Kenneth, *Money, Whence it came, where it went* (Boston, 1975)

GALBRAITH, V. H., *Domesday Book – its place in administrative history* (Oxford, 1974)

GALL, Norman, *American Field Report: Bolivia* (New York, c. 1972)

GARD, Richard A., *Buddhism* (New York, 1962)

GASH, Norman, article in BUTLER, Lord, *The Conservatives* (noticed above)

GAY, Peter, *Weimar Culture* (London, 1968)

GEYL, PIETER, *The Revolt of the Netherlands 1555–1609*, (London, 1932)

GIBBON, Edward, *The History of the Decline and Fall of the Roman Empire* (London, 1969)

GIEDION, Siegfried, *Mechanisation takes Command* (New York, 1948)

GINSBURG, Evgenia, *Into the Whirlwind* (London, 1967)

GIVEN, James McGovern, *Society and Homicide in Thirteenth Century England* (Stanford, 1977)

GLASS, D. V., *Introduction to Malthus* (London, 1953)

GLASS, D. V., and D. E. C. EVERSLEY (editors), *Population in History* (London, 1965)

GLASS, D. V., and Roger REVELLE, *Population and Social Change* (London, 1972)

GLOTZ, Gustave, *The Greek City and its institutions* (London, 1929)

GOBINEAU, *Selected political writings*. Ed. by Michael Biddis (London, 1970)

GOETHE, Johann Wolfgang, *Works* (5 vols) Tr. (New York, 1885)

GOLDSMITH, Oliver, *The Miscellaneous works of* (London, 1923)

GORDON, Harold J., *Hitler and the Beer Hall Putsch* (Princeton, 1972)

GRANT, Michael (editor), *Roman Readings* (London, 1958)

GRAVES, Robert (and Alan HODGE), *The Long Weekend. A Social History of Great Britain 1918–1939* (London, 1940)

GRIFFITH, Edward D. (and Alan W. CLARKE), 'World Coal Production', *Scientific American* (January 1979)

GRIMAL, Pierre, *In Search of Ancient Italy* (Tr.) (London, 1964)

GUILBERT, Y.

GUILLAUME, Pierre (and Jean Pierre POUSSON), *Démographie historique* Paris, 1970)

HALE, John, *The Medici: The pattern of Control* (London, 1977)

HALEVY, Elie, (1) *A history of the English People in the nineteenth century*, 6 volumes (London, 1924–1932)

(2) *The era of tyrannies* (London, 1965)

HALIFAX, Lord (George Savile), *Complete works* (Oxford, 1912)

HALSEY, A. H. (editor), *Trends in British Society since 1900* (London, 1972)

HAMILTON, Earl, *War and Prices in Spain 1651–1800* (Cambridge, Mass., 1947)

HANOTAUX, Gabriel, *Histoire de Richelieu* (2 vols (Paris 1893–1903)

HARRISON, Gordon, *Mosquitoes, malaria and war. A history of the hostilities since 1880* (New York, 1978)

HASKINS, C. H., *Norman Institutions* (Cambridge, Mass., 1918)

HAYEK, F. A., (1) *The Constitution of Liberty* (London, 1960)

(2) *Law, Legislation and Liberty*. 3 vols (London, 1976–79)

(3) *The Road to Serfdom* (London, 1944)

HEER, Friedrich, *The medieval world: Europe 1100–1350* (London, 1961)

HEMARDIQUER, Jean Jacques (ed.), *Pour une histoire de l'alimentation* (Paris, 1970)

HERODOTUS, *The Histories* (Everyman ed.)

HERR, Richard, *The 18th century Revolution in Spain* (Princeton, 1958)

HIGHET, Gilbert, *Poets in a landscape* (London, 1957)

HILLBERG, R., *The destruction of the European Jews* (Chicago, 1961)

HILTON, Rodney, *A mediaeval society* (London, 1966)

HIMES, Norman, *Medical history of Contraception* (Washington, 1936)

HIRSCH, Fred, *Social Limits to Growth* (London, 1977)
HISTORICAL STATISTICS OF THE US (Washington, 1960)
HITLER, Adolf *Tabletalk*. Ed. by H. R. Trevor-Roper (London, 1953)
HOBBES, Thomas, *Leviathan* (Cambridge, 1950)
HOBSBAWM, E. J., *Industry and Empire* (London, 1969)
HOFSTADTER, Richard, *America at 1750* (London, 1972)
HOLLINGTON, Dorothy (ed.) *People and Food tomorrow* (London, 1976)
HOLT, J. C., *Magna Carta* (Cambridge, 1965)
HOMER, *The Odyssey*
HOMO, León, *Roman Political Institutions from city to state* (London, 1929)
HOOVEN, Frederick, 'The Wright Brothers' Flight-Control System', *Scientific American* (November 1978)
HOLDSWORTH, W. H., *History of English Law*, 3 volumes (London 1903–09)
HOURANI, G. F., *Arab Seafaring in the Indian Ocean in ancient and early mediaeval times* (Princeton, 1951)
HOUSMAN, A. E., *Collected Works* (London, 1939)
HOWARD, Michael, (1) Power at Sea, *Adelphi Papers*, no. 124 (London, 1976)
 (2) *War in European History* (Oxford, 1975)
 (3) *The Franco-Prussian War* (London, 1961)
HSÜ, Kenneth J., 'When the Black Sea was drained', *Scientific American* (May 1978)
HUDSON, Kenneth, *The language of modern politics* (London, 1978)
HUFTON, Olwen, *Bayeux in the late eighteenth century* (London, 1967)
HUIZINGA, J., *Homo Ludens: A study of the play element in culture* (London, 1949)
HUNTINGTON, Ellsworth, *Civilisation and climate* (New Haven, 1924)
IRVING, David, *Hitler's War* (London, 1977)
ISAAC, Glynn, 'The Foodsharing behaviour of protohuman hominids', *Scientific American* (April 1978)
JAMES, C. L. R., *The Black Jacobins* (New York, 1963)
JAURES, Jean, *Histoire Socialiste de la révolution francaise* (Paris, 1968)
JEANS, Sir James, *The growth of physical science* (Cambridge, 1950)
JENKS, Leland, *Our Cuban Colony: a study in sugar* (New York, 1928)
JEWKES, John, *A return to free market economics?* (London, 1978)
JOLL, James, (1) *Gramsci* (London, 1977)
 (2) *Intellectuals in politics* (London, 1960)
 (3) *1914, The Unspoken Assumptions* (London, 1968)
JONES, A. H. M., (1) *The Decline of the Ancient World* (London, 1966)
JOSEPHSON, Matthew, *The Robber Barons, the Great American Capitalists* (New York, 1935)
JUNGK, Robert, *Brighter than a thousand suns* (London, 1958)
KAHN, HERMAN, *Towards the year 2000*, (London, 1968)
KAISER, Robert, *Russia, the People and the Power* (London, 1977)
KAPLAN, Martin M. (and Robert G. WEBSTER), 'The Epidemiology of Influenza', *Scientific American* (December, 1977)
KATKOV, George, *Russia 1917* (London, 1967)
KEDOURIE, Elie, (1) *The Chatham House Version* (London, 1970)
 (2) *England and the Middle East* (Cambridge, 1956)
 (3) *Nationalism* (London, 1963)
KEELEY, Lawrence H., 'The functions of palaeolithic Flint tools', *Scientific American* (November 1977)
KENNAN, George, *Russia and the West under Lenin and Stalin* (London, 1961)

KEYNES, J. M. (Lord), *Economic consequences of the Peace* (London, 1919)
   (2) *Economic consequences of the Peace* (London, 1919)
KINDELBERGER, Charles P., *Economic Growth in France and Britain 1851–1950* (Cambridge, Mass., 1964)
KISSINGER, Henry, Interview in *The Economist* (London) 10 February 1979
KLEIN, Julius, *The Mesta* (Cambridge (US), 1920)
KNIGHTLEY, Philip, *The first casualty* (London, 1975)
KRIEGEL, Annie, *Les Communistes francais* (Paris, 1968)
LABAT, Jean Baptiste, *Nouveau voyage aux isles de l'Amérique*. 6 vols (Paris, 1722)
LADURIE, Emmanuel Le Roy, (1) *Montaillou: Cathars and catholics in a French village 1294–1324* (London, 1978)
   (2) *Times of Feast, times of famine* (London, 1972)
LANDUCCI, Luca, *A Florentine Diary* (edited by Iodoco del Badia) (London, 1927)
LAPEYRE, Henri, *Geographie de l'Espagne morisque* (Paris, 1959)
LAQUEUR, Walter, *Terrorism* (London, 1977)
LASLETT, Peter, *The world we have lost* (London, 1965)
LECKY, William, (1) *The Rise and influence of Rationalism in Europe* (London, 1865)
   (2) *A History of European Morals*, 2 vols (London, 1911)
LEONARD, Irving A., *Books of the Brave* (New York, 1964)
LEUCHTENBERG, W. D., *Franklin D. Roosevelt and the New Deal* (London, 1963)
LEWIN, Ronald, *Ultra goes to war: the secret story* (London, 1978)
LEWIS, Bernard, *The Arabs in History* (Revised edn.) (New York, 1967)
LIDDELL HART, Sir Basil, (1) *History of the first world war* (London, 1970)
   (2) *History of the second world war* (London, 1970)
LISÓN TOLOSANO, Carmelo, *Belmonte de los Caballeros* (Oxford, 1966)
LIST, Friedrich, *The National System of political Economy* (Tr. by Sampson Lloyd (London, 1885)
LOOMIS, Robert S., 'Agricultural Systems', *Scientific American*, (September, 1976)
LORENZO, Anselmo, *El Proletariado militante*, New ed. (Mexico, n.d.)
LUDENDORFF, Friedrich Wilhelm, *My War Memories 1914–1918*. 2 vols (Tr) (London, 1919)
LUKACZ, John, *The Last European War* (New York, 1977)
LYNCH, John, *The Spanish American Revolutions* (London, 1973)
LYTTLETON, Adrian, *The Seizure of Power* (London, 1973)
MACAULAY, Lord, (1) *Essays and Lays of Ancient Rome* (London, 1903)
   (2) *The History of England* (London, 1905)
MACK SMITH, Denis, (1) *Italy a modern history* (Ann Arbor, 1959)
   (2) *Mussolini as a military leader* (Reading, 1974)
   (3) *Mussolini's Roman Empire* (London, 1976)
MACMILLAN, Harold, *Tides of Fortune* (London, 1969)
MCBURNEY, C. B. M., *Early man in the Soviet Union* (London, 1970)
MCNEILL, William, *Plagues and Peoples* (Oxford, 1977)
MAINE, Sir Henry, *Ancient Law* (London, n.d.)
MAITLAND, F. W., (1) *Domesday Book and Beyond* (Cambridge, 1921)
   (2) *The Constitutional history of England* (Cambridge, 1926)
MALRAUX, André, *Les Noyers de l'Altenburg* (Paris, 1948)
MANTOUX, Paul, *The industrial revolution in the eighteenth century*. New and revised ed. with preface by T. S. Ashton (London, 1961)
MARCHENKO, Anatoly, *My testimony* (London, 1969)

MARTIN, Calvin, *Keepers of the Game: Indian Animal Relationships and the Fur Trade* (Berkeley, 1978)

MARTIN, George, *The Red Shirt and the Cross of Savoy* (New York, 1969)

MARWICK, Arthur, (1) *Britain in the century of Total war* (London, 1968)
(2) *The Deluge* (London, 1965)
(3) *War and Social Change in the Twentieth Century* (London, 1974)

MARX, Karl, *Capital*. 3 vols (Moscow, 1961)

MASER, Werner, *Hitler's Letters and Notes* (London, 1973)

MAURA, Gabriel, *Historia crítica del reinado de Don Alfonso XIII*. 2 vols (Barcelona, 1919)

MAYER, Arno, *Politics and Diplomacy of Peace-making* (London, 1967).

MEAKER, Gerald H., *The revolutionary left in Spain 1914–1923* (London, 1974)

MEDAWAR, P. B., *The Hope of Progress* (London, 1974)

MEDVEDEV, Roy, *Let History Judge* (London, 1972)

MELLAART, James, *The Neolithic of the Near East* (London, 1975)

MENENDEZ PIDAL, Ramón, *La España del Cid* (5th ed.) (Madrid, 1956)

MERCIER, L. S., *L'habitant de la Guadeloupe* (Paris, 1782)

MESAVOVIC, Mihajlo (and Eduard Pestel), *Mankind at the Turning Point: The Second Report of the Club of Rome* (London, 1975)

MICHEL, Henri, *The Shadow War* (Tr.) (London, 1972)

MICHELS, R., *Political parties* (Tr.) (London, 1915)

MICHELET, Jules, *Histoire de la Revolution francaise*, New ed. (Paris, 1952)

MILIBAND, Ralph, *Marxism and politics* (Oxford, 1977)

The Military Balance 1978 (London, 1978)

MILL, J. S., *Utilitarianism, Liberty and representative government* (Everyman) (London, 1910)

MILWARD, Alan, (1) *The German economy at War* (London, 1965)
(2) *The New Order and the French economy* (Oxford, 1970)

MIQUEL, André, *La géographie humaine du monde musulman* (Paris (Mouton), 1978)

MITCHELL, B. R., *European historical statistics 1750–1970* (London, 1975)

MITCHELL, B. R. (with Phyllis DEANE), *Abstract of British historical Statistics* (Cambridge, 1962)

MOGGRIDGE, D. E., *The Return to Gold 1925* (Cambridge, 1969)

MOLNAR, Peter, and Paul TAPPONNER, 'The Collision between India and Russia' *Scientific American* (April 1977)

MOMIGLIANO, Arnaldo, *Studies in Historiography* (London, 1966)

MONOD, Jacques, *Chance and Necessity* (London, 1972)

MONTAIGNE, Michel de, *Diary of Montaigne's Journey to Italy in 1580 and 1581*. Tr by E. J. Trechmann (London, 1929)

MONTESQUIEU, Charles Louis, Baron de, *Lettres persanes* (Paris, 1897)

MONTET, Pierre, *Eternal Egypt* (Tr. by Doreen Weightman) (London, 1964)

MOORE, Barrington (J. R.), *Social origins of Dictatorships and democracy* (London, 1967)

MORISON, Samuel Eliot, (1) *Christopher Columbus, mariner* (London, 1956)
(2) *The growth of the American Republic* (with COMMAGER) 2 vols (Oxford, 1950)

MORISON, E. E. (ed.) *Letters of Theodore Roosevelt* (Cambridge, Mass., 1951–54)

MORRISON, Philip, and Paul WALKER, 'A new strategy for military spending' *Scientific American* (October, 1978)

MOSKOVITZ, Breyne Arlene, 'The acquisition of language', *Scientific American*

(November, 1978)

MOSSE, George L., *Nazi Culture* (London, 1966)

MOUSNIER, Roland, *The assassination of Henry IV.* Tr. by Joan Spencer (London, 1973)

MULTHAUF, Robert, *Neptune's Gift: a history of Common Salt* (Baltimore, 1978)

MUMFORD, Lewis, (1) *The City in History* (New York, 1961)
(2) *The transformations of Man* (New York, 1956)

MYRDAL, Gunnar, *Asian Drama. An inquiry into the poverty of nations* (3 vols. (London 1968)

NADAL, Jordi, *El fracaso de la revolución industrial en España, 1814–1913* (Barcelona, 1975)

NAMIER, Lewis, 'Anthony Bacon', *Harvard Journal of Economic and Business Studies*, II, no. 1, (November, 1929)

NEEDHAM, Joseph, *Science and civilisation in China.* Vol I (Cambridge, 1954 onwards)

NEF, J. U., *Industry and Government in France and England* (Ithaca, 1957)

NELSON, Lowry, *Rural Cuba* (Minneapolis, 1950)

New York Review of Books, The

NICHOLLS, J. W., *History of Vickers* (London, 1963)

NICHOLS, Peter, *Italia, Italia* (London, 1973)

NICOLSON, Harold, *The Congress of Vienna* (London, 1946)

NIEBUHR, Reinhold, *The Self and the dramas of history* (London, 1956)

NISBET, Robert, *The Twilight of authority* (London, 1976)

NOZICK, Robert, *Anarchy, State and Utopia* (London, 1974)

OLIVER, Roland and J. D. FAGE, *A Short History of Africa* (London, 1974)

OMAN, Sir C., *A history of the Art of War in the Middle Ages* (London, 1924)

ORIEUX, Jean, *Talleyrand, the Art of Survival* (London, 1974)

ORIGO, Iris, *The merchant of Prato* (London, 1957)

ORTIZ, Fernando, (1) *Cuban counterpoint: tobacco and sugar* (New York, 1947)
(2) *Los Negros Esclavos* (Havana, 1916)

ORWIN, C. S. and C. S., *The Open Fields* (Oxford, 1967)

OSSORIO Y GALLARDO, Angel, *Julio de 1909, Declaración de un testigo* (Madrid, 1910)

PABON, J., *Cambó.* 3 vols (Barcelona, 1952 onwards)

PARKER, Geoffrey, *The Army of Flanders and the Spanish Road* (Cambridge, 1972)

PARRY, John, *The Spanish Seaborne Empire* (London, 1966)

PAXTON, Robert O., *Vichy France* (London, 1972)

PECK, J. M., *A new guide for emigrants to the West* (Boston, 1837)

PELHAM, H. F., *Essays* (Oxford, 1911)

PELLING, Henry, *A history of British trade unionism* (London, 1963)

PESTAÑA, Angel, *Lo que aprendí en la vida* (Madrid, 1933)

PETTY, Sir William, *Several essays in political arithmetic* (London, 1755)

PEVSNER, Nikolaus, *An outline of European architecture* (London, 1948)

PHILLIPSON, D. W., 'The spread of the Bantu language', *Scientific American* (April, 1977)

PIPES, Richard, *Russia under the Old Regime* (London, 1974)

PIRENNE, Henri, (1) *Mahomet and Charlemagne* (New York, 1939)
(2) *Mediaeval cities* (Princeton, 1946)

PLATO, *The Republic of Plato* (Tr. with Introduction and Notes) (London, 1941)

PLUMB, J. H., (1) *The death of the past* (London, 1968)
(2) *The growth of political stability in England 1675–1725* (London, 1969)

(3) *Man versus society in eighteenth century England* (London, 1969)

POLE, J. R., *Political representation in England and the origins of the American Republic* (London, 1966)

Policing the Hidden Economy (Report by the Outer Circle Policy Unit) (London, 1978)

'Political Quarterly'.

POLO, Marco, *Travels of* (Tr.) (London, 1958)

POLÁNYI, Károly, *Trade and Market in early empires* (Indian Hills, 1957)

POPPER, Karl, *The Open Society and its enemies.* 2 vols (5th ed.) (London, 1966)

POST, John D., *The Last great subsistence crisis in the Western World* (Baltimore, 1977)

POSTAN, M. M., *An economic history of Western Europe* (London, 1967)

PRICE, M. Philips, *My reminiscences of the Russian Revolution* (London, 1921)

PROUDHON, Pierre Joseph, *Qu'est-ce que la propriété?* (Paris, 1966)

QUENNELL, Peter, *Four Portraits* (London, 1945)

RABB, Theodore K. (and Robert I. ROTBERG), *The Family in History: Interdisciplinary Essays* (New York, 1973)

RADISCHEV, *A Journey from St Petersburg to Moscow* (Tr. by Leo Wiener) (Cambridge, Mass., 1958)

RANGEL, Carlos, *De buen salvaje al buen revolucionario* (Caracas, 1976)

RAUSCHNING, HERMANN, *The Voice of destruction* (New York, 1940)

READ, Herbert, *Anarchy and Order: Essays in Politics* (London, 1954)

REDFORD, Donald, 'The Razed temple of Akhenaten', *Scientific American*, (December, 1978)

REINHARD, Marcel R., with André ARMENGAUD and Jacques DUPAQUIER, *Histoire Générale de la Population Mondiale* (Paris, 1968)

REVEL, Jean Francois, (1) *La Tentation totalitaire* (Paris, 1976)

(2) 'The Trouble with Latin America', *Commentary* (February, 1979)

ROGERS, Thorold, *History of Agriculture & Prices in England* (1259–1795) 7 vols Oxford 1866–1902

ROEDERER, Pierre Louis, *Oeuvres.* 8 vols (Paris 1853–59)

ROOSEVELT, Theodore, *Letters of.* Selected and edited by Elting E. Morison (Cambridge, Mass., 1951–54)

ROSE, J. H., *The Life of Napoleon I.* 6th ed. (London, 1922)

ROSNAY, Jöel de, *Les origines de la vie* (Paris, 1966)

ROSTOW, Walt (edited), *The Economics of 'take off' into self-sustained growth* (Washington, 1963)

ROTH, Cecil, *A short history of the Jewish People* (London, 1947)

ROUSSEAU, Jean Jacques, *A discourse on the origin of inequality* (London, 1952)

RUNICMAN, W. G., *Social Science and Political Theory* (Cambridge, 1969)

RUSKIN, John, *The Stones of Venice.* 3 vols (London, 1873)

RUSSELL, Bertrand, (1) *A history of western philosophy* (London, 1946)

(2) *Freedom and organisation 1815–1914* (London, 1934)

(3) *Practice and theory of Bolshevism* (London, 1920)

RUSSELL, E. John, *The world of the soil* (London, 1961)

RUSSELL, J. C., *Late ancient and mediaeval population* (Philadelphia, 1958)

SAGGS, H. W. F., *The greatness that was Babylon* (London, 1962)

SALAMAN, Redcliffe, *The history of social influence of the Potato* (Cambridge, 1949)

SÁNCHEZ ALBORNOZ, Claudio, *Spain: a historical enigma* (Eng. ed.) 2 vols (Madrid, 1975)

SAUVY, Alfred, *General Theory of Population* (London, 1969)

SAWYER, P. H., *The Age of the Vikings* (London, 1962)

Scandinavian Historical Review, The

SCHAPIRO, Leonard, *The Communist Party of the Soviet Union* (London, 1960)

SCHEVILL, Ferdinand, *The Medici* (London, 1950)

SCHMITT, Bernadotte, *The Coming of the War, 1914.* 2 vols (London, 1930)

SCHLESINGER, Arthur, *The Imperial Presidency* (London, 1973)

SCHMANDT BESSERAT, Denise, 'The earliest precursor of writing', *Scientific American* (June, 1978)

SCHOENBAUM, David, *Hitler's social revolution* (London, 1966)

Scientific American, The

SCOVILLE, Warren, *The Persecution of the Huguenots and French economic development, 1680–1720* (Berkeley, 1960)

SCHOLES, Percy, *The Oxford Companion to Music* (London, 1938)

SCHUMACHER, E. F., *A Guide to the Perplexed,* (London, 1977)

SEERS, Dudley (ed), *Cuba, the Economic and Social Revolution* (Chapel Hill, 1964)

SELTMAN, Charles, *Wine in the ancient world* (London, 1957)

SETON WATSON, Hugh, *The Russian Empire 1801–1917* (London, 1967)

SHAW, Bernard, *The Complete Plays of* (London, 1937)

SHELLEY, Percy Bysshe, *Poetry and Prose* (with an introduction and notes by A. M. D. Hughes) (Oxford, 1931)

SHORTER, Edward, *The Making of the Modern Family* (London, 1976)

SIDGWICK, Henry, *The Development of European Polity* (London, 1903)

SINGER, Charles, and E. Ashworth UNDERWOOD, *A short history of Medicine* (Oxford, 1962)

SINGER, Charles, with E. J. HOLMYARD and A. R. HALL (Editors), *A History of Technology* (Oxford, 1954)

SMITH, Adam, *An enquiry into the nature and causes of the Wealth of Nations .* 2 vols (London, 1910)

SMITH, Hendrick, *The Russians* (London, 1976)

SOBOUL, Albert, *The French Revolution 1787–1799.* 2 vols (London, 1962)

SOLZHENITSYN, Alexander, (1) *The Gulag Archipelago 1918–1956: an experiment in literacy investigation* (London, 1974, 1976, 1978)

(2) *The Nobel Lecture on Literature* (New York, 1972)

SOMBART, Werner, *The Quintessence of Capitalism* (London, 1915)

SOREL, Albert, *Europe and the French Revolution.* Translated by Alfred Cobban and J. W. Hunt (London, 1969)

SOUTHERN, R. W., *The making of the Middle Ages* (London, 1959)

SOUTHGATE, see BUTLER, Lord

SPEER, Albert, *Encounter* (October 1976)

SPEER, Albert, see *Encounter* (October 1976)

SPOONER, Lysander, *No Treason, the Constitution of no authority* (New York, 1870)

STARHEMBERG, Ernst, Prince, *Between Hitler and Mussolini* (New York, 1942)

STEINBERG, S. H., *Five hundred years of printing* (3rd ed.) (London, 1974)

STEINER, George, *After Babel* (London, 1975)

STONE, Lawrence, (1) *Crisis of the Aristocracy* (Oxford, 1965)

(2) *The family, sex and marriage* (London, 1977)

STONE, Norman, *The Eastern Front* (London, 1975)

STOREY, Graham, *Reuters' century 1851–1951* (London, 1951)

STRACHEY, Amy, *St Loe Strachey, his life and his paper (the Spectator)* (London,

1930)

SUTHERLAND, C. H. V., *Gold* (London, 1959)

SZAMUELY, Tibor, *The Russian Tradition* (London, 1974)

TACITUS, Publius Cornelius, *The Histories*. A new translation by Kenneth Wellesley (London, 1964)

TALMON, J. L., *Romanticism and Revolt: Europe 1815–48* (London, 1968)

TANNAHILL, Reay, *Food in History* (London, 1973)

TAYLOR, A. J. P., *From Sarajevo to Potsdam* (London, 1966)

TEC – see SINGER, C., and HOLMYARD, ed. *History of technology*

TERMES, Josep, *Anarquismo y sindicalismo en España* (Esplugues de Llobregat, 1972)

THAPAR, Romila, *A history of India* (London, 1966)

THATCHER, Margaret, *The Ideals of the Open Society*. Speech in London, 8 May 1978

THIRSK, Joan, *English peasant farming* (London, 1957)

THOMAS, Hugh, (1) *Cuba or the Pursuit of Freedom* (London, 1971)
   (2) *John Strachey* (London, 1973)

THOMAS, K. V., *Religion and the decline of magic* (London, 1971)

THOMPSON, E. A., *The Early Germans* (Oxford, 1965)

THOMPSON, E. P., *The making of the English Working class* (London, 1965)

THUCYDIDES, *History of the Peloponnesian War*. (Tr. by Richard Crawley) (London, 1910)

TIERSKY, Ronald, *French Communism* (London, 1974)

TILLY, Charles, Louise and Richard, *The Rebellious century* (London, 1975)

TOBIAS, Henry, *The Jewish Bund in Russia* (Stamford, 1972)

TOCQUEVILLE, Alexis de, (1) *Democracy in America*. 2 vols (New York, 1948)
   (2) *The old Regime and the Revolution*. New tr. by Stuart Gilbert (New York, 1955)

TODD, Emmanuel, *La Chute finale* (Paris, 1977)

TREVELYAN, G. M., (1) *English Social History* (London, 1942)
   (2) *Garibaldi's Defence of the Roman Republic* (London, 1920)

TREVELYAN, George Otto, *The early life of Charles James Fox* (London, 1886)

TREVOR-ROPER, Hugh, *The Rise of Christian Europe* (London, 1966)

TRILLING, Lionel, 'Whitaker Chambers' Journey', *New York Review of Books* (5 April 1975)

TRUETA, J., *The Spirit of Catalonia* (London, 1946)

TUOHY, Frank, *Yeats* (London, 1976)

TUZET, Hélène, *La Sicile au dixhuitième siècle vue par les voyageurs* (Strasburg, 1955)

ULAM, Adam, *Lenin and the Bolsheviks* (London, 1965)

ULLMAN, Walter, *Law and Politics in the Middle Ages* (Cambridge, 1975)

UN Statistical Yearbook, *Annual Survey* (New York, 1973)

UNAMUNO, Miguel de, *The Tragic Sense of Life in men and nations*. Tr. by Anthony Kerrigan (London, 1972)

UTTERSTRÖM, See *Scandinavian Historical Review*

VALENTINE, James H., 'The evolution of multicellular plants and animals', *Scientific American* (September, 1978)

VANSITTART, Lord, *The Mist Procession* (London, 1958)

VASARI, Giorgio, *Lives of the Painters, Sculptors and Architects* (Everyman) (London, 1927)

VILAR, Pierre, *La Catalogue dans l'Espagne Moderne*. 3 vols (Paris, 1962)

VILLANI, Giovanni, *Villani's Chronicle: being selections from the first nine books of the Chroniche fiorentine* (London, 1906)

VINCENT, John, *The formation of the British Liberal Party* (London, 1966)

VOLTAIRE, *Letters of and Frederick the Great* (London, 1927)

WAGNER, Anthony, *English Genealogy* (London, 1972)

WAINWRIGHT, Geoffrey, 'A Celtic farmstead in Southern Britain', *Scientific American* (December 1977)

WASHBURN, Sherwood L. 'The evolution of Man', *Scientific American* (September, 1978)

WEBER, Max, *The Protestant ethic and the spirit of capitalism* (London, 1930)

WESLEY, John, *Standard Sermons* (London, 1921)

WESTOFF, Charles, 'Marriage and fertility in the developed countries', *Scientific American* (December 1978)

WHEELER, Sir Mortimer, *The Indus Civilisation* (Cambridge, 1953)

WHITE, Lynn, *Mediaeval technology and social change* (Oxford, 1966)

WILLIAMS, E. T., *A short history of China* (New York, 1928)

WILLIAMS, Eric, *Capitalism and Slavery* (London, 1964)

WILSON, David Gordon, 'Alternative automobile engines', *Scientific American* (July, 1978)

WITTFOGEL, Karl A., *Oriental despotism* (New Haven, 1957)

WOMACK, John, *Zapata and the Mexican Revolution* (London, 1969)

WORLD BANK, *Report on Cuba* (Washington, 1951)

WORLD ENERGY SUPPLIES 1971–1975

XENOPHON, *Works*. Tr. by H. G. Dakyns (London, 1898)

YATES, P. L., *Forty years of foreign trade* (London, 1959)

YOUNG, J. Z., *An introduction to the Study of Man* (Oxford, 1971)

ZAEHNER, R. C., *The Dawn and Twilight of Zoroastrianism* (London, 1961)

ZAYAS, Alfred, *Nemesis at Potsdam* (London, 1977)

ZELDIN, Theodore, *France 1848–1945*. 2 vols (Oxford, 1973, 1974)

ZEUMER, Frederick E., *A history of domesticated animals* (London, 1963)

ZINSSER, Hans, *Rats, Lice and History* (New York, 1935 and 1965)

Index